ℬEING HUMAN

BEING HUMAN

CORE READINGS IN THE HUMANITIES

READINGS FROM THE PRESIDENT'S
COUNCIL ON BIOETHICS

WASHINGTON, D.C.
DECEMBER 2003

NEW YORK, NEW YORK
JULY 2004

W. W. NORTON • NEW YORK • LONDON

Preface to the Norton Edition copyright © 2004 by Leon R. Kass, M.D.

ISBN 0-393-92639-7 (pbk.)

W. W. Norton & Company, Inc., 500 Fifth Avenue, New York, N.Y. 10110
www.wwnorton.com
W. W. Norton & Company Ltd., Castle House, 75/76 Wells Street,
London WIT 3QT

2 3 4 5 6 7 8 9 0

CONTENTS

CHAPTER 3:
TO HEAL SOMETIMES, TO COMFORT ALWAYS   119

SECTION II:
THE HUMAN BEING
AND THE LIFE CYCLE   165

CHAPTER 4:
ARE WE OUR BODIES?   167

CHAPTER 5:
MANY STAGES, ONE LIFE

CHAPTER 6:
AMONG THE GENERATIONS

PREFACE TO THE NORTON EDITION

What does it mean to *be human?* How can we live *well*, as *human* beings?

Through the ages, these complex and perplexing questions have never been far from our consciousness. They have occupied the lifelong attention of great thinkers; they have captured the intermittent attention of nearly everyone. Philosophers and prophets have elaborated arguments and delivered exhortations on them. In the pursuit of answers, poets, novelists, and playwrights have created powerful portraits and conjured poignant images that show us to ourselves. Biographers and historians have explored them through the depiction of exemplary lives, both noble and base, lived in diverse cultures and under the widest variety of circumstances. And perfectly ordinary people of all ages, in their letters, diaries, and essays, have struggled to articulate their own experiences of the human condition and their own understandings of a worthy life.

Such efforts constitute the core of the humanities, the human effort to understand and negotiate the many remarkable aspects of being human. Today we need the humanities more than ever. For today the powers of technology, having brought great changes in the world, are increasingly being used to influence and alter the structures and functions of human bodies and minds. Are these desirable uses of technological power? What do we hope to gain and what do we stand to lose from applying these powers to ourselves? What vision of human life and well-being should guide us in this brave new age in which technology promises—and threatens—to change fundamentally the meaning of *being human?* This book of readings from the humanities is intended to help us address these newly urgent versions of some very old questions.

Being Human was first produced and published by the President's Council on Bioethics. The enthusiastic response it received from readers and reviewers alike has made it clear that there should be a college edition. Professors in courses ranging from Introduction to Humanities to Bioethics to Freshman Composition have expressed interest in using *Being Human* as a core text. These teachers have realized that the remarkably rich selection of shorter pieces, the clear headnotes that place the work and its central concerns in an engaging context, and the questions that complete each headnote will help students think critically about the large human questions and their implications.

Happily, this new edition, produced in collaboration with W. W. Norton & Company, will bring this remarkable collection into the hands of today's young adults. In selecting the readings, we intentionally avoided concentrating solely on today's much-discussed bioethical issues. Instead, we chose to look at the deeper and more fundamental matters of life and its value, matters that are never far from the surface of twenty-first-century dilemmas. Whether the subject is the pursuit of perfection, the relations among the generations, or the meaning of mortality, the pieces in *Being Human* demonstrate that we have much to learn from great thinkers, whatever their era. We have included selections from works as old as the Book of Job and as new as Malcolm Gladwell's "Drugstore Athlete"; as lyrical as Shakespeare's *As You Like It* and as disturbing as Andrew Niccol's *Gattaca*. Readings span cultures from Homer's Troy to Tolstoy's imperial Russia; from Frederick Douglass's antebellum America to Isaac Bashevis Singer's Jewish ghetto. Whether in Philosophy, Humanities, or Composition and Writing courses, professors and their students will find much from which to choose.

I look forward to having this new edition of *Being Human* reach a wider and younger audience—a generation which, perhaps more than any before it, cannot afford to ignore the issues this book raises. *Being Human* offers students the means to reflect on "'life lived humanly,' [on] birth and death, freedom and dignity, the meaning of suffering," and the many experiences that shape our lives. It is at once introductory and foundational: these readings will expose students to the larger questions and give them the means to consider and evaluate various answers. It is our hope that *Being Human* will provide a base from which young people can more effectively confront the complex issues they face today and with which they will continue to grapple in the coming years.

Leon R. Kass, M.D.
Washington, D.C.
May 2004

MEMBERS OF THE PRESIDENT'S COUNCIL ON BIOETHICS (December 2003)

Leon R. Kass, M.D., Ph.D., Chairman.
Addie Clark Harding Professor, The College and the Committee on Social Thought, University of Chicago. Hertog Fellow, American Enterprise Institute.

Elizabeth H. Blackburn, Ph.D.
Professor, Department of Biochemistry and Biophysics, University of California, San Francisco.

Rebecca S. Dresser, J.D., M.S.
Daniel Noyes Kirby Professor of Law and Professor of Ethics in Medicine, Washington University, St. Louis.

Daniel W. Foster, M.D.
Donald W. Seldin Distinguished Chair in Internal Medicine, Chairman of the Department of Internal Medicine, University of Texas Southwestern Medical School.

Francis Fukuyama, Ph.D.
Dean of the Faculty, Bernard L. Schwartz Professor of International Political Economy, Paul H. Nitze School of Advanced International Studies, Johns Hopkins University.

Michael S. Gazzaniga, Ph.D.
Dean of the Faculty, David T. McLaughlin Distinguished Professor, Professor of Psychological and Brain Sciences, Dartmouth College.

Robert P. George, J.D., D.Phil.
McCormick Professor of Jurisprudence, Director of the James Madison Program in American Ideals and Institutions, Princeton University.

Mary Ann Glendon, J.D., M.Comp.L.
  Learned Hand Professor of Law, Harvard University.

Alfonso Gómez-Lobo, Dr. phil.
  Ryan Family Professor of Metaphysics and Moral Philosophy, Georgetown University.

William B. Hurlbut, M.D.
  Consulting Professor in Human Biology, Stanford University.

Charles Krauthammer, M.D.
  Syndicated Columnist.

William F. May, Ph.D.
  Fellow, Institute for Practical Ethics and Public Life. Visiting Professor, Department of Religious Studies, University of Virginia.

Paul McHugh, M.D.
  University Distinguished Service Professor of Psychiatry, Johns Hopkins School of Medicine. Professor, Department of Mental Health, Bloomberg School of Public Health, Johns Hopkins University.

Gilbert C. Meilaender, Ph.D.
  Phyllis & Richard Duesenberg Professor of Christian Ethics, Valparaiso University.

Janet D. Rowley, M.D.
  Blum-Riese Distinguished Service Professor of Medicine, Molecular Genetics and Cell Biology, and Human Genetics, Pritzker School of Medicine, University of Chicago.

Michael J. Sandel, D.Phil.
  Anne T. and Robert M. Bass Professor of Government, Harvard University.

James Q. Wilson, Ph.D.
  James A. Collins Professor of Management and Public Policy Emeritus, University of California-Los Angeles. Reagan Professor of Public Policy, Pepperdine University.

COUNCIL STAFF AND CONSULTANTS

Dean Clancy
Executive Director

Michelle R. Bell
Staff Assistant

Peter Berkowitz
Senior Consultant

Karen Blackistone
Staff Assistant

Eric Cohen
Senior Research Consultant

Judith E. Crawford
Administrative Director

Diane M. Gianelli
Director of Communications

Laura Harmon, Esq.
Projects Administrator

Emily Jones
Executive Administrator

Yuval Levin
Senior Research Analyst

Michelle Powers
Law Clerk

Richard Roblin, Ph.D.
Scientific Director

Adam Schulman
Research Consultant

O. Carter Snead, Esq.
General Counsel

Catherine Thorp
Staff Assistant/Receptionist

Audrea R. Vann
Information Technology
Specialist

Rachel Flick Wildavsky
Director, Education Project

Lee L. Zwanziger, Ph.D.
Director of Research

ILLUSTRATIONS

Frontispiece, Feeding the Hungry, Antonio Canova
© Cameraphoto Arte, Venice / Art Resource, NY

Landscape with the Fall of Icarus, page 467
Pieter Bruegel (the Elder)
By permission of the Royal Museum of Fine Arts of Belgium

BEING HUMAN: AN INTRODUCTION

by Leon R. Kass, M.D.
Chairman, President's Council on Bioethics

Why another thick book about bioethics? Why a bioethics *reader*? Why a reader on *Being Human*? And why a reader on being human *from the President's Council on Bioethics*? The short answer is this: The Council believes that readings of the sort offered here can contribute to a richer understanding and deeper appreciation of our humanity, necessary for facing the challenges confronting us in a biotechnological age. The longer answer constitutes our introduction to this volume.

We begin at the beginning: What is "bioethics," and why do we need it? Bioethics is a relatively young area of concern and field of inquiry, less than forty years old in its present incarnation—though many of the questions it leads to are in fact ancient. In the mid-1960s, following the disclosure of several abuses here and abroad, ethical attention first focused on the use of human subjects in medical experimentation. Intense public discussion established the importance of voluntary and informed consent, and institutional arrangements were subsequently developed to protect vulnerable patients against the potentially excessive zeal of otherwise worthy experimenters. Around the same time, it also became clear that advances in biomedical science and technology were raising—and would increasingly raise—more far-reaching and profound challenges to familiar human practices and ways of thinking, feeling, and acting.

By 1970, the effects of the so-called biological revolution were beginning to be felt. Oral contraceptives, tranquilizers, and psychedelic drugs were in use, as were cardiac pacemakers, respirators, and kidney dialysis machines. In vitro fertilization of human egg by human sperm had just been achieved and the first heart transplant had just been performed. People were developing a new "definition of death" that looked to brain activity rather than heartbeat or spontaneous breathing as the definitive sign of existing life. Scientists had discovered a "pleasure center" in the brain, and were exploring possible uses of implanted electrodes in this area for purposes of behavior therapy and control. Genetic screening and pre-natal diagnosis had just arrived, and scientific conferences were being held about coming prospects for gene therapy and even about genetically engineered improvements in the human race. There was great excitement about using the new knowledge and techniques to cure disease, overcome infertility, treat mental illness, and relieve much human suffering. Yet at the same time, people sensed that the new possibilities for intervening into the human body and mind would likely raise large questions, not only about safety and efficacy but also about human freedom and dignity, human self-understanding, and the kind of society we were bringing into being. No one had yet heard of bioethics or bioethicists. But their time had arrived.

Actually, the word "bioethics" was coined in 1970 by the biologist Van Rensselaer Potter—to designate a "new ethics" to be built not on philosophical or religious foundations but on the supposedly more solid ground of modern biology. But the term soon came rather to denote a domain of inquiry that examines the ethical implications of advances in biomedical science and technology for everyday life, as well as for law, social institutions, and public policy. Today, "bioethics" also names a specialized academic discipline, granting degrees in major universities and credentialing its practitioners as professional experts in the field.

Over the past thirty years, the field of bioethics has mushroomed. It has entertained discussions and debates on moral and policy issues connected with abortion, fetal tissue implantation, genetic screening (and privacy and discrimination), assisted reproductive technologies, surrogate motherhood, embryo and stem cell research, cloning, gene therapy and genetic "enhancement," the use of mechanical hearts or animal organs in transplantation, the use of performance-enhancing drugs in athletics or psychotropic drugs for modifying and controlling behavior, living wills and "Do Not Resuscitate" orders, assisted suicide and euthanasia, and the merits of hospice care—among many, many others. Ongoing attention to research with human subjects has further refined the principles and procedures needed to safeguard subjects' rights and well-being. Hospital-based ethics committees have been established to deal with difficult end-of-life issues regarding termination of treatment. Professional societies and biotechnology companies employ ethics committees to address specific issues as they arise—say, about whether to practice sex-selection, or how to insure fair access to the fruits of biotechnical innovation. Federal legislation has been enacted both to facilitate organ transplantation and to ban the buying and selling of the organs themselves. Debates continue regarding remedies for the inequities of heath care in the United States or the virtual absence of health care and public health measures in underdeveloped countries abroad. Today, bioethicists teach at most medical schools and universities, advise governments and corporations, and appear frequently in the media. Hardly a day passes without some topic of bioethical significance appearing on the front pages of the newspapers. And the President's Council on Bioethics is but the latest in a series of national bioethics commissions charged with offering advice about this entire set of developments. Bioethics business is booming, and deservedly so, for there is much of importance at stake.

In creating this Council, President George W. Bush gave us a broad mandate and, among other charges, a somewhat unusual responsibility: "to conduct fundamental inquiry into the human and moral significance of developments in biomedical and behavioral science and technology." We are also charged "to facilitate a greater understanding of bioethical issues." Yet, as the Council noted when we first convened in January 2002, many of the deep and broad human implications of the coming age of biotechnology are not today receiving adequate attention. Perhaps it is because the field is so busy attending to the novel problems that emerge almost daily. Perhaps it is because attention to devising guidelines and regulations leaves little time to reflect on the full range of human goods that we should be trying to promote or protect. But it may also be that the concerns and concepts that have come to dominate the discussions of academic and public bioethics, for all their strengths, do not by themselves get to the deepest reaches of our subject.

The major principles of professionalized bioethics, according to the leading textbook in the field, are these: (1) beneficence (or at least "non-maleficence"—in plain English: "do no harm"), (2) respect for persons, and (3) justice. As applied to particular cases, these principles translate mainly into concerns to avoid bodily harm and to do bodily good, to respect patient autonomy and to secure informed consent, and to promote equal access to health care and to provide equal protection against biohazards. So long as no one is hurt, no one's will is violated, and no one is excluded or discriminated against, there may be little to worry about. Fitting well with our society's devotion to health, freedom, and equality, this outlook governs much of today's public bioethical discourse.

Thus, we worry much that human cloning may be unsafe, but little about what it might mean for the relations between the generations should children arise not from the coupling of two but from the replication of one or should procreation come to be seen as manufacture. We worry much about genetic privacy and genetic discrimination, but little about acquiring godlike powers of deciding which genetic defects disqualify one for birth or about how we will regard our own identity should we come to be defined as largely a collection of genes. We worry much about issues of safety or unfairness when athletes use steroids or college students take stimulants, but little about the way these (and other mediating) technologies might distort the character of human activity, severing performance from effort or pleasure from the activity that ordinarily is its foundation. We worry much about the obstacles to living longer, but little about the relation between trying to live longer and living well.

In a word, we are quick to notice dangers to life, threats to freedom, and risks of discrimination or exploitation. But we are slow to think about the need to uphold human dignity and the many ways of doing and feeling and being in the world that make human life rich, deep, and fulfilling. Indeed, it sometimes seems as though our views of the meaning of our humanity have been so transformed by the technological approach to the world that we may be in danger of forgetting what we have to lose, humanly speaking.

To enlarge our vision and deepen our understanding, we need to focus not only on the astonishing new technologies but also on those (in truth, equally astonishing) aspects of "being human" on which the technologies impinge and which they may serve or threaten. For bioethical dilemmas, though generated by novel developments in biomedical science and technology, are not themselves scientific or technological matters. They are human dilemmas—individual, familial, social, political, and spiritual—confronted by human beings at various stages in the human lifespan, embedded in networks of meaning and relation, and informed by varying opinions and beliefs about better and worse, right and wrong, and how we are to live. Often, competing human goods are at stake (for example, seeking cures for disease versus respecting nascent life); in other cases, the evils we seek to avoid are deeply intertwined with the goods we ardently pursue (for example, eliminating genetic defects without stigmatizing those who have them). Moreover, both in practice and in our self-understanding, bioethical issues generally touch matters close to the core of our humanity: birth and death, body and mind, sickness and health, sex and procreation, love and family, identity and individuality, freedom and dignity, aspiration and contentment, the purposes of knowledge, the aim of technology, the meaning of suffering, the quest for meaning. A richer bioethics would attend to these matters directly and keep them central to all bioethical inquiry and judgment. A richer bioethics would feature careful and wisdom-seeking reflection regarding the full range of human goods at stake in bioethical dilemmas.

In all of its work to date, the President's Council on Bioethics has tried to practice and foster such an approach. For the Council, "bioethics" is not an ethics based on biology, but an ethics in the service of *bios*—of a life lived humanly, a course of life lived not merely physiologically, but also mentally, socially, culturally, politically, and spiritually. Even as we have tackled specific issues such as human cloning or the uses of biotechnology that lie "beyond therapy," we have sought to probe the meanings of the intersections of biology and biography, where life as lived experientially encounters the results of life studied scientifically. We have sought as best we can to clarify, promote, and defend "being human."

Where might we seek help in thinking about "life lived humanly," about birth and death, freedom and dignity, the meaning of suffering, or any of the other marks of a genuinely human experience? Since the beginnings of human self-consciousness, these matters have been the subjects of humanistic reflection and writing, capturing the attentions of great thinkers and authors. Works of history, philosophy, poetry, imaginative literature, and religious meditation have pondered and commented upon—and continue to ponder and comment upon—these matters. In the Council's own discussions and reports, we have on several occasions looked to these works for their insights and instruction (roughly a dozen of the works included in this volume have explicitly entered the conversations at our meetings or the pages of our writings). And each of us individually, explicitly or tacitly, relies on what we have learned throughout our lives from texts such as these, as we grapple with the difficult bioethical issues before us. Early recognizing the value of such readings, we have featured many selections "From Our Bookshelf" on the Council's website (www.bioethics.gov). Now, "to facilitate a greater understanding of bioethical issues," we have collected and organized them in this volume in the hope that others may discover for themselves the help that is available from wise, sensitive, and thoughtful authors, many of whom come from other times and places. As we strive to *stay* human in the age of biotechnology in ever-better and fuller ways, we must take whatever help we can get in deepening our appreciation of "*being human.*"

We do not offer these readings as authoritative or as authorities. As readers will discover, they differ too much among themselves to constitute any single coherent teaching. Rather, we offer them in the wisdom-seeking—rather than wisdom-delivering—spirit, as writings that make us think, that challenge our unexamined opinions, expand our sympathies, elevate our gaze, and illuminate important aspects of our lives that we have insufficiently understood or appreciated.

Each reading is accompanied by a brief introduction directing readers toward the bioethical implications of the text, not by drawing conclusions but by asking questions. As any teacher knows, most good books do not teach themselves. We are all frequently lazy readers, who pass off what is puzzling or unfamiliar, and, even worse, who fail to see the depth in what is, by contrast, familiar and congenial. Often our prejudices get in the way. Sometimes, our inexperience blinds us to crucial subtleties and nuances. Accordingly, we have prefaced each reading with some observations and questions designed to make for more active and discerning reading. These questions should be suitable for discussion by groups reading together or for study by individuals reading alone. In some cases, where the text seemed more remote or where we thought it helpful, we have taken a more didactic tone, asking the reader to come at the text with certain questions and concerns in mind. We have done this with mixed feelings; we do not wish to get between author and reader, nor do we wish to imperil understanding of texts written by subtler and greater minds because of our limited understandings and specialized concerns. We thus encourage the readers to use the introductions if they find them helpful, but to treat them with the proverbial grain of salt.

Readers will note, though, that in our choice of readings we have not excluded texts that evince strong moral viewpoints or that are rooted in particular religious faiths. We have welcomed all valuable anthropological or moral insights, regardless of whether they are rooted in religious faith, philosophy, or ordinary personal experience. Respect for American pluralism does not mean excluding deeply held religious (or non-religious) viewpoints or sensibilities. On the contrary, with the deepest human questions on the table, we should be eager to avail ourselves of the wisdom contained in all the great religious, literary, and philosophical traditions.

One of the virtues of an anthology is that readers are free to pick and choose what they wish to read, skipping around in no particular order. Yet, as we will now indicate—and as the introductions to each of the chapters will make even clearer—there is method in our ordering, and we think there is additional advantage in following the text straight through.

It remains, therefore, only to sketch the structure of this volume. The (ninety-five) readings are divided into ten chapters; each chapter opens with a brief introduction, setting forth the topic at hand and providing a synoptic view of the readings that follow. The ten chapters are in turn arranged in three sections.

The first section, "Natural Imperfection and Human Longing," introduces a central human question that lurks beneath the surface of many bioethical issues: Which is the proper human attitude or disposition in the world: molding or beholding? When and to what extent should we strive to change and alter nature and especially our own given nature, in an effort to improve or save it? When and to what extent should we strive to accept and appreciate nature and our own given nature, in an effort to know or savor it? This section, comprising three chapters, also introduces the means we have for acting upon these dueling impulses and longings: biomedical science and the art of medicine, both major players in the dramas of bioethics today.

In Chapter One, "The Search for Perfection," readings explore the age-old human aspiration to improve our native lot, removing our imperfections and bringing our nature closer to our ideal. Does our flourishing depend on our ability to better our form and function? Or does it depend, conversely, on our ability to accept and even celebrate our natural limitations?

In Chapter Two, "Scientific Aspirations," readings from biographies and memoirs of great scientists explore the motives and goals of scientific activity. Both as a mode of inquiry and as a body of knowledge, science has served both human aspirations—beholding and molding—although its utility as the basis of technological innovation is one of the central features of modern science. Yet science is also a human—and ethical—activity, the fulfillment of personal human desires. How do scientists themselves see the relation between theory and practice? What guides their own scientific quest?

In Chapter Three, "To Heal Sometimes, To Comfort Always," we turn from the pursuit of knowledge to the age-old medical dream: by means of such knowledge, to bring healing to the sick and wholeness to the broken, and, in the limit, to perfect our vulnerable and mortal human bodies. Readings explore the purposes of medicine, seen from the perspective of doctor and patient, and examine a vocation not only to heal but also to care and comfort.

The second section, "The Human Being and the Life Cycle," moves from aspirations of and for human beings to questions about human nature itself: What *is* a human being? And what sort of a life have we human beings been given to live? The four chapters comprising this section treat various aspects of these anthropological questions, many of them sorely neglected in much current bioethical discourse: the meaning for our identity of our embodiment; the tension between change and stability as we progress through the life cycle; the place of begetting and belonging in human flourishing, as we live with ancestors and descendants; and the meaning of mortality as the ultimate boundary of any human life. The relevance of these topics to contem-

porary bioethical arenas such as organ transplantation, assisted reproduction and genetic screening, and research to alter aging and the
human lifespan needs only to be mentioned to be seen.

In Chapter Four, "Are We Our Bodies?" readings explore the puzzling question about the relation between our bodies and our minds
(or souls). Are we mostly one or the other? Are we rather only the two
of them together? How are our lofty aspirations related to our "fleshi-
ness"? How crucial is our body to our identity and worth?

In Chapter Five, "Many Stages, One Life," readings ponder what it
means that we live in time, that we both change constantly yet continue always as "ourselves." Is there a shape or meaning to our temporal journey? What sense are we supposed to make of life's various
"stages"? What unites the beginning of our lives with its end?

In Chapter Six, "Among the Generations," we move from the life
cycle of individuals to their connections to those who came before and
those who come after. Readings explore the experience and significance of human procreation and renewal, as well as our obligations to
ancestors and descendants. How important are biological ties to the
work of human parenting and perpetuation? What is the significance
of the family tree? What do the various branches owe to one another?

In Chapter Seven, "Why Not Immortality?" we move from procreation to a more radical response to our finitude: the quest for personal
immortality. The readings consider various expressions of, and responses to, this ancient human longing. How does this longing affect
the way we spend the time of our lives? What does it imply regarding
the goodness of terrestrial life? Is mortality only a burden or also a
blessing? Does the answer depend on the truth about an afterlife?
Would our longing for immortality be satisfied by having "more of the
same"? Do we long for an endless existence or for a perfected one?

The third section, "Living Well," moves from the anthropological
questions to the ethical and spiritual ones, with a special eye on possible excellences that may be enhanced or threatened in the age of
biotechnology. The three chapters in this section deal with some of
the deepest bioethical questions: the value, if any, of vulnerability and
suffering; the importance, for living well, of unmediated and direct
engagement with the world and with our fellow creatures; and the
character of human dignity. Once again, these are matters that tend
to be neglected in current bioethical discussions. Yet on reflection,
their centrality is not difficult to recognize, especially in such matters
as our use of heroic measures to save and extend life, our increased

reliance on psychotropic drugs to handle the trials and tribulations of life, or our attempts to describe and explain human life and human freedom solely in terms of genes, hormones, or neurotransmitters.

In Chapter Eight, "Vulnerability and Suffering," the readings consider the venerable question of why we suffer, and the further question of whether there is anything to be said on suffering's behalf. Would eliminating all suffering be humanly desirable? Could it be that some forms of suffering are essential to our identities and our dignity? Or is this just a rationalizing effort, to make—quite literally—a virtue out of necessity?

In Chapter Nine, "Living Immediately," the readings look closely at the character of human activities when these are engaged in at their peak. Of special interest are instances when we can be at-work in the world wholeheartedly and immediately, unencumbered by pain and suffering and not deflected by technological or other "intermediaries." How can we take advantage of the powers technology bestows on us without hazarding distortions of the very activities these powers are meant to serve? What is required for genuine encounters with the world and with other people—for what some call "real life"—and what are the obstacles to their achievement?

Finally, in Chapter Ten, "Human Dignity," we turn explicitly to the theme that has been tacitly present throughout the volume: the dignity or worth or standing of the human creature. Though the term, "human dignity," has a lofty ring, its content is quite difficult to define. Or rather, to be more precise, many different authors and traditions define it differently, as the readings in this chapter make abundantly clear. Yet they are all struggling to reveal that elusive core of our humanity, those special qualities that make us more than beasts yet less than gods, the encouragement and defense of which may be said, arguably, to be the highest mission of a richer bioethics. Some readings will do so by argument, others by presenting instances and exemplars. Taken together, they should help us see the profoundly special character of human beings and the special virtue to which we may rise—with and without the help of biotechnology.

ACKNOWLEDGMENTS

The Council wishes to express its gratitude to the Council's able staff for its assistance in the preparation of this reader, and in particular to Rachel Wildavsky, Director of the Council's Education Project, who has served as our editor. Over a two-year period, she gathered advice on readings fit for inclusion, conferred with individual Council members, carefully excerpted and organized the final selections, drafted the introductions, and presided over the entire process with grace, skill, and good cheer. Special thanks are also due to Laura Harmon for her excellent work on permissions and production.

SECTION I:
NATURAL IMPERFECTION AND
HUMAN LONGING

CHAPTER 1:
THE SEARCH FOR PERFECTION

NATURE IS FALLIBLE AND her works are imperfect. Human beings are no exceptions; our bodies decay and perish and our powers are limited. Seemingly from the beginning, human beings have been alive to the many ways in which what we have been given falls short of what we can envision and what we desire. We are human, but can imagine gods. We die, but can imagine immortality.

But human beings have more than longings and imaginations. Although we are far from omnipotent, we have extraordinary powers, unique among the earth's creatures, to shape our environment and even ourselves according to our wills. It is perhaps not surprising, therefore, that also from the beginning human beings have struggled with two opposing responses to our lot. Should we try to mold the imperfection we have been given into something closer to our ideal? Or should we content ourselves with beholding and enjoying it as it is? And what about our own natures? Does our ability to flourish as human beings depend on our ability to improve upon the human form or function? Or might the contrary be true: does our flourishing depend on accepting—or even celebrating—our natural limitations?

All the readings in our first chapter explore this ancient and continuing dilemma. Our first reading, however, perhaps captures it best. Nathaniel Hawthorne's great short story "The Birth-mark" is the tale of an otherwise perfectly beautiful woman with a birthmark on her left cheek, "the fatal flaw of humanity which nature in one shape or another stamps ineffaceably on all her productions." This marked woman is married to an idealistic scientist who seeks to remove her blemish, only to discover that it is her "birthmark of mortality" and that removing it removes her from life itself.

The remaining readings in this chapter treat various aspects of the problem Hawthorne's story presents.

The second reading—the Latin poet Ovid's retelling of the legends of

Pygmalion and Myrrha—like "The Birth-mark" concerns a frustrated idealist who creates the perfect woman he desires, with disastrous consequences. The next two readings—Gerard Manley Hopkins's "Pied Beauty" and Lewis Thomas's "The Wonderful Mistake"—are odes to natural imperfection, its beauty and genius. Where Hawthorne's and Ovid's protagonists act upon nature to improve it, Hopkins and Thomas merely contemplate nature to admire it.

Our next four readings consider the various human weaknesses we are most tempted to seek to improve. An excerpt from Andrew M. Niccols's screenplay *Gattaca* imagines a future in which we have improved our natural powers by manipulating our genes. A passage from C. S. Lewis's *That Hideous Strength* addresses the desire to shelter the "purity" of the mind from the corporeality and decay of our bodies. Richard Selzer's "Imelda" is about the desire to perfect the body using plastic surgery. Finally, the epilogue of Stephen Braun's *The Science of Happiness* looks forward to the perfection of the soul and to a more perfect happiness.

THE BIRTH-MARK

by Nathaniel Hawthorne

"The Birth-mark" is the story of a great scientist who applies his vast knowledge to removing a birthmark from the face of his otherwise perfect wife. The scientist succeeds, but leaves his wife dead. The tale of this disastrous assault on "the visible mark of earthly imperfection" explores the troubled relationship between the human condition and the loftiest aims of science.

While the scientist, Aylmer, is wooing Georgiana, he is not troubled by her birthmark, which resembles a tiny red hand in the center of her left cheek. After they marry, though, he becomes obsessed by "the spectral Hand that wrote mortality where he would fain have worshipped." Eventually Georgiana, made miserable by his revulsion, begs him to remove her birthmark "at whatever risk."

Even after Aylmer discovers that the hand "has clutched its grasp into [her] being with a strength of which I had no previous conception," Georgiana remains fixed in her purpose. She even reflects, at this point, on her husband's "honorable love," which would not "make itself contented with an earthlier nature than he had dreamed of." With her last breath, she cautions him not to "repent that with so high and pure a feeling, you have rejected the best the earth could offer."

What is a birthmark? What does it mean to be marked at and by birth? What does Hawthorne suggest is the special significance of Georgiana's birthmark?

What animates Aylmer? What about Georgiana? Why does Georgiana allow her husband to do what he does?

Just before drinking the deadly draught, Georgiana tells Aylmer: "Life is but a sad possession to those who have attained precisely the degree of moral advancement at which I stand." Aylmer replies that she is "fit for heaven without tasting death." What degree of moral advancement has Georgiana reached? What about Aylmer?

Why did Aylmer kiss the birthmark while he waited for it to fade away?

When Aylmer shudders at Georgiana's birthmark, his shudder so distresses her that she faints. Later, she reflects that even if she could survive the erasure of her birthmark and be perfect, as Aylmer hopes, she would "satisfy his highest and deepest conception" only briefly, because for him, "each instant required something that was beyond the scope of the instant before." Yet Georgiana loves and admires her husband. Why? What is the reader to think of Aylmer?

By the end of the story, Aylmer and Georgiana are powerfully bound together. Can the bond they share be called a marriage? Why or why not?

What vision of marriage is suggested in the story's final paragraph? Is it significant that Aylmer and Georgiana have no children? Is the pursuit of perfect beauty sterile?

What are we to make of the close connections that Hawthorne implies between the love of beauty, the desire for control, and the quest for perfection? Are these things necessarily linked?

In the latter part of the last century, there lived a man of science—an eminent proficient in every branch of natural philosophy—who, not long before our story opens, had made experience of a spiritual affinity, more attractive than any chemical one. He had left his laboratory to the care of an assistant, cleared his fine countenance from the furnace-smoke, washed the stain of acids from his fingers, and persuaded a beautiful woman to become his wife. In those days when the comparatively recent discovery of electricity, and other kindred mysteries of nature, seemed to open paths into the region of miracle, it was not unusual for the love of science to rival the love of woman, in its depth and absorbing energy. The higher intellect, the imagination, the spirit, and even the heart, might all find their congenial aliment in pursuits which, as some of their ardent votaries believed, would ascend from one step of powerful intelligence to another, until the philosopher should lay his hand on the secret of creative force, and perhaps make new worlds for himself. We know not whether Aylmer possessed this degree of faith in man's ultimate control over nature. He had devoted himself, however, too unreservedly to scientific studies, ever to be weaned from them by any second passion. His love for his young wife might prove the stronger of the two; but it could only be by intertwining itself with his love of science, and uniting the strength of the latter to its own.

Such a union accordingly took place, and was attended with truly remarkable consequences, and a deeply impressive moral. One day, very soon after their marriage, Aylmer sat gazing at his wife, with a trouble in his countenance that grew stronger, until he spoke.

"Georgiana," said he, "has it never occurred to you that the mark upon your cheek might be removed?"

"No, indeed," said she, smiling; but perceiving the seriousness of his manner, she blushed deeply. "To tell you the truth, it has been so often called a charm, that I was simple enough to imagine it might be so."

"Ah, upon another face, perhaps it might," replied her husband. "But never on yours! No, dearest Georgiana, you came so nearly perfect from the hand of Nature, that this slightest possible defect—which we hesitate whether to term a defect or a beauty—shocks me, as being the visible mark of earthly imperfection."

"Shocks you, my husband!" cried Georgiana, deeply hurt; at first reddening with momentary anger, but then bursting into tears. "Then why did you take me from my mother's side? You cannot love what shocks you!"

To explain this conversation, it must be mentioned, that, in the centre of Georgiana's left cheek, there was a singular mark, deeply interwoven, as it were, with the texture and substance of her face. In the usual state of her complexion,—a healthy though delicate bloom,—the mark wore a tint of deeper crimson, which imperfectly defined its shape amid the surrounding rosiness. When she blushed, it gradually became more indistinct, and finally vanished amid the triumphant rush of blood, that bathed the whole cheek with its brilliant glow. But, if any shifting emotion caused her to turn pale, there was the mark again, a crimson stain upon the snow, in what Aylmer sometimes deemed an almost fearful distinctness. Its shape bore not a little similarity to the human hand, though of the smallest pigmy size. Georgiana's lovers were wont to say, that some fairy, at her birth-hour, had laid her tiny hand upon the infant's cheek, and left this impress there, in token of the magic endowments that were to give her such sway over all hearts. Many a desperate swain would have risked life for the privilege of pressing his lips to the mysterious hand. It must not be concealed, however, that the impression wrought by this fairy sign-manual varied exceedingly, according to the difference of temperament in the beholders. Some fastidious persons—but they were exclusively of her own sex—affirmed that the Bloody Hand, as they chose to call it, quite destroyed the effect of Georgiana's béauty, and rendered her countenance even hideous. But it would be as reasonable to say, that one of those small blue stains, which sometimes occur in the purest statuary marble, would convert the Eve of Powers to a monster. Masculine observers, if the birth-mark did not heighten their admiration, contented themselves with wishing it away, that the world might possess one living specimen of ideal loveliness, without the semblance of a flaw. After his marriage—for he thought little or nothing of the matter before—Aylmer discovered that this was the case with himself.

Had she been less beautiful—if Envy's self could have found aught else to sneer at—he might have felt his affection heightened by the prettiness of this mimic hand, now vaguely portrayed, now lost, now stealing forth again, and glimmering to-and-fro with every pulse of emotion that throbbed within her heart. But, seeing her otherwise so perfect, he found this one defect grow more and more intolerable, with every moment of their united lives. It was the fatal flaw of humanity, which Nature, in one shape or another, stamps ineffaceably on all her productions, either to imply that they are temporary and finite, or that their perfection must be wrought by toil and pain. The Crimson Hand expressed the ineludible gripe, in which mortality clutches the highest and purest of earthly mould, degrading them into kindred with the lowest, and even with the very brutes, like whom their visible frames return to dust. In this manner, selecting it as the symbol of his wife's liability to sin, sorrow, decay, and death, Aylmer's sombre imagination was not long in rendering the birth-mark a frightful object, causing him more trouble and horror than ever Georgiana's beauty, whether of soul or sense, had given him delight.

At all the seasons which should have been their happiest, he invariably, and without intending it—nay, in spite of a purpose to the contrary—reverted to this one disastrous topic. Trifling as it at first appeared, it so connected itself with innumerable trains of thought, and modes of feeling, that it became the central point of all. With the morning twilight, Aylmer opened his eyes upon his wife's face, and recognized the symbol of imperfection; and when they sat together at the evening hearth, his eyes wandered stealthily to her cheek, and beheld, flickering with the blaze of the wood fire, the spectral Hand that wrote mortality, where he would fain have worshipped. Georgiana soon learned to shudder at his gaze. It needed but a glance, with the peculiar expression that his face often wore, to change the roses of her cheek into a deathlike paleness, amid which the Crimson Hand was brought strongly out, like a bas-relief of ruby on the whitest marble.

Late, one night, when the lights were growing dim, so as hardly to betray the stain on the poor wife's cheek, she herself, for the first time, voluntarily took up the subject.

"Do you remember, my dear Aylmer," said she, with a feeble attempt at a smile—"have you any recollection of a dream, last night, about this odious Hand?"

"None!—none whatever!" replied Aylmer, starting; but then he added in a dry, cold tone, affected for the sake of concealing the real depth of his emotion:—"I might well dream of it; for before I fell asleep, it had taken a pretty firm hold of my fancy."

"And you did dream of it," continued Georgiana, hastily; for she dreaded lest a gush of tears should interrupt what she had to say—"A terrible dream! I wonder that you can forget it. Is it possible to forget this one expression?—'It is in her heart now—we must have it out!'—Reflect, my husband; for by all means I would have you recall that dream."

The mind is in a sad note, when Sleep, the all-involving, cannot confine her spectres within the dim region of her sway, but suffers them to break forth, affrighting this actual life with secrets that perchance belong to a deeper one. Aylmer now remembered his dream. He had fancied himself, with his servant Aminadab, attempting an operation for the removal of the birth-mark. But the deeper went the knife, the deeper sank the Hand, until at length its tiny grasp appeared to have caught hold of Georgiana's heart; whence, however, her husband was inexorably resolved to cut or wrench it away.

When the dream had shaped itself perfectly in his memory, Aylmer sat in his wife's presence with a guilty feeling. Truth often finds its way to the mind close-muffled in robes of sleep, and then speaks with un-compromising directness of matters in regard to which we practise an unconscious self-deception, during our waking moments. Until now, he had not been aware of the tyrannizing influence acquired by one idea over his mind, and of the lengths which he might find in his heart to go, for the sake of giving himself peace.

"Aylmer," resumed Georgiana, solemnly, "I know not what may be the cost to both of us, to rid me of this fatal birth-mark. Perhaps its removal may cause cureless deformity. Or, it may be, the stain goes as deep as life itself. Again, do we know that there is a possibility, on any terms, of unclasping the firm gripe of this little Hand, which was laid upon me before I came into the world?"

"Dearest Georgiana, I have spent much thought upon the subject," hastily interrupted Aylmer—"I am convinced of the perfect practicabil-ity of its removal."

"If there be the remotest possibility of it," continued Georgiana, "let the attempt be made, at whatever risk. Danger is nothing to me; for life—while this hateful mark makes me the object of your horror and disgust—life is a burthen which I would fling down with joy. Either re-move this dreadful Hand, or take my wretched life! You have deep sci-ence! All the world bears witness of it. You have achieved great wonders! Cannot you remove this little, little mark, which I cover with the tips of two small fingers? Is this beyond your power, for the sake of your own peace, and to save your poor wife from madness?"

"Noblest—dearest—tenderest wife!" cried Aylmer, rapturously. "Doubt not my power. I have already given this matter the deepest thought—

thought which might almost have enlightened me to create a being less perfect than yourself. Georgiana, you have led me deeper than ever into the heart of science. I feel myself fully competent to render this dear cheek as faultless as its fellow; and then, most beloved, what will be my triumph, when I shall have corrected what Nature left imperfect, in her fairest work! Even Pygmalion, when his sculptured woman assumed life, felt not greater ecstasy than mine will be."

"It is resolved, then," said Georgiana, faintly smiling,—"And, Aylmer, spare me not, though you should find the birth-mark take refuge in my heart at last."

Her husband tenderly kissed her cheek—her right cheek—not that which bore the impress of the Crimson Hand.

The next day, Aylmer apprized his wife of a plan that he had formed, whereby he might have opportunity for the intense thought and constant watchfulness, which the proposed operation would require; while Georgiana, likewise, would enjoy the perfect repose essential to its success. They were to seclude themselves in the extensive apartments occupied by Aylmer as a laboratory, and where, during his toilsome youth, he had made discoveries in the elemental powers of nature, that had roused the admiration of all the learned societies in Europe. Seated calmly in this laboratory, the pale philosopher had investigated the secrets of the highest cloud-region and of the profoundest mines; he had satisfied himself of the causes that kindled and kept alive the fires of the volcano; and had explained the mystery of fountains, and how it is that they gush forth, some so bright and pure, and others with such rich medicinal virtues, from the dark bosom of the earth. Here, too, at an earlier period, he had studied the wonders of the human frame, and attempted to fathom the very process by which Nature assimilates all her precious influences from earth and air, and from the spiritual world, to create and foster Man, her masterpiece. The latter pursuit, however, Aylmer had long laid aside, in unwilling recognition of the truth, against which all seekers sooner or later stumble, that our great creative Mother, while she amuses us with apparently working in the broadest sunshine, is yet severely careful to keep her own secrets, and, in spite of her pretended openness, shows us nothing but results. She permits us indeed, to mar, but seldom to mend, and, like a jealous patentee, on no account to make. Now, however, Aylmer resumed these half-forgotten investigations; not, of course, with such hopes or wishes as first suggested them; but because they involved much physiological truth, and lay in the path of his proposed scheme for the treatment of Georgiana.

As he led her over the threshold of the laboratory, Georgiana was cold and tremulous. Aylmer looked cheerfully into her face, with intent to reassure her, but was so startled with the intense glow of the birth-mark upon the whiteness of her cheek, that he could not restrain a strong convulsive shudder. His wife fainted.

"Aminadab! Aminadab!" shouted Aylmer, stamping violently on the floor.

Forthwith, there issued from an inner apartment a man of low stature, but bulky frame, with shaggy hair hanging about his visage, which was grimed with the vapors of the furnace. This personage had been Aylmer's under-worker during his whole scientific career, and was admirably fitted for that office by his great mechanical readiness, and the skill with which, while incapable of comprehending a single principle, he executed all the practical details of his master's experiments. With his vast strength, his shaggy hair, his smoky aspect, and the indescribable earthiness that incrusted him, he seemed to represent man's physical nature; while Aylmer's slender figure, and pale, intellectual face, were no less apt a type of the spiritual element.

"Throw open the door of the boudoir, Aminadab," said Aylmer, "and burn a pastille."

"Yes, master," answered Aminadab, looking intently at the lifeless form of Georgiana; and then he muttered to himself:—"If she were my wife, I'd never part with that birth-mark."

When Georgiana recovered consciousness, she found herself breathing an atmosphere of penetrating fragrance, the gentle potency of which had recalled her from her deathlike faintness. The scene around her looked like enchantment. Aylmer had converted those smoky, dingy, sombre rooms, where he had spent his brightest years in recondite pursuits, into a series of beautiful apartments, not unfit to be the secluded abode of a lovely woman. The walls were hung with gorgeous curtains, which imparted the combination of grandeur and grace, that no other species of adornment can achieve; and as they fell from the ceiling to the floor, their rich and ponderous folds, concealing all angles and straight lines, appeared to shut in the scene from infinite space. For aught Georgiana knew, it might be a pavilion among the clouds. And Aylmer, excluding the sunshine, which would have interfered with his chemical processes, had supplied its place with perfumed lamps, emitting flames of various hue, but all uniting in a soft, empurpled radiance. He now knelt by his wife's side, watching her earnestly, but without alarm; for he was confident in his science, and felt that he could draw a magic circle round her, within which no evil might intrude.

"Where am I?—Ah, I remember!" said Georgiana, faintly; and she placed her hand over her cheek, to hide the terrible mark from her husband's eyes.

"Fear not, dearest!" exclaimed he. "Do not shrink from me! Believe me, Georgiana, I even rejoice in this single imperfection, since it will be such rapture to remove it."

"Oh, spare me!" sadly replied his wife—"Pray do not look at it again. I never can forget that convulsive shudder."

In order to soothe Georgiana, and, as it were, to release her mind from the burthen of actual things, Aylmer now put in practice some of the light and playful secrets, which science had taught him among its profounder lore. Airy figures, absolutely bodiless ideas, and forms of unsubstantial beauty, came and danced before her, imprinting their momentary footsteps on beams of light. Though she had some indistinct idea of the method of these optical phenomena, still the illusion was almost perfect enough to warrant the belief, that her husband possessed sway over the spiritual world. Then again, when she felt a wish to look forth from her seclusion, immediately, as if her thoughts were answered, the procession of external existence flitted across a screen. The scenery and the figures of actual life were perfectly represented, but with that bewitching, yet indescribable difference, which always makes a picture, an image, or a shadow, so much more attractive than the original. When wearied of this, Aylmer bade her cast her eyes upon a vessel, containing a quantity of earth. She did so, with little interest at first, but was soon startled, to perceive the germ of a plant, shooting upward from the soil. Then came the slender stalk—the leaves gradually unfolded themselves— and amid them was a perfect and lovely flower.

"It is magical!" cried Georgiana, "I dare not touch it."

"Nay, pluck it," answered Aylmer, "pluck it, and inhale its brief perfume while you may. The flower will wither in a few moments, and leave nothing save its brown seed-vessels—but thence may be perpetuated a race as ephemeral as itself."

But Georgiana had no sooner touched the flower than the whole plant suffered a blight, its leaves turning coal-black, as if by the agency of fire.

"There was too powerful a stimulus," said Aylmer thoughtfully.

To make up for this abortive experiment, he proposed to take her portrait by a scientific process of his own invention. It was to be effected by rays of light striking upon a polished plate of metal. Georgiana assented—but, on looking at the result, was affrighted to find the features of the portrait blurred and indefinable; while the minute figure of a hand appeared where the cheek should have been. Aylmer snatched the metallic plate, and threw it into a jar of corrosive acid.

Soon, however, he forgot these mortifying failures. In the intervals of study and chemical experiment, he came to her, flushed and exhausted, but seemed invigorated by her presence, and spoke in glowing language of the resources of his art. He gave a history of the long dynasty of the Alchemists, who spent so many ages in quest of the universal solvent, by which the Golden Principle might be elicited from all things vile and base. Aylmer appeared to believe, that, by the plainest scientific logic, it was altogether within the limits of possibility to discover this long-sought medium; but, he added, a philosopher who should go deep enough to acquire the power, would attain too lofty a wisdom to stoop to the exercise of it. Not less singular were his opinions in regard to the Elixir Vitae. He more than intimated, that it was his option to concoct a liquid that should prolong life for years—perhaps interminably—but that it would produce a discord in nature, which all the world, and chiefly the quaffer of the immortal nostrum, would find cause to curse.

"Aylmer, are you in earnest?" asked Georgiana, looking at him with amazement and fear; "it is terrible to possess such power, or even to dream of possessing it!"

"Oh, do not tremble, my love!" said her husband, "I would not wrong either you or myself by working such inharmonious effects upon our lives. But I would have you consider how trifling, in comparison, is the skill requisite to remove this little Hand."

At the mention of the birth-mark, Georgiana, as usual, shrank, as if a red-hot iron had touched her cheek.

Again Aylmer applied himself to his labors. She could hear his voice in the distant furnace-room, giving directions to Aminadab, whose harsh, uncouth, misshapen tones were audible in response, more like the grunt or growl of a brute than human speech. After hours of absence, Aylmer reappeared, and proposed that she should now examine his cabinet of chemical products, and natural treasures of the earth. Among the former he showed her a small vial, in which, he remarked, was contained a gentle yet most powerful fragrance, capable of impregnating all the breezes that blow across a kingdom. They were of inestimable value, the contents of that little vial; and, as he said so, he threw some of the perfume into the air, and filled the room with piercing and invigorating delight.

"And what is this?" asked Georgiana, pointing to a small crystal globe, containing a gold-colored liquid. "It is so beautiful to the eye, that I could imagine it the Elixir of Life."

"In one sense it is," replied Aylmer, "or rather the Elixir of Immortality. It is the most precious poison that ever was concocted in this world. By its aid, I could apportion the lifetime of any mortal at whom you might point your finger. The strength of the dose would determine whether he were to linger out years, or drop dead in the midst of a breath. No king, on his guarded throne, could keep his life, if I, in my private station, should deem that the welfare of millions justified me in depriving him of it."

"Why do you keep such a terrific drug?" inquired Georgiana in horror.

"Do not mistrust me, dearest!" said her husband, smiling; "its virtuous potency is yet greater than its harmful one. But, see! here is a powerful cosmetic. With a few drops of this, in a vase of water, freckles may be washed away as easily as the hands are cleansed. A stronger infusion would take the blood out of the cheek, and leave the rosiest beauty a pale ghost."

"Is it with this lotion that you intend to bathe my cheek?" asked Georgiana, anxiously.

"Oh, no!" hastily replied her husband—"this is merely superficial. Your case demands a remedy that shall go deeper."

In his interviews with Georgiana, Aylmer generally made minute inquiries as to her sensations, and whether the confinement of the rooms, and the temperature of the atmosphere, agreed with her. These questions had such a particular drift, that Georgiana began to conjecture that she was already subjected to certain physical influences, either breathed in with the fragrant air, or taken with her food. She fancied, likewise—but it might be altogether fancy—that there was a stirring up of her system,—a strange indefinite sensation creeping through her veins, and tingling, half painfully, half pleasurably, at her heart. Still, whenever she dared to look into the mirror, there she beheld herself, pale as a white rose, and with the crimson birth-mark stamped upon her cheek. Not even Aylmer now hated it so much as she.

To dispel the tedium of the hours which her husband found it necessary to devote to the processes of combination and analysis, Georgiana turned over the volumes of his scientific library. In many dark old tomes, she met with chapters full of romance and poetry. They were the works of philosophers of the middle ages, such as Albertus Magnus, Cornelius Agrippa, Paracelsus, and the famous friar who created the prophetic Brazen Head. All these antique naturalists stood in advance of their centuries, yet were imbued with some of their credulity, and therefore were believed, and perhaps imagined themselves, to have acquired from the investigation of nature a power above nature, and from physics a sway over the spiritual world. Hardly less curious and imaginative were the early volumes of the Transactions of the Royal Society, in which the members, knowing little of the limits of natural possibility, were continually recording wonders, or proposing methods whereby wonders might be wrought.

But, to Georgiana, the most engrossing volume was a large folio from her husband's own hand, in which he had recorded every experiment of his scientific career, with its original aim, the methods adopted for its development, and its final success or failure, with the circumstances to which either event was attributable. The book, in truth, was both the history and emblem of his ardent, ambitious, imaginative, yet practical and laborious, life. He handled physical details, as if there were nothing beyond them; yet spiritualized them all, and redeemed himself from materialism, by his strong and eager aspiration towards the infinite. In his grasp, the veriest clod of earth assumed a soul. Georgiana, as she read, reverenced Aylmer, and loved him more profoundly than ever, but with a less entire dependence on his judgment than heretofore. Much as he had accomplished, she could not but observe that his most splendid successes were almost invariably failures, if compared with the ideal at which he aimed. His brightest diamonds were the merest pebbles, and felt to be so by himself, in comparison with the inestimable gems which lay hidden beyond his reach. The volume, rich with achievements that had won renown for its author, was yet as melancholy a record as ever mortal hand had penned. It was the sad confession, and continual exemplification, of the short-comings of the composite man—the spirit burthened with clay and working in matter—and of the despair that assails the higher nature, at finding itself so miserably thwarted by the earthly part. Perhaps every man of genius, in whatever sphere, might recognize the image of his own experience in Aylmer's journal.

So deeply did these reflections affect Georgiana, that she laid her face upon the open volume, and burst into tears. In this situation she was found by her husband.

"It is dangerous to read in a sorcerer's books," said he, with a smile, though his countenance was uneasy and displeased. "Georgiana, there are pages in that volume, which I can scarcely glance over and keep my senses. Take heed lest it prove as detrimental to you!"

"It has made me worship you more than ever," said she.

"Ah! wait for this one success," rejoined he, "then worship me if you will. I shall deem myself hardly unworthy of it. But, come! I have sought you for the luxury of your voice. Sing to me, dearest!"

So she poured out the liquid music of her voice to quench the thirst of his spirit. He then took his leave, with a boyish exuberance of gaiety, assuring her that her seclusion would endure but a little longer, and that the result was already certain. Scarcely had he departed, when Georgiana felt irresistibly impelled to follow him. She had forgotten to inform Aylmer of a symptom, which, for two or three hours past, had begun to excite her attention. It was a sensation in the fatal birth-mark, not painful, but which induced a restlessness throughout her system. Hastening after her husband, she intruded, for the first time, into the laboratory.

The first thing that struck her eye was the furnace, that hot and feverish worker, with the intense glow of its fire, which, by the quantities of soot clustered above it, seemed to have been burning for ages. There was a distilling apparatus in full operation. Around the room were retorts, tubes, cylinders, crucibles, and other apparatus of chemical research. An electrical machine stood ready for immediate use. The atmosphere felt oppressively close, and was tainted with gaseous odors, which had been tormented forth by the processes of science. The severe and homely simplicity of the apartment, with its naked walls and brick pavement, looked strange, accustomed as Georgiana had become to the fantastic elegance of her boudoir. But what chiefly, indeed almost solely, drew her attention, was the aspect of Aylmer himself.

He was pale as death, anxious, and absorbed, and hung over the furnace as if it depended upon his utmost watchfulness whether the liquid, which it was distilling, should be the draught of immortal happiness or misery. How different from the sanguine and joyous mien that he had assumed for Georgiana's encouragement!

"Carefully now, Aminadab! Carefully, thou human machine! Carefully, thou man of clay!" muttered Aylmer, more to himself than his assistant. "Now, if there be a thought too much or too little, it is all over!"

"Hoh! hoh!" mumbled Aminadab—"look, master, look!"

Aylmer raised his eyes hastily, and at first reddened, then grew paler than ever, on beholding Georgiana. He rushed towards her, and seized her arm with a gripe that left the print of his fingers upon it.

"Why do you come hither? Have you no trust in your husband?" cried he impetuously. "Would you throw the blight of that fatal birth-mark over my labors? It is not well done. Go, prying woman, go!"

"Nay, Aylmer," said Georgiana, with the firmness of which she possessed no stinted endowment, "it is not you that have a right to complain. You mistrust your wife! You have concealed the anxiety with which you watch the development of this experiment. Think not so unworthily of me, my husband! Tell me all the risk we run; and fear not that I shall shrink, for my share in it is far less than your own!"

"No, no, Georgiana!" said Aylmer impatiently, "it must not be."

"I submit," replied she calmly. "And, Aylmer, I shall quaff whatever draught you bring me; but it will be on the same principle that would induce me to take a dose of poison, if offered by your hand."

"My noble wife," said Aylmer, deeply moved, "I knew not the height and depth of your nature, until now. Nothing shall be concealed. Know, then, that this Crimson Hand, superficial as it seems, has clutched its grasp into your being, with a strength of which I had no previous conception. I have already administered agents powerful enough to do aught except to change your entire physical system. Only one thing remains to be tried. If that fail us, we are ruined!"

"Why did you hesitate to tell me this?" asked she.

"Because, Georgiana," said Aylmer, in a low voice, "there is danger!"

"Danger? There is but one danger—that this horrible stigma shall be left upon my cheek!" cried Georgiana. "Remove it! remove it!—whatever be the cost, or we shall both go mad!"

"Heaven knows, your words are too true," said Aylmer, sadly. "And now, dearest, return to your boudoir. In a little while, all will be tested."

He conducted her back, and took leave of her with a solemn tenderness, which spoke far more than his words how much was now at stake. After his departure, Georgiana became wrapt in musings. She considered the character of Aylmer, and did it completer justice than at any previous moment. Her heart exulted, while it trembled, at his honorable love, so pure and lofty that it would accept nothing less than perfection, nor miserably make itself contented with an earthlier nature than he had dreamed of. She felt how much more precious was such a sentiment, than that meaner kind which would have borne with the imperfection for her sake, and have been guilty of treason to holy love, by degrading its perfect idea to the level of the actual. And, with her whole spirit, she prayed, that, for a single moment, she might satisfy his highest and deepest conception. Longer than one moment, she well knew, it could not be; for his spirit was ever on the march—ever ascending—and each instant required something that was beyond the scope of the instant before.

The sound of her husband's footsteps aroused her. He bore a crystal goblet containing a liquor colorless as water, but bright enough to be the draught of immortality. Aylmer was pale; but it seemed rather the consequence of a highly wrought state of mind, and tension of spirit, than of fear or doubt.

"The concoction of the draught has been perfect," said he, in answer to Georgiana's look. "Unless all my science have deceived me, it cannot fail."

"Save on your account, my dearest Aylmer," observed his wife, "I might wish to put off this birth-mark of mortality by relinquishing mortality itself, in preference to any other mode. Life is but a sad possession to those who have attained precisely the degree of moral advancement at which I stand. Were I weaker and blinder, it might be happiness. Were I stronger, it might be endured hopefully. But, being what I find myself, methinks I am of all mortals the most fit to die."

"You are fit for heaven without tasting death!" replied her husband. "But why do we speak of dying? The draught cannot fail. Behold its effect upon this plant!"

On the window-seat there stood a geranium, diseased with yellow blotches, which had overspread all its leaves. Aylmer poured a small quantity of the liquid upon the soil in which it grew. In a little time, when the roots of the plant had taken up the moisture, the unsightly blotches began to be extinguished in a living verdure.

"There needed no proof," said Georgiana, quietly. "Give me the goblet. I joyfully stake all upon your word."

"Drink, then, thou lofty creature!" exclaimed Aylmer, with fervid admiration. "There is no taint of imperfection on thy spirit. Thy sensible frame, too, shall soon be all perfect!"

She quaffed the liquid, and returned the goblet to his hand.

"It is grateful," said she, with a placid smile. "Methinks it is like water from a heavenly fountain; for it contains I know not what of unobtrusive fragrance and deliciousness. It allays a feverish thirst, that had parched me for many days. Now, dearest, let me sleep. My earthly senses are closing over my spirit, like the leaves around the heart of a rose, at sunset."

She spoke the last words with a gentle reluctance, as if it required almost more energy than she could command to pronounce the faint and lingering syllables. Scarcely had they loitered through her lips, ere she was lost in slumber. Aylmer sat by her side, watching her aspect with the emotions proper to a man, the whole value of whose existence was involved in the process now to be tested. Mingled with this mood, however, was the philosophic investigation, characteristic of the man of science. Not the minutest symptom escaped him. A heightened flush of the cheek—a slight irregularity of breath—a quiver of the eyelid—a hardly perceptible tremor through the frame—such were the details which, as the moments passed, he wrote down in his folio volume. Intense thought had set its stamp upon every previous page of that volume; but the thoughts of years were all concentrated upon the last.

While thus employed, he failed not to gaze often at the fatal Hand,

and not without a shudder. Yet once, by a strange and unaccountable impulse, he pressed it with his lips. His spirit recoiled, however, in the very act, and Georgiana, out of the midst of her deep sleep, moved uneasily and murmured, as if in remonstrance. Again, Aylmer resumed his watch. Nor was it without avail. The Crimson Hand, which at first had been strongly visible upon the marble paleness of Georgiana's cheek now grew more faintly outlined. She remained not less pale than ever; but the birth-mark, with every breath that came and went, lost somewhat of its former distinctness. Its presence had been awful; its departure was more awful still. Watch the stain of the rainbow fading out of the sky; and you will know how that mysterious symbol passed away.

"By Heaven, it is well nigh gone!" said Aylmer to himself, in almost irrepressible ecstasy. "I can scarcely trace it now. Success! Success! And now it is like the faintest rose-color. The slightest flush of blood across her cheek would overcome it. But she is so pale!"

He drew aside the window-curtain, and suffered the light of natural day to fall into the room, and rest upon her cheek. At the same time, he heard a gross, hoarse chuckle, which he had long known as his servant Aminadab's expression of delight.

"Ah, clod! Ah, earthly mass!" cried Aylmer, laughing in a sort of frenzy. "You have served me well! Matter and Spirit—Earth and Heaven—have both done their part in this! Laugh, thing of senses! You have earned the right to laugh."

These exclamations broke Georgiana's sleep. She slowly unclosed her eyes, and gazed into the mirror, which her husband had arranged for that purpose. A faint smile flitted over her lips, when she recognized how barely perceptible was now that Crimson Hand, which had once blazed forth with such disastrous brilliancy as to scare away all their happiness. But then her eyes sought Aylmer's face, with a trouble and anxiety that he could by no means account for.

"My poor Aylmer!" murmured she.

"Poor? Nay, richest! Happiest! Most favored!" exclaimed he. "My peerless bride, it is successful! You are perfect!"

"My poor Aylmer!" she repeated, with a more than human tenderness. "You have aimed loftily!—you have done nobly! Do not repent, that, with so high and pure a feeling, you have rejected the best that earth could offer. Aylmer—dearest Aylmer—I am dying!"

Alas, it was too true! The fatal Hand had grappled with the mystery of life, and was the bond by which an angelic spirit kept itself in union with a mortal frame. As the last crimson tint of the birth-mark—that sole token of human imperfection—faded from her cheek, the parting breath of the now perfect woman passed into the atmosphere, and her soul, lingering a moment near her husband, took its heavenward flight. Then a hoarse, chuckling laugh was heard again! Thus ever does the gross Fatality of Earth exult in its invariable triumph over the immortal essence, which, in this dim sphere of half-development, demands the completeness of a higher state. Yet, had Alymer reached a profounder wisdom, he need not thus have flung away the happiness, which would have woven his mortal life of the self-same texture with the celestial. The momentary circumstance was too strong for him; he failed to look beyond the shadowy scope of Time, and living once for all in Eternity, to find the perfect Future in the present.

Excerpts from
METAMORPHOSES
Pygmalion and *Myrrha*
by Ovid, translated by A. D. Melville

In Metamorphoses *the Latin poet Ovid tells "of bodies changed to other forms."*
The first part of the excerpt that follows tells of the sculptor Pygmalion's cre-
ation of a perfectly beautiful woman, who is later brought to life for him to
marry. The latter half describes the consequences of this marriage two genera-
tions later.

The excerpt opens with a description of the Propoetides, a race living in
Amathus, Pygmalion's home. The Propoetides offend Venus by their impiety.
Venus, goddess of beauty and erotic love, takes revenge on them by turning
them into prostitutes. Seeing the prostitutes, Pygmalion is so horrified by "the
countless vices nature gives to womankind" that he avoids all women. In-
stead, he carves an ivory woman "more beautiful than ever woman born,"
and falls in love with her.

Pygmalion treats his ivory woman not as an artist treats his creation, but as
a husband treats a wife. Yet despite his attentions to her, she remains hard and
unresponsive. At a festival to honor Venus, "half afraid," Pygmalion beseech-
es the goddess for the ivory woman's "living likeness." When he returns to his
statue, the woman comes to life beneath his fingers, "and shyly raise[s] her
eyes to his and [sees] the world and him." Venus blesses "the union she [has]
made" and a daughter, Paphos, is born.

In the next, "terrible" tale, Paphos' granddaughter, Myrrha, falls in love
with her father, Cinyras, who is Paphos's son. Knowing her love is forbidden
by human laws, she resolves to take her own life. Her nurse, however, discov-
ers that she is planning suicide, and learns why. To save Myrrha's life, the
nurse takes the girl to her father under cloak of darkness. When at last Cinyras
brings in a lamp and learns who she is, he draws his sword.

Myrrha flees and wanders, until it is time for her to give birth to the child of
her father. Then "not knowing what to wish, afraid of death and tired of life,"
she asks to be "expel[led] from both realms" rather than "outrage" either one.
Her prayer is answered. She is turned into a tree.

From Metamorphoses by Ovid, translated and edited by A. D. Melville (1986). By
permission of Oxford University Press.

Myrrha's son, the beautiful Adonis, is born through the bark. He grows up
to "[avenge] his mother's passion" by becoming the mortal love object of Venus. Pursuing him, Venus abandons her previous haunts, including Amathus
and heaven itself.

Why does Pygmalion reject womankind? Why does he create the perfect
statuesque woman as his own "masterwork"? Why does he love her? Why is
Pygmalion not satisfied with his "perfect" creation? What might she have in
common with the Propoetides who repelled him?

Pygmalion is "half afraid" to ask Venus for what he truly wants. He therefore requests the "living likeness" of the woman he has made, not the woman
herself. Why was he afraid to ask that his creation be brought to life? Is there
something wrong with his desire? Why does Venus grant his real wish? Is there
something wrong with her doing so?

Is Pygmalion's wish to vivify and unite with his own artistic creation tantamount to the incestuous union of his descendants, Myrrha and Cinyras?

Is it fitting that Adonis, the descendant of Pygmalion and his creation,
should cause Venus to abandon Amathus, a land that worships her, in fruitless
pursuit of a mortal beloved?

What light does this story cast on the character and hazards of our search
for perfection?

. . . Even so the obscene Propoetides had dared
Deny Venus' divinity. For that
The goddess' rage, it's said, made them the first
Strumpets to prostitute their bodies' charms.
As shame retreated and their cheeks grew hard,
  They turned with little change to stones of flint.

Pygmalion

Pygmalion had seen these women spend
Their days in wickedness, and horrified
At all the countless vices nature gives
To womankind lived celibate and long
Lacked the companionship of married love.
Meanwhile he carved his snow-white ivory
With marvellous triumphant artistry
And gave it perfect shape, more beautiful
Than ever woman born. His masterwork

Fired him with love. It seemed to be alive,
Its face to be a real girl's, a girl
Who wished to move—but modesty forbade.
Such art his art concealed. In admiration
His heart desired the body he had formed.
With many a touch he tries it—is it flesh
Or ivory? Not ivory still, he's sure!
Kisses he gives and thinks they are returned;
He speaks to it, caresses it, believes
The firm new flesh beneath his fingers yields,
And fears the limbs may darken with a bruise.
And now fond words he whispers, now brings gifts
That girls delight in—shells and polished stones,
And little birds and flowers of every hue,
Lilies and coloured balls and beads of amber,
The tear-drops of the daughters of the Sun.
He decks her limbs with robes and on her fingers
Sets splendid rings, a necklace round her neck.
Pearls in her ears, a pendant on her breast;
Lovely she looked, yet unadorned she seemed
In nakedness no whit less beautiful.
He laid her on a couch of purple silk,
Called her his darling, cushioning her head,
As if she relished it, on softest down.
    Venus' day came, the holiest festival
All Cyprus celebrates; incense rose high
And heifers, with their wide horns gilded, fell
Beneath the blade that struck their snowy necks,
Pygmalion, his offering given, prayed
Before the altar, half afraid, "Vouchsafe,
O Gods, if all things you can grant, my bride
Shall be"—he dared not say my ivory girl—
"The living likeness of my ivory girl."
And golden Venus (for her presence graced
Her feast) knew well the purpose of his prayer;
And, as an omen of her favouring power,
Thrice did the flame burn bright and leap up high.
And he went home, home to his heart's delight,
And kissed her as she lay, and she seemed warm;
Again he kissed her and with marvelling touch
Caressed her breast; beneath his touch the flesh

Grew soft, its ivory hardness vanishing,
And yielded to his hands, as in the sun
Wax of Hymettus softens and is shaped
By practised fingers into many forms,
And usefulness acquires by being used.
His heart was torn with wonder and misgiving,
Delight and terror that it was not true!
Again and yet again he tried his hopes—
She was alive! The pulse beat in her veins!
And then indeed in words that overflowed
He poured his thanks to Venus, and at last
His lips pressed real lips, and she, his girl,
Felt every kiss, and blushed, and shyly raised
Her eyes to his and saw the world and him.
The goddess graced the union she had made,
And when nine times the crescent moon had filled
Her silver orb, an infant girl was born,
Paphos, from whom the island takes its name.

Myrrha

Her son was Cinyras, who might have been
Numbered among the fortunate, had he
Been childless. Terrible my tale will be!
Away, daughters! Away, parents! Away!
Or, if my singing charms you, hold *this* tale
In disbelief; suppose the deed not done;
Or, with belief, believe the punishment. . . .
. . . To hate one's father is a crime; this love
A greater crime than hate.
   From everywhere
The eager suitors came; the golden youth
Of all the Orient vied to win her hand.
Choose, Myrrha, one among that company
So long as *one* among them shall not be!
In truth she fought the love she felt was foul.
"What are these thoughts?" she asked herself; "My aim,
What is it? May the gods, may duty's bond,
The sacred rights of parents, stop this crime,
If it is crime. Yet surely duty's bond
They say does not condemn such love as this.

Why, other creatures couple as they choose
Regardless. If a heifer's mounted by
Her father, that's no shame; a horse becomes
His daughter's husband; goats will mate with kids
They've sired themselves; why, even birds conceive
From seed that fathered them. How blest are they
That have such license! Human nicety
Makes spiteful laws. What nature will allow,
Their jealous code forbids. Yet there exist
Peoples, it's said, where sons will marry mothers
And daughters fathers, and their doubled love
Increases duty's bond. But I, poor me,
Was not so lucky—I was not born there.
The chance of birthplace injures me.—Oh, why
Hark back to things like that? Away, away,
Forbidden hopes! He's worthy of my love,
Yes, but as father.—Well then, were I not
Great Cinyras's daughter, I could lie
With Cinyras. But now because he's mine,
He isn't mine! Propinquity itself
Does damage; I'd do better not so near.
I'd wish to go away and leave afar
My native borders, could I flee from crime.
But evil fires hold my heart here, to keep
Beloved Cinyras before my eyes, . . .
      . . . Oh, to see
In him the same mad fire that flames in me!"
   Now Cinyras, confronted with a crowd
Of worthy suitors, doubting what to do,
Asked Myrrha herself, enquiring name by name
Whom she would have for husband. She at first
Was silent, gazing in her father's face, her thoughts
In turmoil, hot tears welling in her eyes.
And Cinyras, who thought her tears were but
A girl's misgiving, told her not to cry,
And dried her cheeks and kissed her on the lips.
His kisses! Joy too thrilling! Then he asked
What kind of husband she would like, and she
Said "One like you." He did not understand
And praised her: "May you never lose your love
So dutiful!" At "dutiful" the girl

Lowered her eyes, too conscious of her guilt.
　　Midnight had come and sleep relaxed the limbs
And cares of men, but Myrrha lay awake,
A prey to ungoverned passion, and resumed
Her frenzied longings, sometimes in despair,
Sometimes resolved to try, at once ashamed
And yearning, vainly groping for some plan.
And as a huge tree, wounded by an axe,
Only the last stroke left, will wait in doubt
Which way to fall and every side's in fear,
So Myrrha's mind, weakened by wound on wound,
Wavered uncertainly this way and that,
Nodding on either side and found no end,
No respite for her love except in death.
Death it shall be! She rises up resolved
To hang herself. . . .

Before she can carry out her plan, Myrrha is discovered by her nurse, who eventually drags from her her awful secret.

　　. . . An icy shudder ran
Through the old woman's frame (she understood)
And every hair upon her snowy head
Stood stiff on end; and many many words
She poured to expel that passion if she could,
So terrible. The girl well knew the truth
Of what she warned; but still her purpose held
To die unless she had her heart's desire.
"Live then," the nurse replied, "and have your—" not
Daring to utter "father," she stopped short
In silence, then she called the gods of heaven
To ratify the promise she had given. . . .

Under cloak of darkness, for many nights, the nurse takes Myrrha to her father's bed. When he at last produces a lamp and discovers who she is, he draws his sword against her.

　　. . . Myrrha fled.
The darkness and the night's blind benison
Saved her from death. Across the countryside
She wandered till she left the palm-fringed lands
Of Araby and rich Panchaia's fields.

Nine times the crescent of the moon returned
And still she roamed, and then she found at last
Rest for her weariness on Saba's soil;
She scarce could bear the burden of her womb.
And then, not knowing what to wish, afraid
Of death and tired of life, she framed these words
Of prayer: "If Powers of heaven are open to
The cries of penitents, I've well deserved—
I'll not refuse—the pain of punishment,
But lest I outrage, if I'm left alive,
The living, or, if I shall die, the dead,
Expel me from both realms; some nature give
That's different; let me neither die nor live!"
Some Power is open to a penitent;
For sure her final prayer found gods to hear.
For, as she spoke, around her legs the earth
Crept up; roots thrusting from her toes
Spread sideways, firm foundations of a trunk;
Her bones gained strength; though marrow still remained,
Blood became sap, her fingers twigs, her arms
Branches, her skin was hardened into bark.
And now the growing tree had tightly swathed
Her swelling womb, had overlapped her breast,
Ready to wrap her neck. She would not wait,
But sinking down to meet the climbing wood,
Buried her face and forehead in the bark.
Though with her body she had forfeited
Her former feelings, still she weeps and down
The tree the warm drops ooze. Those tears in truth
Have honour; from the trunk the weeping myrrh
Keeps on men's lips for aye the name of her.
    The child conceived in sin had grown inside
The wood and now was searching for some way
To leave its mother and thrust forth. The trunk
Swelled in the middle with its burdened womb.
The load was straining, but the pains of birth
Could find no words, nor voice in travail call
Lucina.[1] Yet the tree, in labour, stooped
With groan on groan and wet with falling tears.

---

[1] Goddess of light and birth.

Then, pitying, Lucina stood beside
The branches in their pain and laid her hands
Upon them and pronounced the words of birth.
The tree split open and the sundered bark
Yielded its living load; a baby boy
Squalled, and the Naiads laid him on soft grass
And bathed him in his mother's flowing tears.
Envy herself would praise his looks; for like
The little naked Loves that pictures show
He lay there, give or take the slender bow.

Venus and Adonis

Time glides in secret and his wings deceive;
Nothing is swifter than the years. That son,
Child of his sister and his grandfather,
So lately bark-enswathed, so lately born,
Then a most lovely infant, then a youth,
And now a man more lovely than the boy,
Was Venus' darling (Venus'!) and avenged
His mother's passion. Once, when Venus' son
Was kissing her, his quiver dangling down,
A jutting arrow, unbeknown, had grazed
Her breast.
She pushed the boy away.
In fact the wound was deeper than it seemed,
    Though unperceived at first. Enraptured by
The beauty of a man, she cared no more
For her Cythera's shores nor sought again
Her sea-girt Paphos nor her Cnidos, famed
For fish, nor her ore-laden Amathus.
She shunned heaven too: to heaven she preferred
Adonis. . . .

PIED BEAUTY

by Gerard Manley Hopkins

In this lyric poem the English priest-poet Gerard Manley Hopkins celebrates the beauty of the irregular.

Hopkins joined the Catholic Church at age twenty-two, in 1866. "Pied Beauty" is dated eleven years later, in 1877, the year Hopkins was ordained. In this poem Hopkins chooses to praise God for the beautiful imperfection of nature. Readers, however, need not share his kind of piety to share his admiration for "dappled things."

"Pied" means "of two or more colors in blotches,"[1] and the poem begins with gorgeous and irregular natural sights, notably mottled color. As it progresses, though, it widens to encompass also the "dappled" impressions made on the other senses by man-made things, behavior ("fickle"), and "all things counter, original, spare, strange." The poet sees the beauty, and the divine source, of them all.

"Pied Beauty" sees, and praises. It does not seek to alter, improve, or even understand. Would the appreciation the poet feels be compatible with a more active approach to his subject? Would it be compatible with an impulse to regularize or improve upon the irregular?

How is imperfection related to beauty? Is the relationship different in nature than in man-made things? Is it different in human beings?

Does the beauty of a thing tell us anything meaningful about it?

Hopkins contrasts the irregular beauty of nature to a beauty that is "past change." Is this comparison essential to the point he wishes to make?

Why would a perfect Creator create an imperfect world?

---

[1] Merriam-Webster's Collegiate Dictionary, 10th Edition.

Glory be to God for dappled things—
   For skies of couple-colour as a brinded cow;
      For rose-moles all in stipple upon trout that swim;
Fresh-firecoal chestnut-falls; finches' wings;
   Landscape plotted and pieced—fold, fallow, and plough;
      And áll trádes, their gear and tackle and trim.
All things counter, original, spare, strange;
   Whatever is fickle, freckled (who knows how?)
      With swift, slow; sweet, sour; adazzle, dim;
He fathers-forth whose beauty is past change:
                 Praise him.

THE WONDERFUL MISTAKE

by Lewis Thomas

In this essay from his collection, The Medusa and the Snail: More Notes of a Biology Watcher, *the late Lewis Thomas makes the case that DNA is nature's greatest achievement and that much of DNA's greatness lies in its ability to err.*

Thomas begins by asserting that all DNA on earth today descended from the DNA of the first cell to emerge from the primordial ooze three thousand million years ago. He then tries to imagine what might have occurred had human intelligence attempted to design the mechanism to replicate that first creature. He concludes that humans would have botched the job, because we would have arranged for the mechanism to work perfectly. It is only because of "blunders" by the actual mechanism of DNA replication—duplication errors, spontaneous mutations, etc.—that that creature evolved into the complex life forms we see today.

Is Thomas's thesis generalizable: Are errors, or at least the possibility for error, necessary for progress? Is perfection necessarily static?

In Thomas's account, without blunders life would not have evolved and progressed. Is it possible to imagine progress by other than accidental means?

If error is essential to progress in nature, is it essential to progress in human undertakings as well?

The greatest single achievement of nature to date was surely the invention of the molecule of DNA. We have had it from the very beginning, built into the first cell to emerge, membranes and all, somewhere in the soupy water of the cooling planet three thousand million years or so ago. All of today's DNA, strung through all the cells of the earth, is simply an extension and elaboration of that first molecule. In a fundamental sense we cannot claim to have made progress, since the method used for growth and replication is essentially unchanged.

But we have made progress in all kinds of other ways. Although it is out of fashion today to talk of progress in evolution if you use that word to mean anything like improvement, implying some sort of value judgment beyond the reach of science, I cannot think of a better term to describe what has happened. After all, to have come all the way from a system of life possessing only one kind of primitive microbial cell, living out colorless lives in hummocks of algal mats, to what we see around us today—the City of Paris, the State of Iowa, Cambridge University, Woods Hole, the succession of travertine-lined waterfalls and lakes like flights of great stairs in Yugoslavia's Plitvice, the horse-chestnut tree in my backyard, and the columns of neurones arranged in modules in the cerebral cortex of vertebrates—*has* to represent improvement. We have come a long way on that old molecule.

We could never have done it with human intelligence, even if molecular biologists had been flown in by satellite at the beginning, laboratories and all, from some other solar system. We have evolved scientists, to be sure, and so we know a lot about DNA, but if our kind of mind had been confronted with the problem of designing a similar replicating molecule, starting from scratch, we'd never have succeeded. We would have made one fatal mistake: our molecule would have been perfect. Given enough time, we would have figured out how to do this, nucleotides, enzymes, and all, to make flawless, exact copies, but it would never have occurred to us, thinking as we do, that the thing had to be able to make errors.

The capacity to blunder slightly is the real marvel of DNA. Without this special attribute, we would still be anaerobic bacteria and there would be no music. Viewed individually, one by one, each of the mutations that have brought us along represents a random, totally spontaneous accident, but it is no accident at all that mutations occur; the molecule of DNA was ordained from the beginning to make small mistakes.

If we had been doing it, we would have found some way to correct this, and evolution would have been stopped in its tracks. Imagine the consternation of human scientists, successfully engaged in the letter-perfect replication of prokaryotes, nonnucleated cells like bacteria, when nucleated cells suddenly turned up. Think of the agitated commissions assembled to explain the scandalous proliferation of trilobites all over the place, the mass firings, the withdrawal of tenure.

To err is human, we say, but we don't like the idea much, and it is harder still to accept the fact that erring is biological as well. We prefer sticking to the point, and insuring ourselves against change. But there it is: we are here by the purest chance, and by mistake at that. Somewhere along the line, nucleotides were edged apart to let new ones in; maybe viruses moved in, carrying along bits of other, foreign genomes; radiation from the sun or from outer space caused tiny cracks in the molecule, and humanity was conceived.

And maybe, given the fundamental instability of the molecule, it had to turn out this way. After all, if you have a mechanism designed to keep changing the ways of living, and if all the new forms have to fit together as they plainly do, and if every improvised new gene representing an embellishment in an individual is likely to be selected for the species, and if you have enough time, maybe the system is simply bound to develop brains sooner or later, and awareness.

Biology needs a better word than "error" for the driving force in evolution. Or maybe "error" will do after all, when you remember that it came from an old root meaning to wander about, looking for something.

Excerpt from
GATTACA
written and directed by Andrew M. Niccol

The movie Gattaca, *the screenplay of which is excerpted below, explores the enduring significance of character in a society obsessed with genetically inherited traits.*

Gattaca is set in the future. Our ability to shape the genetic inheritance of children before they are born has become so sophisticated that it is commonplace for parents to design children who are free of defects and whose attributes and abilities they choose. After birth, in this imagined world, it is possible to read an individual's complete genetic profile almost instantly, from any sample of his DNA. Everyone's profile is registered, and one's DNA alone determines one's access to education, jobs, and even marriage partners. Those who were designed at birth therefore have the edge in every way over the dwindling ranks of "naturals."

Inevitably, ambitious individuals with poor DNA engage in identity fraud. They acquire DNA samples from donors who have the genetic endowments essential for success but who lack the ability to use them. They contrive to pass off this DNA as their own, alter their appearances so they resemble their DNA donors, and then enter walks of life otherwise closed to them.

The story concerns Vincent Antonio Luca, a "natural" with a natural defect: a weak heart. Despite this limitation, as Vincent grows, he develops a passion for astronomy and longs to become an astronaut. Knowing he will never be permitted to be one, he arranges to assume the identity of Jerome, a young man who has outstanding DNA but has been paralyzed in an accident and now suffers from alcoholism.

As Gattaca begins, Vincent, living as Jerome, is on the verge of his first, longed-for space flight. He soon becomes romantically involved with Irene, who also has a weak heart but does not know that this is a characteristic they share; she does not know that "Jerome" is a false identity. The authorities begin to suspect Vincent of fraud, however, and he is soon pursued by an Investigator.

In the first excerpt, "Jerome" tells the story of his birth and upbringing as Vincent, alongside his designed brother, Anton. The excerpt culminates as the brothers compete in an ocean swim. In the second excerpt, "Jerome" and Irene have a conversation that exposes important differences between them. In the final excerpt, "Jerome" and the Investigator, who is now revealed to be Vincent's brother, Anton, face off again in the open sea.

Vincent does not correct his parents when they mistakenly believe Anton rescued him from near drowning. "It's okay," he tells Anton. "It's the way they want it." Does this reflect Vincent's own resignation or his parents' true desire? Both? Neither? What is the understanding of perfection that moves Vincent's parents to design their second child? In what ways, if any, is the designed child perfect?

Throughout their lives, Vincent and Irene were told they were sick and incapable. Vincent seems never to have yielded to this, while Irene did. Why do they respond so differently to the same influence? Does the importance Vincent attaches to the value of risk ring true?

Does his willingness to take risks make Vincent more or less perfect?

Does the way we live with our particular capacities and attributes depend on how we acquired them?

Who would be responsible for the actions or products of an altered human, the alterer or the altered? Whom might you consider more perfect?

Excerpt 1

EXT. BEACH. DUSK—THIRTY-ODD YEARS EARLIER[1]

[*A starry sky. The camera tilts down to find palm trees swaying against a setting sun.*]

JEROME (VO)

I was conceived in the Riviera. Not the *French* Riviera.

[*The camera tilts down further to find a Buick Riviera parked in a deserted beachfront parking lot on a polluted stretch of beach.*]

JEROME (VO)

The Detroit variety.

[*Through the car's steamed windows we see Jerome's mother and father, Maria and Antonio, early twenties, making love.*]

---

[1] This screenplay uses the following standard abbreviations: "Ext." for "exterior," "Int." for "interior," and "VO" for "voiceover." Stage directions appear in italics and are bracketed.

JEROME (VO)

They used to say that a child conceived in love, has a greater chance of happiness. They don't say that any more.

INT. FAMILY PLANNING CLINIC. DAY.

[Maria, wearing a medical gown, lies on an examining table, feet in stirrups. A Nurse, forties, wheels an instrument tray towards her. Maria suddenly disengages her feet from the stirrups and swings her legs off the table.]

NURSE

What are you doing?

MARIA

[shaking her head]

I can't do this.

NURSE

[misinterpreting the problem]

I told you, the government pays. It's all taken care of.

MARIA

No, you don't understand. I can't.

[The nurse places a comforting hand on Maria's shoulder.]

NURSE

[reassuring]

The doctor will give you something.

MARIA

[removing the hand, adamant]

I'm not doing it.

NURSE

[trying to make her see reason]

Honey, you've made one mistake—

[The remark stings Maria.]

NURSE

[softening her tone]

I've read your profile. I don't know about the father but you carry enough hereditary factors on your own. [pause] You can have other children.

MARIA

[holding her swollen stomach protectively]

Not like this one.

NURSE

[trying to be diplomatic]

Honey, look around you. The world doesn't want one like that one.

[*Maria gets off the table and reaches for her clothes laying across a chair.*]

MARIA

[*irate*]

You don't know what it will be!

[*The nurse watches Maria as she dresses, genuinely bewildered.*]

NURSE

[*calling out to Maria as she disappears out of the door*]

The child won't thank you!

INT. DELIVERY ROOM. DAY.

[*We focus on a crucifix dangling on a rosary. Tilting up we find the rosary clasped between Maria and Antonio's intertwined hands.*]

JEROME (VO)

Those were early days—days when a priest could still persuade someone to put their faith in God's hands rather than those of the local geneticist.

[*Bathed in sweat, Maria gives a final push on the delivery table. While still attached to his umbilical cord, the heel of the newborn baby boy is immediately pricked by a masked nurse. A minute drop of blood is inserted into an analyzing machine.*

Even as the baby is put into Maria's arms, page after page of data begins to appear on a monitor, pulsing warning signals throughout the spreadsheets.

Two assisting nurses exchange a look. Antonio senses something amiss.]

ANTONIO

What's wrong?

JEROME (VO)

Of course, there was nothing wrong with me. Not so long ago I would have been considered a perfectly healthy, normal baby. Ten fingers, ten toes. That was all that used to matter. But now my immediate well-being was not the sole concern.

[*Antonio turns his attention from his baby to the data appearing on the monitor. We see individual items highlighted amongst the data— "NERVE CONDITION—PROBABILITY 60%", "MANIC DE-PRESSION—42%", "OBESITY—66%", "ATTENTION DEFICIT DISORDER—89%"—*]

JEROME (VO)

My destiny was mapped out before me—all my flaws, predisposi-
tions and susceptibilities—most untreatable to this day. Only
minutes old, the date and cause of my death was already known.

[Antonio focuses on a final highlighted item on the monitor's screen,
"HEART DISORDER—99%—EARLY FATAL POTENTIAL".
"LIFE EXPECTANCY—33 YEARS".]

NURSE

The name?

[typing details into birth certificate]

For the certificate.

MARIA

Antonio—

ANTONIO

[correcting her]

—No, Vincent Antonio.

[With a computer stylus he signs the nurse's handheld screen.]

EXT. TRACT HOME—BACKYARD. DAY.

[2-year-old Jerome (referred to by his given name of "Vincent" for
most of the following flashback) running with a toy rocket falls more
in clumsiness than fatigue. Maria suddenly whisks up the toddler.]

MARIA

[hysterical]

Oh, Vincent, Vincent, Vincent . . . I can't let you out of my sight.

[Maria frantically listens to her young son's heartbeat. For his part,
Vincent appears surprised by the attention. Maria places a portable
oxygen mask over Vincent's mouth.]

JEROME (VO)

I was born Vincent Antonio Luca. And from an early age I came
to think of myself as others thought of me—chronically ill. Every
skinned knee and runny nose treated as if it were life-threatening.

INT. DAY CARE CENTER. DAY.

[Maria and Antonio drop off dark-haired 2-year-old Vincent at a
Day Care Center.]

JEROME (VO)

And my parents soon realized that wherever I went, my genetic
prophecy preceded me.

[While healthy children play outside on tricycles, clamber over jun-
gle-gyms and finger-paint, the pre-school teacher shows Vincent into
a room where children with obvious disabilities sleep on mats.
Maria wheels around and marches out of the center with Vincent in her
arms. Antonio follows close behind, pleading with his wife to see sense.]

JEROME (VO)

They put off having any more children until they could afford not
to gamble—to bring a child into the world in what has become
the "natural" way.

EXT. HOME. DAY.

[Antonio reluctantly shows off his spotless Buick Riviera to a pro-
spective buyer.]

JEROME (VO)

It meant selling the beloved Buick.

[The two men haggle over the price while Maria, holding Vincent in
her arms, looks on. Finally money and a pink slip are exchanged.]

VINCENT (VO)

My father got a good price. After all, the only accident he'd ever
had in that car was me.

[As the buyer drives away, Antonio shrugs to Maria to hide his disappointment.]

EXT. GENETIC COUNSELLING OFFICE BUILDING. DAY.

[Antonio, Maria and 2-year-old Vincent exit a packed commuter
bus and enter a Genetic Counselling office building bearing the sign—
"PRO-CREATION".]

INT. GENETIC COUNSELLING OFFICE. DAY.

[A geneticist stares into a high-powered microscope as Antonio, Maria
and 2-year-old Vincent are shown into the office by a nurse. On the
counter beside the Geneticist is a glass-doored industrial refrigerator
containing petri dishes arranged on racks several feet high.]

GENETICIST

[to the NURSE, without taking his eyes from his binocular micro-
scope]

Put up the dish.

[While Antonio and Maria take a seat in front of a television moni-

*tor, the nurse puts a labelled petri dish under a video-equipped micro-
scope. The Geneticist swings around in his chair to greet his clients.
Four magnified clusters of cells—eight cells on each cluster—appear
on the television screen.]*

GENETICIST

Your extracted eggs . . .

[noting the couple's names from data along the edge of the screen]
. . . *Maria*, have been fertilized with . . . *Antonio's* sperm and we
have performed an analysis of the resulting pre-embryos. After
screening we're left with two healthy boys and two healthy girls.
Naturally, no critical pre-dispositions to any of the major inherita-
ble diseases. All that remains is to select the most compatible
candidate.

[Maria and Antonio exchange a nervous smile.]

GENETICIST

First, we may as well decide on gender. Have you given it any
thought?

MARIA

[referring to the toddler on her knee]
We would like Vincent to have a brother. . . you know, to play
with.

[The Geneticist nods. He scans the data around the edge of the screen.]

GENETICIST

You've already specified blue eyes, dark hair and fair skin. I have
taken the liberty of eradicating any potentially prejudicial conditions—premature baldness, myopia, alcoholism and addictive
susceptibility, propensity for violence and obesity—

MARIA

[interrupting, anxious]
—We didn't want—*diseases*, yes.

ANTONIO

[more diplomatic]
We were wondering if we should leave some things to chance.

GENETICIST

[reassuring]
You want to give your child the best possible start. Believe me, we
have enough imperfection built-in already. Your child doesn't
need any additional burdens. And keep in mind, this child is still
you, simply the *best* of you. You could conceive naturally a thousand times and never get such a result.

ANTONIO

[squeezing Maria's hand]
He's right, Maria. That's right.
[Maria is only half-convinced, but the Geneticist swiftly moves on.]
GENETICIST
Is there any reason you'd want a left-handed child?
ANTONIO
[blank]
Er, no . . .
GENETICIST
[explaining]
Some believe it is associated with creativity, although there's no evidence. Also for sports like baseball it can be an advantage.
ANTONIO
[shrugs]
I like football.
GENETICIST
[injecting a note of levity]
I have to warn you, Mr. Luca, he's going to be at least a head taller than you. Prepare for a crick in the neck in sixteen years time.
[Antonio beams proudly.]
GENETICIST
[scanning the data on the screen]
Anything I've forgotten?
MARIA
[hesitant about broaching the subject]
We want him—we were hoping he would get married and have children. We'd like grandchildren.
GENETICIST
[conspiratorial smile]
I understand. That's already been taken care of.
[an afterthought]
Now you appreciate I can only work with the raw material I have at my disposal but for a little extra . . . I could also attempt to insert sequences associated with enhanced mathematical or musical ability.
MARIA
[suddenly enthused]
Antonio, the choir . . .
GENETICIST
[interjecting, covering himself]
I have to caution you it's not foolproof. With multi-gene traits

there can be no guarantees.

ANTONIO

How much extra?

GENETICIST

It would be five thousand more.

    [Antonio's face falls.]

ANTONIO

I'm sorry, there's no way we can.

GENETICIST

Don't worry. You'll probably do just as well singing to him in the womb.

    [rising to end the appointment]

We can implant the most successful pre-embryo tomorrow afternoon.

    [Maria is staring at the four magnified clumps on the screen.]

MARIA

What will happen to the others?

GENETICIST

    [reassuring]

They are not babies, Maria, merely "human possibilities".

    [Removing the petri dish from beneath the lens of the microscope, he points out the four minuscule specks.]

GENETICIST

Smaller than a grain of sand.

    [DISSOLVE TO]

INT. TRACT HOME. DAY.

[A red pencil draws a mark on a doorway at the height of a child's head. The child moves away and the name, "Anton 11" is written beside the mark by proud father, Antonio.]

JEROME (VO)

That's how my brother, Anton, came into the world—a son my father considered worthy of his name.

    [There is little physical similarity between 11-year-old Anton and 13-year-old Vincent standing beside him, apart from their height. In fact Vincent is mortified to see that his younger brother's mark is a fraction of an inch higher than the mark beside his own name, "Vincent 13". Vincent runs from the room.]

EXT. BEACH. DAY.

[13-year-old Vincent and 11-year-old Anton sit together on a wind-swept beach.

Anton picks up a broken shell and deliberately slices the tip of his thumb with the sharp edge. He hands the shell to Vincent who hesitantly follows suit.]

JEROME (VO)

By the time we were playing at blood brothers I understood that there was something very different flowing through my veins.

[The two brothers press their thumbs together, merging the blood.]

JEROME (VO)

And I'd need an awful lot more than a drop if I was going to get anywhere.

EXT. BEACH. LATER IN THE DAY.

[While Antonio and Maria doze under a beach umbrella, Anton and Vincent enter the water, diving through the waves. From above we watch their two young bodies swimming beside each other beyond the breakers.]

JEROME (VO)

Our favorite game was "chicken". When our parents weren't watching, we used to swim outside the flags, as far out as we dared. It was about who would get scared and turn back first.

[Suddenly Vincent stops swimming, pulling up sharply in the water, exhausted and fearful. He watches Anton swim on into the distance.]

JEROME (VO)

Of course, it was always me. Anton was by far the stronger swimmer and he had no excuse to fail.

INT. SCHOOL—CLASSROOM. DAY.

[A teacher gives a physics lesson. The bespectacled 13-year-old Vincent has his arm energetically raised at each opportunity but is never called upon. Eventually he lowers his arm in defeat.]

JEROME (VO)

My genetic scarlet letter continued to follow me from school to school. When you're told you're prone to learning disabilities, it's sometimes easier not to disappoint anybody.

EXT. STREET. NIGHT.

[13-year-old Vincent stands at a cul-de-sac at the end of a long, straight deserted street. He places a basketball in the middle of the street to represent the Sun and begins to unwind the huge reel of string attached to the ball. 11-year-old Anton walks a pace behind him. Several yards along the trail a bead is threaded through the string to represent the planet Mercury.]

ANTON

How many astronauts are there, anyway?

[Vincent ignores him and continues to reel out the string.]

ANTON

I bet I could be one.

[Vincent stops and regards his younger brother with contempt.]

VINCENT

You're standing on Venus.

[Anton lifts his foot. There is a bead beneath it. . . .]

EXT. BEACH. DAY.

[17-year-old Jerome walks up the beach to find 15-year-old Anton sitting with [a] young woman Vincent had previously dated.]

JEROME (VO)

I didn't blame Anton for his free ride. You can't blame someone for winning the lottery.

[The Young Woman hastily departs.]

LATER

[The two brothers face each other on the sand. Anton is the more statuesque of the two.]

ANTON

[cocky]

You sure you want to do this?

[Vincent's answer is to walk towards the water. Anton smiles mockingly at his brother's grim "game face" and follows.

From an aerial view we watch Vincent and his younger brother, Anton, swim beyond the breakers.]

JEROME (VO)

It was the last time we swam together. Out into the open sea, like always, knowing each stroke towards the horizon was one we had to make back to the shore. Like always, the unspoken contest.

[We watch the two young men swimming stroke for stroke. They swim far out, beyond the point. Suddenly Anton starts to slow, his strokes becoming labored until he becomes motionless in the water. He begins to sink like a stone. Vincent, realizing Anton is no longer beside him, turns back to lend support. Vincent takes him in a life-guard hold and begins to nurse him back to shore. Finally the two boys are coughed up onto the shallows. They collapse, just beyond the waterline, exhausted, gasping for air. Antonio and Maria arrive on the scene. Anton is the first to recover while Vincent clutches his side, his face screwed up in pain. Maria kneels down and starts to administer to Vincent but his father, Antonio, is unable to conceal his anger and contempt for Vincent.]

ANTONIO

Vincent, you damn fool! You could have killed Anton with your ridiculous contest! Why should he risk his life to save yours?! When are you going to get it through your thick head—you can't compete with your brother! Why try?!

[Maria takes Antonio aside. Anton and Vincent exchange a look.]

ANTON

Why didn't you say anything?

VINCENT

Why didn't you?

[staring back at his father knowingly]

It's okay. It's the way they want it.

JEROME (VO)

It confirmed everything in the minds of my parents—that they had taken the right course with my younger brother and the wrong course with me. It would have been so much easier for everyone if I had slipped away that day. I decided to grant them that wish.

INT. HOME. NIGHT.

[Anton stands at the mantelpiece in the dimly-lit living room. He gazes at a framed family portrait—Vincent's face has been torn out of it. He suddenly spies Vincent exiting the front gate, carrying a suit-case. Anton goes to shout Vincent's name but the words don't get out.]

Excerpt 2

Years pass.

INT. IRENE'S APARTMENT. LATER THAT MORNING.

> *[Back in the bedroom, Jerome, partially dressed, holds Irene in bed. She softly touches the scars on his shins[2].]*

IRENE
> *(referring to the shins)*

What happened?

JEROME

You remember the '99 Chrysler LeBaron? It's the exact height of the front fender. *[shrugs]* Looked right instead of left.

IRENE
> *[comforted by the thought]*

So you're not so smart after all. *[awkward about raising the subject]* I want you to know—if it ever came to it—I'd be willing to get an ovum from the Egg Bank. In fact, I'd rather use a donor egg—*(quickly covering herself again)*—if it came to it.

JEROME

But "if it came to it" then it couldn't have your—*(searching for an appropriate body part)*—nose. *(stroking her face)* How perfect does your child have to be?

IRENE
> *[mildly irritated by what she perceives as his mocking]*

You hypocrite. Do you think for one moment you'd be doing what you're doing if it wasn't for who you are—what you are? Don't you get any satisfaction knowing that your children will be able to live to a ripe old age unless they do something foolish?

JEROME

That's precisely what scares me—that they won't do anything foolish or courageous or anything—worth a Goddamn.

> *[Irene is taken aback by Jerome's passion, regarding him in a new light.]*

---

[2] Vincent had deliberately broken his legs to gain the height he needed to transform himself into "Jerome."

Excerpt 3

EXT. BEACH. NIGHT.

[Jerome and Anton walk down a dune together towards the beach not far from Gattaca[3]—an ocean beach pounded by an angry, black sea. Jerome picks up a sharp piece of shell and slices the end of his thumb. A drop of blood oozes out. He offers the shell to Anton but Anton does not take it.

Both men begin to disrobe. The brothers stand beside each other on the sand once again—Anton still the more athletically-built of the two.

Together, they enter the raging surf. Diving through the breaking waves, they begin to swim.

In the moonlit night, we watch their two bodies swimming side by side. They swim a long distance, Anton waiting for his brother to tire. But the pace does not slacken. Anton pulls up in the water. Sensing his brother is no longer beside him, Jerome also pulls up. They tread water several yards apart.]

ANTON

[attempting to conceal his distress]

How are you doing this, Vincent? How have you done any of this?

JEROME

Now is your chance to find out.

[Jerome swims away a second time. Anton is forced to follow once again. Angry now, gritting his teeth, Anton calls upon the same determination we have witnessed during his constant swimming in the pool.[4] He puts on a spurt, slowly reeling in Jerome.

Anton gradually draws alongside Jerome, certain that this effort will demoralize his older brother. But Jerome has been foxing—waiting for him to catch up. Jerome smiles at Anton. With almost a trace of sympathy, he forges ahead again. Anton is forced to go with him. They swim again for a long distance.

It is Anton who gradually becomes demoralized—his strokes weaken, his will draining away. Anton pulls up, exhausted and fearful. Jerome also pulls up. However his face displays none of Anton's anxiety.]

---

[3] The institution for which Jerome works.
[4] Anton has worked out compulsively in a swimming pool since his defeat by Vincent years ago.

They tread water several yards apart. The ocean is choppier now. The view of the lights on the shore is obscured by the peaks of the waves.]

ANTON

[panic starting to show]

Vincent, where's the shore? We're too far out. We have to go back!

JEROME

[calling back]

Too late for that. We're closer to the other side.

[Anton looks towards the empty horizon.]

ANTON

What other side? How far do you want to go?! Do you want to drown us both?

[becoming hysterical]

How are we going to get back?!

[Jerome merely smiles back at his younger brother, a disturbingly serene smile.]

JEROME

[eerily calm]

You wanted to know how I did it. That's how I did it, Anton. I never saved anything for the swim back.

[Anton stares at Jerome, aghast. The two men face each other in silence, treading water several yards apart in the dark, rolling ocean. Jerome turns and heads back towards the shore. Anton is left alone with the terrifying realization. The only sound, the wind and the water. . . .]

Excerpts from
THAT HIDEOUS STRENGTH
by C. S. Lewis

That Hideous Strength *is the third volume of a science fiction trilogy by C. S. Lewis. Set in a futuristic England, it explores what happens when the technological project to master human nature reaches its logical limit.*

One of the novel's central characters is Mark Studdock, a young sociologist who is more or less coerced into working for a secretive government institute (the National Institute for Co-ordinated Experiments, or N.I.C.E.). For his first few weeks at N.I.C.E., Studdock is in the dark about its real work and purpose. In the following excerpt, he and several others equally ignorant are at last enlightened in an after-dinner conversation with a knowledgeable Italian insider named Filostrato.

Filostrato describes his ambition to "shave" the earth of all organic life, including human bodies, because "the impure and the organic are interchangeable conceptions." The body will no longer be necessary. It will be transcended by pure Mind. All will be done for the sake of cleanliness and "civilization," which Filostrato describes as "peace and order and discipline."

Is Filostrato right that "the real filth is what comes from organisms"? Is Filostrato's movement from artificial tree to artificial birdsong and finally to the eradication of the human body the unbroken continuum that he implies it is?

Are Filostrato's assumptions valid?

Is human perfection tantamount to purity?

Is "the conquest of death" tantamount to "the conquest of organic life"?

Is bodiless mind the peak of human flourishing?

Are Filostrato's motives noble? Base? Neither?

At dinner he sat next to Filostrato. There were no other members of the inner circle within earshot. The Italian was in good spirits and talkative. He had just given orders for the cutting down of some fine beech trees in the grounds.

"Why have you done that, Professor?" said a Mr. Winter who sat opposite. "I shouldn't have thought they did much harm at that distance from the house. I'm rather fond of trees myself."

"Oh, yes, yes," replied Filostrato. "The pretty trees, the garden trees. But not the savages. I put the rose in my garden, but not the brier. The forest tree is a weed. But I tell you I have seen the civilised tree in Persia. It was a French attaché who had it because he was in a place where trees do not grow. It was made of metal. A poor, crude thing. But how if it were perfected? Light, made of aluminum. So natural, it would even deceive."

"It would hardly be the same as a real tree," said Winter.

"But consider the advantages! You get tired of him in one place; two workmen carry him somewhere else: wherever you please. It never dies. No leaves to fall, no twigs, no birds building nests, no muck and mess."

"I suppose one or two, as curiosities, might be rather amusing."

"Why one or two? At present, I allow, we must have forests, for the atmosphere. Presently we find a chemical substitute. And then, why *any* natural trees? I foresee nothing but the *art* tree all over the earth. In fact, we *clean* the planet."

"Do you mean," put in a man called Gould, "that we are to have no vegetation at all?"

"Exactly. You shave your face: even, in the English fashion, you shave him every day. One day we shave the planet."

"I wonder what the birds will make of it?"

"I would not have any birds either. On the art tree I would have the art birds all singing when you press a switch inside the house. When you are tired of the singing you switch them off. Consider again the improvement. No feathers dropped about, no nests, no eggs, no dirt."

"It sounds," said Mark, "like abolishing pretty well all organic life."

"And why not? It is simple hygiene. Listen, my friends. If you pick up some rotten thing and find this organic life crawling over it, do you not say, 'Oh, the horrid thing. It is alive,' and then drop it?"

"Go on," said Winter.

"And you, especially you English, are you not hostile to any organic life except your own on your own body? Rather than permit it you have invented the daily bath."

"That's true."

"And what do you call dirty dirt? Is it not precisely the organic? Minerals are clean dirt. But the real filth is what comes from organisms—sweat, spittles, excretions. Is not your whole idea of purity one huge example? The impure and the organic are interchangeable conceptions."

"What are you driving at, Professor?" said Gould. "After all we are organisms ourselves."

"I grant it. That is the point. In us organic life has produced Mind. It has done its work. After that we want no more of it. We do not want the world any longer furred over with organic life, like what you call the blue mould—all sprouting and budding and breeding and decaying. We must get rid of it. By little and little, of course. Slowly we learn how. Learn to make our brains live with less and less body: learn to build our bodies directly with chemicals, no longer have to stuff them full of dead brutes and weeds. Learn how to reproduce ourselves without copulation."

"I don't think that would be much fun," said Winter.

"My friend, you have already separated the Fun, as you call it, from fertility. The Fun itself begins to pass away. Bah! I know that is not what you think. But look at your English women. Six out of ten are frigid, are they not? You see? Nature herself begins to throw away the anachronism. When she has thrown it away, then real civilisation becomes possible. You would understand if you were peasants. Who would try to work with stallions and bulls? No, no; we want geldings and oxen. There will never be peace and order and discipline so long as there is sex. When man has thrown it away, then he will become finally governable. . . . "

. . . "The world I look forward to is the world of perfect purity. The clean mind and the clean minerals. What are the things that most offend the dignity of man? Birth and breeding and death. How if we are about to discover that man can live without any of the three? . . . "

. . . Filostrato turned sharply from him and with a great scraping movement flung back the window curtains. Then he switched off the light. The fog had all gone, the wind had risen. Small clouds were scudding across the stars and the full Moon—Mark had never seen her so bright— stared down upon them. As the clouds passed her she looked like a ball that was rolling through them. Her bloodless light filled the room.

"There is a world for you, no?" said Filostrato. "There is cleanness, purity. Thousands of square miles of polished rock with not one blade of grass, not one fibre of lichen, not one grain of dust. Not even air. Have you thought what it would be like, my friend, if you could walk on that land? No crumbling, no erosion. The peaks of those mountains are real peaks: sharp as needles, they would go through your hand. Cliffs as high as Everest and as straight as the wall of a house. And cast by those cliffs, acres of shadow black as ebony, and in the shadow hundreds of degrees of frost. And then, one step beyond the shadow, light that would pierce your eyeballs like steel and rock that would burn your feet. The temperature is at boiling point. You would die, no? But even then you would not become filth. In a few moments you are a little heap of ash; clean, white powder. And mark, no wind to blow that powder about. Every grain in the little heap would remain in its place, just where you died, till the end of the world . . . but that is nonsense. The universe will have no end."

"Yes. A dead world," said Mark gazing at the Moon.

"No!" said Filostrato. He had come close to Mark and spoke almost in a whisper, the bat-like whisper of a voice that is naturally high-pitched. "No. There is life there."

"Do we *know* that?" asked Mark.

"Oh, *si.* Intelligent life. Under the surface. A great race, further advanced than we. An inspiration. A *pure* race. They have cleaned their world, broken free (almost) from the organic."

"But how—?"

"They do not need to be born and breed and die; only their common people, their *canaglia* do that. The Masters live on. They retain their intelligence: they can keep it artificially alive after the organic body has been dispensed with—a miracle of applied biochemistry. They do not need organic food. You understand? They are almost free of Nature, attached to her only by the thinnest, finest cord."

"Do you mean that all *that,*" Mark pointed to the mottled globe of the Moon, "is their own doing?"

"Why not? If you remove all the vegetation, presently you have not atmosphere, no water."

"But what was the purpose?"

"Hygiene. Why should they have their world all crawling with organisms? And specially, they would banish one organism. Her surface is not all as you see. There are still surface-dwellers—savages. One great dirty patch on the far side of her where there is still water and air and forests—yes, and germs and death. They are slowly spreading their hygiene over their whole globe. Disinfecting her. The savages fight against them. There are frontiers, and fierce wars, in the caves and galleries down below. But the great race presses on. If you could see the other side you would see year by year the clean rock—like this side of the Moon—encroaching: the organic stain, all the green and blue and mist, growing smaller. Like cleaning tarnished silver."

"But how do we know all this?"

"I will tell you all that another time. The Head has many sources of information. For the moment, I speak only to inspire you. I speak that you may know what can be done: what shall be done here. This Institute—*Dio meo*, it is for something better than housing and vaccinations and faster trains and curing the people of cancer. It is for the conquest of death: or for the conquest of organic life, if you prefer. They are the same thing. It is to bring out of that cocoon of organic life which sheltered the babyhood of mind the New Man, the man who will not die, the artificial man, free from Nature. Nature is the ladder we have climbed up by, now we kick her away."

"And you think that some day we shall really find a means of keeping the brain alive indefinitely?"

"We have begun already. The Head himself . . ."

"Go on," said Mark. His heart was beating wildly and he had forgotten both Jane and Wither. This at last was the real thing.

"The Head himself has already survived death, and you shall speak to him this night. . . ."

IMELDA

by Richard Selzer

In this short story by the physician-writer Richard Selzer, an unnamed narrator remembers a disaster that taught a great plastic surgeon the limits of his art.

Before the disaster, the surgeon, Hugh Franciscus, appears like "someone made up of several gods," on account of his personal remoteness, his skill at transforming human flesh, and his ability to read "all the secrets of the world" in the human body. After, he is "a quieter, softer man," one who has lost "perfection" but gained "pain."

The disaster strikes a patient named Imelda, whom Franciscus treats while working on a charitable basis in Honduras. Before this fateful trip, Franciscus appeared to have only two motivations as a doctor. First, he delighted in the exercise of his skill, perhaps even "exalt[ing] activity for its own sake." Second, he feared dishonor. When Franciscus meets Imelda, however, the reader sees the first hint of another motivation: To cure the shame and psychic distress caused by bodily imperfection.

Through no apparent fault of his own, Franciscus's effort to help Imelda results in her death. Her mother's response leads him to an extraordinary action. Why does he undertake it?

What about Imelda awakens the doctor's sensibilities? What about her mother, later, has the same effect?

At first, the narrator perceives Franciscus's action one way; later—after a crisis at a slide presentation—he comes to understand it differently. What changed the narrator's opinion? Which account of Franciscus's action rings truest?

Is the disaster a fitting consequence of Franciscus's initial attitude? Is Franciscus better or worse for it? How important is it for patients to see their doctors as invulnerable and omnipotent?

What did Franciscus learn from his encounters with Imelda, alive and dead?

What does the narrator—and the reader—learn about the aspirations and actual practice of plastic surgery, and about his own expectations of doctors? Are these lessons generalizable?

I heard the other day that Hugh Franciscus had died. I knew him once. He was the Chief of Plastic Surgery when I was a medical student at Albany Medical College. Dr. Franciscus was the archetype of the professor of surgery—tall, vigorous, muscular, as precise in his technique as he was impeccable in his dress. Each day a clean lab coat, monkishly starched, that sort of thing. I doubt that he ever read books. One book only, that of the human body, took the place of all others. He never raised his eyes from it. He read it like a printed page as though he knew that in the calligraphy there just beneath the skin were all the secrets of the world. Long before it became visible to anyone else, he could detect the first sign of granulation at the base of a wound, the first blue line of new epithelium at the periphery that would tell him that a wound would heal, or the barest hint of necrosis that presaged failure. This gave him the appearance of a prophet. "This skin graft will take," he would say, and you must believe beyond all cyanosis, exudation, and inflammation that it would.

He had enemies, of course, who said he was arrogant, that he exalted activity for its own sake. Perhaps. But perhaps it was no more than the honesty of one who knows his own worth. Just look at a scalpel, after all. What a feeling of sovereignty, megalomania even, when you know that it is you and you alone who will make certain use of it. It was said, too, that he was a ladies' man. I don't know about that. It was all rumor. Besides, I think he had other things in mind than mere living. Hugh Franciscus was a zealous hunter. Every fall during the season he drove upstate to hunt deer. There was a glass-front case in his office where he showed his guns. How could he shoot a deer? we asked. But he knew better. To us medical students he was someone heroic, someone made up of several gods, beheld at a distance, and always from a lesser height. If he had grown accustomed to his miracles, we had not. He had no close friends on the staff. There was something a little sad in that. As though once long ago he had been flayed by friendship and now the slightest breeze would hurt. Confidences resulted in dishonor. Perhaps the person in whom one confided would scorn him, betray. Even though he spent his days among those less fortunate, weaker than he—the sick, after all—Franciscus seemed aware of an air of personal harshness in his environment to which he reacted by keeping his own counsel, by a certain remoteness. It was what gave him the appearance of being haughty. With the patients he was forthright. All the facts laid out, every question anticipated and answered with specific information. He delivered good news and bad with the same dispassion.

I was a third-year student, just turned onto the wards for the first time, and clerking on Surgery. Everything—the operating room, the morgue, the emergency room, the patients, professors, even the nurses—was terrifying. One picked one's way among the mines and booby traps of the hospital, hoping only to avoid the hemorrhage and perforation of disgrace. The opportunity for humiliation was everywhere.

It all began on ward rounds. Dr. Franciscus was demonstrating a cross-leg flap graft he had constructed to cover a large fleshy defect in the leg of a merchant seaman who had injured himself in a fall. The man was from Spain and spoke no English. There had been a comminuted fracture of the femur, much soft-tissue damage, necrosis. After weeks of debridement and dressings, the wound had been made ready for grafting. Now the patient was in his fifth postoperative day. What we saw was a thick web of pale blue flesh arising from the man's left thigh, and which had been sutured to the open wound on the right thigh. When the surgeon pressed the pedicle with his finger, it blanched; when he let up, there was a slow return of the violaceous color.

"The circulation is good," Franciscus announced. "It will get better." In several weeks, we were told, he would divide the tube of flesh at its site of origin, and tailor it to fit the defect to which, by then, it would have grown more solidly. All at once, the webbed man in the bed reached out, and gripping Franciscus by the arm, began to speak rapidly, pointing to his groin and hip. Franciscus stepped back at once to disengage his arm from the patient's grasp.

"Anyone here know Spanish? I didn't get a word of that."

"The cast is digging into him up above," I said. "The edges of the plaster are rough. When he moves, they hurt."

Without acknowledging my assistance, Dr. Franciscus took a plaster shears from the dressing cart and with several large snips cut away the rough edges of the cast.

"*Gracias, gracias.*" The man in the bed smiled. But Franciscus had already moved on to the next bed. He seemed to me a man of immense strength and ability, yet without affection for the patients. He did not want to be touched by them. It was less kindness that he showed them than a reassurance that he would never give up, that he would bend every effort. If anyone could, he would solve the problems of their flesh.

Ward Rounds had disbanded and I was halfway down the corridor when I heard Dr. Franciscus's voice behind me.

"You speak Spanish." It seemed a command.

"I lived in Spain for two years," I told him.

"I'm taking a surgical team to Honduras next week to operate on the natives down there. I do it every year for three weeks, somewhere. This year, Honduras. I can arrange the time away from your duties here if you'd like to come along. You will act as interpreter. I'll show you how to use the clinical camera. What you'd see would make it worthwhile."

So it was that, a week later, the envy of my classmates, I joined the mobile surgical unit—surgeons, anesthetists, nurses, and equipment—aboard a Military Air Transport plane to spend three weeks performing plastic surgery on people who had been previously selected by an advance team. Honduras. I don't suppose I shall ever see it again. Nor do I especially want to. From the plane it seemed a country made of clay—burnt umber, raw sienna, dry. It had a dead-weight quality, as though the ground had no buoyancy, no air sacs through which a breeze might wander. Our destination was Comayagua, a town in the Central Highlands. The town itself was situated on the edge of one of the flatlands that were linked in a network between the granite mountains. Above, all was brown, with only an occasional Spanish cedar tree; below, patches of luxuriant tropical growth. It was a day's bus ride from the airport. For hours, the town kept appearing and disappearing with the convolutions of the road. At last, there it lay before us, panting and exhausted at the bottom of the mountain.

That was all I was to see of the countryside. From then on, there was only the derelict hospital of Comayagua, with the smell of spoiling bananas and the accumulated odors of everyone who had been sick there for the last hundred years. Of the two, I much preferred the frank smell of the sick. The heat of the place was incendiary. So hot that, as we stepped from the bus, our own words did not carry through the air, but hung limply at our lips and chins. Just in front of the hospital was a thirsty courtyard where mobs of waiting people squatted or lay in the meager shade, and where, on dry days, a fine dust rose through which untethered goats shouldered. Against the walls of this courtyard, gaunt, dejected men stood, their faces, like their country, preternaturally solemn, leaden. Here no one looked up at the sky. Every head was bent beneath a wide-brimmed straw hat. In the days that followed, from the doorway of the dispensary I would watch the brown mountains sliding about, drinking the hospital into their shadow as the afternoon grew later and later, flattening us by their very altitude.

The people were mestizos, of mixed Spanish and Indian blood. They had flat, broad, dumb museum feet. At first they seemed to me indistinguishable the one from the other, without animation. All the vitality, the hidden sexuality, was in their black hair. Soon I was to know them by the fissures with which each face was graven. But, even so, compared to us, they were masked, shut away. My job was to follow Dr. Franciscus around, photograph the patients before and after surgery, interpret and generally act as aide-de-camp. It was exhilarating. Within days I had decided that I was not just useful, but essential. Despite that we spent all day in each other's company, there were no overtures of friendship from Dr. Franciscus. He knew my place, and I knew it, too. In the afternoon he examined the patients scheduled for the next day's surgery. I would call out a name from the doorway to the examining room. In the court-yard someone would rise. I would usher the patient in, and nudge him to the examining table where Franciscus stood, always, I thought, on the verge of irritability. I would read aloud the case history, then wait while he carried out his examination. While I took the "before" photographs, Dr. Franciscus would dictate into a tape recorder:

"Ulcerating basal-cell carcinoma of the right orbit—six by eight cen-timeters—involving the right eye and extending into the floor of the orbit. Operative plan: wide excision with enucleation of the eye. Later, bone and skin grafting." The next morning we would be in the operat-ing room where the procedure would be carried out.

We were more than two weeks into our tour of duty—a few days to go—when it happened. Earlier in the day I had caught sight of her through the window of the dispensary. A thin, dark Indian girl about fourteen years old. A figurine, orange-brown, terra-cotta, and still attached to the unshaped clay from which she had been carved. An older, sun-weath-ered woman stood behind and somewhat to the left of the girl. The mother was short and dumpy. She wore a broad-brimmed hat with a high crown, and a shapeless dress like a cassock. The girl had long, loose black hair. There were tiny gold hoops in her ears. The dress she wore could have been her mother's. Far too big, it hung from her thin shoul-ders at some risk of slipping down her arms. Even with her in it, the dress was empty, something hanging on the back of a door. Her breasts made only the smallest imprint in the cloth, her hips none at all. All the while, she pressed to her mouth a filthy, pink, balled-up rag as though to stanch a flow or buttress against pain. I knew that what she had come to show us, what we were there to see, was hidden beneath that pink cloth. As I watched, the woman handed down to her a gourd from which the girl drank, lapping like a dog. She was the last patient of the day. They had been waiting in the courtyard for hours.

"Imelda Valdez," I called out. Slowly she rose to her feet, the cloth never leaving her mouth, and followed her mother to the examining-room door. I shooed them in.

"You sit up there on the table," I told her. "Mother, you stand over there, please." I read from the chart:

"This is a fourteen-year-old girl with a complete, unilateral, left-sided cleft lip and cleft palate. No other diseases or congenital defects. Laboratory tests, chest X-ray—negative."

"Tell her to take the rag away," said Dr. Franciscus. I did, and the girl shrank back, pressing the cloth all the more firmly.

"Listen, this is silly," said Franciscus. "Tell her I've got to see it. Either she behaves, or send her away."

"Please give me the cloth," I said to the girl as gently as possible. She did not. She could not. Just then, Franciscus reached up and, taking the hand that held the rag, pulled it away with a hard jerk. For an instant the girl's head followed the cloth as it left her face, one arm still upflung against showing. Against all hope, she would hide herself. A moment later, she relaxed and sat still. She seemed to me then like an animal that looks outward at the infinite, at death, without fear, with recognition only.

Set as it was in the center of the girl's face, the defect was utterly hideous—a nude rubbery insect that had fastened there. The upper lip was widely split all the way to the nose. One white tooth perched upon the protruding upper jaw projected through the hole. Some of the bone seemed to have been gnawed away as well. Above the thing, clear almond eyes and long black hair reflected the light. Below, a slender neck where the pulse trilled visibly. Under our gaze the girl's eyes fell to her lap where her hands lay palms upward, half open. She was a beautiful bird with a crushed beak. And tense with the expectation of more shame.

"Open your mouth," said the surgeon. I translated. She did so, and the surgeon tipped back her head to see inside.

"The palate, too. Complete," he said. There was a long silence. At last he spoke.

"What is your name?" The margins of the wound melted until she herself was being sucked into it.

"Imelda." The syllables leaked through the hole with a slosh and a whistle.

"Tomorrow," said the surgeon, "I will fix your lip. Mañana." It seemed to me that Hugh Franciscus, in spite of his years of experience, in spite of all the dreadful things he had seen, must have been awed by the sight of this girl. I could see it flit across his face for an instant. Perhaps it was her small act of concealment, that he had had to demand that she show him the lip, that he had had to force her to show it to him. Perhaps it was her resistance that intensified the disfigurement. Had she brought her mouth to him willingly, without shame, she would have been for him neither more nor less than any other patient.

He measured the defect with calipers, studied it from different angles, turning her head with a finger at her chin.

"How can it ever be put back together?" I asked.

"Take her picture," he said. And to her, "Look straight ahead." Through the eye of the camera she seemed more pitiful than ever, her humiliation more complete.

"Wait!" The surgeon stopped me. I lowered the camera. A strand of her hair had fallen across her face and found its way to her mouth, becoming stuck there by saliva. He removed the hair and secured it behind her ear.

"Go ahead," he ordered. There was the click of the camera. The girl winced.

"Take three more, just in case."

When the girl and her mother had left, he took paper and pen and with a few lines drew a remarkable likeness of the girl's face. "Look," he said. "If this dot is A, and this one B, this, C and this, D, the incisions are made A to B, then C to D. CD must equal AB. It is all equilateral triangles." All well and good, but then came X and Y and rotation flaps and the rest.

"Do you see?" he asked.

"It is confusing," I told him.

"It is simply a matter of dropping the upper lip into a normal position, then crossing the gap with two triangular flaps. It is geometry," he said.

"Yes," I said. "Geometry." And relinquished all hope of becoming a plastic surgeon.

In the operating room the next morning the anesthesia had already been administered when we arrived from ward rounds. The tube emerging from the girl's mouth was pressed against her lower lip to be kept out of the field of surgery. Already, a nurse was scrubbing the face which swam in a reddish brown lather. The tiny gold earrings were included in the scrub. Now and then, one of them gave a brave flash. The face was washed for the last time, and dried. Green towels were placed over the face to hide everything but the mouth and nose. The drapes were applied.

"Calipers!" The surgeon measured, locating the peak of the distorted Cupid's bow.

"Marking pen!" He placed the first blue dot at the apex of the bow. The nasal sills were dotted; next, the inferior philtral dimple, the vermilion line. The A flap and the B flap were outlined. On he worked, peppering the lip and nose, making sense out of chaos, realizing the lip that lay waiting in that deep essential pink, that only he could see. The last dot and line were placed. He was ready.

"Scalpel!" He held the knife above the girl's mouth.

"Okay to go ahead?" he asked the anesthetist.

"Yes."

He lowered the knife.

"No! Wait!" The anesthetist's voice was tense, staccato. "Hold it!"

The surgeon's hand was motionless.

"What's the matter?"

"Something's wrong. I'm not sure. God, she's hot as a pistol. Blood pressure is way up. Pulse one-eighty. Get a rectal temperature." A nurse fumbled beneath the drapes. We waited. The nurse retrieved the thermometer.

"One hundred seven . . . no . . . eight." There was disbelief in her voice.

"Malignant hyperthermia," said the anesthetist. "Ice! Ice! Get lots of ice!" I raced out the door, accosted the first nurse I saw.

"Ice!" I shouted. "*Hielo!* Quickly! *Hielo!*" The woman's expression was blank. I ran to another. "*Hielo! Hielo!* For the love of God, ice!"

"*Hielo?*" She shrugged. "*Nada.*" I ran back to the operating room.

"There isn't any ice," I reported.

Dr. Franciscus had ripped off his rubber gloves and was feeling the skin of the girl's abdomen. Above the mask his eyes were the eyes of a horse in battle.

"The EKG is wild . . . "

"I can't get a pulse . . . "

"What the hell . . . "

The surgeon reached for the girl's groin. No femoral pulse.

"EKG flat. My God! She's dead!"

"She can't be."

"She is."

The surgeon's fingers pressed the groin where there was no pulse to be felt, only his own pulse hammering at the girl's flesh to be let in.

It was noon, four hours later, when we left the operating room. It was a day so hot and humid I felt steamed-open like an envelope. The woman was sitting on a bench in the courtyard in her dress like a cassock. In one hand she held the piece of cloth the girl had used to conceal her mouth. As we watched, she folded it once neatly, and then again, smoothing it, cleaning the cloth which might have been the head of the girl in her lap that she stroked and consoled.

"I'll do the talking here," he said. He would tell her himself, in what-ever Spanish he could find. Only if she did not understand was I to speak for him. I watched him brace himself, set his shoulders. How could he tell her? I wondered. What? But I knew he would tell her everything, exactly as it had happened. As much for himself as for her, he needed to explain. But suppose she screamed, fell to the ground, attacked him, even? All that hope of love . . . gone. Even in his discomfort I knew that he was teaching me. The way to do it was professionally. Now he was standing above her. When the woman saw that he did not speak, she lifted her eyes and saw what he held crammed in his mouth to tell her. She knew, and rose to her feet.

"Señora," he began, "I am sorry." All at once he seemed to me shorter than he was, scarcely taller than she. There was a place at the crown of his head where the hair had grown thin. His lips were stones. He could hardly move them. The voice dry, dusty.

"No one could have known. Some bad reaction to the medicine for sleeping. It poisoned her. High fever. She did not wake up." The last, a whisper. The woman studied his lips as though she were deaf. He tried, but could not control a twitching at the corner of his mouth. He raised a thumb and forefinger to press something back into his eyes.

"Muerte," the woman announced to herself. Her eyes were human, deadly.

"Sí, muerte." At that moment he was like someone cast, still alive, as an effigy for his own tomb. He closed his eyes. Nor did he open them until he felt the touch of the woman's hand on his arm, a touch from which he did not withdraw. Then he looked and saw the grief corroding her face, breaking it down, melting the features so that eyes, nose, mouth ran together in a distortion, like the girl's. For a long time they stood in silence. It seemed to me that minutes passed. At last her face cleared, the features rearranged themselves. She spoke, the words coming slowly to make certain that he understood her. She would go home now. The next day her sons would come for the girl, to take her home for burial. The doctor must not be sad. God has decided. And she was happy now that the harelip had been fixed so that her daughter might go to Heaven without it. Her bare feet retreating were the felted pads of a great bereft animal.

The next morning I did not go to the wards, but stood at the gate leading from the courtyard to the road outside. Two young men in striped ponchos lifted the girl's body wrapped in a straw mat onto the back of a wooden cart. A donkey waited. I had been drawn to this place as one is

drawn, inexplicably, to certain scenes of desolation—executions, bat-
tlefields. All at once, the woman looked up and saw me. She had taken
off her hat. The heavy-hanging coil of her hair made her head seem
larger, darker, noble. I pressed some money into her hand.

"For flowers," I said. "A priest." Her cheeks shook as though minutes
ago a stone had been dropped into her navel and the ripples were just
now reaching her head. I regretted having come to that place.

"Sí, Sí," the woman said. Her own face was stitched with flies. "The
doctor is one of the angels. He has finished the work of God. My daughter is beautiful."

What could she mean! The lip had not been fixed. The girl had died
before he would have done it.

"Only a fine line that God will erase in time," she said.

I reached into the cart and lifted a corner of the mat in which the girl
had been rolled. Where the cleft had been there was now a fresh line of
tiny sutures. The Cupid's bow was delicately shaped, the vermilion border aligned. The flattened nostril had now the same rounded shape as
the other one. I let the mat fall over the face of the dead girl, but not
before I had seen the touching place where the finest black hairs sprang
from the temple.

"Adiós, adiós . . . " And the cart creaked away to the sound of hooves,
a tinkling bell.

There are events in a doctor's life that seem to mark the boundary
between youth and age, seeing and perceiving. Like certain dreams, they
illuminate a whole lifetime of past behavior. After such an event, a doctor is not the same as he was before. It had seemed to me then to have
been the act of someone demented, or at least insanely arrogant. An
attempt to reorder events. Her death had come to him out of order. It
should have come after the lip had been repaired, not before. He could
have told the mother that, no, the lip had not been fixed. But he did
not. He said nothing. It had been an act of omission, one of those strange
lapses to which all of us are subject and which we live to regret. It must
have been then, at that moment, that the knowledge of what he would
do appeared to him. The words of the mother had not consoled him;
they had hunted him down. He had not done it for her. The dire necessity was his. He would not accept that Imelda had died before he could
repair her lip. People who do such things break free from society. They
follow their own lonely path. They have a secret which they can never
reveal. I must never let on that I knew.

How often I have imagined it. Ten o'clock at night. The hospital of
Comayagua is all but dark. Here and there lanterns tilt and skitter up

and down the corridors. One of these lamps breaks free from the others and descends the stone steps to the underground room that is the morgue of the hospital. This room wears the expression as if it had waited all night for someone to come. No silence so deep as this place with its cargo of newly dead. Only the slow drip of water over stone. The door closes gassily and clicks shut. The lock is turned. There are four tables, each with a body encased in a paper shroud. There is no mistaking her. She is the smallest. The surgeon takes a knife from his pocket and slits open the paper shroud, that part in which the girl's head is enclosed. The wound seems to be living on long after she has died. Waves of heat emanate from it, blurring his vision. All at once, he turns to peer over his shoulder. He sees nothing, only a wooden crucifix on the wall.

He removes a package of instruments from a satchel and arranges them on a tray. Scalpel, scissors, forceps, needle holder. Sutures and gauze sponges are produced. Stealthy, hunched, engaged, he begins. The dots of blue dye are still there upon her mouth. He raises the scalpel, pauses. A second glance into the darkness. From the wall a small lizard watches and accepts. The first cut is made. A sluggish flow of dark blood appears. He wipes it away with a sponge. No new blood comes to take its place. Again and again he cuts, connecting each of the blue dots until the whole of the zigzag slice is made, first on one side of the cleft, then on the other. Now the edges of the cleft are lined with fresh tissue. He sets down the scalpel and takes up scissors and forceps, undermining the little flaps until each triangle is attached only at one side. He rotates each flap into its new position. He must be certain that they can be swung without tension. They can. He is ready to suture. He fits the tiny curved needle into the jaws of the needle holder. Each suture is placed precisely the same number of millimeters from the cut edge, and the same distance apart. He ties each knot down until the edges are apposed. Not too tightly. These are the most meticulous sutures of his life. He cuts each thread close to the knot. It goes well. The vermilion border with its white skin roll is exactly aligned. One more stitch and the Cupid's bow appears as if by magic. The man's face shines with moisture. Now the nostril is incised around the margin, released, and sutured into a round shape to match its mate. He wipes the blood from the face of the girl with gauze that he has dipped in water. Crumbs of light are scattered on the girl's face. The shroud is folded once more about her. The instruments are handed into the satchel. In a moment the morgue is dark and a lone lantern ascends the stairs and is extinguished.

Six weeks later I was in the darkened amphitheater of the Medical School. Tiers of seats rose in a semicircle above the small stage where

Hugh Franciscus stood presenting the case material he had encountered in Honduras. It was the highlight of the year. The hall was filled. The night before, he had arranged the slides in the order in which they were to be shown. I was at the controls of the slide projector.

"Next slide!" he would order from time to time in that military voice which had called forth blind obedience from generations of medical students, interns, residents, and patients.

"This is a fifty-seven-year-old man with a severe burn contracture of the neck. You will notice the rigid webbing that has fused the chin to the presternal tissues. No motion of the head on the torso is possible. . . . Next slide!"

Click, went the projector.

"Here he is after the excision of the scar tissue and with the head in full extension for the first time. The defect was then covered . . . Next slide!"

Click.

". . . with full-thickness drums of skin taken from the abdomen with the Padgett dermatome. Next slide!"

Click.

And suddenly there she was, extracted from the shadows, suspended above and beyond all of us like a resurrection. There was the oval face, the long black hair unbraided, the tiny gold hoops in her ears. And that luminous gnawed mouth. The whole of her life seemed to have been summed up in this photograph. A long silence followed that was the surgeon's alone to break. Almost at once, like the anesthetist in the operating room in Comayagua, I knew that something was wrong. It was not that the man would not speak as that he could not. The audience of doctors, nurses, and students seemed to have been infected by the black, limitless silence. My own pulse doubled. It was hard to breathe. Why did he not call out for the next slide? Why did he not save himself? Why had he not removed this slide from the ones to be shown? All at once I knew that he had used his camera on her again. I could see the long black shadows of her hair flowing into the darker shadows of the morgue. The sudden blinding flash. . . . The next slide would be the one taken in the morgue. He would be exposed.

In the dim light reflected from the slide, I saw him gazing up at her, seeing not the colored photograph, I thought, but the negative of it where the ghost of the girl was. For me, the amphitheater had become Honduras. I saw again that courtyard littered with patients. I could see the dust in the beam of light from the projector. It was then that I knew that she was his measure of perfection and pain—the one lost, the other gained. He, too, had heard the click of the camera, had seen her wince and felt his mercy enlarge. At last he spoke.

"Imelda." It was the one word he had heard her say. At the sound of his voice I removed the next slide from the projector. *Click* . . . and she was gone. *Click* again, and in her place the man with the orbital cancer. For a long moment Franciscus looked up in my direction, on his face an expression that I have given up trying to interpret. Gratitude? Sorrow? It made me think of the gaze of the girl when at last she understood that she must hand over to him the evidence of her body.

"This is a sixty-two-year-old man with a basal-cell carcinoma of the temple eroding into the bony orbit . . ." he began, as though nothing had happened.

At the end of the hour, even before the lights went on, there was loud applause. I hurried to find him among the departing crowd. I could not. Some weeks went by before I caught sight of him. He seemed vaguely convalescent, as though a fever had taken its toll before burning out.

Hugh Franciscus continued to teach for fifteen years, although he operated a good deal less, then gave it up entirely. It was as though he had grown tired of blood, of always having to be involved with blood, of having to draw it, spill it, wipe it away, stanch it. He was a quieter, softer man, I heard, the ferocity diminished. There were no more expeditions to Honduras or anywhere else.

I, too, have not been entirely free of her. Now and then, in the years that have passed, I see that donkey-cart cortege, or his face bent over hers in the morgue. I would like to have told him what I now know, that his unrealistic act was one of goodness, one of those small, persevering acts done, perhaps, to ward off madness. Like lighting a lamp, boiling water for tea, washing a shirt. But, of course, it's too late now.

Excerpt from
THE SCIENCE OF HAPPINESS: UNLOCKING THE MYSTERIES OF MOOD

by Stephen Braun

Modern neuroscience holds out the promise of psychic self-improvement through the use of drugs. In this autobiographical epilogue to his book, The Science of Happiness, *Stephen Braun recounts his "quest," over many years, for "an optimal mood," one reliably "energetic, outgoing, poised [and] lighthearted."*

Braun frankly describes himself as not ill but "basically normal." He is troubled, though, because a review of the journal he has always kept reveals to him that without drugs, he "seem[s] to spend more time in a bleak or simply neutral mood than in a frankly happy mood." Occasionally, he is subject to brief turns for the worse that he calls "microbursts." Although he has long sought to manipulate his mood with, among other tools, alcohol and caffeine, he becomes dissatisfied with those drugs and seeks "a more perfect drug, a better drug."

By the end of this account, after experimenting with several less successful alternatives, he finds a drug that "nudge[s] up" his "happiness set point." Because he is unsure of the "health risks" of continuing to take it for the rest of his life, Braun has resolved only to continue "for now." He concludes, though, by wishing good fortune to the "drug companies" seeking to improve on the products now available.

Braun finally decides to try drugs because during one "microburst" he suddenly and fleetingly thinks of suicide. As quickly as the thought comes, Braun realizes that he doesn't want to die, "not by a long shot." Yet his concern that "my brain somehow generated the thought" leads him to a psychiatrist's office and a prescription. Does a quick consideration and rejection of suicide mean, as Braun says, that one is in "sizeable" part "indifferent" to life?

What might Braun mean by "normal"? Throughout this account, how well is his concept of "normal" serving him?

How much of the way Braun understands himself and his state of mind can be traced to the existence of new diagnostic terms and the availability of new pharmacological remedies?

Has Braun eliminated obstacles to the natural pursuit of his own flourishing? Or has he artificially induced a feeling of flourishing divorced from the activities that could genuinely produce it? Does it matter, and if so, why?

Is "happiness" just a matter of feeling or being in "a good mood"?

Is Braun searching for perfection? Of what sort?

As a young newspaper reporter, Braun notices that his mood fluctuates unpredictably, especially with variations in his patterns of sleep, diet, and exercise, and his use of alcohol and caffeine.

. . . no matter what I tried, my mood inevitably soured. It seemed impossible for me to maintain for long the energetic, outgoing, poised, lighthearted mood I craved. Seemingly at random I would find myself mildly depressed, lethargic, pessimistic, and cross.

These bleak moods never blossomed into full-blown clinical depression, which is a realm of despair, pain, and abject dysfunction that I am most grateful I have never experienced. My mood "disorder" is mild—some might even say trivial—compared to clinical depression. I never lost a day of work because I felt down. I never lost my appetite or my ability to sleep. I didn't lose my friendships or isolate myself pathologically. It's just that when I would review my journal I would repeatedly see that I seemed to spend more time in a bleak or simply neutral mood than in a frankly happy mood.

In addition to a more or less chronic sense of being slightly shy of "good-humored," there are infrequent times when my mood takes a distinctly abrupt turn for the worse. I call these quick eclipses "microbursts" because of their severity and brevity—they usually last no longer than forty-eight hours or so.

Caught in a microburst, I feel emotionally flat, tight, edgy, and hostile. Normally slow to anger, I become impatient and irritable. I find fault with practically everyone around me. I fume at people who don't think quickly enough or get to the point of a conversation fast enough. In the middle of a microburst I am also painfully aware of my own mortality. I feel as though a veil lifts from my eyes—perhaps that rosy gauze provided by nature to encourage us to continue living and, more importantly from our genes' point of view, procreating. Whatever. In a microburst I am convinced that life is fundamentally meaningless and that everybody's hopes and dreams amount to nothing in the cosmic scheme of things. Since I lack even a shred of belief in an afterlife, I am vulnerable to the depressing view that when we die, we die, and that a hundred years after our death, or two hundred or a thousand or ten thousand, depending on the impact we happen to have on those around us—not a trace of us will survive.

This, in any case, is how things appear when I'm nipped by the Black Dog—Winston Churchill's name for the depression that visited him throughout his life.

Unlike Churchill, however, my Black Dog lopes away from me as quickly and mysteriously as he appears. Despite the seeming certainty of my dark beliefs and the apparent clarity of my vision, I usually wake up a day or two after the onset of a microburst and feel better. My former preoccupation with death suddenly doesn't interest me. There is too much fun to be had. Too many people to love. There are children to hug, stars to marvel at, and good wine to enjoy in the company of dear friends.

And as I have observed myself over time, I have noticed that sometimes my microbursts are not as random as they at first appear. Sometimes they occur during a stressful or difficult time in my life. . . .

. . . The difficulty was that for every time a microburst was a helpful siren of an emotional emergency, there would be another time when it was a flagrant false alarm. . . .

Before trying to treat this condition with prescription medication, Braun decides to try eliminating alcohol and caffeine.

. . . And so for about four months I lived a very wholesome life. I quit caffeine and drank only celebratory alcohol. I rode my bicycle every day, ate well, and got enough sleep.

And, at first, I felt great.

I felt calmer, I slept deeply, and a wry sense of humor emerged from time to time that seemed absent when I was "speeding" on caffeine. But slowly the calm began to feel more like lethargy. Despite sleeping well, I felt tired and unproductive in the afternoon. And even with a midday nap, I would start to yawn at about nine-thirty in the evening and be snoring at ten—which didn't leave much time for socializing, much less writing another book. But, more importantly, microbursts became more frequent.

One day I felt a rising sense of tension, irritation, and moodiness. I had no particular reason to be sad. I enjoyed my work, I loved my wife and daughters, I was about to move into a new home, and I was in great health. And yet, as I drove on the highway that evening, I felt more and more vexed and cross. And as I eased off the road and up an exit ramp, a black thought bubbled up from some muck in my brain: "I could just kill myself."

Even as the thought surfaced, another part of me said "How absurd," because I didn't really want to kill myself. Not by a long shot. And yet, there it was. Some apparently sizable part of my marbled personality was shockingly indifferent to everything in my life—including life itself.

I drove on, less concerned with suicide itself than with the fact that my brain somehow generated the thought of suicide. If this was being "natural," I decided, then to hell with it. It occurred to me then that living with my "natural" brain made about as much sense as walking around "naturally" naked. . . .

He visits a psychotherapist, who asks him about his relationship with his wife. He answers that whatever difficulties he and his wife may experience are normal, and that he thinks he could benefit from drugs.

. . . Somewhat to my surprise, she agreed with me. She said she had seen other people do very well on antidepressants—especially people like me with mild symptoms. And then, to my vast relief, she mentioned the "D" word—"dysthymia"—the chronic condition of low mood that has served in the past decade to immeasurably expand the umbrella of "mental illness" to include people like me who used to be considered "normal." Dysthymia was my ticket to drugs. The labeling would make everyone happy. My HMO would have the diagnostic code for billing, the psychiatrist to whom I would be referred would have a label to hang his hat on, and I could use the word to conceptualize my own difficulty. Reducing my highly idiosyncratic and frankly unusual mood irregularity to a common clinical syndrome was a relief in other ways.

As much as I value psychotherapy, part of me breathed a sigh of relief when she mentioned dysthymia. That word meant that the basic problem wasn't that I needed to learn better ways to communicate with my wife or, far worse, that the problem was some fatal flaw in my relationship that I had been denying all this time and for which divorce was the only remedy. Instead of long, hard work learning new skills and hashing through emotional minefields with my wife, the laying on of the dysthymia label promised the ultimate easy fix: a pill. . . .

The therapist sends him to a psychiatrist, who starts him on a round of
experimentation with various medications. Some pills seem to do nothing.
One pill makes him sleepy. At last, he begins to take Celexa.

. . . That was almost six months ago now. This time I have refilled my prescriptions as they have expired. Several times I've thought about stopping, again because everything feels so normal. My mood fluctuates in response to events around me. I can get angry, annoyed, and blue. Life is hardly uninterrupted bliss. And if it were not for my previous trials with other drugs, I might well think the drug I was taking was doing nothing, nothing at all.

But I think I know better now. And I may have succeeded in my quest. I may have actually nudged up my happiness set point—enough for me to participate more fully in life, but not so much as to render me insensible to life events, to the slings and arrows of outrageous fortune. Almost miraculously, a single small white pill taken every day seems to have balanced my mood machinery such that I can look my fate squarely in the eye—hold my own mortality and the existential uncertainties of life firmly in mind—and not flinch, quail, or despair. . . .

. . . And so I'll continue for now. I'll keep using these pharmaceutical "eyeglasses" to correct my mood astigmatism. I'll keep up with the news from the drug companies. I'll remain connected with both my therapist and my psychiatrist. I'll certainly continue to exercise, meditate, deal with relationship issues, and follow other common-sense guidelines for a balanced lifestyle. And despite my profound skepticism toward the claims and tactics of drug companies, I will wish them well in their chase of more perfect drugs, hoping that in a better, clearer understanding of human mood will come pharmacological tools that are safe, effective, and useful to everyone seeking to live a long, healthy, happy life.

CHAPTER 2:
SCIENTIFIC ASPIRATIONS

IN OUR FIRST CHAPTER, we saw how human beings have long struggled with our opposing desires and dispositions: to behold and appreciate the given world, and to shape it into what we would like it to be. In this chapter we turn our attention toward science, a mode of inquiry and body of learning that has served both aspirations with awesome effectiveness. From what does science come? What are its animating impulses? What are its goals?

The readings that follow explore the wellsprings of scientific activity by drawing on histories and memoirs of five great scientists. All of these men have irrevocably affected our lives with the fruits of their labor, rigor, and genius. From these words written by or about them, we can see that all were spurred to greatness by different ambitions and visions.

The first scientist recalled below—by Plutarch, in an excerpt from his "Life of Marcellus"—is the ancient geometrician Archimedes. Archimedes, who disdained applying his discoveries toward practical ends, exemplifies the pursuit of knowledge for its own sake. This view is radically altered by René Descartes, who in his *Discourse on Method* sought a new way of knowing that could make us "like masters and possessors of nature."

Three contemporary scientists follow Archimedes and Descartes, both in our chapter and, to varying extents, in philosophical outlook. Entomologist E. O.Wilson, in an excerpt from his autobiography, *Naturalist*, recounts three episodes in his boyhood that formed him as a "naturalist" who "celebrate[d] . . . animals that can be picked up between thumb and forefinger and brought close for inspection." Two chapters from the autobiography of the late physicist Richard Feynman, *Surely You're Joking, Mr. Feynman*, establish his love of play and especially of solving puzzles. His "puzzle drive" leads Feynman to physics; as a physicist, he is determined to remain playful. Finally, biologist James Watson celebrates the pursuit of scientific glory in an excerpt from *The Double Helix*, the story of his race, with Francis Crick, to discover the structure of DNA. Here, scientific activity is directed as much toward the Nobel Prize that would surely go to the winner as toward the mystery that would be solved or the uses to which the new knowledge might be put.

Excerpt from
THE LIVES OF THE NOBLE GRECIANS AND ROMANS
by Plutarch, translated by John Dryden

This passage from Plutarch's Lives contains a brief portrait of the life, work, and death of the legendary Greek mathematician, Archimedes, known both for his feats of engineering and for his theoretical studies.

The portrait appears in the "Life of Marcellus." Marcellus, a Roman general, is described by Plutarch as "skillful in the art of war, of a strong body, valiant of hand, and by natural inclinations addicted to war." Yet though a consummate soldier, Marcellus was in other respects "modest and obliging, and so far studious of Greek learning and discipline, as to honour and admire those that excelled in it."

The attached passage begins just after Marcellus has assaulted the Sicilian city of Syracuse, the home of Archimedes. Marcellus attacks with a massive force of ships, arms, and missiles. Yet all his weapons are no match for Archimedes and the instruments of war he has devised.

In what follows, Plutarch first explains why Archimedes has designed these machines, despite his sympathy with those, like Plato, who consider mechanics the "corruption and annihilation" of geometry. The passage proceeds to a dazzling account of the terror his machines inflict on Marcellus's men.

Plutarch next writes that, despite Archimedes' worldly success, he still "placed his whole affection and ambition in those purer speculations where there can be no reference to the vulgar needs of life." Then follow stories Plutarch has heard about Archimedes' uncannily single-minded devotion to geometry.

What moves Archimedes? Why does he disdain the inventions and machines he is able to devise on the basis of his geometrical knowledge? Why does he prefer "purer speculations"?

How might Archimedes' way of approaching mathematics be explained by what he sees in it? What might that vision be?

Why did Archimedes refuse to obey the soldier who ordered him to go to Marcellus? Do you admire his reason for refusing?

Why is Marcellus so afflicted by the death of Archimedes? What do the several stories about how he died tell us about the ruling passion of this man of science, and about the relations of the scientific quest to the rest of life?

Can one imagine a man like Archimedes managing the human demands of his own life? His work had the power to transform the lives of others. Is there

75

anything to be feared from a man so capable of affecting others, yet so indifferent to ordinary human needs?

Marcellus attacks Syracuse by land and sea.

. . . The land forces were conducted by Appius: Marcellus, with sixty galleys, each with five rows of oars, furnished with all sorts of arms and missiles, and a huge bridge of planks laid upon eight ships chained together, upon which was carried the engine to cast stones and darts, assaulted the walls, relying on the abundance and magnificence of his preparations, and on his own previous glory; all which, however, were, it would seem, but trifles for Archimedes and his machines.

These machines he had designed and contrived, not as matters of any importance, but as mere amusements in geometry; in compliance with King Hiero's desire and request, some little time before, that he should reduce to practice some part of his admirable speculation in science, and by accommodating the theoretic truth to sensation and ordinary use, bring it more within the appreciation of the people in general. Eudoxus and Archytas had been the first originators of this far-famed and highly-prized art of mechanics, which they employed as an elegant illustration of geometrical truths, and as means of sustaining experimentally, to the satisfaction of the senses, conclusions too intricate for proof by words and diagrams. As, for example, to solve the problem, so often required in constructing geometrical figures, given the two extremes, to find the two mean lines of a proportion, both these mathematicians had recourse to the aid of instruments, adapting to their purpose certain curves and sections of lines. But what with Plato's indignation at it, and his invectives against it as the mere corruption and annihilation of the one good of geometry, which was thus shamefully turning its back upon the unembodied objects of pure intelligence to recur to sensation, and to ask help (not to be obtained without base supervisions and depravation) from matter; so it was that mechanics came to be separated from geometry, and, repudiated and neglected by philosophers, took its place as a military art. Archimedes, however, in writing to King Hiero, whose friend and near relation he was, had stated that given the force, any given weight might be moved, and even boasted, we are told, relying on the strength of demonstration, that if there were another earth, by going into it he could remove this. Hiero being struck with amazement at this, and entreating him to make good this problem by actual experiment, and show some great weight moved by a small engine, he fixed accordingly upon a ship of burden out of the king's arsenal, which could not be drawn out of the dock without great labour and many men; and, loading her with many passengers and a full freight, sitting himself the while far off, with no great endeavour, but only holding the head of the pulley in his hand and drawing the cords by degrees, he drew the ship in a straight line, as smoothly and evenly as if she had been in the sea. The king, astonished at this, and convinced of the power of the art, prevailed upon Archimedes to make him engines accommodated to all the purposes, offensive and defensive, of a siege. These the king himself never made use of, because he spent almost all his life in a profound quiet and the highest affluence. But the apparatus was, in most opportune time, ready at hand for the Syracusans, and with it also the engineer himself.

When, therefore, the Romans assaulted the walls in two places at once, fear and consternation stupefied the Syracusans, believing that nothing was able to resist that violence and those forces. But when Archimedes began to ply his engines, he at once shot against the land forces all sorts of missile weapons, and immense masses of stone that came down with incredible noise and violence; against which no man could stand; for they knocked down those upon whom they fell in heaps, breaking all their ranks and files. In the meantime huge poles thrust out from the walls over the ships sunk some by the great weights which they let down from on high upon them; others they lifted up into the air by an iron hand or beak like a crane's beak and, when they had drawn them up by the prow, and set them on end upon the poop, they plunged them to the bottom of the sea; or else the ships, drawn by engines within, and whirled about, were dashed against steep rocks that stood jutting out under the walls, with great destruction of the soldiers that were aboard them. A ship was frequently lifted up to a great height in the air (a dreadful thing to behold), and was rolled to and fro, and kept swinging, until the mariners were all thrown out, when at length it was dashed against the rocks, or let fall. At the engine that Marcellus brought upon the bridge of ships, which was called *Sambuca*, from some resemblance it had to an instrument of music, while it was as yet approaching the wall, there was discharged a piece of rock of ten talents weight, then a second and a third, which, striking upon it with immense force and a noise like thunder, broke all its foundation to pieces, shook out all its fastenings, and completely dislodged it from the bridge. So Marcellus, doubtful what counsel to pursue, drew off his ships to a safer distance, and sounded a retreat to his forces on land. They then took a resolution of coming up under the walls, if it were possible, in the night; thinking that as Archimedes used ropes stretched at length in playing his engines, the soldiers would now be under the shot, and the darts would, for want of sufficient distance to throw them, fly over their heads without effect. But he, it appeared, had long before framed for such occasions engines accommodated to any distance, and shorter weapons; and had made numerous small openings in the walls, through which, with engines of a shorter range, unexpected blows were inflicted on the assailants. Thus, when they who thought to deceive the defenders came close up to the walls, instantly a shower of darts and other missile weapons was again cast upon them. And when stones came tumbling down perpendicularly upon their heads, and, as it were, the whole wall shot out arrows at them, they retired. And now, again, as they were going off arrows and darts of a longer range inflicted a great slaughter among them, and their ships were driven one against another; while they themselves were not able to retaliate in any way. For Archimedes had provided and fixed most of his engines immediately under the wall; whence the Romans, seeing that indefinite mischief overwhelmed them from no visible means, began to think they were fighting with the gods.

Yet Marcellus escaped unhurt, and deriding his own artificers and engineers, "What," said he, "must we give up fighting with this geometrical Briareus, who plays pitch-and-toss with our ships, and, with the multitude of darts which he showers at a single moment upon us, really outdoes the hundred-handed giants of mythology?" And, doubtless, the rest of the Syracusans were but the body of Archimedes's designs, one soul moving and governing all; for, laying aside all other arms, with this alone they infested the Romans and protected themselves. In fine, when such terror had seized upon the Romans, that, if they did but see a little rope or a piece of wood from the wall, instantly crying out, that there it was again, Archimedes was about to let fly some engine at them, they turned their backs and fled, Marcellus desisted from conflicts and assaults, putting all his hope in a long siege. Yet Archimedes possessed so high a spirit, so profound a soul, and such treasures of scientific knowledge, that though these inventions had now obtained him the renown of more than human sagacity, he yet would not deign to leave behind him any commentary or writing on such subjects; but, repudiating as sordid and ignoble the whole trade of engineering, and every sort of art that lends itself to mere use and profit, he placed his whole affection and ambition in those purer speculations where there can be no reference to the vulgar needs of life; studies, the superiority of which to all others is unquestioned, and in which the only doubt can be whether the beauty and grandeur of the subjects examined, of the precision and cogency of the methods and means of proof, most deserve our admiration. It is not possible to find in all geometry more difficult and intricate questions, or more simple and lucid explanations. Some ascribe this to his natural genius; while others think that incredible effort and toil produced these, to all appearances, easy and unlaboured results. No amount of investigation of yours would succeed in attaining the proof, and yet, once seen, you immediately believe you would have discovered it; by so smooth and so rapid a path he leads you to the conclusion required. And thus it ceases to be incredible that (as is commonly told of him) the charm of his familiar and domestic Siren made him forget his food and neglect his person, to that degree that when he was occasionally carried by absolute violence to bathe or have his body anointed, he used to trace geometrical figures in the ashes of the fire, and diagrams in the oil on his body, being in a state of entire preoccupation, and, in the truest sense, divine possession with his love and delight in science. His discoveries were numerous and admirable; but he is said to have requested his friends and relations that, when he was dead, they would place over his tomb a sphere containing a cylinder, inscribing it with the ratio which the containing solid bears to the contained. . . .

Despite Archimedes' defenses, Marcellus and his army eventually gain access to Syracuse. As they prepare to enter, Marcellus regrets the coming, inevitable destruction of the city he is taking.

. . . But nothing afflicted Marcellus so much as the death of Archimedes, who was then, as fate would have it, intent upon working out some problem by a diagram, and having fixed his mind alike and his eyes upon the subject of his speculation, he never noticed the incursion of the Romans, nor that the city was taken. In this transport of study and contemplation, a soldier, unexpectedly coming up to him, commanded him to follow to Marcellus; which he declining to do before he had worked out his problem to a demonstration, the soldier, enraged, drew his sword and ran him through. Others write that a Roman soldier, running upon him with a drawn sword, offered to kill him; and that Archimedes, looking back, earnestly besought him to hold his hand a little while, that he might not leave what he was then at work upon inconclusive and imperfect; but the soldier, nothing moved by his entreaty, instantly killed him. Others again relate that, as Archimedes was carrying to Marcellus mathematical instruments, dials, spheres, and angles, by which the magnitude of the sun might be measured to the sight, some soldiers seeing him, and thinking that he carried gold in a vessel, slew him. Certain it is that his death was very afflicting to Marcellus; and that Marcellus ever after regarded him that killed him as a murderer; and that he sought for his kindred and honoured them with signal favours.

Excerpt from
DISCOURSE ON METHOD
by René Descartes, translated by Richard Kennington

*In 1636, the great French philosopher-scientist René Descartes published three
scientific treatises,* The Dioptrics, The Meteors, *and his world-shaking* Geometry, *the last providing the basis for all of modern mathematical physics.
As a preface to these three treatises, Descartes wrote his famous* Discourse on
the Method of Conducting One's Reason Well and Seeking Truth in the
Sciences, *popularly known as the* Discourse on Method. *In this* Discourse,
*Descartes presents a synopsis of his entire philosophical system in the form of a
six-part autobiographical history or fable, two excerpts of which are presented
here.*

*In the first, taken from part 1, Descartes gives an account of his early
education, indicating why he rejected all book learning and nearly all the then-
extant sciences: their teachings were either uncertain or useless, or both. This
desire for certain and useful knowledge led him to devise a method that would
yield such knowledge, a method that combined elements of the previously distinct sciences of arithmetic and geometry to form what we today call analytic
geometry (part 2, not reproduced here). Armed with this new mathematics,
Descartes then shows how it could lead to an entirely new science of nature
(physics), one devoted not to discovering the nature of things but to describing
precisely all the material changes they undergo in terms of laws formulable as
equations (part 5, not reproduced here).*

*In the second excerpt, from the beginning of part 6, Descartes in a famous
passage tells the reader why he publishes, despite the great danger that he might
in doing so run afoul of the Inquisition. He has discovered "knowledge very
useful in life," practical knowledge that could enable us to become "like masters and possessors of nature." Such "mastery," Descartes predicts, will enable us to satisfy all basic needs without toil, to conserve health, to make men
wiser and more capable, and even to conquer the infirmities of age: in a word,
to lift the curse which, according to Genesis, was laid on Adam and Eve and
to regain the tree of life by means of the tree of (scientific) knowledge.*

*What moves the soul of Descartes? What is the demand for certainty? For
utility?*

Is there some connection between these motives and the insistence on "me-

Reprinted by permission of the estate of Richard Kennington.

thodical" knowledge?

Is there some connection between these motives and the goals of "mastery and possession of nature"?

Can we have certain knowledge about all the questions that we are inclined to ask, even about the natural world and about human beings?

Who stands to benefit from the new practical science? What is the implied relationship between the scientist and the broader society?

Part I

I was nourished in letters from childhood, and because I was persuaded that by their means one could acquire a clear and assured knowledge of all that is useful for life, I had an extreme desire to learn them. But as soon as I had finished this whole course of studies, at the end of which one is customarily received into the ranks of the learned, I changed my opinion entirely. For I found myself embarrassed with so many doubts and errors that there seemed to me to have been no other benefit in trying to instruct myself except that I discovered more and more my own ignorance. And yet I was in one of the most celebrated schools of Europe, where I thought there must be some learned men if there were any in any place on earth. I had learned there all that the others there had learned; and not being content with those sciences that they taught us, I had even looked through all the books, treating of the most curious and unusual things, that had fallen into my hands. Moreover, I knew the judgments others made of me, and I did not see that I was esteemed inferior to my fellow students, although there were already some among them destined to fill the places of our masters. And finally our age seemed to me as flourishing and as fertile in good minds, as any of the preceding. Therefore I took the liberty of judging all others by myself, and of think-ing that there was no doctrine in the world such as I had been led to hope for.

I did not, however, cease to respect the exercises which occupy one in the schools. I knew that the languages that we learn there are necessary for the understanding of ancient books; that the gracefulness of fables awakens the mind; that the memorable actions of histories elevate it, and if they are read with discretion, they help to form the judgment; that the reading of all good books is like a conversation with the finest men of past ages who are their authors, and even a studied conversation, in which they unfold to us only the best of their thoughts; that eloquence has incomparable powers and beauties; that poetry has most enchanting refinements and sweetness; that mathematics has very subtle discoveries which have great service, whether for contenting our curiosity, or for facilitating the arts and reducing human toil; that the writings which treat of morals contain many teachings and exhortations to virtue which are very useful; that theology teaches us how to get to heaven; that philosophy supplies a means of talking plausibly about everything, and of making one admired by the less learned; that jurisprudence, medicine, and the other sciences afford honors and riches to those who cultivate them; and, finally, that it is good to have examined them all, even the most superstitious and false, in order to know their just worth, and to keep from being deceived by them.

But I believed I had given enough time to languages, and even to the reading of ancient books, to their histories as well as their fables. For conversing with those of other ages is almost the same thing as travelling. It is good to know something of the morals of different peoples, in order to judge more sanely of our own, and not think that what is contrary to our modes is ridiculous, and against reason, as those who have seen nothing usually do. But a man who employs too much time travelling finally becomes a stranger in his own country; and when he becomes too curious about things practiced in past ages he ordinarily remains very ignorant of those practiced in this one. Besides which, fables make us imagine many things as possible which are not; and even the most faithful histories, if they do not change nor augment the value of things, in order to render them more worthy of being read, at least almost always omit the most base and least illustrious circumstances: so that what remains does not appear such as it was, and those who regulate their morals by the examples they draw from them are likely to fall into the extravagances of the knights-errant of our romances, and to conceive purposes that surpass their powers.

I held eloquence in high esteem, and I was enamored of poetry, but I thought that both were gifts of mind, rather than fruits of study. Those who have the strongest reasoning capacity, and who best digest their thoughts in order to make them clear and intelligible, are always the best able to persuade others of what they propose, although they only speak low-Breton, and have never learned rhetoric. And those who have the most agreeable conceits, and who know how to express them with the most adornment and sweetness, would not fail to be the best poets although they are ignorant of the poetic art.

I was above all pleased with the mathematical sciences because of the certitude and evidence of their arguments. But I did not yet perceive their true usage, and, thinking they were only of service to the mechanical arts, I was astonished that since their foundations were so firm and solid, nothing more exalted had been built on them. On the other hand, I compared the moral writings of the ancient pagans to splendid and magnificent palaces built only on sand and mud. They exalt the virtues to the heights, and make them appear more estimable than everything in the world, but they do not sufficiently teach how to know them, and often what they call by such a beautiful name is only insensibility, or pride, or despair, or parricide.

I revered our theology, and aspired as much as any one to reach heaven; but, having learned as an assured thing, that the way to heaven is open to the most ignorant no less than to the most learned, and that the revealed truths, which lead us there, are above our intelligence, I would not have dared to submit them to the feebleness of my reasonings, and I thought that in order to undertake to examine them and to succeed, I would need to have some extraordinary assistance from heaven, and to be more than a man.

I shall say nothing of philosophy except that, seeing that it has been cultivated by the most excellent minds who have lived in many ages, and that nevertheless nothing is found in it which is not in dispute, and consequently which is not doubtful, I did not have enough presumption to hope for better success there than others. And when I considered that there can be diverse opinions about the same matter maintained by learned people, without it being possible for more than one to be true, I regarded almost as false that which was only probable.

Then, as for the other sciences, inasmuch as they draw their principles from philosophy, I judged that nothing solid could have been built on such infirm foundations. And neither the honor nor the gain which they promise was sufficient to incite me to learn them, for I felt that my situation, thanks be to God, did not oblige me to make a trade of science in order to alleviate my fortune. And although I did not make a profession of disdaining glory like the cynics, nevertheless I cared little for what I could hope to gain only by false titles. And finally, as regards evil doctrines, I thought I already knew sufficiently what they were worth, so as not to be deceived by the promises of an alchemist, the predictions of an astrologer, the impostures of a magician, or by the artifices and the boasting of those who make a profession of knowing more than they do.

That is why, as soon as age permitted me to escape the subjection of my preceptors, I gave up the study of letters completely. Resolving to seek no other science but that which could be found in myself, or else in the great book of the world, I used the rest of my youth to travel, to look at courts and armies, to frequent people of diverse humors and conditions, to collect various experiences, to test myself in the encounters that fortune offered me, and everywhere to make such reflection on the things that presented themselves as would profit me. For it seemed to me that I could encounter much more truth in the reasonings that each man makes about the affairs that concern him, and whose outcome must punish him immediately afterwards if he has judged badly, than in those made by a man of letters in his study in speculations that produce no effect, and which have no other consequence for him, except insofar as he will derive more vanity from them the farther they are removed from common sense, because he will have had to employ so much more mind and artifice to render them probable. And I always had an extreme desire to learn to distinguish the true from the false in order to see clearly in my actions, and to walk with assurance in this life.

It is true that while I did nothing but observe the morals of other men, I found scarcely anything there to convince me, and I noticed almost as much diversity in them as I had previously found in the opinions of the philosophers. So that the greatest profit I derived from this was that, seeing many things which, although they seem most extravagant and ridiculous to us, do not fail to be commonly received and approved by other great peoples, I learned not to believe anything too firmly which had persuaded me only by example and custom. And thus I liberated myself little by little from many errors which may obscure our natural light, and render us less capable of listening to reason. But after I had spent several years in thus studying the book of the world and in trying to acquire some experience, I took one day the resolution also to study within myself, and to use all the forces of my mind to choose the paths that I should follow. I succeeded much better in this, it seems to me, than if I had never left either my country or my books. . . .

Part VI

It is now three years since I completed the treatise that contains all these things, and began to review it before putting it in the hands of the printer, when I learned that certain persons to whom I defer, and whose authority over my actions is scarcely less than that of my own reason over my thoughts, had disapproved of a certain opinion in physics, published shortly before by someone else.[1] I do not wish to say that I agreed

---

[1] Galileo.

with it, but since I had noticed nothing in it before their censure which I could imagine to be prejudicial to religion or to the State, or, consequently, which could have prevented me from writing it if reason had so persuaded me, this made me fear that there might be found among my thoughts some one which was mistaken, despite the great care I have always taken not to receive new ones among my beliefs, or of which I did not have very certain demonstrations, and to write nothing which could turn to the disadvantage of anyone. This sufficed to compel me to change the resolution that I had taken to publish them. For although the reasons for it that I had previously taken were very strong, my inclination, which had always made me hate the trade of producing books, immediately made me find enough other reasons to excuse me from it. And these reasons on both sides of the matter are such that not only do I have some interest in stating them, but perhaps the public will also have some in knowing them.

I have never made much of the things which came from my mind, and so long as the only fruits of the method I use were in satisfying myself regarding certain difficulties that belong to the speculative sciences, and in trying to regulate my morals by the reasons that it taught me, I did not believe that I was obliged to write about it. For with regard to morals, each man is so impressed with his own judgment, that there would be found as many reformers as heads, if others besides those whom God has established as sovereigns over his peoples, or to whom he has given enough grace and zeal to be prophets, were permitted to try to change anything. And although my speculations pleased me greatly, I believe that others also had some that pleased them perhaps more. But as soon as I had acquired certain general notions about physics, and after beginning to test them on various particular questions, I had noticed where they might lead, and how much they differed from the principles in use up to the present, I believed that I could not keep them hidden without gravely sinning against the law that obliges us to procure, so much as we can, the general good of all men. For they have made me see that it is possible to attain knowledge which is very useful to life, and in place of that speculative philosophy that is taught in the schools, we can find a practical one, by which, because it knows the force and actions of fire, water, air, stars, the heavens and all the other bodies that environ us, as distinctly as we know the different trades of our artisans, we can employ them in all their proper usages, and thus make ourselves like masters and possessors of nature. This is desirable not only for the invention of an infinity of artifices which would enable us to enjoy, without any pain, the fruits of the earth and all the commodities to be found there, but also and principally for the conservation of health, which is without doubt the primary good and the foundation of all other goods of this life. For even the mind is so dependent on the temperament, and on the disposition of the organs of the body, that if it is possible to find some means that generally renders men more wise and more capable than they have been up to now, I believe that we must seek for it in medicine. It is true that what is now practiced contains little whose utility is very remarkable; but, although I have no intention of deprecating it, I am sure that there is nobody, even among those who make a profession of it, who does not admit that all we now know is almost nothing in comparison with what remains to be known, and that we could be spared an infinity of diseases, of the body as well as of the mind, and even also perhaps the enfeeblement of old age, if we had enough knowledge of their causes and of all the remedies which nature has provided us. And because I intended to use my whole life for the inquiry into such a necessary science, and had found a path by following which it seemed that I must infallibly find it, unless prevented by the brevity of my life or the lack of experiments, I judged that there was no better remedy against these two impediments than to communicate faithfully to the public all the little that I had found, and to urge good minds to try to go further by contributing, each according to his inclination and power, to the experiments required, and also to communicate to the public everything that they learned, in order that later men begin where their predecessors had arrived. Thus we all together would go much further, joining the lives and labors of many, than each in particular could do. . . .

Excerpt from
NATURALIST
by E. O. Wilson

The first three chapters of this memoir by the great contemporary entomologist Edward O. Wilson, from which the attached readings are drawn, relate the experiences he believes formed him as a man and, specifically, as a scientist. The first, Wilson's "embrace of nature," occurred as he roamed free on the gulf shore of Florida at age seven. The second was his early education at a military academy. The third was his encounter with religious faith.

Most people would call Wilson a scientist, and often in this book he calls himself one, too. Yet the title of his memoir is Naturalist, *and he begins it with his experiences at the ocean shore to illustrate "how a naturalist is created."*

Wilson writes that his memories of that experience, when he was seven, are "built around a small collection of dominating images." These images are of the creatures—"monsters"—he found at the water's edge. In this beginning of what would become a lifelong passion for collecting, the young Wilson sought to capture these creatures, the better to behold them.

Why, in this chapter of gathering and gazing, does Wilson say he is describing the creation of a "naturalist"? What is the difference between the boy's gaze at the "impervious" sea and the adult's gaze at insects, which can be taken apart and revealed? How might the injury done to his eyes by one of the creatures at which he is gazing have influenced his memories of the "monsters" he saw that summer, or of his subsequent views of nature?

Wilson and Archimedes share a desire to gaze at the truth. Yet how do their gazes differ?

In the second chapter, a portion of which appears below, the now eight-year-old Wilson is sent to board for one year at the Gulf Coast Military Academy in Gulfport, Mississippi. Although this marked the end of "all dreams of languor and boyhood adventure," he ultimately grew to love the academy for leaving him with "images of a perfect orderliness and lofty purpose." As a result of the academy's training, Wilson developed an intense admiration for those who "concentrate all the courage and self-discipline they possess toward a single worthy goal."

Is greatness in science dependent on or enhanced by devotion to "perfect orderliness and lofty purpose"? Is there any similarity between military self-discipline and the discipline of scientific method? Are the outlooks and beliefs of the naturalist and the scientist the same?

In the third chapter, part of which is attached here, Wilson describes how he was drawn to faith by the powerful Baptist service, and by a pastor who tapped his sensitivity to patriotism and sacrifice. A grandmotherly woman further fired his religious imagination and hope with a story about a miracle.

Yet even when that hope began to fade, Wilson's faith remained strong. It started to crack only at his baptism; the pastor smoked a cigar, and Wilson's immersion in the baptismal water felt "totally physical" and "somehow common."

His growing enchantment with science completed the destruction of his faith, as the physical world "increasingly seemed to me to be the complete world." Yet while he has lost his belief in God, he continues to believe in the religious experiences of men. For these he now seeks a naturalistic explanation, one encompassing everything from "atoms to genes to the human spirit."

Wilson writes at the end of chapter 1 that when his sight and hearing were both diminished, "the turning wheel of my life came to a halt," leaving him to "celebrate" that part of nature which can be "brought close for inspection." For a man like Wilson, where might the "wheel" have stopped had these accidents not halted it when they did?

Wilson attributes his admiration for scientists who work "heroically" to his education at the military academy. Can it also be understood in the light of his early impression that nature is a "tensed malignity" and the source of monsters?

When Wilson became disappointed by religion, and science replaced it for him as "the light and the way," he sought a comprehensive scientific explanation for religion. How might the frustration of his religious hopes have enlarged his scientific quest? Does his science rest on something like a religious faith? Is such a "faith in science" rational? Is it reasonable?

Paradise Beach

What happened, what we *think* happened in distant memory, is built around a small collection of dominating images. In one of my own from the age of seven, I stand in the shallows off Paradise Beach, staring down at a huge jellyfish in water so still and clear that its every detail is revealed as though it were trapped in glass. The creature is astonishing. It existed outside my previous imagination. I study it from every angle I can manage from above the water's surface. Its opalescent pink bell is divided by thin red lines that radiate from center to circular edge. A wall of tentacles falls from the rim to surround and partially veil a feeding tube and other organs, which fold in and out like the fabric of a drawn curtain. I can see only a little way into this lower tissue mass. I want to know more but am afraid to wade in deeper and look more closely into the heart of the creature.

The jellyfish, I know now, was a sea nettle, formal scientific name *Chrysaora quinquecirrha*, a scyphozoan, a medusa, a member of the pelagic fauna that drifted in from the Gulf of Mexico and paused in the place I found it. I had no idea then of these names from the lexicon of zoology. The only word I had heard was *jellyfish*. But what a spectacle my animal was, and how inadequate, how demeaning, the bastard word used to label it. I should have been able to whisper its true name: *scyph-o-zo-an!* Think of it! I have found a scyphozoan. The name would have been a more fitting monument to this discovery.

The creature hung there motionless for hours. As evening approached and the time came for me to leave, its tangled undermass appeared to stretch deeper into the darkening water. Was this, I wondered, an animal or a collection of animals? Today I can say that it was a single animal. And that another outwardly similar animal found in the same waters, the Portuguese man-of-war, is a colony of animals so tightly joined as to form one smoothly functioning superorganism. Such are the general facts I recite easily now, but this sea nettle was special. It came into my world abruptly, from I knew not where, radiating what I cannot put into words except—*alien purpose and dark happenings in the kingdom of deep water.* The scyphozoan still embodies, when I summon its image, all the mystery and tensed malignity of the sea.

The next morning the sea nettle was gone. I never saw another during that summer of 1936. The place, Paradise Beach, which I have revisited in recent years, is a small settlement on the east shore of Florida's Perdido Bay, not far from Pensacola and in sight of Alabama across the water.

There was trouble at home in this season of fantasy. My parents were ending their marriage that year. Existence was difficult for them, but not for me, their only child, at least not yet. I had been placed in the care of a family that boarded one or two boys during the months of the summer vacation. Paradise Beach was paradise truly named for a little boy. Each morning after breakfast I left the small shorefront house to wander alone in search of treasures along the strand. I waded in and out of the dependably warm surf and scrounged for anything I could find in the drift. Sometimes I just sat on a rise to scan the open water. Back in time for lunch, out again, back for dinner, out once again, and, finally, off to bed to relive my continuing adventure briefly before falling asleep.

I have no remembrance of the names of the family I stayed with, what they looked like, their ages, or even how many there were. Most likely they were a married couple and, I am willing to suppose, caring and warmhearted people. They have passed out of my memory, and I have no need to learn their identity. It was the animals of that place that cast a lasting spell. I was seven years old, and every species, large and small, was a wonder to be examined, thought about, and, if possible, captured and examined again.

There were needlefish, foot-long green torpedoes with slender beaks, cruising the water just beneath the surface. Nervous in temperament, they kept you in sight and never let you come close enough to reach out a hand and catch them. I wondered where they went at night, but never found out. Blue crabs with skin-piercing claws scuttled close to shore at dusk. Easily caught in long-handled nets, they were boiled and cracked open and eaten straight or added to gumbo, the spicy seafood stew of the Gulf coast. Sea trout and other fish worked deeper water out to the nearby eelgrass flats and perhaps beyond; if you had a boat you could cast for them with bait and spinners. Stingrays, carrying threatening lances of bone flat along their muscular tails, buried themselves in the bottom sand of hip-deep water in the daytime and moved close to the surf as darkness fell. . . .

. . . How I longed to discover animals each larger than the last, until finally I caught a glimpse of some true giant! I knew there were large animals out there in deep water. Occasionally a school of bottlenose porpoises passed offshore less than a stone's throw from where I stood. In pairs, trios, and quartets they cut the surface with their backs and dorsal fins, arced down and out of sight, and broke the water again ten or twenty yards farther on. Their repetitions were so rhythmic that I could pick the spot where they would appear next. On calm days I sometimes scanned the glassy surface of Perdido Bay for hours at a time in the hope of spotting something huge and monstrous as it rose to the surface. I wanted at least to see a shark, to watch the fabled dorsal fin thrust proud out of the water, knowing it would look a lot like a porpoise at a distance but would surface and sound at irregular intervals. I also hoped for more than sharks, what exactly I could not say: something to enchant the rest of my life.

Almost all that came in sight were clearly porpoises, but I was not completely disappointed. Before I tell you about the one exception, let me say something about the psychology of monster hunting. Giants exist as a state of the mind. They are defined not as an absolute measurement but as a proportionality. I estimate that when I was seven years old I saw animals at about twice the size I see them now. The bell of a sea nettle averages ten inches across, I know that now; but the one I found seemed two feet across—a grown man's two feet. So giants can be real, even if adults don't choose to classify them as such. I was destined to meet such a creature at last. But it would not appear as a swirl on the surface of the open water.

It came close in at dusk, suddenly, as I sat on the dock leading away from shore to the family boathouse raised on pilings in shallow water. In the failing light I could barely see to the bottom, but I stayed perched on the dock anyway, looking for any creature large or small that might be moving. Without warning a gigantic ray, many times larger than the stingrays of common experience, glided silently out of the darkness, beneath my dangling feet, and away into the depths on the other side. It was gone in seconds, a circular shadow, seeming to blanket the whole bottom. I was thunderstruck. And immediately seized with a need to see this behemoth again, to capture it if I could, and to examine it close up. Perhaps, I thought, it lived nearby and cruised around the dock every night.

Late the next afternoon I anchored a line on the dock, skewered a live pinfish on the biggest hook I could find in the house, and let the bait sit in six feet of water overnight. The following morning I rushed out and pulled in the line. The bait was gone; the hook was bare. I repeated the procedure for a week without result, always losing the pinfish. I might have had better luck in snagging a ray if I had used shrimp or crab for bait, but no one gave me this beginner's advice. One morning I pulled in a Gulf toadfish, an omnivorous bottom-dweller with a huge mouth, bulging eyes, and slimy skin. Locals consider the species a trash fish and one of the ugliest of all sea creatures. I thought it was wonderful. I kept my toadfish in a bottle for a day, then let it go. After a while I stopped putting the line out for the great ray. I never again saw it pass beneath the dock.

Why do I tell you this little boy's story of medusas, rays, and sea monsters, nearly sixty years after the fact? Because it illustrates, I think, how a naturalist is created. A child comes to the edge of deep water with a mind prepared for wonder. He is like a primitive adult of long ago, an acquisitive early *Homo* arriving at the shore of Lake Malawi, say, or the Mozambique Channel. The experience must have been repeated countless times over thousands of generations, and it was richly rewarded. The sea, the lakes, and the broad rivers served as sources of food and barriers against enemies. No petty boundaries could split their flat expanse. They could not be burned or eroded into sterile gullies. They were impervious, it seemed, to change of any kind. The waterland was always there, timeless, invulnerable, mostly beyond reach, and inexhaustible. The child is ready to grasp this archetype, to explore and learn, but he has few words to describe his guiding emotions. Instead he is given a compelling image that will serve in later life as a talisman, transmitting a powerful energy that directs the growth of experience and knowledge. He will add complicated details and context from his culture as he grows older. But the core image stays intact. When an adult he will find it curious, if he is at all reflective, that he has the urge to travel all day to fish or to watch sunsets on the ocean horizon.

Hands-on experience at the critical time, not systematic knowledge, is what counts in the making of a naturalist. Better to be an untutored savage for a while, not to know the names or anatomical detail. Better to spend long stretches of time just searching and dreaming. Rachel Carson, who understood this principle well, used different words to the same effect in *The Sense of Wonder* in 1965: "If facts are the seeds that later produce knowledge and wisdom, then the emotions and the impressions of the senses are the fertile soil in which the seeds must grow. The years of childhood are the time to prepare the soil." She wisely took children to the edge of the sea.

The summer at Paradise Beach was for me not an educational exercise planned by adults, but an accident in a haphazard life. I was parked there in what my parents trusted would be a safe and carefree environment. During that brief time, however, a second accident occurred that determined what kind of naturalist I would eventually become. I was fishing on the dock with minnow hooks and rod, jerking pinfish out of the water as soon as they struck the bait. The species, *Lagodon rhomboides*, is small, perchlike, and voracious. It carries ten needlelike spines that stick straight up in the membrane of the dorsal fin when it is threatened. I carelessly yanked too hard when one of the fish pulled on my line. It flew out of the water and into my face. One of its spines pierced the pupil of my right eye.

The pain was excruciating, and I suffered for hours. But being anxious to stay outdoors, I didn't complain very much. I continued fishing. Later, the host family, if they understood the problem at all (I can't remember), did not take me in for medical treatment. The next day the pain had subsided into mild discomfort, and then it disappeared. Several months later, after I had returned home to Pensacola, the pupil of the eye began to cloud over with a traumatic cataract. As soon as my parents noticed the change, they took me to a doctor, who shortly afterward admitted me to the old Pensacola Hospital to have the lens removed. . . .

. . . I was left with full sight in the left eye only. Fortunately, that vision proved to be more acute at close range than average—20/10 on the ophthalmologist's chart—and has remained so all my life. I lost stereoscopy but can make out fine print and the hairs on the bodies of small insects. In adolescence I also lost, possibly as the result of a hereditary defect, most of my hearing in the uppermost registers. Without a hearing aid, I cannot make out the calls of many bird and frog species. So when I set out later as a teenager with Roger Tory Peterson's *Field Guide to the Birds* and binoculars in hand, as all true naturalists in America must at one time or other, I proved to be a wretched birdwatcher. I couldn't hear birds; I couldn't locate them unless they obligingly fluttered past in clear view; even one bird singing in a tree close by was invisible unless someone pointed a finger straight at it. The same was true of frogs. On rainy spring nights my college companions could walk to the mating grounds of frogs guided only by the high-pitched calls of the males. I managed a few, such as the deep-voiced barking tree frog, which sounds like someone thumping a tub, and the eastern spadefoot toad, which wails like a soul on its way to perdition; but from most species all I detected was a vague buzzing in the ears.

In one important respect the turning wheel of my life came to a halt at this very early age. I was destined to become an entomologist, committed to minute crawling and flying insects, not by any touch of idiosyncratic genius, not by foresight, but by a fortuitous constriction of physiological ability. I had to have one kind of animal if not another, because the fire had been lit and I took what I could get. The attention of my surviving eye turned to the ground. I would thereafter celebrate the little things of the world, the animals that can be picked up between thumb and forefinger and brought close for inspection.

Send Us the Boy

Who can say what events formed his own character? Too many occur in the twilight of early childhood. The mind lives in half-remembered experiences of uncertain valence, where self-deception twists memory further from truth with every passing year. But of one event I can be completely sure. It began in the winter of 1937, when my parents, Edward and Inez Freeman Wilson, separated and began divorce proceedings. Divorce was still unusual at that time and in that part of the country, and there must have been a great deal of gossiping and head-shaking among other family members. While my parents untangled their lives, they looked for a place that could offer a guarantee of security to a seven-year-old. They chose the Gulf Coast Military Academy, a private school located on the shore road four miles east of Gulfport, Mississippi. . . . All dreams of languor and boyhood adventure vanished.

GCMA was a carefully planned nightmare engineered for the betterment of the untutored and undisciplined. It was a military academy of the original mold, all gray-wool clothed and ramrod-straight. The school prospectus guaranteed—it did not "offer" or "make available"; it *guaranteed*—a solid traditional education. Some of its graduates went on to civilian colleges and universities across the country. But at heart GCMA was a preparatory school for West Point, Annapolis, and private equivalents such as the Virginia Military Academy whose central purpose was to train America's officer corps. . . .

. . . The Gulf Coast Military Academy was classed each year without fail as an Honor School by the United States War Department. In other words, it was a boot camp. Its regimen was designed to abrade away all the bad qualities inhering in the adolescent male, while building the kind of character that does not flinch at a whiff of grape-shot. "Send Us the Boy and We Will Return the Man" was its motto. The 1937 yearbook, from which my childish face stonily gazes, explains the formula with pitiless clarity:

— The daily work is a systematic routine in which every duty has its place in the day and, therefore, will not be overlooked.

— By association with other cadets, each cadet begins to recognize himself as an integral part of a body and, with this in view, he assumes the correct attitude toward the rights of others.

— By being thrown on his own resources, a boy develops initiative and self-dependence and grows away from the helpless, dependent spirit into which many boys have been coddled.

The systematic routine the author had in mind (and was he, I wonder, square-faced Major Charles W. Chalker, Professor of Military Science and Tactics, whose photograph gazes out at me from the yearbook?) emulated those of the adult service academies. It could be used today, if softened a bit, at the Marine training camp on Parris Island. For seven days a week real bugles, played by cadets proud of their job, led us lockstep through the Schedule. First Call 6:00, Reveille 6:05, Assembly 6:10,

Sick Call 6:30, Police Inspection 6:40, Waiter's Warning 6:45, Assembly and March to Mess 7:00, School Call 7:40. Then, without bugles, came calls to change class, Chapel Assembly 10:20, Intermission 4 minutes, Warning Call, Return to Class. And so tramp forward through the day, finally to dinner. The bugles resumed with Call to Quarters 6:50, Study (no radios!) 7:00, Tattoo 9:15, and Taps 9:30. No talking afterward, or you go on delinquency report.

On Saturday the schedule was similar but lighter, with time off for leisure, athletics, and delinquency reports. On Sunday we really snapped to life: shined our shoes, polished our buttons and belt buckles (uniforms mandatory at all times, formal gray and white on Sunday), and attended church. Then we prepared for Battalion Parade, which kicked off at 3:30. We marched out in formation, to be watched and graded by unit and individual, past officer-instructors, visiting parents, and a few curious, respectful townspeople. The youngest boys, of whom I was one, brought up the rear.

The curriculum was laid before the student in resonant single words: arithmetic, algebra, geometry, physics, chemistry, history, English, foreign language. No art, nature field trips, and certainly no enterprises with wimpy titles like "introduction to chemistry" or "the American experience." Some electives were allowed, but only in cheerless subjects such as Latin, commercial geography, and business ethics. There was an implication that if you could not cut the mustard in the military, there was always commerce. Older cadets were trained in rifle marksmanship, mortar and machine-gun fire, surveying, and military strategy. . . .

. . . Disputes among cadets that could not be talked through were expected to be settled manfully, under adult supervision and in a boxing ring formed by standing cadets. Occasionally fistfights were quietly arranged behind buildings with no instructors or student officers present, but in general all aggression was effectively channeled according to regulations.

Misbehavior of any kind brought time in the bull ring, an activity not mentioned in the brochures. Regular cadets marched with rifles at shoulder arms around a circular track for one to several hours, the length of time depending on the seriousness of the charge. Longer terms were broken up and spread over a succession of days. Junior cadets "marched"— actually, most of the time we just strolled—without rifles. It was a good time to get away from the others and daydream. I was a frequent rule breaker, and spent what seems in retrospect to have been an unconscionable amount of my time at GCMA traveling in circles. As I recall, most of my sins involved talking with other cadets during class. If so, the lesson did not take. Now, as a university professor, I spend almost all of my time talking in class.

In my heart I know that I was a reasonably good kid. I was neither laggard nor rebellious, and time in the bull ring usually came as a surprise. Little or nothing was said to us junior cadets directly about discipline and punishment. We learned mostly by example and word of mouth. Infractions and sentences were posted each Saturday afternoon at 1:50 on the bulletin board next to the mail window, under "Delinquencies." We ran there each time to see who would play and who would march. No further recreation was allowed until all bull-ring time was completed. We heard rumors of legendary sentences imposed on older boys for unspeakable violations.

Wednesday afternoons were for fun, in the GCMA way of thinking. From 1:30 to 5:30, all cadets free of punishment went on leave. Buses conveyed us the four miles west to Gulfport for milkshakes, movies, and just walking around.

This dollop of frivolity was all well and good, but I pined for my beloved Gulf of Mexico, always in full sight from the front lawn of the Academy. . . .

. . . To all this strange new life I adjusted reasonably well. For the first few days after arrival I was seized with confusion and black loneliness, crying myself to sleep when the lights were out—quietly, however, so no one would hear. But after a while I came to feel that I belonged, that GCMA was a family of sorts, one moved by benevolent intention. I hated the place then but came to love it later, savoring it ever more in memory as the years passed and recollections of my distress faded. I stayed just long enough to be transformed in certain qualities of mind. I still summon easily the images of a perfect orderliness and lofty purpose. In one of those least faded, a cadet officer approaches on a Sunday morning as we gather for parade, a teenager mounted on a horse, resplendent in boots, Sam Browne belt, sheathed saber, and a cap cloth-covered in spotless white. He is poised to move in intricate maneuvers. He works his mount slowly through a tight circle, turning, turning, as he speaks to a group of other cadets on foot. He has fallen silent now in my mind, but his visual presence still shines with grace, decent ambition, and high achievement. I ask, What achievement? I cannot say, but no matter; the very ambiguity of his image preserves the power.

I left at the end of the spring term, carrying an inoculum of the military culture. Up to college age I retained the southerner's reflexive deference to elders. Adult males were "sir" and ladies "ma'am," regardless of their station. These salutations I gave with pleasure. I instinctively respect authority and believe emotionally if not intellectually that it should be perturbed only for conspicuous cause. At my core I am a social conservative, a loyalist. I cherish traditional institutions, the more venerable and ritual-laden the better.

All my life I have placed great store in civility and good manners, practices I find scarce among the often hard-edged, badly socialized scientists with whom I associate. Tone of voice means a great deal to me in the course of debate. I try to remember to say "With all due respect" or its equivalent at the start of a rebuttal, and mean it. I despise the arrogance and doting self-regard so frequently found among the very bright.

I have a special regard for altruism and devotion to duty, believing them virtues that exist independent of approval and validation. I am stirred by accounts of soldiers, policemen, and firemen who have died in the line of duty. I can be brought to tears with embarrassing quickness by the solemn ceremonies honoring these heroes. The sight of the Iwo Jima and Vietnam Memorials pierces me for the witness they bear of men who gave so much, and who expected so little in life, and the strength ordinary people possess that held civilization together in dangerous times.

I have always feared I lack their kind of courage. They kept on, took the risk, stayed the course. In my heart I admit I never wanted it; I dreaded the social machine that can grind a young man up, and somehow, irrationally, I still feel that I dropped out. . . .

. . . You will understand, then, that the people I find it easiest to admire are those who concentrate all the courage and self-discipline they possess toward a single worthy goal: explorers, mountain climbers, ultramarathoners, military heroes, and a very few scientists. Science is modern civilization's highest achievement, but it has few heroes. Most is the felicitous result of bright minds at play. Tricksters of the arcane, devising clever experiments in the laboratory when in the mood, chroniclers of the elegant insight, travelers to seminars in Palo Alto and Heidelberg. For it is given unto you to be bright, and play is one of the most pleasurable of human activities, and all that is well and good; but for my own quite possibly perverse reasons I prefer those scientists who drive toward daunting goals with nerves steeled against failure and a readiness to accept pain, as much to test their own character as to participate in the scientific culture. . . .

. . . There are certain experiences in childhood that surge up through the limbic system to preempt the thinking brain and hold fast for a lifetime to shape value and motivation. For better or for worse, they are what we call character.

I have told you of two such early formative experiences, the embracing of Nature and military discipline in turn, very different from each other in quality and strangely juxtaposed. There were three such episodes during my early childhood. I now come to the last, which in the genesis of a scientist may seem the most peculiar of them all.

A Light in the Corner

Wilson describes the stirring Baptist service, which tapped his sensitivity to patriotism and sacrifice and affected him powerfully. This impression was enhanced by Belle Raub, a family friend with whom, at 8, he lived for a while.

. . . Belle Raub, Mother Raub as I quickly came to call her, lived on East Lee Street in Pensacola with her husband, E. J., a retired carpenter. She was a heavyset, bosomy woman in her late fifties. She eschewed makeup and favored long, floral-print dresses. She wore a cougar-claw pendant that I found fascinating. ("Where did you get it? Where are cougars found? What do they do?" Monsters of the land.)

Mother Raub was in fact the perfect grandmother. She was forever cheerily working in and around the house, from before I woke in the morning to after I fell asleep, gardening, cleaning, cooking, and crocheting spokewheel-patterned bedspreads that she gave to friends and neighbors. She was attentive to my every need and listened carefully to every story of my life, which I considered to have been both long and filled with meaning. I gave her no problems with my manners or discipline; the Gulf Coast Military Academy had taken care of that. . . .

. . . Mother Raub was a woman with a steadfast heart and a mystic soul. Holiness was for her a state to be ardently sought. She told me a story about a very religious friend who wished to unite with Jesus through prayer. One day this good woman looked up from her devotions and saw a strange light in the room. It was a sign from God.

"Where in the room?" I interrupted.

"Well, in the corner."

"Where in the corner?"

"Well . . . in the upper part of the corner, next to the ceiling."

My mind raced. Her friend had seen God! Or, at least, she had received a Sign. Therefore, she must have been a chosen person. Maybe the light gives you the answer to everything, whatever that is. It was the *Grail!* The leap was possible if you prayed in some special way.

So I prayed long and hard many evenings after that, glancing around occasionally to see if the light had arrived or if any other change had occurred in the room. Nothing happened. I decided I just wasn't up to bringing God into my life, at least not yet. I would have to wait, maybe grow a little more.

At the end of that school year I left Mother Raub, this time to rejoin my father. My interest in the mysterious light faded. Perhaps (I cannot remember exactly) I stopped believing altogether in the existence of the light. But I never lost faith in the immanence of the Lord. He would come soon as a light unto the world.

In the fall of 1943, when I was fourteen, I came back to spend another year with Belle Raub. I was old enough to be baptized and born again by my own free will. No one counseled me to take this step; I could have waited for years before the weekly altar call struck home. One evening it just happened. Mother Raub and I had walked over to the McReynolds School to attend a recital of gospel hymns sung a cappella by a traveling tenor soloist. I have forgotten his repertoire as a whole. But one song, delivered in measured, somber tones, deeply moved me. It was a dissonant piece that gripped the listener in Pentecostal embrace:

> Were you there when they crucified my Lord?
> Were you there when they nailed Him to the cross?
> Sometimes it makes me to tremble, tremble.
> Were you there when they crucified my Lord?

An otherwise restless and free-spirited adolescent, I wept freely in response to the tragic evocation. I wanted to do something decisive. I felt emotion as though from the loss of a father, but one retrievable by redemption through the mystic union with Christ—that is, if you believed, if you really believed; and I did so really believe, and it was time for me to be baptized.

Dressed in my Sunday clothes and accompanied by Mother Raub, I called on the Reverend Wallace Rogers at the First Baptist Church to announce my decision and to select a time for baptism. For a teenager to meet the pastor of a large congregation was an exceptional event. I was tense and nervous as we walked into Rogers' office. He rose from his desk to greet us.

He was dressed in sports clothes and *smoking a cigar*. A cigar! In his friendly, casual way he congratulated me on my decision, and together we chose a date for the baptism. I filled out the application form as he watched and drew on his cigar. Mother Raub said nothing, then or later, about his transgression. But I knew what was on her mind!

One Sunday evening in February 1944, I stood in the line of the newly converted in a room behind the pulpit. While the congregation watched, we came out one by one to join the pastor in a large tank of chest-deep water in the choir loft at the front of the church. I was dressed in a light gown over my undershorts. When my turn came Rogers recited the baptismal dedication and bent me over once like a ballroom dancer, backward and downward, until my entire body and head dipped beneath the surface.

Later, as I dried off and rejoined the congregation, I reflected on how totally physical, how somehow common, the rite of passage had been, like putting on swimming trunks and jumping off the tower at the Pensacola Bay bathhouse the way it was done in 1943, letting your toes squish in the bottom mud for a moment before you kicked back up to the surface. I had felt embarrassed and uncomfortable during the baptism itself. Was the whole world completely physical, after all? I worried over Dr. Rogers' comfortable clothing and cigar. And something small somewhere cracked. I had been holding an exquisite, perfect spherical jewel in my hand, and now, turning it over in a certain light, I discovered a ruinous fracture.

The still faithful might say I never truly knew grace, never had it; but they would be wrong. The truth is that I found it and abandoned it. In the years following I drifted away from the church, and my attendance became desultory. My heart continued to believe in the light and the way, but increasingly in the abstract, and I looked for grace in some other setting. By the time I entered college at the age of seventeen, I was absorbed in natural history almost to the exclusion of everything else. I was enchanted with science as a means of explaining the physical world, which increasingly seemed to me to be the complete world. In essence, I still longed for grace, but rooted solidly on Earth.

My fictional heroes in late adolescence were the protagonists of *Arrowsmith*, *The Sea Wolf*, and *Martin Eden*, the Nietzschean loners and seekers. I read Trofim D. Lysenko's *Heredity and Its Variability*, a theory officially sanctioned by Stalin as sound Marxist-Leninist doctrine, and wrote an excited essay about it for my high school science class. Imagine, I scribbled, if Lysenko was right (and he must be, because otherwise why would traditional geneticists be up in arms against him?), biologists could change heredity in any direction they wished! It was rank pseudoscience, of course, but I didn't know it at the time. And I didn't care by then; I had tasted the sweet fruit of intellectual rebellion.

I was exhilarated by the power and mystery of nuclear energy. Robert Oppenheimer was another far-removed science hero. I was especially impressed by a *Life* magazine photograph of him in a porkpie hat taken as he spoke with General Leslie Groves at ground zero following the first nuclear explosion. Here was Promethean intellect triumphant. Oppenheimer was a slight man, as I was a slight boy. He was vulnerable in appearance like me, but smilingly at ease in the company of a general; and the two stood there together because the physicist was master of arcane knowledge that had tamed for human use the most powerful force in nature.

Shortly afterward, during my first year at college, someone lent me a book that was creating a sensation among biologists, Erwin Schrödinger's *What Is Life?* The great scientist argued not only that life was entirely a physical process, but that biology could be explained by the principles of physics and chemistry. Imagine: biology transformed by the same mental effort that split the atom! I fantasized being Schrödinger's student and joining the great enterprise. Then, as an eighteen-year-old sophomore, I read Ernst Mayr's *Systematics and the Origin of Species.* It was a cornerstone of the Modern Synthesis of evolutionary theory, one of the books that combined genetics with Darwin's theory of evolution by natural selection. Mayr's writing reinforced in my mind the philosophy implicit in Schrödinger. He showed that variety among plants and animals is created through stages that can be traced by the study of ordinary nature around us. Mayr's text told me that I could conduct scientific research of a high order with the creatures I already knew and loved. I didn't need to journey to a faraway place and sit at the feet of a Schrödinger or a Mayr in order to enter the temple of science.

Science became the new light and the way. But what of religion? What of the Grail, and the revelation of purest ray serene that gives wholeness and meaning to life? There must be a scientific explanation for religion, moral precepts, the rites of passage, and the craving for immortality. Religion, I knew from personal experience, is a perpetual fountainhead of human emotion. It cannot be dismissed as superstition. It cannot be compartmentalized as the manifestation of some separate world. From the beginning I never could accept that science and religion are separate domains, with fundamentally different questions and answers. Religion had to be explained as a material process, from the bottom up, atoms to genes to the human spirit. It had to be embraced by the single grand naturalistic image of man.

That conviction still grips me, impelled and troubled as I am by emotions I confess I do not even now fully understand. There was one instructive moment when the subterranean feelings surfaced without warning. The occasion was the visit of Martin Luther King, Sr., to Harvard in January 1984. He came under the auspices of a foundation devoted to the improvement of race relations at the university. Its director, Allen Counter, an old friend with a similar Southern Baptist background, invited me to attend a service conducted by the father of the martyred civil rights leader, and to join a small group at a reception afterward.

It was the first Protestant service I had sat through in forty years. It was held in Harvard's Memorial Church. Reverend King gave a quiet hortatory address organized around scripture and moral principle. He omitted the altar call—this was, after all, Harvard. But at the end a choir of black Harvard students surprised me by singing a medley of old-time gospel hymns, with a professionalism equaling anything I ever heard in the churches of my youth. To my even greater surprise, I wept quietly as I listened. My people, I thought. My people. And what else lay hidden deep within my soul?

Excerpt from
SURELY YOU'RE JOKING,
MR. FEYNMAN
by Richard P. Feynman (as told to Ralph Leighton)

While some great scientists are driven by personal ambition, or a desire to behold the truth, or a passion to discover cures for human suffering, Nobel Prize-winning physicist Richard P. Feynman was driven by the love of play. The passages that follow are from Surely You're Joking, Mr. Feynman, *his memoir as told to Ralph Leighton.*

In the first of these passages, Feynman recounts his boyhood adventures tinkering with radios and introduces what he calls the "puzzle drive," which will not let him abandon any problem until he has solved it. Feynman's "puzzle drive" first directs him to tinker with electrical circuits, then radios, then mathematical problems and theorems.

In the second attached passage, the adult Feynman has just finished working on the Manhattan Project in Los Alamos, New Mexico, where the atom bomb was developed. Although he is still young, he has recently lost his wife (to tuberculosis). He has accepted a professorship at Cornell University, but finds himself at loose ends, personally and professionally. For reasons he does not initially understand, ideas fail to come to him. He feels like a fraud.

Feynman is brought out of his funk when he remembers that he loves to play and used to consider physics the greatest of all playgrounds. He decides to resume playing with physics, with no thought for the consequences. Great consequences result, nonetheless.

How does a puzzle differ from a question? How does tackling a puzzle differ from pursuing an answer to a question? What is it that is satisfied by and satisfying about solving a puzzle? What is it that is satisfied by and satisfying about finding the answer to a question? How does solving a puzzle compare with uncovering and beholding a truth?

How might a science based on solving puzzles differ from a science based on asking questions and seeking to answer them? Solving puzzles is one kind of

*play, but it is not the only kind. Is Feynman solving a puzzle when he begins to
play with the problem of the plate?*

*It is often said that play is done for its own sake. When Feynman plays with
the plate, he refuses even to consider the possible "importance" of what he is
doing. For Archimedes, too, science was important for its own sake (and not,
for instance, for the useful things it could produce). Can Archimedes be said
to have been "playing" with geometry? If not, what is the difference between
his approach and Feynman's?*

*Archimedes and Feynman approach the mysteries of nature in two differ-
ent ways. Will they feel differently about what they reveal, as well?*

How do hard work, play, and happiness merge for a man like Feynman?

He Fixes Radios by Thinking!

When I was about eleven or twelve I set up a lab in my house. It consisted of an old wooden packing box that I put shelves in. I had a heater,
and I'd put in fat and cook french-fried potatoes all the time. I also had
a storage battery, and a lamp bank.

To build the lamp bank I went down to the five-and-ten and got
some sockets you can screw down to a wooden base, and connected
them with pieces of bell wire. By making different combinations of
switches—in series or parallel—I knew I could get different voltages.
But what I hadn't realized was that a bulb's resistance depends on its
temperature, so the results of my calculations weren't the same as the
stuff that came out of the circuit. But it was all right, and when the
bulbs were in series, all half-lit, they would *gloooooooooow*, very pretty—it was great!

I had a fuse in the system so if I shorted anything, the fuse would
blow. Now I had to have a fuse that was weaker than the fuse in the
house, so I made my own fuses by taking tin foil and wrapping it around
an old burnt-out fuse. Across my fuse I had a five-watt bulb, so when my
fuse blew, the load from the trickle charger that was always charging the
storage battery would light up the bulb. The bulb was on the switchboard behind a piece of brown candy paper (it looks red when a light's
behind it)—so if something went off, I'd look up to the switchboard and
there would be a big red spot where the fuse went. It was *fun!*

I enjoyed radios. I started with a crystal set that I bought at the store, and I used to listen to it at night in bed while I was going to sleep, through a pair of earphones. When my mother and father went out until late at night, they would come into my room and take the earphones off—and worry about what was going into my head while I was asleep.

About that time I invented a burglar alarm, which was a very simple-minded thing: it was just a big battery and a bell connected with some wire. When the door to my room opened, it pushed the wire against the battery and closed the circuit, and the bell would go off.

One night my mother and father came home from a night out and very, very quietly, so as not to disturb the child, opened the door to come into my room to take my earphones off. All of a sudden this tremendous bell went off with a helluva racket—BONG BONG BONG BONG BONG!!! I jumped out of bed yelling, "It worked! It worked!"

I had a Ford coil—a spark coil from an automobile—and I had the spark terminals at the top of my switchboard. I would put a Raytheon RH tube, which had argon gas in it, across the terminals, and the spark would make a purple glow inside the vacuum—it was just great! . . .

. . . I also did some things with electric motors and built an amplifier for a photo cell that I bought that could make a bell ring when I put my hand in front of the cell. I didn't get to do as much as I wanted to, because my mother kept putting me out all the time, to play. But I was often in the house, fiddling with my lab.

I bought radios at rummage sales. I didn't have any money, but it wasn't very expensive—they were old, broken radios, and I'd buy them and try to fix them. Usually they were broken in some simple-minded way—some obvious wire was hanging loose, or a coil was broken or partly unwound—so I could get some of them going. On one of these radios one night I got WACO in Waco, Texas—it was tremendously exciting! . . .

. . . One day I got a telephone call: "Mister, are you Richard Feynman?"

"Yes."

"This is a hotel. We have a radio that doesn't work, and would like it repaired. We understand you might be able to do something about it."

"But I'm only a little boy," I said. "I don't know how—"

"Yes, we know that, but we'd like you to come over anyway."

It was a hotel that my aunt was running, but I didn't know that. I went over there with—they still tell the story—a big screwdriver in my back pocket. Well, I was small, so *any* screwdriver looked big in my back pocket.

I went up to the radio and tried to fix it. I didn't know anything about it, but there was also a handyman at the hotel, and either he noticed, or I noticed, a loose knob on the rheostat—to turn up the volume—so that it wasn't turning the shaft. He went off and filed something, and fixed it up so it worked.

The next radio I tried to fix didn't work at all. That was easy: it wasn't plugged in right. As the repair jobs got more and more complicated, I got better and better, and more elaborate. . . .

. . . Sometimes it took quite a while. I remember one particular time when it took the whole afternoon to find a burned-out resistor that was not apparent. That particular time it happened to be a friend of my mother, so I *had* time—there was nobody on my back saying, "What are you doing?" Instead, they were saying, "Would you like a little milk, or some cake?" I finally fixed it because I had, and still have, persistence. Once I get on a puzzle, I can't get off. If my mother's friend had said, "Never mind, it's too much work," I'd have blown my top, because I want to beat this damn thing, as long as I've gone this far. I can't just leave it after I've found out so much about it. I have to keep going to find out ultimately what is the matter with it in the end.

That's a puzzle drive. It's what accounts for my wanting to decipher Mayan hieroglyphics, for trying to open safes. . . .

. . . We had a thing at high school called the algebra team, which consisted of five kids, and we would travel to different schools as a team and have competitions. We would sit in one row of seats and the other team would sit in another row. A teacher, who was running the contest, would take out an envelope, and on the envelope it says "forty-five seconds." She opens it up, writes the problem on the blackboard, and says, "Go!"—so you really have more than forty-five seconds because while she's writing you can think. Now the game was this: You have a piece of paper, and on it you can write anything, you can *do* anything. The only thing that counted was the answer. If the answer was "six books," you'd have to write "6," and put a big circle around it. If what was in the circle was right, you won; if it wasn't, you lost.

One thing was for sure: It was practically impossible to do the problem in any conventional, straightforward way, like putting "A is the number of red books, B is the number of blue books," grind, grind, grind, until you get "six books." That would take you fifty seconds, because the people who set up the timings on these problems had made them all a trifle short. So you had to think, "Is there a way to *see* it?" Sometimes you could see it in a flash, and sometimes you'd have to invent another way to do it and then do the algebra as fast as you could. It was wonderful practice, and I got better and better, and I eventually got to be the head of the team. So I learned to do algebra very quickly, and it came in handy in college. When we had a problem in calculus, I was very quick to see where it was going and to do the algebra—fast.

Another thing I did in high school was to invent problems and theorems. I mean, if I were doing any mathematical thing at all, I would find some practical example for which it would be useful. I invented a set of right-triangle problems. But instead of giving the lengths of two of the sides to find the third, I gave the difference of the two sides. A typical example was: There's a flagpole, and there's a rope that comes down from the top. When you hold the rope straight down, it's three feet longer than the pole, and when you pull the rope out tight, it's five feet from the base of the pole. How high is the pole?

I developed some equations for solving problems like that, and as a result I noticed some connection—perhaps it was $\sin^2 + \cos^2 = 1$—that reminded me of trigonometry. Now, a few years earlier, perhaps when I was eleven or twelve, I had read a book on trigonometry that I had checked out from the library, but the book was by now long gone. I remembered only that trigonometry had something to do with relations between sines and cosines. So I began to work out all the relations by drawing triangles, and each one I proved by myself. I also calculated the sine, cosine, and tangent of every five degrees, starting with the sine of five degrees as given, by addition and half-angle formulas that I had worked out.

A few years later, when we studied trigonometry in school, I still had my notes and I saw that my demonstrations were often different from those in the book. Sometimes, for a thing where I didn't notice a simple way to do it, I went all over the place till I got it. Other times, my way was most clever—the standard demonstration in the book was much more complicated! So sometimes I had 'em beat, and sometimes it was the other way around. . . .

. . . I had also invented a set of symbols for the typewriter, like FOR-TRAN has to do, so I could type equations. I also fixed typewriters, with paper clips and rubber bands (the rubber bands didn't break down like they do here in Los Angeles), but I wasn't a professional repairman; I'd just fix them so they would work. But the whole problem of discovering what was the matter, and figuring out what you have to do to fix it—that was interesting to me, like a puzzle. . . .

The Dignified Professor

The adult Feynman has been made a professor at Cornell University.

. . . Anyway, I began to teach the course in mathematical methods in physics, and I think I also taught another course—electricity and magnetism, perhaps. I also intended to do research. Before the war, while I was getting my degree, I had many ideas: I had invented new methods of doing quantum mechanics with path integrals, and I had a lot of stuff I wanted to do.

At Cornell, I'd work on preparing my courses, and I'd go over to the library a lot and read through the *Arabian Nights* and ogle the girls that would go by. But when it came time to do some research, I couldn't get to work. I was a little tired; I was not interested; I couldn't do research! This went on for what I felt was a few years, but when I go back and calculate the timing, it couldn't have been that long. Perhaps nowadays I wouldn't think it was such a long time, but then, it seemed to go on for a *very* long time. I simply couldn't get started on any problem: I remember writing one or two sentences about some problem in gamma rays and then I couldn't go any further. I was convinced that from the war and everything else (the death of my wife) I had simply burned myself out.

I now understand it much better. First of all, a young man doesn't realize how much time it takes to prepare good lectures, for the first time, especially—and to give the lectures, and to make up exam problems, and to check that they're sensible ones. I was giving good courses, the kind of courses where I put a lot of thought into each lecture. But I didn't realize that that's a *lot* of work! So here I was, "burned out," reading the *Arabian Nights* and feeling depressed about myself.

During this period I would get offers from different places—universities and industry—with salaries higher than my own. And each time I got something like that I would get a little more depressed. I would say to myself, "Look, they're giving me these wonderful offers, but they don't realize that I'm burned out! Of course I can't accept them. They expect me to accomplish something, and I can't accomplish anything! I have no ideas. . . ."

The head of Feynman's laboratory tells him not to worry about research accomplishment, releasing him from his "feeling of guilt."

. . . Then I had another thought: Physics disgusts me a little bit now, but I used to *enjoy* doing physics. Why did I enjoy it? I used to *play* with it. I used to do whatever I felt like doing—it didn't have to do with whether it was important for the development of nuclear physics, but whether it was interesting and amusing for me to play with. When I was in high school, I'd see water running out of a faucet growing narrower, and wonder if I could figure out what determines that curve. I found it was rather easy to do. I didn't *have* to do it; it wasn't important for the future of science; somebody else had already done it. That didn't make any difference: I'd invent things and play with things for my own entertainment.

So I got this new attitude. Now that I *am* burned out and I'll never accomplish anything, I've got this nice position at the university teaching classes which I rather enjoy, and just like I read the *Arabian Nights* for pleasure, I'm going to *play* with physics, whenever I want to, without worrying about any importance whatsoever.

Within a week I was in the cafeteria and some guy, fooling around, throws a plate in the air. As the plate went up in the air I saw it wobble, and I noticed the red medallion of Cornell on the plate going around. It was pretty obvious to me that the medallion went around faster than the wobbling.

I had nothing to do, so I start to figure out the motion of the rotating plate. I discover that when the angle is very slight, the medallion rotates twice as fast as the wobble rate—two to one. It came out of a complicated equation! Then I thought, "Is there some way I can see in a more fundamental way, by looking at the forces or the dynamics, why it's two to one?"

I don't remember how I did it, but I ultimately worked out what the motion of the mass particles is, and how all the accelerations balance to make it come out two to one.

I still remember going to Hans Bethe and saying, "Hey, Hans! I noticed something interesting. Here the plate goes around so, and the reason it's two to one is . . ." and I showed him the accelerations.

He says, "Feynman, that's pretty interesting, but what's the importance of it? Why are you doing it?"

"Hah!" I say. "There's no importance whatsoever. I'm just doing it for the fun of it." His reaction didn't discourage me; I had made up my mind I was going to enjoy physics and do whatever I liked.

I went on to work out equations of wobbles. Then I thought about how electron orbits start to move in relativity. Then there's the Dirac Equation in electrodynamics. And then quantum electrodynamics. And before I knew it (it was a very short time) I was "playing"—working, really—with the same old problem that I loved so much, that I had stopped working on when I went to Los Alamos: my thesis-type problems; all those old-fashioned, wonderful things.

It was effortless. It was easy to play with these things. It was like uncorking a bottle: Everything flowed out effortlessly. I almost tried to resist it! There was no importance to what I was doing, but ultimately there was. The diagrams and the whole business that I got the Nobel Prize for came from that piddling around with the wobbling plate.

Excerpt from

THE DOUBLE HELIX: A PERSONAL ACCOUNT OF THE DISCOVERY OF THE STRUCTURE OF DNA

by James D. Watson

The Double Helix *relates the discovery of the structure of DNA in 1953 through the eyes of one of the two men who achieved it.*

Watson and his partner, Francis Crick, long to penetrate and reveal "the secret of life." They succeed, in what Watson describes as "an adventure characterized both by youthful arrogance and by the belief that the truth, once found, would be simple as well as pretty."

In the beginning of the story (not attached), Watson, an American, be-comes interested in DNA after seeing a photograph of it, taken by the English X-ray crystallographer Maurice Wilkins. The photo revealed that the mole-cule was not "irregular," as Watson had feared, but rather that it was entirely ordered and highly regular. Inspired, Watson found a position in the Cavend-ish Laboratory of Cambridge University in England, where he hoped he could begin work on DNA.

Also at Cavendish was Crick, a physicist who had recently begun working in biology. Crick's "shattering bang" of a laugh was one among several reasons why the lab's director, Sir Lawrence Bragg, hoped soon to dispatch him to America. Yet "immediately" upon arriving, Watson writes, he "discovered the fun of talking to Francis Crick."

Just previously, the great American chemist Linus Pauling had partly solved the mystery of the structure of proteins through his discovery of the alpha helix. Pauling owed his breakthrough to a technique called model-building. Watson had expected to use crystallography to decode DNA. Crick soon convinced him, though, that while crystallography would be useful, they should emulate Pauling. Pauling's achievement, Crick believed, "was the product of common sense, not the result of complicated mathematical reasoning. . . . [T]he essen-tial trick . . . was to ask which atoms like to sit next to each other. In place of pencil and paper, the main working tools were a set of molecular models super-

ficially resembling the toys of preschool children. . . . [A]ll we had to do was construct a set of molecular models and begin to play. . . ."

But the search for the structure of DNA was more than play. It was a serious race, not only for priority but also for the Nobel Prize that would surely accompany it. Pauling, fresh from his triumph with the alpha helix, was also known to be after the big prize. Within days of meeting, Watson and Crick had a plan: to "imitate Linus Pauling and beat him at his own game." They would have to tread carefully, however. Scientific etiquette gave researchers who started first a proprietary claim on the subjects they were investigating, and Wilkins and his colleague Rosalind Franklin, both of King's College, London, had prior stakes. Worsening the potential for rivalry, Maurice and "Rosy" were committed to crystallography.

The first of the attached excerpts begins near the end of 1952, when Pauling's son Peter—a student in the Cavendish labs and a friend of Watson's—reveals that his father may be close to a breakthrough. To its glee, the English team soon discovers that the great Pauling has made an elementary mistake.

The second excerpt begins just a few months later, after Watson and Crick have made their discovery. It describes the reactions of their competitors as word of their triumph trickles out and they move toward their momentous publication.

Given how the spirit of competition spurred these researchers forward, how can one explain their coming together when the truth was found?

What moves Watson as a scientist? How do his aspirations compare with those of Archimedes or Wilson or Feynman? How does the desire for priority, recognition, and lasting fame (the Nobel Prize) help or hinder the scientific quest for knowledge?

What assumptions about scientific truth guide Watson's efforts? Are those assumptions themselves "scientific"?

Why might Rosalind Franklin have believed the structure was "too pretty not to be true?" What gave Watson his initial confidence that the truth would be "simple" and "pretty"?

Wilson has written that most science is "the felicitous result of bright minds at play," adding that "play is one of the most pleasurable of human activities." Does Watson's account support those assertions?

And what did the twenty-five-year-old Watson mean when—on the heels of his historic accomplishment—he declared himself "too old to be unusual"?

Excerpt 1

The Pauling paper arrives in England in the first week of February.

Two copies, in fact, were dispatched to Cambridge—one to Sir Lawrence,[1] the other to Peter.[2] Bragg's response upon receiving it was to put it aside. Not knowing that Peter would also get a copy, he hesitated to take the manuscript down to Max's[3] office. There Francis[4] would see it and set off on another wild-goose chase. Under the present timetable there were only eight months more of Francis' laugh to bear. That is, if his thesis was finished on schedule. Then for a year, if not more, with Crick in exile in Brooklyn, peace and serenity would prevail.

While Sir Lawrence was pondering whether to chance taking Crick's mind off his thesis, Francis and I were poring over the copy that Peter brought in after lunch. Peter's face betrayed something important as he entered the door, and my stomach sank in apprehension at learning that all was lost. Seeing that neither Francis nor I could bear any further suspense, he quickly told us that the model was a three-chain helix with the sugar-phosphate backbone in the center. This sounded so suspiciously like our aborted effort of last year that immediately I wondered whether we might already have had the credit and glory of a great discovery if Bragg had not held us back. Giving Francis no chance to ask for the manuscript, I pulled it out of Peter's outside coat pocket and began reading. By spending less than a minute with the summary and the introduction, I was soon at the figures showing the locations of the essential atoms.

At once I felt something was not right. I could not pinpoint the mistake, however, until I looked at the illustrations for several minutes. Then I realized that the phosphate groups in Linus' model were not ionized, but that each group contained a bound hydrogen atom and so had no net charge. Pauling's nucleic acid in a sense was not an acid at all. Moreover, the uncharged phosphate groups were not incidental features. The hydrogens were part of the hydrogen bonds that held together the three intertwined chains. Without the hydrogen atoms, the chains would immediately fly apart and the structure vanish.

Everything I knew about nucleic-acid chemistry indicated that phos-

---

[1] Sir Lawrence Bragg, Director of the Cavendish and a founder of crystallography.
[2] Peter Pauling, Linus Pauling's son.
[3] Max Perutz, crystallographer.
[4] Francis Crick, Watson's partner.

phate groups never contained bound hydrogen atoms. No one had ever questioned that DNA was a moderately strong acid. Thus, under physiological conditions, there would always be positively charged ions like sodium or magnesium lying nearby to neutralize the negatively charged phosphate groups. All our speculations about whether divalent ions held the chains together would have made no sense if there were hydrogen atoms firmly bound to the phosphates. Yet somehow Linus, unquestionably the world's most astute chemist, had come to the opposite conclusion.

When Francis was amazed equally by Pauling's unorthodox chemistry, I began to breathe slower. By then I knew we were still in the game. Neither of us, however, had the slightest clue to the steps that had led Linus to his blunder. If a student had made a similar mistake, he would be thought unfit to benefit from Cal Tech's chemistry faculty. Thus, we could not but initially worry whether Linus' model followed from a revolutionary re-evaluation of the acid-base properties of very large molecules. The tone of the manuscript, however, argued against any such advance in chemical theory. No reason existed to keep secret a first-rate theoretical breakthrough. Rather, if that had occurred Linus would have written two papers, the first describing his new theory, the second showing how it was used to solve the DNA structure.

The blooper was too unbelievable to keep secret for more than a few minutes. I dashed over to Roy Markham's[5] lab to spurt out the news and to receive further reassurance that Linus' chemistry was screwy. Markham predictably expressed pleasure that a giant had forgotten elementary college chemistry. He then could not refrain from revealing how one of Cambridge's great men had on occasion also forgotten his chemistry. Next I hopped over to the organic chemists', where again I heard the soothing words that DNA was an acid.

By teatime I was back in the Cavendish, where Francis was explaining to John[6] and Max that no further time must be lost on this side of the Atlantic. When his mistake became known, Linus would not stop until he had captured the right structure. Now our immediate hope was that his chemical colleagues would be more than ever awed by his intellect and not probe the details of his model. But since the manuscript had already been dispatched to the *Proceedings of the National Academy,* by mid-March at the latest Linus' paper would be spread around the world. Then it would be only a matter of days before the error would be

---

[5] The English biochemist in whose lab Watson nominally worked.
[6] John Kendrew, one of two crystallographers in charge of Crick's lab.

discovered. We had anywhere up to six weeks before Linus again was in full-time pursuit of DNA.

Though Maurice[7] had to be warned, we did not immediately ring him. The pace of Francis' words might cause Maurice to find a reason for terminating the conversation before all the implications of Pauling's folly could be hammered home. Since in several days I was to go up to London to see Bill Hayes,[8] the sensible course was to bring the manuscript with me for Maurice's and Rosy's[9] inspection.

Then, as the stimulation of the last several hours had made further work that day impossible, Francis and I went over to the Eagle. The moment its doors opened for the evening we were there to drink a toast to the Pauling failure. Instead of sherry, I let Francis buy me a whiskey. Though the odds still appeared against us, Linus had not yet won his Nobel.

Excerpt 2

Watson and Crick have made their discovery and show it to their competitors.

Maurice needed but a minute's look at the model to like it. He had been forewarned by John that it was a two-chain affair, held together by the A-T and G-C base pairs, and so immediately upon entering our office he studied its detailed features. That it had two, not three, chains did not bother him since he knew the evidence never seemed clear-cut. While Maurice silently stared at the metal object, Francis stood by, sometimes talking very fast about what sort of X-ray diagram the structure should produce, then becoming strangely noiseless when he perceived that Maurice's wish was to look at the double helix, not to receive a lecture in crystallographic theory which he could work out by himself. There was no questioning of the decision to put guanine and thymine in the keto form. Doing otherwise would destroy the base pairs. . . .

. . . The next scientific step was to compare seriously the experimental X-ray data with the diffraction pattern predicted by our model. Maurice went back to London, saying that he would soon measure the critical reflections. There was not a hint of bitterness in his voice, and I felt quite relieved. Until the visit I had remained apprehensive that he would

---

[7] Maurice Wilkins, English X-ray crystallographer.
[8] Microbiologist.
[9] Rosalind Franklin of King's College, London.

look gloomy, being unhappy that we had seized part of the glory that should have gone in full to him and his younger colleagues. But there was no trace of resentment on his face, and in his subdued way he was thoroughly excited that the structure would prove of great benefit to biology.

He was back in London only two days before he rang up to say that both he and Rosy found that their X-ray data strongly supported the double helix. They were quickly writing up their results and wanted to publish simultaneously with our announcement of the base pairs. *Nature* was a place for rapid publication, since if both Bragg and Randall[10] strongly supported the manuscripts they might be published within a month of their receipt. However, there would not be only one paper from King's. Rosy and Gosling[11] would report their results separately from Maurice and his collaborators.

Two letters from Pasadena that week brought the news that Pauling was still way off base. The first came from Delbrück,[12] saying that Linus had just given a seminar during which he described a modification of his DNA structure. Most uncharacteristically, the manuscript he had sent to Cambridge had been published before his collaborator, R. B. Corey, could accurately measure the interatomic distances. When this was finally done, they found several unacceptable contacts that could not be overcome by minor jiggling. Pauling's model was thus also impossible on straightforward stereochemical grounds. . . .

Pauling learns of Watson and Crick's discovery. His "reaction was one of genuine thrill." As news of the discovery trickles out to other labs, it rapidly becomes apparent that all evidence supports it. Watson and Crick write up their findings and move toward publication.

. . . Sir Lawrence was shown the paper in its nearly final form. After suggesting a minor stylistic alteration, he enthusiastically expressed his willingness to post it to *Nature* with a strong covering letter. The solution to the structure was bringing genuine happiness to Bragg. That the result came out of the Cavendish and not Pasadena was obviously a factor. More important was the unexpectedly marvelous nature of the answer, and the fact that the X-ray method he had developed forty years before was at the heart of a profound insight into the nature of life itself.

---

[10] Prof. J. T. Randall, Wilkins's boss.
[11] R. G. Gosling, Rosy's student.
[12] Theoretical physicist Max Delbrück, a colleague of Pauling's.

The final version was ready to be typed on the last weekend of March. Our Cavendish typist was not on hand, and the brief job was given to my sister. There was no problem persuading her to spend a Saturday afternoon this way, for we told her that she was participating in perhaps the most famous event in biology since Darwin's book. Francis and I stood over her as she typed the nine-hundred-word article that began, "We wish to suggest a structure for the salt of deoxyribose nucleic acid (DNA). This structure has novel features which are of considerable biological interest." On Tuesday the manuscript was sent up to Bragg's office and on Wednesday, April 2, went off to the editors of *Nature*.

Linus arrived in Cambridge on Friday night. On his way to Brussels for the Solvay meeting, he stopped off both to see Peter and to look at the model. Unthinkingly Peter arranged for him to stay at Pop's.[13] Soon we found that he would have preferred a hotel. The presence of foreign girls at breakfast did not compensate for the lack of hot water in his room. Saturday morning Peter brought him into the office, where, after greeting Jerry with Cal Tech news, he set about examining the model. Though he still wanted to see the quantitative measurements of the King's lab, we supported our argument by showing him a copy of Rosy's original B photograph. All the right cards were in our hands and so, gracefully, he gave his opinion that we had the answer.

Bragg then came in to get Linus so that he could take him and Peter to his house for lunch. That night both Paulings, together with Elizabeth[14] and me, had dinner with the Cricks at Portugal Place. Francis, perhaps because of Linus' presence, was mildly muted and let Linus be charming to my sister and Odile.[15] Though we drank a fair amount of Burgundy, the conversation never got animated and I felt that Pauling would rather talk to me, clearly an unfinished member of the younger generation, than to Francis. The talk did not last long, since Linus, still on California time, was becoming tired, and the party was over at midnight.

Elizabeth and I flew off the following afternoon to Paris, where Peter would join us the next day. Ten days hence she was sailing to the States on her way to Japan to marry an American she had known in college. These were to be our last days together, at least in the carefree spirit that had marked our escape from the Middle West and the American culture it was so easy to be ambivalent about. Monday morning we went over to

[13] Watson liked this "high class boarding house," which served an attractive clientele.
[14] Watson's sister.
[15] Crick's wife.

the Faubourg St. Honoré for our last look at its elegance. There, peering in at a shop full of sleek umbrellas, I realized one should be her wedding present and we quickly had it. Afterwards she searched out a friend for tea while I walked back across the Seine to our hotel near the Palais du Luxembourg. Later that night with Peter we would celebrate my birthday. But now I was alone, looking at the long-haired girls near St. Germain des Prés and knowing they were not for me. I was twenty-five and too old to be unusual.

CHAPTER 3:
TO HEAL SOMETIMES,
TO COMFORT ALWAYS

WE HAVE CONSIDERED THE enduring human dream of perfecting nature. We have seen how some great scientists perceive the potential of the methodical pursuit of useful knowledge to make this dream a reality, even as others seek to shield scientific inquiry from utilitarian purposes. In our third chapter we turn to medicine, where we see, among other things, the dream of using knowledge to achieve perfect wholeness applied to the vulnerable, mortal human body.

This is a dream that comes naturally both to doctors, who see first-hand the suffering brought by disease and death, and to the sick and dying, who seek deliverers. But can doctors serve this desire for deliverance from the "natural shocks that flesh is heir to"? Is that all they do? Is it what they should do? Readings in this chapter explore the purposes of medicine, from the point of view of both doctor and patient. Taken together, they explore a vocation summoned to the work of healing and comforting.

Our readings begin with the Hippocratic oath, which for centuries encapsulated the ideals of medical purpose and physicianly conduct. Fittingly, the oath begins and ends with an attempt to locate the practice of medicine and the doctor himself within the greater order.

But human beings have always wondered about the source of healing and the relation between the doctor and the divine, and Hippocrates' word on these questions was not to be the last. Our next two readings— one from the Book of Sirach, which appears in the Catholic Bible, and one from Albert Camus's *The Plague*—further explore these mysteries.

Our fourth reading, "The Surgeon as Priest," by surgeon and writer Richard Selzer, offers a doctor's view of what it means to practice medicine. W. H. Auden follows with the point of view of a patient, in this case a patient eulogizing a beloved practitioner in "The Art of Healing."

A doctor, however, does not always heal. A physician confronts perhaps his hardest task when he knows he cannot be the deliverer for whom his patient hopes. What are his obligations when the news is bad? In the next three readings—"To One Shortly to Die," by Walt Whitman, and excerpts from Thomas Mann's *Buddenbrooks* and George Eliot's *Middlemarch*—we find doctors (or others) confronting the continuing illnesses or certain deaths of those in their care. What should be done for the patients themselves? What should be said to their families?

Finally, doctors stand in a privileged relation to their patients, and the privilege is fraught with danger for both. In our final reading, "Invasions," doctor and writer Perri Klass ruminates on one such privilege: the necessary invasion of the patient's privacy.

THE HIPPOCRATIC OATH

translated by Leon R. Kass, M.D.

This oath, the oldest and best-known expression of a medical ethic, was for centuries regarded as the guide for proper medical conduct. Although the accomplishments of modern medicine appear to have taken the discipline far from its ancient roots, the oath continues to offer a powerful account of what it means to be a doctor.

The oath begins by invoking ancient Greek deities. The specific deities invoked are Apollo, (here, "Apollo Physician"), the god associated with light, truth, and prophecy; Asclepius, child of Apollo, the "father" of medicine; Hygieia (whose name means "health," "living well") and Panaceia ("all heal"), both daughters of Asclepius and associated with what modern readers might call "prevention" and "treatment." The oath concludes with a plea, acknowledging that the physician's fortunes depend on his fulfillment of its terms.

The six substantive paragraphs in between address first (in the oath's longest paragraph) how the physician should comport himself with respect to his teachers, as well as his teacher's offspring, his own, and all other students of medicine. Physicians are here, literally, called into fraternity with one another; the gift of the medical art is equated with the gift of life. The five subsequent paragraphs indicate how the physician should conduct himself with respect to his patients and their households. The first three deal with the ends and means of treatment, appropriate and inappropriate, the last two with decorum.

Why begin the oath with an invocation of the gods? Why these gods? What does this beginning suggest about the powers of the physician and their source?

Parents, rightly, often resent the authority teachers have over their children. Yet, here, physician-teachers are explicitly equated with fathers, medical students with their sons. Is this equation or analogy justifiable? Why or why not?

What attitude toward the medical arts is expressed in the oath's five paragraphs on ends, means, and conduct toward patients and families?

What, according to the oath, is the true purpose of medicine?

Can you explain and justify the limits the oath places upon the uses of medical technique?

Except to say that a doctor must neither kill nor suggest killing, the oath is silent on the subject of death. What can one infer from the oath about a doctor's obligations to the hopelessly ill?

The Oath

I swear by Apollo Physician and Asclepius and Hygieia and Panaceia and all the gods and goddesses, making them my witnesses, that I will fulfil according to my ability and judgment this oath and this covenant:

To hold the one who has taught me this art as equal to my parents and to live my life in partnership with him, and if he is in need of money to give him a share of mine, and to regard his offspring as equal to my brothers in male lineage and to teach them this art—if they desire to learn it—without fee and covenant; to give a share of precepts and oral instruction and all the other learning to my sons and to the sons of him who has instructed me and to pupils who have signed the covenant and have taken an oath according to the medical law, but to no one else.

I will apply dietetic measures for the benefit of the sick according to my ability and judgment; I will keep them from harm and injustice.

I will neither give a deadly drug to anybody if asked for it, nor will I make a suggestion to this effect. Similarly I will not give to a woman an abortive remedy. In purity and holiness I will guard my life and my art.

I will not use the knife, not even on sufferers from stone, but will withdraw in favor of such men as are engaged in this work.

Into whatever houses I may enter, I will come for the benefit of the sick, remaining clear of all voluntary injustice and of other mischief and of sexual deeds upon bodies of females and males, be they free or slave.

Things I may see or hear in the course of the treatment or even outside of treatment regarding the life of human beings, things which one should never divulge outside, I will keep to myself holding such things unutterable [or "shameful to be spoken"].

If I fulfil this oath and do not violate it, may it be granted to me to enjoy life and art, being honored with fame among all men for all time to come; if I transgress it and swear falsely, may the opposite of all this be my lot.

Excerpt from

THE BOOK OF SIRACH

prepared by the Catholic Biblical Association of Great Britain

What is the true source of healing? For centuries, people have wondered whether healing comes from faith or art, from divine power or human skill. What is the relation between the doctor and the divine? And what about the medicines we take?

The following passage from the Book of Sirach asserts that "healing comes from the Most High," but identifies the physician as a divinely gifted instrument of that power. Because the physician is part of the holy gift of healing, he should be honored, and indeed is admired "in the presence of great men."

The opening words of this passage exhort readers to honor the physician "with the honour due him," and also "according to your need of him." What does it mean to honor the physician according to the honorer's need? Are these two exhortations in tension with each other? Why should the "honour due" to the physician be measured according to the honorer's need?

The physician should be honored and given his place, but because of the heavenly source of healing, the sick should also "pray to the Lord" and "offer a sweet-smelling sacrifice." Does this advice imply, also, its corollary: that illness is a result of sin? If one believes the source of healing is divine, must this inevitably affect one's understanding of illness?

In his final words, Sirach commends him "who sins before his Maker" to "the care of a physician." What does this suggest about the relation between the physician and the divine?

Honour the physician with the
      honour due him, according
      to your need of him,
   for the Lord created him;
for healing comes from the Most
      High,
   and he will receive a gift from
      the king.
The skill of the physician lifts up
      his head,
   and in the presence of great
      men he is admired.
The Lord created medicines from
      the earth,
   and a sensible man will not
      despise them.
Was not water made sweet with a
      tree
   in order that his power might
      be known?
And he gave skill to men
   that he might be glorified in
      his marvellous works.
By them he heals and takes away
      pain;
   the pharmacist makes of them
      a compound.
His works will never be finished;
My son, when you are sick do not
      be negligent,
   but pray to the Lord, and he
      will heal you.
Give up your faults and direct your
      hands aright,
   and cleanse your heart from all
      sin.
Offer a sweet-smelling sacrifice,

and a memorial portion of
   fine flour,
and pour oil on your offering,
   as much as you can afford.
And give the physician his place,
   for the Lord created him;
let him not leave you, for there
   is need of him.
There is a time when success lies
   in the hands of physicians,
for they too will pray to the Lord
that he should grant them success
   in diagnosis
and in healing, for the sake of
   preserving life.
He who sins before his Maker,
   may he fall into the care of a
   physician.

Excerpt from
THE PLAGUE
by Albert Camus, translated by Stuart Gilbert

*In Albert Camus's novel, an Algerian town is stricken by a deadly and myste-
rious plague. The population of the town is quarantined and, in its isolation,
struggles both to survive and to understand its strange fate.[1] In chronicling his
characters' search for understanding, the author explores the theological questions raised by suffering, death, and, sometimes, recovery.*

*The following excerpt consists of a conversation between the physician, Dr.
Rieux, and one Mr. Tarrou, a journalist who was trapped in the ailing town
by the quarantine.*

*Tarrou appears at Rieux's home at night and offers to help. The weary and
overburdened Rieux accepts at once but asks Tarrou if he "has weighed the
dangers" of his offer—exposure and death. Tarrou responds with a question of
his own, about a recently preached sermon that suggested the plague might be
a spiritual opportunity. Tarrou's question provokes a searching and intimate
conversation between the two men about why someone who lacks faith might
risk his own life to help others fight death.*

*Under questioning by Tarrou, Rieux confesses that he is at best uncertain
about the existence of God. He is certain, though, that "the order of the world
is shaped by death." Death causes suffering, which he cannot "get used to."
Indeed, Rieux's "idea of his profession" is, as he says, "more or less" to fight
"against creation as he found it."*

*Hippocrates and Sirach see the divine as the source of healing and believe
the doctor's role is to work with this gift. Rieux believes "the world is shaped by
death" and wonders whether, if there is a God, He might not want us to
"struggle with all our might" against it. Are these two views of medicine incompatible? Do they necessarily imply different understandings of the human
body? Do they necessarily imply different understandings of the obligations of
physicians?*

[1] Although *The Plague* is widely understood to be an allegory concerning a devastat-
ing political evil, the novel makes perfect sense if the plague is treated, literally, for
the medical problem it is.

Would either Hippocrates or Sirach have physicians comport themselves in a way different from Rieux, if faced with a deadly plague?

Should we believe the confessions of Dr. Rieux? Should we admire him?

An Algerian town has been stricken by a deadly and mysterious plague, and is under quarantine. The weary doctor, Rieux, is for the moment at home.

The doorbell rang. The doctor gave his mother a smile and went to open the door. In the dim light on the landing Tarrou[2] looked like a big gray bear. Rieux gave his visitor a seat facing his desk, while he himself remained standing behind the desk chair. Between them was the only light in the room, a desk lamp.

Tarrou came straight to the point. "I know," he said, "that I can talk to you quite frankly."

Rieux nodded.

"In a fortnight, or a month at most," Tarrou continued, "you'll serve no purpose here. Things will have got out of hand."

"I agree."

"The sanitary department is inefficient—understaffed, for one thing—and you're worked off your feet."

Rieux admitted this was so.

"Well," Tarrou said, "I've heard that the authorities are thinking of a sort of conscription of the population, and all men in good health will be required to help in fighting the plague."

"Your information was correct. But the authorities are in none too good odor as it is, and the Prefect can't make up his mind."

"If he daren't risk compulsion, why not call for voluntary help?"

"It's been done. The response was poor."

"It was done through official channels, and half-heartedly. What they're short on is imagination. Officialdom can never cope with something really catastrophic. And the remedial measures they think up are hardly adequate for a common cold. If we let them carry on like this they'll soon be dead, and so shall we."

"That's more than likely," Rieux said. "I should tell you, however, that they're thinking of using the prisoners in the jails for what we call the 'heavy work.'"

---

[2] A journalist trapped in town by the quarantine.

"I'd rather free men were employed."

"So would I. But might I ask why you feel like that?"

"I loathe men's being condemned to death."

Rieux looked Tarrou in the eyes.

"So—what?" he asked.

"It's this I have to say. I've drawn up a plan for voluntary groups of helpers. Get me empowered to try out my plan, and then let's sidetrack officialdom. In any case the authorities have their hands more than full already. I have friends in many walks of life; they'll form a nucleus to start from. And, of course, I'll take part in it myself."

"I need hardly tell you," Rieux replied, "that I accept your suggestion most gladly. One can't have too many helpers, especially in a job like mine under present conditions. I undertake to get your plan approved by the authorities. Anyhow, they've no choice. But—" Rieux pondered. "But I take it you know that work of this kind may prove fatal to the worker. And I feel I should ask you this; have you weighed the dangers?"

Tarrou's gray eyes met the doctor's gaze serenely.

"What did you think of Paneloux's sermon, doctor?"

The question was asked in a quite ordinary tone, and Rieux answered in the same tone.

"I've seen too much of hospitals to relish any idea of collective punishment. But, as you know, Christians sometimes say that sort of thing without really thinking it. They're better than they seem."

"However, you think, like Paneloux, that the plague has its good side; it opens men's eyes and forces them to take thought?"

The doctor tossed his head impatiently.

"So does every ill that flesh is heir to. What's true of all the evils in the world is true of plague as well. It helps men to rise above themselves. All the same, when you see the misery it brings, you'd need to be a madman, or a coward, or stone blind, to give in tamely to the plague."

Rieux had hardly raised his voice at all; but Tarrou made a slight gesture as if to calm him. He was smiling.

"Yes." Rieux shrugged his shoulders. "But you haven't answered my question yet. Have you weighed the consequences?"

Tarrou squared his shoulders against the back of the chair, then moved his head forward into the light.

"Do you believe in God, doctor?"

Again the question was put in an ordinary tone. But this time Rieux took longer to find his answer.

"No—but what does that really mean? I'm fumbling in the dark, struggling to make something out. But I've long ceased finding that original."

"Isn't that it—the gulf between Paneloux and you?"

"I doubt it. Paneloux is a man of learning, a scholar. He hasn't come in contact with death; that's why he can speak with such assurance of the truth—with a capital T. But every country priest who visits his parishioners and has heard a man gasping for breath on his deathbed thinks as I do. He'd try to relieve human suffering before trying to point out its excellence." Rieux stood up; his face was now in shadow. "Let's drop the subject," he said, "as you won't answer."

Tarrou remained seated in his chair; he was smiling again.

"Suppose I answer with a question."

The doctor now smiled, too.

"You like being mysterious, don't you? Yes, fire away."

"My question's this," said Tarrou. "Why do you yourself show such devotion, considering you don't believe in God? I suspect your answer may help me to mine."

His face still in shadow, Rieux said that he'd already answered: that if he believed in an all-powerful God he would cease curing the sick and leave that to Him. But no one in the world believed in a God of that sort; no, not even Paneloux, who believed that he believed in such a God. And this was proved by the fact that no one ever threw himself on Providence completely. Anyhow, in this respect Rieux believed himself to be on the right road—in fighting against creation as he found it.

"Ah," Tarrou remarked. "So that's the idea you have of your profession?"

"More or less." The doctor came back into the light.

Tarrou made a faint whistling noise with his lips, and the doctor gazed at him.

"Yes, you're thinking it calls for pride to feel that way. But I assure you I've no more than the pride that's needed to keep me going. I have no idea what's awaiting me, or what will happen when all this ends. For the moment I know this; there are sick people and they need curing. Later on, perhaps, they'll think things over; and so shall I. But what's wanted now is to make them well. I defend them as best I can, that's all."

"Against whom?"

Rieux turned to the window. A shadow-line on the horizon told of the presence of the sea. He was conscious only of his exhaustion, and at the same time was struggling against a sudden, irrational impulse to unburden himself a little more to his companion; an eccentric, perhaps, but who, he guessed, was one of his own kind.

"I haven't a notion, Tarrou; I assure you I haven't a notion. When I entered this profession, I did it 'abstractedly,' so to speak; because I had a desire for it, because it meant a career like another, one that young men often aspire to. Perhaps, too, because it was particularly difficult for a workman's son, like myself. And then I had to see people die. Do you know that there are some who *refuse* to die? Have you ever heard a woman scream 'Never!' with her last gasp? Well, I have. And then I saw that I could never get hardened to it. I was young then, and I was out-raged by the whole scheme of things, or so I thought. Subsequently I grew more modest. Only, I've never managed to get used to seeing people die. That's all I know. Yet after all—"

Rieux fell silent and sat down. He felt his mouth dry.

"After all—?" Tarrou prompted softly.

"After all," the doctor repeated, then hesitated again, fixing his eyes on Tarrou, "it's something that a man of your sort can understand most likely, but, since the order of the world is shaped by death, mightn't it be better for God if we refuse to believe in Him and struggle with all our might against death, without raising our eyes toward the heaven where He sits in silence."

Tarrou nodded.

"Yes. But your victories will never be lasting; that's all."

Rieux's face darkened.

"Yes, I know that. But it's no reason for giving up the struggle."

"No reason, I agree. Only, I now can picture what this plague must mean for you."

"Yes. A never ending defeat."

Tarrou stared at the doctor for a moment, then turned and tramped heavily toward the door. Rieux followed him and was almost at his side when Tarrou, who was staring at the floor, suddenly said:

"Who taught you all this, doctor?"

The reply came promptly:

"Suffering."

THE SURGEON AS PRIEST
by Richard Selzer

What is the human body to a doctor, and how should he approach it? Here surgeon and writer Richard Selzer thinks aloud about these questions.

First, after confessing that he shares the sense that "one must not gaze into the body," Selzer takes the reader on an imaginary tour of the "forbidden" interior of the human body. Next, he recalls a patient who refused surgery to repair a cancer-eaten, brain-exposing hole in his skull, but recovered after applying holy water. Third, reflecting on the brain, Selzer observes that the surgeon "knows the landscape of the brain, yet does not know how a thought is made." Surgeons who fail to understand the mystery of the brain commit acts against it "violent as rape." Selzer next imagines the temple of Asclepius, the ancient Greek god of medicine, to which the sick came to be cured. In his mind's eye he sees a patient in the temple reaching to touch a healing vision. Finally, in a most moving and astonishing account, he describes witnessing a diagnostic consultation based almost entirely on palpation of the pulse. Selzer notes that "I, who have palpated a hundred thousand pulses, have not felt a single one."

What do all these episodes have in common? What attitude toward the human body do they reveal, convey, or recommend?

What is Selzer's bond with Vesalius, the pioneer of the autopsy? Do surgeons have, or need, "dark desires"? How can it be "priestly" to transgress the taboo against visualizing the inner parts of someone's body?

In his discussion of the miraculous recovery of his patient, Joe Riker, Selzer notes, "How often it seems that the glory leaves as soon as the wound is healed?" What does this mean?

Why might the modern surgeon, who enters the body "like an exile returning at last to his hearth," want his heart to be buried in the temple of Asclepius, where the patient reaches for the healing touch in a dream?

What did Selzer admire about Yeshi Dhonden's approach to his patient? Why does he envy the patient of such a physician?

What might it mean to suggest that a surgeon (or a physician) is a priest? What god or religion or sacred being does he serve? What exactly is priestly about the medical vocation?

In the foyer of a great medical school there hangs a painting of Vesalius. Lean, ascetic, possessed, the anatomist stands before a dissecting table upon which lies the naked body of a man. The flesh of the two is silvery. A concentration of moonlight, like a strange rain of virus, washes them. The cadaver has dignity and reserve; it is distanced by its death. Vesalius reaches for his dissecting knife. As he does so, he glances over his shoulder at a crucifix on the wall. His face wears an expression of guilt and melancholy and fear. He knows that there is something wrong, forbidden in what he is about to do, but he cannot help himself, for he is a fanatic. He is driven by a dark desire. To see, to feel, to discover is all. His is a passion, not a romance.

I understand you, Vesalius. Even now, after so many voyages within, so much exploration, I feel the same sense that one must not gaze into the body, the same irrational fear that it is an evil deed for which punishment awaits. Consider. The sight of our internal organs is denied us. To how many men is it given to look upon their own spleens, their hearts, and live? The hidden geography of the body is a Medusa's head one glimpse of which would render blind the presumptuous eye. Still, rigid rules are broken by the smallest inadvertencies: I pause in the midst of an operation being performed under spinal anesthesia to observe the face of my patient, to speak a word or two of reassurance. I peer above the screen separating his head from his abdomen, in which I am most deeply employed. He is not asleep, but rather stares straight upward, his attention riveted, a look of terrible discovery, of wonder upon his face. Watch him. This man is violating a taboo. I follow his gaze upward, and see in the great operating lamp suspended above his belly the reflection of his viscera. There is the liver, dark and turgid above, there the loops of his bowel winding slow, there his blood runs extravagantly. It is that which he sees and studies with so much horror and fascination. Something primordial in him has been aroused—a fright, a longing. I feel it, too, and quickly bend above his open body to shield it from his view. How dare he look within the Ark! Cover his eyes! But it is too late; he has already *seen*; that which no man should; he has trespassed. And I am no longer a surgeon, but a hierophant who must do magic to ward off the punishment of the angry gods.

I feel some hesitation to invite you to come with me into the body. It seems a reckless, defiant act. Yet there is more than dread reflected from these rosy coasts, these restless estuaries of pearl. And it is time to share it, the way the catbird shares the song which must be a joy to him and is a living truth to those who hear it. So shall I make of my fingers, words; of my scalpel, a sentence; of the body of my patient, a story.

One enters the body in surgery, as in love, as though one were an exile returning at last to his hearth, daring uncharted darkness in order to reach home. Turn sideways, if you will, and slip with me into the cleft I have made. Do not fear the yellow meadows of fat, the red that sweats and trickles where you step. Here, give me your hand. Lower between the beefy cliffs. Now rest a bit upon the peritoneum. All at once, gleaming, the membrane parts . . . and you are *in*.

It is the stillest place that ever was. As though suddenly you are struck deaf. Why, when the blood sluices fierce as Niagara, when the brain teems with electricity, and the numberless cells exchange their goods in ceaseless commerce—why is it so quiet? Has some priest in charge of these rites uttered the command "Silence"? This is no silence of the vacant stratosphere, but the awful quiet of ruins, of rainbows, full of expectation and holy dread. Soon you shall know surgery as a Mass served with Body and Blood, wherein disease is assailed as though it were sin.

Touch the great artery. Feel it bound like a deer in the might of its lightness, and know the thunderless boil of the blood. Lean for a bit against this bone. It is the only memento you will leave to the earth. Its tacitness is everlasting. In the hush of the tissue wait with me for the shaft of pronouncement. Press your ear against this body, the way you did as a child holding a seashell and heard faintly the half-remembered, longed-for sea. Now strain to listen *past* the silence. In the canals, cilia paddle quiet as an Iroquois canoe. Somewhere nearby a white whipslide of tendon bows across a joint. Fire burns here but does not crackle. Again, listen. Now there *is* sound—small splashings, tunneled currents of air, slow gaseous bubbles ascend through dark, unlit lakes. Across the diaphragm and into the chest . . . here at last it is all noise; the whisper of the lungs, the *lubdup, lubdup* of the garrulous heart.

But it is good you do not hear the machinery of your marrow lest it madden like the buzzing of a thousand coppery bees. It is frightening to lie with your ear in the pillow, and hear the beating of your heart. Not that it beats . . . but that it might stop, even as you listen. For anything that moves must come to rest; no rhythm is endless but must one day lurch . . . then halt. Not that it is a disservice to a man to be made mindful of his death, but—at three o'clock in the morning it is less than philosophy. It is Fantasy, replete with dreadful images forming in the smoke of alabaster crematoria. It is then that one thinks of the bristlecone pines, and envies them for having lasted. It is their slowness, I think. Slow down, heart, and drub on.

What is to one man a coincidence is to another a miracle. It was one or the other of these that I saw last spring. While the rest of nature was in flux, Joe Riker remained obstinate through the change of the seasons. "No operation," said Joe. "I don't want no operation."

Joe Riker is a short-order cook in a diner where I sometimes drink coffee. Each week for six months he had paid a visit to my office, carrying his affliction like a pet mouse under his hat. Every Thursday at four o'clock he would sit on my examining table, lift the fedora from his head, and bend forward to show me the hole. Joe Riker's hole was as big as his mouth. You could have dropped a plum in it. Gouged from the tonsured top of his head was a mucky puddle whose meaty heaped edge rose above the normal scalp about it. There was no mistaking the announcement from this rampart.

The cancer had chewed through Joe's scalp, munched his skull, then opened the membranes underneath—the dura mater, the pia mater, the arachnoid—until it had laid bare this short-order cook's brain, pink and gray, and pulsating so that with each beat a little pool of cerebral fluid quivered. Now and then a drop would manage the rim to run across his balding head, and Joe would reach one burry hand up to wipe it away, with the heel of his thumb, the way such a man would wipe away a tear.

I would gaze then upon Joe Riker and marvel. How dignified he was, as though that tumor, gnawing him, denuding his very brain, had given him a grace that a lifetime of good health had not bestowed.

"Joe," I say, "let's get rid of it. Cut out the bad part, put in a metal plate, and you're cured." And I wait.

"No operation," says Joe. I try again.

"What do you mean, 'no operation'? You're going to get meningitis. Any day now. And die. That thing is going to get to your brain."

I think of it devouring the man's dreams and memories. I wonder what they are. The surgeon knows all the parts of the brain, but he does not know his patient's dreams and memories. And for a moment I am tempted . . . to take the man's head in my hands, hold it to my ear, and listen. But his dreams are none of my business. It is his flesh that matters.

"No operation," says Joe.

"You give me a headache," I say. And we smile, not because the joke is funny anymore, but because we've got something between us, like a secret.

"Same time next week?" Joe asks. I wash out the wound with peroxide, and apply a dressing. He lowers the fedora over it.

"Yes," I say, "same time." And the next week he comes again.

There came the week when Joe Riker did not show up; nor did he the week after that, nor for a whole month. I drive over to his diner. He is behind the counter, shuffling back and forth between the grill and the sink. He is wearing the fedora. He sets a cup of coffee in front of me.

"I want to see your hole," I say.

"Which one?" he asks, and winks.

"Never mind that," I say. "I want to see it." I am all business.

"Not here," says Joe. He looks around, checking the counter, as though I have made an indecent suggestion.

"My office at four o'clock," I say.

"Yeah," says Joe, and turns away.

He is late. Everyone else has gone for the day. Joe is beginning to make me angry. At last he arrives.

"Take off your hat," I say, and he knows by my voice that I am not happy. He does, though, raise it straight up with both hands the way he always does, and I see . . . that the wound has healed. Where once there had been a bitten-out excavation, moist and shaggy, there is now a fragile bridge of shiny new skin.

"What happened?" I manage.

"You mean that?" He points to the top of his head. "Oh well," he says, "the wife's sister, she went to France, and brought me a bottle of water from Lourdes. I've been washing it out with that for a month."

"Holy water?" I say.

"Yeah," says Joe. "Holy water."

I see Joe now and then at the diner. He looks like anything but a fleshly garden of miracles. Rather, he has taken on a terrible ordinariness—Eden after the Fall, and minus its most beautiful creatures. There is a certain slovenliness, a dishevelment of the tissues. Did the disease ennoble him, and now that it is gone, is he somehow diminished? Perhaps I am wrong. Perhaps the only change is just the sly wink with which he greets me, as though to signal that we have shared something furtive. Could such a man, I think as I sip my coffee, could such a man have felt the brush of wings? How often it seems that the glory leaves as soon as the wound is healed. But then it is only saints who bloom in martyrdom, becoming less and less the flesh that pains, more and more ghost-colored weightlessness.

It was many years between my first sight of the living human brain and Joe Riker's windowing. I had thought then, long ago: Could this one-pound loaf of sourdough be the pelting brain? *This*, along whose busy circuitry run Reason and Madness in perpetual race—a race that most often ends in a tie? But the look deceives. What seems a fattish snail drowzing in its shell, in fact lives in quickness, where all is dart and stir and rapids of electricity.

Once again to the operating room . . .

How to cut a paste that is less solid than a cheese—Brie, perhaps? And not waste any of it? For that would be a decade of remembrances and wishes lost there, wiped from the knife. Mostly it is done with cautery, burning the margins of the piece to be removed, coagulating with the fine electric current these blood vessels that course everywhere. First a spot is burned, then another alongside the first, and the cut is made between. One does not stitch—one cannot sew custard. Blood is blotted with little squares of absorbent gauze. These are called patties. Through each of these a long black thread has been sewn, lest a blood-soaked patty slip into some remote fissure, or flatten against a gyrus like a starfish against a coral reef, and go unnoticed come time to close the incision. A patty abandoned brainside does not benefit the health, or improve the climate of the intelligence. Like the bodies of slain warriors, they must be retrieved from the field, and carried home, so they do not bloat and mortify, poisoning forever the plain upon which the battle was fought. One pulls them out by their black thread and counts them.

Listen to the neurosurgeon: "Patty, buzz, suck, cut," he says. Then "Suck, cut, patty, buzz." It is as simple as a nursery rhyme.

The surgeon knows the landscape of the brain, yet does not know how a thought is made. Man has grown envious of this mystery. He would master and subdue it electronically. He would construct a computer to rival or surpass the brain. He would harness Europa's bull to a plow. There are men who implant electrodes into the brain, that part where anger is kept—the rage center, they call it. They press a button, and a furious bull halts in mid-charge, and lopes amiably to nuzzle his matador. Anger has turned to sweet compliance. Others sever whole tracts of brain cells with their knives, to mollify the insane. Here is surgery grown violent as rape. These men cannot know the brain. They have not the heart for it.

I last saw the brain in the emergency room. I wiped it from the shoulder of a young girl to make her smashed body more presentable to her father. Now I stand with him by the stretcher. We are arm in arm, like brothers. All at once there is that terrible silence of discovery. I glance at him, follow his gaze and see that there is more brain upon her shoulder, newly slipped from the cracked skull. He bends forward a bit. He must make certain. It *is* her brain! I watch the knowledge expand upon his face, so like hers. I, too, stare at the fragment flung wetly, now drying beneath the bright lights of the emergency room, its cargo of thoughts evaporating from it, mingling for this little time with his, with mine, before dispersing in the air.

On the east coast of the Argolid, in the northern part of the Peloponnesus, lies Epidaurus. O bury my heart there, in that place I have never seen, but that I love as a farmer loves his home soil. In a valley nearby, in the fourth century b.c., there was built the temple of Asclepius, the god of medicine. To a great open colonnaded room, the abaton, came the sick from all over Greece. Here they lay down on pallets. As night fell, the priests, bearing fire for the lamps, walked among them, commanding them to sleep. They were told to dream of the god, and that he would come to them in their sleep in the form of a serpent, and that he would heal them. In the morning they arose cured. . . .

Walk the length of the abaton; the sick are in their places, each upon his pallet. Here is one that cannot sleep. See how his breath rises and falls against some burden that presses upon it. At last, he dozes, only to awaken minutes later, unrefreshed. It is toward dawn. The night lamps flicker low, casting snaky patterns across the colonnade. Already the chattering swallows swoop in and out among the pillars. All at once the fitful eyes of the man cease their roving, for he sees between the candle-lamp and the wall the shadow of an upraised serpent, a great yellow snake with topaz eyes. It slides closer. It is arched and godlike. It bends above him, swaying, the tongue and the lamplight flickering as one. Exultant, he raises himself upon one arm, and with the other, reaches out for the touch that heals.

On the bulletin board in the front hall of the hospital where I work, there appeared an announcement. "Yeshi Dhonden," it read, "will make rounds at six o'clock on the morning of June 10." The particulars were then given, followed by a notation: "Yeshi Dhonden is Personal Physician to the Dalai Lama." I am not so leathery a skeptic that I would knowingly ignore an emissary from the gods. Not only might such sangfroid be inimical to one's earthly well-being, it could take care of eternity as well. Thus, on the morning of June 10, I join the clutch of whitecoats waiting in the small conference room adjacent to the ward selected for the rounds. The air in the room is heavy with ill-concealed dubiety and suspicion of bamboozlement. At precisely six o'clock, he materializes, a short, golden, barrelly man dressed in a sleeveless robe of saffron and maroon. His scalp is shaven, and the only visible hair is a scanty black line above each hooded eye.

He bows in greeting while his young interpreter makes the introduc-tion. Yeshi Dhonden, we are told, will examine a patient selected by a member of the staff. The diagnosis is as unknown to Yeshi Dhonden as it is to us. The examination of the patient will take place in our presence, after which we will reconvene in the conference room where Yeshi Dhonden will discuss the case. We are further informed that for the past two hours Yeshi Dhonden has purified himself by bathing, fasting, and prayer. I, having breakfasted well, performed only the most desultory of ablutions, and given no thought at all to my soul, glance furtively at my fellows. Suddenly, we seem a soiled, uncouth lot.

The patient had been awakened early and told that she was to be examined by a foreign doctor, and had been asked to produce a fresh specimen of urine, so when we enter her room, the woman shows no surprise. She has long ago taken on that mixture of compliance and resignation that is the facies of chronic illness. This was to be but another in an endless series of tests and examinations. Yeshi Dhonden steps to the bedside while the rest stand apart, watching. For a long time he gazes at the woman, favoring no part of her body with his eyes, but seem-ing to fix his glance at a place just above her supine form. I, too, study her. No physical sign nor obvious symptom gives a clue to the nature of her disease.

At last he takes her hand, raising it in both of his own. Now he bends over the bed in a kind of crouching stance, his head drawn down into the collar of his robe. His eyes are closed as he feels for her pulse. In a moment he has found the spot, and for the next half hour he remains thus, suspended above the patient like some exotic golden bird with folded wings, holding the pulse of the woman beneath his fingers, cra-dling her hand in his. All the power of the man seems to have been drawn down into this one purpose. It is palpation of the pulse raised to the state of ritual. From the foot of the bed, where I stand, it is as though he and the patient have entered a special place of isolation, of apartness, about which a vacancy hovers, and across which no violation is possi-ble. After a moment the woman rests back upon her pillow. From time to time, she raises her head to look at the strange figure above her, then sinks back once more. I cannot see their hands joined in a correspon-dence that is exclusive, intimate, his fingertips receiving the voice of her sick body through the rhythm and throb she offers at her wrist. All at once I am envious—not of him, not of Yeshi Dhonden for his gift of beauty and holiness, but of her. I want to be held like that, touched so, *received*. And I know that I, who have palpated a hundred thousand pulses, have not felt a single one.

At last Yeshi Dhonden straightens, gently places the woman's hand upon the bed, and steps back. The interpreter produces a small wooden bowl and two sticks. Yeshi Dhonden pours a portion of the urine specimen into the bowl, and proceeds to whip the liquid with the two sticks. This he does for several minutes until a foam is raised. Then, bowing above the bowl, he inhales the odor three times. He sets down the bowl and turns to leave. All this while, he has not uttered a single word. As he nears the door, the woman raises her head and calls out to him in a voice at once urgent and serene. "Thank you, doctor," she says, and touches with her other hand the place he had held on her wrist, as though to recapture something that had visited there. Yeshi Dhonden turns back for a moment to gaze at her, then steps into the corridor. Rounds are at an end.

We are seated once more in the conference room. Yeshi Dhonden speaks now for the first time, in soft Tibetan sounds that I have never heard before. He has barely begun when the young interpreter begins to translate, the two voices continuing in tandem—a bilingual fugue, the one chasing the other. It is like the chanting of monks. He speaks of winds coursing through the body of the woman, currents that break against barriers, eddying. These vortices are in her blood, he says. The last spendings of an imperfect heart. Between the chambers of her heart, long, long before she was born, a wind had come and blown open a deep gate that must never be opened. Through it charge the full waters of her river, as the mountain stream cascades in the springtime, battering, knocking loose the land, and flooding her breath. Thus he speaks, and is silent.

"May we now have the diagnosis?" a professor asks.

The host of these rounds, the man who knows, answers. "Congenital heart disease," he says. "Interventricular septal defect, with resultant heart failure."

A gateway in the heart, I think. That must not be opened. Through it charge the full waters that flood her breath. So! Here then is the doctor listening to the sounds of the body to which the rest of us are deaf. He is more than doctor. He is priest.

I know . . . I know . . . the doctor to the gods is pure knowledge, pure healing. The doctor to man stumbles, must often wound; his patient must die, as must he.

Now and then it happens, as I make my own rounds, that I hear the sounds of his voice, like an ancient Buddhist prayer, its meaning long since forgotten, only the music remaining. Then a jubilation possesses me, and I feel myself touched by something divine.

THE ART OF HEALING (IN MEMORIAM DAVID PROTECH, M.D.)

by W. H. Auden

In this eulogy to his personal physician, who was "what all doctors should be, but few are," English poet W. H. Auden considers the failings to which most doctors are subject and the qualities that make a few great.

The poem begins with what "most" patients believe: that their doctors are immune to death as well as to the vulnerabilities and needs conveyed by our nakedness and served by marriage. The poet, however, we quickly learn, has been saved from this common error by being the son of a doctor, and of one, moreover, who understood both the true nature and the pitfalls of his profession.

Prepared by this early teaching, Auden early recognized the man in the doctor he now eulogizes. Far from the seeming immortal preferred by most patients, this doctor was himself ailing, not only from a natural illness but also from an "arrogant" therapy that overreached and made his condition worse. Understanding, then, both sickness and the need for circumspection in treating it, this doctor, though "difficult," could be trusted.

The poet's father cautioned him that healing is not a "science" but "the intuitive art / of wooing Nature." What does this mean? Is it true? If so, what does this suggest about the teachability of medicine?

The poet's physician-father further observed that patients have unforeseeable "prejudices" that prevent them from reacting as beasts and plants do, "according to the common / whim of their species." Are human prejudices and nature really the opposing forces the poet here suggests? If so, how can a doctor accommodate both? Should he try?

The poet praises his physician for knowing, as Novalis did, that "Every sickness / is a musical problem" and "every cure / a musical solution." Is this an apt metaphor? What does it mean?

Auden also praises his doctor for treating his own small "ailments" well, and leaving his "major vices" alone. Is the capacity to do this necessarily praiseworthy in a doctor? Should not the physician care for "the whole person," his vices as well as his ailments? How might the Hippocratic physician respond to this question?

Most patients believe
dying is something they do,
not their physician,
that white-coated sage,
never to be imagined
naked or married.

Begotten by one,
I should know better. 'Healing,'
Papa would tell me,
'is not a science,
but the intuitive art
of wooing Nature.

Plants, beasts, may react
according to the common
whim of their species,
but all humans have
prejudices of their own
which can't be foreseen.

To some, ill-health is
a way to be important,
others are stoics,
a few fanatics,
who won't feel happy until
they are cut open.'

Warned by him to shun
the sadist, the nod-crafty,
and the fee-conscious,
I knew when we met,
I had found a consultant
who thought as he did,

yourself a victim
of medical engineers
and their arrogance,
when they atom-bombed
your sick pituitary
and over-killed it.

'Every sickness
is a musical problem,'
so said Novalis,
'and every cure
a musical solution':
You knew that also.

Not that in my case
you heard any shattering
discords to resolve:
to date my organs
still seem pretty sure of their
self-identity.

For my small ailments
you, who were mortally sick,
prescribed with success:
my major vices,
my mad addictions, you left
to my own conscience.

Was it your very
predicament that made me
sure I could trust you,
if I were dying,
to say so, not insult me
with soothing fictions?

Must diabetics
all contend with a nisus
to self-destruction?
One day you told me:
'It is only bad temper
that keeps me going.'

But neither anger
nor lust are omnipotent,
nor should we even
want our friends to be
superhuman. Dear David,
dead one, rest in peace,

having been what all
doctors should be, but few are,
and, even when most
difficult, condign
of our biassed affection
and objective praise.

TO ONE SHORTLY TO DIE

by Walt Whitman

*In this poem, the speaker—unidentified by profession or precise relation-
ship to the listener—singles his listener out "from all the rest . . . , having a
message for you."*

*Whoever the speaker may be, his message of painful truth—that his listener
is dying—is one doctors are often called upon to deliver. What is to be learned
from the way this mysterious emissary approaches the task?*

*He begins by confronting the truth, head-on: "You are to die . . . / I am
exact and merciless, but I love you." After this the emissary offers touch—not
an active touch, but mere contact, and with his right hand. He provides quiet
and faithful companionship, spiritual reassurance communicated in silence.*

*"The sun bursts through," and the dying one appears cheered by an insight
he has received. He begins to separate himself from the living, with their preoccupation with his illness, their hopes for a cure, and their grief.*

*Does the exactitude of the speaker make him also merciless? What is the
meaning and force of the "but" in "I am exact and merciless, but I love you"?
What is the relation between the speaker's abrupt "You are to die" and his
love? For what does the speaker offer congratulations with his final words? He
began truthfully; does he end that way?*

Who is the speaker? Does it matter?

*Why might nurse, parent, or neighbor be inadequate, at the end of life?
How ought we to speak "to one shortly to die?"*

From all the rest I single out you, having a message for you,
You are to die—let others tell you what they please, I cannot
    prevaricate,
I am exact and merciless, but I love you—There is no escape for
    you.

Softly I lay my right hand upon you, you just feel it,
I do not argue, I bend my head close and half envelop it,
I sit quietly by, I remain faithful,
I am more than nurse, more than parent or neighbor,

I absolve you from all except yourself spiritual bodily, that is
eternal, you yourself will surely escape,
The corpse you will leave will be but excrementitious.

The sun bursts through in unlooked-for directions,
Strong thoughts fill you and confidence, you smile,
You forget you are sick, as I forget you are sick,
You do not see the medicines, you do not mind the weeping
friends, I am with you,
I exclude others from you, there is nothing to be commiserated,
I do not commiserate, I congratulate you.

Excerpt from
BUDDENBROOKS
Death of the Frau Consul

by Thomas Mann, translated by H. T. Lowe-Porter

Should a doctor always preserve life, at any cost? The death of the Frau Consul, from Thomas Mann's novel Buddenbrooks, *invites readers to consider whether every patient is well-served by strict "vitalism."*

The Frau Consul is the matriarch of a prosperous German mercantile family of the nineteenth century. She has raised her children, welcomed her grandchildren, and buried her husband. Now she herself is dying.

At first she feels unready to die, having still the "tenacious clutch" on life habitual to her, and having been attacked by disease while in the full vigor of health. In her "naive hatred" of her illness, the Frau Consul gives her full attention to her doctors. Spiritual preparations for death distract her only temporarily. She shows greater interest in her symptoms and the course of her treatment even than in her grandson, who is presented to her at her bedside.

Still, she declines, and eventually passes through a transformation typical of the dying, after which "[she] is not as [she] was," and which seems to "cut off [her] retreat back to life." Once her physical suffering becomes acute, the Frau Consul begs for mercy. But her doctors refuse her the "sleeping draught" she requests and even take steps that prolong her miserable struggle. Why do the doctors insist on preserving her life? Are they right to try to do so?

When the Frau Consul's children express dismay at her suffering, the doctor assures them "in a tone of authority" that she is aware of nothing. Yet "a child could have seen," notes Mann, "that she realized everything." Why does the doctor say what he does? Should he have spoken differently?

When the Frau Consul wants treatment, she seems satisfied by what her doctors provide, despite its lack of success. Once she is prepared to die, what is she entitled to expect from them? Does she receive it?

146

The Frau Consul required constant attendance at her bedside. The worse her condition grew, the more she bent all her thoughts and all her energies upon her illness, for which she felt a naïve hatred. Nearly all her life she had been a woman of the world, with a quiet, native, and permanent love of life and good living. Yet she had filled her latter years with piety and charitable deeds: largely out of loyalty toward her dead husband, but also, perhaps, by reason of an unconscious impulse which bade her make her peace with Heaven for her own strong vitality, and induce it to grant her a gentle death despite the tenacious clutch she had always had on life. But the gentle death was not to be hers. Despite many a sore trial, her form was quite unbowed, her eyes still clear. She still loved to set a good table, to dress well and richly, to ignore events that were unpleasant, and to share with complacency in the high regard that was everywhere felt for her son. And now this illness, this inflammation of the lungs, had attacked her erect form without any previous warning, without any preparation to soften the blow. There had been no spiritual anticipation, none of that mining and sapping of the forces which slowly, painfully estranges us from life and rouses in us the sweet longing for a better world, for the end, for peace. No, the old Frau Consul, despite the spiritual courses of her latter years, felt scarce prepared to die; and she was filled with agony of spirit at the thought that if this were indeed the end, then this illness, of itself, in awful haste, in the last hour, must, with bodily torments, break down her spirit and bring her to surrender.

She prayed much; but almost more she watched, as often as she was conscious, over her own condition: felt her pulse, took her temperature, and fought her cough. But the pulse was poor, the temperature mounted after falling a little, and she passed from chills to fever and delirium; her cough increased, bringing up a blood-impregnated mucous, and she was alarmed by the difficulty she had in breathing. It was accounted for by the fact that now not only a lobe of the right lung, but the whole right lung, was affected, with even distinct traces of a process in the left, which Dr. Langhals, looking at his nails, called hepatization, and about which Dr. Grabow said nothing at all. The fever wasted the patient relentlessly. The digestion failed. Slowly, inexorably, the decline of strength went on.

She followed it. She took eagerly, whenever she could, the concentrated nourishment which they gave her. She knew the hours for her medicines better than the nurse; and she was so absorbed in watching the progress of her case that she hardly spoke to any one but the physicians, and displayed actual interest only when talking with them. Callers had been admitted in the beginning, and the old ladies of her social circle, pastors' wives and members of the Jerusalem evenings, came to see her; but she received them with apathy and soon dismissed them. Her relatives felt the difference in the old lady's greeting: it was almost disdainful, as though she were saying to them: "You can't do anything for me." Even when little Hanno came, in a good hour, she only stroked his cheek and turned away. Her manner said more plainly than words: "Children, you are all very good—but—perhaps—I may be dying!" She received the two physicians, on the other hand, with very lively interest, and went into the details of her condition.

One day the Gerhardt ladies appeared, the descendants of Paul Gerhardt. They came in their mantles, with their flat shepherdess hats and their provision-baskets, from visiting the poor, and could not be prevented from seeing their sick friend. They were left alone with her, and God only knows what they said as they sat at her bedside. But when they departed, their eyes and their faces were more gentle, more radiant, more blissfully remote than ever; while the Frau Consul lay within, with just such eyes and just such an expression, quite still, quite peaceful, more peaceful than ever before; her breath came very softly and at long intervals, and she was visibly declining from weakness to weakness. Frau Permaneder murmured a strong word in the wake of the Gerhardt ladies, and sent at once for the physicians. The two gentlemen had barely entered the sick-chamber when a surprising alteration took place in the patient. She stirred, she moved, she almost sat up. The sight of her trusted and faithful professional advisers brought her back to earth at a bound. She put out her hands to them and began: "Welcome, gentlemen. To-day, in the course of the day—"

The illness had attacked both lungs—of that there was no more room for doubt.

"Yes, my dear Senator," Dr. Grabow said, and took Thomas Buddenbrook by the hand, "it is now both lungs—we have not been able to prevent it. That is always serious, you know as well as I do. I should not attempt to deceive you. No matter what the age of the patient, the condition is serious; and if you ask me again to-day whether in my opinion your brother should be written to—or perhaps a telegram would be better—I should hesitate to deter you from it. How is he, by the way? A good fellow, Christian; I've always liked him immensely.—But for Heaven's sake, my dear Senator, don't draw any exaggerated conclusions from what I say. There is no immediate danger—I am foolish to take the word in my mouth! But still—under the circumstances, you know, one must reckon with the unexpected. We are very well satisfied with your mother as a patient. She helps all she can, she doesn't leave us in the lurch; no, on my word, she is an incomparable patient! So there is still great hope, my dear sir. And we must hope for the best."

But there is a moment when hope becomes something artificial and insincere. There is a change in the patient. He alters—there is something strange about him—he is not as he was in life. He speaks, but we do not know how to reply: what he says is strange, it seems to cut off his retreat back to life, it condemns him to death. And when that moment comes, even if he is our dearest upon this earth, we do not know how to wish him back. If we could bid him arise and walk, he would be as frightful as one risen from his coffin.

Dreadful symptoms of the coming dissolution showed themselves, even though the organs, still in command of a tenacious will, continued to function. It had now been weeks since Frau Consul first took to her bed with a cold; and she began to have bed sores. They would not heal, and grew worse and worse. She could not sleep, because of pain, coughing and shortness of breath, and also because she herself clung to consciousness with all her might. Only for minutes at a time did she lose herself in fever; but now she began, even when she was conscious, to talk to people who had long been dead. One afternoon, in the twilight, she said suddenly, in a loud, fervent, anxious voice, "Yes, my dear Jean, I am coming!" And the immediacy of the reply was such that one almost thought to hear the voice of the deceased Consul calling her.

Christian arrived. He came from Hamburg, where he had been, he said, on business. He only stopped a short time in the sick-room, and left it, his eyes roving wildly, rubbing his forehead, and saying "It's frightful—it's frightful—I can't stand it any longer."

Pastor Pringsheim came, measured Sister Leandra with a chilling glance, and prayed with a beautifully modulated voice at the bedside.

Then came the brief "lightening": the flickering up of the dying flame. The fever slackened; there was a deceptive return of strength, and a few plain, hopeful words, that brought tears of joy to the eyes of the watchers at the bedside.

"Children, we shall keep her; you'll see, we shall keep her after all!" cried Thomas Buddenbrook. "She will be with us next Christmas!"

But even in the next night, shortly after Gerda and her husband had gone to bed, they were summoned back to Meng Street by Frau Permaneder, for the mother was struggling with death. A cold rain was falling, and a high wind drove it against the window-panes.

The bed-chamber, as the Senator and his wife entered it, was lighted by two sconces burning on the table; and both physicians were present. Christian too had been summoned from his room, and sat with his back to the bed and his forehead bowed in his hands. They had sent for the dying woman's brother, Justus Kröger, and he would shortly be here. Frau Permaneder and Erica were sobbing softly at the foot of the bed; Sister Leandra and Mamsell Severin had nothing more to do, and stood gazing in sadness on the face of the dying.

The Frau Consul lay on her back, supported by a quantity of pillows. With both her blue-veined hands, once so beautiful, now so emaciated, she ceaselessly stroked the coverlet in trembling haste. Her head in the white nightcap moved from side to side with dreadful regularity. Her lips were drawn inward, and opened and closed with a snap at every tortured effort to breathe, while the sunken eyes roved back and forth or rested with an envious look on those who stood about her bed, up and dressed and able to breathe. They were alive, they belonged to life; but they could help her no more than this, to make the sacrifice that consisted in watching her die. . . . And the night wore on, without any change.

"How long can it go on, like this?" asked Thomas Buddenbrook, in a low tone, drawing Dr. Grabow away to the bottom of the room, while Dr. Langhals was undertaking some sort of injection to give relief to the patient. Frau Permaneder, her handkerchief in her hand, followed her brother.

"I can't tell, my dear Senator," answered Dr. Grabow, "Your dear mother may be released in the next few minutes, or she may live for hours. It is a process of strangulation: an oedema—"

"I know," said Frau Permaneder, and nodded while the tears ran down her cheeks. "It often happens in cases of inflammation of the lungs—a sort of watery fluid forms, and when it gets very bad the patient cannot breathe any more. Yes, I know."

The Senator, his hands folded, looked over at the bed.

"How frightfully she must suffer," he whispered.

"No," Dr. Grabow said, just as softly, but in a tone of authority, while his long, mild countenance wrinkled more than ever. "That is a mistake, my dear friend, believe me. The consciousness is very clouded. These are largely reflex motions which you see; depend upon it." And Thomas answered: "God grant it"—but a child could have seen from the Frau Consul's eyes that she was entirely conscious and realized everything.

They took their places again. Consul Kröger came and sat bowed over his cane at the bedside, with reddened eyelids.

The movements of the patient increased. This body, delivered over to death, was possessed by a terrible unrest, an unspeakable craving, an abandonment of helplessness, from head to foot. The pathetic, imploring eyes now closed with the rustling movement of the head from side to side, now opened with a heart-breaking expression, so wide that the little veins of the eyeballs stood out blood-red. And she was still conscious!

A little after three, Christian got up. "I can't stand it any more," he said, and went out, limping, and supporting himself on the furniture on his way to the door. Erica Weinschenk and Mamsell Severin had fallen asleep to the monotonous sound of the raucous breathing, and sat rosy with slumber on their chairs.

About four it grew much worse. They lifted the patient and wiped the perspiration from her brow. Her breathing threatened to stop altogether. "Let me sleep," she managed to say. "Give me a sleeping-draught." Alas, they could give her nothing to make her sleep.

Suddenly she began again to reply to voices which the others could not hear. "Yes, Jean, not much longer now." And then, "Yes, dear Clara, I am coming."

The struggle began afresh. Was this a wrestling with death? Ah, no, for it had become a wrestling with life for death, on the part of the dying woman. "I want—," she panted, "I want—I cannot—let me sleep! Have mercy, gentlemen—let me sleep!"

Frau Permaneder sobbed aloud as she listened, and Thomas groaned softly, clutching his head a moment with both hands. But the physicians knew their duty: they were obliged, under all circumstances, to preserve life just as long as possible; and a narcotic would have effected an unresisting and immediate giving-up of the ghost. Doctors were not made to bring death into the world, but to preserve life at any cost. There was a religious and moral basis for this law, which they had known once, though they did not have it in mind at the moment. So they strengthened the heart action by various devices, and even improved the breathing by causing the patient to retch.

By five the struggle was at its height. The Frau Consul, erect in convulsions, with staring eyes, thrust wildly about her with her arms as though trying to clutch after some support or to reach the hands which she felt stretching toward her. She was answering constantly in every direction to voices which she alone heard, and which evidently became more numerous and urgent. Not only her dead husband and daughter, but her parents, parents-in-law, and other relatives who had passed before her into death, seemed to summon her; and she called them all by name—

though the names were some of them not familiar to her children. "Yes," she cried, "yes, I am coming now—at once—a moment—I cannot—oh, let me sleep!"

At half-past five there was a moment of quiet. And then over her aged and distorted features there passed a look of ineffable joy, a profound and quivering tenderness; like lightning she stretched up her arms and cried out, with an immediate suddenness swift as a blow, so that one felt there was not a second's space between what she heard and what she answered, with an expression of absolute submission and a boundless and fervid devotion: "Here I am!" and parted.

They were all amazed. What was it? Who had called her? To whose summons had she responded thus instantly?

Some one drew back the curtains and put out the candles, and Dr. Grabow gently closed the eyes of the dead.

They all shivered in the autumn dawn that filled the room with its sallow light. Sister Leandra covered the mirror of the toilet table with a cloth.

Excerpts from
MIDDLEMARCH
by George Eliot

Sometimes a doctor is the bearer of good news, when he brings a therapy or a favorable prognosis to a family in distress. But what is a doctor to say or do when such reassurance is not warranted? How is he to speak to the sick individual and his family?

In this passage from George Eliot's Middlemarch, Dr. Lydgate is called upon to inform a household struck by disease that it must adapt itself to a new way of living and an uncertain outcome. Does he rise to the task?

The young and blooming Dorothea Brooke has made a strange marriage, baffling to those who love her: She has given herself to an aging, bloodless man, a researcher of the antiquities who is regarded by most as "scholarly and uninspired, ambitious and timid, scrupulous and dimsighted." Though his research bears no visible fruit, Dorothea's husband, Casaubon, cares for little else; though neither is happy, Dorothea is determined to be a good wife.

In the passage that follows, Dorothea and Casaubon quarrel, shortly after which Casaubon suffers a heart attack. Dorothea is overwhelmed by fear for her husband's health, and by remorse for the argument that preceded the attack.

The physician, Dr. Lydgate, is called. He examines his patient, both by using a then-novel instrument (his stethoscope) and by quiet observation. He calls for a cure more painful to Casaubon than any other: Casaubon must work less.

Lydgate then speaks to Dorothea, both to tell her of the grim outlook he sees for her husband, and also to indulge his curiosity about her and her marriage.

Before speaking to Dorothea, Lydgate resolves to avoid a "momentous prophecy" that might be disproven by events, despite his interest in seeing how such a prediction might affect her. Instead, he simply advises her to "be very watchful" over her husband's exertions. Dorothea, however, ever perceptive, hears what Lydgate does not say and begs him to tell her the worst, so that she might be spared future regret over preventive measures she did not take. He agrees that forestalling such regret is "one's function as a medical man," and tells her bluntly what the worst outcome might be. He also tells her, though, that he plans not to "enlighten" Casaubon, fearing that anxiety would be unhealthy for the patient.

Does Lydgate's strategy do justice to either Dorothea or Casaubon? Should he have acted differently?

As Lydgate is leaving, Dorothea appeals to him in an outburst, "from soul to soul." Eliot tells us that "for years after Lydgate remembered the impression produced in him by this involuntary appeal. But what should he say now except that he should see Mr. Casaubon again tomorrow?" What, indeed, should he have said? Should he—could he—have said or done anything more comforting?

Dorothea joins her husband in the library after breakfast.

Dorothea had learned to read the signs of her husband's mood, and she saw that the morning had become more foggy there during the last hour. She was going silently to her desk when he said, in that distant tone which implied that he was discharging a disagreeable duty—

"Dorothea, here is a letter for you, which was enclosed in one addressed to me."

It was a letter of two pages, and she immediately looked at the signature.

"Mr Ladislaw! What can he have to say to me?" she exclaimed, in a tone of pleased surprise. "But," she added, looking at Mr Casaubon, "I can imagine what he has written to you about."

"You can, if you please, read the letter," said Mr Casaubon, severely pointing to it with his pen, and not looking at her. "But I may as well say beforehand, that I must decline the proposal it contains to pay a visit here. I trust I may be excused for desiring an interval of complete freedom from such distractions as have been hitherto inevitable, and especially from guests whose desultory vivacity makes their presence a fatigue."

There had been no clashing of temper between Dorothea and her husband since that little explosion in Rome, which had left such strong traces in her mind that it had been easier ever since to quell emotion than to incur the consequence of venting it. But this ill-tempered anticipation that she could desire visits which might be disagreeable to her husband, this gratuitous defence of himself against selfish complaint on her part, was too sharp a sting to be meditated on until after it had been resented. Dorothea had thought that she could have been patient with John Milton, but she had never imagined him behaving in this way; and for a moment Mr Casaubon seemed to be stupidly undiscerning and odiously unjust. Pity, that "newborn babe" which was by-and-by to rule many a storm within her, did not "stride the blast" on this occasion. With her first words, uttered in a tone that shook him, she startled Mr Casaubon into looking at her, and meeting the flash of her eyes.

"Why do you attribute to me a wish for anything that would annoy you? You speak to me as if I were something you had to contend against. Wait at least till I appear to consult my own pleasure apart from yours."

"Dorothea, you are hasty," answered Mr Casaubon, nervously. Decidedly, this woman was too young to be on the formidable level of wifehood—unless she had been pale and featureless and taken everything for granted.

"I think it was you who were first hasty in your false suppositions about my feeling," said Dorothea, in the same tone. The fire was not dissipated yet, and she thought it was ignoble in her husband not to apologise to her.

"We will, if you please, say no more on this subject, Dorothea. I have neither leisure nor energy for this kind of debate."

Here Mr Casaubon dipped his pen and made as if he would return to his writing, though his hand trembled so much that the words seemed to be written in an unknown character. There are answers which, in turning away wrath, only send it to the other end of the room, and to have a discussion coolly waived when you feel that justice is all on your own side is even more exasperating in marriage than in philosophy.

Dorothea left Ladislaw's two letters unread on her husband's writing-table and went to her own place, the scorn and indignation within her rejecting the reading of these letters, just as we hurl away any trash towards which we seem to have been suspected of mean cupidity. She did not in the least divine the subtle sources of her husband's bad temper about these letters: she only knew that they had caused him to offend her. She began to work at once, and her hand did not tremble; on the contrary, in writing out the quotations which had been given to her the day before, she felt that she was forming her letters beautifully, and it seemed to her that she saw the construction of the Latin she was copying, and which she was beginning to understand, more clearly than usual. In her indignation there was a sense of superiority, but it went out for the present in firmness of stroke, and did not compress itself into an inward articulate voice pronouncing the once "affable archangel" a poor creature.

There had been this apparent quiet for half an hour, and Dorothea had not looked away from her own table, when she heard the loud bang of a book on the floor, and turning quickly saw Mr Casaubon on the library-steps clinging forward as if he were in some bodily distress. She started up and bounded towards him in an instant: he was evidently in great straits for breath. Jumping on a stool she got close to his elbow and said with her whole soul melted into tender alarm—

"Can you lean on me, dear?"

He was still for two or three minutes, which seemed endless to her, unable to speak or move, gasping for breath. When at last he descended the three steps and fell backward in the large chair which Dorothea had drawn close to the foot of the ladder, he no longer gasped but seemed helpless and about to faint. Dorothea rang the bell violently, and presently Mr Casaubon was helped to the couch: he did not faint, and was gradually reviving, when Sir James Chettam came in, having been met in the hall with the news that Mr Casaubon had "had a fit in the library."

"Good God! this is just what might have been expected," was his immediate thought. If his prophetic soul had been urged to particularise, it seemed to him that "fits" would have been the definite expression alighted upon. He asked his informant, the butler, whether the doctor had been sent for. The butler never knew his master want the doctor before, but would it not be right to send for a physician?

When Sir James entered the library, however, Mr Casaubon could make some signs of his usual politeness, and Dorothea, who in the reaction from her first terror had been kneeling and sobbing by his side, now rose and herself proposed that some one should ride off for a medical man.

"I recommend you to send for Lydgate," said Sir James. "My mother has called him in, and she has found him uncommonly clever. She has had a poor opinion of the physicians since my father's death."

Dorothea appealed to her husband, and he made a silent sign of approval. So Mr Lydgate was sent for and he came wonderfully soon. . . .

. . . Mr Casaubon had no second attack of equal severity with the first, and in a few days began to recover his usual condition. But Lydgate seemed to think the case worth a great deal of attention. He not only used his stethoscope (which had not become a matter of course in practice at that time), but sat quietly by his patient and watched him. To Mr Casaubon's questions about himself, he replied that the source of the illness was the common error of intellectual men—a too eager and monotonous application: the remedy was, to be satisfied with moderate work, and to seek variety of relaxation. Mr Brooke, who sat by on one occasion, suggested that Mr Casaubon should go fishing, as Cadwallader did, and have a turning-room, make toys, table-legs, and that kind of thing.

"In short you recommend me to anticipate the arrival of my second childhood," said poor Mr Casaubon, with some bitterness. "These things," he added, looking at Lydgate, "would be to me such relaxation as tow-picking is to prisoners in a house of correction."

"I confess," said Lydgate, smiling, "amusement is rather an unsatisfactory prescription. It is something like telling people to keep up their spirits. Perhaps I had better say, that you must submit to be mildly bored rather than to go on working. . . ."

. . . Lydgate had determined on speaking to Dorothea. She had not been present while her uncle was throwing out his pleasant suggestions as to the mode in which life at Lowick might be enlivened, but she was usually by her husband's side, and the unaffected signs of intense anxiety in her face and voice about whatever touched his mind or health, made a drama which Lydgate was inclined to watch. He said to himself that he was only doing right in telling her the truth about her husband's probable future, but he certainly thought also that it would be interesting to talk confidentially with her. A medical man likes to make psychological observations, and sometimes in the pursuit of such studies is too easily tempted into momentous prophecy which life and death easily set at nought. Lydgate had often been satirical on this gratuitous prediction, and he meant now to be guarded.

He asked for Mrs Casaubon, but being told that she was out walking, he was going away, when Dorothea and Celia appeared, both glowing from their struggle with the March wind. When Lydgate begged to speak with her alone, Dorothea opened the library door which happened to be the nearest, thinking of nothing at the moment but what he might have to say about Mr Casaubon. It was the first time she had entered this room since her husband had been taken ill, and the servant had chosen not to open the shutters. But there was light enough to read by from the narrow upper panes of the windows.

"You will not mind this sombre light," said Dorothea, standing in the middle of the room. "Since you forbade books, the library has been out of the question. But Mr Casaubon will soon be here again, I hope. Is he not making progress?"

"Yes, much more rapid progress than I at first expected. Indeed, he is already nearly in his usual state of health."

"You do not fear that the illness will return?" said Dorothea, whose quick ear had detected some significance in Lydgate's tone.

"Such cases are peculiarly difficult to pronounce upon," said Lydgate.

"The only point on which I can be confident is that it will be desirable to be very watchful on Mr Casaubon's account, lest he should in any way strain his nervous power."

"I beseech you to speak quite plainly," said Dorothea, in an imploring tone. "I cannot bear to think that there might be something which I did not know, and which, if I had known it, would have made me act differently." The words came out like a cry: it was evident that they were the voice of some mental experience which lay not very far off.

"Sit down," she added, placing herself on the nearest chair, and throwing off her bonnet and gloves, with an instinctive discarding of formality where a great question of destiny was concerned.

"What you say now justifies my own view," said Lydgate. "I think it is one's function as a medical man to hinder regrets of that sort as far as possible. But I beg you to observe that Mr Casaubon's case is precisely of the kind in which the issue is most difficult to pronounce upon. He may possibly live for fifteen years or more, without much worse health than he has had hitherto."

Dorothea had turned very pale, and when Lydgate paused she said in a low voice, "You mean if we are very careful."

"Yes—careful against mental agitation of all kinds, and against excessive application."

"He would be miserable, if he had to give up his work," said Dorothea, with a quick prevision of that wretchedness.

"I am aware of that. The only course is to try by all means, direct and indirect, to moderate and vary his occupations. With a happy concurrence of circumstances, there is, as I said, no immediate danger from that affection of the heart which I believe to have been the cause of his late attack. On the other hand, it is possible that the disease may develop itself more rapidly: it is one of those cases in which death is sometimes sudden. Nothing should be neglected which might be affected by such an issue."

There was silence for a few moments, while Dorothea sat as if she had been turned to marble, though the life within her was so intense that her mind had never before swept in brief time over an equal range of scenes and motives.

"Help me, pray," she said, at last, in the same low voice as before. "Tell me what I can do."

"What do you think of foreign travel? You have been lately in Rome, I think."

The memories which made this resource utterly hopeless were a new current that shook Dorothea out of her pallid immobility.

"Oh, that would not do—that would be worse than anything," she said with a more childlike despondency, while the tears rolled down. "Nothing will be of any use that he does not enjoy."

"I wish that I could have spared you this pain," said Lydgate, deeply touched, yet wondering about her marriage. Women just like Dorothea had not entered into his traditions.

"It was right of you to tell me. I thank you for telling me the truth."

"I wish you to understand that I shall not say anything to enlighten Mr Casaubon himself. I think it desirable for him to know nothing more than that he must not overwork himself, and must observe certain rules. Anxiety of any kind would be precisely the most unfavourable condition for him."

Lydgate rose, and Dorothea mechanically rose at the same time, unclasping her cloak and throwing it off as if it stifled her. He was bowing and quitting her, when an impulse which if she had been alone would have turned into a prayer, made her say with a sob in her voice—

"Oh, you are a wise man, are you not? You know all about life and death. Advise me. Think what I can do. He has been labouring all his life and looking forward. He minds about nothing else. And I mind about nothing else—"

For years after Lydgate remembered the impression produced in him by this involuntary appeal—this cry from soul to soul, without other consciousness than their moving with kindred natures in the same embroiled medium, the same troublous fitfully-illuminated life. But what could he say now except that he should see Mr Casaubon again tomorrow?

INVASIONS

by Perri Klass

*In this essay, pediatrician and writer Perri Klass reflects on how modern rela-
tions between doctors and patients tend to dehumanize both. Although Klass is
specifically concerned with doctors' necessary but troubling violations of their
patients' privacy, her essay points to other erosions of human dignity as well,
when ailing individuals submit themselves to the inevitable complexities of a big
hospital.*

*Klass begins by recounting the case of "Mr. Z," whom she saw as a medical
student. She took Mr. Z's history when he was admitted to the hospital. With
difficulty, she extracted from him personal information that his doctors needed
to know but that embarrassed him. The doctors later used the information for
both medical and (privately) ribald purposes.*

*Klass then recalls taking another history and meticulously recording the
whole of it, including the patient's past use of illegal drugs. But later—reflecting that the drug use might not be pertinent to the case, and worried about the
potential repercussions of recording it—she erased this information from the
patient's record.*

*In the second case, Klass tries to limit the doctors' knowledge of the patient
to the narrow facts needed to solve the patient's immediate problem. Is such
practice, in general, a good rule of thumb? Might such close circumscription of
a case, however well-intentioned, create a different kind of problem for doctor
or patient?*

*Klass notes that patients tend to cooperate with the processes that dehu-
manize them. But so, it seems, does she herself. Patients, she notes, "give up
their privacy in exchange for some hope—sometimes strong, sometimes faint—
of the alleviation of pain, the curing of disease." For physicians, however,
there is no such exchange: the sense that one is being intrusive, "that feeling of
amazement, that feeling that you are not entitled," as she says, simply "scars
over." Is the hardening—corruption?—of the physician's sensibilities necessary and inevitable? Would one want physicians to be any different? Can they
be?*

Morning rounds in the hospital. We charge along, the resident leading the way, the interns following, the two medical students last, pushing the cart that holds the patients' charts. The resident pulls up in front of a patient's door, the interns stop as well, and we almost run them over with the chart cart. It's time to present the patient, a man who came into the hospital late last night. I did the workup—interviewed him, got his medical history, examined him, wrote a six-page note in his chart, and (at least in theory) spent a little while in the hospital library, reading up on his problems.

"You have sixty seconds, go!" says the resident, looking at his watch. I am of course thinking rebelliously that the interns take as long as they like with their presentations, that the resident himself is long-winded and full of pointless anecdotes—but at the same time I am swinging into my presentation, talking as fast as I can to remind my listeners that no time is being wasted, using the standard hospital turns of phrase. "Mr. Z. is a seventy-eight-year-old white male who presents with dysuria and intermittent hematuria of one week's duration." In other words, for the past week Mr. Z. has experienced pain with urination, and has occasionally passed blood. I rocket on, thinking only about getting through the presentation without being told off for taking too long, without being reprimanded for including nonessential items—or for leaving out crucial bits of data. Of course, fair is fair, my judgment about what is critical and what is not is very faulty. Should I include in this very short presentation (known as a "bullet") that Mr. Z. had gonorrhea five years ago? Well, yes, I decide, and include it in my sentence, beginning, "Pertinent past medical history includes . . ." I don't even have a second to remember how Mr. Z. told me about his gonorrhea, how he made me repeat the question three times last night, my supposedly casual question dropped in between "Have you ever been exposed to tuberculosis?" and "Have you traveled out of the country recently?"

"Five years ago?" The resident interrupts me. "When he was seventy-three? Well, good for him!"

Feeling almost guilty, I think of last night, of how Mr. Z.'s voice dropped to a whisper when he told me about the gonorrhea, how he then went on, as if he felt he had no choice, to explain that he had gone to a convention and "been with a hooker—excuse me, miss, no offense," and how he had then infected his wife, and so on. I am fairly used to this by now, the impulse people sometimes have to confide everything to the person examining them as they enter the hospital. I don't know whether they are frightened by suggestions of disease and mortality, or just accepting me as a medical professional and using me as a comfortable re-

pository for secrets. I have had people tell me about their childhoods
and the deaths of their relatives, about their jobs, about things I have
needed to ask about and things that have no conceivable bearing on
anything that concerns me.

In we charge to examine Mr. Z. The resident introduces himself and
the other members of the team, and then he and the interns listen to
Mr. Z.'s chest, feel his stomach. As they pull up Mr. Z.'s gown to examine his genitals; the resident says heartily, "Well now, I understand you
had a little trouble with VD not so long ago." And immediately I feel
like a traitor; I am sure that Mr. Z. is looking at me reproachfully. I have
betrayed the secret he was so hesitant to trust me with.

I am aware that my scruples are ridiculous. It is possibly relevant that
Mr. Z. had gonorrhea; it is certainly relevant to know how he was treated, whether he might have been reinfected. And in fact, when I make
myself meet his eyes, he does not look nearly as distressed at being examined by three people and asked this question in a loud booming voice
as he seemed last night with my would-be-tactful inquiries.

In fact, Mr. Z. is getting used to being in the hospital. And in the
hospital, as a patient, you have no privacy. The privacy of your body is of
necessity violated constantly by doctors and nurses (and the occasional
medical student), and details about your physical condition are discussed
by the people taking care of you. And your body is made to give up its
secrets with a variety of sophisticated techniques, from blood tests to X
rays to biopsies—the whole point is to deny your body the privacy that
pathological processes need in order to do their damage. Everything must
be brought to light, exposed, analyzed, and noted in the chart. And all
this is essential for medical care, and even the most modest patients are
usually able to come to terms with it, exempting medical personnel from
all the most basic rules of privacy and distance.

So much for the details of the patient's physical condition. But the
same thing can happen to details of the patient's life. For the remainder
of Mr. Z.'s hospital stay, my resident was fond of saying to other doctors,
"Got a guy on our service, seventy-eight, got gonorrhea when he was
seventy-three, from a showgirl. Pretty good, huh?" He wouldn't ever
have said such a thing to Mr. Z.'s relatives, of course, or to any nondoc-
tor. But when it came to his fellow doctors, he saw nothing wrong with
it.

I remember another night, 4:00 A.M. in the hospital and I had finally
gone to sleep after working-up a young woman with a bad case of stomach cramps and diarrhea. Gratefully, I climbed into the top bunk in the
on-call room, leaving the bottom bunk for the intern, who might never

get to bed, and who, if she did, would have to be ready to leap up at a moment's notice if there was an emergency. Me, I hoped that, emergency or not, I would be overlooked in the top bunk and allowed to sleep out the next two hours and fifty-five minutes in peace (I reserved five minutes to pull myself together before rounds). I lay down and closed my eyes, and something occurred to me. With typical medical student compulsiveness, I had done what is called a "mega-workup" on this patient. I had asked her every possible question about her history and conscientiously written down all her answers. And suddenly I realized that I had written in her chart careful details of all her drug use, cocaine, amphetamines, hallucinogens, all the things she had said she had once used but didn't anymore. She was about my age and had talked to me easily, cheerfully, once her pain was relatively under control, telling me she used to be really into this and that, but now she didn't even drink. And I had written all the details in her chart. I couldn't go to sleep, thinking about those sentences. There was no reason for them. There was no reason everyone had to know all this. There was no reason it had to be written in her official chart, available for legal subpoena. It was four in the morning and I was weary and by no means clear-headed; I began to fantasize one scenario after another in which my careless remarks in this woman's record cost her a job, got her thrown into jail, discredited her forever. And as I dragged myself out of the top bunk and out to the nurses' station to find her chart and cross out the offending sentences with such heavy black lines that they could never be read, I was conscious of an agreeable sense of self-sacrifice—here I was, smudging my immaculate mega-writeup to protect my patient. On rounds, I would say, "Some past drug use," if it seemed relevant.

Medical records are tricky items legally. Medical students are always being reminded to be discreet about what they write—the patient can demand to see the record, the records can be subpoenaed in a trial. Do not make jokes. If you think a serious mistake has been made, do not write that in the record—that is not for you to judge, and you will be providing ammunition for anyone trying to use the record against the hospital. And gradually, in fact, you learn a set of evasions and euphemisms with which doctors comment in charts on differences of opinion, misdiagnoses, and even errors. "Unfortunate complication of usually benign procedure." That kind of thing. The chart is a potential source of damage; damage to the patient, as I was afraid of doing, or damage to the hospital and the doctor.

Medical students and doctors have a reputation for crude humor; some is merely off-color, which comes naturally to people who deal all day with sick bodies. Other jokes can be more disturbing; I remember a patient whose cancer had destroyed her vocal cords so she could no longer talk. In taking her history from her daughter we happened to find out that she had once been a professional musician, singing and playing the piano in supper clubs. For the rest of her stay in the hospital, the resident always introduced her case, when discussing it with other doctors, by saying, "Do you know Mrs. Q.? She used to sing and play the piano—now she just plays the piano."

As you learn to become a doctor, there is a frequent sense of surprise, a feeling that you are not entitled to the kind of intrusion you are allowed into patients' lives. Without arguing, they permit you to examine them; it is impossible to imagine, when you do your very first physical exam, that someday you will walk in calmly and tell a man your grandfather's age to undress, and then examine him without thinking about it twice. You get used to it all, but every so often you find yourself marveling at the access you are allowed, at the way you are learning from the bodies, the stories, the lives and deaths of perfect strangers. They give up their privacy in exchange for some hope—sometimes strong, sometimes faint—of the alleviation of pain, the curing of disease. And gradually, with medical training, that feeling of amazement, that feeling that you are not entitled, scars over. You begin to identify more thoroughly with the medical profession—of course you are entitled to see everything and know everything; you're a doctor, aren't you? And as you accept this as your right, you move further from your patients, even as you penetrate more meticulously and more confidently into their lives.

SECTION II:
THE HUMAN BEING
AND THE LIFE CYCLE

CHAPTER 4:
ARE WE OUR BODIES?

WHAT IS A HUMAN being? And what sort of life have we been given to live? In the next several chapters we turn our attention to our selves and our natural life cycle.

We begin in this chapter by acknowledging that we have both corporeal and noncorporeal aspects. We are embodied spirits and inspirited bodies, (or, if you will, embodied minds and minded bodies). This alleged duality, easy to assert, is, however, hard to understand. Many are tempted to resolve the difficulty by belittling the significance of one or the other aspect, declaring instead that either our minds (or souls) or our bodies are the seats of our "real" identities.

But does either declaration do justice to everything we are? Are we or are we not "double" creatures? In what does our identity reside? Just what do I mean when I say "me"?

Our first reading in this chapter, Galway Kinnell's "The Fly," expresses some of the disquiet we may feel as creatures with lofty longings who are burdened by being bound to our flesh. Our second reading, from Plato's *Symposium*, invites us to wonder whether one of our deepest longings—love—is a bodily thing. Our third and fourth readings—"What The Body Knows," by Chitra Divakaruni, and a pair of excerpts from Leo Tolstoy's *War and Peace*—explore the powerfully corporeal basis of our spiritual experience by considering the complex aftermath of surgery.

The trio of readings that follows presents various attempts to separate the body and the mind. St. Augustine, in an excerpt from his autobiographical *Confessions*, attempts to renounce the desires of his body in the name of celibacy and piety. One American poet, Walt Whitman, asserts joyously that "the body is the soul" in "I Sing the Body Electric," and another, Delmore Schwartz in "The Heavy Bear," expresses the anguish of a soul who longs to be free of his body and its inescapable appetites.

Our ninth and tenth readings describe remarkable accomplishments of the "pure" mind and "pure" body. Remarks by a former political prisoner, Vladimir Bukovsky, relate the mind's ability to triumph over the body under the stress of torture. In an excerpt from *Late Innings*, Roger Angell introduces us to a pitcher who accomplishes great physical feats on a baseball diamond.

Our eleventh writer, poet John Ciardi, considers the importance of ritual when touching the body in his "Washing Your Feet." Richard Selzer's enigmatic story "Whither Thou Goest" invites us to wonder whether a body and its separate parts are one and the same. Finally, writer and undertaker Thomas Lynch reflects on the meaning of the dead body in his essay "Good Grief," suggesting that it deserves funeral rites and an escort by those who loved it in life to its final place of rest.

THE FLY

by Galway Kinnell

In this brief poem Kinnell uses two superficially similar but very different creatures to explore the separation between our fleshy, earthbound selves and our longing for the beautiful.

What does it mean to say that the flesh-eating fly is "starved for the soul"?

What does singing "of fulfillment only" have to do with stinging and dying? What does the fly sing of?

In the final stanza, the poet repeats the word "last" five times; in the next-to-final repetition he uses the phrase "the absolute last," and "last" is the last word of the poem. What might be the reason for this emphasis? What does this mean for our love of the bee?

1

The fly
I've just brushed
from my face keeps buzzing
about me, flesh-
eater
starved for the soul.
One day I may learn to suffer
his mizzling, sporadic stroll over eyelid and cheek,
even be glad of his burnt singing.

2

The bee is beautiful.
She is the fleur-de-lis in the flesh.
She has a tuft of the sun on her back.

She brings sexual love to the narcissus flower.
She sings of fulfillment only
and stings and dies.
And everything she ever touches
is opening! opening!

And yet we say our last goodbye
to the fly last,
the flesh-fly last,
the absolute last,
the naked dirty reality of him last.

Excerpt from
THE SYMPOSIUM
by Plato, translated by Seth Benardete

Plato's Symposium *is an account of a small private party at which several members of the Athenian intellectual elite make speeches in praise of Eros, god of love. The attached excerpt is the famous speech Plato has placed in the mouth of Aristophanes, the great comic poet (playwright). To explain the place of Eros in human life, Aristophanes invents a mythical history of our original human nature and the radical transformation it suffered at the hands of the gods.*

Originally, he explains, each human being was a self-contained, unified, spherical being, with four arms and four legs, two faces (each looking in the opposite direction) on a single head, and two sets of genitalia facing outward from the two "backs." These original beings did not mate with each other, but reproduced in the earth, "like cicadas."

The poet relates how the "circle-men" were "awesome in their strength" and "made an attempt on the gods." To diminish their strength, Zeus had each creature cut in two, and turned each face around to the soft-bellied front. The resulting creatures, now with our human form, spent all their energies seeking their "missing other half." Each would cling so desperately to its complement that the race was in danger of dying out. In pity, Zeus rearranged them, moving their genitals to the front, enabling them to generate during erotic embrace and allowing the race to continue.

It is for this reason, according to the myth, that each human being—now as then—seeks its other half. "Love," Aristophanes concludes, "is the name for the desire and pursuit of the whole." Of all the gods, Eros "benefits us the most by leading us to what is our own; and in the future he offers the greatest hopes."

What, according to this account, do lovers seek from each other? Is love a "bodily thing"? Only a bodily thing? Why is it that the lovers are presented as silent and speechless—even incapable of answering Hephaestus' question about what they are truly longing for?

Is love, according to this account, self-forgetting and generous or self-centered and egoistic? What does love have to do with generation or procreation?

Aristophanes begins by describing Eros as "a physician dealing with an illness the healing of which would result in the greatest happiness for the human race." What illness does love treat? Can love, as described here, succeed in healing our wound?

If love were to succeed in its aspiration, would we still be human? Were the original "circle-men" human?

"Well, Eryximachus," Aristophanes said, "I do intend to speak in a somewhat different vein from that in which you and Pausanias spoke. Human beings, in my opinion, have been entirely unaware of the power of Eros, since if they were aware of it, they would have provided the greatest sanctuaries and altars for him, and would be making him the greatest sacrifices, and not act as they do now when none of this happens to him, though it most certainly should. For Eros is the most philanthropic of gods, a helper of human beings as well as a physician dealing with an illness the healing of which would result in the greatest happiness for the human race. So I shall try to initiate you into his power; and you will be the teachers of everyone else. But you must first understand human nature and its afflictions. Our nature in the past was not the same as now but of a different sort. First of all, the races of human beings were three, not two as now, male and female; for there was also a third race that shared in both, a race whose name still remains, though it itself has vanished. For at that time one race was androgynous, and in looks and name it combined both, the male as well as the female; but now it does not exist except for the name that is reserved for reproach. Secondly, the looks of each human being were as a whole round, with back and sides in a circle. And each had four arms, and legs equal in number to his arms, and two faces alike in all respects on a cylindrical neck, but there was one head for both faces— they were set in opposite directions—and four ears, and two sets of genitals, and all the rest that one might conjecture from this. Each used to walk upright too, just as one does now, in whatever direction he wanted; and whenever he had the impulse to run fast, then just as tumblers with their legs straight out actually move around as they tumble in a circle, so did they, with their eight limbs as supports, quickly move in a circle. It is for this reason that the races were three and of this sort: because the male was in origin the offspring of the sun; the female, of the earth; and the race that shared in both, of the moon—since the moon also shares in both. And they themselves were globular, as was their manner of walking, because they were like their parents. Now, they were awesome in their strength and robustness, and they had great and proud thoughts, so they made an attempt on the gods. And what Homer says about Ephialtes and Otus, is said about them—that they attempted to make an ascent into the sky with a view to assaulting the gods. Then Zeus and the other gods deliberated as to what they should do with them. And they were long perplexed, for the gods knew neither how they could kill them and (just as they had struck the giants with lightning) obliterate the race—for, in that case, their own honors and sacrifices from human beings would vanish—nor how they could allow them to continue to behave licentiously. Then Zeus thought hard and says, 'In my own opinion,' he said, 'I have a device whereby human beings would continue to exist and at the same time, having become weaker, would stop their licentiousness. I shall now cut each of them in two,' he said; 'and they will be both weaker and more useful to us through the increase in their numbers. And they will walk upright on two legs. But if they are thought to behave licentiously still, and are unwilling to keep quiet, then I shall cut them again in two,' he said, 'so that they will go hopping on one leg.' As soon as he said this he began to cut human beings in two, just like those who cut sorb-apples in preparation for pickling, or those who cut eggs with hairs. And whenever he cut someone he had Apollo turn the face and half the neck around to face this cut, so that in beholding his own cutting the human being might be more orderly; and he had him heal all the rest. Apollo turned the face around; and by drawing together the skin from everywhere toward what is now called the belly (just like drawstring bags) he made one opening, which he tied off in the middle of the belly, and that is what they call the navel. He shaped up the chest and smoothed out many of the other wrinkles, with somewhat the same kind of tool as shoemakers use in smoothing the wrinkles in leather on the last; but he left a few wrinkles, those on the belly itself and the navel, to be a reminder of our ancient affliction. When its nature was cut in two, each—desiring its own half—came together; and throwing their arms around one another and entangling themselves with one another in their desire to grow together, they began to die off due to hunger and the rest of their inactivity, because they were unwilling to do anything apart from one another; and whenever one of the halves did die and the other was left, the one that was left tried to seek out another and entangle itself with that, whether it met the half of the whole woman—and that is what we now call a woman—or of a man; and so they continued to perish. But Zeus took pity on them and supplies another device: He rearranges their genitals toward the front—for up till then they had them on the outside, and they generated and gave birth not in one another but in the earth, like cicadas—and for this purpose, he changed this part of them toward the front, and by this means made generation possible in one another, by means of the male in the female; so that in embracing, if a man meets with a woman, they might generate and the race continue; and if male meets with male, there might at least be satiety in their being together; and they might pause and turn to work and attend to the rest of their livelihood. So it is really from such early times that human beings have had, inborn in themselves, Eros for one another—Eros, the bringer-together of their ancient nature, who tries to make one out of two and to heal their human nature. Each of us, then, is a token of a human being, because we are sliced like fillets of sole, two out of one; and so each is always in search of his own token. Now all who are the men's slice from the common genus, which was then called androgynous, are lovers of women; and many adulterers have been of this genus; and, in turn, all who are women of this genus prove to be lovers of men and adulteresses. And all women who are sliced off from woman hardly pay attention to men but are rather turned toward women, and lesbians arise from this genus. But all who are male slices pursue the males; and while they are boys—because they are cutlets of the male—they are friendly to men and enjoy lying down together with and embracing men; and these are the best of boys and lads, because they are naturally the manliest. Some, to be sure, assert that such boys are shameless, but they lie. For it is not out of shame-lessness that they do this but out of boldness, manliness, and mascu-linity, feeling affection for what is like to themselves. And there is a great proof of this, for once they have reached maturity, only men of this kind go off to political affairs. When they are fully grown men, they are pederasts and naturally pay no attention to marriage and pro-creation, but are compelled to do so by the law; whereas they would be content to live unmarried with one another. Now it is one of this sort who wholly becomes a pederast and passionate lover, always feeling affection for what is akin to himself. And when the pederast or anyone else meets with that very one who is his own half, then they are won-drously struck with friendship, attachment, and love, and are just about unwilling to be apart from one another even for a short time. And here you have those who continue through life with one another, though they could not even say what they want to get for themselves from one another. For no one would be of the opinion that it was sexual intercourse that was wanted, as though it were for this reason—of all things—that each so enjoys being with the other in great earnestness; but the soul of each plainly wants something else. What it is, it is incapable of saying, but it divines what it wants and speaks in riddles. If Hephaestus with his tools were to stand over them as they lay in the same place and were to ask, 'What is it that you want, human beings, to get for yourselves from one another?'—and if in their perplexity he were to ask them again, 'Is it this you desire, to be with one another in the very same place, as much as is possible, and not to leave one another night and day? For if you desire that, I am willing to fuse you and make you grow together into the same thing, so that—though two—you would be one; and as long as you lived, you would both live together just as though you were one; and when you died, there again in Hades you would be dead together as one instead of as two. So see if you love this and would be content if you got it.' We know that there would not be even one who, if he heard this, would refuse, and it would be self-evident that he wants nothing else than this; and he would quite simply believe he had heard what he had been desiring all along: in conjunction and fusion with the beloved, to become one from two. The cause of this is that this was our ancient nature and we were wholes. So love is the name for the desire and pursuit of the whole. And previously, as I say, we were one; but now through our injustice we have been dispersed by the god, just as the Arcadians were dispersed by the Spartans. There is the fear, then, that if we are not orderly in our behavior to the gods, we shall be split again and go around like those who are modeled in relief on stelae, sawed through our nostrils, like dice. For this reason every real man must be exhorted to be pious toward the gods in all his acts, so that we may avoid the one result and get the other, as Eros is our guide and general. Let no one act contrary to Eros—and he acts contrary whoever incurs the enmity of the gods—for if we become friends and reconciled to the gods, we shall find out and meet with our own favorites, which few at the moment do. And please don't let Eryximachus suppose, in making a comedy of my speech, that I mean Pausanias and Agathon—perhaps they have found their own and are both naturally born males. For whatever the case may be with them, I am referring to all men and women: our race would be happy if we were to bring our love to a consummate end, and each of us were to get his own favorite on his return to his ancient nature. And if this is the best, it must necessarily be the case that, in present circumstances, that which is closest to it is the best; and that is to get a favorite whose nature is to one's taste. And were we to hymn the god who is the cause of this we should justly hymn Eros, who at the present time benefits us the most by leading us to what is our own; and in the future he offers the greatest hopes, while we offer piety to the gods, to restore us to our ancient nature and by his healing make us blessed and happy."

WHAT THE BODY KNOWS

by Chitra Banerjee Divakaruni

"Some things can't be spoken," thinks the young mother in this story. "The body alone knows them. It holds them patiently in its silent, intelligent cells, until you are ready to see." Divakaruni's story invites readers to ponder just what the body knows, what the mind knows, and which knowledge, if either, is true.

Aparna believes she is prepared to have a baby. She is not prepared, though, for what follows: life-threatening complications from a Caesarean delivery. Back in the hospital after the baby's birth, she is overwhelmed by despair over her separation from her newborn, and by physical pain.

A second surgery to remove a deadly growth of scar tissue corrects Aparna's physical problem, but she has lost her will to live. This she recovers only after touching the face of the surgeon who describes to her how he "touched the innermost crevices of her body." Her recovery, though, is marked by emotional turmoil and fluctuation, as she rebuilds her fractured attachment to her husband and son, and learns to see her doctor differently.

Some of what the body knows, it knows through touch. What varieties of touch does Aparna experience? Are some more truthful than others? Do different touches express different truths? What did Aparna finally "see" through her body and its touchings?

Does the body owe all of its knowledge to touch?

Aparna's brush with death appears to teach her a kind of wisdom about her body. What has she learned? Can this be learned without a life-threatening crisis?

Aparna thinks, consciously, about "the body" and what "it knows." How does her mind interact with this "it"? Is Aparna's body independent of her mind? Is it subject to her mind?

If Aparna's body has knowledge of which she is not aware, who and where is Aparna?

When her water breaks, Aparna is standing on a chair in the baby's room, hanging up the ceramic flying-fish mobile Umesh and she had purchased the day before. As the wetness gushes out of her, warm and unpleasantly sticky, she notes for one wondering moment the instinctive reactions of her body—the panic drying her mouth, the legs clamping together as though by doing so they could prevent loss. Then terror takes over, sour and atavistic—just what she had been determined not to succumb to, all through the carefully planned months of doctors visits and iron pills and baby-care books and Lamaze classes. It floods her brain and she cannot think.

She drops the mobile and hears it hit the tile floor with a splintery crash. Somewhere in the back of her mind there is regret, but her body has suddenly grown clumsy, and all her energies must go into getting down from the chair. She negotiates the newly dangerous floor to the kitchen where Umesh is fixing an omelette just the way she likes it, with lots of onions and sliced green chilies. She can smell their crisp, buttery odor. She opens her mouth to say he's the best husband—No, it's something else she must tell him, only she can't recall what.

But already he's abandoned the omelette and rushed across the room.

"Aparna, sweetheart, are you okay? You look awfully pale." And then, as she holds her stomach, the words still lost, "No, it can't be! It's only July—three weeks too early. Are you sure? Does it hurt?"

His face is so scrunched up with anxiety, his eyes so eloquent with guilt, she has to laugh. His fear lessens hers. She puts out her hand to him and the flood in her brain recedes, leaving only a few muddy patches behind. "I'm fine," she says. "My water broke."

She likes the way he fusses over her, making her lie down on the sofa, arranging pillows under her feet. Her long hair falls over the edge of the sofa, glossy and dramatic hair that might belong to the heroine of a tragedy. Only this isn't a tragedy, it's the happiest event in their lives. Maybe it's a comedy—the way, in his hurry, he misdials the hospital number, getting a Texaco instead. He's sweating by the time he gets the labor ward, shouting into the phone. She smiles. In her mind she's already making up the story she will tell her son. *Do you know what your father did, the day you were born?* She thinks of the hospital bag, has she packed everything the Lamaze instructor listed? Yes, even the sourballs she is supposed to suck on during labor—she picked them up on her last trip to the grocery, just in case. She feels pleased about that.

All through the ride to the hospital the sky is a scrubbed-clean, holiday blue, echoing the Niles lilies that fill the neighboring gardens. She allows her mind the luxury of wandering. Panic comes at her in waves, but she makes her body loose, the way a sea swimmer might, and feels it pass beneath her. How is it she's never noticed all these roses, red and white and a golden yellow the same shade as the baby outfit that lies folded in tissue at the bottom of her hospital bag? She chose green sour-balls, lime flavor. They make her mouth pucker in pleasant anticipation. The air is soft against her face, like a baby's cheek.

Later she would wonder, was it better that way, not knowing when death looked over your shoulder? Was it better to confound its breath with the scent of roses? To take that perfect moment and squander it because you were sure you had a thousand more?

They're all talking about stocks, she can hear them quite clearly, although they've draped a curtain of sorts between her and them. Her gynecologist prefers the blue chip kind. IBM, he says as he starts cutting. The anesthesiologist, a young man with a jolly mustache who shook her hand before inserting the needle into her spine, disagrees. The thing is to invest in a good start-up before it goes public. "There's a bunch of them right here in the Valley, right under our noses," he says, and rattles off names.

"I hope you're taking notes," Aparna whispers with mock-seriousness to Umesh. "It'll put the kid through college." Then she shudders as the doctor slices into a particularly stubborn piece of tissue.

Umesh's hands on her arm are slick with sweat. She can see the thin red traceries of veins in his eyes. He has been biting his lips ever since they said they'd have to operate, the baby's heartbeats didn't sound so good. She feels an illogical need to comfort him.

"Are you hurting?" he leans forward to ask. "Shall I ask them to do something about it?"

She shakes her head. Through all the pulling and cutting, her flesh being rent apart and then stitched together like old leather, there's an amazing absence of pain. But the body knows, she thinks. You can't fool the body. It knows what's being done to it. At the right time, it will take revenge.

Now they're laying the baby on her chest, the compact solidness of him, the face red and worried, like his father's. But beautiful, not discolored and cone-shaped from being pushed out of the birth-tunnel as in the Lamaze videos, so that she feels a bit better about having the C-section. She thinks of the name she chose for him. Aashish. Blessing. Even though the spinal is wearing off and pain begins to flex its muscles, she holds on to that word.

Unlike the squalling infants in the birth videos she's watched, her baby gazes at her with self-possession. She's been told that newborns can't focus, but she knows better. Her baby sees her, and likes what he sees. If only they would leave the two of them alone to get to know each other. But a uniformed somebody swoops him up out of her arms with foolish, clucking sounds. Umesh is saying something equally foolish about bringing him back when she's rested. Can't they see she's quite rested and wants him *now?* She hates hospitals, she thinks with a sudden star-burst of energy, always has. She can't wait to get out of this one and never come back.

The night she returns home, Aparna wakes in the dark, early hours with a sentence running through her head. *I think of pain as the most faithful of my friends.* It takes her a while to place it. It's from a diary, a woman writer she read in a long-ago class in early American literature. She didn't trust that woman, forgot her name as soon as she could.

But now Aparna must admit she knows what the writer had meant. Pain is with Aparna constantly, lurking beneath the lavender-scented sheets of the king-size bed she and Aashish have taken over. Different from the ache she felt in the hospital, it gnaws at her like a giant rat.

"How lovely!" the visitors say. "Look at the roses in her cheeks! It's wonderful to see someone so happy!"

She snaps at Umesh when he feels her hot, dry forehead and asks if he can get her something. When he calls, the doctor says pain is normal—just as normal as new fathers worrying too much.

She will conquer pain by ignoring it, Aparna resolves. For three shim-mery days of learning to breast-feed Aashish, she focuses on the shape of him in the crook of her arm, the blunt tug of his gums on her swollen nipples. But one morning when she climbs out of bed to try to use the toilet, which is becoming increasingly difficult, she falls and cannot get up.

She will always remember the moment when she swims up out of delirium, which spreads around her like a bottomless lake, shining like mercury. It's hard to focus her eyes, but driven by an unnamed fear she forces herself to do so. It's evening. She's in the hospital. In the very same room where she was before. Has all this in-between time been a dream, then? But the space next to her bed where the bassinet stood, against the cheerful peach wall, is empty. *Where's my baby?* she screams, *what did you do with my baby?* The words come out as gurgles through the tubes in her nose and mouth. The nurse bends over her, so cow-faced in her ignorance that Aparna must shake some sense into her—until they tie down her hands and give her a shot.

Then Umesh is there, explaining that she was too ill to take care of Aashish, so he's at a friend's house while the doctors try to figure out what's wrong with her. He understands her meaningless grunts and sobs. "Please don't worry, we'll all be fine," he says, stroking the insides of her elbows, the thin ache of needles plunged in and taped over, until she stops trembling and her eyes don't dart around as much. "Calm down, sweetheart, I'll hold you till you sleep." He tells her how well Aashish is doing, gaining weight every day, how he turns his head at sounds, how hard he can kick. She even smiles a little as she falls asleep in the middle of a question she wants to ask, *When can I go home?* In sleep she thinks she hears his murmured answer. *Soon, darling.* His voice is cool and breathable, like night mist. But when she wakes, she's in the middle of the mercury lake. She flails her way up, there's that gaping space by her bed again, and she screams.

Aparna has never been an angry person. It amazes her, therefore, when in the brief moments of clarity between panic and the dull cottony stupor of medication, she feels fury swelling her organs, as tangible as all the fluids her body has forgotten how to get rid of. She's been here for two weeks now, with test after inconclusive test being run on her. Everything in this hospital enrages her. The gluey odor of the walls. The chalky liquid she has to choke down so machines can take a clearer picture of her insides. The pretty, polished faces of the young nurses who chose the obstetrics ward so they would have happy patients. Her gynecologist's smile as he says they'll soon have her good as new. Aparna wants to punch his teeth in. She wants a lawyer who'll sue him for every stock he owns. She wants a hit man who'll wipe that smile off the face of the earth.

When they tell her she has to have a second surgery, she cries in great, gulping sobs, letting the snot and tears mingle on her face. She's too tired to wipe them away, and, besides, what's the point? She's ugly, she knows it, with her hair matted and smelly around her face. Ugly as sin, having to wear that hospital gown which exposes her backside. Having them hold her head when, periodically, she throws up bowlfuls of greenish scum. Having them clean her up afterward. That's the worst, somehow, the dispassionate way in which a stranger's hand moves over her body, doing its job. She's defeated by pain, she finally admits it. That evening when Umesh comes to visit, she turns her head away and won't look at the Polaroid photos he's taken of Aashish being given his bath.

Although the surgery has been successful, and the intestinal adhesions that had caused all the problems have been removed, Aparna's recovery is not going well. They're worried about it. She knows this from the flurries of whispers when the doctors come to see her each day. There's a whole team of them, her gynecologist, the surgeon who performed the second surgery, an immunologist, and even a social worker, a gnatlike woman who has informed Aparna that she is one of her cases now. They poke and prod, examine her stitches and her charts, ask questions which she doesn't answer. Until they walk away, she keeps her eyes tightly closed against them. This way, if she ever gets better and meets them, say, in a shopping mall, she won't know who they are. She'll walk right past them with the polite, powerful unconcern only a stranger is capable of.

Once she hears the night nurse talking to Umesh about her. This nurse is an older woman, not foolishly chirpy like the others. In her pre-hospital days, when she had energy for such things, Aparna would have equipped her with a complete, imagined life: She had lost her family, husband and all four children, in the Los Angeles earthquake, and moved to the Bay Area, where she now worked nights because she couldn't stand to be home alone. Or perhaps she'd been in Vietnam and seen things the young nurses couldn't even imagine. That's why she watched them with that slightly sardonic expression as they cooed over their patients, bringing cranberry juice and tucking down comforters. But the present, eroded Aparna only knows that the night nurse is comfortable with death. She knows it from the way the nurse sometimes comes in after lights-out and massages Aparna's feet, leaning there in a dark that smells thick and sticky, like hospital lotion, without speaking a single word.

But now, outside the door, the nurse is speaking to Umesh. "She's lost the will to live," she says in her dour, gravelly way.

"But why?" asks Umesh. His voice is high and bewildered, like a child's. "How can she, when she has so much to live for?"

"It happens."

"I won't let it," Umesh says angrily. "I won't. There must be something I can do."

Aparna listens with faint curiosity, the way one might to a TV soap playing in the next room. Does the wise nurse have a solution which will revitalize the dispirited young mother and unite her once more with her caring husband and helpless infant?

"You must—" says the nurse. But what he must do is drowned in the excited exclamations of a family who arrive just then in the room next to Aparna's to view their newest member.

She should have known what they were planning. But the medication has turned her mind soft, like butter left out overnight, so that the things she wants to hold on to—questions and suspicions—sink into it and disappear. Still, she shouldn't have been so utterly shocked when her friend walked in carrying Aashish.

A few times before this, Umesh had tried to get her to see Aashish. But each time he suggested it, she wept so vehemently that her temperature went up and the nurse had to give her a shot. Afterward, he would stroke the ragged ends of her hair with distressed hands and say, "Please, please, Aparna. Don't act this way. Be reasonable." She did not want to be reasonable. He had no right to ask her to be. An enormous, thwarted emotion ballooned inside her chest whenever she thought of her lost baby—*lost,* yes, that was the right word. She felt it pushing into her lungs, displacing air, long after Umesh gave up and left.

She watches them now, her friend who looks anxious as she sets the car seat down and picks up Aashish. Aashish in a little red two-piece outfit that Aparna didn't buy for him. Aashish looking so grown and cheerful that Aparna can hardly believe he's hers. But that's it, he *isn't* her baby. Something terrible happened to her own baby because she was in the hospital and couldn't take care of him, and they're afraid to tell her. So they've brought in this . . . this little impostor. *Where's my baby?* she wants to ask. *What did you do with my baby?* Instead she says, in a gray, toneless voice, "Take him away."

"At least hold him once," her friend says, and she bends over Aparna to move the tubes out of the way so she can lay the baby beside her. Her eyelashes are spiky with tears. Aparna can smell, in her friend's hair, the woodsy fragrance of Clairol Herbal Essence. It's the same shampoo Aparna used when she was pregnant. Suddenly she longs for the slow, steady green of it pooling in her palm, the relaxing steam of the shower, her fingers—her own fingers—on her scalp, knowing just where to rub deep and where to lighten up.

But here against her side is this baby, kicking his legs, batting at her with his small, fat arms. When she offers him a finger, he grabs it and gives an unexpected, gurgly laugh. Her friend has stepped outside, leaving a bottle of baby formula on the nightstand. "Baby," she whispers—she isn't ready, yet, to speak the name that will claim him as hers—and he laughs again. The sound tugs at the corners of her stiff, unaccustomed mouth until she's laughing, too. His gums are the color of the pink oleanders she planted in her backyard.

Then he's hungry, suddenly and absolutely, the way babies are. He's starting to fuss, in a minute he'll begin crying, she can tell from the way he's squinching up his face. She reaches, hurriedly, for the bottle, then stops, struck by an idea so compelling she can hardly breathe. She glances guiltily at the doorway, but it's empty, so she pulls at her hospital gown until she uncovers a breast and holds it to Aashish's mouth.

Why does Aparna do this? She's aware that she has no milk, although exactly how that occurred is obscured by the cottony fog which hangs over the first few days of her readmission to the hospital. Perhaps this is a test, offering her breast to the baby: *If he's my true, true son, he'll take it.* Perhaps it's the hope of a miracle. She remembers, vaguely, old Indian tales where milk spurts from a mother's breasts when she is reunited with her long-lost children. But mostly it's her body crying out to feel, once more, the hard, focused clamp of those gums.

Aashish will have none of it. He howls, face splotched with red, his body gone rigid. He refuses to be consoled by pats or clucking sounds, so Aparna must reach for the bottle with shaking fingers, afraid that someone will rush in and demand to know just what she's done to the poor child and take him away. In her haste she knocks over the bottle, which rolls under the bed, beyond the reach of her tube-restricted arms. And she must lie there next to her son's crying, a sound that jabs at her like a burning needle, until her friend does, indeed, rush in and take him from her.

Later, when all this is over and Aparna has settled back into the familiar rhythms of her life—but, no, her life, bisected by almost-death into Before and After, will never be familiar again. She will find it subtly altered, like a known melody into which a new instrument has been inserted. Anyhow, when she has settled back, people will ask her, *But what finally made you better?* She will give them different answers. "It was the new antibiotic," she might say, "the Cipro." Or, with a shrug, "I was lucky." Only once will she say, to a friend—not the one who had taken care of her baby; somehow they drifted apart after Aparna got better—she will say, looking out the window and blushing a little, "Love saved me."

"Of course," the friend will reply, nodding her sympathy. "I understand!" But Aparna herself will not be sure if she has been referring to her husband and son, as the friend has surmised, or to something quite different.

A few days after the disastrous baby episode, Aparna opens her eyes to find a man in her room. He startles her in his clean-shaven, blond boyishness, this stranger in a T-shirt and jeans. "I'm Dr. Byron Michaels," he says, extending a hand which she ignores. It takes her several minutes to recognize him as the man who performed her second surgery. In his street clothes, he looks so different from the times when he visited her with the rest of the squad that she doesn't close her eyes and turn away, as she originally intended. And though she doesn't return his smile, when he pulls up a chair and settles himself next to her, she watches him with a certain interest.

"I want to tell you," he says, "about your surgery. I think you need to know."

Before she can say, *No, thank you very much*, he has started.

"The other surgeons," he says, talking in the clipped tones of a man who's grown used to being always busy, "didn't want to operate on you. They thought you'd die on the table. But I took it as a challenge. Maybe it was foolish. When I opened you up and saw everything stuck together, I thought, I can't do it. The guy working with me wanted me to stitch you up again. But I was damned if I was going to leave you there to die."

Dr. Michaels's voice slows down. He's looking at her, but Aparna feels he's seeing something else. As he speaks, his hands make small, plucking movements in the air. "I started cleaning the organs, wiping the gunk off them, cutting away the cocoon that covered your intestines. It took hours. I was sweating like crazy. The nurse had to keep wiping my face. Afterward, she had to help me off with my gloves. My legs were shaking so much I had to sit down. But I'd done it."

Through the window, sunlight catches the golden hairs of the surgeon's forearm. His biceps are smooth and convex, like a high school athlete's. Aparna wonders if she is one of his first serious cases.

"And now," he says bitterly, "you're just throwing it all away."

The sunlight is on his cheek now, glowing and insistent. It strikes her that in all her life she's never touched a man's face except for her husband's. She would like to know, before she dies, how this pink, American skin feels. She puts out her hand—she has so little to lose that she isn't embarrassed—and touches his face. It's unexpectedly hot. She thinks she senses a pricking in her fingertips, the slight, tingly pain of circulation returning to a limb. A blush springs up under his skin, but perhaps Byron—through the rest of her hospital stay, that's how she'll think of him, a Romantic poet resurrected in surgical greens—understands, for he sits very still and allows her finger to circle the hollow between his jaw and cheekbone.

Something has changed. Where before Aparna refused to step out of bed, she now goes for walks, shuffling in badly fitting foam hospital slippers alongside a nurse who pushes her IV machine. Where she barely endured with indifference the quick swipe of a washcloth, now she wants to be helped to the bathroom so she can wash her face properly. She asks a delighted Umesh to bring her makeup bag, and each morning with unsteady fingers she applies lipstick and eyeliner and rubs jasmine oil behind her earlobes. When Umesh holds her hands in his and tells her how beautiful she looks, how thankful he is that she's taken such a turn for the better, she smiles distractedly. One night when he kisses her before leaving, murmuring how lonely it is in bed, she finds herself imagining that it is Byron who says this. And thus she is forced to admit to herself the motivation for her improvement.

Byron's visits to her are brief and irregular, sandwiched between surgeries and other, sicker patients. She waits for him with an eagerness that she recognizes as excessive. She does not touch him again, but against her will she finds herself fantasizing about it—and worse. This is humiliating, particularly since he seems to feel nothing but professional interest toward her as he examines her stitches and compliments her on her recovery process.

Aparna tells herself she's behaving stupidly. She's degenerating into a stereotype, the female patient infatuated with her doctor. Surely she's more intelligent than that? She thinks she catches an amused look, once or twice, in a nurse's eye. Stop it! she commands herself. Yet there she is next morning, sitting up in bed lipsticked and ready, trying to comb the knots out of her hair, which she has made the nurse shampoo for her. When the curtain moves, she looks up with her sultriest smile. But it is only Umesh, who wanted to surprise her on his way to work with a bouquet of irises from their garden, and who is baffled by the sulky monosyllables with which she answers him.

It's Byron's idea to bring the baby back. Aparna is reluctant and scared. She blurts out that the previous visit was a disaster, though she cannot bear to share its painful details even with him.

"Try it one more time," he says. He puts a hand on her shoulder. "Try it for me."

This time it's a lot better, once she gets over how big Aashish has grown. He looks nothing like the tiny, swaddled baby she's held on to so tightly inside her head. He doesn't recognize her at all. But that's almost a relief, because now she doesn't have to behave like a mother—she's not sure she'd know how to, after all this time. It's okay for her to be, instead, her awkward, prickly self.

But Aashish has a way of deprickling her. Maybe it's his willingness to be amused by the finger games she invents. He likes it when she brings her face close to his and makes strange noises. When she runs out of noises to make, he watches her unblinkingly—"as though my face were the most interesting thing in the universe," she says in laughing amazement to Umesh.

That intent, considering gaze, that looking out at the world with a pure and complete attention. She is delighted and humbled by it. She, too, wants to learn it. And if (as she fears) she's too old for that, then she wants to be close to her son and learn it through him. So she practices over and over with the breath-blower the nurses have given her, the little balls inside plastic tubes which are supposed to strengthen her lungs. She forces herself to walk a little farther down the corridor each day. She even tries the visualization exercises in the book one of her friends brought, shutting her eyes and willing herself to feel her body glowing with disks of light. She still makes up her face every morning for Byron, still enjoys seeing him. But sometimes as they talk, she finds her mind straying. Those footsteps outside, could that be Umesh, bringing Aashish a little earlier today?

Miraculously, the day of her discharge arrives. The nurses make a special occasion of it, chipping in to buy her a baby outfit and a pair of hand puppets. They blow on noisemakers and clap as they wheel her down the corridor for the last time. From the back of the car, she waves at them with one hand as she holds tight to Aashish's car seat with the other. When the car turns the corner, she realizes that she is crying.

Byron came in that morning for a final checkup and pronounced her cured. This isn't exactly true. She still finds it tiring to walk the length of the corridor and back. She has to lower herself into a chair with aggravating slowness.

Though she longs for a nice chili curry, she has been placed on a strict diet: interminable wastelands of applesauce and white bread loom ahead of her. Still, her heart leaped like a fish that had been tossed back into the lake.

Byron held out his hand. She touched it lightly. It was the first time she was touching him since the afternoon he told her how he'd saved her life. She wanted to say something to him about that, about love. But he was telling her he hoped to see her in his office in a week's time, telling her to call his secretary, telling her to watch that diet. He filled up the space between them with mundaneness. When he stopped, she didn't have anything left to say.

Quick and slim in a black T-shirt and shorts, Aparna moves through the children's section of Macy's, picking up items for Aashish's first birthday. In her cart, in addition to goody-bag gifts for the children she has invited, is a large purple Barney, Aashish's favorite TV character, and a red silk kite in the shape of a fish. She has worked hard to gain back her pre-pregnancy body and has, her friends claim enviously, even more energy than before. There's a new impatience about her, too. At times it makes them uneasy. *Get to the point,* it seems to say. *You don't have as much time as you think.*

Aparna has managed to forget most of what she wanted to forget about her illness. There are a few things. She'll drive a mile out of her way so she doesn't have to pass the squat gray building where she spent a month of her life. She can't stand certain colors—cheery yellow, innocuous peach, cute pink. A particular hour of evening, when shadows the color of bruises cluster under windowsills, makes her stomach clench with anxiety. But she chalks these up as minor costs.

She flings a wave of dark hair over her shoulder and makes for the cash register, a beautiful woman with such confident eyes that people would never guess what she's been through. At that moment she sees Dr. Michaels. He, too, is heading toward the cashier with something bunched up in his hand—a pullover, she thinks, but she is lightheaded with an anguish she thought she had done with, and thus not sure.

She never did go back to see him. She told Umesh it was too painful, all those negative associations. Did he suspect other reasons? If so, he didn't bring them up. There was a wary gentleness to how he handled her requests in those first days, as though she were a glass window. Any refusal would be a rock thrown into it. Thankfully, she thinks with a smile, recalling their energetic arguments about the birthday party, that didn't last too long.

Aparna's first impulse is to duck behind the enormous display of floral bedsheets across the way. But that would be cowardly. Besides, Dr. Michaels has spotted her already and walks up to her with his head slightly cocked, as though he isn't quite sure that she's who she is. She's afraid he'll be accusing or, worse still, sentimental, but he only puts out the hand she knows so intimately—the way we know objects out of our childhood, or our dreams—and touches her on the elbow.

"I'm so glad to see you," he says. "How have you been? And your baby? A boy, wasn't it?"

Aparna struggles to find an intelligent answer. But that touch—it disturbs her, bringing back that long-ago afternoon, her hand on his sun-tinted cheek. The embarrassment she had not felt then floods her face. Then she notices how he's looking at her. Her strong, slender legs, the sheen in her newly washed hair—he gazes at them with the marvel-ing eyes of someone who lives each day with bodies broken by disease.

She feels a rush inside her, but it is different from the clutching, shame-ful emotion she felt toward him in the hospital. It dizzies her. When she looks up, everything—his face, the bedsheet display, the ceiling of Ma-cy's—is tinged with a tender gold. She wants to tell him that he will always be unique in her life, the man who opened her up and touched the innermost crevices of her body. Who traveled with her, Orpheus-like, the dusky alleyway between life and death.

"I'd love to hear all your news," Dr. Michaels is saying. "Do you have time for coffee?" He's holding her hand in a proprietorial fashion. As though she were still in the hospital, and he still in charge, thinks Apar-na with slight annoyance. The look in his eyes has changed, and is eas-ier to read. Once she had sat up in her sickbed, rubbing lipstick into cracked lips, darkening sunken eyes with shaky fingers, longing for such a look from him. Now it fills her with sadness because it reveals him to be no different from other men.

Aparna has time. The party isn't until next week, and being a com-pulsive planner she has already organized the major details. Aashish, who is at the house of a friend with whom she exchanges child care twice a week, doesn't need to be picked up until afternoon. But she whispers an apology and frees her hand from Dr. Michaels's.

"Maybe at another time, then?" he says. "That might be better—some afternoon when we aren't rushed. For lunch, or maybe drinks? We could go up to San Francisco . . ." He takes out a card, writes a number on the back. "My cell phone," he says. "Call me . . . ?"

She takes the card and inclines her head slightly. It is a gesture not of assent—as he takes it to be, she can tell by his pleased, boyish grin—but of acceptance. The acceptance of frailty—hers and his, their different, inevitable frailties. She will never tell him—or anyone—about how, just a moment ago, everything was touched with gold. Some things can't be spoken. The body alone knows them. It holds them patiently, in its silent intelligent cells, until you are ready to see.

When, with a jaunty wave, Dr. Michaels turns the corner, she drops his card—but gently—into a garbage can. At the cash register, laying her purchases on the counter, she closes her eyes for a moment. *What, then, are we to do?* No answers come. Only an image: a hillside brown as a lion's skin, her husband running with a spool, her son yelling his ex-citement as she releases the kite. The fabric unfurling above them into the brief, vivid shape of human joy.

Excerpts from
WAR AND PEACE
Cannon Fodder and The Operating Tent
by Leo Tolstoy, translated by Aylmer and Louise Maude

Tolstoy's War and Peace *follows the lives of various Russian noblemen from the onset of the war against Napoleon until after its conclusion. The two excerpts that follow concern the wealthy and high-born Prince Andrew Bolkón-ski. In both excerpts, Andrew is abruptly confronted with human corporeality, but under very different circumstances and with very different effects.*

Andrew enters the war in his late twenties, full of expectations about it and of dreams of glory for himself. Months later, disabused of his illusions and war-weary, he returns home, arriving just as his wife dies in childbirth. A few years later, his fiancée, Countess Natásha Rostóva, the inspiring young woman with whom he fell in love after his wife's death, is seduced and abandoned by a shallow and despicable man. Andrew severs his ties with Natásha and returns to the war, determined to hunt down and kill the rake who seduced her.

The first excerpt begins as the Russian army, having abandoned the important city of Smolénsk, is in retreat. Andrew, in command of a retreating regiment, passes near Bald Hills, the Bolkónski family estate where he grew up. In a passage not reproduced here, Andrew leaves the regiment briefly to view the devastation of his home.

When he rejoins his men, he finds them bathing happily in a dirty pond, and is disgusted and horrified by the sight of so much naked flesh flailing about in the muddy water.

In the second excerpt, Andrew's regiment is under fire and he has been badly wounded. Despite his recent unhappiness, when he knew he was about to be hit he was seized by a "passionate love of life" and a desire not to die.

Now, in great physical distress, Andrew is taken to the operating tent, where amid the profusion of bodies he is once again struck by "the same flesh" that had "filled the dirty pond." In this tent he both witnesses and experiences the horror of nineteenth-century battlefield surgery. In the aftermath of this ordeal, Andrew observes an excruciating amputation occurring on the table next to his own, and recognizes the sufferer as the man he has been pursuing:

the seducer of his beloved Natásha.

Andrew feels "disgust and horror" because of "that immense number of bodies splashing about in the dirty pond." Why? What evokes this response? Why does it extend to his own flesh?

When Andrew sees the "naked, bleeding human bodies" in the surgical tent, he believes he sees "the same flesh" that had disturbed him in the pond. Is it the same flesh? Does he regard it in the same way? Why or why not?

Why does the amputee beg to see the leg that has been taken from him?

In the operating tent Andrew experiences fear for his own life, terrible pain, tender care, and the sight of acute human suffering. What accounts for the revelation that comes to him? What does flesh have to do with it?

What does human flesh teach Andrew about the human soul?

Excerpt 1

From Smolénsk the troops continued to retreat, followed by the enemy. On the tenth of August the regiment Prince Andrew commanded was marching along the highroad past the avenue leading to Bald Hills. Heat and drought had continued for more than three weeks. Each day fleecy clouds floated across the sky and occasionally veiled the sun, but toward evening the sky cleared again and the sun set in reddish-brown mist. Heavy night dews alone refreshed the earth. The unreaped corn was scorched and shed its grain. The marshes dried up. The cattle lowed from hunger, finding no food on the sun-parched meadows. Only at night and in the forests while the dew lasted was there any freshness. But on the road, the highroad along which the troops marched, there was no such freshness even at night or when the road passed through the forest; the dew was imperceptible on the sandy dust churned up more than six inches deep. As soon as day dawned the march began. The artillery and baggage wagons moved noiselessly through the deep dust that rose to the very hubs of the wheels, and the infantry sank ankle-deep in that soft, choking, hot dust that never cooled even at night. Some of this dust was kneaded by the feet and wheels, while the rest rose and hung like a cloud over the troops, settling in eyes, ears, hair, and nostrils, and worst of all in the lungs of the men and beasts as they moved along that road. The higher the sun rose the higher rose that cloud of dust, and through the screen of its hot fine particles one could look with naked eye at the sun, which showed like a huge crimson ball in the unclouded sky. There was no wind, and the men choked in that motionless atmosphere. They marched with handkerchiefs tied over their noses and mouths. When they passed through a village they all rushed to the wells and fought for the water and drank it down to the mud.

Prince Andrew was in command of a regiment, and the management of that regiment, the welfare of the men and the necessity of receiving and giving orders, engrossed him. The burning of Smolénsk and its abandonment made an epoch in his life. A novel feeling of anger against the foe made him forget his own sorrow. He was entirely devoted to the affairs of his regiment and was considerate and kind to his men and officers. In the regiment they called him "our prince," were proud of him and loved him. But he was kind and gentle only to those of his regiment, to Timókhin and the like—people quite new to him, belonging to a different world and who could not know and understand his past. As soon as he came across a former acquaintance or anyone from the staff, he bristled up immediately and grew spiteful, ironical, and contemptuous. Everything that reminded him of his past was repugnant to him, and so in his relations with that former circle he confined himself to trying to do his duty and not to be unfair. . . .

. . . Prince Andrew was somewhat refreshed by having ridden off the dusty highroad along which the troops were moving. But not far from Bald Hills he again came out on the road and overtook his regiment at its halting place by the dam of a small pond. It was past one o'clock. The sun, a red ball through the dust, burned and scorched his back intolerably through his black coat. The dust always hung motionless above the buzz of talk that came from the resting troops. There was no wind. As he crossed the dam Prince Andrew smelled the ooze and freshness of the pond. He longed to get into that water, however dirty it might be, and he glanced round at the pool from whence came sounds of shrieks and laughter. The small, muddy, green pond had risen visibly more than a foot, flooding the dam, because it was full of the naked white bodies of soldiers with brick-red hands, necks, and faces, who were splashing about in it. All this naked white human flesh, laughing and shrieking, floundered about in that dirty pool like carp stuffed into a watering can, and the suggestion of merriment in that floundering mass rendered it specially pathetic.

One fair-haired young soldier of the third company, whom Prince Andrew knew and who had a strap round the calf of one leg, crossed himself, stepped back to get a good run, and plunged into the water; another, a dark noncommissioned officer who was always shaggy, stood up to his waist in the water joyfully wriggling his muscular figure and snorted with satisfaction as he poured the water over his head with hands blackened to the wrists. There were sounds of men slapping one another, yelling, and puffing.

Everywhere on the bank, on the dam, and in the pond, there was healthy, white, muscular flesh. The officer, Timókhin, with his red little nose, standing on the dam wiping himself with a towel, felt confused at seeing the prince, but made up his mind to address him nevertheless.

"It's very nice, your excellency! Wouldn't you like to?" said he.

"It's dirty," replied Prince Andrew, making a grimace.

"We'll clear it out for you in a minute," said Timókhin, and, still undressed, ran off to clear the men out of the pond.

"The prince wants to bathe."

"What prince? Ours?" said many voices, and the men were in such haste to clear out that the prince could hardly stop them. He decided that he would rather souse himself with water in the barn.

"Flesh, bodies, cannon fodder!" he thought, and he looked at his own naked body and shuddered, not from cold but from a sense of disgust and horror he did not himself understand, aroused by the sight of that immense number of bodies splashing about in the dirty pond.

Excerpt 2

The militiamen carried Prince Andrew to the dressing station by the wood, where wagons were stationed. The dressing station consisted of three tents with flaps turned back, pitched at the edge of a birch wood. In the wood, wagons and horses were standing. The horses were eating oats from their movable troughs and sparrows flew down and pecked the grains that fell. Some crows, scenting blood, flew among the birch trees cawing impatiently. Around the tents, over more than five acres, blood-stained men in various garbs stood, sat, or lay. Around the wounded stood crowds of soldier stretcher-bearers with dismal and attentive faces, whom the officers keeping order tried in vain to drive from the spot. Disregarding the officers' orders, the soldiers stood leaning against their stretchers and gazing intently, as if trying to comprehend the difficult problem of what was taking place before them. From the tents came now loud angry cries and now plaintive groans. Occasionally dressers ran out to fetch water, or to point out those who were to be brought in next. The wounded men awaiting their turn outside the tents groaned, sighed, wept, screamed, swore, or asked for vodka. Some were delirious. Prince Andrew's bearers, stepping over the wounded who had not yet been bandaged, took him, as a regimental commander, close up to one of the tents and there stopped, awaiting instructions. Prince Andrew opened his eyes and for a long time could not make out what was going on around him. He remembered the meadow, the wormwood, the field, the whirling black ball, and his sudden rush of passionate love of life. Two steps from him, leaning against a branch and talking loudly and attracting general attention, stood a tall, handsome, black-haired non-commissioned officer with a bandaged head. He had been wounded in the head and leg by bullets. Around him, eagerly listening to his talk, a crowd of wounded and stretcher-bearers was gathered.

"We kicked *him* out from there so that he chucked everything, we grabbed the King himself!" cried he, looking around him with eyes that glittered with fever. "If only reserves had come up just then, lads, there wouldn't have been nothing left of him! I tell you surely. . . ."

. . . Like all the others near the speaker, Prince Andrew looked at him with shining eyes and experienced a sense of comfort. "But isn't it all the same now?" thought he. "And what will be there, and what has there been here? Why was I so reluctant to part with life? There was something in this life I did not and do not understand."

One of the doctors came out of the tent in a bloodstained apron, holding a cigar between the thumb and little finger of one of his small bloodstained hands, so as not to smear it. He raised his head and looked about him, but above the level of the wounded men. He evidently wanted a little respite. After turning his head from right to left for some time, he sighed and looked down.

"All right, immediately," he replied to a dresser who pointed Prince Andrew out to him, and he told them to carry him into the tent.

Murmurs arose among the wounded who were waiting.

"It seems that even in the next world only the gentry are to have a chance!" remarked one.

Prince Andrew was carried in and laid on a table that had only just been cleared and which a dresser was washing down. Prince Andrew could not make out distinctly what was in that tent. The pitiful groans from all sides and the torturing pain in his thigh, stomach, and back distracted him. All he saw about him merged into a general impression of naked, bleeding human bodies that seemed to fill the whole of the low tent, as a few weeks previously, on that hot August day, such bodies had filled the dirty pond beside the Smolénsk road. Yes, it was the same flesh, the same *chair à canon*, the sight of which had even then filled him with horror, as by a presentiment.

There were three operating tables in the tent. Two were occupied, and on the third they placed Prince Andrew. For a little while he was left alone and involuntarily witnessed what was taking place on the other two tables. On the nearest one sat a Tartar, probably a Cossack, judging by the uniform thrown down beside him. Four soldiers were holding him, and a spectacled doctor was cutting into his muscular brown back.

"Ooh, ooh, ooh!" grunted the Tartar, and suddenly lifting up his swarthy snub-nosed face with its high cheekbones, and baring his white teeth, he began to wriggle and twitch his body and utter piercing, ringing, and prolonged yells. On the other table, round which many people were crowding, a tall well-fed man lay on his back with his head thrown back. His curly hair, its color, and the shape of his head seemed strangely familiar to Prince Andrew. Several dressers were pressing on his chest to hold him down. One large, white, plump leg twitched rapidly all the time with a feverish tremor. The man was sobbing and choking convulsively. Two doctors—one of whom was pale and trembling—were silently doing something to this man's other, gory leg. When he had finished with the Tartar, whom they covered with an overcoat, the spectacled doctor came up to Prince Andrew, wiping his hands.

He glanced at Prince Andrew's face and quickly turned away.

"Undress him! What are you waiting for?" he cried angrily to the dressers.

His very first, remotest recollections of childhood came back to Prince Andrew's mind when the dresser with sleeves rolled up began hastily to undo the buttons of his clothes and undressed him. The doctor bent down over the wound, felt it, and sighed deeply. Then he made a sign to someone, and the torturing pain in his abdomen caused Prince Andrew to lose consciousness. When he came to himself the splintered portions of his thighbone had been extracted, the torn flesh cut away, and the wound bandaged. Water was being sprinkled on his face. As soon as Prince Andrew opened his eyes, the doctor bent over, kissed him silently on the lips, and hurried away.

After the sufferings he had been enduring, Prince Andrew enjoyed a blissful feeling such as he had not experienced for a long time. All the best and happiest moments of his life—especially his earliest childhood, when he used to be undressed and put to bed, and when leaning over him his nurse sang him to sleep and he, burying his head in the pillow, felt happy in the mere consciousness of life—returned to his memory, not merely as something past but as something present.

The doctors were busily engaged with the wounded man the shape of whose head seemed familiar to Prince Andrew: they were lifting him up and trying to quiet him.

"Show it to me . . . Oh, ooh . . . Oh! Oh, ooh!" his frightened moans could be heard, subdued by suffering and broken by sobs.

Hearing those moans Prince Andrew wanted to weep. Whether because he was dying without glory, or because he was sorry to part with life, or because of those memories of a childhood that could not return, or because he was suffering and others were suffering and that man near him was groaning so piteously—he felt like weeping childlike, kindly, and almost happy tears.

The wounded man was shown his amputated leg stained with clotted blood and with the boot still on.

"Oh! Oh, ooh!" he sobbed, like a woman.

The doctor who had been standing beside him, preventing Prince Andrew from seeing his face, moved away.

"My God! What is this? Why is he here?" said Prince Andrew to himself.

In the miserable, sobbing, enfeebled man whose leg had just been amputated, he recognized Anatole Kurágin.[1] Men were supporting him in their arms and offering him a glass of water, but his trembling, swollen lips could not grasp its rim. Anatole was sobbing painfully. "Yes, it is he! Yes, that man is somehow closely and painfully connected with me," thought Prince Andrew, not yet clearly grasping what he saw before him. "What is the connection of that man with my childhood and my life?" he asked himself without finding an answer. And suddenly a new unexpected memory from that realm of pure and loving childhood presented itself to him. He remembered Natásha as he had seen her for the first time at the ball in 1810, with her slender neck and arms and with a frightened happy face ready for rapture, and love and tenderness for her, stronger and more vivid than ever, awoke in his soul. He now remembered the connection that existed between himself and this man who was dimly gazing at him through tears that filled his swollen eyes. He remembered everything, and ecstatic pity and love for that man overflowed his happy heart.

Prince Andrew could no longer restrain himself and wept tender loving tears for his fellow men, for himself, and for his own and their errors.

"Compassion, love of our brothers, for those who love us and for those who hate us, love of our enemies; yes, that love which God preached on earth and which Princess Mary taught me and I did not understand— that is what made me sorry to part with life, that is what remained for me had I lived. But now it is too late. I know it!"

---

[1] Andrew's worst enemy, the seducer of Natásha, his beloved fiancée.

Excerpt from
CONFESSIONS
by St. Augustine, translated by Henry Chadwick

In this celebrated passage from Augustine's autobiography, the author recalls the moment when, after years of hesitation and torment, he gives himself wholly to God, resolving from that time forward to follow the injunction from Romans to "make no provision for the flesh in its lusts." This moving account of St. Augustine's conversion raises many questions about the interaction between the body and the spirit, and about the seat of human identity.

Confessions, which is addressed to God, dates to the late fourth century. Augustine, thirty-one at the time of this excerpt, is a teacher. Thanks in part to the influence of his mother, a devout Christian, he has long wrestled with Christian belief and practice, and feels powerfully drawn to it. Augustine believes that if he is to give himself wholeheartedly to God as he wishes to do, he must be celibate. Yet he cannot bring himself to give up women.

Augustine has lived for many years with a woman he loves dearly and by whom he has had a child. Now Augustine's mother has arranged for him a socially advantageous marriage to a girl who will not be of legal age for another two years. When he becomes engaged, the woman with whom he lives is "torn away from [his] side." Augustine writes: "My heart which was deeply attached was cut and wounded, and left a trail of blood." Lonely, and with his marriage still two years off, he takes another lover. He finds that this makes the "wound" of the first separation not better, but worse.

Just before this excerpt begins, Augustine and his friend Alypius are visited by a court official named Ponticianus. When Ponticianus discovers Augustine's interest in Christianity, he reveals that he is a Christian. He then begins to talk about holy men and to tell of two conversions that have recently taken place, nearly before his eyes.

This story provokes the crisis that has long been brewing within Augustine. After Ponticianus leaves, at the start of this excerpt, the crisis breaks over him with full force. Before the day is finished and after hearing, at a crucial moment, a voice he interprets as "divine command"—Augustine has become a Christian too, and has brought Alypius with him. Together they tell Augustine's mother.

From *Confessions*, by St. Augustine, Book VIII. Translated by Henry Chadwick. By permission of Oxford University Press.

Why might Augustine believe that the spiritual life for which he longs requires celibacy? Does this tell you more about Augustine or about the spiritual life?

Augustine recalls the prayer in which he worried that "you [God] might too rapidly heal me of the disease of lust which I preferred to satisfy." Is lust a disease? Might Augustine have regarded lust differently had he been married to the woman he loved?

Augustine's conversion is marked by physical distress, including tears and "physical gestures of the kind men make when they want to achieve something and lack the strength." What does bodily turmoil have to do with spiritual rebirth?

At the moment of his greatest despair, Augustine hears a voice. The voice may or may not be "real," but his immediate perception is that it is, and that he receives it with his actual body (in his ears). Why might it take this seemingly physical experience to provoke his spiritual change? What does this say about the power of the body? About the desire to renounce the body?

How can it be that the conversion of Alypius occurs "without any agony of hesitation" and with no physical distress?

At the news that her son will not marry, Augustine's mother experiences a joy "dearer and more chaste than she expected when she looked for grandchildren begotten of my body." Why might the spiritual change in her son offer a "dearer" joy than new life from his body? Must one be a devout Christian to appreciate or accept this?

Augustine's repudiation of his own sexuality is the outward sign that he is a new man. In what way(s), if any, might we, nevertheless, regard him as the same man?

A visitor, Ponticianus, has told Augustine and his friend Alypius about some recent conversions to Christianity by young men in the civil service. Augustine is deeply moved by what he has heard.

This was the story Ponticianus told. But while he was speaking, Lord, you turned my attention back to myself. You took me up from behind my own back where I had placed myself because I did not wish to observe myself (Ps. 20: 13),[1] and you set me before my face (Ps. 49: 21) so that I should see how vile I was, how twisted and filthy, covered in sores

---

[1] Citations to pertinent passages from Scripture appear throughout this text.

and ulcers. And I looked and was appalled, but there was no way of escaping from myself. If I tried to avert my gaze from myself, his story continued relentlessly, and you once again placed me in front of myself; you thrust me before my own eyes so that I should discover my iniquity and hate it. I had known it, but deceived myself, refused to admit it, and pushed it out of my mind.

But at that moment the more ardent my affection for those young men of whom I was hearing, who for the soul's health had given them-selves wholly to you for healing, the more was the detestation and ha-tred I felt for myself in comparison with them. Many years of my life had passed by—about twelve—since in my nineteenth year I had read Cice-ro's *Hortensius*, and had been stirred to a zeal for wisdom. But although I came to despise earthly success, I put off giving time to the quest for wisdom. For 'it is not the discovery but the mere search for wisdom which should be preferred even to the discovery of treasures and to ruling over nations and to the physical delights available to me at a nod.' But I was an unhappy young man, wretched as at the beginning of my adolescence when I prayed you for chastity and said: 'Grant me chastity and conti-nence, but not yet.' I was afraid you might hear my prayer quickly, and that you might too rapidly heal me of the disease of lust which I pre-ferred to satisfy rather than suppress. I had gone along 'evil ways' (Ec-clus. 2: 10) with a sacrilegious superstition, not indeed because I felt sure of its truth but because I preferred it to the alternatives, which I did not investigate in a devout spirit but opposed in an attitude of hostility.

I supposed that the reason for my postponing 'from day to day' (Ec-clus. 5: 8) the moment when I would despise worldly ambition and fol-low you was that I had not seen any certainty by which to direct my course. But the day had now come when I stood naked to myself, and my conscience complained against me: 'Where is your tongue? You were saying that, because the truth is uncertain, you do not want to abandon the burden of futility. But look, it is certain now, and the burden still presses on you. Yet wings are won by the freer shoulders of men who have not been exhausted by their searching and have not taken ten years or more to meditate on these matters.' This is how I was gnawing at my inner self. I was violently overcome by a fearful sense of shame during the time that Ponticianus was telling his story. When he had ended his talk and settled the matter for which he came, he went home and I was left to myself. What accusations against myself did I not bring? With what verbal rods did I not scourge my soul so that it would follow me in my attempt to go after you! But my soul hung back. It refused, and had no excuse to offer. The arguments were exhausted, and all had been refuted. The only thing left to it was a mute trembling, and as if it were facing death it was terrified of being restrained from the treadmill of habit by which it suffered 'sickness unto death' (John 11: 4).

Then in the middle of that grand struggle in my inner house, which I had vehemently stirred up with my soul in the intimate chamber of my heart, distressed not only in mind but in appearance, I turned on Alyp-ius and cried out: 'What is wrong with us? What is this that you have heard? Uneducated people are rising up and capturing heaven (Matt. 11: 12), and we with our high culture without any heart—see where we roll in the mud of flesh and blood. Is it because they are ahead of us that we are ashamed to follow? Do we feel no shame at making not even an attempt to follow?' That is the gist of what I said, and the heat of my passion took my attention away from him as he contemplated my condi-tion in astonished silence. For I sounded very strange. My uttered words said less about the state of my mind than my forehead, cheeks, eyes, colour, and tone of voice.

Our lodging had a garden. We had the use of it as well as of the entire house, for our host, the owner of the house, was not living there. The tumult of my heart took me out into the garden where no one could interfere with the burning struggle with myself in which I was engaged, until the matter could be settled. You knew, but I did not, what the outcome would be. But my madness with myself was part of the process of recovering health, and in the agony of death I was coming to life. I was aware how ill I was, unaware how well I was soon to be. So I went out into the garden. Alypius followed me step after step. Although he was present, I felt no intrusion on my solitude. How could he abandon me in such a state? We sat down as far as we could from the buildings. I was deeply disturbed in spirit, angry with indignation and distress that I was not entering into my pact and covenant with you, my God, when all my bones (Ps. 34: 10) were crying out that I should enter into it and were exalting it to heaven with praises. But to reach that destination one does not use ships or chariots or feet. It was not even necessary to go the distance I had come from the house to where we were sitting. The one necessary condition, which meant not only going but at once arriv-ing there, was to have the will to go—provided only that the will was strong and unqualified, not the turning and twisting first this way, then that, of a will half-wounded, struggling with one part rising up and the other part falling down.

Finally in the agony of hesitation I made many physical gestures of the kind men make when they want to achieve something and lack the strength, either because they lack the actual limbs or because their limbs are fettered with chains or weak with sickness or in some way hindered. If I tore my hair, if I struck my forehead, if I intertwined my fingers and clasped my knee, I did that because to do so was my will. But I could have willed this and then not done it if my limbs had not possessed the power to obey. So I did many actions in which the will to act was not equalled by the power. Yet I was not doing what with an incomparably greater longing I yearned to do, and could have done the moment I so resolved. For as soon as I had the will, I would have had a wholehearted will. At this point the power to act is identical with the will. The willing itself was performative of the action. Nevertheless, it did not happen. The body obeyed the slightest inclination of the soul to move the limbs at its pleasure more easily than the soul obeyed itself, when its supreme desire could be achieved exclusively by the will alone.

What is the cause of this monstrous situation? Why is it the case? May your mercy illuminate me as I ask if perhaps an answer can be found in the hidden punishments and secret tribulations that befall the sons of Adam? What causes this monstrous fact? and why is it so? The mind commands the body and is instantly obeyed. The mind commands itself and meets resistance. The mind commands the hand to move, and it is so easy that one hardly distinguishes the order from its execution. Yet mind is mind, and hand is body. The mind orders the mind to will. The recipient of the order is itself, yet it does not perform it. What causes this monstrosity and why does this happen? Mind commands, I say, that it should will, and would not give the command if it did not will, yet does not perform what it commands. The willing is not wholehearted, so the command is not wholehearted. The strength of the command lies in the strength of will, and the degree to which the command is not performed lies in the degree to which the will is not engaged. For it is the will that commands the will to exist, and it commands not another will but itself. So the will that commands is incomplete, and therefore what it commands does not happen. If it were complete, it would not need to command the will to exist, since it would exist already. Therefore there is no monstrous split between willing and not willing. We are dealing with a morbid condition of the mind which, when it is lifted up by the truth, does not unreservedly rise to it but is weighed down by habit. So there are two wills. Neither of them is complete, and what is present in the one is lacking to the other.

'Let them perish from your presence' (Ps. 67: 3) O God, as do 'empty talkers and seducers' of the mind (Titus 1: 10) who from the dividing of the will into two in the process of deliberation, deduce that there are two minds with two distinct natures, one good, the other bad. They really are evil themselves when they entertain these evil doctrines. Yet the very same people would be good if they held to the true doctrines and assented to the truth. As your apostle says to them 'You were at one time darkness, but now are light in the Lord' (Eph. 5: 8). But they wish to be light not in the Lord but in themselves because they hold that the nature of the soul is what God is. They have in fact become a thicker darkness in that by their horrendous arrogance they have withdrawn further away from you—from you who are 'the true light illuminating every man coming into this world' (John 1: 9). They should give heed to what you say and blush: 'Come to him and be illuminated, and your faces will not blush' (Ps. 33: 6).

In my own case, as I deliberated about serving my Lord God (Jer. 30: 9) which I had long been disposed to do, the self which willed to serve was identical with the self which was unwilling. It was I. I was neither wholly willing nor wholly unwilling. So I was in conflict with myself and was dissociated from myself. The dissociation came about against my will. Yet this was not a manifestation of the nature of an alien mind but the punishment suffered in my own mind. And so it was 'not I' that brought this about 'but sin which dwelt in me' (Rom. 7: 17, 20), sin resulting from the punishment of a more freely chosen sin, because I was a son of Adam.

If there are as many contrary natures as there are wills in someone beset by indecision, there will be not two wills but many. If a person is deliberating whether to go to the Manichees' conventicle or to the theatre, they cry: 'Here are two natures, a good one leads one way, a bad one leads the other way. How otherwise explain the opposition of two wills to one another?' But I affirm that they are both evil, both the will to attend their meeting and the will to go to the theatre. They think that the intention to go along to them can only be good. What then? If one of us Catholic Christians were deliberating and, with two wills quarrelling with one another, fluctuated between going to the theatre or to our Church, surely the Manichees would be quite undecided what to say about that. Either they will have to concede that to go to our Church is an act of good will, as is the case with those worshippers who are initiated into its sacraments and feel the obligation thereby imposed, or they will have to think two evil natures and two evil minds are in conflict within a single person. This argument will prove untrue their usual assertion that one is good, the other bad. The alternative for them will be to be converted to the true view and not to deny that in the process of deliberation a single soul is wavering between different wills.

Accordingly, when they note two wills in one person in conflict with each other, let them no more say that two conflicting minds are derived from two rival substances, and that two conflicting principles are in contention, one good, the other evil. God of truth, you condemn them and refute and confound them. For both wills are evil when someone is deliberating whether to kill a person by poison or by a dagger; whether to encroach on one estate belonging to someone else or a different one, when he cannot do both; whether to buy pleasure by lechery or avariciously to keep his money; whether to go to the circus or the theatre if both are putting on a performance on the same day, or (I add a third possibility) to steal from another person's house if occasion offers, or (I add a fourth option) to commit adultery if at the same time the chance is available. Suppose that all these choices are confronted at one moment of time, and all are equally desired, yet they cannot all be done simultaneously. They tear the mind apart by the mutual incompatibility of the wills—four or more according to the number of objects desired. Yet they do not usually affirm that there is such a multiplicity of diverse substances.

The same argument holds for good wills. For I ask them whether it is good to delight in a reading from the apostle, or if it is good to take pleasure in a sober psalm, or if it is good to discourse upon the gospel. In each case they will reply 'good'. What then? If all these offer equal delight at one and the same time, surely the divergent wills pull apart the human heart while we are deliberating which is the most attractive option to take? All are good and yet are in contention with each other until the choice falls on one to which is then drawn the entire single will which was split into many. So also when the delight of eternity draws us upwards and the pleasure of temporal good holds us down, the identical soul is not wholehearted in its desire for one or the other. It is torn apart in a painful condition, as long as it prefers the eternal because of its truth but does not discard the temporal because of familiarity.

Such was my sickness and my torture, as I accused myself even more bitterly than usual. I was twisting and turning in my chain until it would break completely: I was now only a little bit held by it, but I was still held. You, Lord, put pressure on me in my hidden depths with a severe mercy wielding the double whip of fear and shame, lest I should again succumb, and lest that tiny and tenuous bond which still remained should not be broken, but once more regain strength and bind me even more firmly. Inwardly I said to myself: Let it be now, let it be now. And by this phrase I was already moving towards a decision; I had almost taken it, and then I did not do so. Yet I did not relapse into my original condition, but stood my ground very close to the point of deciding and recovered

my breath. Once more I made the attempt and came only a little short
of my goal; only a little short of it—yet I did not touch it or hold on to it.
I was hesitating whether to die to death and to live to life. Ingrained evil
had more hold over me than unaccustomed good. The nearer approached
the moment of time when I would become different, the greater the
horror of it struck me. But it did not thrust me back nor turn me away,
but left me in a state of suspense.

Vain trifles and the triviality of the empty-headed, my old loves, held
me back. They tugged at the garment of my flesh and whispered: 'Are
you getting rid of us?' And 'from this moment we shall never be with you
again, not for ever and ever'. And 'from this moment this and that are
forbidden to you for ever and ever.' What they were suggesting in what
I have called 'this and that'—what they were suggesting, my God, may
your mercy avert from the soul of your servant! What filth, what dis-
graceful things they were suggesting! I was listening to them with much
less than half my attention. They were not frankly confronting me face
to face on the road, but as it were whispering behind my back, as if they
were furtively tugging at me as I was going away, trying to persuade me
to look back. Nevertheless they held me back. I hesitated to detach
myself, to be rid of them, to make the leap to where I was being called.
Meanwhile the overwhelming force of habit was saying to me: 'Do you
think you can live without them?'

Nevertheless it was now putting the question very half-heartedly. For
from that direction where I had set my face and towards which I was
afraid to move, there appeared the dignified and chaste Lady Conti-
nence, serene and cheerful without coquetry, enticing me in an honourable manner to come and not to hesitate. To receive and embrace me
she stretched out pious hands, filled with numerous good examples for
me to follow. There were large numbers of boys and girls, a multitude of
all ages, young adults and grave widows and elderly virgins. In every one
of them was Continence herself, in no sense barren but 'the fruitful
mother of children' (Ps. 112: 9), the joys born of you, Lord, her husband.
And she smiled on me with a smile of encouragement as if to say: 'Are
you incapable of doing what these men and women have done? Do you
think them capable of achieving this by their own resources and not by
the Lord their God? Their Lord God gave me to them. Why are you
relying on yourself, only to find yourself unreliable? Cast yourself upon
him, do not be afraid. He will not withdraw himself so that you fall.
Make the leap without anxiety; he will catch you and heal you.'

I blushed with embarrassment because I was still listening to the mut-
terings of those vanities, and racked by hesitations I remained undecid-

ed. But once more it was as if she said: ' "Stop your ears to your impure members on earth and mortify them" (Col. 3: 5). They declare delights to you, but "not in accord with the law of the Lord your God" ' (Ps. 118: 85). This debate in my heart was a struggle of myself against myself. Alypius stood quite still at my side, and waited in silence for the outcome of my unprecedented state of agitation.

From a hidden depth a profound self-examination had dredged up a heap of all my misery and set it 'in the sight of my heart' (Ps. 18: 15). That precipitated a vast storm bearing a massive downpour of tears. To pour it all out with the accompanying groans, I got up from beside Alypius (solitude seemed to me more appropriate for the business of weeping), and I moved further away to ensure that even his presence put no inhibition upon me. He sensed that this was my condition at that moment. I think I may have said something which made it clear that the sound of my voice was already choking with tears. So I stood up while in profound astonishment he remained where we were sitting. I threw myself down somehow under a certain figtree, and let my tears flow freely. Rivers streamed from my eyes, a sacrifice acceptable to you (Ps. 50: 19), and (though not in these words, yet in this sense) I repeatedly said to you: 'How long, O Lord? How long, Lord, will you be angry to the uttermost? Do not be mindful of our old iniquities.' (Ps. 6: 4). For I felt my past to have a grip on me. It uttered wretched cries: 'How long, how long is it to be?' 'Tomorrow, tomorrow.' 'Why not now? Why not an end to my impure life in this very hour?'

As I was saying this and weeping in the bitter agony of my heart, suddenly I heard a voice from the nearby house chanting as if it might be a boy or a girl (I do not know which), saying and repeating over and over again 'Pick up and read, pick up and read.' At once my countenance changed, and I began to think intently whether there might be some sort of children's game in which such a chant is used. But I could not remember having heard of one. I checked the flood of tears and stood up. I interpreted it solely as a divine command to me to open the book and read the first chapter I might find. For I had heard how Antony happened to be present at the gospel reading, and took it as an admonition addressed to himself when the words were read: 'Go, sell all you have, give to the poor, and you shall have treasure in heaven; and come, follow me' (Matt. 19: 21). By such an inspired utterance he was immediately 'converted to you' (Ps. 50: 15). So I hurried back to the place where Alypius was sitting. There I had put down the book of the apostle when I got up. I seized it, opened it and in silence read the first passage on which my eyes lit: 'Not in riots and drunken parties, not in eroticism and indecencies, not in strife and rivalry, but put on the Lord Jesus Christ and make no provision for the flesh in its lusts' (Rom. 13: 13–14).

I neither wished nor needed to read further. At once, with the last words of this sentence, it was as if a light of relief from all anxiety flooded into my heart. All the shadows of doubt were dispelled.

Then I inserted my finger or some other mark in the book and closed it. With a face now at peace I told everything to Alypius. What had been going on in his mind, which I did not know, he disclosed in this way. He asked to see the text I had been reading. I showed him, and he noticed a passage following that which I had read. I did not know how the text went on; but the continuation was 'Receive the person who is weak in faith' (Rom. 14: 1). Alypius applied this to himself, and he made that known to me. He was given confidence by this admonition. Without any agony of hesitation he joined me in making a good resolution and affirmation of intention, entirely congruent with his moral principles in which he had long been greatly superior to me. From there we went in to my mother, and told her. She was filled with joy. We told her how it had happened. She exulted, feeling it to be a triumph, and blessed you who 'are powerful to do more than we ask or think' (Eph. 3: 20). She saw that you had granted her far more than she had long been praying for in her unhappy and tearful groans.

The effect of your converting me to yourself was that I did not now seek a wife and had no ambition for success in this world. I stood firm upon that rule of faith on which many years before you had revealed me to her. You 'changed her grief into joy' (Ps. 29: 12) far more abundantly than she desired, far dearer and more chaste than she expected when she looked for grandchildren begotten of my body.

I SING THE BODY ELECTRIC

by Walt Whitman

Here Whitman, a nineteenth-century American poet, offers a profound appreciation of the human body, even suggesting that the body is the soul.

In "One's Self I Sing," Whitman's inscription to the volume in which this poem appears, he declares that "Not physiognomy alone nor brain alone is worthy for the / Muse, I say the Form complete is worthier far. . . ."

True to this assertion, in the poem reproduced below Whitman admires the human body, male and female, in its every aspect: in form, in gesture, as a whole, part by part, clothed, naked, in the face, in the body, in motion, in repose, in itself, and as the bearer of bodies to come. In the center of this panegyric is a brief against slavery, which had only recently been abolished in the United States when he wrote.

Whitman ends the first section with a question: "And if the body were not the soul, what is the soul?" He ends the poem asserting the answer: "I say now these [the body's parts] are the soul." What is the basis of his answer? Is this poetic exaggeration? Is he serious? Is he right?

In section 1, Whitman asks, "Was it doubted that those who corrupt their own bodies conceal themselves?" In section 8, after discussing the slave auction, he rails against "the fool that corrupted his own live body," and asserts that such fools "cannot conceal themselves." What might he mean by "corruption" and "concealment?"

Whitman appreciates the human body aesthetically and sexually. His sexual appreciation includes both a narrowly erotic response and admiration for the fertility of the body. Do these responses overwhelm his perception of human individuality?

In his inscription, "One's Self I Sing," Whitman also declares his political intentions. He writes that he will sing of "a simple separate person," and will "utter the word Democratic, the word En-Masse." In the center of this poem, he directly addresses the political implications of his belief in the body when he condemns the slave auction. How do Whitman's views about body and soul relate to his democratic ideals?

Is the "poetry of the body" the body's or the poet's? Which body part "sings the body electric?"

1

I sing the body electric,
The armies of those I love engirth me and I engirth them,
They will not let me off till I go with them, respond to them,
And discorrupt them, and charge them full with the charge
    of the soul.

Was it doubted that those who corrupt their own bodies
    conceal themselves?
And if those who defile the living are as bad as they who
    defile the dead?
And if the body does not do fully as much as the soul?
And if the body were not the soul, what is the soul?

2

The love of the body of man or woman balks account,
    the body itself balks account,
That of the male is perfect, and that of the female is perfect.
The expression of the face balks account,
But the expression of a well-made man appears not only
    in his face,
It is in his limbs and joints also, it is curiously in the joints
    of his hips and wrists,
It is in his walk, the carriage of his neck, the flex of his
    waist and knees, dress does not hide him,
The strong sweet quality he has strikes through the cotton
    and broadcloth,
To see him pass conveys as much as the best poem, perhaps
    more,
You linger to see his back, and the back of his neck and
    shoulder-side.
The sprawl and fulness of babes, the bosoms and heads of
women, the folds of their dress, their style as we pass in
the street, the contour of their shape downwards,
The swimmer naked in the swimming-bath, seen as he swims
    through the transparent green-shine, or lies with his face
    up and rolls silently to and fro in the heave of the water,
The bending forward and backward of rowers in row-boats,
    the horseman in his saddle,

Girls, mothers, house-keepers, in all their performances,
The group of laborers seated at noon-time with their open
   dinner-kettles, and their wives waiting,
The female soothing a child, the farmer's daughter in the
   garden or cow-yard,
The young fellow hoeing corn, the sleigh-driver driving his
   six horses through the crowd,
The wrestle of wrestlers, two apprentice-boys, quite grown,
   lusty, good-natured, native-born, out on the vacant lot at
   sundown after work,
The coats and caps thrown down, the embrace of love and
   resistance,
The upper-hold and under-hold, the hair rumpled over and
   blinding the eyes;
The march of firemen in their own costumes, the play of
   masculine muscle through clean-setting trowsers and
   waist-straps,
The slow return from the fire, the pause when the bell
   strikes suddenly again, and the listening on the alert,
The natural, perfect, varied attitudes, the bent head, the
   curv'd neck and the counting;
Such-like I love—I loosen myself, pass freely, am at the
   mother's breast with the little child,
Swim with the swimmers, wrestle with wrestlers, march in
   line with the firemen, and pause, listen, count.

3

I knew a man, a common farmer, the father of five sons,
And in them the fathers of sons, and in them the fathers of
   sons.

This man was of wonderful vigor, calmness, beauty of
   person,
The shape of his head, the pale yellow and white of his hair
   and beard, the immeasurable meaning of his black eyes,
   the richness and breadth of his manners,
These I used to go and visit him to see, he was wise also,
He was six feet tall, he was over eighty years old, his sons
   were massive, clean, bearded, tan-faced, handsome,

They and his daughters loved him, all who saw him loved
    him,
They did not love him by allowance, they loved him with
    personal love,
He drank water only, the blood show'd like scarlet through
    the clear-brown skin of his face,
He was a frequent gunner and fisher, he sail'd his boat
    himself, he had a fine one presented to him by a
    ship-joiner, he had fowling-pieces presented to him by
    men that loved him,
When he went with his five sons and many grand-sons to
    hunt or fish, you would pick him out as the most
    beautiful and vigorous of the gang,
You would wish long and long to be with him, you would
    wish to sit by him in the boat that you and he might
    touch each other.

4

I have perceiv'd that to be with those I like is enough,
To stop in company with the rest at evening is enough,
To be surrounded by beautiful, curious, breathing,
    laughing flesh is enough,
To pass among them or touch any one, or rest my arm ever
    so lightly round his or her neck for a moment, what is this
    then?
I do not ask any more delight, I swim in it as in a sea.
There is something in staying close to men and women and
    looking on them, and in the contact and odor of them, that
    pleases the soul well,
All things please the soul, but these please the soul well.

5

This is the female form,
A divine nimbus exhales from it from head to foot,
It attracts with fierce undeniable attraction,
I am drawn by its breath as if I were no more than a
    helpless vapor, all falls aside but myself and it,
Books, art, religion, time, the visible and solid earth, and
    what was expected of heaven or fear'd of hell, are now

consumed,
Mad filaments, ungovernable shoots play out of it, the
      response likewise ungovernable,
Hair, bosom, hips, bend of legs, negligent falling hands all
      diffused, mine too diffused,
Ebb stung by the flow and flow stung by the ebb, love-flesh
      swelling and deliciously aching,
Limitless limpid jets of love hot and enormous, quivering
      jelly of love, white-blow and delirious juice,
Bridegroom night of love working surely and softly into
      the prostrate dawn,
Undulating into the willing and yielding day,
Lost in the cleave of the clasping and sweet-flesh'd day.
This the nucleus—after the child is born of woman, man is
      born of woman,
This the bath of birth, this the merge of small and large,
      and the outlet again.
Be not ashamed women, your privilege encloses the rest,
      and is the exit of the rest,
You are the gates of the body, and you are the gates of the
      soul.
The female contains all qualities and tempers them,
She is in her place and moves with perfect balance,
She is all things duly veil'd, she is both passive and active,
She is to conceive daughters as well as sons, and sons as
      well as daughters.
As I see my soul reflected in Nature,
As I see through a mist, One with inexpressible
      completeness, sanity, beauty,
See the bent head and arms folded over the breast, the
Female I see.

6

The male is not less the soul nor more, he too is in his place,
He too is all qualities, he is action and power,
The flush of the known universe is in him,
Scorn becomes him well, and appetite and defiance become
      him well,
The wildest largest passions, bliss that is utmost, sorrow
      that is utmost become him well, pride is for him,

The full-spread pride of man is calming and excellent to
    the soul,
Knowledge becomes him, he likes it always, he brings every
    thing to the test of himself,
Whatever the survey, whatever the sea and the sail he strikes
    soundings at last only here,
(Where else does he strike soundings except here?)
The man's body is sacred and the woman's body is sacred,
No matter who it is, it is sacred—is it the meanest one in
    the laborers' gang?
Is it one of the dull-faced immigrants just landed on the
    wharf?
Each belongs here or anywhere just as much as the well-off,
    just as much as you,
Each has his or her place in the procession.
(All is a procession,
The universe is a procession with measured and perfect
    motion.)
Do you know so much yourself that you call the meanest
    ignorant?
Do you suppose you have a right to a good sight, and he or
    she has no right to a sight?
Do you think matter has cohered together from its diffuse
    float, and the soil is on the surface, and water runs and
    vegetation sprouts,
For you only, and not for him and her?

7

A man's body at auction,
(For before the war I often go to the slave-mart and watch
    the sale,)
I help the auctioneer, the sloven does not half know his
    business.
Gentlemen look on this wonder,
Whatever the bids of the bidders they cannot be high
    enough for it,
For it the globe lay preparing quintillions of years without
    one animal or plant,
For it the revolving cycles truly and steadily roll'd.
In this head the all-baffling brain,

In it and below it the makings of heroes.
Examine these limbs, red, black, or white, they are cunning
    in tendon and nerve,
They shall be stript that you may.
Exquisite senses, life-lit eyes, pluck, volition,
Flakes of breast-muscle, pliant backbone and neck, flesh
    not flabby, good-sized arms and legs,
And wonders within there yet.
Within there runs blood,
The same old blood! the same red-running blood!
There swells and jets a heart, there all passions, desires,
    reachings, aspirations,
(Do you think they are not there because they are not
    express'd in parlors and lecture-rooms?)
This is not only one man, this the father of those who shall
    be fathers in their turns,
In him the start of populous states and rich republics,
Of him countless immortal lives with countless
    embodiments and enjoyments.
How do you know who shall come from the offspring of
    his offspring through the centuries?
(Who might you find you have come from yourself, if you
    could trace back through the centuries?)

8

A woman's body at auction,
She too is not only herself, she is the teeming mother of
    mothers,
She is the bearer of them that shall grow and be mates to
    the mothers.
Have you ever loved the body of a woman?
Have you ever loved the body of a man?
Do you not see that these are exactly the same to all in all
    nations and times all over the earth?

If any thing is sacred the human body is sacred,
And the glory and sweet of a man is the token of manhood
    untainted,
And in man or woman a clean, strong, firm-fibred body, is
    more beautiful than the most beautiful face.

Have you seen the fool that corrupted his own live body?
  or the fool that corrupted her own live body?
For they do not conceal themselves, and cannot conceal
  themselves.

9

O my body! I dare not desert the likes of you in other men
  and women, nor the likes of the parts of you,
I believe the likes of you are to stand or fall with the likes
  of the soul, (and that they are the soul,)
I believe the likes of you shall stand or fall with my poems,
  and that they are my poems,
Man's, woman's, child's, youth's, wife's, husband's,
  mother's, father's, young man's, young woman's poems,
Head, neck, hair, ears, drop and tympan of the ears,
Eyes, eye-fringes, iris of the eye, eyebrows, and the waking
  or sleeping of the lids,
Mouth, tongue, lips, teeth, roof of the mouth, jaws,
  and the jaw-hinges,
Nose, nostrils of the nose, and the partition,
Cheeks, temples, forehead, chin, throat, back of the neck,
  neck-slue,
Strong shoulders, manly beard, scapula, hind-shoulders,
  and the ample side-round of the chest,
Upper-arm, armpit, elbow-socket, lower-arm, arm-sinews,
  armbones,
Wrist and wrist-joints, hand, palm, knuckles, thumb,
  forefinger, finger-joints, finger-nails,
Broad breast-front, curling hair of the breast, breast-bone,
  breast-side,
Ribs, belly, backbone, joints of the backbone,
Hips, hip-sockets, hip-strength, inward and outward round,
  man-balls, man-root,
Strong set of thighs, well carrying the trunk above,
Leg-fibres, knee, knee-pan, upper-leg, under-leg,
Ankles, instep, foot-ball, toes, toe-joints, the heel;
All attitudes, all the shapeliness, all the belongings of my or
  your body or of any one's body, male or female,
The lung-sponges, the stomach-sac, the bowels sweet
  and clean,

The brain in its folds inside the skull-frame,
Sympathies, heart-valves, palate-valves, sexuality,
    maternity,
Womanhood, and all that is a woman, and the man that
    comes from woman,
The womb, the teats, nipples, breast-milk, tears, laughter,
    weeping, love-looks, love-perturbations and risings,
The voice, articulation, language, whispering, shouting
    aloud,
Food, drink, pulse, digestion, sweat, sleep, walking,
    swimming,
Poise on the hips, leaping, reclining, embracing, arm-curving
    and tightening,
The continual changes of the flex of the mouth, and around
    the eyes,
The skin, the sunburnt shade, freckles, hair,
The curious sympathy one feels when feeling with the hand
    the naked meat of the body,
The circling rivers the breath, the breathing it in and out,
The beauty of the waist, and thence of the hips, and thence
    downward toward the knees,
The thin red jellies within you or within me, the bones and
    the marrow in the bones,
The exquisite realization of health;
O I say these are not the parts and poems of the body only,
    but of the soul,
O I say now these are the soul!

THE HEAVY BEAR

by Delmore Schwartz

In this sad poem, Schwartz likens his body to a "heavy bear who goes with me," distorting or thwarting the finer self he longs to present.

"That heavy animal" is a creature of crude appetites, for "candy, anger and sleep." He is a "show-off," but fears death. He interposes himself between the poet and the woman he would like to love in a better way. In the end, the poem widens to encompass not just the individual problem of the poet's appetites, but also "the scrimmage of appetite everywhere."

The poet has a will that is not expressed by his physical self. Is he unhappy to have his particular body, or to have a body at all?

What would the poet like to be?

What is the word that would "bare my heart and make me clear"? Why does he not speak?

Is the poet fair to the body? To "himself"? Could there be poetry in the absence of "the heavy bear?"

"the withness of the body"—WHITEHEAD

The heavy bear who goes with me,
A manifold honey to smear his face,
Clumsy and lumbering here and there,
The central ton of every place,
The hungry beating brutish one
In love with candy, anger, and sleep,
Crazy factotum, dishevelling all,
Climbs the building, kicks the football,
Boxes his brother in the hate-ridden city.

Breathing at my side, that heavy animal,
That heavy bear who sleeps with me,

Howls in his sleep for a world of sugar,
A sweetness intimate as the water's clasp,
Howls in his sleep because the tight-rope
Trembles and shows the darkness beneath.
—The strutting show-off is terrified,
Dressed in his dress-suit, bulging his pants,
Trembles to think that his quivering meat
Must finally wince to nothing at all.

That inescapable animal who walks with me,
Has followed me since the black womb held,
Moves where I move, distorting my gesture,
A caricature, a swollen shadow,
A stupid clown of the spirit's motive,
Perplexes and affronts with his own darkness,
The secret life of belly and bone,
Opaque, too near, my private, yet unknown,
Stretches to embrace the very dear
With whom I would walk without him near,
Touches her grossly, although a word
Would bare my heart and make me clear,
Stumbles, flounders, and strives to be fed
Dragging me with him in his mouthing care,
Amid the hundred million of his kind,
The scrimmage of appetite everywhere.

ACCOUNT OF TORTURE

by Vladimir Bukovsky

For more than twelve years, beginning in 1963, dissident Vladimir Bukovsky was held as a political prisoner in the former USSR and periodically tortured. In 1976, following years of international pressure, he was released to the West and freedom. At a forum at the University of Chicago in October 1986, he recalled the episode from his imprisonment that is described below.

In response to questions, Bukovsky explained that sometime around 1971, a friend of his was facing trial and wanted a lawyer. Soviet authorities refused to provide one, because this individual was Bukovsky's friend. Bukovsky, in protest, began a hunger strike. As the date of the trial approached, Bukovsky's jailers became "nasty" and decided to force-feed him, by violent and brutal means.

In the remarks reproduced below, Bukovsky describes this torture and his technique for coping with it—a technique he says is used by "many people" because with its help, "you just don't feel it."

What might account for the success of Bukovsky's extraordinary act of pretending? Do you think an individual who did not believe himself to be morally right, as Bukovsky did, could be equally powerful?

What does the success of Bukovsky's pretense suggest about the power of the mind over the body?

Bukovsky's torturers assaulted and injured his body. Did they assault and injure Bukovsky?

They started feeding me forcibly through the nostril. By a rather thick rubber tube with a metal end on it . . . The procedure will be that four or five KGB guys will come to my cell, take me to a medical unit, put a straitjacket on me, tie me up to a table, and somebody will be still holding, even so I was tied down, holding my shoulders and head and legs, and one will be pushing this thing through my nostril. And of course it

From remarks by Vladimir Bukovsky in October 1986 at the University of Chicago, following a lecture sponsored by the John M. Olin Center for Inquiry into the Theory and Practice of Democracy.

doesn't go. Unless it just bursts all these cartilages and others and it's a very unpleasant thing because the blood starts bubbling out of your nostrils and it goes down and you start suffocating and you have exact feeling that you just will die of suffocation and it's painful like hell I must tell you, because for some reason nose is very sensitive part of body and the tears will be filling your eyes and sort of streaming down because it's so painful, and—awful thing. Then they would pour down some liquid food through this rubber tube. And leave it for a while. And then they will remove from your nostril this tube, which is also quite painful the other way as it is this way, and then they will sort of bring you back to yourself. And the next day, just when it will start healing and covering with you know, sort of—all this crust, they will take you again and it will be even narrower than it used to be and they will force it through again and so I went and in and out for twelve days.

Now in twelve days it happened to be Sunday, and I'd sort of—I developed a technique which many people develop, under these conditions—you just pretend it doesn't happen to you, you pretend it's somewhere outside of you, you just externalize the pain, it's just somewhere over here, it's not here. And it does help. You just don't feel it that way.

Excerpt from
LATE INNINGS
by Roger Angell

In this excerpt from Angell's baseball appreciation, Late Innings, *catcher Ted Simmons talks to the author about what it takes to hit a ball pitched at upwards of 90 miles per hour.*

Though Simmons explains the art of hitting as well as anyone can, the author reaches the point where he can no longer understand what Simmons is saying. Then Simmons takes another pass at putting this extraordinary "physical art" into words.

Why is it hard to express bodily experiences in words?

Simmons says hitting is "mostly a matter of feel" and that a slump results from having "lost the feel of making solid contact with the ball on the thick part of the bat." He also describes minute differences in the appearances of various pitches in the brief time in which they are airborne.

In Simmons's account, does a great hitter "know" with his body, or with his mind? In what does his success lie?

As a hitter, is Simmons his body?

Late Innings

Simmons, a switch-hitting catcher, moved from the Cardinals to the Brewers during the off-season as part of a complicated multi-player trade; he batted .298 during his eleven years with the Cards, and he hits with enough power to have twice batted in over a hundred runs in a season. A lot of baseball people think that his acquisition by the Brewers will take them all the way to a pennant this year. Simmons has a square-jawed, alert face (he looks very much like an Ivy League football player from the eighteen-nineties), and he talks baseball as articulately as anyone I know. By this time, however, I had begun to sense an overload in

my hitting comprehension. The more I heard about it, the more difficult and impossible it had begun to seem to me. I said something to this
effect to Simmons.

"Well, hitting is a physical art, and that's never easy to explain," he
said. "And it's hard. It's one hard way to make a living if you're not good
at it. Hitting is mostly a matter of feel, and it's abstract as hell. If I'm in
a slump, it's because I've lost the feel of making solid contact with the
ball on the thick part of the bat, and I get a pitcher and go out and take
extra batting practice until that feeling comes back—maybe ten minutes, maybe half an hour: for as long as it takes. I've made some kind of
physical adjustment in order to attain a better mental state, a better
psychic condition. You have to feel good if you're going to hit aggressively and with confidence. But I *know* I can hit—I've been doing it all
my life—and that breeds confidence, too."

I asked Simmons about batters' picking up the spin on the pitch—the
part of hitting that most startled me when I first heard batters mention
it. Simmons said that Carl Yastrzemski had once told him that the players who hit the ball hardest and most often are simply the ones who are
quickest to see the spin and identify it. Some pitches can be read before
they leave the pitcher's hand, Simmons said—the curveball, much of
the time, because it is delivered from a wider angle (I recalled Billy Williams saying that a ball delivered from the upper, outer limits of a pitcher's reach which was headed for his chin was almost surely a curve,
"because big-league pitchers just ain't that wild")—but most pitches are
identified by the precise appearance of the ball in mid-flight. The fastball has a blurry, near-vertical spin. The curveball spins on a slight axis.
The slider—well, there is more than one kind of slider.

"If a pitcher holds the ball with his forefinger and middle finger between the wide part of the seams, out at that horseshoe-shaped part of
the ball, you see a big, wide white spot when it's pitched—sort of a flickering," Simmons said. "The better slider comes when he grabs the ball
where the seams are close together. Then the red laces on the ball make
a little red spot out there. That's because the ball is spiralling so hard
that it's like the tip of a football that's just been passed. The seams make
a little circle—that red dot—and you think, *Slider!* The red-dot sliders
are the hard ones to hit—like J. R. Richard's. The white ones tend to
hang. You can read the white one when it's about three feet out of the
pitcher's hand. The red dot I can pick up about five feet from his hand."

"I still can't believe it," I said.

"It's just data," Simmons said. "You learn it and you use it. What's
much harder—what makes the biggest disadvantage for any hitter—is

not knowing the pitchers. If you see a batter facing a pitcher for the first time ever, the odds are way, way in the pitcher's favor. It's not just knowing what the pitcher has—sinker, slider, a riding fastball; whether he has a change; whether he'll throw you a breaking ball when he's behind in the count—but what kind of speeds he throws them with. That identifies him in your mind. That's his pitcher's character. Without that, you're at a gross disadvantage. I'll be up against that for the first few weeks this year, because this is a new league for me. It's more of a breaking-ball league than the National League. But it doesn't take *that* long to learn it, because you compare every pitcher with someone you've faced before. Just a couple of at-bats against him, and you begin to say to yourself, 'O.K., you pitch like Sutton.' Or 'Your fastball is a little like Seaver's.' Or 'You come at a batter like Jerry Reuss.' And then it's all a lot easier. Your data grows. That's why a young pitcher will do so well sometimes in his first year in the majors. He might win ten or fifteen games out there—because the batters don't know him yet—and then he's never heard of again. The hitters have caught up."

WASHING YOUR FEET

by John Ciardi

This rueful poem reflects on what it is like to wash one's feet after one has gotten fat.

The poet recalls what it was like for him to wash his feet when he was "lithe," and what foot-washing might still be for one more artistic or holier than he. He wishes that to touch his own or any body were, as he says it should be, "ritual": "memorial, meditative, immortal." Instead, the ritual is "wheezy and a bit ridiculous."

What does it mean to say: "To touch any body anywhere" or "one's own body anywhere should be ritual?"

The poet tells us that he wishes he could "paint like Degas" or "believe like Mary," and that he has gotten fat. What can one infer about him from this information?

What does the poet seem to think of his own longings? Is he mocking his desire to ritualize touch?

How can it be that the body, which is "ridiculous" and gets fat, should be touched ritually?

The poet attributes his problem to having gotten fat. Would foot-washing be different for him, now, if he lost weight?

Washing your feet is hard when you get fat.
          ***

In lither times the act was unstrained and pleasurable.
          ***

You spread the toes for signs of athlete's foot.
          ***

You used creams, and rubbing alcohol, and you powdered.
          ***

You bent over, all in order, and did everything.
          ***

Mary Magdalene made a prayer meeting of it.

***

She, of course, was not washing her feet but God's.

***

Degas painted ladies washing their own feet.

***

Somehow they also seem to be washing God's feet.

***

To touch any body anywhere should be ritual.

***

To touch one's own body anywhere should be ritual.

***

Fat makes the ritual wheezy and a bit ridiculous.

***

Ritual and its idea should breathe easy.

***

They are memorial, meditative, immortal.

***

Toenails keep growing after one is dead.

***

Washing my feet, I think of immortal toenails.

***

What are they doing on these ten crimped polyps?

***

I reach to wash them and begin to wheeze.

***

I wish I could paint like Degas or believe like Mary.

***

It is sad to be naked and to lack talent.

***

It is sad to be fat and to have dirty feet.

WHITHER THOU GOEST

by Richard Selzer

This short story by surgeon and writer Richard Selzer uses a modern capability—organ transplantation—to examine timeless questions about the connection between the body and the soul, and the true seat of human identity.

A young husband, Sam, is brutally shot while trying to perform a good deed. He is pronounced brain-dead and his wife, Hannah, is urged to allow his organs to be "harvested" for transplantation. "That way," the doctor tells her, "your husband will live on. He will not really have died."

After she has granted permission and Sam's organs have been given away, Hannah is tormented by doubts about whether he is really dead. Uncertain whether she is a widow or a wife, she cannot move forward.

Following a wild and portentous storm, Hannah realizes in a dream that to "heal" herself, she must find the man who has received Sam's heart, and listen to it. With great difficulty Hannah does find and hear Sam's heart, now beating in another man's chest. As she foresaw, she is comforted by this and gains the strength to move forward with her life.

After watching a butcher cut apart a chicken, Hannah becomes convinced that what's in the cemetery is not really Sam. Why do the parts of Sam seem to her so different from the whole?

Is Hannah's desire to listen again to her late husband's heart simply weird? Does the heart still bear any portion of her late husband's identity?

Would your attitude be different if the transplanted part were a face or hands? Kidney or liver? Is the heart special in any important way?

What explains the conduct of the heart recipient, Henry Pope? Is his identity changed by the transplant? By his encounter with Hannah?

Whose heart is it?

"Brain-dead," said the doctor. "There is no chance that he will wake up. Ever. Look here." And he unrolled a scroll of paper onto her lap.

"This is the electroencephalograph. It's nothing but a flat line. No blips." Hannah bowed her head over the chart. The doctor cleared his throat, took one of her hands in both of his, and leaned toward her as though about to tell a secret. Hannah submitted to what under any other circumstance she might have considered presumption, submitted because she thought she ought to. It was expected of her. The formality of the occasion and all.

"Hannah, it is three weeks since your husband was shot in the head. The only thing keeping him alive is the respirator."

Hannah waited for the walls of the solarium to burst.

"I'm asking you to let us put an end to it, unplug the machinery, let him go. There is just no sense in prolonging a misfortune." Hannah felt that she should say something, not just sit there, but for the life of her she couldn't think what. The doctor was speaking again.

"But before we do that, we would like your permission to harvest Sam's organs for transplantation."

"Harvest?" said Hannah. "Like the gathering in of wheat?"

"Yes," said the doctor. "That is what we call it when we take the organs. It is for a good cause. That way your husband will live on. He will not really have died. . . ."

"Dead is dead," said Hannah.

"I know, I know," said the doctor. And he looked down at his feet for relief. Hannah noticed that he was wearing oxblood wing-tip shoes of a large size. They were the shoes of power.

A week later she received a letter from the doctor.

> Dear Mrs. Owen,
>   You will be pleased and comforted to know that because of your generosity and thanks to the miracle of modern science, seven people right here in the state of Texas are living and well with all their faculties restored to them. Your husband's liver has gone to a lady in Abilene; the right kidney is functioning in Dallas; the left kidney was placed in a teenaged girl in Galveston; the heart was given to a man just your husband's age in a little town near Arkansas; the lungs are in Fort Worth; and the corneas were used on two people right here in Houston. . . .

. . . Hannah folded the letter and put it back in its envelope and then into the bottom drawer of the desk without reading to the end. There was no need. She already knew what had become of the rest of Sam. She had buried it in the family plot of the Evangelical Baptist Church cemetery.

That was three years ago. And still, she had only to close her eyes to have the whole of the horror spring vividly before her, as though it had been painted on the inside of her eyelids. For Sam's thirty-third birthday they had spent the weekend at the beach. Now they were in the pickup truck on the way back to Houston. Hannah had fallen asleep. It was the sudden stop that woke her up.

"We couldn't be there already," she murmured.

"No," said Sam. "I'm just going to change that lady's tire." Hannah sat up and saw the green Buick pulled off to the side of the road. The right rear tire was flat. An elderly woman sitting behind the wheel looked up and smiled when she saw Sam walking toward her with a car jack in one hand and the tire iron in the other. Hannah got out of the truck and went over to talk. "Bless you," the woman said. Sam hadn't given that jack more than half a dozen pumps when a man—he looked Mexican—appeared out of nowhere with a gun in his hand.

"Sam?" Hannah had said in that low, questioning voice that always made him turn to see if she was upset. For a long moment Sam stayed where he was, crouched over the jack. When at last he stood, he had the tire iron in his hand.

"What do you want, mister?" he said. The Mexican made a gesture as if to turn a key and nodded at the pickup.

"The keys are in the truck," said Sam. The Mexican made no move. Perhaps he did not understand? Sam raised his arm to point. The Mexican fired. It took a long time for the echo of that shot to peter out. When it had, the truck and the Mexican were gone, and Sam lay on his back wearing a halo of black blood. He was still holding the tire iron. Something pink squeezed slowly out of the middle of his forehead.

"Dead is dead," she had told that doctor. But now, three years later, she wasn't so sure. For Hannah had begun to have doubts. Incidents occurred, like the time months ago when she had gone to the butcher's. Just ahead of her at the counter a woman had ordered a chicken. "I want it in parts," she heard the woman say. Hannah had watched as the butcher scooped out the entrails, cleaved the carcass through the middle of the breast, and hacked off its thighs, legs, and wings. The heart, gizzard, neck, and liver he put in a small plastic bag.

"You can keep the feet," said the woman. And then it was Hannah's turn.

"What'll it be?" said the butcher. And wiped the clots from his fingers onto his apron.

"What do you call that?" she asked, trying not to look at his bloody hands. As though they were his privates.

"What do you call what?"

"What you just did, cutting up the chicken. What is the name for it?" The butcher stared at her blankly.

"It's called 'cleaning a chicken.' Why?"

"Cleaning?"

"Look, miss," said the butcher, "I'm real busy. What'll it be?" But Hannah had already turned to leave.

It was after that that she stopped going to the cemetery to visit the grave. It wasn't Sam in that cemetery, not by a long shot. It was only parts of Sam, the parts that nobody needed. The rest of him was scattered all over Texas. And, unless she had been misinformed, very much alive. And where did that leave her? God knows it was hard enough to be a widow at the age of thirty-three, and her sympathies were all with those women whose husbands had truly, once and for all, died. But widowhood, bleak as it might be, seemed preferable by a whole lot to the not-here, not-there condition into which she had been thrust by "the miracle of modern science." At least if your husband were all dead you could one day get over it and go on with your life. But this! This state of bafflement. Maybe, she thought, maybe it was a matter of percentage—if more than 50 percent of your husband was dead, you were a widow. Whom could she ask?

Along with doubt came resentment. Oh, not just at the doctors. They simply do what they want to anyway, without really thinking. Doctors, she decided, don't think. They just *do*, and cover it all up with language. *Harvest. Transplantation.* The soft words of husbandry and the soil. Even they cannot bear to speak the real names of their deeds—dismemberment, evisceration. What was worse, she had begun to resent Samuel. Here she was, living in this sort of limbo, while he, Sam, was participating in not one but seven lives, none of which had anything to do with her. It wasn't fair. Even if he hadn't chosen it, it wasn't fair.

Hannah's cousin Ivy Lou was also her best friend. Lately she had taken to bringing her lunch over to eat at Hannah's house. One day when she got there, Hannah was standing at the kitchen window, looking out into the backyard. Over the radio came the pitched monotone of a preacher. The subject was the resurrection of the flesh.

"And it says right here in First Corinthians, chapter fifteen: 'For the trumpet shall sound, and the dead shall be raised incorruptible.'

"And here it is again in Romans, chapter eight, verse eleven: 'If the Spirit of him who raised Jesus from the dead dwells in you, he who raised Christ Jesus from the dead will give life to your mortal bodies. . . .'"

"Turn that damn fool off," said Hannah.

"For goodness' sake!" said Ivy Lou. "What's got into you?" Four years ago Ivy Lou had been born again.

"It's a big lie," said Hannah. "It's the way the preachers swindle you."

"I'm sure I don't know what you are talking about," said Ivy Lou.

"There is no such thing as the resurrection of the flesh," said Hannah. "Just tell me at what stage of life we are supposed to be on the day of resurrection, so-called? Do we look as we did when we were babies? At age forty? Or as we are when we die, old and wasted? And tell me this: What about Samuel Owen on your resurrection day? Here he is scattered all over Texas, breathing in Fort Worth, urinating in Dallas *and* Galveston, digesting or whatever it is the liver does in Abilene. They going to put him back together again when the day comes, or is it to the recipients belong the spoils? Tell me that."

"Well," said Ivy Lou. "I don't have the least idea about any of that, but I do know that you are committing the sin of blasphemy. Hannah, I'm real worried about you. Don't you believe in God anymore?" Hannah looked out the window and was silent for a long moment.

"About God," she said at last, "I have only the merest inkling. That's all anyone can have."

Hannah could not have said exactly when the idea first occurred to her. Later, she thought it might have been on the day of the tornado. From the kitchen window her eye had been caught by a frenzy of leaves in the live oak. All that August morning it had been sultry and still, until all at once it turned dark as twilight. Then lightning came to tear open the clouds. And the air, as if desperate to announce great tidings, broke its silence and turned to wind. But such a wind! At the height of the storm Hannah opened the back door and stood to receive the force of the rain on her face, her hair. It stung like pebbles. The violence lasted but a few minutes, after which it settled into a steady drizzle. Then, as abruptly as it had come, the storm passed and the sun came out, leaving Hannah with the feeling that something more than the humidity had been relieved. Something, a pressure that had been building inside her, had boiled its way to the surface, then broke.

That very night she awoke suddenly and sat bolt upright in bed, and she clapped her hand over her mouth as if to hold back what threatened to burst forth from it. A scream? Laughter? She didn't know what. But what she did know, beyond any doubt, as though it had been a revelation, was what it was she must do.

She had been dreaming, and in her dream, she saw two men lying on narrow tables next to each other. One of them was Samuel; the other she could not see clearly. His features were blurred, out of focus. Both of the men were stripped to the waist, and their chests were open in the middle, the halves of their rib cages raised like cellar doors. A surgeon was there, dressed in a blue scrub suit, mask, and cap. As she watched, the surgeon reached his hands into Samuel's chest and lifted forth his heart, held it up like some luminous prize. At that moment, Hannah could see into the chests of both men, see that they were both empty. Then the surgeon turned away from Samuel and lowered the incandescent, glowing heart into the chest of the other man, who promptly sat up, put on his shirt, and walked away.

What was instantly made clear to her—it was so simple—was that she must go to find that man who was carrying Samuel's heart. If she could find him, and listen once more to the heart, she would be healed. She would be able to go on with her life.

In the morning, the idea seemed quite mad. She wondered whether she was losing her mind. And she began to interrogate herself. Why would she do such a thing? What good would it do? To say nothing of the intrusion on the life of a perfect stranger. What made her think he would agree to let her do it? How could she explain it to him when she could not even explain it to herself? What would she say? Would it be like a pilgrim visiting a shrine? No, it had nothing to do with worship. Although, it might be a bit like going to the Delphic oracle for advice. But that wasn't it either. Did she just want to make sure that Sam's heart had found a good home? For God's sake, it wasn't a dog that she had given away. Nor was she the least bit curious about the man himself, other than to know how to find him. "No," Hannah said aloud, addressing the nameless, faceless man of her dream. "Thou shalt be unto my hand as a banister upon a dark staircase, to lead me up to the bright landing above. Once having climbed, I shall most willingly let thee go." The more she thought about it, the more she felt like a woman whose husband had been declared missing in action in a war. What would she have done if that were the case? Why, she would bend every effort to find him—living or dead—even travel to Vietnam or Laos, wherever, and she wouldn't leave until she knew, one way or the other.

Perhaps it *was* a phantom she was chasing, a phantom that would dissolve when she drew near. But she would have to take that chance. Hannah remembered the time, a year after they were married, when she and Samuel were lying in bed and she had said: "Let's tell each other a secret. You first." And Sam had told her about when he was twelve years old and his father had died suddenly of a heart attack. For a long time afterward he would think that he saw his father on the streets of the city.

It was always from the back, so he couldn't be sure. But the man was wearing the same gray fedora and holding the cigarette the same way. The more Sam looked, the more certain he became that it was his father whom he saw walking downtown, that he had not really died, but had gone away or been taken away for some reason, and now here he was. And Samuel would quicken his pace, then break into a run to catch up, calling out "Daddy! Daddy!" in his excitement. And each time, when the man turned around to see, it wasn't, no it wasn't, and there was that fresh wave of desolation. One day, a policeman came to the door and told his mother that Sam had been following men on the street and that one of them had reported him, said he might be a pickpocket, or worse.

"Is it true?" asked his mother. When he didn't answer, she asked him why. But he couldn't or wouldn't say why because no one would believe him or understand, and they would think he was crazy.

"Well, don't you dare do it ever again," said his mother in front of the policeman. But he couldn't stop, because the next day he thought he saw his father again and he followed him. After a year it stopped happening and Sam felt a mixture of relief and disappointment. Relief, because at last he had laid to rest his father's ghost; disappointment, because the wild possibility no longer existed. Sam had never told anyone about this before, he said. It was the first time he had ever mentioned it. When he had finished, Hannah hugged him and kissed him and cried and cried for the young boy who couldn't let go of his father.

"You're so pretty," Sam had said after a while to make her stop.

But Sam had been a young boy, and she was a grown woman. No matter—even if it turned out that she, too, was chasing a phantom.

Hannah went to the cupboard where three years before she had placed the doctor's letter, the one telling her about the seven transplantations. She read it again, this time to the end, and made a list. The kidneys, liver, and lungs, she decided, were inaccessible—hidden away in the deepest recesses of the bodies of those who had received them. How could she get to them? And the corneas just didn't seem right. She didn't think she could relate to a cornea. That left the heart. A heart can be listened to. A heart can be felt. And besides, there had been her dream. She would seek to follow the heart. But then there was that man, that other, who had lain on the table next to Samuel and whose face she had not been able to see. What if he refused her, mistook her intentions? No, she would explain it to him, write it all in a letter, and then he would agree. He would have to. In the letter she would tell what happened that night on the highway, how Sam had raised his arm to point to the truck, still holding the tire iron, how the Mexican had fired, and what the doctor had said to her in the hospital.

"That way your husband will not really have died," he had said. And that she had said to him, "Dead is dead," but that now she was not so sure. And how, ever since, she had been living in this gray place, unable to grieve or get on with her life because she no longer knew who or even what she was. All this she would tell him in the letter and he would let her come. He must.

Once she had decided, it was not difficult to get his name and address, a few of the facts of his illness. Hospital records, she learned, were scandalously accessible to whoever might want to see them, whatever the hospitals swore to the contrary. Anyone who really tried could get to see them—lawyers hunting for malpractice suits, legal assistants, reporters, detectives, graduate students gathering statistics, nurses, insurance companies. It was in this last guise that Hannah called the record librarian of the university hospital and made an appointment. She had followed it up with a letter on official stationery of the Aetna Casualty and Life Insurance Company.

She had had to take Ivy Lou into her confidence; Ivy Lou worked as a secretary for Aetna.

Ivy Lou was appalled. "I don't like it one bit. No good will come of it." And at first she had refused. "I just don't see what you could possibly hope to get out of it." And then, when Hannah didn't answer, "Why? Just tell me why."

"I don't know why," said Hannah. How could she say why, when she really didn't know herself? Perhaps it was something like the way a flower can't help but face the sun, or the way a moth goes to the flame.

"Hannah, you're going to get burned," said Ivy Lou as though she had read her mind. "Besides," she went on, "it's not only sick, it's in the grossest ill taste." Ivy Lou set down her teacup and walked to the door, shaking her head.

But then, there was poor Hannah, and in the end Ivy Lou gave in.

"Just don't tell anyone where you got it," she said when she brought the stationery.

The next week at the hospital, the record librarian welcomed her with a smile and showed her to a cubicle where the chart was waiting for her. POPE, HENRY, she read. AGE: 33. NEXT OF KIN: MRS. INEZ POPE. CHILDREN: NONE. ADDRESS: 8 ORCHARD ROAD, AVERY, TEXAS. DIAGNOSIS: CARDIOMYOPATHY, VIRAL. SURGERY: HEART TRANSPLANT. Reading on, she learned of his "intractable heart failure," that his prognosis had been "hopeless"—he had been given an estimated life expectancy of a few months "at most."

And then she came to the part about the operation, which occupied the bulk of the fat chart, and none of which she read. There was no need.

"That didn't take long," said the librarian as Hannah walked by her desk.

"No," said Hannah. "I'm quick."

Avery, Texas. Hannah and Ivy Lou looked for it on a map.

"There it is," said Ivy Lou. "Way up almost into Arkansas."

"How far away is that?"

"Maybe a couple of hundred miles, but, Hannah, I'm telling you—don't. You are making the biggest mistake of your life."

That night, Hannah sat at her kitchen table with a pen and a blank sheet of paper. "Dear Mr. Pope," she wrote, then set down the pen. There was something absurd about that Mr., considering that she had been married for seven years to a significant part of the man. But she would let it stand. The situation called for tact, patience, diplomacy. There would be plenty of time for "Dear Henry," if and when. She picked up the pen and continued.

> My name is Hannah Owen. Could the name mean anything to you? Doubtless not, considering the decorum with which these things are done. I am the wife (some say widow) of Samuel Owen, the man whose heart is even now beating in your chest.
>
> Perhaps you will forgive a woman's curiosity? I am writing to ask how you are since the operation. Your early discharge from the intensive-care unit, and even from the hospital itself—three weeks! It might be a record of some kind and would seem to show that you had an uneventful recovery. It would follow that you have continued to improve and that by now, three years later, you have completely regained your health? I surely do hope so. It is my dearest wish that the heart is doing as good a job for you as it did for Sam and for me too. Do let me hear from you, please.
>
> Yours truly,
> Hannah Owen

There, she thought. That should do it. Nothing whatever to arouse suspicion or to make anyone wonder. Only the shock of who she was. After that, just an expression of well-meaning concern. When she dropped the letter in the slot at the post office and heard the soft siffle as it went down the chute, she sighed. It had begun.

It was two weeks before she saw the envelope in her mailbox written in neat handwriting in black ink. It was postmarked Avery, Texas. How it shook in her hand.

Dear Mrs. Owen,
    It was very kind of you to write asking after my husband's health. He is not much of a letter writer and has asked me to tell you that he is stronger and healthier than he has been in years. He says he is the luckiest man on earth. By the way, however did you get hold of our name and address? I had thought such information might be protected, under the circumstances, but—I guess not. Thank you for your interest.

Sincerely,
(Mrs.) Inez Pope

Dear Mr. Pope,
    I don't know any other way to say it than to just take a deep breath and come right out with it. What I am going to ask will seem at first quite insane. But I assure you I am no maniac. I want to come and listen to your heart for the space of one hour at a time when it is convenient for you. While I know that at first this request will seem strange to you, I pray that you will say yes. You have no idea how important it is to me.

Yours truly,
Hannah Owen

Dear Mrs. Owen,
    My husband and I have tried to understand your position. But we feel that it would not be at all wise for you to come here. Not that we aren't grateful and all of that, but you have to admit it is a little on the bizarre side. So this is good-bye.

Sincerely,
(Mrs.) Henry Pope

P.S. We have consulted with our doctor, who says it is a terrible idea and perhaps you should get some professional attention to get over it. No offense meant.

Dear Mr. Pope,
    Your wife does not wish to let me come. I can understand her hesitation. The awkwardness and all. And perhaps it is only human nature, a touch of suspicion. Perhaps I have ulterior motives? I assure you, Mr. Pope, that I do not. As for my interest in you personally, it is limited to you as the carrier of something I used to possess and which I for one reason or another would like to see again. Or rather, hear again. For that is all I want to do—to listen to your heart for the space of one hour. The way a person would like to go back to visit the house where he had grown up. You are in a sense that house. Your doctor doesn't think it is a good idea? Mr. Pope, the doctors don't think. They are unaccustomed to it. Doctors just do whatever they want to, without thinking. If they had thought, perhaps they might have foreseen the predicament into which the "miracle of modern science" has placed me. No, speak to me not of doctors. They haven't the least idea about the human heart except to move it from place to place.

Yours truly,
Hannah Owen

Dear Mrs. Owen,
    I am very sorry. But the answer is still no. And that is final. Ever since I got your first letter, I've been feeling awful. Like ungrateful or something. But I know in my heart it wouldn't be a good thing for you either.

Sincerely yours,
Henry Pope

Dear Mr. Pope,
    The circumstances of my husband's death were violent and shocking. In case you do not know, he was shot in the head by a

bandit on the highway where he had stopped to help an old lady
with a flat tire. I was there. After three weeks on the respirator,
they came and told me it was no use, and could they disconnect
the respirator? But just before they did that, could they take
parts of his body (*harvest* is the word) to transplant to other
people? I said yes, and so they took his liver, lungs, heart, corneas, and kidneys. There are seven of you out there. You, Mr. Pope,
got the heart, or more exactly, *my* heart, as under the law, I had
become the owner of my husband's entire body at the time that
he became "brain-dead." Don't worry—I don't want it back. But I
do ask you to let me come to Avery for one hour to listen to your
heart. It is such a small thing, really, to ask in return for the dona-
tion of a human heart. Just to listen. For one hour. That is all,
really all. The reasons are private, and anyway, even if I wanted to
tell you why, I don't know if I could put it into words. If you see fit
to let me come, I will never bother you again, and you will have
repaid me in full. Do please let me know when I can come.

Yours truly,
Hannah Owen

P.S. Of course your wife can be in the room all the time. Although, frankly, I would prefer otherwise. Mrs. Pope, what I want
to do is no more than what dozens of nurses have done—listen
to your husband's heart. Only the reason is different. Couldn't
you look at it as just another medical checkup?

Dear Mrs. Owen,
   You said there were seven of us recipients. Why me? Or do
you plan a statewide reunion with all your husband's organs?
And the answer is NO! Please do not keep writing, as it is an-
noying to say the least, and it is making my wife nervous.

Sincerely,
Henry Pope

Dear Mr. Pope,
   You ask "Why me?" And you are right to ask. It is because
you have the heart. The others—the liver, lungs, kidneys—are

hidden away. I can't get to them. As for the corneas, well, I just can't relate to corneas somehow. But the heart! A heart can be felt. It can be listened to. You can hear a heart. A heart is reachable. That's why *you*.

Yours truly,
Hannah Owen

When there had been no reply for two weeks, Hannah wrote again.

Dear Mr. Pope,
    Please.

Yours truly,
Hannah Owen

Dear Mrs. Owen,
    No, goddammit, and if you don't stop this business and get the hell out of my life, I'm going to notify the police.

Sincerely yours,
Henry Pope

Dear Mr. Pope,
    And so your answer is still No. Oh, can you imagine how sad I am? Now I am the one who is disheartened. Never mind. I will try to accept it, as I have no alternative. You said I can't come and so I won't. I shall not be bothering you and your wife again. You can relax. I can't resist saying one more time, although it doesn't matter anymore, that I was the owner of the heart. It was mine to give. I think I did mention to you that the body of the deceased is the property of the next of kin. It wasn't Samuel who was the donor at all. It was me. But that is all water over the dam. Now may I ask you for a much smaller favor? I would like to have a photograph of you for my scrapbook. Nothing, for goodness' sake, posed or formal. Just a casual snapshot would be fine. Chalk it up to foolish sentiment. Thank you and good-bye.

Yours truly,
Hannah Owen

For three weeks Hannah prowled the house, smoking the cigarettes of disappointment, settling into her despair. Ivy Lou was frankly worried. But she knew better than to suggest a psychiatrist, or a minister, for that matter.

"Hannah," she said. "You have got to pull yourself together and get over it. It was a lousy idea in the first place. What's going to be the end of it?"

"I really don't know," said Hannah and waited for Ivy Lou to go away.

And then there it was, lying at the bottom of her mailbox like a dish of cream waiting to be lapped up. No need to look at the postmark—she could tell that handwriting anywhere. Stifling her excitement, she waited till she was back in her kitchen, sitting at the table, before she opened it. The sole content was a snapshot. No letter.

Hannah studied the photograph. It was three by four inches, black-and-white. The next size up from passport. It showed, at some distance, a thin, dark-haired man slouched against the trunk of a tree, his right knee flexed at right angles, with the sole of his foot braced against the tree. A live oak, she guessed, judging by the girth. His hands bulged the pockets of a zip-up jacket. He wore a baseball cap and was looking off to the left, the head turned almost in profile. The face, what she could see of it, was unremarkable, the eyes, shaded by the peak of the cap, giving away nothing. Only the dark seam of a mouth expressed suffering. Even with the help of a magnifying glass, she could read no more on that face. It was possessed of no mystery. Compared to the large color photograph of Samuel that she kept on the mantel in the parlor, with its generous smile that held nothing back, the snapshot in her hand was of a sick man who had known pain and expected more of it. He looked twenty years older than Samuel, although she knew they were the same age. This was taken before the operation, she decided.

But that he had sent it! Actually looked for and found the photograph, then put it in an envelope and *mailed* it. That heart is *working*, she thought. Hannah smiled and fixed herself a tuna-salad sandwich and a glass of milk.

She waited exactly two weeks—it wasn't easy—before she answered.

Dear Mr. Pope,

Thank you so much for the photo. I have put it in my scrapbook. My friend Ivy Lou, who is sort of an actuary, has calculated that your face occupies 2.1 percent of the picture and what with the peaked cap, you are a bit hard to make out. But, still. I like your backyard, is it? Are those azaleas on the right of the live oak you are leaning against? I have a live oak in my back-yard too.

Sincerely yours,
Hannah Owen

Six weeks later, another letter arrived.

Dear Mrs. Owen,
My wife Inez will be in Little Rock visiting her parents on the weekend of October 20th. If you still want to come, I don't see why not, so long as you just stay for one hour. I will expect you at the house at ten o'clock Saturday morning. You know where it is, I'm sure.

Yours truly,
Henry Pope

"I wouldn't drive, if I were you," said Ivy Lou. "Not wound as tight as you are. Why, you're as nervous as a bride. See if there's a bus." It was the first piece of Ivy Lou's advice Hannah thought she should take. She didn't trust herself to drive. Besides, she wanted the time to think, to prepare herself. Like a bride, she agreed, but she quickly shooed that notion out of her mind. There was an early-morning bus that got to Avery at nine-thirty, and the next day, before dawn, Hannah was on it. But once on the bus, she couldn't think, only reached up now and then to touch her right ear, which, when the bus stopped in Avery, would become a mollusk that would attach itself to the rock of Henry Pope's chest and cling through whatever crash of the sea.

Number eight was one of a dozen identical single-family ranch hous-es that made up the dead end that was Orchard Road, only this one was ennobled by the big live oak at the back, which fringed and softened the flat roof. At precisely ten o'clock Hannah unlatched the front gate and walked up to the door. Before she could ring the bell, the door opened halfway.

"Come in," he said, keeping himself out of sight until the door was closed behind her. The house was in darkness, every shade and blind drawn and shut. It had the same furtive, tense look she saw on the face of the man standing before her.

"No need to call attention," he said. "It would be hard to explain if anyone saw you come in." He was, she saw, a healthy man who looked even younger than she knew him to be. He had put on at least twenty pounds since that picture had been taken. His hair was light brown, almost blond, and curly. He was wearing jeans and a white T-shirt.

He's nervous as a cat, thought Hannah, and that makes two of us.

Hannah followed him into a small room, a den furnished with a sofa, an upholstered easy chair, and a television set. One wall was lined with bookshelves. She guessed that he had spent his convalescence in this room.

"It's your show," he said. "How do you want me?" When she didn't answer, he reached up with both arms and pulled the T-shirt over his head.

"I suppose you want this off," he said. Then Hannah saw on his chest the pale violet stripe that marked the passage of her husband's heart into this man. She felt her pulse racing. She might faint.

"Well, it's your show," he said again. "How do you want to do this? Come on, let's just get it over with. One hour, you said."

"Best, I think, for you to lie down flat," she said. "I'll sit on the edge and lean over." She had gone over it so many times in her mind.

He lay down and slid a small pillow beneath his head, then shifted as far as he could to give her room to sit. When she did, he rose abruptly to his elbows.

"Where is your stethoscope?"

"I don't have a stethoscope."

"How are you going to listen to my heart without a stethoscope?"

"They didn't always have them," she said. "I'm going to listen with my ear." She gave her right ear two short taps. "I have very acute hearing," she added, because he looked dubious, as though he might call the whole thing off. But he didn't, just lay back down and stared straight up at the ceiling with his arms at his sides, as though he were still a patient at the hospital awaiting some painful procedure.

Then Hannah bent her head, turning toward the left, and lowered first to her elbows, then all the way, lowering her ear toward his left, his secret-sharing, nipple. When she touched his skin, she could feel him wince.

Oh, it was Samuel's heart, all right. She knew the minute she heard it. She could have picked it out of a thousand. It wasn't true that you couldn't tell one heart from another by the sound of it. This one was Sam's. Hadn't she listened to it just this way often enough? When they were lying in bed? Hadn't she listened with her head on his chest, just this way, and heard it slow down after they had made love? It was like a little secret that she knew about his body and it had always made her smile to think of the effect she had on him.

Hannah settled and gave herself up to the labor of listening. Closing her eyes, she drew herself down, down into that one sense of hearing, shedding sight and touch and all her other senses, peeling away everything that was not pure hearing until the entire rest of her body was an adjunct to her right ear and she was oblivious to whatever else might be in the world. She listened and received the deep regular beat, the emphatic *lub-dup*, *lub-dup* to which with all her own heart she surrendered. Almost at once, she felt a sense of comfort that she had not known in three years. She could have stayed there forever, bathed in the sound and touch of that heart. Thus she lay, until her ear and the chest of the man had fused into a single bridge of flesh across which marched, one after the other, in cadence, the parade of that mighty heart. Her own pulse quieted to match it beat for beat. And now it was no longer sound that entered and occupied her, but blood that flowed from one to the other, her own blood driven by the heart that lay just beneath the breast, whose slow rise and fall she rode as though it were a small boat at anchor in a tranquil sea, and she a huddled creature waiting to be born.

At last Hannah opened her eyes and raised her head. Never, never had she felt such a sense of consolation and happiness. Had it been a dream? Had she fallen asleep? It was a moment before she felt his arm about her shoulders. How long, she wondered, had she lain encircled and unaware? She looked up to see that he was smiling down at her. Angels must smile like that, she thought.

"You were trembling," he explained. "It was like holding a bird."

Gently, Hannah disengaged herself and stood, but listening still, cocking her ear for scraps of sound, echoes. And it seemed to her in the darkened room that light emanated from the naked torso of the man and that the chest upon which she had laid her head was a field of golden wheat in which, for this time, it had been given to her to go gleaning.

Henry Pope followed her to the door.

"Will you want to come again, Hannah?" he asked. How soft and low his voice as he uttered her name.

"No," said Hannah. "There will be no need." And she stepped out into the golden kingdom of October with the certainty that she had at last been retrieved from the shadows and set down once more upon the bright lip of her life. All the way home on the bus a residue of splendor sang in her ears.

Excerpts from
GOOD GRIEF: AN UNDERTAKER'S REFLECTIONS
by Thomas Lynch

*At no time is the question, "Are we our bodies?" more perplexing and trou-
bling than in death. The dead body is clearly and uniquely the mortal remains
of the one who has died, yet it is also just as clearly no longer he (or she). Is the
body, then, "just a shell," distinct from the real person? What do we owe that
dead body and the life it once led? How does the way we treat the dead body
reveal our attitude toward life, and how does it address what we have lost to
death? These questions are powerfully raised in this poignant essay by Thomas
Lynch, an undertaker who considers why a funeral, which includes the body of
the deceased, might be preferable to a memorial service, which does not.*

*Lynch considers this question in the context of his own, Christian, faith. As
death is universal, however, so is the problem of how best to dispatch the dead.
Much of what Lynch writes, therefore, should interest even readers who do
not share his religious beliefs.*

*The author begins with the widely accepted premise that "the good death
engages our entire humanity—both what is permanent and what is passing."
A good funeral, he goes on to say, also deals with both aspects of death, "not
just the idea but also the sad and actual fact of the matter—the dead body." If
the needs of the dead body are neglected at the funeral, Lynch suggests, mourners
cannot fulfill their "fundamental obligations" to "bear witness to the life that
was lived and the death that has occurred." He concludes by recalling clergy-
men who have fulfilled this obligation well, by standing with the mourners by
the side of the coffin, and accompanying them and it to the crematory or the
grave.*

*Lynch makes much of the need for "witnesses" at a grave. To what are they
bearing witness? Why do so many people prefer to say goodbye without the
body present? Are their reasons sound? What does a dead body "say" to the
living? Is Lynch persuasive?*

It's sunny and 70 at Chapel Hill. I'm speaking to Project Compassion, an advocacy group for end-of-life issues, on an unlikely trinity of oxymorons—the *good* death, *good* grief and the *good* funeral. "What," most people reasonably ask, "can ever be good about death or grief or funerals?" The 150 people in this room understand. They are mostly women—clergy, hospice and social workers, doctors, nurses and funeral directors—and they work, so to speak, in the deep end of the pool, with the dying, the dead and the bereaved.

We begin by agreeing that the good death is the one that happens when we are among our own, surrounded not by beeping meters and blinking monitors but by the faces of family and people who care. It is the death of a whole person, not an ailing part. It is neither a failure nor an anomaly; it is less science and more serenity. The good death, like the good life, does not happen in isolation. It is not only or entirely a medical event, nor only or entirely a social or spiritual or retail one. The good death engages our entire humanity—both what is permanent and what is passing. So I am thanking these women for the power of their presence—as nurses and doctors and hospice volunteers, as pastors and rabbis, priests and imams, as mothers and daughters, sisters and wives—for their willingness to stand in the room where someone is dying, without an easy answer, without a cure or false hopes, with only their own humanity, to bear witness and to be present. The power of being there is that it emboldens others—family and friends—to be present too to the glorious and sorrowful mysteries.

And grief, *good* grief, we further concur, is something about which we have little choice. It is the tax we pay on the loves of our lives, our habits and attachments. And like every other tax there is this dull math to it—if you love, you grieve. So the question is not so much whether or not, but rather how well, how completely, how meaningfully we mourn. And though we do not grieve as those who have no faith grieve, as people of faith we grieve nonetheless. We talk about the deeper meanings we sometimes find in the contemplation of these things and how we sometimes feel God's presence there, and sometimes God's absence.

And everything is going very well. We are all nodding in warm consensus. It's like preaching to the choir—until I come to the part where I talk about a good funeral.

A good funeral, I tell them, serves the living by caring for the dead. It tends to both—the living and dead—because a death in the family happens to both. A good funeral transports the newly deceased and the newly bereaved to the borders of a changed reality. The dead are disposed of in a way that says they mattered to us, and the living are brought to the edge of a life they will lead without the one who has died. We deal with death by dealing with the dead, not just the idea but also the sad and actual fact of the matter—the dead body.

Here is where some of the audience stops nodding. Brows furrow, eyes narrow into squints, as if something doesn't exactly compute. The idea of death is one thing. A dead body is quite another. An Episcopal priest in the third row raises her hand to ask, "Why do we need the body there? Isn't it, after all, just a shell?" . . .

. . . Human beings are bodies and souls. And souls, made in the image and likeness of God, are eternal and essential, whereas bodies are mortal and impermanent. "There is," the scripture holds, "a natural body and a spiritual body." In life, we are regarded as one—a whole being, body and soul, flesh and blood and spirit. And we are charged with the care and maintenance of both. We feed the flesh and the essence. We pamper the wounds and strive to improve the condition of both body and soul. We read and run wind sprints, we fast and pray, confide in our pastors and medicos, and seek communion, spiritual and physical, with other members of our species. "Know ye not," Paul asks the Corinthians, "that ye are the temple of God, and that the Spirit of God dwelleth in you?"

But in death, the good priest in the third row seemed to be saying, the temple becomes suddenly devalued, suddenly irrelevant, suddenly negligible and disposable—"just a shell" from which we ought to seek a hurried and most often unseen riddance.

Like many of her fellow clergy, she finds the spiritual bodies more agreeable than the natural ones. The spirits are well intentioned and faultless; the bodies are hungry, lustful, greedy and weak. The soul is the sanctuary of faith, the body full of doubts and despairs. The soul sees the straight and narrow path, whereas the body wants the easier, softer way. The corruptible bleeds and belches and dies, and the incorruptible is perfect and perpetual. Souls are just easier all around. Which is why for years she's been officiating at memorial services instead of funerals. They are easier, more convenient and more cost-efficient. They are notable for their user-friendliness. They can be scheduled around the churches' priorities—the day care and Stephen Ministries, the Bible studies and rummage sales—and around a pastor's all-too-busy schedule. A quick and private disposal of the dead removes the sense of emergency and immediacy from a death in the family. No need, as W. H. Auden wrote, to:

> Stop all the clocks, cut off the telephone,
> Prevent the dog from barking with a juicy bone,

Silence the pianos and with muffled drum
Bring out the coffin, let the mourners come.
(*from "Funeral Blues"*)

There is no bother with coffins at all. The dead are secreted off to the crematory or grave while the living go about their business. Where a dead body requires more or less immediate attention, riddance of "just the shell" can hold grief off for a few days, or a week, or a season. No cutting short the pastor's too brief vacation, no rushing home from a ministerial conference to deal with a death in the parish family. The eventual "celebration" will be a lovely and, needless to say, "life-affirming" event to which everyone is invited—except, of course, the one who has died. The talk is determinedly uplifting, the finger food and memorabilia are all in good taste, the music more purposefully cheering than poignant, the bereaved most likely on their best behavior, less likely to "break down," "fall apart" or "go to pieces"—they will be brave and faithful. And "closure," if not achieved, is nonetheless proclaimed, often just before the Merlot runs out. . . .

The author discusses problems in the funeral industry.

. . . These funerary fashion blunders make most people more than a little wary. Too often, however, to avoid the fashions, the fundamental obligations are neglected—to bear witness to the life that was lived and the death that has occurred. Too often the body is dispatched by cell phone and gold card to the grave unaccompanied by clergy, family or the company of those who care. It is a function performed by functionaries—quick, clean, cheap, convenient and ultimately meaningless.

A good funeral is not about how much we spend or how much we save. Rather it is about what we do—to act out our faith, our hopes, our loves and losses. Pastoral care is not about making death easier, or grief less keenly felt or funerals cheaper or more convenient. It is about bringing the power of faith to bear on the human experience of dying, death and bereavement. And our faith is not for getting around grief or past it, but for getting through it. It is not for denying death, but for confronting it. It is not for dodging our dead, but for bearing us up as we bear them to the grave or tomb or fire at the edge of which we give them back to God.

Among the several blessings of my work as a funeral director is that I have seen the power of such faith in the face of death. I remember the churchman at the deathbed of a neighbor—it was four in the morning in the middle of winter—who gathered the family around to pray, then helped me guide the stretcher through the snow out to where our hearse was parked. Three days later, after the services at church, he rode with me in the hearse to the grave, committed the body with a handful of earth and then stood with the family and friends as the grave was filled, reading from the psalms—the calm in his voice and the assurance of the words making the sad and honorable duties bearable.

I remember the priest I called to bury one of our town's indigents—a man without family or friends or finances. He, the gravediggers and I carried the casket to the grave. The priest incensed the body, blessed it with holy water and read from the liturgy for 20 minutes, then sang In Paradisum—that gorgeous Latin for "May the angels lead you into Paradise"—as we lowered the poor man's body into the ground. When I asked him why he'd gone to such trouble he said these are the most important funerals—even if only God is watching—because it affirms the agreement between "all God's children" that we will witness and remember and take care of each other.

And I remember the Presbyterian pastor, a woman of strength and compassion who assisted a young mother whose baby had died in placing the infant's body into a tiny casket. She held the young woman as she placed a cross in the baby's hands and a teddy bear at the baby's side and then, because the mother couldn't, the pastor carefully closed the casket lid. They stood and prayed together—"God grant us the serenity to accept the things we cannot change"—then drove with me to the crematory.

Or the Baptist preacher called to preach the funeral of one of our famously imperfect citizens who drank and smoked and ran a little wild, contrary to how his born-again parents had raised him. Instead of damnation and altar calls, the pastor turned the service into a lesson in God's love and mercy and forgiveness. After speaking about the man's Christian youth, he allowed as how he had "gone astray" after he'd left home and joined the army. "It seems he couldn't keep his body and his soul aligned," the young pastor said, and seemed a little lost for words until he left the pulpit, walked over and opened the casket, took out a harmonica and began to play "Just As I Am" while everyone in the congregation nodded and wept and smiled, some of them mouthing the words of promise and comfort to themselves.

In each case these holy people treated the bodies of the dead neither as a bother or embarrassment, nor an idol or icon, nor just a shell. They treated the dead like one of our own, precious to the people who loved them, temples of the Holy Spirit, neighbors, family, fellow pilgrims. They stand—these local heroes, these saints and sinners, these men and women of God—in that difficult space between the living and the dead, between faith and fear, between humanity and Christianity and say out loud, "Behold, I show you a mystery."

CHAPTER 5:
MANY STAGES, ONE LIFE

IN THE PREVIOUS CHAPTER we saw that we are embodied beings. But that is not our whole story. We are also embodied beings living in time and changing continuously as it passes. The physical changes we undergo are all too easy to see. But what becomes of our noncorporeal identities as our bodies age and our experiences accumulate? How do our minds develop, from cradle to grave? In what ways do we remain the same?

And what are we to make of the complete span of a human life, from beginning to end? Does it tell a coherent story? Does it advance? What meaning is to be found in its distinctive shape? Though each life is different, what might each individual's movement through childhood, youth, maturity, and old age share with every other's?

Our readings in this chapter begin with three attempts to describe the progress of a life from its beginning, or near its beginning, to its end. In a celebrated passage from *The Rhetoric*, Aristotle considers the differences between youth, old age, and manhood in its prime. Francis Bacon compares two of these stages in "On Youth and Old Age," and William Shakespeare, in a famous speech, traces the seven "acts" of a man's life.

The series of readings that follows presents portraits of various life stages. It begins with childhood, as seen by J. M. Barrie in his great children's novel, *Peter Pan*. Next, in the first of several excerpts from Tolstoy's *War and Peace*, we are introduced to a youth, Nicholas, and two of his friends. In the following excerpt, we meet Nicholas again, this time as a mature man. An excerpt from Thomas Mann's *Buddenbrooks* then shows us another man in his prime, but one who feels his power and vitality beginning to slip. We then return to *War and Peace* to meet an old woman who is living out her last days in the care of her children. What might it mean to be sensible of this inexorable trajectory? An excerpt from novelist Vladimir Nabokov's memoir *Speak, Memory* considers the significance of our awareness of time.

Not every life is fully played out, from beginning to shapely end. Our next reading, Robert Louis Stevenson's "Ordered South," offers two

views—one by a youth, and one by the same man in his middle years—
of a life cut short by mortal illness. We follow this with an excerpt from
Willa Cather's *The Professor's House*, in which we see that not only one's
physical health, but one's mental state as well, can confound the expected course of a life.

We conclude with "Life," a story by Liam O'Flaherty about the peculiar and powerful bond between a new-born boy and his old and demented grandfather. What is the source of this bond? What unites the
beginning of life with its end?

Excerpt from
THE RHETORIC OF ARISTOTLE
translated by Lane Cooper

As most of us realize, we change as we age, and not only biologically. Time and experience alter our appetites and, often, our outlooks, attitudes, and aspirations as well. In this famous account of the young, the old, and those in their prime, Aristotle offers a capsule summary of the most common characteristics found in each of these stages of life.

Every reader will recall individuals who do not fit the pattern Aristotle describes. The existence of exceptions, though, should not prevent most readers from finding much that is familiar in Aristotle's account.

Aristotle considers the young and the old to suffer from excesses that tend in opposite directions. These excesses produce, in each, characteristic qualities and defects. The qualities and defects common to the young are largely mirror images of those common to the old, while a man in his prime, he claims, strikes the "fitting mean" between them.

Is Aristotle's account accurate? Is this account gender-specific, or does it apply equally well to men and women? How young are the "young" that Aristotle describes? How old are the "old"? Are these stages merely chronological?

What causes the changes Aristotle observes between youth and the prime of life, and between the prime and old age?

Do the changes Aristotle describes constitute progress, or deterioration, over the course of a life?

Wisdom is often said to come with old age. Does it, in this account?

Are all of these stages necessary to a full or complete life? Is there something to be said for each of them?

If Aristotle is correct about the changes that come with advancing age, then what can we conclude about the coherence and goodness of our lives?

In what sense do we remain the same person, despite these age-dependent changes in character?

Excerpt from THE RHETORIC OF ARISTOTLE, translated by Lane Cooper, by permission of Pearson Education.

Let us now discuss the various types of human character in relation to the emotions and moral states, to the several periods of life and the varieties of fortune. By emotions are meant anger, desire, and the like—which we have already discussed.

By moral states are meant virtues and vices; and these, too, have already been treated, along with the characteristic choices, and characteristic acts, of the men who are subject to them. By periods of life are meant youth, the prime of life, and old age; by varieties of fortune [states or conditions of life] are meant health, wealth, power [in its several kinds], and their opposites—in a word, good fortune and bad.

We shall begin with the characteristics of youth. Young men have strong desires, and whatever they desire they are prone to do. Of the bodily desires the one they let govern them most is the sexual; here they lack self-control. They are shifting and unsteady in their desires, which are vehement for a time, but soon relinquished; for the longings of youth are keen rather than deep—are like sick people's fits of hunger and thirst. The young are passionate, quick to anger, and apt to give way to it. And their angry passions get the better of them; for, since they wish to be honored, young men cannot put up with a slight; they are resentful if they only imagine that they are unfairly treated. Fond of honor, they are even fonder of victory, for youth likes to be superior, and winning evinces superiority. They love both honor and victory more than they love money. Indeed, they care next to nothing about money, for they have not yet learned what the want of it means; the point is brought out in the saying of Pittacus about Amphiaraus. The young think no evil [are not cynical], but believe in human goodness, for as yet they have not seen many examples of vice. They are trustful, for as yet they have not been often deceived. And they are sanguine; for young men glow with a natural heat as drinkers are heated with wine, while as yet their failures have not been many. They live their lives for the most part in hope [anticipation], as hope is of the future and memory of the past; and for young men the future is long, the past but short; on the first day of life there is nothing to remember, everything to expect. They are easily deceived, and for the same reason, since they are quick to hope. Being passionate as well as hopeful, they are relatively brave; the passion excludes fear, and the hope inspires confidence—no one is afraid when he is angry, and an anticipation of good makes one confident. And they are shy; for as yet they have no independent standard of good conduct, but only the conventional standards in which they were reared. They are

high-minded [have lofty aspirations]; first, because they have not yet
been humbled by life, nor come to know the force of circumstances; and
secondly, because high-mindedness means thinking oneself fitted for great
things, and this again is characteristic of the hopeful. In their actions
they prefer honor to expediency; for their lives are rather lives of good
impulse [moral instinct or feeling] than of calculation [reason]; and calculation aims at the expedient, virtue at the honorable. They are fond
of their friends, intimates, and associates—more so than are men in the
other two periods of life; this comes from their love of company, and
from the fact that as yet they judge nothing, and hence do not judge
their friends, by the standard of expediency. All their mistakes are on
the side of intensity and excess, running counter to the maxim of Chilon
['Moderation in all things']. They carry everything too far: they love to
excess, they hate to excess—and so in all else. They think they know
everything, and are positive about everything; indeed, this is why they
always carry their doings too far. When they wrong other people, the
injuries are wanton [insolent], not malicious. The young are prone to
pity, because they think every one good, or at all events better than
people really are. That is, they judge their fellow man by their own guile-
lessness, and hence assume that his sufferings are undeserved. They are
fond of laughter, and therefore facetious, facetiousness being a subdued
insolence.

Such, then, is the character of the young. As for elderly men—men
who are past their prime—we may say that their characteristics for the
most part are the opposite of these. The old have lived long, have been
often deceived, have made many mistakes of their own; they see that
more often than not the affairs of men turn out badly. And so they are
positive about nothing; in all things they err by an extreme moderation.
They 'think'—they never 'know'; and in discussing any matter they always subjoin 'perhaps'—'possibly.' Everything they say is put thus doubtfully—nothing with firmness. They think evil [are cynical]; that is, they
are disposed to put the worse construction on everything. Further, they
are suspicious because they are distrustful, and distrustful from sad experience. As a result, they have no strong likings or hates; rather, illustrat-
ing the precept of Bias, they love as men ready some day to hate, and
hate as ready to love. They are mean-souled [small-minded], because
they have been humbled by life. Thus they aspire to nothing great or
exalted, but crave the mere necessities and comforts of existence. And
they are not generous. Property, as they know, is one of the necessities,
and they have learned by experience how hard it is to acquire, how easy
to lose. They are cowards, apprehensive about everything—in tempera-

ment just the opposite of youth; for they are grown cold, as youth is hot, so that advancing age has paved the way to cowardice, since fear in itself is a species of chill. They cling to life, and all the more as the latter end of it comes nearer; for, as the object of all desire is the absent, so the thing they most lack will be the thing they most desire. They are unduly selfish [their self-love exceeds the right measure]—another trait of the mean-souled. And through selfishness they live their lives with too much regard for the expedient, too little for honor; by expediency we mean what is good for oneself, by honor what is good absolutely. They are not shy, but tend to be shameless; because they have less regard for honor than for expediency, they do not care what people think of them. They are slow to hope; partly from experience—since things generally go wrong, or at all events seldom turn out well; and partly, too, from cowardice. They live in memory rather than anticipation; for the part of life remaining to them is but small, while the part that is past is large—and hope is of the future, memory of the past. Here, again, is the reason for their garrulity; they are for ever talking of bygone events, which they thus enjoy in recollection. Their fits of passion, though quick, are feeble; as for their desires of sense, these have either wholly failed, or are weakened. Accordingly, the old are not characterized by passion, and their actions are governed, not by impulse, but by the love of gain. And hence men in this period of life are thought to be temperate [appear to have the virtue of self-control]; the truth is that their desires have slackened, and they themselves are mastered by the love of gain. Their lives are rather lives of calculation than of moral bias; for calculation aims at expediency, whereas the object of morality is virtue. When they wrong others, the injuries are done out of malice, and not from insolence. Old men, too, as well as young men, tend to feel pity, but not for the same reason. Young men feel pity out of human kindness, old men out of their infirmity. Because they are weak, they take all possible sufferings to be near them; and this, as we saw, is the state of mind in which pity is felt. And hence they are querulous, not given to jesting or laughter; for the querulous disposition is just the opposite of the mirthful.

Such, then, are the characteristics of young men and of the elderly. . . .

. . . As for men in the prime of life, their character evidently will be intermediate between these two, exempt from the excess of either young or old. They will be neither excessively confident—which means confident to the point of rashness—nor yet too timid; they will be both confident and cautious. They will neither trust every one nor distrust every one; rather they will judge each case by the facts. Their rule of life will be neither honor alone, nor expediency alone; they will duly observe both standards. And so with regard to parsimony and prodigality: their economy will be fit and proper. So, too, with regard to passion and desire: they will combine self-control with valor, and valor with self-control. In the young and the old these qualities are not combined; young men are brave, but lack self-control, and old men, while temperate, are cowardly. To put it generally: all the valuable qualities which youth and age divide between them are joined in the prime of life; and between the respective excesses and defects of youth and age, in every case it strikes the fitting mean. The body is in its prime from thirty years of age to five-and-thirty, and the soul about forty-nine.

OF YOUTH AND AGE

by Francis Bacon

Like Aristotle, Francis Bacon believes one's temperament changes as one grows older, in characteristic and even predictable ways. In this essay he turns his attention in part to the strengths, but mostly to the weaknesses, typical of youth and age.

Bacon begins by noting that occasionally someone bypasses the weaknesses of youth, but that this is rare. Generally, the minds of the young, and not just their years, are different. Because of their propensity to "vision," Bacon twice suggests that the young may be "nearer to God than the old."

Because of their differences, Bacon argues, for each stage of life there is a fitting kind of work. With few exceptions, "Young men are fitter to invent than to judge, fitter for execution than for counsel, and fitter for new projects than for settled business."

Also like Aristotle, Bacon sees in the old the mirror image of the strengths and weaknesses of the young. After describing the work best suited to each age, Bacon recommends employing both, "because the virtues of either age may correct the defects of both."

Bacon suggests not only that it is normal but also that it is best for a life to develop as he says it usually does. He demonstrates this by describing the characteristic infirmities of the three types of men who bypass the weaknesses of youth, having what he calls "an over-early ripeness in their years."

Is Bacon's account of youth and age true? Is it more accurate or better than Aristotle's? What might we infer from his omission of a "prime" of life?

If a weakness is normal to one's age, can it be considered a defect?

Why are those closest to God said to be least suited for "judgment" and "counsel"?

If Bacon is right about youth and age, what should we think about our own process of aging? If Bacon is right, how might the character of society be affected by major changes in the age structure of its population, either toward a preponderance of the old or a preponderance of the young?

A man that is young in years may be old in hours, if he have lost no time; but that happeneth rarely. Generally, youth is like the first cogitations, not so wise as the second; for there is a youth in thoughts as well as in ages; and yet the invention of young men is more lively than that of old, and imaginations stream into their minds better, and, as it were, more divinely. Natures that have much heat, and great and violent desires and perturbations, are not ripe for action till they have passed the meridian of their years: as it was with Julius Caesar and Septimius Severus; of the latter of whom it is said, He passed his youth full of errors, of madness, even; and yet he was the ablest emperor, almost, of all the list; but reposed natures may do well in youth, as it is seen in Augustus Caesar, Cosmus Duke of Florence, Gaston de Foix, and others. On the other side, heat and vivacity in age is an excellent composition for business. Young men are fitter to invent than to judge, fitter for execution than for counsel, and fitter for new projects than for settled business; for the experience of age, in things that fall within the compass of it, directeth them; but in new things abuseth them. The errors of young men are the ruin of business; but the errors of aged men amount but to this, that more might have been done, or sooner.

Young men, in the conduct and manage of actions, embrace more than they can hold; stir more than they can quiet; fly to the end, without consideration of the means and degrees; pursue some few principles which they have chanced upon absurdly; care not to innovate, which draws unknown inconveniences; use extreme remedies at first; and that, which doubleth all errors, will not acknowledge or retract them, like an unready horse, that will neither stop nor turn. Men of age object too much, consult too long, adventure too little, repent too soon, and seldom drive business home to the full period, but content themselves with a mediocrity of success. Certainly it is good to compound employments of both; for that will be good for the present, because the virtues of either age may correct the defects of both; and good for succession, that young men may be learners, while men in age are actors; and, lastly, good for externe accidents, because authority followeth old men, and favor and popularity youth; but, for the moral part, perhaps, youth will have the pre-eminence, as age hath for the politic. A certain rabbin, upon the text, Your young men shall see visions, and your old men shall dream dreams, inferreth that young men are admitted nearer to God than old, because vision is a clearer revelation than a dream; and, certainly, the more a man drinketh of the world, the more it intoxicateth; and age doth profit rather in the powers of understanding than in the virtues of the will and affections. There be some have an over-early ripeness in their years, which fadeth betimes; these are, first, such as have brittle wits, the edge whereof is soon turned; such as was Hermogenes the rhetorician, whose books are exceedingly subtle; who afterwards

waxed stupid. A second sort is of those that have some natural dispositions, which have better grace in youth than in age; such as is a fluent
and luxuriant speech, which becomes youth well, but not age; so Tully
saith of Hortensius: He remained the same, though it was no longer
becoming. The third is of such as take too high a strain at the first, and
are magnanimous more than tract of years can uphold; as was Scipio
Africanus, of whom Livy saith, in effect, *His last deeds did not equal his
first*.

Excerpt from

AS YOU LIKE IT

by William Shakespeare

The following famous speech, from Shakespeare's comedy As You Like It, *is delivered by Jaques, a confirmed bachelor and cosmopolite, who is living with the exiled Duke Senior and his courtiers in the idyllic Forest of Arden.*

After declaring that "All the world's a stage, / And all the men and women merely players," Jaques describes seven "acts" or stages that comprise a man's life. He has a caustic remark for each of the "parts" a man plays: infant, schoolboy, lover, soldier, justice, "pantaloon," and lastly, "second childishness and mere oblivion."

Is it true to say that we are all merely players? Is life really like play-acting? If it is a performance, for whom is it performed?

Is Jaques's characterization of each of these stages or parts of human life accurate?

Do the seven parts cohere with each other?

Does the life so described progress? Does it lead up to anything?

Is Jaques's portrait of the human drama complete? Is any important stage, or "part," missing? If so, what difference does it make for the wholeness of a life?

JAQUES
   All the world's a stage,
   And all the men and women merely players ;
   They have their exits and their entrances,
   And one man in his time plays many parts,
   His acts being seven ages. At first, the infant,
   Mewling and puking in the nurse's arms.
   Then the whining schoolboy, with his satchel
   And shining morning face, creeping like snail

Unwillingly to school. And then the lover,
Sighing like furnace, with a woeful ballad
Made to his mistress' eyebrow. Then a soldier,
Full of strange oaths and bearded like the pard,
Jealous in honor, sudden and quick in quarrel,
Seeking the bubble reputation
Even in the cannon's mouth. And then the justice,
In fair round belly with good capon lined,
With eyes severe and beard of formal cut,
Full of wise saws and modern instances ;
And so he plays his part. The sixth age shifts
Into the lean and slippered pantaloon,
With spectacles on nose and pouch on side ;
His youthful hose, well saved, a world too wide
For his shrunk shank, and his big manly voice,
Turning again toward childish treble, pipes
And whistles in his sound. Last scene of all,
That ends this strange eventful history,
Is second childishness and mere oblivion,
Sans teeth, sans eyes, sans taste, sans everything.

Excerpts from
PETER PAN
by J. M. Barrie

J. M. Barrie's Peter Pan *is well known as a children's novel. To the adult reader, though, it has much to teach about the movement of a life from childhood to adulthood to parenthood, and about our eventual replacement by our children. By offering a particularly rich account of the distinctive character of childhood,* Peter Pan *reminds adults of a world no longer accessible to them.*

Mr. and Mrs. Darling live at No. 14 with their children, Wendy, John, and Michael, and the children's nurse, Nana, a dog. "There never was a simpler happier family," Barrie tells us, *"until the coming of Peter Pan," the magical boy who refuses to grow up.*

The first of the two excerpts below describes Peter's appearance at No. 14. Before he arrives, though, Mrs. Darling finds a portent that he will come in her children's minds, which she "tidies up" at night while they sleep. A child's mind, Barrie tells us, *is an island, called the Neverland, where Peter lives (with the "lost boys," who are there because they have no mothers).*

After Peter's arrival, in a part of the story not reproduced here, he teaches the children to fly and takes them away with him to the Neverland, leaving their parents bereft. In the Neverland, Wendy acts as his mother, and plans to become his wife.

The second excerpt consists of the concluding pages of the book. The children have returned and Mr. and Mrs. Darling have adopted the lost boys. Peter, though, refuses to be adopted. Instead, he goes back to the Neverland, arranging to return for Wendy once each year. But Peter, who has no sense of time and little memory, forgets to return, and Wendy and the boys grow up.

After a long while Peter does return, and finds Wendy an adult with a daughter of her own. When he sees what has become of her he feels fear and pain, emotions almost unknown to him. He recovers, though, when he discovers that Wendy's daughter can now take her mother's place. She—and also her daughters after her—fly away to the Neverland and become the keepers of his stories.

What is the Neverland? Why are there no parents there? What is the meaning of Mrs. Darling's effort to "tidy up" her children's minds? Can she, or any mother, succeed? Should she even try?

Peter's arrival terrifies Mrs. Darling. Why do adults fear the approach of the Neverland, though children do not? Are adults right to fear it?

Why has Peter no sense of time, and so little memory? What effect does this have on his character? Why is he afraid when he sees Wendy fully grown?

Can all children fly? Is it true that only children can fly? Is childhood necessarily age-specific?

Excerpt 1

Mrs. Darling first heard of Peter when she was tidying up her children's minds. It is the nightly custom of every good mother after her children are asleep to rummage in their minds and put things straight for next morning, repacking into their proper places the many articles that have wandered during the day. If you could keep awake (but of course you can't) you would see your own mother doing this, and you would find it very interesting to watch her. It is quite like tidying up drawers. You would see her on her knees, I expect, lingering humorously over some of your contents, wondering where on earth you had picked this thing up, making discoveries sweet and not so sweet, pressing this to her cheek as if it were as nice as a kitten, and hurriedly stowing that out of sight. When you wake in the morning, the naughtiness and evil passions with which you went to bed have been folded up small and placed at the bottom of your mind; and on the top, beautifully aired, are spread out your prettier thoughts, ready for you to put on.

I don't know whether you have ever seen a map of a person's mind. Doctors sometimes draw maps of other parts of you, and your own map can become intensely interesting, but catch them trying to draw a map of a child's mind, which is not only confused, but keeps going round all the time. There are zigzag lines on it, just like your temperature on a card, and these are probably roads in the island; for the Neverland is always more or less an island, with astonishing splashes of colour here and there, and coral reefs and rakish-looking craft in the offing, and savages and lonely lairs, and gnomes who are mostly tailors, and caves through which a river runs, and princes with six elder brothers, and a hut fast going to decay, and one very small old lady with a hooked nose. It would be an easy map if that were all; but there is also first day at school, religion, fathers, the round pond, needlework, murders, hang-

ings, verbs that take the dative, chocolate pudding day, getting into brac-
es, say ninety-nine, three-pence for pulling out your tooth yourself, and
so on; and either these are part of the island or they are another map
showing through, and it is all rather confusing, especially as nothing
will stand still.

Of course the Neverlands vary a good deal. John's, for instance, had a
lagoon with flamingoes flying over it at which John was shooting, while
Michael, who was very small, had a flamingo with lagoons flying over it.
John lived in a boat turned upside down on the sands, Michael in a
wigwam, Wendy in a house of leaves deftly sewn together. John had no
friends, Michael had friends at night, Wendy had a pet wolf forsaken by
its parents; but on the whole the Neverlands have a family resemblance,
and if they stood in a row you could say of them that they have each
other's nose, and so forth. On these magic shores children at play are
forever beaching their coracles. We too have been there; we can still
hear the sound of the surf, though we shall land no more.

Of all delectable islands the Neverland is the snuggest and most compact; not large and sprawly, you know, with tedious distance between
one adventure and another, but nicely crammed. When you play at it by
day with the chairs and table-cloth, it is not in the least alarming, but in
the two minutes before you go to sleep it becomes very nearly real. That
is why there are night-lights.

Occasionally in her travels through her children's minds Mrs. Darling found things she could not understand, and of these quite the most
perplexing was the word Peter. She knew of no Peter, and yet he was
here and there in John and Michael's minds, while Wendy's began to be
scrawled all over with him. The name stood out in bolder letters than
any of the other words, and as Mrs. Darling gazed she felt that it had an
oddly cocky appearance.

"Yes, he is rather cocky," Wendy admitted with regret. Her mother
had been questioning her.

"But who is he, my pet?"

"He is Peter Pan, you know, mother."

At first Mrs. Darling did not know, but after thinking back into her
childhood she just remembered a Peter Pan who was said to live with
the fairies. There were odd stories about him; as that when children died
he went part of the way with them, so that they should not be frightened. She had believed in him at the time, but now that she was married
and full of sense she quite doubted whether there was any such person.

"Besides," she said to Wendy, "he would be grown up by this time."

"Oh no, he isn't grown up," Wendy assured her confidently, "and he is just my size." She meant that he was her size in both mind and body; she didn't know how she knew it, she just knew it.

Mrs. Darling consulted Mr. Darling, but he smiled pooh-pooh. "Mark my words," he said, "it is some nonsense Nana has been putting into their heads; just the sort of idea a dog would have. Leave it alone, and it will blow over."

But it would not blow over; and soon the troublesome boy gave Mrs. Darling quite a shock.

Children have the strangest adventures without being troubled by them. For instance, they may remember to mention, a week after the event happened, that when they were in the wood they met their dead father and had a game with him. It was in this casual way that Wendy one morning made a disquieting revelation. Some leaves of a tree had been found on the nursery floor, which certainly were not there when the children went to bed, and Mrs. Darling was puzzling over them when Wendy said with a tolerant smile:

"I do believe it is that Peter again!"

"Whatever do you mean, Wendy?"

"It is so naughty of him not to wipe," Wendy said, sighing. She was a tidy child.

She explained in quite a matter-of-fact way that she thought Peter sometimes came to the nursery in the night and sat on the foot of her bed and played on his pipes to her. Unfortunately she never woke, so she didn't know how she knew, she just knew.

"What nonsense you talk, precious. No one can get into the house without knocking."

"I think he comes in by the window," she said.

"My love, it is three floors up."

"Were not the leaves at the foot of the window, mother?"

It was quite true; the leaves had been found very near the window.

Mrs. Darling did not know what to think, for it all seemed so natural to Wendy that you could not dismiss it by saying she had been dreaming.

"My child," the mother cried, "why did you not tell me of this before?"

"I forgot," said Wendy lightly. She was in a hurry to get her breakfast.

Oh, surely she must have been dreaming.

But, on the other hand, there were the leaves. Mrs. Darling examined them carefully; they were skeleton leaves, but she was sure they did not come from any tree that grew in England. She crawled about the floor, peering at it with a candle for marks of a strange foot. She rattled the poker up the chimney and tapped the walls. She let down a tape from the window to the pavement, and it was a sheer drop of thirty feet, without so much as a spout to climb up by.

Certainly Wendy had been dreaming.

But Wendy had not been dreaming, as the very next night showed, the night on which the extraordinary adventures of these children may be said to have begun.

On the night we speak of all the children were once more in bed. It happened to be Nana's evening off, and Mrs. Darling had bathed them and sung to them till one by one they had let go her hand and slid away into the land of sleep.

All were looking so safe and cosy that she smiled at her fears now and sat down tranquilly by the fire to sew.

It was something for Michael, who on his birthday was getting into shirts. The fire was warm, however, and the nursery dimly lit by three night-lights, and presently the sewing lay on Mrs. Darling's lap. Then her head nodded, oh, so gracefully. She was asleep. Look at the four of them, Wendy and Michael over there, John here, and Mrs. Darling by the fire. There should have been a fourth night-light.

While she slept she had a dream. She dreamt that the Neverland had come too near and that a strange boy had broken through from it. He did not alarm her, for she thought she had seen him before in the faces of many women who have no children. Perhaps he is to be found in the faces of some mothers also. But in her dream he had rent the film that obscures the Neverland, and she saw Wendy and John and Michael peeping through the gap.

The dream by itself would have been a trifle, but while she was dreaming the window of the nursery blew open, and a boy did drop on the floor. He was accompanied by a strange light, no bigger than your fist, which darted about the room like a living thing; and I think it must have been this light that wakened Mrs. Darling.

She started up with a cry, and saw the boy, and somehow she knew at once that he was Peter Pan. If you or I or Wendy had been there we should have seen that he was very like Mrs. Darling's kiss. He was a lovely boy, clad in skeleton leaves and the juices that ooze out of trees; but the most entrancing thing about him was that he had all his first teeth. When he saw she was a grown-up, he gnashed the little pearls at her.

Excerpt 2

*The children have returned from the Neverland with Peter and the lost boys.
The lost boys have been adopted by the Darlings, but Peter refuses to be
adopted and to grow up to be a man. Instead, he pleads with Wendy to
return with him to the Neverland, to live in a little house in the treetops.*

"Well, then, come with me to the little house."

"May I, mummy?"

"Certainly not. I have got you home again, and I mean to keep you."

"But he does so need a mother."

"So do you, my love."

"Oh, all right," Peter said, as if he had asked her from politeness merely;
but Mrs. Darling saw his mouth twitch, and she made this handsome
offer: to let Wendy go to him for a week every year to do his spring
cleaning. Wendy would have preferred a more permanent arrangement;
and it seemed to her that spring would be long in coming; but this promise sent Peter away quite gay again. He had no sense of time, and was so
full of adventures that all I have told you about him is only a halfpenny-
worth of them. I suppose it was because Wendy knew this that her last
words to him were these rather plaintive ones:

"You won't forget me, Peter, will you, before spring-cleaning time
comes?"

Of course Peter promised; and then he flew away. He took Mrs. Darling's kiss with him. The kiss that had been for no one else Peter took
quite easily. Funny. But she seemed satisfied.

Of course all the boys went to school; and most of them got into Class
III, but Slightly was put first into Class IV and then into Class V. Class I
is the top class. Before they had attended school a week they saw what
goats they had been not to remain on the island; but it was too late now,
and soon they settled down to being as ordinary as you or me or Jenkins
minor. It is sad to have to say that the power to fly gradually left them.
At first Nana tied their feet to the bed-posts so that they should not fly
away in the night; and one of their diversions by day was to pretend to
fall off 'buses; but by and by they ceased to tug at their bonds in bed, and
found that they hurt themselves when they let go of the 'bus. In time
they could not even fly after their hats. Want of practice, they called it;
but what it really meant was that they no longer believed.

Michael believed longer than the other boys, though they jeered at
him; so he was with Wendy when Peter came for her at the end of the

first year. She flew away with Peter in the frock she had woven from leaves and berries in the Neverland, and her one fear was that he might notice how short it had become; but he never noticed, he had so much to say about himself.

She had looked forward to thrilling talks with him about old times, but new adventures had crowded the old ones from his mind.

"Who is Captain Hook?" he asked with interest when she spoke of the arch enemy.

"Don't you remember," she asked, amazed, "how you killed him and saved all our lives?"

"I forget them after I kill them," he replied carelessly.

When she expressed a doubtful hope that Tinker Bell would be glad to see her he said, "Who is Tinker Bell?"

"O Peter," she said, shocked; but even when she explained he could not remember.

"There are such a lot of them," he said. "I expect she is no more."

I expect he was right, for fairies don't live long, but they are so little that a short time seems a good while to them.

Wendy was pained too to find that the past year was but as yesterday to Peter; it had seemed such a long year of waiting to her. But he was exactly as fascinating as ever, and they had a lovely spring-cleaning in the little house on the tree tops.

Next year he did not come for her. She waited in a new frock because the old one simply would not meet; but he never came.

"Perhaps he is ill," Michael said.

"You know he is never ill."

Michael came close to her and whispered, with a shiver, "Perhaps there is no such person, Wendy!" and then Wendy would have cried if Michael had not been crying.

Peter came next spring cleaning; and the strange thing was that he never knew he had missed a year.

That was the last time the girl Wendy ever saw him. For a little longer she tried for his sake not to have growing pains; and she felt she was untrue to him when she got a prize for general knowledge. But the years came and went without bringing the careless boy; and when they met again Wendy was a married woman, and Peter was no more to her than a little dust in the box in which she had kept her toys. Wendy was grown up. You need not be sorry for her. She was one of the kind that likes to grow up. In the end she grew up of her own free will a day quicker than other girls.

All the boys were grown up and done for by this time; so it is scarcely worth while saying anything more about them. You may see the twins and Nibs and Curly any day going to an office, each carrying a little bag and an umbrella. Michael is an engine-driver. Slightly married a lady of title, and so he became a lord. You see that judge in a wig coming out at the iron door? That used to be Tootles. The bearded man who doesn't know any story to tell his children was once John.

Wendy was married in white with a pink sash. It is strange to think that Peter did not alight in the church and forbid the banns.

Years rolled on again, and Wendy had a daughter. This ought not to be written in ink but in a golden splash.

She was called Jane, and always had an odd inquiring look, as if from the moment she arrived on the mainland she wanted to ask questions. When she was old enough to ask them they were mostly about Peter Pan. She loved to hear of Peter, and Wendy told her all she could remember in the very nursery from which the famous flight had taken place. It was Jane's nursery now, for her father had bought it at the three per cents. from Wendy's father, who was no longer fond of stairs. Mrs. Darling was now dead and forgotten.

There were only two beds in the nursery now, Jane's and her nurse's; and there was no kennel, for Nana also had passed away. She died of old age, and at the end she had been rather difficult to get on with; being very firmly convinced that no one knew how to look after children except herself.

Once a week Jane's nurse had her evening off; and then it was Wendy's part to put Jane to bed. That was the time for stories. It was Jane's invention to raise the sheet over her mother's head and her own, thus making a tent, and in the awful darkness to whisper:

"What do we see now?"

"I don't think I see anything to-night," says Wendy, with a feeling that if Nana were here she would object to further conversation.

"Yes, you do," says Jane, "you see when you were a little girl."

"That is a long time ago, sweetheart," says Wendy. "Ah me, how time flies!"

"Does it fly," asks the artful child, "the way you flew when you were a little girl?"

"The way I flew! Do you know, Jane, I sometimes wonder whether I ever did really fly."

"Yes, you did."

"The dear old days when I could fly!"

"Why can't you fly now, mother?"

"Because I am grown up, dearest. When people grow up they forget the way."

"Why do they forget the way?"

"Because they are no longer gay and innocent and heartless. It is only the gay and innocent and heartless who can fly."

"What is gay and innocent and heartless? I do wish I was gay and innocent and heartless."

Or perhaps Wendy admits that she does see something.

"I do believe," she says, "that it is this nursery."

"I do believe it is," says Jane. "Go on."

They are now embarked on the great adventure of the night when Peter flew in looking for his shadow.

"The foolish fellow," says Wendy, "tried to stick it on with soap, and when he could not he cried, and that woke me, and I sewed it on for him."

"You have missed a bit," interrupts Jane, who now knows the story better than her mother. "When you saw him sitting on the floor crying, what did you say?"

"I sat up in bed and I said, 'Boy, why are you crying?'"

"Yes, that was it," says Jane, with a big breath.

"And then he flew us all away to the Neverland and the fairies and the pirates and the redskins and the mermaids' lagoon, and the home under the ground, and the little house."

"Yes! which did you like best of all?"

"I think I liked the home under the ground best of all."

"Yes, so do I. What was the last thing Peter ever said to you?"

"The last thing he ever said to me was, 'Just always be waiting for me, and then some night you will hear me crowing.'"

"Yes."

"But, alas, he forgot all about me." Wendy said it with a smile. She was as grown up as that.

"What did his crow sound like?" Jane asked one evening.

"It was like this," Wendy said, trying to imitate Peter's crow.

"No, it wasn't," Jane said gravely, "it was like this;" and she did it ever so much better than her mother.

Wendy was a little startled. "My darling, how can you know?"

"I often hear it when I am sleeping," Jane said.

"Ah yes, many girls hear it when they are sleeping, but I was the only one who heard it awake."

"Lucky you," said Jane.

And then one night came the tragedy. It was the spring of the year, and the story had been told for the night, and Jane was now asleep in her bed. Wendy was sitting on the floor, very close to the fire, so as to see to darn, for there was no other light in the nursery; and while she sat darning she heard a crow. Then the window blew open as of old, and Peter dropped on the floor.

He was exactly the same as ever, and Wendy saw at once that he still had all his first teeth.

He was a little boy, and she was grown up. She huddled by the fire not daring to move, helpless and guilty, a big woman.

"Hullo, Wendy," he said, not noticing any difference, for he was thinking chiefly of himself; and in the dim light her white dress might have been the nightgown in which he had seen her first.

"Hullo, Peter," she replied faintly, squeezing herself as small as possible. Something inside her was crying "Woman, woman, let go of me."

"Hullo, where is John?" he asked, suddenly missing the third bed.

"John is not here now," she gasped.

"Is Michael asleep?" he asked, with a careless glance at Jane.

"Yes," she answered; and now she felt that she was untrue to Jane as well as to Peter.

"That is not Michael," she said quickly, lest a judgment should fall on her.

Peter looked. "Hullo, is it a new one?"

"Yes."

"Boy or girl?"

"Girl."

Now surely he would understand; but not a bit of it.

"Peter," she said, faltering, "are you expecting me to fly away with you?"

"Of course; that is why I have come." He added a little sternly, "Have you forgotten that this is spring-cleaning time?"

She knew it was useless to say that he had let many spring-cleaning times pass.

"I can't come," she said apologetically, "I have forgotten how to fly."

"I'll soon teach you again."

"O Peter, don't waste the fairy dust on me."

She had risen; and now at last a fear assailed him. "What is it?" he cried, shrinking.

"I will turn up the light," she said, "and then you can see for yourself."

For almost the only time in his life that I know of, Peter was afraid. "Don't turn up the light," he cried.

She let her hands play in the hair of the tragic boy. She was not a little girl heart-broken about him; she was a grown woman smiling at it all, but they were wet smiles.

Then she turned up the light, and Peter saw. He gave a cry of pain; and when the tall beautiful creature stooped to lift him in her arms he drew back sharply.

"What is it?" he cried again.

She had to tell him.

"I am old, Peter. I am ever so much more than twenty. I grew up long ago."

"You promised not to!"

"I couldn't help it. I am a married woman, Peter."

"No, you're not."

"Yes, and the little girl in the bed is my baby."

"No, she's not."

But he supposed she was; and he took a step towards the sleeping child with his dagger upraised. Of course he did not strike. He sat down on the floor instead and sobbed; and Wendy did not know how to comfort him, though she could have done it so easily once. She was only a woman now, and she ran out of the room to try to think.

Peter continued to cry, and soon his sobs woke Jane. She sat up in bed, and was interested at once.

"Boy," she said, "why are you crying?"

Peter rose and bowed to her, and she bowed to him from the bed.

"Hullo," he said.

"Hullo," said Jane.

"My name is Peter Pan," he told her.

"Yes, I know."

"I came back for my mother," he explained, "to take her to the Neverland."

"Yes, I know," Jane said, "I have been waiting for you."

When Wendy returned diffidently she found Peter sitting on the bedpost crowing gloriously, while Jane in her nighty was flying round the room in solemn ecstasy.

"She is my mother," Peter explained; and Jane descended and stood by his side, with the look on her face that he liked to see on ladies when they gazed at him.

"He does so need a mother," Jane said.

"Yes, I know," Wendy admitted rather forlornly; "no one knows it so well as I."

"Good-bye," said Peter to Wendy; and he rose in the air, and the shameless Jane rose with him; it was already her easiest way of moving about.

Wendy rushed to the window.

"No, no," she cried.

"It is just for spring-cleaning time," Jane said; "he wants me always to do his spring cleaning."

"If only I could go with you," Wendy sighed.

"You see you can't fly," said Jane.

Of course in the end Wendy let them fly away together.

Our last glimpse of her shows her at the window, watching them receding into the sky until they were as small as stars.

As you look at Wendy you may see her hair becoming white, and her figure little again, for all this happened long ago. Jane is now a common grown-up, with a daughter called Margaret; and every spring-cleaning time, except when he forgets, Peter comes for Margaret and takes her to the Neverland, where she tells him stories about himself, to which he listens eagerly. When Margaret grows up she will have a daughter, who is to be Peter's mother in turn; and thus it will go on, so long as children are gay and innocent and heartless.

Excerpt from
WAR AND PEACE
The Young Nicholas

by Leo Tolstoy, translated by Aylmer and Louise Maude

Tolstoy's War and Peace *follows the lives of various Russian noblemen from the onset of the war against Napoleon until after its conclusion. The following excerpt concerns seventeen-year-old Count Nicholas Rostóv, who has joined the hussars (a cavalry unit) to fight for the motherland and his own great glory.*

In this excerpt, Nicholas, between battles, rides to a neighboring camp to visit Borís Drubetskóy, a childhood friend who is holding letters and money from home for him. Borís has joined the Guards, and is serving under members of the imperial family. Nicholas and Borís grew up together in the same large household and know one another well. Borís is quartered with Berg, another acquaintance from home.

The three young men have entered the war under different circumstances. Nicholas is both titled and rich enough to want for nothing. Borís is "from one of the best families in Russia," but is penniless and making his own way in life. Berg, a middle-class German determined to establish himself comfortably in Russian society, must also arrange for his own future.

The reunion of these three goes less than smoothly from the start, for each is eager to impress the others. It falls apart, though, with the arrival of Prince Andrew Bolkónski. Andrew, both wealthy and high-born, is more than ten years older than Nicholas and Borís, and is an adjutant, or personal assistant, to an important general (Kutúzov). Andrew has come to do a favor for Borís, but finds Nicholas there. Before he leaves he has an unpleasant exchange with the young hussar.

Nicholas and Borís have entered military service with dissimilar ambitions. Is this entirely due to the disparity in their circumstances? Can Berg's approach to his career be explained by his circumstances?

Borís and Nicholas are about the same age. Do they seem to be? Is one more appealing than the other?

Berg is delighted to tell Nicholas and Borís how he bested the Grand Duke by remaining silent when challenged. How would Nicholas have been likely to respond to the Grand Duke? How would Borís?

Borís displays precocious tact in the potentially unpleasant meeting between Nicholas and Berg. Why does his tact fail him when Nicholas meets Andrew?

Andrew urges Nicholas "as a man older than you" to let their disagreement drop. Why does he raise the difference in their ages, in so urging?

What does Nicholas discover when he realizes he would like Andrew for a friend?

How do these young people compare to the portraits of youth found in Aristotle and Bacon?

. . . On receiving Borís' letter [Nicholas] rode with a fellow officer to Olmütz, dined there, drank a bottle of wine, and then set off alone to the Guards' camp to find his old playmate. Rostóv had not yet had time to get his uniform. He had on a shabby cadet jacket, decorated with a soldier's cross, equally shabby cadet's riding breeches lined with worn leather, and an officer's saber with a sword knot. The Don horse he was riding was one he had bought from a Cossack during the campaign, and he wore a crumpled hussar cap stuck jauntily back on one side of his head. As he rode up to the camp he thought how he would impress Borís and all his comrades of the Guards by his appearance—that of a fighting hussar who had been under fire.

The Guards had made their whole march as if on a pleasure trip, parading their cleanliness and discipline. They had come by easy stages, their knapsacks conveyed on carts, and the Austrian authorities had provided excellent dinners for the officers at every halting place. . . .

. . . Berg and Borís, having rested after yesterday's march, were sitting, clean and neatly dressed, at a round table in the clean quarters allotted to them, playing chess. Berg held a smoking pipe between his knees. Borís, in the accurate way characteristic of him, was building a little pyramid of chessmen with his delicate white fingers while awaiting Berg's move, and watched his opponent's face, evidently thinking about the game as he always thought only of whatever he was engaged on.

"Well, how are you going to get out of that?" he remarked.

"We'll try to," replied Berg, touching a pawn and then removing his hand.

At that moment the door opened.

"Here he is at last!" shouted Rostóv. "And Berg too! Oh, you *petisen-*

fans, allay cushay dormir!" [1] he exclaimed, imitating his Russian nurse's French, at which he and Borís used to laugh long ago.

"Dear me, how you have changed!"

Borís rose to meet Rostóv, but in doing so did not omit to steady and replace some chessmen that were falling. He was about to embrace his friend, but Nicholas avoided him. With that peculiar feeling of youth, that dread of beaten tracks, and wish to express itself in a manner different from that of its elders which is often insincere, Nicholas wished to do something special on meeting his friend. He wanted to pinch him, push him, do anything but kiss him—a thing everybody did. But notwithstanding this, Borís embraced him in a quiet, friendly way and kissed him three times.

They had not met for nearly half a year and, being at the age when young men take their first steps on life's road, each saw immense changes in the other, quite a new reflection of the society in which they had taken those first steps. Both had changed greatly since they last met and both were in a hurry to show the changes that had taken place in them.

"Oh, you damned dandies! Clean and fresh as if you'd been to a fete, not like us sinners of the line," cried Rostóv, with martial swagger and with baritone notes in his voice, new to Borís, pointing to his own mud-bespattered breeches. The German landlady, hearing Rostóv's loud voice, popped her head in at the door.

"Eh, is she pretty?" he asked with a wink.

"Why do you shout so? You'll frighten them!" said Borís. "I did not expect you today," he added. "I only sent you the note yesterday by Bolkónski—an adjutant of Kutúzov's, who's a friend of mine. I did not think he would get it to you so quickly. . . . Well, how are you? Been under fire already?" asked Borís.

Without answering, Rostóv shook the soldier's Cross of St. George fastened to the cording of his uniform and, indicating a bandaged arm, glanced at Berg with a smile.

"As you see," he said.

"Indeed? Yes, yes!" said Borís, with a smile. "And we too have had a splendid march. You know, of course, that His Imperial Highness rode with our regiment all the time, so that we had every comfort and every advantage. What receptions we had in Poland! What dinners and balls! I can't tell you. And the Tsarévich was very gracious to all our officers."

And the two friends told each other of their doings, the one of his hussar revels and life in the fighting line, the other of the pleasures and

---

[1] A Russian nurse's attempt to say in French: "Little children, go to bed and sleep."—A.M.

advantages of service under members of the Imperial family.

"Oh, you Guards!" said Rostóv. "I say, send for some wine."

Borís made a grimace.

"If you really want it," said he.

He went to his bed, drew a purse from under the clean pillow, and sent for wine.

"Yes, and I have some money and a letter to give you," he added.

Rostóv took the letter and, throwing the money on the sofa, put both arms on the table and began to read. After reading a few lines, he glanced angrily at Berg, then, meeting his eyes, hid his face behind the letter.

"Well, they've sent you a tidy sum," said Berg, eying the heavy purse that sank into the sofa. "As for us, Count, we get along on our pay. I can tell you for myself. . . ."

"I say, Berg, my dear fellow," said Rostóv, "when you get a letter from home and meet one of your own people whom you want to talk everything over with, and I happen to be there, I'll go at once, to be out of your way! Do go somewhere, anywhere . . . to the devil!" he exclaimed, and immediately seizing him by the shoulder and looking amiably into his face, evidently wishing to soften the rudeness of his words, he added, "Don't be hurt, my dear fellow; you know I speak from my heart as to an old acquaintance."

"Oh, don't mention it, Count! I quite understand," said Berg, getting up and speaking in a muffled and guttural voice.

"Go across to our hosts: they invited you," added Borís.

Berg put on the cleanest of coats, without a spot or speck of dust, stood before a looking glass and brushed the hair on his temples upwards, in the way affected by the Emperor Alexander, and, having assured himself from the way Rostóv looked at it that his coat had been noticed, left the room with a pleasant smile.

"Oh dear, what a beast I am!" muttered Rostóv, as he read the letter.

"Why?"

"Oh, what a pig I am, not to have written and to have given them such a fright! Oh, what a pig I am!" he repeated, flushing suddenly. "Well, have you sent Gabriel for some wine? All right let's have some!"

In the letter from his parents was enclosed a letter of recommendation to Bagratión[2] which the old countess at Anna Mikháylovna's[3] advice had obtained through an acquaintance and sent to her son, asking him to take it to its destination and make use of it.

"What nonsense! Much I need it!" said Rostóv, throwing the letter

---

[2] Prince Bagratión, a Russian commander.

[3] Borís's mother, who is an old friend of Nicolas's family.

under the table.

"Why have you thrown that away?" asked Borís.

"It is some letter of recommendation . . . what the devil do I want it for!"

"Why 'What the devil'?" said Borís, picking it up and reading the address. "This letter would be of great use to you."

"I want nothing, and I won't be anyone's adjutant."

"Why not?" inquired Borís.

"It's a lackey's job!"

"You are still the same dreamer, I see," remarked Borís, shaking his head.

"And you're still the same diplomatist! But that's not the point. . . . Come, how are you?" asked Rostóv.

"Well, as you see. So far everything's all right, but I confess I should much like to be an adjutant and not remain at the front."

"Why?"

"Because when once a man starts on military service, he should try to make as successful a career of it as possible."

"Oh, that's it!" said Rostóv, evidently thinking of something else.

He looked intently and inquiringly into his friend's eyes, evidently trying in vain to find the answer to some question.

Old Gabriel brought in the wine.

"Shouldn't we now send for Berg?" asked Borís. "He would drink with you. I can't."

"Well, send for him . . . and how do you get on with that German?" asked Rostóv, with a contemptuous smile.

"He is a very, very nice, honest, and pleasant fellow," answered Borís.

Again Rostóv looked intently into Borís' eyes and sighed. Berg returned, and over the bottle of wine conversation between the three officers became animated. The Guardsmen told Rostóv of their march and how they had been made much of in Russia, Poland, and abroad. They spoke of the sayings and doings of their commander, the Grand Duke, and told stories of his kindness and irascibility. Berg, as usual, kept silent when the subject did not relate to himself, but in connection with the stories of the Grand Duke's quick temper he related with gusto how in Galicia he had managed to deal with the Grand Duke when the latter made a tour of the regiments and was annoyed at the irregularity of a movement. With a pleasant smile Berg related how the Grand Duke had ridden up to him in a violent passion, shouting: "Arnauts!" [4] (Arnauts was the Tsarévich's

[4] Arnauts is a Turkish name for the Albanians, who supplied the Turks with irregular cavalry.—A.M.

favorite expression when he was in a rage) and called for the company commander.

"Would you believe it, Count, I was not at all alarmed, because I knew I was right. Without boasting, you know, I may say that I know the Army Orders by heart and know the Regulations as well as I do the Lord's Prayer. So, Count, there never is any negligence in my company, and so my conscience was at ease. I came forward. . . ." (Berg stood up and showed how he presented himself, with his hand to his cap, and really it would have been difficult for a face to express greater respect and self-complacency than his did.) "Well, he stormed at me, as the saying is, stormed and stormed and stormed! It was not a matter of life but rather of death, as the saying is. 'Albanians!' and 'devils!' and "To Siberia!' " said Berg with a sagacious smile. "I knew I was in the right so I kept silent; was not that best, Count? . . . 'Hey, are you dumb?' he shouted. Still I remained silent. And what do you think, Count? The next day it was not even mentioned in the Orders of the Day. That's what keeping one's head means. That's the way, Count," said Berg, lighting his pipe and emitting rings of smoke.

"Yes, that was fine," said Rostóv, smiling.

But Borís noticed that he was preparing to make fun of Berg, and skillfully changed the subject. He asked him to tell them how and where he got his wound. This pleased Rostóv and he began talking about it, and as he went on became more and more animated. He told them of his Schön Grabern affair, just as those who have taken part in a battle generally do describe it, that is, as they would like it to have been, as they have heard it described by others, and as sounds well, but not at all as it really was. Rostóv was a truthful young man and would on no account have told a deliberate lie. He began his story meaning to tell everything just as it happened, but imperceptibly, involuntarily, and inevitably he lapsed into falsehood. If he had told the truth to his hearers—who like himself had often heard stories of attacks and had formed a definite idea of what an attack was and were expecting to hear just such a story—they would either not have believed him or, still worse, would have thought that Rostóv was himself to blame since what generally happens to the narrators of cavalry attacks had not happened to him. He could not tell them simply that everyone went at a trot and that he fell off his horse and sprained his arm and then ran as hard as he could from a Frenchman into the wood. Besides, to tell everything as it really happened, it would have been necessary to make an effort of will to tell only what happened. It is very difficult to tell the truth, and young people are rarely capable of it. His hearers expected a story of how beside himself and all aflame with excitement, he had flown like a storm at the square, cut his way in, slashed right and left, how his saber had tasted flesh and he had fallen exhausted, and so on. And so he told them all that.

In the middle of his story, just as he was saying: "You cannot imagine what a strange frenzy one experiences during an attack," Prince Andrew, whom Borís was expecting, entered the room. Prince Andrew, who liked to help young men, was flattered by being asked for his assistance and being well disposed toward Borís, who had managed to please him the day before, he wished to do what the young man wanted. Having been sent with papers from Kutúzov to the Tsarévich, he looked in on Borís, hoping to find him alone. When he came in and saw an hussar of the line recounting his military exploits (Prince Andrew could not endure that sort of man), he gave Borís a pleasant smile, frowned as with half-closed eyes he looked at Rostóv, bowed slightly and wearily, and sat down languidly on the sofa: he felt it unpleasant to have dropped in on bad company. Rostóv flushed up on noticing this, but he did not care, this was a mere stranger. Glancing, however, at Borís, he saw that he too seemed ashamed of the hussar of the line.

In spite of Prince Andrew's disagreeable, ironical tone, in spite of the contempt with which Rostóv, from his *fighting* army point of view, regarded all these little adjutants on the staff, of whom the newcomer was evidently one, Rostóv felt confused, blushed, and became silent. Borís inquired what news there might be on the staff, and what, without indiscretion, one might ask about our plans.

"We shall probably advance," replied Bolkónski, evidently reluctant to say more in the presence of a stranger.

Berg took the opportunity to ask, with great politeness, whether, as was rumored, the allowance of forage money to captains of companies would be doubled. To this Prince Andrew answered with a smile that he could give no opinion on such an important government order, and Berg laughed gaily.

"As to your business," Prince Andrew continued, addressing Borís, "we will talk of it later" (and he looked round at Rostóv). "Come to me after the review and we will do what is possible."

And, having glanced round the room, Prince Andrew turned to Rostóv, whose state of unconquerable childish embarrassment now changing to anger he did not condescend to notice, and said: "I think you were talking of the Schön Grabern affair? Were you there?"

"I was there," said Rostóv angrily, as if intending to insult the aide-de-camp.

Bolkónski noticed the hussar's state of mind, and it amused him. With a slightly contemptuous smile, he said: "Yes, there are many stories now told about that affair!"

"Yes, stories!" repeated Rostóv loudly, looking with eyes suddenly grown furious, now at Borís, now at Bolkónski. "Yes, many stories! But our stories are the stories of men who have been under the enemy's fire! Our stories have some weight, not like the stories of those fellows on the staff who get rewards without doing anything!"

"Of whom you imagine me to be one?" said Prince Andrew, with a quiet and particularly amiable smile.

A strange feeling of exasperation and yet of respect for this man's self-possession mingled at that moment in Rostóv's soul.

"I am not talking about you," he said, "I don't know you and, frankly, I don't want to. I am speaking of the staff in general."

"And I will tell you this," Prince Andrew interrupted in a tone of quiet authority, "you wish to insult me, and I am ready to agree with you that it would be very easy to do so if you haven't sufficient self-respect, but admit that the time and place are very badly chosen. In a day or two we shall all have to take part in a greater and more serious duel, and besides, Drubetskóy, who says he is an old friend of yours, is not at all to blame that my face has the misfortune to displease you. However," he added rising, "you know my name and where to find me, but don't forget that I do not regard either myself or you as having been at all insulted, and as a man older than you, my advice is to let the matter drop. Well then, on Friday after the review I shall expect you, Drubetskóy. *Au revoir!*" exclaimed Prince Andrew, and with a bow to them both he went out.

Only when Prince Andrew was gone did Rostóv think of what he ought to have said. And he was still more angry at having omitted to say it. He ordered his horse at once and, coldly taking leave of Borís, rode home. Should he go to headquarters next day and challenge that affected adjutant, or really let the matter drop, was the question that worried him all the way. He thought angrily of the pleasure he would have at seeing the fright of that small and frail but proud man when covered by his pistol, and then he felt with surprise that of all the men he knew there was none he would so much like to have for a friend as that very adjutant whom he so hated.

Excerpt from
WAR AND PEACE
The Mature Nicholas

by Leo Tolstoy, translated by Aylmer and Louise Maude

In the previous selection from War and Peace, *we met Count Nicholas Rostóv at seventeen as the carefree and honor-driven count went to war. In the excerpt that follows we see an older and very different Nicholas.*

By the war's end, everything has changed for him. The Rostóv family home (Otrádnoe) and fortune are gone; Nicholas's father and younger brother are dead; and Nicholas is left solely responsible for his shattered mother and her dependent niece, Sonya.

But Nicholas—who has served, been wounded, and witnessed the devastation of his country—has grown up. He makes a home for his mother and cousin, voluntarily assumes responsibility for his father's many debts, and goes to work.

His loneliness and difficulty in this period end with his marriage to the wealthy Princess Mary Bolkonskaya. This selection, excerpted from the first epilogue, begins as Nicholas and Mary move to her family's country estate, Bald Hills, of which Nicholas is now master.

Nicholas, who once dreamt of being a soldier, has become a devoted farmer, and a notably successful one. He cares for the estate as a whole and remembers at all times his ultimate goal for it: production, for the benefit of his family.

Unlike the young Nicholas, the mature man waits to exercise the authority given to him until he has equipped himself to do so.[1] He studies and learns

---

[1] Nicholas is a Russian landowner in the era of serfdom, so his authority over those who serve him goes far beyond what we as modern readers accept. Yet Nicholas's insights concerning the centrality of labor to the success of an enterprise remain recognizably true, despite the very great differences between the social arrangements of his time and those of our own. Similarly, Nicholas's close attention to the characters of those who work for him, and his grasp of the importance of working conditions and of a standard of justice, would be marks of excellence in an employer or manager of any era.

from those who know more than he does, undeterred by their lower rank. In dispensing justice, he is guided by a "standard" he cannot articulate, but which is "quite firm and definite in his own mind;" he knows he must not yield to his mere inclinations.

The success of Nicholas's marriage rests in good part on his understanding of where he should and should not be guided by his wife; this understanding, in turn, rests on a clear knowledge of their respective strengths and weaknesses.

According to Aristotle, a man in his prime is "confident and cautious," is guided by the love of honor and expediency both, and is neither "parsimonious" nor "prodigal." He neither trusts nor distrusts everyone, but judges "each case by the facts." Would Aristotle regard Nicholas as a man in the prime of his life? Or is he past his peak of vitality, vigor, and aspiration?

The Nicholas in this excerpt is obviously different from the Nicholas we met at seventeen. Are the two Nicholases utterly disconnected? Is it possible to see in the mature Nicholas the same boy who joined the hussars and went to war?

Is it possible to predict what Nicholas will be like as an old man?

In the winter of 1813 Nicholas married Princess Mary and moved to Bald Hills with his wife, his mother, and Sónya.

Within four years he had paid off all his remaining debts without selling any of his wife's property, and having received a small inheritance on the death of a cousin he paid his debt to Pierre[2] as well.

In another three years, by 1820, he had so managed his affairs that he was able to buy a small estate adjoining Bald Hills and was negotiating to buy back Otrádnoe—that being his pet dream.

Having started farming from necessity, he soon grew so devoted to it that it became his favorite and almost his sole occupation. Nicholas was a plain farmer: he did not like innovations, especially the English ones then coming into vogue. He laughed at theoretical treatises on estate management, disliked factories, the raising of expensive products, and the buying of expensive seed corn, and did not make a hobby of any particular part of the work on his estate. He always had before his mind's eye the estate as a whole and not any particular part of it. The chief thing in his eyes was not the nitrogen in the soil, nor the oxygen in the air, nor manures, nor special plows, but that most important agent by which nitrogen, oxygen, manure, and plow were made effective—the peasant laborer. When Nicholas first began farming and

---

2 His wealthy brother-in-law, from whom he has borrowed money.

began to understand its different branches, it was the serf who especially attracted his attention. The peasant seemed to him not merely a tool, but also a judge of farming and an end in himself. At first he watched the serfs, trying to understand their aims and what they considered good and bad, and only pretended to direct them and give orders while in reality learning from them their methods, their manner of speech, and their judgment of what was good and bad. Only when he had understood the peasants' tastes and aspirations, had learned to talk their language, to grasp the hidden meaning of their words, and felt akin to them did he begin boldly to manage his serfs, that is, to perform toward them the duties demanded of him. And Nicholas' management produced very brilliant results.

Guided by some gift of insight, on taking up the management of the estates he at once unerringly appointed as bailiff, village elder, and delegate, the very men the serfs would themselves have chosen had they had the right to choose, and these posts never changed hands. Before analyzing the properties of manure, before entering into the *debit* and *credit* (as he ironically called it), he found out how many cattle the peasants had and increased the number by all possible means. He kept the peasant families together in the largest groups possible, not allowing the family groups to divide into separate households. He was hard alike on the lazy, the depraved, and the weak, and tried to get them expelled from the commune.

He was as careful of the sowing and reaping of the peasants' hay and corn as of his own, and few landowners had their crops sown and harvested so early and so well, or got so good a return, as did Nicholas.

He disliked having anything to do with the domestic serfs—the "drones" as he called them—and everyone said he spoiled them by his laxity. When a decision had to be taken regarding a domestic serf, especially if one had to be punished, he always felt undecided and consulted everybody in the house; but when it was possible to have a domestic serf conscripted instead of a land worker he did so without the least hesitation. He never felt any hesitation in dealing with the peasants. He knew that his every decision would be approved by them all with very few exceptions.

He did not allow himself either to be hard on or punish a man, or to make things easy for or reward anyone, merely because he felt inclined to do so. He could not have said by what standard he judged what he should or should not do, but the standard was quite firm and definite in his own mind.

Often, speaking with vexation of some failure or irregularity, he would say: "What can one do with our Russian peasants?" and imagined that he could not bear them.

Yet he loved "our Russian peasants" and their way of life with his whole soul, and for that very reason had understood and assimilated the one way and manner of farming which produced good results.

Countess Mary was jealous of this passion of her husband's and regretted that she could not share it; but she could not understand the joys and vexations he derived from that world, to her so remote and alien. She could not understand why he was so particularly animated and happy when, after getting up at daybreak and spending the whole morning in the fields or on the threshing floor, he returned from the sowing or mowing or reaping to have tea with her. She did not understand why he spoke with such admiration and delight of the farming of the thrifty and well-to-do peasant Matthew Ermíshin, who with his family had carted corn all night; or of the fact that his (Nicholas') sheaves were already stacked before anyone else had his harvest in. She did not understand why he stepped out from the window to the veranda and smiled under his mustache and winked so joyfully, when warm steady rain began to fall on the dry and thirsty shoots of the young oats, or why when the wind carried away a threatening cloud during the hay harvest he would return from the barn, flushed, sunburned, and perspiring, with a smell of wormwood and gentian in his hair and, gleefully rubbing his hands, would say: "Well, one more day and my grain and the peasants' will all be under cover."

Still less did she understand why he, kindhearted and always ready to anticipate her wishes, should become almost desperate when she brought him a petition from some peasant men or women who had appealed to her to be excused some work; why he, that kind Nicholas, should obstinately refuse her, angrily asking her not to interfere in what was not her business. She felt he had a world apart, which he loved passionately and which had laws she had not fathomed.

Sometimes when, trying to understand him, she spoke of the good work he was doing for his serfs, he would be vexed and reply: "Not in the least; it never entered my head and I wouldn't do that for their good! That's all poetry and old wives' talk—all that doing good to one's neighbor! What I want is that our children should not have to go begging. I must put our affairs in order while I am alive, that's all. And to do that, order and strictness are essential. . . . That's all about it!" said he, clenching his vigorous fist. "And fairness, of course," he added, "for if the peasant is naked and hungry and has only one miserable horse, he can do no good either for himself or for me."

And all Nicholas did was fruitful—probably just because he refused to allow himself to think that he was doing good to others for virtue's sake. His means increased rapidly; serfs from neighboring estates came to beg him to buy them, and long after his death the memory of his administration was devoutly preserved among the serfs. "He was a master . . . the peasants' affairs first and then his own. Of course he was not to be trifled with either—in a word, he was a real master!"

One matter connected with his management sometimes worried Nicholas, and that was his quick temper together with his old hussar habit of making free use of his fists. At first he saw nothing reprehensible in this, but in the second year of his marriage his view of that form of punishment suddenly changed.

Once in summer he had sent for the village elder from Boguchárovo, a man who had succeeded to the post when Dron died and who was accused of dishonesty and various irregularities. Nicholas went out into the porch to question him, and immediately after the elder had given a few replies the sound of cries and blows was heard. On returning to lunch Nicholas went up to his wife, who sat with her head bent low over her embroidery frame, and as usual began to tell her what he had been doing that morning. Among other things he spoke of the Boguchárovo elder.

Countess Mary turned red and then pale, but continued to sit with head bowed and lips compressed and gave her husband no reply.

"Such an insolent scoundrel!" he cried, growing hot again at the mere recollection of him. "If he had told me he was drunk and did not see . . . But what is the matter with you, Mary?" he suddenly asked. Countess Mary raised her head and tried to speak, but hastily looked down again and her lips puckered.

"Why, whatever is the matter, my dearest?"

The looks of the plain Countess Mary always improved when she was in tears. She never cried from pain or vexation, but always from sorrow or pity, and when she wept her radiant eyes acquired an irresistible charm.

The moment Nicholas took her hand she could no longer restrain herself and began to cry.

"Nicholas, I saw it . . . he was to blame, but why do you . . . Nicholas!" and she covered her face with her hands.

Nicholas said nothing. He flushed crimson, left her side, and paced up and down the room. He understood what she was weeping about, but could not in his heart at once agree with her that what he had regarded from childhood as quite an everyday event was wrong. "Is it just sentimentality, old wives' tales, or is she right?" he asked himself. Before he had solved that point he glanced again at her face filled with love and pain, and he suddenly realized that she was right and that he had long been sinning against himself.

"Mary," he said softly, going up to her, "it will never happen again; I give you my word. Never," he repeated in a trembling voice like a boy asking for forgiveness.

The tears flowed faster still from the countess' eyes. She took his hand and kissed it.

"Nicholas, when did you break your cameo?" she asked to change the subject, looking at his finger on which he wore a ring with a cameo of Laocoön's head.

"Today—it was the same affair. Oh, Mary, don't remind me of it!" and again he flushed. "I give you my word of honor it shan't occur again, and let this always be a reminder to me," and he pointed to the broken ring.

After that, when in discussions with his village elders or stewards the blood rushed to his face and his fists began to clench, Nicholas would turn the broken ring on his finger and would drop his eyes before the man who was making him angry. But he did forget himself once or twice within twelvemonth, and then he would go and confess to his wife, and would again promise that this should really be the very last time.

"Mary, you must despise me!" he would say. "I deserve it."

"You should go, go away at once, if you don't feel strong enough to control yourself," she would reply sadly, trying to comfort her husband.

Among the gentry of the province Nicholas was respected but not liked. He did not concern himself with the interests of his own class, and consequently some thought him proud and others thought him stupid. The whole summer, from spring sowing to harvest, he was busy with the work on his farm. In autumn he gave himself up to hunting with the same businesslike seriousness—leaving home for a month, or even two, with his hunt. In winter he visited his other villages or spent his time reading. The books he read were chiefly historical, and on these he spent a certain sum every year. He was collecting, as he said, a serious library, and he made it a rule to read through all the books he bought. He would sit in his study with a grave air, reading—a task he first imposed upon himself as a duty, but which afterwards became a habit affording him a special kind of pleasure and a consciousness of being occupied with serious matters. In winter, except for business excursions, he spent most of his time at home making himself one with his family and entering into all the details of his children's relations with their mother. The harmony between him and his wife grew closer and closer and he daily discovered fresh spiritual treasures in her.

Excerpt from
BUDDENBROOKS
Thomas Buddenbrooks

by Thomas Mann, translated by H. T. Lowe-Porter

In this excerpt from Thomas Mann's novel Buddenbrooks, *we see a man widely assumed to be in his prime, but privately aware that he is declining— that something within him has begun to slip.*

Senator Thomas Buddenbrooks is the head of a prosperous German mercantile family in the late-middle nineteenth century. He has just built himself a magnificent house—more magnificent than that of his longtime rival, Herman Hagenström. There he lives with his sophisticated wife, Gerda, and their young son, Hanno. Buddenbooks is concerned about Hanno, who has been slow to develop.

Before this excerpt begins, Buddenbrooks's sister, Frau Permaneder (Tony), arrives at the new house to bring Thomas bad news. Tony, who lives to see her family triumph, is at first cheered by the magnificence in which her brother is living. Yet she soon remembers that she has come to tell him that their sister Clara, who lives in a distant city with her husband, is dying. Discussing this, Tony and Thomas together recall that their brother, Christian, too, is hospitalized with little hope.

Moved by this bad news to unburden himself, Thomas tells his sister about his troubles.

Of the various things that Thomas speaks about—his business, the completion of his house, his child, etc.—which one most accounts for his falling spirits? Why does be not regard himself as a "success"?

Can Thomas's failure to take comfort in his son be traced entirely to the child's frailty? Could thriving children be expected to make a difference for a man in his position? Could the birth of a child possibly contribute to someone's waning enthusiasm for life?

Does the course of Thomas's maturation seem healthy? Normal? If not, why not? How would the problem he describes be handled today?

*Tony has just told her brother, Senator Thomas Buddenbrooks, that their
sister Clara is dying.*

"Yes," said the Senator, quietly. "It seems as if one thing just followed on
another."

She put her arm for an instant across his shoulders.

"But *you* mustn't give way, Tom. This is no time for you to be down-
hearted. You need all your courage—"

"Yes, God knows I need it."

"What do you mean, Tom? Tell me, why were you so quiet Thursday
afternoon at dinner, if I may ask?"

"Oh—business, my child. I had to sell no very small quantity of grain
not very advantageously—or, rather, I had to sell a large quantity very
much at a loss."

"Well, that happens, Tom. You sell at a loss to-day, and to-morrow
you make it good again. To get discouraged over a thing of that kind—"

"Wrong, Tony," he said, and shook his head. "My courage does not go
down to zero because I have a piece of bad luck. It's the other way on. I
believe in that, and events show it."

"But what is the matter with it, then?" she asked, surprised and alarmed.
"One would think you have enough to make you happy, Tom. Clara is
alive, and with God's help she will get better. And as for everything
else—here we are, walking about, in your own garden, and it all smells
so sweet—and yonder is your house, a dream of a house—Hermann
Hagenström's is a dog-kennel beside it! And you have done all that—"

"Yes, it is almost too beautiful, Tony. I'll tell you—it is too new. It jars
on me a little—perhaps that is what is the matter with me. It may be
responsible for the bad mood that comes over me and spoils everything.
I looked forward immensely to all this; but the anticipation was the best
part of it—it always is. Everything gets done too slowly—so when it is
finished the pleasure is already gone."

"The pleasure is gone, Tom? At your age?"

"A man is as young, or as old, as he feels. And when one gets one's
wish too late, or works too hard for it, it comes already weighted with all
sorts of small vexatious drawbacks—with all the dust of reality upon it,
that one did not reckon with in fancy. It is so irritating—so irritating—"

"Oh yes.—But what do you mean by 'as old as you feel?'"

"Why, Tony—it is a mood, certainly. It may pass. But just now I feel
older than I am. I have business cares. And at the Directors' meeting of

the Buchen Railway yesterday, Consul Hagenström simply talked me down, refuted my contentions, nearly made me appear ridiculous. I feel that could not have happened to me before. It is as though something had begun to slip—as though I haven't the firm grip I had on events.— What is success? It is an inner, and indescribable force, resourcefulness, power of vision; a consciousness that I am, by my mere existence, exerting pressure on the movement of life about me. It is my belief in the adaptability of life to my own ends. Fortune and success lie with ourselves. We must hold them firmly—deep *within* us. For as soon as something begins to slip, to relax, to get tired, within us, then everything without us will rebel and struggle to withdraw from our influence. One thing follows another, blow after blow—and the man is finished. Often and often, in these days, I have thought of a Turkish proverb; it says, 'When the house is finished, death comes.' It doesn't need to be death. But the decline, the falling-off, the beginning of the end. You know, Tony," he went on, in a still lower voice, putting his arm underneath his sister's, "when Hanno was christened, you said: 'It looks as if quite a new life would dawn for us all!' I can still hear you say it, and I thought then that you were right, for I was elected Senator, and was fortunate in my business, and this house seemed to spring up out of the ground. But the 'Senator' and this house are superficial after all. I know, from life and from history, something you have not thought of: often, the outward and visible material signs and symbols of happiness and success only show themselves when the process of decline has already set in. The outer manifestations take time—like the light of that star up there, which may in reality be already quenched, when it looks to us to be shining its brightest."

He ceased to speak, and they walked for a while in silence, while the fountain gently murmured, and a whispering sounded from the top of the walnut tree. Then Frau Permaneder breathed such a heavy sigh that it sounded like a sob.

"How sadly you talk, Tom. You never spoke so sadly before. But it is good to speak out, and it will help you to put all that kind of thoughts out of your mind."

"Yes, Tony, I must try to do that, I know, as well as I can. And now give me the enclosures from Clara and the Pastor. It will be best, won't it, for me to take over the matter, and speak to-morrow morning with Mother? Poor Mother! If it is really tuberculosis, one may as well give up hope."

Excerpt from

WAR AND PEACE
The Countess Rostóva

by Leo Tolstoy, translated by Aylmer and Louise Maude

*This selection from Tolstoy's epic novel shows us Countess Rostóva, mother of
Nicholas (see Nicholas Rostóv, above), at the last stage of her life.*

*In Tolstoy's earlier descriptions of the countess, she appears resilient, real-
istic in her hopes and expectations, and perceptive about life and the changes it
inevitably brings. Now, after the war, her family raised, her home and fortune
lost, and her husband and youngest son dead, the countess is living out her
final years with her son and his family at their estate in the country, remote
from society.*

*As the excerpt begins, the countess's daughter and son-in-law, Natásha
and Pierre, are in the middle of a visit of some months' duration, with their
children. Pierre has just returned from St. Petersburg, bringing back with him
gifts and news, all of which he is eager to share. But some of this must await
the countess's needs.*

*These needs, while compelling, are now aimless. The countess cries, talks,
thinks, and is angry not as the occasion merits, but as she feels the need. She is
irritable, repetitive, and unable to take an interest in anything new.*

*How do the countess's children treat her, and why? Do we admire their
conduct toward her? How might the presence of their own children affect their
relation to the countess?*

*The countess cannot remember from one conversation to the next what has
happened in the lives of her old friends and acquaintances. How might her
failing memory be related to her irritability and her waning interest in the present
and the future?*

*What is responsible for the countess's outlook and moodiness? Were she
younger, do you think she could have been more resilient?*

How might Aristotle's account of the elderly shed light on the aged countess?

The countess was sitting with her companion Belóva, playing grand-patience as usual, when Pierre and Natásha came into the drawing room with parcels under their arms.

The countess was now over sixty, was quite gray, and wore a cap with a frill that surrounded her face. Her face had shriveled, her upper lip had sunk in, and her eyes were dim.

After the deaths of her son and husband in such rapid succession, she felt herself a being accidentally forgotten in this world and left without aim or object for her existence. She ate, drank, slept, or kept awake, but did not *live*. Life gave her no new impressions. She wanted nothing from life but tranquillity, and that tranquillity only death could give her. But until death came she had to go on living, that is, to use her vital forces. A peculiarity one sees in very young children and very old people was particularly evident in her. Her life had no external aims—only a need to exercise her various functions and inclinations was apparent. She had to eat, sleep, think, speak, weep, work, give vent to her anger, and so on, merely because she had a stomach, a brain, muscles, nerves, and a liver. She did these things not under any external impulse as people in the full vigor of life do, when behind the purpose for which they strive that of exercising their functions remains unnoticed. She talked only because she physically needed to exercise her tongue and lungs. She cried as a child does, because her nose had to be cleared, and so on. What for people in their full vigor is an aim was for her evidently merely a pretext.

Thus in the morning—especially if she had eaten anything rich the day before—she felt a need of being angry and would choose as the handiest pretext Belóva's deafness.

She would begin to say something to her in a low tone from the other end of the room.

"It seems a little warmer today, my dear," she would murmur.

And when Belóva replied: "Oh yes, they've come," she would mutter angrily: "O Lord! How stupid and deaf she is!"

Another pretext would be her snuff, which would seem too dry or too damp or not rubbed fine enough. After these fits of irritability her face would grow yellow, and her maids knew by infallible symptoms when Belóva would again be deaf, the snuff damp, and the countess' face yellow. Just as she needed to work off her spleen so she had sometimes to exercise her still-existing faculty of thinking—and the pretext for that was a game of patience. When she needed to cry, the deceased count would be the pretext. When she wanted to be agitated, Nicholas and his health would be the pretext, and when she felt a need to speak spiteful-ly, the pretext would be Countess Mary. When her vocal organs needed exercise, which was usually toward seven o'clock when she had had an after-dinner rest in a darkened room, the pretext would be the retelling of the same stories over and over again to the same audience.

The old lady's condition was understood by the whole household though no one ever spoke of it, and they all made every possible effort to satisfy her needs. Only by a rare glance exchanged with a sad smile be-tween Nicholas, Pierre, Natásha, and Countess Mary was the common understanding of her condition expressed.

But those glances expressed something more: they said that she had played her part in life, that what they now saw was not her whole self, that we must all become like her, and that they were glad to yield to her, to restrain themselves for this once precious being formerly as full of life as themselves, but now so much to be pitied. "*Memento mori*," said these glances.

Only the really heartless, the stupid ones of that household, and the little children failed to understand this and avoided her.

When Pierre and his wife entered the drawing room the countess was in one of her customary states in which she needed the mental exertion of playing patience, and so—though by force of habit she greeted him with the words she always used when Pierre or her son returned after an absence: "High time, my dear, high time! We were all weary of waiting for you. Well, thank God!" and received her presents with another cus-tomary remark: "It's not the gift that's precious, my dear, but that you give it to me, an old woman . . ."—yet it was evident that she was not pleased by Pierre's arrival at that moment when it diverted her atten-tion from the unfinished game.

She finished her game of patience and only then examined the pre-sents. They consisted of a box for cards, of splendid workmanship, a bright-blue Sèvres tea cup with shepherdesses depicted on it and with a lid, and a gold snuffbox with the count's portrait on the lid which Pierre had had done by a miniaturist in Petersburg. The countess had long wished for such a box, but as she did not want to cry just then she glanced indifferently at the portrait and gave her attention chiefly to the box for cards.

"Thank you, my dear, you have cheered me up," said she as she always did. "But best of all you have brought yourself back—for I never saw anything like it, you ought to give your wife a scolding! What are we to do with her? She is like a mad woman when you are away. Doesn't see anything, doesn't remember anything," she went on, repeating her usual phrases. "Look, Anna Timoféevna," she added to her companion, "see what a box for cards my son has brought us!"

Belóva admired the presents and was delighted with her dress material.

Though Pierre, Natásha, Nicholas, Countess Mary, and Denísov[1] had much to talk about that they could not discuss before the old countess—not that anything was hidden from her, but because she had dropped so far behindhand in many things that had they begun to converse in her presence they would have had to answer inopportune questions and to repeat what they had already told her many times: that so-and-so was dead and so-and-so was married, which she would again be unable to remember—yet they sat at tea round the samovar in the drawing room from habit, and Pierre answered the countess' questions as to whether Prince Vasíli had aged and whether Countess Mary Alexéevna had sent greetings and still thought of them, and other matters that interested no one and to which she herself was indifferent.

Conversation of this kind, interesting to no one yet unavoidable, continued all through teatime. . . . Pierre sat between his wife and the old countess. He spoke of what he knew might interest the old lady and that she could understand. He told her of external social events and of the people who had formed the circle of her contemporaries and had once been a real, living, and distinct group, but who were now for the most part scattered about the world and like herself were garnering the last ears of the harvests they had sown in earlier years. But to the old countess those contemporaries of hers seemed to be the only serious and real society. Natásha saw by Pierre's animation that his visit had been interesting and that he had much to tell them but dare not say it before the old countess. Denísov, not being a member of the family, did not understand Pierre's caution and being, as a malcontent, much interested in what was occurring in Petersburg, kept urging Pierre to tell them about what had happened in the Semënovsk regiment, then about Arakchéev, and then about the Bible Society.[2] Once or twice Pierre was carried away and began to speak of these things, but Nicholas and Natásha always brought him back to the health of Prince Iván and Countess Mary Alexéevna.

"Well, and all this idiocy—Gossner[3] and Tatáwinova?"[4] Denísov asked.

---

[1] An old family friend.

[2] A Russian Bible Society founded by A. N. Golitsyn in December, 1812, had political influence.

[3] Johann Gossner was a Catholic priest and mystic around whom a pietist group formed in Munich.

[4] Ekaterína Filíppovna Tatárinova founded a mystical sect in Petersburg, in 1817.

"Is that weally still going on?"

"Going on?" Pierre exclaimed. "Why more than ever! The Bible Society is the whole government now!"

"What is that, *mon cher ami?*" asked the countess, who had finished
her tea and evidently needed a pretext for being angry after her meal.
"What are you saying about the government? I don't understand."

"Well, you know, *Maman*," Nicholas interposed, knowing how to translate things into his mother's language, "Prince Alexander Golítsyn has
founded a society and in consequence has great influence, they say."

"Arakchéev and Golítsyn," incautiously remarked Pierre, "are now
the whole government! And what a government! They see treason every where and are afraid of everything."

"Well, and how is Prince Alexander to blame? He is a most estimable
man. I used to meet him at Mary Antónovna's," said the countess in an
offended tone; and still more offended that they all remained silent, she
went on: "Nowadays everyone finds fault. A Gospel Society! Well, and
what harm is there in that?" and she rose (everybody else got up too)
and with a severe expression sailed back to her table in the sitting room.

The melancholy silence that followed was broken by the sounds of
the children's voices and laughter from the next room. Evidently some
jolly excitement was going on there.

Excerpt from
SPEAK, MEMORY
by Vladimir Nabokov

In this beautifully crafted memoir, Russian-born novelist Vladimir Nabokov presents life as a passage from the timeless darkness that precedes it to the timeless darkness after, through the "radiant" time in between.

For Nabokov, time is a prison, "spherical and without exits." Yet he also believes it is our perception of this element that defines us as human.

In the beginning of his opening chapter, attached below, Nabokov describes himself as a lifelong "rebel" against the reality that life is "a brief crack of light between two eternities of darkness." He then recalls his discovery, at four, of the differences between his age and the ages of his parents, a discovery that taught him that he was living in the "mobile medium" of time.

This insight—made when time seemed "boundless"—was like "a second baptism . . . more divine" than the first, as it was "the birth of sentient life." Man shares the "spatial world" with "apes and butterflies;" the awareness of time is his own.

How can awareness of the passage of time give rise to human self-awareness and identity?

Nabokov rebels at the thought that his consciousness of time must end. How would the distinctively human life he cherishes change if he could succeed in breaking through to the "free world of timelessness"?

Nabokov says that "the first creatures on earth to become aware of time were also the first to smile." At what do we smile, why, and in what spirit?

Part 1

The cradle rocks above an abyss, and common sense tells us that our existence is but a brief crack of light between two eternities of darkness. Although the two are identical twins, man, as a rule, views the prenatal abyss with more calm than the one he is heading for (at some forty-five hundred heartbeats an hour). I know, however, of a young chronophobiac who experienced something like panic when looking for the first time at homemade movies that had been taken a few weeks before his birth. He saw a world that was practically unchanged—the same house, the same people—and then realized that he did not exist there at all and that nobody mourned his absence. He caught a glimpse of his mother waving from an upstairs window, and that unfamiliar gesture disturbed him, as if it were some mysterious farewell. But what particularly frightened him was the sight of a brand-new baby carriage standing there on the porch, with the smug, encroaching air of a coffin; even that was empty, as if, in the reverse course of events, his very bones had disintegrated.

Such fancies are not foreign to young lives. Or, to put it otherwise, first and last things often tend to have an adolescent note—unless, possibly, they are directed by some venerable and rigid religion. Nature expects a full-grown man to accept the two black voids, fore and aft, as stolidly as he accepts the extraordinary visions in between. Imagination, the supreme delight of the immortal and the immature, should be limited. In order to enjoy life, we should not enjoy it too much.

I rebel against this state of affairs. I feel the urge to take my rebellion outside and picket nature. Over and over again, my mind has made colossal efforts to distinguish the faintest of personal glimmers in the impersonal darkness on both sides of my life. That this darkness is caused merely by the walls of time separating me and my bruised fists from the free world of timelessness is a belief I gladly share with the most gaudily painted savage. I have journeyed back in thought—with thought hopelessly tapering off as I went—to remote regions where I groped for some secret outlet only to discover that the prison of time is spherical and without exits. Short of suicide, I have tried everything. I have doffed my identity in order to pass for a conventional spook and steal into realms that existed before I was conceived. I have mentally endured the degrading company of Victorian lady novelists and retired colonels who remembered having, in former lives, been slave messengers on a Roman road or sages under the willows of Lhasa. I have ransacked my oldest dreams for keys and clues—and let me say at once that I reject completely the vulgar, shabby, fundamentally medieval world of Freud, with its crankish quest for sexual symbols (something like searching for Baconian acrostics in Shakespeare's works) and its bitter little embryos spying, from their natural nooks, upon the love life of their parents.

Initially, I was unaware that time, so boundless at first blush, was a prison. In probing my childhood (which is the next best to probing one's eternity) I see the awakening of consciousness as a series of spaced flashes, with the intervals between them gradually diminishing until bright blocks of perception are formed, affording memory a slippery hold. I had learned numbers and speech more or less simultaneously at a very early date, but the inner knowledge that I was I and that my parents were my parents seems to have been established only later, when it was directly associated with my discovering their age in relation to mine. Judging by the strong sunlight that, when I think of that revelation, immediately invades my memory with lobed sun flecks through overlapping patterns of greenery, the occasion may have been my mother's birthday, in late summer, in the country, and I had asked questions and had assessed the answers I received. All this is as it should be according to the theory of recapitulation; the beginning of reflexive consciousness in the brain of our remotest ancestor must surely have coincided with the dawning of the sense of time.

Thus, when the newly disclosed, fresh and trim formula of my own age, four, was confronted with the parental formulas, thirty-three and twenty-seven, something happened to me. I was given a tremendously invigorating shock. As if subjected to a second baptism, on more divine lines than the Greek Catholic ducking undergone fifty months earlier by a howling, half-drowned half-Victor (my mother, through the half-closed door, behind which an old custom bade parents retreat, managed to correct the bungling archpresbyter, Father Konstantin Vetvenitski), I felt myself plunged abruptly into a radiant and mobile medium that was none other than the pure element of time. One shared it—just as excited bathers share shining seawater—with creatures that were not oneself but that were joined to one by time's common flow, an environment quite different from the spatial world, which not only man but apes and butterflies can perceive. At that instant, I became acutely aware that the twenty-seven-year-old being, in soft white and pink, holding my left hand, was my mother, and that the thirty-three-year-old being, in hard white and gold, holding my right hand, was my father. Between them, as they evenly progressed, I strutted, and trotted, and strutted again, from sun fleck to sun fleck, along the middle of a path, which I easily identify today with an alley of ornamental oaklings in the park of our country estate, Vyra, in the former Province of St. Petersburg, Russia. Indeed, from my present ridge of remote, isolated, almost uninhabited time, I see my diminutive self as celebrating, on that August day 1903, the birth of sentient life. If my left-hand-holder and my right-hand-holder had both been present before in my vague infant world, they had been so under the mask of a tender incognito; but now my father's attire, the resplendent uniform of the Horse Guards, with that smooth golden swell of cuirass burning upon his chest and back, came out like the sun, and for several years afterward I remained keenly interested in the age of my parents and kept myself informed about it, like a nervous passenger asking the time in order to check a new watch.

My father, let it be noted, had served his term of military training long before I was born, so I suppose he had that day put on the trappings of his old regiment as a festive joke. To a joke, then, I owe my first gleam of complete consciousness—which again has recapitulatory implications, since the first creatures on earth to become aware of time were also the first creatures to smile.

Excerpt from
ORDERED SOUTH
by Robert Louis Stevenson

Not everyone's years form a shapely span from infancy to old age and the grave. Robert Louis Stevenson's "Ordered South" is a meditation on premature decline and death, and invites us to consider the character of a foreshortened life.

Much of the essay views invalidism and the threat of death from the perspective of one who experiences them young. At the end is a three-paragraph amendment added years later, because "a slightly greater age teaches us a slightly different wisdom."

In the late nineteenth century, when Stevenson fell ill with tuberculosis, the "cure" was to send the patient, if he had the means to go, to a "healthier" climate. For northern Europeans, this often meant the Mediterranean. Stevenson describes such a journey.

What he will later call the "falling aside" from "the mid race of active life" begins on the train, which hurtles past the lives of others, offering glimpses of them, but not altering or even disturbing them. When the voyage ends, the invalid first feels the pleasant anticipation of having arrived in a beautiful, beloved spot, only to discover that while it has not changed, he has, and in such a way that it can no longer be what it was to him. Eventually, he accepts his status as a bystander, and even sees in "this dullness of the senses . . . a gentle preparation for the final insensibility of death."

This invalid is still attached to the world, though, by "many and kindly" ties: the sight of children not his own; his longstanding, undiminished humanitarian hopes; the thought of his friends, in whose hearts he knows he will live on.

While he did not live to old age, Stevenson lived longer than he expected to when he wrote this essay. In the years that followed its writing, he brought a woman and children into his life. The note at the end of "Ordered South" therefore addresses the differences between facing death as a footloose youth and facing it as a family man.

Stevenson's humanitarian ideals and the belief that he might have made a difference to the greater world helped to console him as he confronted death as a young man. As a mature man, he sees these as dreams, and cares far more for his actual obligations to particular people who need him.

Stevenson's attachment to the world appears to have grown narrower as he matured. Did it grow deeper as well?

It pleased Stevenson, the youth, to think that he would live on in the hearts of his friends. It distressed Stevenson, the adult, to leave his parents, wife, and children, though no doubt they, too, would remember him. Why was the one idea so different from the other? What might this difference say about the nature of the ties that bind one to life?

Unlike Aristotle, Bacon, or Shakespeare's Jaques, Stevenson explicitly considers the effect of parenthood on a man in his prime. How does this consideration affect his account of one's prime?

Stevenson found it more painful to die in midlife than in his youth, and felt that he and others paid a heavier price for it. But by managing to survive he accomplished a great deal, much of it of lasting value. For him, was it good to live as long as he could? Was each year a gift? Would that be true for everyone?

By a curious irony of fate, the places to which we are sent when health deserts us are often singularly beautiful. Often, too, they are places we have visited in former years, or seen briefly in passing by, and kept ever afterwards in pious memory; and we please ourselves with the fancy that we shall repeat many vivid and pleasurable sensations, and take up again the thread of our enjoyment in the same spirit as we let it fall. We shall now have an opportunity of finishing many pleasant excursions, interrupted of yore before our curiosity was fully satisfied. It may be that we have kept in mind, during all these years, the recollection of some valley into which we have just looked down for a moment before we lost sight of it in the disorder of the hills; it may be that we have lain awake at night, and agreeably tantalised ourselves with the thought of corners we had never turned, or summits we had all but climbed: we shall now be able, as we tell ourselves, to complete all these unfinished pleasures, and pass beyond the barriers that confined our recollections.

The promise is so great, and we are all so easily led away when hope and memory are both in one story, that I daresay the sick man is not very inconsolable when he receives sentence of banishment, and is inclined to regard his ill-health as not the least fortunate accident of his life. Nor is he immediately undeceived. The stir and speed of the journey, and the restlessness that goes to bed with him as he tries to sleep between two days of noisy progress, fever him, and stimulate his dull nerves into something of their old quickness and sensibility. And so he can enjoy the faint autumnal splendour of the landscape, as he sees hill and plain, vineyard and forest, clad in one wonderful glory of fairy gold, which the first great winds of winter will transmute, as in the fable, into withered leaves. And so too he can enjoy the admirable brevity and simplicity of such little glimpses of country and country ways as flash upon him through the windows of the train; little glimpses that have a character all their own; sights seen as a travelling swallow might see them from the wing, or Iris as she went abroad over the land on some Olympian errand. Here and there, indeed, a few children huzzah and wave their hands to the express; but for the most part it is an interruption too brief and isolated to attract much notice; the sheep do not cease from browsing; a girl sits balanced on the projecting tiller of a canal boat, so precariously that it seems as if a fly or the splash of a leaping fish would be enough to over-throw the dainty equilibrium, and yet all these hundreds of tons of coal and wood and iron have been precipitated roaring past her very ear, and there is not a start, not a tremor, not a turn of the averted head, to indicate that she has been even conscious of its passage. Herein, I think, lies the chief attraction of railway travel. The speed is so easy, and the train disturbs so little the scenes through which it takes us, that our heart becomes full of the placidity and stillness of the country; and while the body is borne forward in the flying chain of carriages, the thoughts alight, as the humour moves them, at unfrequented stations; they make haste up the poplar alley that leads toward the town; they are left behind with the signalman as, shading his eyes with his hand, he watches the long train sweep away into the golden distance. . . .

. . . It is only after he is fairly arrived and settled down in his chosen corner, that the invalid begins to understand the change that has befall-en him. Everything about him is as he had remembered, or as he had anticipated. Here, at his feet, under his eyes, are the olive gardens and the blue sea.

Nothing can change the eternal magnificence of form of the naked Alps behind Mentone; nothing, not even the crude curves of the rail-way, can utterly deform the suavity of contour of one bay after another along the whole reach of the Riviera. And of all this, he has only a cold head knowledge that is divorced from enjoyment. He recognises with his intelligence that this thing and that thing is beautiful, while in his heart of hearts he has to confess that it is not beautiful for him. It is in vain that he spurs his discouraged spirit; in vain that he chooses out points of view, and stands there, looking with all his eyes, and waiting for some return of the pleasure that he remembers in other days, as the sick folk may have awaited the coming of the angel at the pool of Be-thesda. He is like an enthusiast leading about with him a stolid, indifferent tourist. There is some one by who is out of sympathy with the scene, and is not moved up to the measure of the occasion; and that some one is himself. The world is disenchanted for him. He seems to himself to touch things with muffled hands, and to see them through a veil. His life becomes a palsied fumbling after notes that are silent when he has found and struck them. He cannot recognise that this phlegmatic and unimpressionable body with which he now goes burthened, is the same that he knew heretofore so quick and delicate and alive. . . .

. . . For it is not altogether ill with the invalid, after all. If it is only rarely that anything penetrates vividly into his numbed spirit, yet, when anything does, it brings with it a joy that is all the more poignant for its very rarity. . . .

. . . It is not in such numbness of spirit only that the life of the invalid resembles a premature old age. Those excursions that he had promised himself to finish, prove too long or too arduous for his feeble body; and the barrier-hills are as impassable as ever. Many a white town that sits far out on the promontory, many a comely fold of wood on the mountain side, beckons and allures his imagination day after day, and is yet as inaccessible to his feet as the clefts and gorges of the clouds. The sense of distance grows upon him wonderfully; and after some feverish efforts and the fretful uneasiness of the first few days, he falls contentedly in with the restrictions of his weakness. His narrow round becomes pleasant and familiar to him as the cell to a contented prisoner. Just as he has fallen already out of the mid race of active life, he now falls out of the little eddy that circulates in the shallow waters of the sanatorium. He sees the country people come and go about their everyday affairs, the foreigners stream out in goodly pleasure parties; the stir of man's activity is all about him, as he suns himself inertly in some sheltered corner; and he looks on with a patriarchal impersonality of interest, such as a man may feel when he pictures to himself the fortunes of his remote descendants, or the robust old age of the oak he has planted over-night.

In this falling aside, in this quietude and desertion of other men, there is no inharmonious prelude to the last quietude and desertion of the grave; in this dulness of the senses there is a gentle preparation for the final insensibility of death. And to him the idea of mortality comes in a shape less violent and harsh than is its wont, less as an abrupt catastrophe than as a thing of infinitesimal gradation, and the last step on a long decline of way. As we turn to and fro in bed, and every moment the movements grow feebler and smaller and the attitude more restful and easy, until sleep overtakes us at a stride and we move no more, so desire after desire leaves him; day by day his strength decreases, and the circle

of his activity grows ever narrower; and he feels, if he is to be thus tenderly weaned from the passion of life, thus gradually inducted into the
slumber of death, that when at last the end comes, it will come quietly
and fitly. If anything is to reconcile poor spirits to the coming of the last
enemy, surely it should be such a mild approach as this; not to hale us
forth with violence, but to persuade us from a place we have no further
pleasure in. It is not so much, indeed, death that approaches as life that
withdraws and withers up from round about him. He has outlived his
own usefulness, and almost his own enjoyment; and if there is to be no
recovery; if never again will he be young and strong and passionate, if
the actual present shall be to him always like a thing read in a book or
remembered out of the far-away past; if, in fact, this be veritably nightfall, he will not wish greatly for the continuance of a twilight that only
strains and disappoints the eyes, but steadfastly await the perfect darkness. He will pray for Medea: when she comes, let her either rejuvenate
or slay.

And yet the ties that still attach him to the world are many and kindly. The sight of children has a significance for him such as it may have
for the aged also, but not for others. If he has been used to feel humane-
ly, and to look upon life somewhat more widely than from the narrow
loophole of personal pleasure and advancement, it is strange how small
a portion of his thoughts will be changed or embittered by this proxim-
ity of death. He knows that already, in English counties, the sower follows the ploughman up the face of the field, and the rooks follow the
sower; and he knows also that he may not live to go home again and see
the corn spring and ripen, and be cut down at last, and brought home
with gladness. And yet the future of this harvest, the continuance of
drought or the coming of rain unseasonably, touch him as sensibly as
ever. For he has long been used to wait with interest the issue of events
in which his own concern was nothing; and to be joyful in a plenty, and
sorrowful for a famine, that did not increase or diminish, by one half
loaf, the equable sufficiency of his own supply. Thus there remain unal-
tered all the disinterested hopes for mankind and a better future which
have been the solace and inspiration of his life. These he has set beyond
the reach of any fate that only menaces himself; and it makes small
difference whether he die five thousand years, or five thousand and fifty
years, before the good epoch for which he faithfully labours. He has not
deceived himself; he has known from the beginning that he followed
the pillar of fire and cloud, only to perish himself in the wilderness, and
that it was reserved for others to enter joyfully into possession of the
land. And so, as everything grows grayer and quieter about him, and

slopes towards extinction, these unfaded visions accompany his sad decline, and follow him, with friendly voices and hopeful words, into the very vestibule of death. The desire of love or of fame scarcely moved him, in his days of health, more strongly than these generous aspirations move him now; and so life is carried forward beyond life, and a vista kept open for the eyes of hope, even when his hands grope already on the face of the impassable.

Lastly, he is bound tenderly to life by the thought of his friends; or shall we not say rather, that by their thought for him, by their unchangeable solicitude and love, he remains woven into the very stuff of life, beyond the power of bodily dissolution to undo? In a thousand ways will he survive and be perpetuated. Much of Etienne de la Boetie survived during all the years in which Montaigne continued to converse with him on the pages of the ever-delightful essays. Much of what was truly Goethe was dead already when he revisited places that knew him no more, and found no better consolation than the promise of his own verses, that soon he too would be at rest. Indeed, when we think of what it is that we most seek and cherish, and find most pride and pleasure in calling ours, it will sometimes seem to us as if our friends, at our decease, would suffer loss more truly than ourselves. As a monarch who should care more for the outlying colonies he knows on the map or through the report of his vicegerents, than for the trunk of his empire under his eyes at home, are we not more concerned about the shadowy life that we have in the hearts of others, and that portion in their thoughts and fancies which, in a certain far-away sense, belongs to us, than about the real knot of our identity—that central metropolis of self, of which alone we are immediately aware—or the diligent service of arteries and veins and infinitesimal activity of ganglia, which we know (as we know a proposition in Euclid) to be the source and substance of the whole? At the death of every one whom we love, some fair and honourable portion of our existence falls away, and we are dislodged from one of these dear provinces; and they are not, perhaps, the most fortunate who survive a long series of such impoverishments, till their life and influence narrow gradually into the meagre limit of their own spirits, and death, when he comes at last, can destroy them at one blow.

NOTE—*To this essay I must in honesty append a word or two of qualification; for this is one of the points on which a slightly greater age teaches us a slightly different wisdom:*

A youth delights in generalities, and keeps loose from particular obligations; he jogs on the footpath way, himself pursuing butterflies, but courteously lending his applause to the advance of the human species and the coming of the kingdom of justice and love. As he grows older, he begins to think more narrowly of man's action in the general, and perhaps more arrogantly of his own in the particular. He has not that same unspeakable trust in what he would have done had he been spared, seeing finally that that would have been little; but he has a far higher notion of the blank that he will make by dying. A young man feels himself one too many in the world; his is a painful situation: he has no calling; no obvious utility; no ties, but to his parents, and these he is sure to disregard. I do not think that a proper allowance has been made for this true cause of suffering in youth; but by the mere fact of a prolonged existence, we outgrow either the fact or else the feeling. Either we become so callously accustomed to our own useless figure in the world, or else—and this, thank God, in the majority of cases—we so collect about us the interest or the love of our fellows, so multiply our effective part in the affairs of life, that we need to entertain no longer the question of our right to be.

And so in the majority of cases, a man who fancies himself dying, will get cold comfort from the very youthful view expressed in this essay. He, as a living man, has some to help, some to love, some to correct; it may be, some to punish. These duties cling, not upon humanity, but upon the man himself. It is he, not another, who is one woman's son and a second woman's husband and a third woman's father. That life which began so small, has now grown, with a myriad filaments, into the lives of others. It is not indispensable; another will take the place and shoulder the discharged responsibility; but the better the man and the nobler his purposes, the more will he be tempted to regret the extinction of his powers and the deletion of his personality. To have lived a generation, is not only to have grown at home in that perplexing medium, but to have assumed innumerable duties. To die at such an age, has, for all but the entirely base, something of the air of a betrayal. A man does not only reflect upon what he might have done in a future that is never to be his; but beholding himself so early a deserter from the fight, he eats his heart for the good he might have done already. To have been so useless and now to lose all hope of being useful any more—there it is that death and memory assail him. And even if mankind shall go on, founding heroic cities, practising heroic virtues, rising steadily from strength to strength; even if his work shall be fulfilled, his friends consoled, his wife remarried by a better than he; how shall this alter, in one jot, his estimation of a career which was his only business in this world, which was so fitfully pursued, and which is now so ineffectively to end?

Excerpt from
THE PROFESSOR'S HOUSE
by Willa Cather

A stage of life is not only a matter of years, or of physical capability. It is a state of mind, too. This excerpt from Willa Cather's The Professor's House *describes the state of mind of a man who, though not old, feels he is approaching the end of his life.*

The novel takes place a few years after the First World War. Godfrey St. Peter is a professor of history at a midwestern college. His believes his life's work is complete. St. Peter wrote a history of the exploration of the American southwest; it is done and he misses the joy it gave him. His best student, a native of the southwest named Tom Outland, died in the war. St. Peter's two daughters are grown and married; the problems that trouble them now are no longer the sort with which he can help, and the family is now largely in the hands of his sons-in-law. Although he lives amicably with his wife, Lillian, St. Peter no longer feels close to her.

As this excerpt begins, Lillian is traveling in France with one of their two daughters and the daughter's husband, Louie. St. Peter is home alone for the summer and living in the house he and his wife have occupied for years. He hopes to use the summer to complete a small scholarly task. When his family returns, they will expect him to move into a new house they have bought. He doesn't want to go.

"The Professor knew," we are told, "that adolescence grafted a new creature into the original one, and that the complexion of a man's life was largely determined by how well or how ill his original self and his nature as modified by sex rubbed on together." What does he mean? Is it true?

What has St. Peter begun to understand about the senile grandfather he remembers from his boyhood?

The "recognitions" of this, his second boyhood, give St. Peter "a kind of sad pleasure." Why sorrow and pleasure both?

St. Peter's sense that he is near death arises from his realization that he is "indifferent" to his life. Yet when the doctor tells him there is nothing wrong with him, and suggests he continue "doing nothing," he is "well satisfied."

Does St. Peter want to die? Is he enjoying this stage of life, with its indifference and its "sad pleasures"?

How might St. Peter's frame of mind be affected by the disappointments he has experienced? Does he feel "done" with life because his work is finished, or does he feel that his work is finished because he is done with life? If St. Peter still loved his wife, might he feel differently about continuing to live?

Is St. Peter's frame of mind a function of his time of life or his experiences—his disappointments, losses, etc.? What insights does St. Peter, at this stage of his life, share with the boyhood self he remembers? Why is he capable of these insights only now? In what sense, if any, does the Professor have a whole or unified life?

All those summer days, while the Professor was sending cheerful accounts of his activities to his family in France, he was really doing very little. . . .

. . . When the first of August came round, the Professsor realized that he had pleasantly trifled away nearly two months at a task which should have taken little more than a week. But he had been doing a good deal besides—something he had never before been able to do.

St. Peter had always laughed at people who talked about "day-dreams," just as he laughed at people who naïvely confessed that they had "an imagination." All his life his mind had behaved in a positive fashion. When he was not at work, or being actively amused, he went to sleep. He had no twilight stage. But now he enjoyed this half-awake loafing with his brain as if it were a new sense, arriving late, like wisdom teeth. He found he could lie on his sand-spit by the lake for hours and watch the seven motionless pines drink up the sun. In the evening, after dinner, he could sit idle and watch the stars, with the same immobility. He was cultivating a novel mental dissipation—and enjoying a new friendship. Tom Outland had not come back again through the garden door (as he had so often done in dreams!), but another boy had: the boy the Professor had long ago left behind him in Kansas, in the Solomon Valley—the original, unmodified Godfrey St. Peter.

This boy and he had meant, back in those far-away days, to live some sort of life together and to share good and bad fortune. They had not shared together, for the reason that they were unevenly matched. The young St. Peter who went to France to try his luck, had a more active mind than the twin he left behind in the Solomon Valley. After his adoption into the Thierault household, he remembered that other boy very rarely, in moments of home-sickness. After he met Lillian Ornsley, St. Peter forgot that boy had ever lived.

But now that the vivid consciousness of an earlier state had come back to him, the Professor felt that life with this Kansas boy, little as there had been of it, was the realest of his lives, and that all the years between had been accidental and ordered from the outside. His career, his wife, his family, were not his life at all, but a chain of events which had happened to him. All these things had nothing to do with the person he was in the beginning.

The man he was now, the personality his friends knew, had begun to grow strong during adolescence, during the years when he was always consciously or unconsciously conjugating the verb "to love"—in society and solitude, with people, with books, with the sky and open country, in the lonesomeness of crowded city streets. When he met Lillian, it reached its maturity. From that time to this, existence had been a catching at handholds. One thing led to another and one development brought on another, and the design of his life had been the work of this secondary social man, the lover. It had been shaped by all the penalties and responsibilities of being and having been a lover. Because there was Lillian, there must be marriage and a salary. Because there was marriage, there were children. Because there were children, and fervour in the blood and brain, books were born as well as daughters. His histories, he was convinced, had no more to do with his original ego than his daughters had; they were a result of the high pressure of young manhood.

The Kansas boy who had come back to St. Peter this summer was not a scholar. He was a primitive. He was only interested in earth and woods and water. Wherever sun sunned and rain rained and snow snowed, wherever life sprouted and decayed, places were alike to him. He was not nearly so cultivated as Tom's old cliff-dwellers must have been—and yet he was terribly wise. He seemed to be at the root of the matter; Desire under all desires, Truth under all truths. He seemed to know, among other things, that he was solitary and must always be so; he had never married, never been a father. He was earth, and would return to earth. When white clouds blew over the lake like bellying sails, when the seven pine-trees turned red in the declining sun, he felt satisfaction and said to himself merely: "That is right." Coming upon a curly root that thrust itself across his path, he said: "That is it." When the maple-leaves along the street began to turn yellow and waxy, and were soft to the touch,—like the skin on old faces,—he said: "That is true; it is time." All these recognitions gave him a kind of sad pleasure.

When he was not dumbly, deeply recognizing, he was bringing up out of himself long-forgotten, unimportant memories of his early childhood, of his mother, his father, his grandfather. His grandfather, old Napoleon Godfrey, used to go about lost in profound, continuous meditation, sometimes chuckling to himself. Occasionally, at the family dinner-table, the old man would try to rouse himself, from motives of politeness, and would ask some kindly question—nearly always absurd and often the same one he had asked yesterday. The boys used to shout with laughter and wonder what profound matters could require such deep meditation, and make a man speak so foolishly about what was going on under his very eyes. St. Peter thought he was beginning to understand what the old man had been thinking about, though he himself was but fifty-two, and Napoleon had been well on in his eighties. There are only a few years, at the last, in which man can consider his estate, and he thought he might be quite as near the end of his road as his grandfather had been in those days.

The Professor knew, of course, that adolescence grafted a new creature into the original one, and that the complexion of a man's life was largely determined by how well or ill his original self and his nature as modified by sex rubbed on together.

What he had not known was that, at a given time, that first nature could return to a man, unchanged by all the pursuits and passions and experiences of his life; untouched even by the tastes and intellectual activities which have been strong enough to give him distinction among his fellows and to have made for him, as they say, a name in the world. Perhaps this reversion did not often occur, but he knew it had happened to him, and he suspected it had happened to his grandfather. He did not regret his life, but he was indifferent to it. It seemed to him like the life of another person.

Along with other states of mind which attended his realization of the boy Godfrey, came a conviction (he did not see it coming, it was there before he was aware of its approach) that he was nearing the end of his life. This conviction took its place so quietly, seemed so matter-of-fact, that he gave it little thought. But one day, when he realized that all the while he was preparing for the fall term he didn't in the least believe he would be alive during the fall term, he thought he might better see a doctor.

The family doctor knew all about St. Peter. It was summer, moreover, and he had plenty of time. He devoted several mornings to the Professor and made tests of the most searching kind. In the end he of course told St. Peter there was nothing the matter with him.

"What made you come to me, any discomfort or pain?"

"None. I simply feel tired all the time."

Dr. Dudley shrugged. "So do I! Sleep well?"

"Almost too much."

"Eat well?"

"In every sense of the word, well. I am my own *chef*."

"Always a *gourmet*, and never anything wrong with your digestive tract! I wish you'd ask me to dine with you some night. Any of that sherry left?"

"A little. I use it plentifully."

"I'll bet you do! But why did you think there was something wrong with you? Low in your mind?"

"No, merely low in energy. Enjoy doing nothing. I came to you from a sense of duty."

"How about travel?"

"I shrink from the thought of it. As I tell you, I enjoy doing nothing."

"Then do it! There's nothing the matter with you. Follow your inclination."

St. Peter went home well satisfied. He did not mention to Dr. Dudley the real reason for his asking for a medical examination. One doesn't mention such things. The feeling that he was near the conclusion of his life was an instinctive conviction, such as we have when we waken in the dark and know at once that it is near morning; or when we are walking across the country and suddenly know that we are near the sea.

Letters came every week from France. Lillian and Louie alternated, so that one or the other got off a letter to him on every fast boat. Louie told him that wherever they went, when they had an especially delightful day, they bought him a present. At Trouville, for instance, they had laid in dozens of the brilliant rubber casquettes he liked to wear when he went swimming. At Aix-les-Bains they found a gorgeous dressing-gown for him in a Chinese shop. St. Peter was happy in his mind about them all. He was glad they were there, and that he was here. Their generous letters, written when there were so many pleasant things to do, certainly deserved more than one reading. He used to carry them out to the lake to read them over again. After coming out of the water he would lie on the sand, holding them in his hand, but somehow never taking his eyes off the pine-trees, appliquéd against the blue water, and their ripe yellow cones, dripping with gum and clustering on the pointed tips like a mass of golden bees in swarming-time. Usually he carried his letters home unread.

His family wrote constantly about their plans for next summer, when they were going to take him over with them. Next summer? The Professor wondered. . . . Sometimes he thought he would like to drive up in front of Notre Dame, in Paris, again, and see it standing there like the Rock of Ages, with the frail generations breaking about its base. He hadn't seen it since the war.

But if he went anywhere next summer, he thought it would be down into Outland's country, to watch the sunrise break on sculptured peaks and impassable mountain passes—to look off at those long, rugged, untamed vistas dear to the American heart. Dear to all hearts, probably—at least, calling to all. Else why had his grandfather's grandfather, who had tramped so many miles across Europe into Russia with the Grande Armée, come out to the Canadian wilderness to forget the chagrin of his Emperor's defeat?

The fall term of the university opened, and now the Professor went to his lectures instead of to the lake. He supposed he did his work, he heard no complaints from his assistants, and the students seemed interested. He found, however, that he wasn't willing to take the trouble to learn the names of several hundred new students. It wasn't worth while. He felt that his relations with them would be of short duration.

The McGregors[1] got home from their vacation in Oregon, and Scott was much amused to find the Professor so doggedly anchored in the old house.

"It never struck me, Doctor, that you were a man who would be keeping up two establishments. They'll be coming home pretty soon, and then you'll have to decide where you are going to live."

"I can't leave my study, Scott. That's flat."

"Don't, then! Darn it, you've a right to two houses if you want 'em."

This encounter took place on the street in front of the house. The Professor went wearily upstairs and lay down on the couch, his refuge from this ever-increasing fatigue. He really didn't see what he was going to do about the matter of domicile. He couldn't make himself believe that he was ever going to live in the new house again. He didn't belong there. He remembered some lines of a translation from the Norse he used to read long ago in one of his mother's few books, a little two-volume Ticknor and Fields edition of Longfellow, in blue and gold, that used to lie on the parlour table:

---

[1] St. Peter's other daughter and son-in-law.

For thee a house was built
Ere thou wast born;
For thee a mould was made
Ere thou of woman camest.

Lying on his old couch, he could almost believe himself in that house already. The sagging springs were like the sham upholstery that is put in coffins. Just the equivocal American way of dealing with serious facts, he reflected. Why pretend that it is possible to soften that last hard bed?

He could remember a time when the loneliness of death had terrified him, when the idea of it was insupportable. He used to feel that if his wife could but lie in the same coffin with him, his body would not be so insensible that the nearness of hers would not give it comfort. But now he thought of eternal solitude with gratefulness; as a release from every obligation, from every form of effort. It was the Truth.

LIFE

by Liam O'Flaherty

In his short story "Life," Irish writer Liam O'Flaherty shines his light on the relation between old age and infancy. The story begins with the birth of an unnamed infant to an aging mother who knows that this child—her fourteenth—will be her last. The infant grows and is weaned as his aged grandfather, a member of the same household, declines towards death.

The grandfather, though infirm, "emerges from his witless state" when the baby awakens and cries. He recognizes the child, with delight, as "a man of my blood." Similarly, the infant emerges into awareness—his "resplendent soul shone out through his eyes"—as he consciously strives to imitate the gestures of the old man. When the old man dies, it is in the spring, alongside the baby, while the two are together enjoying the spectacle of birds leaping and fighting for their food.

What do the baby and the old man have in common? What do they recognize in each other?

Do the women and the old man understand "life" in the same way? Why is the mother of the infant sad that she will never again bring forth life, when it is so hard for her to provide for the lives she has already created? Why does the family begrudge the old man what it joyfully provides for the infant?

What, according to this story, is "life"?

The mother lay flat on her back, with her eyes closed and her arms stretched out to their full length above the bedclothes. Her hands kept turning back and forth in endless movement. Her whole body was exhausted after the great labour of giving birth.

Then the infant cried. She opened her eyes as soon as she heard the faint voice. She seized the bedclothes fiercely between her fingers. She raised her head and looked wildly towards the grandmother, who was tending the new-born child over by the fireplace.

The old woman noticed the mother's savage look. She burst out laughing.

"For the love of God," she said to the two neighbouring women that were helping her, "look at herself and she as frightened as a young girl on her wedding night. You'd think this is her first child instead of her last."

She took the infant by the feet, raised him up high and smacked him quite hard on the rump with her open palm.

"Shout now, in God's name," she said, "and put the devil out of your carcass."

The child started violently under the impact of the blow. He screamed again. Now there was power in his voice.

"Upon my soul!" said one of the neighbouring women.

"I don't blame her at all for being conceited about a young fellow like that."

She spat upon the infant's naked stomach.

"I never laid eyes on a finer new-born son than this one, 'faith," she said in a tone of deep conviction.

"A fine lad, God bless him," said the other woman as she made the sign of the Cross over the child. "Begob, he has the makings of a hero in him, by all appearances."

"He has, indeed," said the grandmother. "He has the makings of a man in him, all right."

A deep sadness fell upon the mother when she heard the old woman say that this child would be the last to come from her womb. She was now forty-three. The years had already brought silver to her hair. She knew very well that she would never again bring life, by the miraculous power of God, from the substance of her body. She had done that fourteen times already. Except for the first time, when the intoxication of love was still strong in her blood, she got little comfort from giving birth. As the holy seed of life multiplied under her roof, so also did misfortune and hunger multiply. It was so hard for a poor couple like her husband and herself, with only a few acres of stony land, to feed and care for so many little bodies and souls.

Yet she now felt miserably sad at the thought that her womb would henceforth be without fruit. She closed her eyes once more, crossed her hands on her bosom and began a prayer to Almighty God, asking for divine help on the hard road that lay ahead of her.

When the infant and the mother were put in order, the father was allowed to enter the bedroom. He was still in his prime, even though he was nearly fifty years of age, most of which time had been spent in drudgery on the land. He uncovered his head when he came into the presence of the new-born. He crossed himself and bent a knee in homage to the new life.

"May God bless you," he said to the child.

Then he went over to the bed and bowed to his wife in the same way.
"Thank God," he said to her gently, "you have that much past you."
She smiled faintly as she looked at him.

"I'm glad," she said, "that it was a son I gave you as my last child."

"May God reward you for it!" he said fervently as he again bowed to her.

The old woman brought the child to the bed and laid him against the
mother's bosom.

"Here you are now," she said. "Here is the newest little jewel in your
house."

All trace of sorrow departed from the mother's soul, as she put her
hands about the infant's little body and felt the strong young heart beating behind the ribs. She got a lump in her throat and tears flowed down
her cheeks.

"Praised be the great God of glory!" she cried fervently.

The cock began to crow out in the barn. Its voice rose high and sharp
above the roar of the November wind that was tearing through the sky.

"May the hand of God protect my child!" cried the mother when she
heard the crowing of the cock.

All the village cocks kept joining in the crowing until they were of
one voice saluting the dawn.

"May God preserve the little one!" said the other women.

Far away the sound of the waves was loud as they lashed the great
southern cliffs.

"Safe from sickness," prayed the mother, "safe from blemish, safe from
misfortune, safe in body and soul."

After a while, the other children were allowed to enter the room, so
that they might make the acquaintance of their youngest little brother.
There were seven of them. Four of the fourteen had already died. Another three had gone out into the world in search of a livelihood. All
that remained were between the ages of fifteen and three. They became
silent with wonder when they caught sight of the baby. They stood about
the bed with their mouths open, holding one another by the hand.

Then the grandfather was allowed into the room. He was far from
being silent. He began to babble foolishly when he caught sight of his
youngest grandson.

"Aie! Aie!" he said. "Everything is more lasting than man. Aie! The
Virgin Mary have pity on me! Look at me now and I only the wreck of a
man. Yet there was a day. . . ."

He was very old. A few years previously, the sun hurt him while he
was asleep in a field on a warm day. He was practically a cripple since

then, having lost the use of his limbs almost entirely. He was doting. His body shrank from day to day. Now he was no heavier than a little boy. His head was so stooped that one would think it was tethered to his ankles like that of a wicked ass. He trembled like a leaf.

"Aie! Aie!" he said bitterly. "There was a day when I wasn't afraid of any man, I don't care what man it was, from east or west, that might challenge me, looking for fight or for trouble. 'Faith, I'd let no man take the sway from me, for I was that sort of a man, that never looked for a fight and never ran from one. That was the class of a man I was, a man that could stand his ground without fear or favour. . . ."

The old woman had to take hold of him and carry him out of the room.

"Come on down out of this," she said, "and don't be bothering the people with your foolish talk."

"Ah! God help me!" said one of the neighbouring women. "The longest journey from the womb to the grave is only a short one after all."

When the baby took up residence in his cradle by the kitchen hearth, he was like a king in the house. The whole family waited on him. It was thankless work. The newborn was entirely unaware that the slightest favour was being conferred on him. He was completely unaware of all but the solitary instinct that he had brought with him from the womb. That was to maintain and strengthen the life that was in him.

When he awoke, he screamed savagely until he was given hold of his mother's breast. Then he became silent at once. His toothless jaws closed firmly on the swollen teat. His little body shivered with voluptuous pleasure when he felt the first stream of warm milk pouring on to his tongue. He sucked until he was replete. Then again he fell asleep. When he felt unwell, from stomach-ache or some other trivial complaint, he yelled outrageously. He went on yelling in most barbarous fashion until they began to rock the cradle. They had to keep rocking until his pain had gone.

They sang to him while they rocked.

"Oh! My darling! My darling! My darling!" they sang to him. "Oh! My darling, you're the love of my heart."

Far different was their conduct towards the old man. There was little respect for him. When they waited on him, it was through charity and not because it gave them pleasure. They begrudged him the smallest favour that they conferred on him.

"Look at that old devil," they used to say. "Neither God nor man can get any good out of him and he sitting there in the chimney corner from morning till night. You'd be better off begging your bread than waiting on him."

True enough, it was hard to blame them for complaining. It was very unpleasant work having to wait upon the poor old man. They had to take him from his sleeping place each morning. They had to clean and dress him and put him seated on a little stool in the chimney corner. They had to tie a horsehair rope around his waist, lest he might fall into the fire. At mealtimes, they had to mash his food and put it in his mouth with a spoon.

He was dependent on them in every way exactly like the infant.

"Aie! The filthy thing!" they used to say. "It would be a great kindness to the people of this house if God would call him."

The grandfather remained tied in his chimney corner all day, between sleep and wake, jabbering, threatening imaginary people with his stick, scolding enemies that were long since dead, making idiotic conversation with the creatures of his folly about people and places.

He only emerged from his witless state when he heard the infant cry on awaking from sleep.

"Who is this?" he would say with his ear cocked. "Who is squealing like this?"

When the mother took the baby from the cradle and gave it suck in the opposite corner, the old man's eyes would brighten and he would recognise the child.

"Ho! Ho!" he would cry in delight. "It's yourself that's in it. Ho! My lovely one! That's a pretty young man I see over opposite me and no doubt about it."

Then he would try to reach the infant. He would get angry when he failed to go farther than the length of his horsehair rope.

"Let me at him," he would cry, struggling to leave his stool. "Let go this rope, you pack of devils. He is over there, one of my kindred. Let me at him. He is a man of my blood. Let me go to him."

His rage never lasted long. He would get overcome with delight on seeing the infant stretch and shudder voluptuously as he sucked.

"Bravo! Little one," the old man then cried as he jumped up and down on his stool. "Throw it back, my boy. Don't leave a drop of it. Ho! You are a man of my blood, all right. Drink, little one. More power to you!"

Winter was almost spent before the infant recognised anybody. Until then he only knew his mother's breasts and the warmth of his cradle by means of touch. Even though he often watched what was happening about him, there was no understanding in his big staring blue eyes. Then the day came at last when the resplendent soul shone out through his eyes.

He was lying on his belly across his mother's lap, suffering a little from stomach-ache owing to having drunk too much, when he took note of the old man's foolish gestures in the opposite corner. He smiled at first. Then he began to clap hands and to leap exactly like the old man. He uttered a little jovial yell.

"Praised be the great God of Glory!" said the mother.

The household gathered round. They all stood looking at the infant and at the old man, who were imitating one another's foolish gestures across the hearth. Everybody laughed gaily except the grandmother. It was now she began to weep out loud.

"Aie! My Lord God!" she wailed. "The foolishness of infancy is a lovely thing to behold, but it's pitiful to see an old person that has out-lived his reason."

From that day onward, the old man and the baby spent long spells playing together, clapping hands, jabbering and drivelling. It would be hard to say which of them was the more foolish. When the infant was weaned, it was with the same mash they were both fed.

According as the infant grew strong from day to day the old man weakened. He got bronchitis in spring and they thought that his end had come. He received Extreme Unction. Yet he recovered from that attack. He was soon able to leave his bed and resume his position in the hearth corner. Now he was merely a shadow of his former self. They could lift him with one hand.

A day came early in May when there was a big spring tide and the whole family went to pick carrigeen moss along the shore. The grand-mother was left to take care of the house, the infant and the old man. It was a fine sunny day.

"Take me out into the yard," the old man said to his wife. "I'd like to see the sun before I die."

She did as he asked her. She put him sitting in a straw chair outside the door. She herself sat on a stool near him, with the infant on her bosom. She began to call the fowls.

"Tiuc! Tiuc!" she cried. "Fit! Fit! Beadai! Beadai! Beadai!"

They all came running to her at top speed, hens and ducks and geese. She threw them scraps of food from a big dish. The birds began to fight for the food, as they leaped and screamed and prodded one another with their beaks.

The infant took delight in the tumult of the birds. He began to clap his hands and to leap, as he watched the fierce struggle of the winged creatures. He screamed with glee in answer to their harsh croaking.

"Ho! Ho! Ho!" he cried, while the spittle ran from his mouth.

The old man got equally excited and he imitated the gestures of the infant. He began to clap hands and to hop on his chair and to babble unintelligibly.

"Musha, God help the two of you!" the old woman said.

The old man became silent all of a sudden. She glanced anxiously in his direction. She saw him half erect and leaning forward. Then he fell to the ground head foremost. She rushed to him with the child under her arm. When she stooped over him, she heard the death rattle in his throat. Then there was nothing at all to be heard from him.

She stood up straight and began the lamentation for the newly dead.

"Och! Ochon!" she wailed. "It was with you I walked through the delight and sorrow of life. Now you are gone and I'll soon be following you. Och! Ochon! My love! It was you that was lovely on the day of our marriage. . . ."

When the neighbours came, the old woman sat lamenting on her stool by the corpse with the child within her arms, while the birds still leaped and fought savagely for the food in the dish.

The infant hopped up and down, shouting merrily as he struggled to touch the bright feathers of the rushing birds with his outstretched hands.

The strong young heart was unaware that the tired old heart had just delivered up the life that made it beat.

CHAPTER 6:
AMONG THE GENERATIONS

WE BEGAN THIS SECTION by considering our embodiment. Then, in the last chapter, we read about the progress of our embodied lives, beginning with childhood, and moving through youth, maturity, and old age to death. In the final image of that chapter, at the conclusion of Liam O'Flaherty's "Life," a very old man lay lifeless on the ground.

In this chapter we address the question that naturally follows such an image: What, then, is left to us? Is human life nothing more than the relentless movement toward death?

That the human race has not been crippled by despair over this question is thanks largely to our faith—not universal but widespread—that we are not only bodies. Death is the end of the corporeal individual, but throughout history and around the world, human beings have held fast to the belief that our non-embodied selves, or souls, are eternal.

However, our embodiment, too, offers its own promise of eternity, one that is at odds neither with religious faith nor with the lack of it. This promise is of renewal, and it, too, is eloquently expressed at the end of "Life," as his infant grandson hops beside the dead old man, "shouting merrily." Like most of us, before he died the old man had generated. He did not live and perish alone; rather, he made himself a link in the branching chain of generations, a link distinct from his ancestors and descendants but connected to them.

Readings in this chapter are about the experience and the meaning of human renewal, and our obligations to those who came before us and those who will come after.

Renewal, of course, produces a new individual and is not the same as replacement. We bring our children into the world, but we do not determine who they will be. In our first reading, from Leo Tolstoy's *Anna Karenina*, we see that even well-prepared parents can be caught off guard by this reality. Our second reading, from George Eliot's *Silas Marner*, reminds us that it is not necessary to give birth to a child to participate in the great work of transmitting the wisdom of one generation to the next. The renewal of life and the assurance of its continuance is not a labor of a few hours, but a task for many years, and is shared by adoptive parents as well. Our third reading, however, returns to the act of procreation and the creation of a family. What do the parents in Galway Kinnell's "After Making Love We Hear Footsteps" really hear?

In our last three readings, adults look backward to their progenitors, as well as forward to their children. In an excerpt from his memoir, *The Duke of Deception*, Geoffrey Wolff struggles with the memory of a father he could not trust, while trying to be a different sort of father to his own two sons. A pregnant new wife in an excerpt from Sigrid Undset's *Kristin Lavransdatter* begins to perceive a connection between her husband's failure to preserve his inherited estate for his children and his ignorance of his family's past. Finally, two excerpts from *The Iliad* of Homer illustrate the importance of knowing and honoring one's ancestors for finding one's own place in the world, and for forging a place for one's children, as well.

Excerpt from
ANNA KARENINA
Childbirth

by Leo Tolstoy, translated by Aylmer and Louise
Maude

Leo Tolstoy's Anna Karenina *tells the stories of two families: Anna's, which
ends tragically, and Constantine Levin's, which ends happily. In the much-
quoted opening line, the author tells us: "All happy families resemble one another, but each unhappy family is unhappy in its own way." Following Tolstoy's
lead, readers are often far more interested in the tumultuous turnings of Anna's
adulterous love for the dashing Vronsky than we are in the ripening love of
Levin for Kitty. Yet their seemingly ordinary marriage is punctuated by extraordinary moments, moments that are "like openings in that usual life through
which something higher [becomes] visible."*

*One such moment, the birth of their son, is the subject of this excerpt. It
begins as Levin awakens and learns that Kitty is in labor, recounts the subsequent suffering, terror, and strain they each undergo, and ends more than
twenty-two hours later—more like one hundred years, according to Levin—
with the "bold, clamorous" wails of the newborn infant and the different responses of his new parents.*

*What are Levin's and Kitty's initial thoughts and feelings regarding their
son? Why does Levin respond so differently from Kitty? How does witnessing
Kitty's suffering in childbirth affect his subsequent reaction as a husband and a
father? How does Kitty's ordeal affect her subsequent reaction as a mother, a
wife, and a daughter? Should we be surprised by their different responses?*

*What might their responses betoken regarding their views of fatherhood and
motherhood? Why is Levin moved to compare what was happening to Kitty to
what he witnessed the year before at the deathbed of his brother? Have modern
interventions to ease the ordeal of labor and childbirth altered the meaning of
bringing a child into the world?*

First published by Oxford University Press 1918. Anna Karenina, by Leo Tolstoy,
Aylmer and Louise Maude, translators. Published by Oxford University Press.
Reprinted by permission of Oxford University Press.

There are no conditions of life to which a man cannot accustom himself, especially if he sees that every one around him lives in the same way. Three months previously Levin would not have believed that he could quietly fall asleep under the circumstances in which he now found himself: that while leading an aimless, senseless life, one moreover that was above his means; after tippling (he could call what had happened in the club by no other name), after showing unsuitable friendship to the man with whom his wife had once been in love, and after a still more unsuitable visit to a woman who could only be called a fallen woman[1], and after being allured by her and having grieved his wife—that in such circumstances he could quietly fall asleep. But under the influence of weariness, a sleepless night, and the wine he had drunk, he slept soundly and peacefully.

At five in the morning the creak of an opening door awoke him. He jumped up and looked round. Kitty was not in the bed beside him. But on the other side of the partition a light was moving, and he heard her step.

'What is it? What is it? . . .' he muttered, not yet quite awake. 'Kitty, what is it?'

'Nothing,' said she, coming candle in hand from beyond the partition. 'I only felt a little unwell,' she added with a peculiarly sweet and significant smile.

'What? Has it begun? Has it?' he asked in a frightened voice. 'We must send . . .' And he began to dress hurriedly.

'No, no,' she said smiling, holding him back with her hand. 'I'm sure it's nothing. I only felt slightly unwell; but it is over now.'

She came back to her bed, put out the candle, lay down, and remained quiet. Though that quietness, as if she were holding her breath, and especially the peculiar tenderness and animation with which, returning from the other side of the partition, she had said: 'It's nothing!' seemed to him suspicious, yet he was so sleepy that he fell asleep at once. Only afterwards he remembered that bated breath, and realized all that had passed in her dear sweet soul while she lay motionless by his side, awaiting the greatest event of a woman's life.

At seven o'clock he was awakened by her touch on his shoulder and a soft whisper. She seemed to hesitate between regret at waking him and a desire to speak to him.

---

1 Levin had visited Anna and her adulterous lover.

'Kostya, don't be frightened. It's nothing, but I think . . . We must send for Mary Vlasevna.'

The candle was burning again. She was sitting on the bed holding in her hands some knitting she had lately been doing.

'Please don't be frightened! It's nothing. I'm not a bit afraid,' she said on seeing his alarmed face, and she pressed his hand to her breast and then to her lips.

He jumped up hastily, hardly aware of himself, and without taking his eyes off her put on his dressing-gown and stood still, gazing at her. It was necessary for him to go, but he could not tear himself away from the sight of her. He had loved that face and known all its expressions and looks, but he had never seen her as she was now. How vile and despicable he appeared to himself before her as she now was, when he recollected the grief he had caused her yesterday! Her flushed face surrounded with soft hair that had escaped from beneath her nightcap shone with joy and resolution.

Little as there was of affectation and conventionality in Kitty's general character, yet Levin was astonished at what was revealed to him now that every veil had fallen and the very kernel of her soul shone through her eyes. And in this simplicity, this nakedness of soul, she whom he loved was more apparent than ever. She looked at him smilingly, but suddenly her eyebrows twitched, she raised her head, and coming quickly to him she took hold of his hand and clinging close she enveloped him in her hot breath. She was suffering, and seemed to be complaining to him of her pain. And for a moment from force of habit he felt as if he were in fault. But her look expressed a tenderness which told him that she not only did not blame him, but loved him because of those sufferings. 'If I am not to blame for it, who is?' he thought, involuntarily seeking a culprit to punish for these sufferings; but there was no culprit. She suffered, complained, triumphed in her sufferings, rejoiced in them and loved them. He saw that something beautiful was taking place in her soul, but what it was he could not understand. It was above his comprehension.

'I have sent for Mama. And you, go quickly and fetch Mary Vlasevna. . . . Kostya! . . . No, it's nothing. It's past.'

She moved away from him and rang.

'Well, go now. Pasha is coming. I am all right.'

And Levin saw with amazement that she again took up the knitting which she had fetched in the night, and recommenced work.

As Levin went out at one door he heard the maid enter at the other. He stopped at the door and heard Kitty give detailed instructions to the maid, and with her help herself move the bed.

He dressed, and while the horse was being harnessed—for it was early, and no *izvoshchiks* were about yet—he ran back to the bedroom not on tiptoe but, as it seemed to him, on wings. Two maids were busy moving something in the bedroom. Kitty was walking up and down and knitting, rapidly throwing the thread over the needle and giving orders.

'I am going straight to the doctor's. They have already gone for Mary Vlasevna, but I will call there too. Is anything else wanted? Oh yes, to Dolly!'[2]

She looked at him, evidently not listening to what he was saying.

'Yes, yes! Go,' she said rapidly, frowning and motioning him away with her hand.

He was already on his way through the drawing-room when suddenly a piteous moan, that lasted only a moment, reached him from the bedroom. He stopped and for a moment could not understand it.

'Yes, it was she,' he said and, clasping his head with his hands, he ran downstairs.

'Lord have mercy! Pardon and help us!' he repeated the words that suddenly and unexpectedly sprang to his lips. And he, an unbeliever, repeated those words not with his lips only. At that instant he knew that neither his doubts nor the impossibility of believing with his reason—of which he was conscious—at all prevented his appealing to God. It all flew off like dust. To whom should he appeal, if not to Him in whose hands he felt himself, his soul, and his love, to be? . . .

On the midwife's instructions, Levin gets opium from the chemist's, and calls for the doctor. He then returns home.

. . . From the moment when he woke up and understood what was the matter Levin had braced himself to endure what might await him, without reasoning and without anticipating anything—firmly suppressing all his thoughts and feelings, determined not to upset his wife but on the contrary to calm and support her. Not allowing himself even to think of what was about to happen and how it would end, judging by inquiries he had made as to the time such affairs usually lasted, Levin mentally prepared himself to endure and to keep his heart under restraint for something like five hours, which seemed to him within his power. But when he returned from the doctor's and again saw her sufferings, he began repeating more and more often: 'God pardon and help us!' sighing and

[2] Kitty's sister.

lifting his head, afraid lest he should not be able to bear the strain and should either burst into tears or run away, so tormenting was it for him. And only one hour had passed!

But after that hour another passed, a second, a third, and all the five hours that he had set himself as the longest term of possible endurance, and still the situation was unchanged; and he went on enduring, for there was nothing else to do but to endure—thinking every moment that he had reached the utmost limit of endurance and that in a moment his heart would burst with pity.

But the minutes went by, and the hours, and other hours, and his suffering and terror and strain grew tenser.

The ordinary conditions of life, without which nothing can be imagined, no longer existed for Levin. He lost the sense of time. Sometimes minutes—those minutes when she called him to her and he held her moist hand, now pressing his with extraordinary strength and now pushing him away—seemed to him like hours; and then again hours seemed but minutes. He was surprised when Mary Vlasevna asked him to light a candle behind the partition, and he learnt that it was already five o'clock in the evening. Had he been told it was ten in the morning he would not have been more astonished. He had just as little idea of where he was at that time as he had of when it all took place. He saw her burning face, now bewildered and full of suffering, and now smiling and soothing him. He saw the Princess[3] red, overwrought, her grey hair out of curl, and with tears which she energetically swallowed, biting her lips. He saw Dolly, he saw the doctor smoking thick cigarettes, and Mary Vlasevna with a firm, resolute, and tranquillizing look on her face, and the old Prince[4] pacing up and down the ballroom and frowning. But he did not know how they came and went, nor where they were. The Princess was one moment in the bedroom with the doctor, and the next in the study, where a table laid for a meal had made its appearance; and next it was not the Princess, but Dolly. Afterwards Levin remembered being sent somewhere. Once he was told to fetch a table and a sofa. He did it with zeal, believing that it was necessary for her sake, and only later discovered that he had been preparing a sleeping-place for himself. Then he was sent to the study to ask the doctor about something. The doctor answered him, and then began talking about the scenes in the city Duma. Then he was sent to fetch an icon with silver-gilt mounts from the Princess's bedroom, and he and the Princess's old lady's maid climbed on a

[3] Kitty's mother.
[4] Kitty's father.

cupboard to get down the icon, and he broke the little lamp that burned
before it, and the old servant tried to comfort him about his wife and
about the lamp. He brought the icon back with him, and put it at the
head of Kitty's bed, carefully pushing it in behind the pillows. But where,
when, and why all this was done he did not know. Nor did he understand why the Princess took his hand, and looking pitifully at him, en-
treated him to be calm; nor why Dolly tried to persuade him to eat
something and led him out of the room; nor why even the doctor looked
seriously and sympathizingly at him, offering him some drops.

He only knew and felt that what was happening was similar to what
had happened the year before in the hotel of the provincial town on the
deathbed of his brother Nicholas. Only that was sorrow and this was joy.
But that sorrow and this joy were equally beyond the usual conditions of
life: they were like openings in that usual life through which something
higher became visible. And, as in that case, what was not being accomplished came harshly, painfully, incomprehensibly; and while watching
it, the soul soared, as then, to heights it had never known before, at
which reason could not keep up with it.

'Lord, pardon and help us!' he kept repeating incessantly to himself,
appealing to God, in spite of a long period of apparently complete es-
trangement, just as trustingly and simply as in the days of childhood and
early youth.

During the whole of that time he was alternately in two different
moods. One day when not in her presence: when with the doctor, who
smoked one thick cigarette after another and extinguished them against
the rim of the overflowing ashpan; when with Dolly and the Prince,
where they talked about dinner, politics, or Mary Petrovna's illness, and
when Levin suddenly quite forgot for an instant what was happening
and felt just as if he was waking up; and the other was in her presence, by
her pillow, where his heart was ready to burst with pity and yet did not
burst, and there he prayed unceasingly to God. And every time when
the screams that came from the bedroom roused him from momentary
forgetfulness he succumbed to the same strange error that had possessed
him in the first moments: every time, on hearing the scream, he jumped
up and ran to justify himself, but recollected on the way that he was not
to blame and that he longed to protect and help her. But when, looking
at her, he again saw that to help was impossible, he was seized with
horror and said, 'Lord, pardon and help us!' And the longer it lasted the
stronger grew both his moods: out of her presence he became calmer,
quite forgetting her, and at the same time both her sufferings and his
feeling of the impossibility of helping her became more and more poign-

ant. He would jump up, wishing to run away somewhere, but ran to her instead.

Sometimes when she had called him again and again, he was half-inclined to blame her. But seeing her meek smiling face and hearing her say, 'I have worn you out,' he blamed God; but the thought of God made him at once pray for forgiveness and mercy.

He did not know whether it was late or early. The candles were all burning low. Dolly had just entered the study and suggested that the doctor should lie down. Levin sat listening to the doctor's stories of a quack magnetizer and staring at the ash of the doctor's cigarette. It was an interval of rest and oblivion. He had quite forgotten what was going on. He listened to the doctor's tale and understood it. Suddenly there was a scream unlike anything he had ever heard. The scream was so terrible that Levin did not even jump up, but looked breathlessly with a frightened and inquiring glance at the doctor, who bent his head on one side to listen and smiled approvingly. Everything was so out of the ordinary that nothing any longer surprised Levin. 'Probably it had to be so,' thought he and remained sitting still. 'But who was it screaming?' He jumped up and rushed into the bedroom on tiptoe, past Mary Vlasevna and the Princess, and stopped at his place at the head of the bed. The screaming had ceased, but there was a change; what it was he could not make out or understand, nor did he want to understand it; but he read it in Mary Vlasevna's face. She looked pale and stern, and as resolute as before, though her jaw trembled a little and her eyes were fixed intently on Kitty. Kitty's burning face, worn with suffering, with a lock of hair clinging to her clammy forehead, was turned toward him trying to catch his eye. Her raised hands asked for his. Seizing his cold hands in her perspiring ones she pressed them to her face.

'Don't go! Don't go! I am not afraid, I am not afraid!' she said rapidly. 'Mama! Take off my earrings, they are in the way! You are not afraid? Soon, Mary Vlasevna, soon . . . !'

She spoke very rapidly and tried to smile, but all at once her face became distorted and she pushed him away.

'No, this is awful! I shall die . . . die! . . . Go! Go!' she cried, and again he heard that scream unlike any other cry.

Levin clasped his head in his hands and ran out of the room.

'It's all right, it's all right! All goes well!' Dolly called after him.

But say what they might, he knew that now all was lost. Leaning his head against the door-post he stood in the next room, and heard some one shrieking and moaning in a way he had never heard till then, and he knew that these sounds were produced by what once was Kitty. He had long ceased wishing for a child, and now he hated that child. He did not now even wish her to live, but only longed that these terrible sufferings should end.

'Doctor, what is it? What is it? Oh, my God!' he cried, grasping the hand of the doctor who had just entered.

'It's coming to an end,' said the doctor, with a face so serious that Levin thought that *end* meant death.

Quite beside himself, he rushed into her room. The first thing he saw was Mary Vlasevna's face. It was still more frowning and stern. Kitty's face was not there. In its place was something terrible, both because of its strained expression and because of the sounds which proceeded from it. He let his head drop upon the wood of the bedstead, feeling that his heart was breaking. The terrible screaming did not cease, but grew yet more awful until, as if it had reached the utmost limit of horror, it suddenly ceased. Levin could scarcely believe his ears, but there was no room for doubt. The screaming had ceased, and he heard a sound of movement, of rustling, of accelerated breathing, and her voice, faltering, living, tender, and happy, as it said, 'It's over.'

He raised his head. With her arms helplessly outstretched upon the quilt, unusually beautiful and calm she lay, gazing silently at him, trying unsuccessfully to smile.

And suddenly, out of the mysterious, terrible, and unearthly world in which he had been living for the last twenty-two hours, Levin felt himself instantaneously transported back to the old everyday world, but now radiant with the light of such new joy that it was insupportable. The taut strings snapped, and sobs and tears of joy that he had not in the least anticipated arose within him, with such force that they shook his whole body and long prevented his speaking.

Falling on his knees by her bedside he held his wife's hand to his lips, kissing it, and that hand, by a feeble movement of the fingers, replied to the kisses. And meanwhile at the foot of the bed, like the flame of a lamp, flickered in Mary Vlasevna's skilful hands the life of a human being who had never before existed: a human being who, with the same right and the same importance to himself, would live and would procreate others like himself.

'Alive! Alive! And a boy! Don't be anxious,' Levin heard Mary Vlasevna say, as she slapped the baby's back with a shaking hand.

'Mama, is it true?' asked Kitty.

The Princess could only sob in reply.

And amid the silence, as a positive answer to the mother's question, a voice quite unlike all the restrained voices that had been speaking in the room made itself heard. It was a bold, clamorous voice that had no consideration for anything, it was the cry of the human being who had so incomprehensibly appeared from some unknown realm.

Before that, if Levin had been told that Kitty was dead, and that he had died with her, that they had angel children, and that God was there present with them—he would not have been astonished. But now, having returned to the world of actuality, he had to make great efforts to understand that she was alive and well, and that the creature that was yelling so desperately was his son. Kitty was alive, her sufferings were over; and he was full of unspeakable bliss. This he comprehended, and it rendered him entirely happy. But the child? Whence and why had he come? Who was he? . . . He could not at all accustom himself to the idea. It seemed something superfluous, something overflowing, and for a long time he was unable to get used to it.

Toward ten o'clock the old Prince, Koznyshev, and Oblonsky were with Levin, and having talked about the young mother they had begun discussing other matters. Levin listened to them and at the same time involuntarily thought of the past and of what had been going on before that morning, remembering himself as he had been yesterday before this event. A hundred years seemed to have elapsed since then. He felt as if he were on some unattainable height, from which he painstakingly descended in order not to hurt the feelings of those with whom he was conversing. He talked, but never ceased thinking of his wife, of the details of her present condition, and of his son—to the idea of whose existence he painstakingly tried to accustom himself. That feminine world which since his marriage had received a new and unsuspected significance for him, now rose so high in his estimation that his imagination could not grasp it. He heard a conversation about yesterday's dinner at the club and thought, 'What is happening to her now? Is she asleep? How is she? What is she thinking about? Is our son, Dmitry, crying?' And in the middle of the conversation, in the middle of a phrase, he suddenly jumped up and left the room.

'Send and let me know whether I may see her,' said the old Prince.

'All right, directly!' answered Levin, and, without pausing, went to her room.

She was not asleep, but was talking quietly with her mother, making plans for the christening.

Made neat, her hair brushed, a smart cap trimmed with something blue on her head, she lay on her back with her arms outside the quilt, and met his look with a look which drew him toward her. That look, already bright, grew still brighter as he approached. On her face was the same change from the earthly to that which was beyond earth, as is seen on the faces of the dead; but in their case it is a farewell, in hers it was a welcome. Again an agitation, similar to that which he had felt at the moment of the birth, gripped his heart. She took his hand and asked whether he had slept. He could not answer and, conscious of his weakness, turned away.

'And I have been dozing, Kostya!' she said. 'And now I feel so comfortable.'

She was gazing at him, but suddenly her face changed.

'Let me have him, Mary Vlasevna, and he will see him too!'

'Well then, we'll let Papa have a look,' said Mary Vlasevna, lifting something red, strange, and quivering and bringing it nearer. 'But wait a bit, let's first get dressed,' and Mary Vlasevna put the quivering red object on the bed, and began unwrapping it and then swaddling it again, raising and turning it with one finger, and powdering it with something.

Levin, gazing at this tiny piteous being, vainly searched his soul for some indications of paternal feeling. He felt nothing for it but repulsion. But when it was stripped and he caught a glimpse of thin, thin, little arms and legs saffron-coloured, but with fingers and toes, and even with thumbs distinguishable from the rest; and when he saw how, as though they were soft springs, Mary Vlasevna bent those little arms which stuck up, and encased them in linen garments, he was so filled with pity for that being, and so alarmed lest she should hurt it, that he tried to restrain her hand.

Mary Vlasevna laughed.

'Don't be afraid, don't be afraid!'

When the baby had been swaddled and made into a firm doll, Mary Vlasevna turned it over as if proud of her work, and stepped aside that Levin might see his son in all his beauty.

Kitty turned her eyes and gazed fixedly in the same direction. 'Let me have him, let me have him!' she said, and was even going to raise herself.

'What are you doing, Catherine Alexandrovna? You must not move like that! Wait a moment, I'll give him to you. Let's show Papa what a fine fellow we are!'

And Mary Vlasevna held out to Levin on one hand (the other merely supporting the nape of the shaky head) this strange, limp, red creature, that hid its head in its swaddling clothes. But there was also a nose, blinking eyes, and smacking lips.

'A beautiful baby!' said Mary Vlasevna.

Levin sighed bitterly. This beautiful baby only inspired him with a sense of repulsion and pity. These were not at all the feelings he had expected.

He turned away while Mary Vlasevna laid the child to the unaccustomed breast.

Suddenly a laugh made him lift his head. It was Kitty laughing. The baby had taken the breast.

'Well, that's enough! That's enough!' said Mary Vlasevna; but Kitty would not part with the baby. He fell asleep in her arms.

'Now look at him,' said Kitty, turning him so that Levin could see him. The old-looking little face wrinkled up still more and the baby sneezed.

Smiling, and hardly able to keep back tears of tenderness, Levin kissed his wife and quitted the darkened room.

What he felt toward this little creature was not at all what he had anticipated. There was nothing merry or joyful in it; on the contrary, there was a new and distressing sense of fear. It was the consciousness of another vulnerable region. And this consciousness was at first so painful, the fear lest that helpless being should suffer was so strong, that it quite hid the strange feeling of unreasoning joy and even pride which he experienced when the baby sneezed.

Excerpts from
SILAS MARNER

by George Eliot

George Eliot's Silas Marner *is the story of an isolated and suffering miser, a weaver named Marner. In the course of the novel, Marner is "saved" from his dismal fate by the arrival of a child. In telling his story, Eliot explores the part of parenthood that transcends a biological connection. She beautifully represents, too, not just the duties parents and children bear toward one another, but also the blessings that flow to each from meeting these obligations.*

In a part of the novel not reproduced here, the young Marner, then a religious man, suffers a shattering betrayal that destroys his faith. He moves from Lantern Yard, the scene of the betrayal, to the village of Raveloe. There he works at his loom, his money accumulates, and gradually it becomes his sole reason for living.

After fifteen years Marner's money is stolen, and this second blow threatens to destroy him altogether. Then one winter night, as he stands stock-still in a trance, a strange woman freezes to death in the snow, and her child, Eppie, wanders into Marner's home. Rejuvenated by her presence, Marner decides to keep Eppie and to rear her. For the next sixteen years she lives with him as his daughter.

Marner's dedication to her care returns him to the human family, restoring him to his community and his lost faith. But as Eppie approaches the brink of womanhood, her natural father, the wealthy and childless Godfrey Cass, makes himself known and seeks to take her back. Despite his offer of two powerful inducements—wealth and his blood relationship as her biological father—Eppie chooses to stay with Marner.

Two excerpts follow. The first describes Marner's new life as Eppie's father, and the many ways she broadens his narrow existence. The second relates what happens, years later, when Cass and his wife, Nancy, appear in Marner's home and propose adopting Eppie.

What does it mean—or what does it really take—to be a parent? How important are biological bonds in the relations between children and their parents? How do those relations link adults—"men and women with parental looks and tones"—to each other?

Why is Marner not placated by the prospect that Eppie, if taken from his home, would visit him? What decision would you have counseled Eppie to make? What, if anything, does Eppie owe to her biological father?

Excerpt 1

Marner has announced his intention to keep the toddler, Eppie, who has wandered into his home and his life. A neighbor, Dolly Winthrop, gives him practical advice about the child's care and presses him to have her christened, despite the possibility that this has already been done.

. . . Baby *was* christened, the rector deciding that a baptism was a lesser risk to incur; and on this occasion Silas, making himself as clean and tidy as he could, appeared for the first time within the church, and shared in the observances held sacred by his neighbours. He was quite unable, by means of anything he heard or saw, to identify the Raveloe religion with his old faith; if he could at any time in his previous life have done so, it must have been by the aid of a strong feeling ready to vibrate with sympathy, rather than by a comparison of phrases and ideas: and now for long years that feeling had been dormant. He had no distinct idea about the baptism and the church-going, except that Dolly had said it was for the good of the child; and in this way, as the weeks grew to months, the child created fresh and fresh links between his life and the lives from which he had hitherto shrunk continually into narrower isolation. Unlike the gold which needed nothing, and must be worshipped in close-locked solitude—which was hidden away from the daylight, was deaf to the song of birds, and started to no human tones—Eppie was a creature of endless claims and ever-growing desires, seeking and loving sunshine, and living sounds, and living movements; making trial of everything, with trust in new joy, and stirring the human kindness in all eyes that looked on her. The gold had kept his thoughts in an ever-repeated circle, leading to nothing beyond itself; but Eppie was an object compacted of changes and hopes that forced his thoughts onward, and carried them far away from their old eager pacing towards the same blank limit—carried them away to the new things that would come with the coming years, when Eppie would have learned to understand how her father Silas cared for her; and made him look for images of that time in the ties and charities that bound together the families of his neighbours. The gold had asked that he should sit weaving longer and longer, deafened and blinded more and more to all things except the monotony of his loom and the repetition of his web; but Eppie called him away from his weaving, and made him think all its pauses a holiday, reawakening his senses with her fresh life, even to the old winter-flies that came crawling forth in the early spring sunshine, and warming him into joy because *she* had joy. . . .

. . . Notwithstanding the difficulty of carrying her and his yarn or linen at the same time, Silas took her with him in most of his journeys to the farm-houses, unwilling to leave her behind at Dolly Winthrop's, who was always ready to take care of her; and little curly-headed Eppie, the weaver's child, became an object of interest at several out-lying home-steads, as well as in the village. Hitherto he had been treated very much as if he had been a useful gnome or brownie—a queer and unaccount-able creature, who must necessarily be looked at with wondering curios-ity and repulsion and with whom one would be glad to make all greetings and bargains as brief as possible, but who must be dealt with in a propi-tiatory way, and occasionally have a present of pork or garden stuff to carry home with him, seeing that without him there was no getting the yarn woven. But now Silas met with open smiling faces and cheerful questioning, as a person whose satisfactions and difficulties could be understood. Everywhere he must sit a little and talk about the child, and words of interest were always ready for him: "Ah, Master Marner, you'll be lucky if she takes the measles soon and easy!"—or, "Why, there isn't many lone men 'ud ha' been wishing to take up with a little un like that: but I reckon the weaving makes you handier than men as do outdoor work—you're partly as handy as a woman, for weaving comes next to spinning." Elderly masters and mistresses, seated observantly in large kitchen arm-chairs, shook their heads over the difficulties attendant on rearing children, felt Eppie's arms and legs, and pronounced them re-markably firm, and told Silas that, if she turned out well (which, howev-er, there was no telling), it would be a fine thing for him to have a steady lass to do for him when he got helpless. Servant maidens were fond of carrying her out to look at the hens and chickens, or to see if any cher-ries could be shaken down in the orchard; and the small boys and girls approached her slowly, with cautious movement and steady gaze, like little dogs face to face with one of their own kind, till attraction had reached the point at which the soft lips were put out for a kiss. No child was afraid of approaching Silas when Eppie was near him: there was no repulsion around him now, either for young or old, for the little child had come to link him once more with the whole world. There was love between him and the child that blent them into one, and there was love between the child and the world—from men and women with parental looks and tones, to the red lady-birds and the round pebbles.

Silas began now to think of Raveloe life entirely in relation to Eppie:

she must have everything that was a good in Raveloe; and he listened docilely, that he might come to understand better what this life was, from which, for fifteen years, he had stood aloof as from a strange thing, with which he could have no communion: as some man who has a precious plant to which he would give a nurturing home in a new soil, thinks of the rain and sunshine, and all influences, in relation to his nursling, and asks industriously for all knowledge that will help him to satisfy the wants of the searching roots, or to guard leaf and bud from invading harm. The disposition to hoard had been utterly crushed at the very first by the loss of his long-stored gold: the coins he earned afterwards seemed as irrelevant as stones brought to complete a house suddenly buried by an earthquake; the sense of bereavement was too heavy upon him for the old thrill of satisfaction to arise again at the touch of the newly-earned coin. And now something had come to replace his hoard which gave a growing purpose to the earnings, drawing his hope and joy continually onward beyond the money.

In old days there were angels who came and took men by the hand and led them away from the city of destruction. We see no white-winged angels now. But yet men are led away from threatening destruction; a hand is put into theirs, which leads them forth gently towards a calm and bright land, so that they look no more backward; and the hand may be a little child's. . . .

Excerpt 2

Sixteen years pass and Marner's gold is found. Cass reveals to his wife, Nancy, that Eppie is his child. The couple, having no children of their own, decide to adopt her. They appear in Marner's home and without explanation, offer to take Eppie, promising to make her their daughter and heir and to marry her to a man of their class. The unhappy Silas leaves the decision to Eppie, who refuses. Cass then reveals his "natural claim": Eppie, he announces, is his daughter.

. . . Eppie had given a violent start, and turned quite pale. Silas, on the contrary, who had been relieved, by Eppie's answer, from the dread lest his mind should be in opposition to hers, felt the spirit of resistance in him set free, not without a touch of parental fierceness. "Then, sir," he answered, with an accent of bitterness that had been silent in him since the memorable day when his youthful hope had perished[1]—"then, sir, why didn't you say so sixteen year ago, and claim her before I'd come to

---

[1] The early betrayal that cost him his faith.

love her, i'stead o' coming to take her from me now, when you might as well take the heart out o' my body? God gave her to me because you turned your back upon her, and He looks upon her as mine; you've no right to her! When a man turns a blessing from his door, it falls to them as take it in."

"I know that, Marner. I was wrong. I've repented of my conduct in that matter," said Godfrey, who could not help feeling the edge of Silas's words.

"I am glad to hear it, sir," said Marner, with gathering excitement; "but repentance doesn't alter what's been going on for sixteen year. Your coming now and saying 'I'm her father,' doesn't alter the feelings inside us. It's me she's been calling her father ever since she could say the word."

"But I think you might look at the thing more reasonably, Marner," said Godfrey, unexpectedly awed by the weaver's direct truth-speaking. "It isn't as if she was to be taken quite away from you, so that you'd never see her again. She'll be very near you, and come to see you very often. She'll feel just the same towards you."

"Just the same?" said Marner, more bitterly than ever. "How'll she feel just the same for me as she does now, when we eat o' the same bit, and drink o' the same cup, and think o' the same things from one day's end to another? Just the same? that's idle talk. You'd cut us i' two."

Godfrey, unqualified by experience to discern the pregnancy of Marner's simple words, felt rather angry again. It seemed to him that the weaver was very selfish (a judgment readily passed by those who have never tested their own power of sacrifice) to oppose what was undoubtedly for Eppie's welfare; and he felt himself called upon, for her sake, to assert his authority.

"I should have thought, Marner," he said, severely—"I should have thought your affection for Eppie would have made you rejoice in what was for her good, even if it did call upon you to give up something. You ought to remember your own life's uncertain, and she's at an age now when her lot may soon be fixed in a way very different from what it would be in her father's home: she may marry some low working-man, and then, whatever I might do for her, I couldn't make her well-off. You're putting yourself in the way of her welfare; and though I'm sorry to hurt you after what you've done, and what I've left undone, I feel now it's my duty to insist on taking care of my own daughter. I want to do my duty."

It would be difficult to say whether it were Silas or Eppie that was most deeply stirred by this last speech of Godfrey's. Thought had been very busy in Eppie as she listened to the contest between her old long-loved father and this new unfamiliar father who had suddenly come to fill the place of that black featureless shadow which had held the ring and placed it on her mother's finger. Her imagination had darted backward in conjectures, and forward in previsions, of what this revealed fatherhood implied; and there were words in Godfrey's last speech which helped to make the previsions especially definite. Not that these thoughts, either of past or future, determined her resolution—that was determined by the feelings which vibrated to every word Silas had uttered; but they raised, even apart from these feelings, a repulsion towards the offered lot and the newly-revealed father.

Silas, on the other hand, was again stricken in conscience, and alarmed lest Godfrey's accusation should be true—lest he should be raising his own will as an obstacle to Eppie's good. For many moments he was mute, struggling for the self-conquest necessary to the uttering of the difficult words. They came out tremulously.

"I'll say no more. Let it be as you will. Speak to the child. I'll hinder nothing."

Even Nancy, with all the acute sensibility of her own affections, shared her husband's view, that Marner was not justifiable in his wish to retain Eppie, after her real father had avowed himself. She felt that it was a very hard trial for the poor weaver, but her code allowed no question that a father by blood must have a claim above that of any foster-father. Besides, Nancy, used all her life to plenteous circumstances and the privileges of "respectability," could not enter into the pleasures which early nurture and habit connect with all the little aims and efforts of the poor who are born poor: to her mind, Eppie, in being restored to her birthright, was entering on a too long withheld but unquestionable good. Hence she heard Silas's words with relief, and thought, as Godfrey did, that their wish was achieved.

"Eppie, my dear," said Godfrey, looking at his daughter, not without some embarrassment, under the sense that she was old enough to judge him, "it'll always be our wish that you should show your love and gratitude to one who's been a father to you so many years, and we shall want to help you to make him comfortable in every way. But we hope you'll come to love us as well; and though I haven't been what a father should have been to you all these years, I wish to do the utmost in my power for you for the rest of my life, and provide for you as my only child. And you'll have the best of mothers in my wife—that'll be a blessing you haven't known since you were old enough to know it."

"My dear, you'll be a treasure to me," said Nancy, in her gentle voice. "We shall want for nothing when we have our daughter."

Eppie did not come forward and curtsy, as she had done before. She held Silas's hand in hers, and grasped it firmly—it was a weaver's hand, with a palm and finger-tips that were sensitive to such pressure—while she spoke with colder decision than before.

"Thank you, ma'am—thank you, sir, for your offers—they're very great, and far above my wish. For I should have no delight i' life any more if I was forced to go away from my father, and knew he was sitting at home, a-thinking of me and feeling lone. We've been used to be happy together every day, and I can't think o' no happiness without him. And he says he'd nobody i' the world till I was sent to him, and he'd have nothing when I was gone. And he's took care of me and loved me from the first, and I'll cleave to him as long as he lives, and nobody shall ever come between him and me."

"But you must make sure, Eppie," said Silas, in a low voice—"you must make sure as you won't ever be sorry, because you've made your choice to stay among poor folks, and with poor clothes and things, when you might ha' had everything o' the best."

His sensitiveness on this point had increased as he listened to Eppie's words of faithful affection.

"I can never be sorry, father," said Eppie. "I shouldn't know what to think on or to wish for with fine things about me, as I haven't been used to. And it 'ud be poor work for me to put on things, and ride in a gig, and sit in a place at church, as 'ud make them as I'm fond of think me unfitting company for 'em. What could I care for then?"

Nancy looked at Godfrey with a pained questioning glance. But his eyes were fixed on the floor, where he was moving the end of his stick, as if he were pondering on something absently. She thought there was a word which might perhaps come better from her lips than from his.

"What you say is natural, my dear child—it's natural you should cling to those who've brought you up," she said, mildly; "but there's a duty you owe to your lawful father. There's perhaps something to be given up on more sides than one. When your father opens his home to you, I think it's right you shouldn't turn your back on it."

"I can't feel as I've got any father but one," said Eppie, impetuously, while the tears gathered. "I've always thought of a little home where he'd sit i' the corner, and I should tend and do everything for him: I can't think o' no other home. I wasn't brought up to be a lady, and I can't turn my mind to it. I like the working-folks, and their houses, and their ways. And," she ended passionately, while the tears fell, "I'm promised to marry a working-man, as'll live with father, and help me to take care of him."

Godfrey looked up at Nancy with a flushed face and a smarting dilation of the eyes. This frustration of a purpose towards which he had set out under the exalted consciousness that he was about to compensate in some degree for the greatest demerit of his life, made him feel the air of the room stifling.

"Let us go," he said, in an undertone.

"We won't talk of this any longer now," said Nancy, rising. "We're your well-wishers, my dear—and yours too, Marner. We shall come and see you again. It's getting late now."

In this way she covered her husband's abrupt departure, for Godfrey had gone straight to the door, unable to say more.

Nancy and Godfrey walked home under the starlight in silence. When they entered the oaken parlour, Godfrey threw himself into his chair, while Nancy laid down her bonnet and shawl, and stood on the hearth near her husband, unwilling to leave him even for a few minutes, and yet fearing to utter any word lest it might jar on his feeling. At last Godfrey turned his head towards her, and their eyes met, dwelling in that meeting without any movement on either side. That quiet mutual gaze of a trusting husband and wife is like the first moment of rest or refuge from a great weariness or a great danger—not to be interfered with by speech or action which would distract the sensations from the fresh enjoyment of repose.

But presently he put out his hand, and as Nancy placed hers within it, he drew her towards him, and said—"That's ended!"

She bent to kiss him, and then said, as she stood by his side, "Yes, I'm afraid we must give up the hope of having her for a daughter. It wouldn't be right to want to force her to come to us against her will. We can't alter her bringing up and what's come of it."

"No," said Godfrey, with a keen decisiveness of tone, in contrast with his usually careless and unemphatic speech—"there's debts we can't pay like money debts, by paying extra for the years that have slipped by. While I've been putting off and putting off, the trees have been growing—it's too late now. Marner was in the right in what he said about a man's turning away a blessing from his door: it falls to somebody else. I wanted to pass for childless once, Nancy[2]—I shall pass for childless now against my wish."

---

[2] When he first learned of his illegitimate daughter.

AFTER MAKING LOVE WE HEAR FOOTSTEPS

by Galway Kinnell

Galway Kinnell's poem invites us to ponder the procreative meaning of love-making by focusing on the mysterious bonds between a child and his parents and between the parents themselves in relation to their child. The poet describes how his son Fergus, ever a sound sleeper, imperturbable even by his father's raucous noises, is uncannily roused from sleep by the sounds of his parents' love-making and comes running to "flop down" between them in the marital bed. The poem concludes by recounting the reaction of the parents/ lovers to Fergus's "return" into their embrace.

We are moved to ask many questions, about both child and parents. What sort of a boy is Fergus? Why do only these sounds "sing [him] awake"? Why does he come running? What is the "habit of memory" that propels him "to the ground of his making"? Why is it that, lying beneath his parents' arms and snuggled back to sleep, his face is "gleam[ing] with satisfaction at being this very child"?

Fergus's face may beam satisfaction, but his parents smile. They can sense how important their presence is to him; but he cannot know what he means to them. What does the poet mean by calling the sounds of love-making "mortal sounds," and in what senses are they capable of "singing awake" the sleeping child? Is it only their son's footsteps that the love-makers hear, or do they also hear footsteps of the "grim reaper," as it were, "behind" them? Would immortal beings hear footsteps? Would their sexual activity be "making love"? What enables the parents to see Fergus as a blessing, as "this blessing," and as a "gift of love"—and do they see rightly? In the last line, what is the meaning of "again"? When did their embrace first accept the gift of Fergus?

Does this understanding of the meaning of love-making require hearing (or being prepared to hear) the footsteps of one's own child?

For I can snore like a bullhorn
Or play loud music
or sit up talking with any reasonably sober Irishman
and Fergus will only sink deeper
into his dreamless sleep, which goes by all in one flash,
but let there be that heavy breathing
or a stifled come-cry anywhere in the house
and he will wrench himself awake
and make for it on the run—as now, we lie together,
after making love, quiet, touching along the length of our bodies,
familiar touch of the long-married,
and he appears—in his baseball pajamas, it happens,
the neck opening so small
he has to screw them on, which one day may make him wonder
about the mental capacity of baseball players—
and flops down between us and hugs us and snuggles himself to
sleep,
his face gleaming with satisfaction at being this very child.
In the half darkness we look at each other
and smile
and touch arms across his little, startlingly muscled body—
this one whom habit of memory propels to the ground of his
making,
sleeper only the mortal sounds can sing awake,
this blessing love gives again into our arms.

Excerpts from
THE DUKE OF DECEPTION
by Geoffrey Wolff

The Duke of Deception, by Geoffrey Wolff, is a son's memoir of his late
father, a lifelong con man who saw the core facts of his identity as "ideas" he
could manipulate. What does a child owe to a parent who has let him down?

  The first of the attached excerpts is the introduction, in which Wolff learns
of his father's death and responds with words that shock his listeners and himself. The second is from the opening chapter, in which he introduces his father
and announces his intention—per what he imagines to have been his father's
wish—to tell the truth about him. The third is an excerpt from the book's
closing chapter. Here Wolff returns to the night when he learned his father was
gone, describes what followed his outburst, and attempts to sort out what he
thinks of the man who had never "seen in my face intimations of his own
mortality."

  "I am his creature, as well as his get . . ." Wolff writes, "trained as his
instrument of perpetuation." Wolff believes he was expected to perpetuate his
father by writing about him. Yet this story about his father begins and ends
with desperate expressions of love for his own sons, and of his desire to shield
them from harm. Why does Wolff's solicitude for his children take center stage
in this story about his father? Every child is his or her parents' "instrument of
perpetuation," but does Wolff see his "instruments" differently from the way
his father saw him?

  Recounting a friend's memorable warning about the perils of writing about
one's father, Wolff resolves to avoid "mere piety." Should a son avoid piety in
publishing his father's life story? Wolff says he believes his father would respect
his wish to tell the truth. Is Wolff deceiving himself?

  When his father dies, Wolff struggles with his feelings for his father. Why
are we so powerfully driven to love our parents, even when they are deeply
flawed?

  Wolff praises his father for never seeing in him "intimations of his own
mortality." Does Wolff see these intimations in his own children? Might his
father have been a better parent if he had seen them in Wolff?

From THE DUKE OF DECEPTION: MEMORIES OF MY FATHER by Geoffrey
Wolff, copyright © 1979 by Geoffrey Wolff. Used by permission of Random House,
Inc.

What, finally, is Wolff's assessment of his father and the gifts he received? Is his account, in the end, an act of love and piety?

Opening The Door

On a sunny day in a sunny humor I could sometimes think of death as mere gossip, the ugly rumor behind that locked door over there. This was such a day, the last of July at Narragansett on the Rhode Island shore.

My wife's grandmother was a figure of legend in Rhode Island, a tenacious grandam near ninety with a classic New Englander's hooked and broken beak, six feet tall in her low-heeled, sensible shoes. A short time ago she had begun a career as a writer; this had brought her satisfaction and some small local celebrity. She spent her summers in Narragansett surrounded by the houses of her five children and by numberless cousins and grandchildren and great-grandchildren. One of these, my son Nicholas, not quite four, had just left for a ride with her. As old as she was she liked to drive short distances in her black Ford sedan, but she maintained a lively regard for her survival, and had cinched in her seat belt, tight.

Nicholas's little brother Justin was with his mother at the beach. I was with my wife's brother-in-law on a friend's shaded terrace. Kay's house was old and shingled, impeccably neglected. It was almost possible to disbelieve in death that day, to put out of mind a son's unbuckled seat belt and the power of surf at the water's edge. I looked past trimmed hedges at the rich lawn; beyond the lawn a shelf of clean rocks angled to the sea. Sitting in an overstuffed wicker chair, gossiping with Kay and a couple of her seven children, protected from the sun, glancing at sailboats beating out to Block Island, listening to bees hum, smelling roses and fresh-cut grass, I felt drowsy, off-guard.

We had been drinking rum. Not too much, but enough; our voices were pitched low. Usually the house was loud with laughter and recorded music—all those children, after all—but this was a subdued moment. We were drinking black rum with tonic and lime; I remember chewing the lime's tart flesh.

In my memory now, as in some melodrama, I hear the phone ring, but I didn't hear it then. The phone in that house seemed always to be ringing. My wife's brother-in-law John was called to the telephone; I guessed it was my wife's sister, fetching us home to our mother-in-law's. We always lingered too long with Kay.

John returned to the terrace. He stood thirty feet from where I sat supporting my drink on my shirt. I remember the icy feel of the glass against my chest. John was smirking, shifting from one foot to the other. John was a man to stand still, with fixed serenity, and my chest cramped. As I stared down the terrace at him, Kay and her children quit talking, and John's cheeks began to dance. I looked at the widow Kay, she looked away, and I knew what I knew. I walked down that terrace to learn which of my boys was dead.

Justin was as sturdy as a fireplug: he once ate an orange-juice glass down to its stem; it didn't seem to trouble him. Another time was different: Running across a meadow he tripped, gave a choked cry, nothing out of the way. We walked toward him casually, paying no attention. We were annoyed to find him face forward in the mud. His mother said, "Get up," but he didn't. He liked to tease us. I rolled him over, and his face was gray patched with pale green. His eyes had rolled back in his head: His brother began to cry; he had understood before we had, and his rage was awful. I tried to breathe life into my son, but in my clumsiness I neglected to pinch shut his nose. I blew and wept into his mouth, and tried to pry it open wider, just to do something, but mostly I wept on his face. My wife shouted at no one to call a doctor, but she knew it was useless. He was dead, any fool could see, and we didn't know why. Then he opened his eyes, went stiff with fear, began to cry. And upon the stroke of our deliverance I began to tremble. We are naked, all of us, I know, and it is cold. But Justin, it seemed then, was invulnerable.

So it was Nicholas.

John said: "Your father is dead."

And I said: "Thank God."

John recoiled from my words. I heard someone behind me gasp. The words did not then strike a blow above my heart but later they did, and there was no calling them back, there is no calling them back now. All I can do now is try to tell what they meant.

Chapter 1

I listen for my father and I hear a stammer. This was explosive and unashamed, not a choking on words but a spray of words. His speech was headlong, edgy, breathless: there was neither room in his mouth nor time in the day to contain what he burned to utter. I have a remnant of that stammer, and I wish I did not; I stammer and blush, my father would stammer and grin. He depended on a listener's good will. My father depended excessively upon people's good will.

As he spoke straight at you, so did he look at you. He could stare down anyone, though this was a gift he rarely practiced. To me, everything about him seemed outsized. Doing a school report on the Easter Islanders I found in an encyclopedia pictures of their huge sculptures, and there he was, massive head and nose, nothing subtle or delicate. He was in fact (and how diminishing those words, *in fact,* look to me now) an inch or two above six feet, full bodied, a man who lumbered from here to there with deliberation. When I was a child I noticed that people were respectful of the cubic feet my father occupied; later I understood that I had confused respect with resentment.

I recollect things, a gentleman's accessories, deceptively simple fabrications of silver and burnished nickel, of brushed Swedish stainless, of silk and soft wool and brown leather. I remember his shoes, so meticulously selected and cared for and used, thin-soled, with cracked uppers, older than I was or could ever be, shining dully and from the depths. Just a pair of shoes? No: I knew before I knew any other complicated thing that for my father there was nothing he possessed that was "just" something. His pocket watch was not "just" a timepiece, it was a miraculous instrument with a hinged front and a representation on its back of porcelain ducks rising from a birch-girt porcelain pond. It struck the hour unassertively, musically, like a silver tine touched to a crystal glass, no hurry, you might like to know it's noon.

He despised black leather, said black shoes reminded him of black attaché cases, of bankers, lawyers, look-before-you-leapers anxious not to offend their clients. He owned nothing black except his dinner jacket and his umbrella. His umbrella doubled as a shooting-stick, and one afternoon at a polo match at Brandywine he was sitting on it when a man asked him what he would do if it rained, sit wet or stand dry? I laughed. My father laughed also, but tightly, and he did not reply; nor did he ever again use this quixotic contraption. He took things, *things,* seriously.

My father, called Duke, taught me skills and manners; he taught me to shoot and to drive fast and to read respectfully and to box and to handle a boat and to distinguish between good jazz music and bad jazz music. He was patient with me, led me to understand for myself why Billie Holiday's understatements were more interesting than Ella Fitzgerald's complications. His codes were not novel, but they were rigid, the rules of decorum that Hemingway prescribed. A gentleman kept his word, and favored simplicity of sentiment; a gentleman chose his words with care, as he chose his friends. A gentleman accepted responsibility for his acts, and welcomed the liberty to act unambiguously. A gentleman was a stickler for precision and punctilio; life was no more than an inventory of small choices that together formed a man's character, entire. A gentleman was this, and not that; a *man* did, did not, said, would not say.

My father could, however, be coaxed to reveal his bona fides. He had been schooled at Groton and passed along to Yale. He was just barely prepared to intimate that he had been tapped for "Bones," and I remember his pleasure when Levi Jackson, the black captain of Yale's 1948 football team, was similarly honored by that secret society. He was proud of Skull and Bones for its hospitality toward the exotic. He did sometimes wince, however, when he pronounced Jackson's Semitic Christian name, and I sensed that his tolerance for Jews was not inclusive; but I never heard him indulge express bigotry, and the first of half a dozen times he hit me was for having called a neighbor's kid a guinea.

There was much luxury in my father's affections, and he hated what was narrow, pinched, or mean. He understood exclusion, mind you, and lived his life believing the world to be divided between a few *us's* and many *thems*, but I was to understand that aristocracy was a function of taste, courage, and generosity. About two other virtues—candor and reticence—I was confused, for my father would sometimes proselytize the one, sometimes the other.

If Duke's preoccupation with bloodlines was finite, this did not cause him to be unmindful of his ancestors. He knew whence he had come, and whither he meant me to go. I saw visible evidence of this, a gold signet ring which I wear today, a heavy bit of business inscribed arsy-turvy with lions and flora and a motto, *nulla vestigium retrorsit*. "Don't look back" I was told it meant.

After Yale—class of late nineteen-twenty something, or early nineteen-thirty something—my father batted around the country, living a high life in New York among school and college chums, flying as a test pilot, marrying my mother, the daughter of a rear admiral. I was born a year after the marriage, in 1937, and three years after that my father went to England as a fighter pilot with Eagle Squadron, a group of American volunteers in the Royal Air Force. Later he transferred to the OSS, and was in Yugoslavia with the partisans; just before the Invasion he was parachuted into Normandy, where he served as a sapper with the Resistance, which my father pronounced *ray-zee-staunce*.

His career following the war was for me mysterious in its particulars; in the service of his nation, it was understood, candor was not always possible. This much was clear: my father mattered in the world, and was satisfied that he mattered, whether or not the world understood precise-ly why he mattered.

A pretty history for an American clubman. Its fault is that it was not true. My father was a bullshit artist. True, there were many boarding schools, each less pleased with the little Duke than the last, but none of them was Groton. There was no Yale, and by the time he walked from a room at a mention of Skull and Bones I knew this, and he knew that I knew it. No military service would have him; his teeth were bad. So he had his teeth pulled and replaced, but the Air Corps and Navy and Army and Coast Guard still thought he was a bad idea. The ring I wear was made according to his instructions by a jeweler two blocks from Schwab's drugstore in Hollywood, and was never paid for. The motto, engraved backwards so that it would come right on a red wax seal, is dog Latin and means in fact "leave no trace behind," but my father did not believe me when I told him this.

My father was a Jew. This did not seem to him a good idea, and so it was his notion to disassemble his history, begin at zero, and re-create himself. His sustaining line of work till shortly before he died was as a confidence man. If I now find his authentic history more surprising, more interesting, than his counterfeit history, he did not. He would not make peace with his actualities, and so he was the author of his own circumstances, and indifferent to the consequences of this nervy pro-gram.

There were some awful consequences, for other people as well as for him. He was lavish with money, with others' money. He preferred to stiff institutions: jewelers, car dealers, banks, fancy hotels. He was, that is, a thoughtful buccaneer, when thoughtfulness was convenient. But people were hurt by him. Much of his mischief was casual enough: I lost a tooth when I was six, and the Tooth Fairy, "financially inconvenienced" or "temporarily out of pocket," whichever was then his locution, left under my pillow an IOU, a sight draft for two bits, or two million. . . .

. . . Well, I'm left behind. One day, writing about my father with no want of astonishment and love, it came to me that I am his creature as well as his get. I cannot now shake this conviction, that I was trained as his instrument of perpetuation, put here to put him into the record. And that my father knew this, calculated it to a degree. How else ex-plain his eruption of rage when I once gave up what he and I called "writing" for journalism? I had taken a job as the book critic of *The Washington Post*, was proud of myself; it seemed then like a wonderful job, honorable and enriching. My father saw it otherwise: "You have failed me," he wrote, "you have sold yourself at discount," he wrote to me, his prison number stamped below his name.

He was wrong then, but he was usually right about me. He would listen to anything I wished to tell him, but would not tell me only what I wished to hear. He retained such solicitude for his clients. With me he was strict and straight, except about himself. And so I want to be strict and straight with him, and with myself. Writing to a friend about this book, I said that I would not now for anything have had my father be other than what he was, except happier, and that most of the time he was happy enough, cheered on by imaginary successes. He gave me a great deal, and not merely life, and I didn't want to bellyache; I wanted, I told my friend, to thumb my nose on his behalf at everyone who had limited him. My friend was shrewd, though, and said that he didn't believe me, that I couldn't mean such a thing, that if I followed out its implications I would be led to a kind of ripe sentimentality, and to mere piety. Perhaps, he wrote me, you would not have wished him to lie to himself, to lie about being a Jew. Perhaps you would have him fool others but not so deeply trick himself. "In writing about a father," my friend wrote me about our fathers, "one clambers up a slippery mountain, carrying the balls of another in a bloody sack, and whether to eat them or worship them or bury them decently is never cleanly decided."

So I will try here to be exact. I wish my father had done more headlong, more elegant inventing. I believe he would respect my wish, be willing to speak with me seriously about it, find some nobility in it. But now he is dead, and he had been dead two weeks when they found him. And in his tiny flat at the edge of the Pacific they found no address book, no batch of letters held with a rubber band, no photograph. Not a thing to suggest that he had ever known another human being. . . .

Through the Open Door

In his final chapter, the author returns to the afternoon when he learned of his father's death.

. . . Now, driving home from Kay's terrace where I had just learned of my father's death, trying to think of my father, I thought instead of Kay's husband. He wore a wooden leg, got around well on it, elaborated jokes about it. He had flown wearing it in the Air Corps, and had escaped from a German POW camp wearing it. People who knew this man loved him, while he was alive. But he shot himself in a spectacularly cruel way, perhaps not calculated to do maximum hurt to his four children and three stepchildren, but having that end, and the damage he did to his wife was incalculable. Driving to my in-laws' house I thought of that suicide. Why would anyone choose so casually to empty so much life from himself? . . .

. . . From my in-laws' house I telephoned my mother, and told her as much as I knew, and for the first time I heard my mother weep. . . . When I had finished with the telephone about suppertime, Priscilla asked me if I wanted to eat. I said I wasn't hungry. She said she was sleepy, and would go to bed. I followed her to the guest room, expecting her to mourn with me. She wouldn't. I grew angry to the point of violence. I didn't understand her coldness, but I do now.

I had felt ashamed of my father in her father's house, and now I was ashamed of my shame, and ashamed to be there at all, under that roof. It was as though to accept their hospitality were to collaborate in their judgment of my father. I thought I knew what they thought of him, and I knew what they thought of me. Sometimes in that house I felt Priscilla look at me through her parents' eyes, and I thought that house in Narragansett was a place where my father would not have been made to feel welcome. I tried to forget the night of his death that neither had he been welcome those past ten years in my own house, and in my eagerness to forget this I repudiated all of them, my wife and her parents, and now Priscilla says she has never seen me so cold or so angry. She withdrew, would not dishonor any of us by seeming to feel what she did not. I wanted her to love my father now. I wanted to love my father now. How could she, if I could not? She had never seen him, had heard his voice once across telephone wires. We had promised him and ourselves a visit to California, but we never went. Every time we settled on a date to show my father his first grandson, and then his second, something happened, he got put away again or pulled a fast move on me or we decided we'd rather visit Madrid, ski in Austria.

I think that for a few hours that night I hated my wife. I drove to a seedy Narragansett roadhouse, a rough bar with a tropical motif where surfers hung out. I wanted a fight. I sat at the bar drinking whiskey chased by beer, scowling and muttering at friendly strangers wearing cut-offs and clean, jokey T-shirts. The beachboys were tan, pacific, easy; surfers had no beef with me. I shut the place down and drove flat out to Kay's house. I wanted to explain to her, at once, why I had thanked God that my father was dead. I wanted her to know that my words were not an atheist's unfelt exclamation, and that they did not only display relief that my children were alive. They also meant what they seemed to mean, that I thanked someone that my father had been delivered from the world, and I had been delivered from him.

I woke my friend three hours before dawn. . . .

The author and Kay reminisce about his late father and her late husband, and he is consoled.

. . . I had felt betrayed by my father, and wanted to betray him. Kay turned my course. She had the authority of someone who had passed through the worst of fires. I listened to her. I saw again what I had seen when I was a child, in love with my father as with no one else. He had never repudiated me or seen in my face intimations of his own mortality. He had never let me think he wished to be rid of me or the burden of my judgment, even when I had hounded him about his history, had quibbled with its details like a small-print artist, like a reviewer, for God's sake! He didn't try to form me in his own image. How could he? Which image to choose? He had wanted me to be happier than he had been, to do better. He had taught me many things, some of which were important, some of which he meant, some of which were true. The things he told me were the right things to tell a son, usually, and by the time I understood their source in mendacity they had done what good they could. I had been estranged from my father by my apprehension of other people's opinions of him, and by a compulsion to be free of his chaos and destructions. I had forgotten I loved him, mostly, and mostly now I missed him. I miss him.

When I finally left Kay's house I felt these things, some for the first time. I drove home slowly, and stopped at stop signs. The door to the room I shared with Priscilla was open when I came in, but I didn't go through that door that night. I went to my children's room. I stood above Justin, looking down at him. And then my son Nicholas began to moan, quietly at first. They did not know their grandfather was dead; they knew nothing about their grandfather. There would be time for that. I resolved to tell them what I could, and hoped they would want to know as much as I could tell. Nicholas cried out in his sleep, as he had so many times before, dragging me out of nightmares about his death with his own nightmares about his death, his dreams of cats with broken legs, broken-winged screaming birds, deer caught in traps, little boys hurt and crying, beyond the range of their parents' hearing. Sometimes I dreamt of my son bleeding to death from some simple wound I had neglected to learn to mend.

Now I smoothed his forehead as my father had smoothed mine when I was feverish. Justin breathed deeply. I crawled in bed beside my sweet Nicholas and took him in my arms and began to rock him in time to

Justin's regular breaths. I stunk of whiskey and there was blood on my face from a fall leaving Kay's house, but I knew I couldn't frighten my son. He ceased moaning, and I rocked him in my arms till light came down on us, and he stirred awake in my arms as I, in his, fell into a sleep free of dreams.

Excerpt from
THE MISTRESS OF HUSABY (KRISTIN LAVRANSDATTER, VOL. 2)

by Sigrid Undset, translated by Charles Archer

Sigrid Undset's Kristin Lavransdatter is the life story, in three volumes, of a fictional noblewoman from fourteenth-century Norway. The excerpts that follow invite readers to consider the associations between one's behavior in the present, one's regard for one's ancestors, and one's regard for generations to come.

At the end of the first volume the heroine, Kristin, marries a high-ranking nobleman named Erlend Nikulausson. Although her father, Lavrans Bjorgulfson, ultimately permits this wedding, the heedless Erlend was not the man he had chosen or would have chosen for Kristin, and he is unhappy about the marriage.

His fears are prophetic. In the early days of what is to be a troubled marriage, Kristin discovers the depth and reach of her husband's carelessness.

Though Erlend loves Kristin, he has lived a dissolute life. By the time he met her, an adulterous affair had already cost him his reputation and a significant portion of his inherited wealth. Unbeknownst to anyone but her, Kristin is pregnant with Erlend's child when she is married. She therefore begins her wedded life burdened by guilt, and by fear that her unborn child will be punished for her sin. (The child is born healthy.)

The attached passage, from the opening of volume 2, describes the newlyweds' arrival at Erlend's manor, Husaby, which is to be their married home. Already Kristin is beginning to think about preserving her children's inheritance from further erosion. During the several days of festivities that mark their homecoming, she notices with dismay the neglect into which the property has been permitted to fall, and compares her husband's home to the orderly and prosperous one she has just left.

How is the care of a household connected to care for those within it? In disregarding his property, what else has Erlend disregarded? Is there any signif-

icance to the relationship between the words "husband" and "husbandry"? What does Erlend's husbandry augur for his fatherhood?

Like any new wife—and certainly like any pregnant wife—Kristin becomes curious about her husband's forbears. She discovers, though, that he knows next to nothing about them. Again, the homesick bride cannot help comparing her new husband to her father, who honored his ancestors.

How might respect for ancestors—filial piety—be related to spiritual piety? To reverence for life?

Is there a connection between one's attitude toward the past and how one lives in the present? Is there a connection between how one lives in the present and one's attitude toward the future?

Erlend at last discovers Kristin's pregnancy. What passions guide his reaction? How might a different sort of man have reacted?

. . . On the third day the guests began to break up, and by the hour of nones on the fifth day the last of them were gone, and Kristin was alone with her husband at Husaby.

The first thing she did was to bid the serving-folk take all the bed-gear out of the bed, wash it and the walls round about it with lye, and carry out and burn up the straw. Then she had the bedstead filled with fresh straw, and above it made up the bed with bed-clothes from the store she had brought with her. It was late in the night before this work was at an end. But Kristin gave order that the same should be done with all the beds on the place, and that the skin rugs should be well baked in the bath-house—the maids must set to the work in the morning the first thing, and get as much done towards it as they could before the Sunday holiday. Erlend shook his head and laughed—she was a housewife indeed! But he was not a little ashamed.

For Kristin had not had much sleep the first night, even though the priests had blessed her bed. 'Twas spread above with silken pillows, with sheets of linen and the bravest rugs and furs; but beneath was dirty, mouldy straw, and there were lice in the bed-clothes and in the splendid black bearskin that was spread over all.

Many things had she seen already in these few days. Behind the costly tapestry hangings, the unwashed walls were black with dirt and soot. At the feast there had been masses of food, but much of it spoilt with ill dressing and ill service. And to make up the fires they had had naught but green and wet logs, that would scarce catch fire, and that filled the hall with smoke. Everywhere she had seen ill husbandry, when on the second day she went round with Erlend and looked over the manor and farm. By the time the feasting was over, little would be left in barn and storehouse; the corn-bins were all but swept clean. And she could not understand how Erlend could think to keep all the horses and so many cattle through the winter on the little hay and straw that was in the barns—of leaf-fodder there was not enough even for the sheep and goats.

But there was a loft half full of flax that had been left lying unused— there must have been the greatest part of many years' harvest. And then a storehouse full of old, old unwashed and stinking wool, some in sacks and some lying loose in heaps. When Kristin took up a handful, a shower of little brown eggs fell from it—moth and maggots had got into it.

The cattle were wretched, lean, galled and scabby; and never had she seen so many aged beasts together, in one place. Only the horses were comely and well-tended. But, even so, there was no one of them that was the equal of Guldsveinen or of Ringdrotten, the stallion her father had now. Slöngvanbauge, the horse he had given her to take along with her from home, was the fairest beast in the Husaby stables. When she came to him, she had to go and throw her arms round his neck and press her face against his cheek.

She thought on her father's face, when the time came for her to ride away with Erlend and he lifted her to the saddle. He had put on an air of gladness, for many folk were standing round them; but she had seen his eyes. He stroked her arm downwards, and held her hand in his for farewell. At the moment, it might be, she had thought most how glad she was that she was to get away at last. But now it seemed to her that as long as she lived her soul would be wrung with pain when she remembered her father's eyes at that hour.

And so Kristin Lavransdatter began to guide and order all things in her house. She was up at cock-crow every morning, though Erlend raised his voice against it, and made as though he would keep her in bed by force—surely no one expected a newly-married wife to rush about from house to house long before 'twas daylight. When she saw in what an ill way all things were here, and how much there was for to set her hand to, a thought shot through her clear and hard; if she had burdened her soul with sin that she might come hither, let it even be so—but 'twas no less sin to deal with God's gifts as they had been dealt with here. Shame upon the folk that had had the guidance of things here, and on all them that had let Erlend's goods go so to waste! There had been no fit steward at Husaby for the last two years; Erlend himself had been much away from home in that time, and besides, he understood but little of the management of the estate. 'Twas no more than was to be looked for, then, that his bailiffs in the outlying parishes should cheat him, as she was sure they did, and that the serving-folk at Husaby should work only as much as they pleased, and when and how it chanced to suit them. 'Twould be no light task for her to put things right again.

One day she talked of these things with Ulf Haldorssön, Erlend's own henchman. They ought to have had the threshing done by now, at least of the corn from the home farm—and there was none too much of it either—before the time came to slaughter for winter meat. Ulf said: ". . . I can well believe it, Kristin—that you will have no easy task this winter . . . "'Twere no easy thing for any woman," he went on, "to come hither to this house—after all that has come and gone. And yet, Mistress Kristin, I deem that you will win through it better than most could have done. You are not the woman to sit down and moan and whimper; but you will set your thoughts on saving your children's inheritance yourself, since none else here takes thought for such things. . . ."

She questioned Erlend about the life here at Husaby in ancient days. But he knew strangely little. Things were thus and thus, he had heard; but he could not remember so nicely. King Skule had owned the manor and built on it—'twas said he had meant to make Husaby his dwelling-place, when he gave away Rein for a nunnery. Erlend was right proud of his descent from the Duke, whom he always called King, and from Bishop Nikulaus; the Bishop was the father of his grandfather, Munan Bishopsson. But it seemed to Kristin that he knew no more of these men than she herself knew already from her father's tales. At home it was otherwise. Neither her father nor her mother was overproud of the power of their forbears and the high esteem they had enjoyed. But they spoke often of them; held up the good that they knew of them as a pattern, and told of their faults and the evil that had come of them as a warning. And they had little tales of mirth too—of Ivar Gjesling the Old and his quarrel with King Sverre; of Ivar Provst's quick and witty sallies; of Haavard Gjesling's huge bulk; and of Ivar Gjesling the Young's wonderful luck in the chase. Lavrans told of his grandfather's brother that carried off the Folkunga maid from Vreta cloister; of his grandfather's mother Ramborg Sunesdatter, who longed always for her home in Wester Gothland and at last went through the ice and was lost, when driving on Lake Vener one time she was staying with her brother at Solberga. He told of his father's prowess in arms, and of his unspeakable sorrow over his young first wife, Kristin Sigurdsdatter, that died in childbirth when Lavrans was born. And he read, from a book, of his ancestress the holy Lady Elin of Skövde, who was given grace to be one of God's blood-witnesses. Her father had often spoken of making a pilgrimage with Kristin to the grave of this holy widow. But it had never come to pass.

In her fear and distress, Kristin tried to pray to this saint that she herself was linked to by the tie of blood. She prayed to St. Elin for her child, kissing the reliquary that she had had of her father; in it was a shred of the holy lady's shroud. But Kristin was afraid of St. Elin, now when she had brought such shame on her race. When she prayed to St. Olav and St. Thomas for their intercession, she often felt that her complaints found a way to living ears and merciful hearts. These two martyrs for righteousness her father loved above all other saints; above even St. Laurentius himself, though this was the saint he was called after, and in honour of whose day in the late summer he always held a great drinking-feast and gave richly in alms. St. Thomas her father had himself seen in his dreams one night when he lay wounded outside Baagahus. No tongue could tell how lovely and venerable he was to look on, and Lavrans himself had been able to say naught but "Lord! Lord!" But the radiant figure in the Bishop's raiment had gently touched his wounds and promised that he should have his life and the use of his limbs, so that he should see again his wife and his daughter, according to his prayer. But at that time no man had believed that Lavrans Björgulfsön could live the night through.

Aye, said Erlend. One heard of such things. Naught of the kind had ever befallen him, and to be sure 'twas not like that it should—for he had never been a pious man, such as Lavrans was.

Then Kristin asked of all the folk who had been at their homecoming feast. Erlend had not much to say of them either. It seemed to Kristin that her husband was not much like the folks of this country-side. They were comely folk, many of them, fair and ruddy of hue, with round hard heads and bodies strong and heavily built—many of the older folks were hugely fat. Erlend looked like a strange bird among his guests. He was a head taller than most of the men, slim and lean, with slender limbs and fine joints. And he had black silky hair and was pale brown of hue—but with light-blue eyes under coal-black brows and long black eyelashes. His forehead was high and narrow, the temples hollow, the nose somewhat too great and the mouth something too small and weak for a man— but he was comely none the less; she had seen no man that was half so fair as Erlend. Even his mellow, quiet voice was unlike the others' thick full-fed utterance.

Erlend laughed and said his forbears were not of these parts either— only his grandfather's mother, Ragnfrid Skulesdatter. Folks said he was much like his mother's father, Gaute Erlendssön of Skogheim. Kristin asked what he knew about this grandfather. But it proved to be almost nothing.

One night Erlend and Kristin were undressing in the hall. Erlend could not get his shoe-latchet unloosed; as he cut it, the knife slipped and gashed his hand. He bled much and swore savagely. Kristin fetched a piece of linen from her chest. She was in her shift. As she was binding up his hand, Erlend passed his other arm around her waist.

Of a sudden he looked down into her face with fear and confusion in his eyes, and his face grew red as fire. Kristin bowed her head. Erlend took away his arm, saying nothing—then Kristin went off in silence and crept into the bed. Her heart beat with hard dull strokes against her ribs. Now and again she looked over at her husband. He had turned his back to her, and was slowly drawing off one garment after another. At last he came to the bed and lay down.

Kristin waited for him to speak. She waited so, that at times, 'twas as though her heart no longer beat, but only stood still and quivered in her breast.

But Erlend said no word. Nor did he take her in his arms. At last, falteringly, he laid a hand across her breast and pressed his chin down on her shoulder so strongly that the stubble of his beard pricked her skin. As he still spoke not a word, Kristin turned to the wall.

It was as though she were sinking, sinking. Not a word could he find to give her—now when he knew that she had borne his child within her all this long weary time. She clenched her teeth hard in the dark. Never would she beg and beseech—if he chose to be silent, she would be silent too, even, if need be, till the day she bore his child. Bitterness surged through her heart; but she lay stock-still against the wall. And Erlend too lay still in the dark. Hour after hour they lay thus, and each knew that the other was not sleeping. At last she heard by his even breathing that he had fallen asleep; and then she let the tears flow as they would, in sorrow and bitterness and shame. Never, it seemed to her, could she forgive him this.

Excerpts from
THE ILIAD OF HOMER
Meeting of Glaukos and Diomedes and
Meeting of Hektor and Andromache
translated by Richmond Lattimore

Homer's ancient epic The Iliad *tells the story of heroes immersed in the war between the Achaians (Greeks) and the Trojans. The poem recounts how heroes, human beings who are descended from gods and thus acutely conscious of their own mortality, seek to cheat death by winning immortal glory on the battlefield. This they accomplish by testing their strength and courage in hand-to-hand combat with worthy opponents—men of similar lineage and prowess.*

The two exerpts that follow, both taken from book 6, invite reflection on the importance of lineage to these heroes. The first rehearses the meeting on the battlefield of Diomedes, son of Tydeus (a Greek) and Glaukos, son of Hippolochus (a Trojan. Because of the importance of lineage, heroes are seldom announced without their patronymics). As they approach one another in the heat of battle, Diomedes remembers a story about the fate of men who fight against gods, and asks Glaukos to identify himself. Glaukos responds by sketching a remarkable image of leaves and trees. The image conveys his awareness that one might pass through life undifferentiated from other men and leaving no trace behind. Nonetheless, Glaukos then offers a history of his family, in which men did distinguish themselves.

Diomedes, in turn, is prompted to recall his own ancestry. In so doing he notes with delight that his grandfather had played host to Glaukos', and that the two had exchanged gifts. As a result, he proposes that he and Glaukos not fight each other, but instead exchange armor as a token of their inherited friendship.

How important are family ties and lineage to knowing who we are and to finding a meaningful place in the world? How important are our own singular deeds? Is a human being—who can describe the generations and his place among them—like a leaf? Do the answers to these questions ring true only for heroes descended from gods?

Finally, Glaukos' and Diomedes' exchange of armor was uneven. How does that compare to the exchange their grandfathers made? What does that say about what each man has inherited, and how he values it?

While the first excerpt tells of the sons of great fathers, the second tells of a great father and his son. Hektor, the mainstay of the Trojans, has met his wife, Andromache, and their infant, Astyanax, atop the wall that divides the city and the battlefield. Both husband and wife, then, are temporarily dislocated. Andromache beseeches Hektor to take greater care for his safety, out of pity for her and their son. Hektor refuses, arguing that holding back would shame him, that he longs for glory, and that if Troy falls—as he fears—she will suffer a terrible fate. Astyanax at first shrinks in terror from his helmeted father, but when Hektor removes his headgear, the infant accepts his embrace. Before leaving, Hektor prays for his son and beseeches his wife to "go back to our house."

Is the desire to avoid disgrace and to win glory—and more generally, the desire to fulfill any great ambition—necessarily incompatible with having and caring for children? What is the view of fatherhood implicit in Hektor's prayer? How does Hektor's prayer for his son compare to what Glaukos and Diomedes felt for their forbears? Does it change your view of Hektor to know that his failure to heed Andromache's advice does, in fact, doom Troy and his son?

Excerpt 1

Now Glaukos, sprung of Hippolochos, and the son of Tydeus[1]
came together in the space between the two armies, battle-bent.
Now as these advancing came to one place and encountered,
first to speak was Diomedes of the great war cry:
'Who among mortal men are you, good friend? Since never
before have I seen you in the fighting where men win glory,
yet now you have come striding far out in front of all others
in your great heart, who have dared stand up to my spear far-shadow-
    ing.
Yet unhappy are those whose sons match warcraft against me.
But if you are some one of the immortals come down from the bright
    sky,

---

[1] Diomedes.

know that I will not fight against any god of the heaven,
since even the son of Dryas, Lykourgos the powerful, did not
live long; he who tried to fight with the gods of the bright sky,
who once drove the fosterers of rapturous Dionysos
headlong down the sacred Nyseian hill, and all of them
shed and scattered their wands on the ground, stricken with an ox-
    goad
by murderous Lykourgos, while Dionysos in terror
dived into the salt surf, and Thetis took him to her bosom,
frightened, with the strong shivers upon him at the man's blustering.
But the gods who live at their ease were angered with Lykourgos,
and the son of Kronos struck him to blindness, nor did he live long
afterwards, since he was hated by all the immortals.
Therefore neither would I be willing to fight with the blessed
gods; but if you are one of those mortals who eat what the soil yields,
come nearer, so that sooner you may reach your appointed destruction.

Then in turn the shining son of Hippolochos answered:
'High-hearted son of Tydeus, why ask of my generation?
As is the generation of leaves, so is that of humanity.
The wind scatters the leaves on the ground, but the live timber
burgeons with leaves again in the season of spring returning.
So one generation of men will grow while another
dies. Yet if you wish to learn all this and be certain
of my genealogy: there are plenty of men who know it.
There is a city, Ephyre, in the corner of horse-pasturing
Argos; there lived Sisyphos, that sharpest of all men,
Sisyphos, Aiolos' son, and he had a son named Glaukos[2],
and Glaukos in turn sired Bellerophontes the blameless.
To Bellerophontes the gods granted beauty and desirable
manhood; but Proitos[3] in anger devised evil things against him,
and drove him out of his own domain, since he was far greater,
from the Argive country Zeus[4] had broken to the sway of his sceptre.
Beautiful Anteia the wife of Proitos was stricken
with passion to lie in love with him, and yet she could not
beguile valiant Bellerophontes, whose will was virtuous.
So she went to Proitos the king and uttered her falsehood:

---

[2] Great-grandfather of the Glaukos who is speaking.
[3] King of Ephyre.
4 Most powerful of the gods.

"Would you be killed, o Proitos? Then murder Bellerophontes
who tried to lie with me in love, though I was unwilling."
So she spoke, and anger took hold of the king at her story.
He shrank from killing him, since his heart was awed by such action,
but sent him away to Lykia, and handed him murderous symbols,
which he inscribed in a folding tablet, enough to destroy life,
and told him to show it to his wife's father, that he might perish.
Bellerophontes went to Lykia in the blameless convoy
of the gods; when he came to the running stream of Xanthos, and
    Lykia,
the lord of wide Lykia tendered him full-hearted honour.
Nine days he entertained him with sacrifice of nine oxen,
but afterwards when the rose fingers of the tenth dawn showed, then
he began to question him, and asked to be shown the symbols,
whatever he might be carrying from his son-in-law, Proitos.
Then after he had been given his son-in-law's wicked symbols
first he sent him away with orders to kill the Chimaira
none might approach; a thing of immortal make, not human,
lion-fronted and snake behind, a goat in the middle,
and snorting out the breath of the terrible flame of bright fire.
He killed the Chimaira, obeying the portents of the immortals.
Next after this he fought against the glorious Solymoi,
and this he thought was the strongest battle with men that he entered;
but third he slaughtered the Amazons, who fight men in battle.
Now as he came back the king spun another entangling
treachery; for choosing the bravest men in wide Lykia
he laid a trap, but these men never came home thereafter
since all of them were killed by blameless Bellerophontes.
Then when the king knew him for the powerful stock of the god,
he detained him there, and offered him the hand of his daughter,
and gave him half of all the kingly privilege. Thereto
the men of Lykia cut out a piece of land, surpassing
all others, fine ploughland and orchard for him to administer.
His bride bore three children to valiant Bellerophontes,
Isandros and Hippolochos and Laodameia.
Laodameia lay in love beside Zeus of the counsels
and bore him godlike Sarpedon of the brazen helmet.
But after Bellerophontes was hated by all the immortals,
he wandered alone about the plain of Aleios, eating
his heart out, skulking aside from the trodden track of humanity.
As for Isandros his son, Ares the insatiate of fighting

killed him in close battle against the glorious Solymoi,
while Artemis of the golden reins killed the daughter in anger.
But Hippolochos begot me, and I claim that he is my father;
he sent me to Troy, and urged upon me repeated injunctions,
to be always among the bravest, and hold my head above others,
not shaming the generation of my fathers, who were
the greatest men in Ephyre and again in wide Lykia.
Such is my generation and the blood I claim to be born from.'

He spoke, and Diomedes of the great war cry was gladdened.
He drove his spear deep into the prospering earth, and in winning
words of friendliness he spoke to the shepherd of the people:
'See now, you are my guest friend from far in the time of our fathers.
Brilliant Oineus[5] once was host to Bellerophontes
the blameless, in his halls, and twenty days he detained him,
and these two gave to each other fine gifts in token of friendship.
Oineus gave his guest a war belt bright with the red dye,
Bellerophontes a golden and double-handled drinking-cup,
a thing I left behind in my house when I came on my journey.
Tydeus, though, I cannot remember, since I was little
when he left me, that time the people of the Achaians perished
in Thebe. Therefore I am your friend and host in the heart of Argos;
you are mine in Lykia, when I come to your country.
Let us avoid each other's spears, even in the close fighting.
There are plenty of Trojans and famed companions in battle for me
to kill, whom the god sends me, or those I run down with my swift
    feet,
many Achaians for you to slaughter, if you can do it.
But let us exchange our armour, so that these others may know
how we claim to be guests and friends from the days of our fathers.'
So they spoke, and both springing down from behind their horses
gripped each other's hands and exchanged the promise of friendship;
but Zeus the son of Kronos stole away the wits of Glaukos
who exchanged with Diomedes the son of Tydeus armour
of gold for bronze, for nine oxen's worth the worth of a hundred.

---

[5] Diomedes' grandfather.

Excerpt 2

So the housekeeper spoke,[6] and Hektor hastened from his home
backward by the way he had come through the well-laid streets. So
as he had come to the gates on his way through the great city,
the Skaian gates, whereby he would issue into the plain, there
at last his own generous wife came running to meet him,
Andromache, the daughter of high-hearted Eëtion;
Eëtion, who had dwelt underneath wooded Plakos,
in Thebe below Plakos, lord over the Kilikian people.

It was his daughter who was given to Hektor of the bronze helm.
She came to him there, and beside her went an attendant carrying
the boy in the fold of her bosom, a little child, only a baby,
Hektor's son, the admired, beautiful as a star shining,
whom Hektor called Skamandrios, but all of the others
Astyanax—lord of the city; since Hektor alone saved Ilion.
Hektor smiled in silence as he looked on his son, but she,
Andromache, stood close beside him, letting her tears fall,
and clung to his hand and called him by name and spoke to him:
    'Dearest,
your own great strength will be your death, and you have no pity
on your little son, nor on me, ill-starred, who soon must be your
    widow;
for presently the Achaians, gathering together,
will set upon you and kill you; and for me it would be far better
to sink into the earth when I have lost you, for there is no other
consolation for me after you have gone to your destiny—
only grief; since I have no father, no honoured mother.
It was brilliant Achilleus who slew my father, Eëtion,
when he stormed the strong-founded citadel of the Kilikians,
Thebe of the towering gates. He killed Eëtion
but did not strip his armour, for his heart respected the dead man,
but burned the body in all its elaborate war-gear
and piled a grave mound over it, and the nymphs of the mountains,
daughters of Zeus of the aegis, planted elm trees about it.
And they who were my seven brothers in the great house all went
upon a single day down into the house of the death god,
for swift-footed brilliant Achilleus slaughtered all of them

---

[6] Telling Hektor where he could find his wife.

as they were tending their white sheep and their lumbering oxen;
and when he had led my mother, who was queen under wooded
    Plakos,
here, along with all his other possessions, Achilleus
released her again, accepting ransom beyond count, but Artemis
of the showering arrows struck her down in the halls of her father.
Hektor, thus you are father to me, and my honoured mother,
you are my brother, and you it is who are my young husband.
Please take pity upon me then, stay here on the rampart,
that you may not leave your child an orphan, your wife a widow,
but draw your people up by the fig tree, there where the city
is openest to attack, and where the wall may be mounted.
Three times their bravest came that way, and fought there to storm it
about the two Aiantes and renowned Idomeneus,
about the two Atreidai and the fighting son of Tydeus.
Either some man well skilled in prophetic arts had spoken,
or the very spirit within themselves had stirred them to the on-
    slaught.'
Then tall Hektor of the shining helm answered her: 'All these
things are in my mind also, lady; yet I would feel deep shame
before the Trojans, and the Trojan women with trailing garments,
if like a coward I were to shrink aside from the fighting;
and the spirit will not let me, since I have learned to be valiant
and to fight always among the foremost ranks of the Trojans,
winning for my own self great glory, and for my father.
For I know this thing well in my heart, and my mind knows it:
there will come a day when sacred Ilion shall perish,
and Priam, and the people of Priam of the strong ash spear.
But it is not so much the pain to come of the Trojans
that troubles me, not even of Priam the king nor Hekabe,
not the thought of my brothers who in their numbers and valour
shall drop in the dust under the hands of men who hate them,
as troubles me the thought of you, when some bronze-armoured
Achaian leads you off, taking away your day of liberty,
in tears; and in Argos you must work at the loom of another,
and carry water from the spring Messeis or Hypereia,
all unwilling, but strong will be the necessity upon you;
and some day seeing you shedding tears a man will say of you:
"This is the wife of Hektor, who was ever the bravest fighter
of the Trojans, breakers of horses, in the days when they fought about
    Ilion."

So will one speak of you; and for you it will be yet a fresh grief,
to be widowed of such a man who could fight off the day of your
    slavery.
But may I be dead and the piled earth hide me under before I
hear you crying and know by this that they drag you captive.'
So speaking glorious Hektor held out his arms to his baby,
who shrank back to his fair-girdled nurse's bosom
screaming, and frightened at the aspect of his own father,
terrified as he saw the bronze and the crest with its horse-hair,
nodding dreadfully, as he thought, from the peak of the helmet.
Then his beloved father laughed out, and his honoured mother,
and at once glorious Hektor lifted from his head the helmet
and laid it in all its shining upon the ground. Then taking
up his dear son he tossed him about in his arms, and kissed him,
and lifted his voice in prayer to Zeus and the other immortals:
'Zeus, and you other immortals, grant that this boy, who is my son,
may be as I am, pre-eminent among the Trojans,
great in strength, as am I, and rule strongly over Ilion;
and some day let them say of him: "He is better by far than his father,"
as he comes in from the fighting; and let him kill his enemy
and bring home the blooded spoils, and delight the heart of his
    mother.'
So speaking he set his child again in the arms of his beloved
wife, who took him back again to her fragrant bosom
smiling in her tears; and her husband saw, and took pity upon her,
and stroked her with his hand, and called her by name and spoke to
    her:
'Poor Andromache! Why does your heart sorrow so much for me?
No man is going to hurl me to Hades, unless it is fated,
but as for fate, I think that no man yet has escaped it
once it has taken its first form, neither brave man nor coward.
Go therefore back to our house, and take up your own work,
the loom and the distaff, and see to it that your handmaidens
ply their work also; but the men must see to the fighting,
all men who are the people of Ilion, but I beyond others.'

CHAPTER 7:
WHY NOT IMMORTALITY?

IN THE PREVIOUS CHAPTER, we saw how renewal—having children—is one response to our finitude. Another response, though, would be to conquer the effects of time and continue life, either much longer than is now possible, or even indefinitely. For this—for immortality—human beings have longed since the beginning of recorded history, and for all we know, longer. For many, this longing is to be satisfied in a promised life hereafter. For many others, it is to be satisfied here on earth, by means of technological progress.

Just how far biomedical technology can take us in the direction of bodily immortality remains to be seen. Yet we need not wait for this promise to mature to consider what it would mean to live forever, or even just to live significantly longer than we do now. Our present lives are largely defined by our awareness that we will die, and die some time within the approximately four-score limit natural to our species. How might unending life, or even significantly longer life, affect us? Would it make a difference whether we continued to age, or remained youthful in our additional years? And what about our children? How would our own immortality, or the great lengthening of the lives we live now, affect our relations with those we expect to follow us? Surely the intergenerational effects of profound changes in the human lifespan would go beyond costlier Social Security payrolls.

Our readings in this chapter consider all these questions and more. They begin, appropriately, with a direct consideration of the existential problem. In our first excerpt, the hero of Homer's *Odyssey* confronts a stark choice between human life and immortality in paradise. What might human life—with its perils, shortcomings, and culmination in the grave—have to place on the scales against deathless perfection? In our second excerpt, from the *Book of Revelation*, we are shown a competing vision: a glimpse of heaven, presented as a new Jerusalem, in which death itself has passed away and all human suffering is redeemed.

Our next three excerpts address the fear of death. First, the Roman poet Lucretius, consistent with his materialist philosophy, attempts to dispose of the fear of death by confronting the facts about it, in an excerpt from *On the Nature of Things*. Next, Francis Bacon attempts the same task but goes further, adding reasons why one might welcome death. In the last of these three, a letter by the Stoic philosopher Seneca offers advice on preparing oneself mentally to "[meet] death cheerfully."

Our next four excerpts consider immortality. First, an excerpt from the ancient *Epic of Gilgamesh* features a hero who travels to the land of the gods in search of endless life. There he is counseled to abandon his quest in favor of a finite human life. Next, the hero of Jonathan Swift's *Gulliver's Travels* discovers a land where some do live forever, and is disabused of his notions about what such a life might be like. After this, the heroine of a contemporary children's novel, *Tuck Everlasting*, meets a family of immortals who both differ from and resemble Swift's. Finally, modernist American poet E. E. Cummings celebrates a naturalistic view of what it might mean to live forever.

We conclude with five meditations on death itself. Philosopher Hans Jonas begins these readings with his essay on "The Burden and Blessing of Mortality." Next, Mark Twain, in the final chapter of his *Autobiography*, is compelled by the loss of a beloved child to confront death squarely for what it is; his judgment of it may surprise readers. In two famous poems—"Fern Hill" and "Do Not Go Gentle into That Good Night"—Welsh poet Dylan Thomas ponders the postures toward mortality typical of the young and the old. Three classical Japanese poets—Murasaki Shikibu, Sôku, and Dogen—consider the relationship between death and beauty. Lastly, William Shakespeare, in his twelfth sonnet, questions whether that which is destined to die can be beautiful at all, and identifies only one "defense" against "Time's scythe."

Excerpt from

THE ODYSSEY OF HOMER
Odysseus and Kalypso

translated by Richmond Lattimore

This excerpt from Homer's Odyssey invites us to compare mortal life in a human home to eternal life in paradise, and to think about why one might be preferred to the other.

The excerpt begins after the Greek king Odysseus is shipwrecked on his way home from the Trojan War. Kalypso, a beautiful and immortal nymph, has rescued Odysseus, brought him to her island, and compelled him to remain as her lover. So happy is Kalypso that she hopes to win immortality for Odysseus and keep him forever. Yet Odysseus, now after seven years with her, does not share her desire. Kalypso is "no longer pleasing" to him, and he pines to go home to his wife and son.

As the passage opens, the goddess Athene appeals to the god Zeus to liberate the captive warrior. Zeus replies that Kalypso must be told of "our absolute purpose: the homecoming of enduring Odysseus."

Hermes, the divine courier, is sent to tell Kalypso. He finds her island so beautiful that even he, a god, "stood and admired it." Yet despite the pleasures of the island, Odysseus is gazing at the ocean, "breaking his heart in tears."

Kalypso releases Odysseus, but not before warning him that many hardships lie before him, and inviting him one last time to "be the lord of this household and be an immortal." Odysseus acknowledges that the ageless goddess far surpasses his wife, Penelope, in beauty. Still, he is determined to return home and willing to endure suffering to do so.

While Odysseus fears that he is trapped on her island forever, he can take no pleasure in the nymph, but "would lie beside her of necessity." Once he learns that he is leaving, the two "enjoy themselves in love." Why does desire fade at the prospect of eternity?

Why does Odysseus choose a life of struggle over ease, life with an aging woman over life with an eternally youthful nymph, and mortal life at home instead of eternal life in paradise? In short, why does he choose to die? Would you make the same choice?

Now Dawn rose from her bed, where she lay by haughty Tithonos,
carrying light to the immortal gods and to mortals,
and the gods came and took their places in session, and among them
Zeus who thunders on high, and it is his power that is greatest,
and Athene spoke to them of the many cares of Odysseus,
remembering. Though he was in the nymph's house, she still thought
    of him:
'Father Zeus, and all other blessed gods everlasting,
no longer now let one who is a sceptered king be eager
To be gentle and kind, be one whose thought is schooled in justice,
but let him always rather be harsh, and act severely,
seeing the way no one of the people he was lord over
remembers godlike Odysseus, and he was kind, like a father.
But now he lies away on an island suffering strong pains
in the palace of the nymph Kalypso, and she detains him
by constraint, and he cannot make his way to his country,
for he has not any ships by him, nor any companions
who can convey him back across the sea's wide ridges. . . .

Zeus replies to Athene, then speaks to the god Hermes.

    . . . 'Hermes, since for other things also you are our messenger,
announce to the nymph with the lovely hair[1] our absolute purpose:
the homecoming of enduring Odysseus, that he shall come back
by the convoy neither of the gods nor of mortal people,
but he shall sail on a jointed raft and, suffering hardships,
on the twentieth day make his landfall on fertile Scheria
at the country of the Phaiakians who are near the gods in origin,
and they will honor him in their hearts as a god, and send him
back, by ship, to the beloved land of his fathers.
bestowing bronze and gold in abundance upon him, and clothing,
more than Odysseus could ever have taken away from Troy, even
if he had escaped unharmed with his fair share of the plunder.
For so it is fated that he shall see his people and come back
to his house with the high roof and to the land of his fathers.'
    He spoke, nor disobeyed him the courier Argeïphontes.[2]
Immediately he bound upon his feet the fair sandals,

[1] Kalypso.
[2] Hermes.

golden and immortal, that carried him over the water
as over the dry boundless earth abreast of the wind's blast.
He caught up the staff, with which he mazes the eyes of those mortals
whose eyes he would maze, or wakes again the sleepers. Holding
this in his hands, strong Argeïphontes winged his way onward.
He stood on Pieria and launched himself from the bright air
across the sea and sped the wave tops, like a shearwater
who along the deadly deep ways of the barren salt sea
goes hunting fish and sprays quick-beating wings in the salt brine.
In such a likeness Hermes rode over much tossing water.
But after he had made his way to the far-lying island,
he stepped then out of the dark blue sea, and walked on over
the dry land, till he came to the great cave, where the lovely-haired
nymph was at home, and he found that she was inside. There was
a great fire blazing on the hearth, and the smell of cedar
split in billets, and sweetwood burning, spread all over
the island. She was singing inside the cave with a sweet voice
as she went up and down the loom and wove with a golden shuttle.
There was a growth of grove around the cavern, flourishing,
alder was there, and the black poplar, and fragrant cypress,
and there were birds with spreading wings who made their nests in it,
little owls, and hawks, and birds of the sea with long beaks
who are like ravens, but all their work is on the sea water;
and right about the hollow cavern extended a flourishing
growth of vine that ripened with grape clusters. Next to it
there were four fountains, and each of them ran shining water,
each next to each, but turned to run in sundry directions;
and round about there were meadows growing soft with parsley
and violets, and even a god who came into that place
would have admired what he saw, the heart delighted within him.
There the courier Argeïphontes stood and admired it.
But after he had admired all in his heart, he went in
to the wide cave, nor did the shining goddess Kalypso
fail to recognize him when she saw him come into her presence;
for the immortal gods are not such as to go unrecognized
by one another, not even if one lives in a far home.
But Hermes did not find great-hearted Odysseus indoors,
but he was sitting out on the beach, crying, as before now
he had done, breaking his heart in tears, lamentation, and sorrow,
as weeping tears he looked out over the barren water.
But Kalypso, shining among goddesses, questioned Hermes

when she had seated him on a chair that shone and glittered:
'How is it, Hermes of the golden staff, you have come to me?
I honor you and love you; but you have not come much before this.
Speak what is in your mind. My heart is urgent to do it
if I can, and if it is a thing that can be accomplished.
But come in with me, so I can put entertainment before you.'
   So the goddess spoke, and she set before him a table
which she had filled with ambrosia, and mixed red nectar for him.
The courier, Hermes Argeïphontes, ate and drank then,
but when he had dined and satisfied his hunger with eating,
then he began to speak, answering what she had asked him:
'You, a goddess, ask me, a god, why I came, and therefore
I will tell you the whole truth of the tale. It is you who ask me.
It was Zeus who told me to come here. I did not wish to.
Who would willingly make the run across this endless
salt water? And there is no city of men nearby, nor people
who offer choice hecatombs to the gods, and perform sacrifice.
But there is no way for another god to elude the purpose
of aegis-bearing Zeus or bring it to nothing. He says
you have with you the man who is wretched beyond all the other
men of all those who fought around the city of Priam
for nine years, and in the tenth they sacked the city and set sail
for home, but on the voyage home they offended Athene,
who let loose an evil tempest and tall waves against them.
Then all the rest of his excellent companions perished,
but the wind and the current carried him here and here they drove him.
Now Zeus tells you to send him on his way with all speed.
It is not appointed for him to die here, away from his people.
It is still his fate that he shall see his people and come back
to his house with the high roof and to the land of his fathers.'
   So he spoke, and Kalypso, shining among divinities,
shuddered, and answered him in winged words and addressed him:
'You are hard-hearted, you gods, and jealous beyond all creatures
beside, when you are resentful toward the goddesses for sleeping
openly with such men as each has made her true husband.
So when Dawn of the rosy fingers chose out Orion,
all you gods who live at your ease were full of resentment,
until chaste Artemis of the golden throne in Ortygia
came with a visitation of painless arrows and killed him;
and so it was when Demeter of the lovely hair, yielding
to her desire, lay down with Iasion and loved him

in a thrice-turned field, it was not long before this was made known
to Zeus, who struck him down with a cast of the shining thunderbolt.
So now, you gods, you resent it in me that I keep beside me
a man, the one I saved when he clung astride of the keel board
all alone, since Zeus with a cast of the shining thunderbolt
had shattered his fast ship midway on the wine-blue water.
Then all the rest of his excellent companions perished,
but the wind and the current carried him here and here they drove
     him,
and I gave him my love and cherished him, and I had hopes also
that, I could make him immortal and all his days to be endless.
But since there is no way for another god to elude the purpose
of aegis-bearing Zeus or bring it to nothing, let him go,
let him go, if he himself is asking for this and desires it,
out on the barren sea; but I will not give him conveyance,
for I have not any ships by me nor any companions
who can convey him back across the sea's wide ridges;
but I will freely give him my counsel and hold back nothing,
so that all without harm he can come back to his own country.'
     Then in turn the courier Argeïphontes answered her:
'Then send him accordingly on his way, and beware of the anger
of Zeus, lest he hold a grudge hereafter and rage against you.'
     So spoke powerful Argeïphontes, and there he left her,
while she, the queenly nymph, when she had been given the message
from Zeus, set out searching after great-hearted Odysseus,
and found him sitting on the seashore, and his eyes were never
wiped dry of tears, and the sweet lifetime was draining out of him,
as he wept for a way home, since the nymph was no longer pleasing
to him. By nights he would lie beside her, of necessity,
in the hollow caverns, against his will, by one who was willing,
but all the days he would sit upon the rocks, at the seaside,
breaking his heart in tears and lamentation and sorrow
as weeping tears he looked out over the barren water.
She, bright among divinities, stood near and spoke to him:
'Poor man, no longer mourn here beside me nor let your lifetime
fade away, since now I will send you on, with a good will.
So come, cut long timbers with a bronze ax and join them
to make a wide raft, and fashion decks that will be on the upper
side, to carry you over the misty face of the water.
Then I will stow aboard her bread and water and ruddy
wine, strength-giving goods that will keep the hunger from you,

and put clothing on you, and send a following stern wind after,
so that all without harm you can come back to your own country,
if only the gods consent. It is they who hold wide heaven.
And they are more powerful than I to devise and accomplish.'

So she spoke to him, but long-suffering great Odysseus
shuddered to hear, and spoke again in turn and addressed her:
'Here is some other thing you devise, O goddess; it is not
conveyance, when you tell me to cross the sea's great open
space on a raft. That is dangerous and hard. Not even
balanced ships rejoicing in a wind from Zeus cross over.
I will not go aboard any raft without your good will,
nor unless, goddess, you can bring yourself to swear me a great oath
that this is not some painful trial you are planning against me.'

So he spoke, and Kalypso, shining among divinities,
smiled and stroked him with her hand and spoke to him and named him:
'You are so naughty, and you will have your own way in all things.
See how you have spoken to me and reason with me.
Earth be my witness in this, and the wide heaven above us,
and the dripping water of the Styx, which oath is the biggest
and most formidable oath among the blessed immortals,
that this is no other painful trial I am planning against you,
but I am thinking and planning for you just as I would do it
for my own self, if such needs as yours were to come upon me;
for the mind in me is reasonable, and I have no spirit
of iron inside my heart. Rather, it is compassionate.'

So she spoke, a shining goddess, and led the way swiftly,
and the man followed behind her walking in the god's footsteps.
They made their way, the man and the god, to the hollow cavern,
and he seated himself upon the chair from which Hermes lately
had risen, while the nymph set all manner of food before him
to eat and drink, such things as mortal people feed upon.
She herself sat across the table from godlike Odysseus,
and her serving maids set nectar and ambrosia before her.
They put their hands to the good things that lay ready before them.
But after they had taken their pleasure in eating and drinking,
the talking was begun by the shining goddess Kalypso;
'Son of Laertes and seed of Zeus, resourceful Odysseus,
are you still all so eager to go on back to your own house
and the land of your fathers? I wish you well, however you do it,
but if you only knew in your own heart how many hardships
you were fated to undergo before getting back to your country,

you would stay here with me and be the lord of this household
and be an immortal, for all your longing once more to look on
that wife for whom you are pining all your days here. And yet
I think that I can claim that I am not her inferior
either in build or stature, since it is not likely that mortal
women can challenge the goddesses for build and beauty.'

Then resourceful Odysseus spoke in turn and answered her:
'Goddess and queen, do not be angry with me. I myself know
that all you say is true and that circumspect Penelope
can never match the impression you make for beauty and stature.
She is mortal after all, and you are immortal and ageless.
But even so, what I want and all my days I pine for
is to go back to my house and see my day of homecoming.
And if some god batters me far out on the wine-blue water,
I will endure it keeping a stubborn spirit inside me,
for already I have suffered much and done much hard work
on the waves and in the fighting. So let this adventure follow.'

So he spoke, and the sun went down and the darkness came over.
These two, withdrawn in the inner recess of the hollowed cavern,
enjoyed themselves in love and stayed all night by each other,
But when the young Dawn showed again with her rosy fingers,
Odysseus wrapped himself in an outer cloak and a tunic,
while she, the nymph, mantled herself in a gleaming white robe
fine-woven and delightful, and around her waist she fastened
a handsome belt of gold, and on her head was a wimple.
She set about planning the journey for great-hearted Odysseus.

THE BOOK OF REVELATION, 21:1-22:5

King James Translation

Some who hope for immortality hope simply that the lives they know will continue indefinitely. Others, though, hope for an eternal life that is not more of the same, but is qualitatively different from the known human life, not an earthly life but a heavenly one. Western writings offer many splendid portraits of such a heavenly life, from the last Canto of Dante's Paradiso *to the concluding chapter of C. S. Lewis's* The Last Battle, *the final volume in his* Chronicles of Narnia. *One of the oldest and most famous visions of heavenly life is offered in this excerpt from the biblical Book of Revelation (as revealed to St. John the Divine, the speaker in this reading). In John's vision, the life hereafter is lived in the new Jerusalem, where death itself is no more and all human suffering is redeemed.*

The passage reproduced below begins after the "second death," in which all people are judged "according to their works" and the evil are eternally damned. But those who are written in "the book of life" pass into the new Jerusalem, where, God tells John, "I make all things new."

The new Jerusalem is lighted by the glory of God. There is no sun or moon, and no alteration of night with day to mark the passage of time. Is eternity, in this vision, endless time or the end of time? What difference might this make for the character of eternity and our experience of life?

In the new Jerusalem there is life; the fountain of the water of life is there, and the tree of life grows in it and bears fruit. Yet there is no evil or suffering in the new Jerusalem; the "curse" that has afflicted mankind is gone. Is this, then, human life, or something different? Something better than human?

Is life in the new Jerusalem static or dynamic, a life of unchanging contemplation or of continuing "growth"? Does it matter?

Why in a portrait of a new Jerusalem, beyond time, is there so much attention to physical detail?

The new Jerusalem is a paradise whose inhabitants have passed through death and will die no more. How does it differ from the immortal paradise Homer shows us on Kalypso's island? Do you think Odysseus would reject an invitation to this paradise?

And I saw a new heaven and a new earth: for the first heaven and the first earth were passed away; and there was no more sea.

2 And I John saw the holy city, new Jerusalem, coming down from God out of heaven, prepared as a bride adorned for her husband.

3 And I heard a great voice out of heaven saying, Behold, the tabernacle of God *is* with men, and he will dwell with them, and they shall be his people, and God himself shall be with them, *and be* their God.

4 And God shall wipe away all tears from their eyes; and there shall be no more death, neither sorrow, nor crying, neither shall there be any more pain: for the former things are passed away.

5 And he that sat upon the throne said, Behold, I make all things new. And he said unto me, Write: For these words are true and faithful.

6 And he said unto me, It is done. I am Alpha and Omega, the beginning and the end. I will give unto him that is athirst of the fountain of the water of life freely.

7 He that overcometh shall inherit all things; and I will be his God, and he shall be my son.

8 But the fearful, and unbelieving, and the abominable, and murderers, and whoremongers, and sorcerers, and idolaters, and all liars, shall have their part in the lake which burneth with fire and brimstone: which is the second death.

9 And there came unto me one of the seven angels which had the seven vials full of the seven last plagues, and talked with me, saying, Come hither, I will show thee the bride, the Lamb's wife.

10 And he carried me away in the spirit to a great and high mountain, and showed me that great city, the holy Jerusalem, descending out of heaven from God,

11 Having the glory of God: and her light *was* like unto a stone most precious, even like a jasper stone, clear as crystal;

12 And had a wall great and high, *and* had twelve gates, and at the gates twelve angels, and names written thereon, which are *the names* of the twelve tribes of the children of Israel:

13 On the east three gates; on the north three gates; on the south three gates; and on the west three gates.

14 And the wall of the city had twelve foundations, and in them the names of the twelve apostles of the Lamb.

15 And he that talked with me had a golden reed to measure the city, and the gates thereof, and the wall thereof.

16 And the city lieth foursquare, and the length is as large as the breadth: and he measured the city with the reed, twelve thousand furlongs. The length and the breadth and the height of it are equal.

17 And he measured the wall thereof, a hundred *and* forty *and* four cubits, *according to* the measure of a man, that is, of the angel.

18 And the building of the wall of it was *of* jasper: and the city *was* pure gold, like unto clear glass.

19 And the foundations of the wall of the city *were* garnished with all manner of precious stones. The first foundation *was* jasper; the second, sapphire; the third, a chalcedony; the fourth, an emerald;

20 The fifth, sardonyx; the sixth, sardius; the seventh, chrysolite; the eighth, beryl; the ninth, a topaz; the tenth, a chrysoprasus; the eleventh, a jacinth; the twelfth, an amethyst.

21 And the twelve gates *were* twelve pearls; every several gate was of one pearl: and the street of the city *was* pure gold, as it were transparent glass.

22 And I saw no temple therein: for the Lord God Almighty and the Lamb are the temple of it.

23 And the city had no need of the sun, neither of the moon, to shine in it: for the glory of God did lighten it, and the Lamb *is* the light thereof.

24 And the nations of them which are saved shall walk in the light of it: and the kings of the earth do bring their glory and honor into it.

25 And the gates of it shall not be shut at all by day: for there shall be no night there.

26 And they shall bring the glory and honor of the nations into it.

27 And there shall in no wise enter into it any thing that defileth, neither *whatsoever* worketh abomination, or *maketh* a lie: but they which are written in the Lamb's book of life.

And he showed me a pure river of water of life, clear as crystal, proceeding out of the throne of God and of the Lamb.

2 In the midst of the street of it, and on either side of the river, *was there* the tree of life, which bare twelve *manner of* fruits, *and* yielded her fruit every month: and the leaves of the tree *were* for the healing of nations.

3 And there shall be no more curse: but the throne of God and of the Lamb shall be in it; and his servants shall serve him:

4 And they shall see his face; and his name *shall be* in their foreheads.

5 And there shall be no night there; and they need no candle, neither light of the sun; for the Lord God giveth them light; and they shall reign for ever and ever.

Excerpt from
ON THE NATURE OF THINGS, BOOK III
by Lucretius, translated by Cyril Bailey

On The Nature of Things, *a long poem by the great Roman poet Titus Lucretius Carus (born around 100 B.C.), is the only surviving complete work of the ancient atomists or materialists, people who believed that all that exists is finally nothing more than atoms and empty space. One of the main targets of this teaching was the fear of death, and in particular, the fear of an afterlife in which we might be punished for the way we lived. In this excerpt, Lucretius makes explicit his attack on the fear of death.*

Lucretius argues that death, being nothingness, is nothing to be afraid of. Life, being limited, offers at best slight and repetitive pleasures. Even the greatest human beings have died, so who are we to complain?

Finally, Lucretius urges perspective. Even if we could extend our lives, death is an eternity: "Nor in truth by prolonging life do we take away a jot from the time of death."

Do you find any of these arguments persuasive? Might they work on the fear of death without curing the desire to continue to stay alive?

Lucretius tries to cure the fear of death by urging his readers to confront the facts about it. Might there be another way to mitigate the fear of death? Is there a way of living that might ease its sting?

What arguments might Lucretius offer against technological efforts to enable us to live to 150 or 200, or even indefinitely? What is Lucretius' answer to "Why Not Immortality?"

Death, then, is nought to us, nor does it concern us a whit, inasmuch as the nature of the mind is but a mortal possession. And even as in the time gone by we felt no ill, when the Poeni came from all sides to the shock of battle, when all the world, shaken by the tremorous turmoil of war, shuddered and reeled beneath the high coasts of heaven, in doubt to which people's sway must fall all human power by land and sea; so, when we shall be no more, when there shall have come the parting of

From On The Nature of Things, by Lucretius, translated by Cyril Bailey. Reprinted by permission of Oxford University Press.

body and soul, by whose union we are made one, you may know that nothing at all will be able to happen to us, who then will be no more, or stir our feeling; no, not if earth shall be mingled with sea, and sea with sky. And even if the nature of mind and the power of soul has feeling, after it has been rent asunder from our body, yet it is nought to us, who are made one by the mating and marriage of body and soul. Nor, if time should gather together our substance after our decease and bring it back again as it is now placed, if once more the light of life should be vouchsafed to us, yet, even were that done, it would not concern us at all, when once the remembrance of our former selves were snapped in twain. And even now we care not at all for the selves that we once were, not at all are we touched by any torturing pain for them. For when you look back over all the lapse of immeasurable time that now is gone, and think how manifold are the motions of matter, you could easily believe this too, that these same seeds, whereof we now are made, have often been placed in the same order as they are now; and yet we cannot recall that in our mind's memory; for in between lies a break in life, and all the motions have wandered everywhere far astray from sense. For, if by chance there is to be grief and pain for a man, he must needs himself too exist at that time, that ill may befall him. Since death forestalls this, and prevents the being of him on whom these misfortunes might crowd, we may know that we have nought to fear in death, and that he who is no more cannot be wretched, and that it were no whit different if he had never at any time been born, when once immortal death has stolen away mortal life.

And so, when you see a man chafing at his lot, that after death he will either rot away with his body laid in earth, or be destroyed by flames or the jaws of wild beasts, you may be sure that his words do not ring true, and that deep in his heart lies some secret pang, however much he deny himself that he believes that he will have any feeling in death. For he does not, I think, grant what he professes, nor the grounds of his profession, nor does he remove and cast himself root and branch out of life, but all unwitting supposes something of himself to live on. For when in life each man pictures to himself that it will come to pass that birds and wild beasts will mangle his body in death, he pities himself; for neither does he separate himself from the corpse, nor withdraw himself enough from the outcast body, but thinks that it is he, and, as he stands watching, taints it with his own feeling. Hence he chafes that he was born mortal, and sees not that in real death there will be no second self, to live and mourn to himself his own loss, or to stand there and be pained that he lies mangled or burning. For if it is an evil in death to be mauled by the jaws and teeth of wild beasts, I cannot see how it is not sharp pain to be laid upon hot flames and cremated, or to be placed in honey and stifled, and to grow stiff with cold, lying on the surface on the top of an icy rock, or to be crushed and ground by a weight of earth above.

'Now no more shall thy glad home welcome thee, nor thy good wife and sweet children run up to snatch the first kisses, and touch thy heart with a silent thrill of joy. No more shalt thou have power to prosper in thy ways, or to be a sure defence to thine own. Pitiful thou art,' men say, 'and pitifully has one malignant day taken from thee all the many prizes of life. Yet to this they add not: 'nor does there abide with thee any longer any yearning for these things.' But if they saw this clearly in mind, and followed it out in their words, they would free themselves from great anguish and fear of mind. 'Thou, indeed, even as thou art now fallen asleep in death, shalt so be for all time to come, released from every pain and sorrow. But 'tis we who have wept with tears unquenchable for thee, as thou wert turned to ashes hard by us on the awesome place of burning, and that unending grief no day shall take from our hearts.' But of him who speaks thus we should ask what there is so exceeding bitter, if it comes at the last to sleep and rest, that anyone should waste away in never-ending lamentation.

This too men often do, when they are lying at the board, and hold their cups in their hands, and shade their brows with garlands: they say from the heart, 'Brief is this enjoyment for us puny men: soon it will be past, nor ever thereafter will it be ours to call it back.' As though in death this were to be foremost among their ills, that thirst would burn the poor wretches and parch them with its drought, or that there would abide with them a yearning for any other thing. For never does any man long for himself and life, when mind and body alike rest in slumber. For all we care sleep may then be never-ending, nor does any yearning for ourselves then beset us. And yet at that time those first-beginnings stray not at all far through our frame away from the motions that bring sense, when a man springs up from sleep and gathers himself together. Much less then should we think that death is to us, if there can be less than what we see to be nothing; for at our dying there follows a greater scattering abroad of the turmoil of matter, nor does anyone wake and rise again whom the chill breach of life has once overtaken.

Again, suppose that the nature of things should of a sudden lift up her voice, and thus in these words herself rebuke some one of us: 'Why is death so great a thing to thee, mortal, that thou dost give way overmuch to sickly lamentation? why groan and weep at death? For if the life that is past and gone has been pleasant to thee, nor have all its blessings, as

though heaped in a vessel full of holes, run through and perished unenjoyed why dost thou not retire like a guest sated with the banquet of life,
and with calm mind embrace, thou fool, a rest that knows no care? But
if all thou hast reaped hath been wasted and lost, and life is a stumbling-
block, why seek to add more, all to be lost again foolishly and pass away
unenjoyed; why not rather make an end of life and trouble? For there is
nought more which I can devise or discover to please thee: all things are
ever as they were. If thy body is not yet wasted with years, nor thy limbs
worn and decayed, yet all things remain as they were, even if thou shouldst
live on to overpass all generations, nay rather, if thou shouldst never
die.' What answer can we make, but that nature brings a just charge
against us, and sets out in her pleading a true plaint? But if now some
older man, smitten in years, should make lament, and pitifully bewail
his decease more than is just, would she not rightly raise her voice and
chide him in sharp tones? 'Away hence with tears, thou rascal, set a
bridle on thy laments. Thou hast enjoyed all the prizes of life and now
dost waste away. But because thou yearnest ever for what is not with
thee, and despisest the gifts at hand, uncompleted and unenjoyed thy
life has slipped from thee, and, ere thou didst think it, death is standing
by thy head, before thou hast the heart to depart filled and sated with
good things. Yet now give up all these things so ill-fitted for thy years,
and with calm mind, come, yield them (to thy sons): for so thou must.'
She would be right, I think, in her plea, right in her charge and chiding.
For the old ever gives place, thrust out by new things, and one thing
must be restored at the expense of others: nor is anyone sent down to
the pit and to black Tartarus. There must needs be substance that the
generations to come may grow; yet all of them too will follow thee, when
they have had their fill of life; yea, just as thyself, the generations have
passed away before now, and will pass away again. So one thing shall
never cease to rise up out of another, and life is granted to none for
freehold, to all on lease. Look back again to see how the past ages of
everlasting time, before we are born, have been as nought to us. These
then nature holds up to us as a mirror of the time that is to come, when
we are dead and gone. Is there ought that looks terrible in this, ought
that seems gloomy? Is it not a calmer rest than any sleep?

   Now we may be sure, all those things, which stories tell us exist in the
depths of Acheron, are in our life. Neither does wretched Tantalus fear
the great rock that hangs over him in the air, as the tale tells, numbed
with idle terror; but rather 'tis in life that the vain fear of the gods threatens mortals; they fear the fall of the blow which chance may deal to
each. Nor do birds make their way into Tityos, as he lies in Acheron, nor

can they verily in all the length of time find food to grope for deep in his huge breast. However vast the mass of his outstretched body, though he cover not only nine acres with his sprawling limbs, but the whole circle of earth, yet he will not be able to endure everlasting pain, nor for ever to supply food from his own body. But for us on earth Tityos is he whom as he lies smitten with love the birds mangle, yea, aching anguish devours him, or care cuts him deep through some other passion. The Sisyphus in our life too is clear to see, he who open-mouthed seeks from the people the rods and cruel axes, and evermore comes back conquered and dispirited. For to seek for a power, which is but in name, and is never truly given, and for that to endure for ever grinding toil, this is to thrust uphill with great effort a stone, which after all rolls back from the topmost peak, and headlong makes for the levels of the plain beneath. Then to feed for ever the ungrateful nature of the mind, to fill it full with good things, yet never satisfy it, as the seasons of the year do for us, when they come round again, and bring their fruits and their diverse delights, though we are never filled full with the joys of life, this, I think, is the story of the maidens in the flower of youth, who pour the water into the vessel full of holes, which yet can in no way be filled full. Cerberus and the Furies, moreover, and the lack of light, Tartarus, belching forth awful vapours from his jaws, these are not anywhere, nor verily can be. But it is fear of punishment for misdeeds in life—fear notable as the deeds are notable—and the atonement for crime, the dungeon and the terrible hurling down from the rock, scourgings, executioners, the rack, pitch, the metal plate, torches; for although they are not with us, yet the conscious mind, fearing for its misdeeds, sets goads to itself, and sears itself with lashings, nor does it see meanwhile what end there can be to its ills, or what limit at last to punishment, yea, and it fears that these same things may grow worse after death. Here after all on earth the life of fools becomes a hell.

This too you might say to yourself from time to time: 'Even Ancus the good closed his eyes on the light of day, he who was a thousand times thy better, thou knave. And since him many other kings and rulers of empires have fallen, who held sway over mighty nations. Even he himself, who once paved a way over the great sea, and made a path for his legions to pass across the deep, and taught them on foot to pass over the salt pools, and made nought of the roarings of ocean, prancing upon it with his horses, yet lost the light of day, and breathed out his soul from his dying body. The son of the Scipios, thunderbolt of war, terror of Carthage, gave his bones to earth, even as though he had been the meanest house-slave. Yes and the inventors of sciences and delightful arts, yes

and the comrades of the sisters of Helicon: among whom Homer, who
sat alone, holding his sceptre, has fallen into the same sleep as the rest.
Again, after a ripe old age warned Democritus that the mindful motions
of his memory were waning, of his own will he met death and offered her
up his head. Epicurus himself died, when he had run his course in the
light of life, Epicurus, who surpassed the race of men in understanding
and quenched the light of all, even as the sun rising in the sky quenches
the stars. Wilt thou then hesitate and chafe to meet thy doom? thou,
whose life is wellnigh dead while thou still livest and lookest on the
light, who dost waste in sleep the greater part of thy years and snore
when wide awake, nor ever cease to see dream-visions, who hast a mind
harassed with empty fear, nor canst discover often what is amiss with
thee, when like a sot thou art beset, poor wretch, with countless cares on
every side, and dost wander drifting on the shifting currents of thy mind.'

If only men, even as they clearly feel a weight in their mind, which
wears them out with its heaviness, could learn too from what causes that
comes to be, and whence so great a mass, as it were, of ill lies upon their
breast, they would not pass their lives, as now for the most part we see
them; knowing not each one of them what he wants, and longing ever
for change of place, as though he could thus lay aside the burden. The
man who is tired of staying at home, often goes out abroad from his great
mansion, and of a sudden returns again, for indeed abroad he feels no
better. He races to his country home, furiously driving his ponies, as
though he were hurrying to bring help to a burning house; he yawns at
once, when he has set foot on the threshold of the villa, or sinks into a
heavy sleep and seeks forgetfulness, or even in hot haste makes for town,
eager to be back. In this way each man struggles to flee from himself: yet,
despite his will he clings to the self, which, we may be sure, in fact he
cannot escape, and hates himself, because in his sickness he knows not
the cause of his malady; but if he saw it clearly, every man would leave
all else, and study first to learn the nature of things, since it is his state
for all eternity, and not for a single hour, that is in question, the state in
which mortals must expect all their being, that is to come after their
death.

Again, what evil craving for life is this which constrains us with such
force to live so restlessly in doubt and danger? Verily, a sure end of life is
ordained for mortals, nor can we avoid death, but we must meet it. Moreover, we move and ever spend our time amid the same things, nor by
length of life is any new pleasure hammered out. But so long as we have
not what we crave, it seems to surpass all else; afterward, when that is
ours, we crave something else, and the same thirst for life besets us ever,

open-mouthed. It is uncertain too what fortune time to come may carry to us, or what chance may bring us, or what issue is at hand. Nor in truth by prolonging life do we take away a jot from the time of death, nor can we subtract anything whereby we could be perchance less long dead. Therefore you may live on to close as many generations as you will: yet no whit the less that everlasting death will await you, nor will he for a less long time be no more, who has made an end of life with today's light, than he who perished many months or years ago.

OF DEATH

by Francis Bacon

Here Bacon offers many reasons not to fear death, and a few reasons why one might welcome it.

Bacon begins by belittling the fear of death, comparing it to a child's fear of the dark and asserting that it is "increased with tales." He then seeks to dispose of some of these: that death will be painful or terrible. He considers the circumstances in which men actually welcome death, and notes how little changed many are by the nearness of the end. Bacon suggests that there is a way of life that makes death sweet: "when a man hath obtained worthy ends and expectations."

Does Bacon adequately dispose of the fear of death? Are there reasons for it beyond the ones he raises and refutes?

"A man would die," writes Bacon, "only upon a weariness to do the same thing so oft over and over." Does this mean, necessarily, that immortality would be boring?

Bacon ends on an ironical note: that when we die, our reputations improve. What view of life does this imply? What does this remark tell us about Bacon, and how might it help us understand his attitude toward death?

Does Bacon's account neglect the question of what happens to us after death? Does this matter to his argument?

Men fear death as children fear to go in the dark; and as that natural fear in children is increased with tales, so is the other. Certainly, the contemplation of death, as the wages of sin, and passage to another world, is holy and religious; but the fear of it, as a tribute due unto nature, is weak. Yet in religious meditations there is sometimes mixture of vanity and of superstition. You shall read in some of the friars' books of mortification, that a man should think with himself, what the pain is, if he have but his finger's end pressed or tortured; and thereby imagine what the pains of death are, when the whole body is corrupted and dissolved; when many times death passeth with less pain than the torture of a limb, for the most vital parts are not the quickest of sense. And by him that spake only as a philosopher and natural man, it was well said, *The*

1. innocence   7. wise

2. growth

3. ~~sponge~~ sponge brain

4. immature

5. change

6. success

trappings of death are more terrifying than death itself. Groans and convulsions, and a discolored face, and friends weeping, and blacks and obsequies, and the like, show death terrible. It is worthy the observing that there is no passion in the mind of man so weak but it mates and masters the fear of death; and therefore death is no such terrible enemy when a man hath so many attendants about him that can win the combat of him. Revenge triumphs over death; love slights it; honor aspireth to it; grief flieth to it; fear preoccupateth it; nay, we read, after Otho the Emperor had slain himself, pity (which is the tenderest of affections) provoked many to die out of mere compassion to their sovereign, and as the truest sort of followers. Nay Seneca adds niceness and satiety: *Consider how long you have done the same thing; a man may wish to die not only because he is brave or miserable, but because he is discriminating.* A man would die, though he were neither valiant nor miserable, only upon a weariness to do the same thing so oft over and over. It is no less worthy to observe how little alteration in good spirits the approaches of death make, for they appear to be the same men till the last instant. Augustus Caesar died in a compliment: *Farewell, Livia, forget not the days of our marriage;* Tiberius in dissimulation, as Tacitus saith of him, *His bodily strength was gone, but not his duplicity;* Vespasian in a jest, sitting upon the stool, *It seems I am becoming a god;* Galba with a sentence, *Strike, if it be for the good of the Roman people,* holding forth his neck, Septimus Severus in dispatch, *Hurry, if there is anything more,* and the like. Certainly, the Stoics bestowed too much cost upon death, and by their great preparations made it appear more fearful. Better, saith he, *who reckons the close of life as one of the boons of nature.* It is as natural to die as to be born; and to a little infant, perhaps, the one is as painful as the other. He that dies in an earnest pursuit is like one that is wounded in hot blood who, for the time, scarce feels the hurt; and therefore a mind fixed and bent upon somewhat that is good doth avert the dolors of death; but, above all, believe it, the sweetest canticle is *Nunc dimittis,* when a man hath obtained worthy ends and expectations. Death hath this also, that it openeth the gate to good fame, and extinguisheth envy: *When dead, the same man shall be loved.*

MORAL EPISTLES:
ON MEETING DEATH CHEERFULLY

by Lucius Annaeus Seneca, translated by Richard M. Gummere

"To have lived long enough," writes the Roman Stoic philosopher Seneca, "depends neither upon our years nor upon our days, but upon our minds." In this letter to an old friend, he explains what state of mind leads him to conclude "I have had my fill. I await death."

One has lived long enough, Seneca suggests, when one has grasped and overcome a defect of life: that something in it will always seem to be lacking. He himself has risen above this condition through an extraordinary effort of will. He has resolved not only to accept the inevitable frustration of his desires, but to attempt to overcome them. This mental effort he calls his "task," to which he is dedicating "my days and my nights."

One of the desires Seneca struggles to overcome is the desire to avoid death. As this desire is doomed to frustration, he resolves to neutralize death's sting by embracing it: "He who takes orders gladly escapes the bitterest part of slavery." Seneca's determination to "die well" spills back upon the quality of his life. "I shall enjoy life," he writes, "just because I am not over-anxious as to the future date of my departure."

Seneca writes: "We must make ready for death before we make ready for life." Is his advice about confronting death intended for the young? Is it feasible for the young? Is it feasible for most people, at any age? For you?

Seneca seems to say both that people fear death, and that people are chronically unsatisfied with their lives. What does it say about life, or about us, that we do not respond to chronic dissatisfaction by welcoming death?

Is Seneca merely making a virtue out of necessity? What answer would he give to the question, "Why not immortality?"—especially were immortality, or indefinite prolongation of healthy life, possible?

Let us cease to desire that which we have been desiring. I, at least, am doing this: in my old age I have ceased to desire what I desired when a boy. To this single end my days and my nights are passed; this is my task, this the object of my thoughts,—to put an end to my chronic ills. I am endeavouring to live every day as if it were a complete life. I do not indeed snatch it up as if it were my last; I do regard it, however, as if it might even be my last. The present letter is written to you with this in mind as if death were about to call me away in the very act of writing. I am ready to depart, and I shall enjoy life just because I am not over-anxious as to the future date of my departure.

Before I became old I tried to live well; now that I am old, I shall try to die well; but dying well means dying gladly. See to it that you never do anything unwillingly: That which is bound to be a necessity if you rebel, is not a necessity if you desire it. This is what I mean: he who takes his orders gladly, escapes the bitterest part of slavery,—doing what one does not want to do. The man who does something under orders is not unhappy; he is unhappy who does something against his will. Let us therefore so set our minds in order that we may desire whatever is de-manded of us by circumstances, and above all that we may reflect upon our end without sadness. We must make ready for death before we make ready for life. Life is well enough furnished, but we are too greedy with regard to its furnishings; something always seems to us lacking, and will always seem lacking. To have lived long enough depends neither upon our years nor upon our days, but upon our minds. I have lived, my dear friend Lucilius, long enough. I have had my fill. I await death. Farewell.

Excerpt from
THE EPIC OF GILGAMESH
translated by N. K. Sandars

This epic poem, which dates from the third millennium B.C., treats a timeless
subject: the fruitless search for everlasting life.
    The poem relates the adventures of Gilgamesh, a great hero whom the gods
made perfect and who accomplished magnificent deeds. Yet when he witnesses
the death of his friend Enkidu, Gilgamesh is seized by terror and despair at the
thought that he, too, must die. He sets off in search of immortality.
    Although he does not find it, Gilgamesh does succeed in entering the land of
the immortals (the gods). There, in the passage reproduced below, he meets
the winemaker, Siduri, who counsels him to abandon his quest, because "when
the gods created man they allotted him to death."
    In arriving in the land of the immortals, Gilgamesh is aware that he has
accomplished what no other mortal ever has. He is acutely aware, too, of his
other larger-than-life exploits; he boasts of them to Siduri as if he knows she
has heard of them, and indeed it seems she has. A man who has achieved what
Gilgamesh has can expect to win immortal fame. For the heroes of the Hom-
eric epics, this is perhaps enough. Why is it not enough for Gilgamesh? Why
does his terror of the earth and the darkness and the worm retain its hold on
him?
    Why does Siduri emphasize life's simple pleasures—food and merriment?
Why does she tell him to cherish his child? Could her words possibly assuage
fears like Gilgamesh's? Like ours?

There was the garden of the gods; all round him stood bushes bearing
gems. Seeing it he went down at once, for there was fruit of carnelian
with the vine hanging from it, beautiful to look at; lapis lazuli leaves
hung thick with fruit, sweet to see. For thorns and thistles there were
haematite and rare stones, agate, and pearls from out of the sea. While
Gilgamesh walked in the garden by the edge of the sea Shamash saw

him, and he saw that he was dressed in the skins of animals and ate their flesh. He was distressed, and he spoke and said, 'No mortal man has gone this way before, nor will, as long as the winds drive over the sea.' And to Gilgamesh he said, 'You will never find the life for which you are searching.' Gilgamesh said to glorious Shamash, 'Now that I have toiled and strayed so far over the wilderness, am I to sleep, and let the earth cover my head for ever? Let my eyes see the sun until they are dazzled with looking. Although I am no better than a dead man, still let me see the light of the sun.'

Beside the sea she lives, the woman of the vine, the maker of wine; Siduri sits in the garden at the edge of the sea, with the golden bowl and the golden vats that the gods gave her. She is covered with a veil; and where she sits she sees Gilgamesh coming towards her, wearing skins, the flesh of the gods in his body, but despair in his heart, and his face like the face of one who has made a long journey. She looked, and as she scanned the distance she said in her own heart, 'Surely this is some felon; where is he going now?' And she barred her gate against him with the cross-bar and shot home the bolt. But Gilgamesh, hearing the sound of the bolt, threw up his head and lodged his foot in the gate; he called to her, 'Young woman, maker of wine, why do you bolt your door; what did you see that made you bar your gate? I will break in your door and burst in your gate, for I am Gilgamesh who seized and killed the Bull of Heaven, I killed the watchman of the cedar forest, I overthrew Humbaba who lived in the forest, and I killed the lions in the passes of the mountain.'

Then Siduri said to him, 'If you are that Gilgamesh who seized and killed the Bull of Heaven, who killed the watchman of the cedar forest, who overthrew Humbaba that lived in the forest, and killed the lions in the passes of the mountain, why are your cheeks so starved and why is your face so drawn? Why is despair in your heart and your face like the face of one who has made a long journey? Yes, why is your face burned from heat and cold, and why do you come here wandering over the pastures in search of the wind?'

Gilgamesh answered her, 'And why should not my cheeks be starved and my face drawn? Despair is in my heart and my face is the face of one who has made a long journey, it was burned with heat and with cold. Why should I not wander over the pastures in search of the wind? My friend, my younger brother, he who hunted the wild ass of the wilderness and the panther of the plains, my friend, my younger brother who seized and killed the Bull of Heaven and overthrew Humbaba in the cedar forest, my friend who was very dear to me and who endured dangers beside me, Enkidu my brother, whom I loved, the end of mortality has overtaken him. I wept for him seven days and nights till the worm fastened on him. Because of my brother I am afraid of death, because of my brother I stray through the wilderness and cannot rest. But now, young woman, maker of wine, since I have seen your face do not let me see the face of death which I dread so much.'

She answered, 'Gilgamesh, where are you hurrying to? You will never find that life for which you are looking. When the gods created man they allotted to him death, but life they retained in their own keeping. As for you, Gilgamesh, fill your belly with good things; day and night, night and day, dance and be merry, feast and rejoice. Let your clothes be fresh, bathe yourself in water, cherish the little child that holds your hand, and make your wife happy in your embrace; for this too is the lot of man.'

Excerpt from
GULLIVER'S TRAVELS
by Jonathan Swift

In Jonathan Swift's best-known novel, the protagonist, Gulliver, recalls his travels to fantastical foreign lands. In the following excerpt, Gulliver recounts his visit to Luggnagg, where every few years a child is born with a distinctive mark that signifies he or she will never die.

Until he went to Luggnagg, Gulliver had regarded death as "the universal calamity of human nature." This view changes when he learns the truth about the immortal "struldbrugs."

When Gulliver first learns about the struldbrugs from mortal Luggnaggians, he is "struck with inexpressible delight." Prompted by them to describe how he would have lived, had he been one, he imagines perpetual study, ever-growing wisdom, service to humanity, and the comfortable fellowship of his own kind. His interlocutors laugh and set him straight. Though they are immortal, the struldbruggs enjoy neither perpetual youth nor perpetual prosperity and health. They live anything but enviable lives.

When Gulliver imagines himself as an immortal, he sees himself growing to accept the ongoing loss of mortal acquaintances with as little regret as mortals feel for the withering of annual flowers. He also sees himself remaining engaged in solving the problems of the human race. Is he realistic in imagining that these two attitudes could coexist?

Were the struldbrugs to remain healthy and prosperous as they aged, would they necessarily be happy? Does Gulliver's interpreter fully understand what ails them?

Marriages among struldbruggs are dissolved when the spouses reach eighty, and the only mention made of the children of these marriages is that they take their inheritances at that time (and are themselves likely to be mortal). What might the experiences of the struldbrugs suggest about the relation between marriage, children, and mortality?

Mortal Luggnaggians are human; are the struldbrugs? If not, what crucial human attributes do they lack?

The Luggnaggians are a polite and generous people, and although they are not without some share of that pride which is peculiar to all eastern countries, yet they shew themselves courteous to strangers, especially such who are countenanced by the court. I had many acquaintances among persons of the best fashion, and being always attended by my interpreter, the conversation we had was not disagreeable.

One day, in much good company, I was asked by a person of quality, whether I had seen any of their struldbrugs, or immortals. I said I had not; and desired he would explain to me what he meant by such an appellation, applied to a mortal creature. He told me, that sometimes, though very rarely, a child happened to be born in a family with a red circular spot in the forehead, directly over the left eye-brow, which was an infallible mark that it should never die. The spot, as he described it, was about the compass of a silver three-pence, but in the course of time grew larger, and changed its colour; for at twelve years old it became green, so continued till five and twenty, then turned to a deep blue; at five and forty it grew coal black, and as large as an English shilling; but never admitted any farther alteration. He said these births were so rare, that he did not believe there could be above eleven hundred struldbrugs of both sexes in the whole kingdom, of which he computed about fifty in the metropolis, and, among the rest, a young girl born, about three years ago; that these productions were not peculiar to any family, but a mere effect of chance; and the children of the struldbrugs themselves were equally mortal with the rest of the people.

I freely own myself to have been struck with inexpressible delight upon hearing this account: and the person who gave it me happening to understand the Balnibarbian language, which I spoke very well, I could not forbear breaking out into expressions, perhaps a little too extravagant. I cried out as in a rapture: "Happy nation, where every child hath at least a chance of being immortal! Happy people, who enjoy so many living examples of ancient virtue, and have masters ready to instruct them in the wisdom of all former ages! But happiest beyond all comparison are those excellent struldbrugs, who, born exempt from that universal calamity of human nature, have their minds free and disengaged, without the weight and depression of spirits caused by the continual apprehension of death." I discovered my admiration that I had not observed any of these illustrious persons at court; the black spot on the forehead being so remarkable a distinction, that I could not have easily overlooked it; and it was impossible that his Majesty, a most judicious prince, should not provide himself with a good number of such wise and able councilors. Yet perhaps the virtue of those reverend sages was too strict for the corrupt and libertine manners of a court. And we often find by experience, that young men are too opinionative and volatile to be guided by the sober dictates of their seniors. However, since the king was pleased to allow me access to his royal person, I was resolved, upon the very first occasion, to deliver my opinion to him on this matter freely, and at large, by the help of my interpreter; and whether he would please to take my advice or no, yet in one thing I was determined, that, his Majesty having frequently offered me an establishment in this country, I would with great thankfulness accept the favour, and pass my life here in the conversation of those superior beings, the struldbrugs, if they would please to admit me.

The gentlemen to whom I addressed my discourse, because (as I have already observed) he spoke the language of Balnibarbi, said to me with a sort of a smile, which usually ariseth from pity to the ignorant, that he was glad of any occasion to keep me among them, and desired my permission to explain to the company what I had spoke. He did so, and they talked together for some time in their own language, whereof I understood not a syllable, neither could I observe by their countenances, what impression my discourse had made on them. After a short silence, the same person told me, that his friends and mine (so he thought fit to express himself) were very much pleased with the judicious remarks I had made on the great happiness and advantages of immortal life, and they were desirous to know in a particular manner, what scheme of living I should have formed to myself, if it had fallen to my lot to have been born a struldbrug.

I answered, it was easy to be eloquent on so copious and delightful a subject, especially to me, who have been often apt to amuse myself with visions of what I should do, if I were a king, a general, or a great lord: and, upon this very case, I had frequently run over the whole system how I should employ myself, and pass the time, if I were sure to live for ever.

That, if it had been my good fortune to come into the world a struldbrug, as soon as I could discover my own happiness, by understanding the difference between life and death, I would first resolve, by all arts and methods whatsoever, to procure myself riches. In the pursuit of which, by thrift and management, I might reasonably expect, in about two hundred years, to be the wealthiest man in the kingdom. In the second place, I would from my earliest youth apply myself to the study of arts and sciences, by which I should arrive in time to excel all others in learning. Lastly, I would carefully record every action and event of consequence that happened in the public, impartially draw the characters of the several successions of princes, and great ministers of state, with my own observations on every point. I would exactly set down the several changes in customs, language, fashions of dress, diet and diversions. By all which acquirements, I should be a living treasury of knowledge and wisdom, and certainly become the oracle of the nation.

I would never marry after threescore, but live in an hospitable manner, yet still on the saving side. I would entertain myself in forming and directing the minds of hopeful young men, by convincing them from my own remembrance, experience and observation, fortified by numerous examples, of the usefulness of virtue in public and private life. But my choice and constant companions should be a set of my own immortal brotherhood, among whom I would elect a dozen from the most ancient, down to my own contemporaries. Where any of these wanted fortunes, I would provide them with convenient lodges round my own estate, and have some of them always at my table, only mingling a few of the most valuable among you mortals, whom length of time would harden me to lose, with little or no reluctance, and treat your posterity after the same manner; just as a man diverts himself with the annual succession of pinks and tulips in his garden, without regretting the loss of those which withered the preceding year.

These struldbrugs and I would mutually communicate our observations and memorials through the course of time; remark the several gradations by which corruption steals into the world, and oppose it in every step, by giving perpetual warning and instruction to mankind; which, added to the strong influence of our own example, would probably prevent that continual degeneracy of human nature, so justly complained of in all ages.

Add to all this, the pleasure of seeing the various revolutions of states and empires; the changes in the lower and upper world; ancient cities in ruins, and obscure villages become the seats of kings; famous rivers lessening into shallow brooks; the ocean leaving one coast dry, and overwhelming another; the discovery of many countries yet unknown; barbarity over-running the politest nations, and the most barbarous become civilized. I should then see the discovery of the longitude, the perpetual motion, the universal medicine, and many other great inventions brought to the utmost perfection.

What wonderful discoveries should we make in astronomy, by outliving and confirming our own predictions, by observing the progress and return of comets, with the changes of motion in the sun, moon, and stars.

I enlarged upon many other topics, which the natural desire of endless life and sublunary happiness could easily furnish me with. When I had ended, and the sum of my discourse had been interpreted, as before, to the rest of the company, there was a good deal of talk among them in the language of the country, not without some laughter at my expense. At last, the same gentleman who had been my interpreter said he was desired by the rest to set me right in a few mistakes, which I had fallen into through the common imbecility of human nature, and, upon that allowance, was less answerable for them. That this breed of struldbrugs was peculiar to their country, for there were no such people, either in Balnibarbi or Japan, where he had the honour to be ambassador from his Majesty, and found the natives in both those kingdoms very hard to believe that the fact was possible; and it appeared from my astonishment, when he first mentioned the matter to me, that I received it as a thing wholly new, and scarcely to be credited. That in the two kingdoms above mentioned, where, during his residence, he had conversed very much, he observed long life to be the universal desire and wish of mankind. That whoever had one foot in the grave, was sure to hold back the other as strongly as he could. That the oldest had still hopes of living one day longer, and looked on death as the greatest evil, from which Nature always prompted him to retreat; only in this island of Luggnagg the appetite for living was not so eager, from the continual example of the struldbrugs before their eyes.

That the system of living, contrived by me, was unreasonable and unjust, because it supposed a perpetuity of youth, health, and vigour, which no man could be so foolish to hope, however extravagant he may be in his wishes. That the question therefore was not whether a man would choose to be always in the prime of youth, attended with prosperity and health; but how he would pass a perpetual life under all the usual disadvantages which old age brings along with it. For although few men will avow their desires of being immortal upon such hard conditions, yet in the two kingdoms before mentioned, of Balnibarbi and Japan he observed that every man desired to put off death for some time longer, let it approach ever so late; and he rarely heard of any man who died willingly, except he were incited by the extremity of grief or torture. And he appealed to me, whether in those countries I had travelled, as well as my own, I had not observed the same general disposition.

After this preface, he gave me a particular account of the struldbrugs among them. He said they commonly acted like mortals, till about thirty years old, after which, by degrees, they grew melancholy and dejected, increasing in both till they came to fourscore. This he learned from their own confession; for otherwise, there not being above two or three of that species born in an age, they were too few to form a general observation by. When they came to fourscore years, which is reckoned the extremity of living in this country, they had not only all the follies and infirmities of other old men, but many more, which arose from the dreadful prospects of never dying. They were not only opinionative, peevish, covetous, morose, vain, talkative; but incapable of friendship, and dead to all natural affection, which never descended below their grandchildren. Envy and impotent desires are their prevailing passions. But those objects, against which their envy seems principally directed, are the vices of the younger sort, and the deaths of the old. By reflecting on the former, they find themselves cut off from all possibility of pleasure; and whenever they see a funeral, they lament and repine that others are gone to an harbour of rest, to which they themselves never can hope to arrive. They have no remembrance of anything but what they learned and observed in their youth and middle age, and even that is very imperfect. And, for the truth or particulars of any fact, it is safer to depend on common traditions, than upon their best recollections. The least miserable among them appear to be those who turn to dotage, and entirely lose their memories; these meet with more pity and assistance, because they want many bad qualities, which abound in others.

If a struldbrug happen to marry one of his own kind, the marriage is dissolved of course, by the courtesy of the kingdom, as soon as the younger of the two comes to be fourscore. For the law thinks it reasonable indulgence, that those who are condemned, without any fault of their own, to a perpetual continuance in the world, should not have their misery doubled by the load of a wife.

As soon as they have completed the term of eighty years, they are looked on as dead in law; their heirs immediately succeed to their estates, only a small pittance is reserved for their support; and the poor ones are maintained at the public charge. After that period they are held incapable of any employment of trust or profit, they cannot purchase lands, or take leases, neither are they allowed to be witnesses in any cause, either civil or criminal, not even for the decision of meers and bounds.

At ninety they lose their teeth and hair; they have at that age no distinction of taste, but eat and drink whatever they can get, without relish or appetite. The diseases they were subject to still continue, without increasing or diminishing. In talking, they forget the common appellation of things, and the names of persons, even of those who are their nearest friends and relations. For the same reason they never can amuse themselves with reading, because their memory will not serve to carry them from the beginning of a sentence to the end; and, by this defect, they are deprived of the only entertainment whereof they might otherwise be capable.

The language of this country being always upon the flux, the struldbrugs of one age do not understand those of another; neither are they able, after two hundred years, to hold any conversation (farther than by a few general words) with their neighbours, the mortals; and thus they lie under the disadvantage of living like foreigners in their own country.

This was the account given me of the struldbrugs, as near as I can remember. I afterwards saw five or six of different ages, the youngest not above two hundred years old, who were brought to me at several times, by some of my friends; but although they were told that I was a great traveller, and had seen all the world, they had not the least curiosity to ask me a question; only desired I would give them *slumskudask*, or a token of remembrance; which is a modest way of begging, to avoid the law that strictly forbids it, because they are provided for by the public, although, indeed, with a very scanty allowance.

They are despised and hated by all sorts of people; when one of them is born, it is reckoned ominous, and their birth is recorded very particularly; so that you may know their age, by consulting the register; which, however, hath not been kept above a thousand years past, or, at least, hath been destroyed by time, or public disturbances. But the usual way of computing how old they are, is, by asking them what kings or great persons they can remember, and then consulting history; for, infallibly, the last prince in their mind did not begin his reign after they were fourscore years old.

They were the most mortifying sight I ever beheld; and the women more horrible than the men. Besides the usual deformities in extreme old age, they acquired an additional ghastliness, in proportion to their number of years, which is not to be described; and, among half a dozen, I soon distinguished which was the eldest, although there was not above a century or two between them.

The reader will easily believe that from what I had heard and seen, my keen appetite for perpetuity of life was much abated. I grew heartily ashamed of the pleasing visions I had formed; and thought no tyrant could invent a death into which I would not run with pleasure from such a life. The king heard of all that had passed between me and my friends upon this occasion, and rallied me very pleasantly; wishing I would send a couple of struldbrugs to my own country, to arm our people against the fear of death; but this, it seems, is forbidden by the fundamental laws of the kingdom, or else I should have been well content with the trouble and expense of transporting them.

I could not but agree that the laws of this kingdom, relative to the struldbrugs, were founded upon the strongest reasons, and such as any other country would be under the necessity of enacting in the like circumstances. Otherwise, as avarice is the necessary consequent of old age, those immortals would in time become proprietors of the whole nation, and engross the civil power; which, for want of abilities to manage, must end in the ruin of the public.

Excerpts from
TUCK EVERLASTING
by Natalie Babbitt

In this children's novel, Natalie Babbitt imagines what immortality might be like, and suggests reasons why we might be better off without it.

Eighty-seven years ago, the four members of the Tuck family drank from a secret spring. Twenty years after doing so, they discovered that its waters had made them ageless and immortal. When a child, Winnie, also discovers the spring, the family kidnaps her and tries to convince her not to betray the secret.

In the first of the following two excerpts, the father of the Tuck family takes the kidnapped Winnie rowing on a pond. There he draws her attention to the life all around them, and to its constant movement and change. He compares life to a moving stream, which though it seems unchanging is "never the same two minutes together." One who does not die, Tuck tells Winnie, is "dropped off" or "left behind."

In the second excerpt Winnie goes out in the rowboat again, this time with Tuck's son, Miles. Miles was twenty-two when he drank from the spring. Before he knew its effect on him, he married and had two children. His wife and children left him when they began to perceive that he did not age.

Now Miles is taking Winnie fishing. This reminds him of his daughter. As he and Winnie float, they discuss how "mixed up and peculiar" it would have been had he taken his family to the spring after he came to understand its strange power. They discuss what Miles might do with the endless time before him. They talk about killing and eating and dying, and then they catch a fish, distressing Winnie.

"You can't have living without dying," Tuck tells Winnie, adding that the members of his family "just are, we just be, like rocks beside the road." Is he right?

Unlike Swift's immortal struldbrugs, the Tuck family lives forever without aging or infirmity. What does their way of living "in the prime of youth" suggest regarding the relative blessings and burdens of healthy immortality?

Why might Babbitt, in a story that "makes the case" for death, have wanted readers to see Winnie's distress at the death of a fish?

Excerpt 1

The sky was a ragged blaze of red and pink and orange, and its double trembled on the surface of the pond like color spilled from a paintbox. The sun was dropping fast now, a soft red sliding egg yolk, and already to the east there was a darkening to purple. Winnie, newly brave with her thoughts of being rescued, climbed boldly into the rowboat. The hard heels of her buttoned boots made a hollow banging sound against its wet boards, loud in the warm and breathless quiet. Across the pond a bull-frog spoke a deep note of warning. Tuck climbed in, too, pushing off, and, settling the oars into their locks, dipped them into the silty bottom in one strong pull. The rowboat slipped from the bank then, silently, and glided out, tall water grasses whispering away from its sides, releas-ing it.

Here and there the still surface of the water dimpled, and bright rings spread noiselessly and vanished. "Feeding time," said Tuck softly. And Winnie, looking down, saw hosts of tiny insects skittering and skating on the surface. "Best time of all for fishing," he said, "when they come up to feed."

He dragged on the oars. The rowboat slowed and began to drift gently toward the farthest end of the pond. It was so quiet that Winnie almost jumped when the bullfrog spoke again. And then, from the tall pines and birches that ringed the pond, a wood thrush caroled. The silver notes were pure and clear and lovely.

"Know what that is, all around us, Winnie?" said Tuck, his voice low. "Life. Moving, growing, changing, never the same two minutes togeth-er. This water, you look out at it every morning, and it *looks* the same, but it ain't. All night long it's been moving, coming in through the stream back there to the west, slipping out through the stream down east here, always quiet, always new, moving on. You can't hardly see the current, can you? And sometimes the wind makes it look like it's going the other way. But it's always there, the water's always moving on, and someday, after a long while, it comes to the ocean."

They drifted in silence for a time. The bullfrog spoke again, and from behind them, far back in some reedy, secret place, another bullfrog an-swered. In the fading light, the trees along the banks were slowly losing their dimensions, flattening into silhouettes clipped from black paper and pasted to the paling sky. The voice of a different frog, hoarser and not so deep, croaked from the nearest bank.

"Know what happens then?" said Tuck. "To the water? The sun sucks some of it up right out of the ocean and carries it back in clouds, and then it rains, and the rain falls into the stream, and the stream keeps moving on, taking it all back again. It's a wheel, Winnie. Everything's a wheel, turning and turning, never stopping. The frogs is part of it, and the bugs, and the fish, and the wood thrush, too. And people. But never the same ones. Always coming in new, always growing and changing, and always moving on. That's the way it's supposed to be. That's the way it *is.*"

The rowboat had drifted at last to the end of the pond, but now its bow bumped into the rotting branches of a fallen tree that thrust thick fingers into the water. And though the current pulled at it, dragging its stern sidewise, the boat was wedged and could not follow. The water slipped past it, out between clumps of reeds and brambles, and gurgled down a narrow bed, over stones and pebbles, foaming a little, moving swiftly now after its slow trip between the pond's wide banks. And, farther down, Winnie could see that it hurried into a curve, around a leaning willow, and disappeared.

"It goes on," Tuck repeated, "to the ocean. But this rowboat now, it's stuck. If we didn't move it out ourself, it would stay here forever, trying to get loose, but stuck. That's what us Tucks are, Winnie. Stuck so's we can't move on. We ain't part of the wheel no more. Dropped off, Winnie. Left behind. And everywhere around us, things is moving and growing and changing. You, for instance. A child now, but someday a woman. And after that, moving on to make room for the new children."

Winnie blinked, and all at once her mind was drowned with understanding of what he was saying. For she—yes, even she—would go out of the world willy-nilly someday. Just go out, like the flame of a candle, and no use protesting. It was a certainty. She would try very hard not to think of it, but sometimes, as now, it would be forced upon her. She raged against it, helpless and insulted, and blurted at last, "I don't want to die."

"No," said Tuck calmly. "Not now. Your time's not now. But dying's part of the wheel, right there next to being born. You can't pick out the pieces you like and leave the rest. Being part of the whole thing, that's the blessing. But it's passing us by, us Tucks. Living's heavy work, but off to one side, the way *we* are, it's useless, too. It don't make sense. If I knowed how to climb back on the wheel, I'd do it in a minute. You can't have living without dying. So you can't call it living, what we got. We just *are*, we just *be*, like rocks beside the road."

Tuck's voice was rough now, and Winnie, amazed, sat rigid. No one had ever talked to her of things like this before. "I want to grow again," he said fiercely, "and change. And if that means I got to move on at the end of it, then I want that, too. Listen, Winnie, it's something you don't find out how you feel until afterwards. If people knowed about the spring down there in Treegap, they'd all come running like pigs to slops. They'd trample each other, trying to get some of that water. That'd be bad enough, but afterwards—can you imagine? All the little ones little forever, all the old ones old forever. Can you picture what that means? *Forever?* The wheel would keep on going round, the water rolling by to the ocean, but the people would've turned into nothing but rocks by the side of the road. 'Cause they wouldn't know till after, and then it'd be too late." He peered at her, and Winnie saw that his face was pinched with the effort of explaining. "Do you see, now, child? Do you understand? Oh, Lord, I just got to make you understand!"

There was a long, long moment of silence. Winnie, struggling with the anguish of all these things, could only sit hunched and numb, the sound of the water rolling in her ears. It was black and silky now; it lapped at the sides of the rowboat and hurried on around them into the stream.

Excerpt 2

This time, Winnie was careful not to make a noise when she climbed into the rowboat. She made her way to her seat in the stern, and Miles handed her two old cane poles—"Watch out for the hooks!" he warned—and a jar of bait: pork fat cut into little pieces. A big brown night moth fluttered out from under the oar blades propped beside her on the seat, and wobbled off toward nowhere through the fragrant air. And from the bank, something plopped into the water. A frog! Winnie caught just a glimpse of it as it scissored away from shore. The water was so clear that she could see tiny brown fish near the bottom, flicking this way and that.

Miles pushed the rowboat off and sprang in, and soon they were gliding up toward the near end of the pond, where the water came in from the stream. The locks grated as the oars dipped and swung, but Miles was skillful. He rowed without a single splash. The dripping from the blades, as they lifted, sent rows of overlapping circles spreading silently behind them. It was very peaceful. "They'll take me home today," thought Winnie. She was somehow certain of this, and began to feel quite cheerful. She had been kidnapped, but nothing bad had happened, and now it was almost over. Now, remembering the visits of the night before, she smiled—and found that she loved them, this most peculiar family. They were her friends, after all. And hers alone.

"How'd you sleep?" Miles asked her.

"All right," she said.

"That's good. I'm glad. Ever been fishing before?"

"No," she told him.

"You'll like it. It's fun." And he smiled at her.

The mist was lifting now, as the sun poked up above the trees, and the water sparkled. Miles guided the rowboat near a spot where lily pads lay like upturned palms on the surface. "We'll let her drift some here," he said. "There'll be trout down in those weeds and stems. Here—give me the poles and I'll bait the hooks for us."

Winnie sat watching him as he worked. His face was like Jesse's, and yet not like. It was thinner, without Jesse's rounded cheeks, and paler, and his hair was almost straight, clipped neatly below the ears. His hands were different, too, the fingers thicker, the skin scrubbed-looking, but black at the knuckles and under the nails. Winnie remembered then that he worked sometimes as a blacksmith, and indeed his shoulders, under his threadbare shirt, were broad and muscled. He looked solid, like an oar, whereas Jesse—well, she decided, Jesse was like water: thin, and quick.

Miles seemed to sense that she was watching him. He looked up from the bait jar and his eyes, returning her gaze, were soft. "Remember I told you I had two children?" he asked. "Well, one of 'em was a girl. I took her fishing, too." His face clouded then, and he shook his head. "Her name was Anna. Lord, how sweet she was, that child! It's queer to think she'd be close to eighty now, if she's even still alive. And my son—he'd be eighty-two."

Winnie looked at his young, strong face, and after a moment she said, "Why didn't you take them to the spring and give them some of the special water?"

"Well, of course, we didn't realize about the spring while we was still on the farm," said Miles. "Afterwards, I thought about going to find them. I wanted to, heaven knows. But, Winnie, how'd it have been if I had? My wife was nearly forty by then. And the children—well, what was the use? They'd have been near growed theirselves. They'd have had a pa close to the same age they was. No, it'd all have been so mixed up and peculiar, it just wouldn't have worked. Then Pa, he was dead-set against it, anyway. The fewer people know about the spring, he says, the fewer there are to tell about it. Here—here's your pole. Just ease the hook down in the water. You'll know when you get a bite."

Winnie clutched her pole, sitting sidewise in the stern, and watched the baited hook sink slowly down. A dragonfly, a brilliant blue jewel, darted up and paused over the lily pads, then swung up and away. From the nearest bank, a bullfrog spoke.

"There certainly are a lot of frogs around here," Winnie observed.

"That's so," said Miles. "They'll keep coming, too, long as the turtles stay away. Snappers, now, they'll eat a frog soon as look at him."

Winnie thought about this peril to the frogs, and sighed. "It'd be nice," she said, "if nothing ever had to die."

"Well, now, I don't know," said Miles. "If you think on it, you come to see there'd be so many creatures, including people, we'd all be squeezed in right up next to each other before long."

Winnie squinted at her fishing line and tried to picture a teeming world. "Mmm," she said, "yes, I guess you're right."

Suddenly the cane pole jerked in her hands and bent into an arch, its tip dragged down nearly to the water's surface. Winnie held on tight to the handle, her eyes wide.

"Hey!" cried Miles. "Look there! You got a bite. Fresh trout for breakfast, Winnie."

But just as suddenly the pole whipped straight again and the line went slack. "Shucks," said Miles. "It got away."

"I'm kind of glad," Winnie admitted, easing her rigid grip on the butt of the pole. "*You* fish, Miles. I'm not so sure I want to."

And so they drifted for a little longer. The sky was blue and hard now, the last of the mist dissolved, and the sun, stepping higher above the trees, was hot on Winnie's back. The first week of August was reasserting itself after a good night's sleep. It would be another searing day.

A mosquito appeared and sat down on Winnie's knee. She slapped at it absently, thinking about what Miles had said. If all the mosquitoes lived forever—and if they kept on having babies!—it would be terrible. The Tucks were right. It was best if no one knew about the spring, including the mosquitoes. She would keep the secret. She looked at Miles, and then she asked him, "What will you do, if you've got so much time?"

"Someday," said Miles, "I'll find a way to do something important."

Winnie nodded. That was what *she* wanted.

"The way I see it," Miles went on, "it's no good hiding yourself away, like Pa and lots of other people. And it's no good just thinking of your own pleasure, either. People got to do something useful if they're going to take up space in the world."

"But what will you *do?*" Winnie persisted.

"I don't know yet," said Miles. "I ain't had no schooling or nothing, and that makes it harder." Then he set his jaw and added, "I'll find a way, though. I'll locate something."

Winnie nodded. She reached out and ran her fingers across a lily pad that lay on the water beside the boat. It was warm and very dry, like a blotter, but near its center was a single drop of water, round and perfect. She touched the drop and brought her fingertip back wet; but the drop of water, though it rolled a little, remained as round and perfect as before.

And then Miles caught a fish. There it flopped, in the bottom of the boat, its jaw working, its gills fanning rapidly. Winnie drew up her knees and stared at it. It was beautiful, and horrible too, with gleaming, rainbow-colored scales, and an eye like a marble beginning to dim even as she watched it. The hook was caught in its upper lip, and suddenly Winnie wanted to weep. "Put it back, Miles," she said, her voice dry and harsh. "Put it back right away."

Miles started to protest, and then, looking at her face, he picked up the trout and gently worked the barbed hook free. "All right, Winnie," he said. He dropped the fish over the edge of the boat. It flipped its tail and disappeared under the lily pads.

"Will it be all right?" asked Winnie, feeling foolish and happy both at once.

"It'll be all right," Miles assured her. And then he said, "People got to be meat-eaters sometimes, though. It's the natural way. And that means killing things."

"I know," said Winnie weakly. "But still."

"Yes," said Miles. "I know."

TWO POEMS
by E. E. Cummings

In these two poems, modernist poet E. E. Cummings offers naturalistic thoughts about death.

In the first, numbered "3," Cummings describes the return of life to earth and, through it, to new life. He says this process will begin "when god lets my body be." Does he mean to suggest that the death and rebirth he describes is God's plan? Why might he describe death as "let[ting his] body be"?

The poet's beloved, we are told, is touched by the wings of the bird that grows from his body. Does he mean by this to suggest that his death has not separated them, that he is, in some sense, still alive?

The second poem, numbered "5," laments human attempts to understand the earth through philosophy, science, and religion. To all these seekers the poet declares that the earth is silent, but for its annual renewal of life in the spring.

Why is death a "rhythmic" lover? Why is the earth his couch? How is spring an answer "true" to death?

Do either of these naturalistic accounts of the cycle of life and death adequately address the fear of death, the loss of a loved one, or the desire for immortality? What does your answer imply for the meaning of any individual's life?

3

when god lets my body be

From each brave eye shall sprout a tree
fruit that dangles therefrom

the purpled world will dance upon
Between my lips which did sing

a rose shall beget the spring
that maidens whom passion wastes

will lay between their little breasts
My strong fingers beneath the snow

Into strenuous birds shall go
my love walking in the grass

their wings will touch with her face
and all the while shall my heart be

With the bulge and nuzzle of the sea

5

O sweet spontaneous
earth how often have
the
doting

      fingers of
prurient philosophers pinched
and
poked

thee
,has the naughty thumb
of science prodded
thy

    beauty   .how
often have religions taken
thee upon their scraggy knees
squeezing and

buffeting thee that thou mightest conceive
gods
    (but
true

to the incomparable
couch of death thy
rhythmic
lover

    thou answerest

them only with

      spring)

THE BURDEN AND BLESSING OF MORTALITY

by Hans Jonas

What is the burden and what is the blessing of mortality? In this essay, philosopher Hans Jonas seeks to identify both.

In the first part, Jonas maintains that the ever-present threat of death is an essential and defining attribute of life, and ponders why life is worth living, despite this "burden." In the second part, he considers the certainty that each of us must die at some point, and finds in this aspect of mortality a "blessing."

Jonas begins with metabolism, which he identifies as "the defining property of all life." As such, he argues, metabolism has two implications regarding the life of any organism. First, "the peril of cessation is with the organism from the beginning," because the need for nourishment requires "the compliance of an environment that can either be granted or denied." Second, metabolism grants the organism "a sort of freedom with respect to its own substance;" its materials are constantly being replaced, while its identity remains the same. While free in this sense, the organism is nonetheless bound by necessity or need. Hence, the existence of a living form amid matter, Jonas writes, is "paradoxical, unstable, precarious, finite, and in intimate company with death."

Jonas then asks the ancient question: "Is it worth the candle?" He notes that "life says 'yes' to itself." Because it could not do this unless it were possible to say "no," Jonas argues, mortality is what makes value possible. The value life has bought "with the coin of mortality," is subjective inwardness, conscious inner experience, or, in a word, feeling. Although feeling can be painful, history has shown that human beings consider its continuation worth the suffering it costs.

In the second part of the essay, Jonas turns to the eventual certainty of death for each living individual. Here Jonas introduces the term "natality"—the facts of giving birth and being born—which he says is "as essential an attribute of the human condition as is mortality." Natality, he writes, "gets its scope from mortality," as the old die to make room for the young, and to spare themselves from becoming "walking anachronisms who have outlived themselves."

Jonas asserts that "there is a finite space" in the human mind for the memories and impressions that make up our individual identities. If the lifespan

By permission of The Hastings Center and Mrs. Eleonore Jonas.

413

could be significantly increased, he writes, the mind would have to be cleared out to make room for new contents. Is this necessarily true? Must our minds "sooner or later call a halt" to new impressions, if the deterioration of our bodies could be arrested?

According to Jonas, history shows that people value "subjective inward-ness" for its own sake, despite their sufferings. Is his account persuasive?

Do you agree with Jonas that mortality is not only a burden, but also a blessing? Would immortality be a still greater—and burdenless—blessing?

Since time immemorial, mortals have bewailed their mortality, have longed to escape it, groped for some hope of eternal life. I speak, of course, of human mortals. Men alone of all creatures know that they must die; men alone mourn their dead, bury their dead, remember their dead. So much is mortality taken to mark the human condition, that the attribute "mortal" has tended to be monopolized for man: in Homeric and later Greek usage, for example, "mortals" is almost a synonym for "men," con-trasting them to the envied, ageless immortality of the gods. *Memento mori* rings through the ages as a persistent philosophical and religious admonition in aid of a truly human life. As Psalm 90 puts it, "Teach us to number our days, that we may get a heart of wisdom."

Over this incurably anthropocentric emphasis, not much thought was spent on the obvious truth that we share the lot of mortality with our fellow creatures, that all life is mortal, indeed that death is coextensive with life. Reflection shows that this must be so; that you cannot have the one without the other. Let this be our first theme: mortality as an essential attribute of life as such—only later to focus on specifically hu-man aspects of it.

Two meanings merge in the term *mortal*: that the creature so called *can* die, is exposed to the constant possibility of death; and that, eventu-ally, it *must* die, is destined for the ultimate necessity of death. In the continual possibility I place the burden, in the ultimate necessity I place the blessing of mortality. The second of these propositions may sound strange. Let me argue both.

I.

I begin with mortality as the ever-present *potential* of death for every-thing alive, concurrent with the life process itself. This "potential" means more than the truism of being destructible, which holds for every composite material structure, dead or alive. With sufficient force, even the diamond can be crushed, and everything alive can be killed by any number of outside causes, prominent among them other life. However, the inmost relation of life to possible death goes deeper than that: it resides in the organic constitution as such, in its very mode of being. I have to spell out this mode to lay bare the roots of mortality in life itself. To this end I now beg you to keep me company on a stretch of ontological inquiry. By this, we philosophers mean an inquiry into the manner of being characteristic of entities of one kind or another—in our case, of the kind called "organism," as this is the sole physical form in which, to our knowledge, life exists. What is the way of being of an organism?

Our opening observation is that organisms are entities whose being is their own doing. That is to say that they exist only in virtue of what they do. And this in the radical sense that the being they earn from this doing is not a possession they then own in separation from the activity by which it was generated, but is the continuation of that very activity itself, made possible by what it has just performed. Thus, to say that the being of organisms is their own doing is also to say that doing what they do is their being itself; being for them consists in doing what they have to do in order to go on to be. It follows directly that to cease doing it means ceasing to be; and since the requisite doing depends not on themselves alone, but also on the compliance of an environment that can either be granted or denied, the peril of cessation is with the organism from the beginning. Here we have the basic link of life with death, the ground of mortality in its very constitution.

What we have couched so far in the abstract terms of being and doing, the language of ontology, can now be called by its familiar name: *metabolism*. This concretely is the "doing" referred to in our opening remark about entities whose being is their own doing, and metabolism can well serve as the defining property of life: all living things have it, no nonliving thing has it. What it denotes is this: to exist by way of exchanging matter with the environment, transiently incorporate it, use it, excrete it again. The German *Stoffwechsel* expresses it nicely. Let us realize how unusual, nay unique a trait this is in the vast world of matter. How does an ordinary physical thing—a proton, a molecule, a stone, a planet—endure? Well, just by being there. Its being now is the sufficient reason for its also being later, if perhaps in a different place. This is so because of the constancy of matter, one of the prime laws of nature ever since, soon after the Big Bang, the exploding chaos solidified into discrete, highly durable units. In the universe hence evolving, the single stubborn particle, say a proton, is simply and fixedly what it is, identical with itself over time, and with no need to maintain that identity by anything it does. Its conservation is mere remaining, not a reassertion of being from moment to moment. It is there once and for all. Saying, then, of a composite, macroscopic body—this stone in our collection—that it is the same as yesterday amounts to saying that it still consists of the same elementary parts as before.

Now by this criterion a living organism would have no identity over time. Repeated inspections would find it to consist less and less of the initial components, more and more of new ones of the same kind that have taken their place, until the two compared states have perhaps no components in common anymore. Yet no biologist would take this to mean that he is not dealing with the same organic individual. On the contrary, he would consider any other finding incompatible with the sameness of a living entity qua living: if it showed the same inventory of parts after a long enough interval, he would conclude that the body in question has soon after the earlier inspection ceased to live and is in that decisive respect no longer "the same," that is, no longer a "creature" but a corpse. Thus we are faced with the ontological fact of an identity totally different from inert physical identity, yet grounded in transactions among items of that simple identity. We have to ponder this highly intriguing fact.

It presents something of a paradox. On the one hand, the living body is a composite of matter, and at any one time its reality totally coincides with its contemporary stuff—that is, with one definite manifold of individual components. On the other hand, it is not identical with this or any such simultaneous total, as this is forever vanishing downstream in the flow of exchange; in this respect it is different from its stuff and not the sum of it. We have thus the case of a substantial entity enjoying a sort of *freedom* with respect to its own substance, an independence from that same matter of which it nonetheless wholly consists. However, though independent of the sameness of this matter, it is dependent on the exchange of it, on its progressing permanently and sufficiently, and there is no freedom in this. Thus, the exercise of the freedom which the living thing enjoys is rather a stern *necessity*. This necessity we call "need," which has a place only where existence is unassured and its own continual task.

With the term *need* we have come upon a property of organic being unique to life and unknown to all the rest of reality. The atom is self-sufficient and would continue to exist if all the world around it were annihilated. By contrast, nonautarky is of the very essence of organism. Its power to use the world, this unique prerogative of life, has its precise reverse in the necessity of having to use it, on pain of ceasing to be. The dependence here in force is the cost incurred by primeval substance in venturing upon the career of organic—that is, self-constituting—identity instead of merely inert persistence. Thus the need is with it from the beginning and marks the existence gained in this way as a hovering between being and not-being. The "not" lies always in wait and must be averted ever anew. Life, in other words, carries death within itself.

Yet if it is true that with metabolizing existence not-being made its appearance in the world as an alternative embodied in the existence itself, it is equally true that thereby to be first assumes an emphatic sense: intrinsically qualified by the threat of its negative it must affirm itself, and existence affirmed is existence as a *concern*. Being has become a task rather than a given state, a possibility ever to be realized anew in opposition to its ever-present contrary, not-being, which inevitably will engulf it in the end.

With the hint at inevitability, we are ahead of our story. As told so far in these musings of mine, we can sum up the inherent dialectics of life somewhat like this: committed to itself, put at the mercy of its own performance, life must depend on conditions over which it has no control and which may deny themselves at any time. Thus dependent on the favor or disfavor of outer reality, life is exposed to the world from which it has set itself off and by means of which it must yet maintain itself. Emancipated from the identity with matter, life is yet in need of it; free, yet under the whip of necessity; separate, yet in indispensable contact; seeking contact, yet in danger of being destroyed by it and threatened no less by its want—imperiled thus from both sides, importunity and aloofness of the world, and balanced on the narrow ridge between the two. In its process, which must not cease, liable to interference; in the straining of its temporality always facing the imminent no-more: thus does the living form carry on its separatist existence in matter— paradoxical, unstable, precarious, finite, and in intimate company with death. The fear of death, with which the hazard of this existence is charged, is a never-ending comment on the audacity of the original venture upon which substance embarked in turning organic.

But we may well ask at this point: Is it worth the candle? Why all the toil? Why leave the safe shore of self-sufficient permanence for the troubled waters of mortality in the first place? Why venture upon the anxious gamble of self-preservation at all? With the hindsight of billions of years and the present witness of our inwardness, which surely is part of the evidence, we are not without clues for a speculative guess. Let us dare it.

The basic clue is that life says "yes" to itself. By clinging to itself it declares that it values itself. But one clings only to what can be taken away. From the organism, which has being strictly on loan, it can be taken and will be unless from moment to moment reclaimed. Continued metabolism is such a reclaiming, which ever reasserts the value of Being against its lapsing into nothingness. Indeed to say "yes," so it seems, requires the copresence of the alternative to which to say "no." Life has in it the sting of death that perpetually lies in wait, ever again to be staved off, and precisely the challenge of the "no" stirs and powers the "yes." Are we then, perhaps, allowed to say that mortality is the narrow gate through which alone *value*—the addressee of a "yes"—could enter the otherwise indifferent universe? That the same crack in the massive unconcern of matter that gave value an opening had also to let in the fear of losing it? We shall presently have to say something about the kind of value purchased at this cost. First allow me one further step in this speculation that roams beyond proof. Is it too bold to conjecture that in the cosmically rare opportunity of organismic existence, when at last it was offered on this planet by lucky circumstance, the secret essence of Being, locked in matter, seized the long-awaited chance to affirm itself, and in doing so to make itself more and more worth affirming? The fact and course of evolution point that way. Then organisms would be the manner in which universal Being says "yes" to itself. We have learned that it can do so only by also daring the risk of not-being, with whose possibility it is now paired. Only in confrontation with ever-possible not-being could Being come to feel itself, affirm itself, make itself its own purpose. Through negated not-being, "to be" turns into a constant choosing of itself. Thus, it is only an apparent paradox that it should be death and holding it off by acts of self-preservation which set the seal upon the self-affirmation of Being.

If this is the burden life was saddled with from the start, what then is its reward? What *is* the value paid for with the coin of mortality? *What* in the outcome was there to affirm? We alluded to it when we said that, in organisms, Being came to "feel" itself. Feeling is the prime condition for anything to be possibly worthwhile. It can be so only as the datum for a feeling and as the feeling of this datum. The presence of feeling as such, whatever its content or mode, is infinitely superior to the total absence of it. Thus, the capacity for feeling, which arose in organisms, is the mother-value of all values. With its arising in organic evolution, reality gained a dimension it lacked in the form of bare matter and which also thereafter remains confined to this narrow foothold in biological entities: the dimension of subjective inwardness. Perhaps aspired to since creation, such inwardness found its eventual cradle with the advent of metabolizing life. Where in its advance to higher forms that mysterious dimension actually opened we cannot know. I am inclined to suspect the infinitesimal beginning of it in the earliest self-sustaining and self-replicating cells—a germinal inwardness, the faintest glimmer of diffused subjectivity long before it concentrated in brains as its specialized organs. Be that as it may. Somewhere in the ascent of evolution, at the latest with the twin rise of perception and motility in animals, that invisible inner dimension burst forth into the bloom of ever more conscious, subjective life: inwardness externalizing itself in behavior and shared in communication.

The gain is double-edged, like every trait of life. Feeling lies open to pain as well as to pleasure, its keenness cutting both ways; lust has its match in anguish, desire in fear; purpose is either attained or thwarted, and the capacity for enjoying the one is the same as that for suffering from the other. In short, the gift of subjectivity only sharpens the yes-no polarity of all life, each side feeding on the strength of the other. Is it, in the balance, still a gain, vindicating the bitter burden of mortality to which the gift is tied, which it makes even more onerous to bear? This is a question of the kind that cannot be answered without an element of personal decision. As part of my pleading for a "yes" to it, I offer two comments.

The first is about the relation of means and ends in an organism's equipment for living. Biologists are wont to tell us (and, I think, with excellent reasons) that this or that organ or behavior pattern has been "selected" out of chance mutations for the *survival* advantage it bestowed on its possessors. Accordingly, the evolution of consciousness must bespeak its utility in the struggle for survival. Survival as such would be the end, consciousness an incremental means thereto. But that implies its having causal power over behavior, and such a power is—by the canons of natural science—attributable only to the physical events in the brain, not to the subjective phenomena accompanying them; and those brain events in turn must be wholly the consequence of physical antecedents. Causes must be as objective throughout as the effects—so decrees a materialist axiom. In terms of causality, therefore, a nonconscious robot mechanism with the same behavioral output could do as well and would have sufficed for natural excerpt. In other words, evolutionary mechanics, as understood by its proponents, explains the evolution of brains, but not of consciousness. Nature, then, is credited with throwing in a redundancy, the free gift of consciousness, now debunked as useless and, moreover, as deceptive in its causal pretense.

There is but one escape here from absurdity, and that is to trust the self-testimony of our subjective inwardness, namely, that it is (to a degree) causally effective in governing our behavior, therefore indeed eligible for natural selection as one more *means* of survival. But with the same act of trust, we have also endorsed its inherent claim that, beyond all instrumentality, it is for its own sake and an end in itself. There is a lesson in this about the general relation of means and ends in organic existence.

To secure survival is indeed one end of organic endowment, but when we ask "Survival of what?" we must often count the endowment itself among the intrinsic goods it helps to preserve. Faculties of the psychological order are the most telling cases in point. Such "means" of survival as perception and emotion, understanding and will, command of limbs and discrimination of goals are never to be judged as means merely, but also as qualities of the life to be preserved and therefore as aspects of the end. It is the subtle logic of life that it employs means which modify the end and themselves become part of it. The feeling animal strives to preserve itself as a feeling, not just metabolizing, creature. That is, it strives to continue the very activity of feeling; the perceiving animal strives to preserve itself as a perceiving creature . . . and so on. Even the sickest of us, if he wants to live on at all, wants to do so thinking and sensing, not merely digesting. Without these subject faculties that emerged in animals, there would be much less to preserve, and this less of what is to be preserved is the same as the less wherewith it is preserved. The self-rewarding experience of the means in action make the preservation they promote more worthwhile. Whatever the changing contents, whatever the tested utility, awareness as such proclaims its own supreme worth.

But must we assent? This question leads over to my second comment. What if the sum of suffering in the living world forever exceeds the sum of enjoyment? What if, especially in the human world, the sum of misery is so much greater than that of happiness as the record of the ages seems to suggest? I am inclined in this matter to side with the verdict of the pessimists. Most probably the balance sheet, if we could really assemble it, would look bleak. But would that be a valid ground to deny the worth of awareness, that things would be better if it were not in the world at all? There one should listen to the voice of its victims, those least bribed by the tasting of pleasures. The votes of those least lucky may be ignored, but those of the suffering unlucky count double in weight and authority. And there we find that almost no amount of misery dims the "yes" to sentient selfhood. Greatest suffering still clings to it, rarely is the road of suicide taken, never is there a "survival" without feeling wished for. The very record of suffering mankind teaches us that the partisanship of inwardness for itself invincibly withstands the balancing of pains and pleasures and rebuffs our judging it by this standard.

More important still, something in us protests against basing a metaphysical judgment on hedonistic grounds. The presence of any worthwhileness in the universe at all—and we have seen that this is bound to feeling—immeasurably outweighs any cost of suffering it exacts. Since it is in the last resort mortality which levies that cost, but is equally the condition for such to exist that can pay it, and existence of this sort is the sole seat of meaning in the world, the burden of mortality laid on all of us is heavy and meaningful at once.

II.

Up to this point we have been dealing with mortality as the *possibility* of death lurking in all life at all times and countered continually by acts of self-preservation. Ultimate *certainty* of death, intrinsic limitation of individual life spans, is a different matter, and that is the meaning we have mostly in mind when we speak of our own "mortality." We are then speaking of death as the terminal point on the long road of *aging*. That word has so far not appeared in our discourse; and indeed, familiar and seemingly self-evident as the phenomenon is to us, aging—that is, internal organic attrition by the life process itself—is not a universal biological trait, not even in quite complex organisms. It is surprising to learn how many and how diverse species are nonsenescent, for example, in groups such as bony fishes, sea anemones, and bivalve mollusks. Attrition there is left entirely to extrinsic causes of death, which suffice to balance population numbers in the interplay with reproduction and amount to certainty of death for each individual within a time frame typical for the species. However, throughout the higher biological orders, aging at a species-determined rate that ends in dying is the pervasive rule (without exception, for example, in warm-blooded animals) and it must have some adaptive benefits, else evolution would not have let it arise. What these benefits are is a subject of speculation among biologists. On principle, they may derive either directly from the trait itself or from some other traits to which senescence is linked as their necessary price. We will not join in this debate, but rather say a word about the general evolutionary aspect of death and dying in their remorseless actuality, whether from extrinsic or intrinsic necessity. The term *evolution* itself already reveals the *creative* role of individual finitude, which has decreed that whatever lives *must* also die. For what else is natural excerpt with its survival premium, this main engine of evolution, than the use of death for the promotion of novelty for the favoring of diversity, and for the singling out of higher forms of life with the blossoming forth of subjectivity? At work to this effect—so we saw—is a mixture of death by extrinsic causes (foremost the merciless feeding of life on life) and the organically programmed dying of parent generations to make room for their offspring. With the advent and ascent of man, the latter kind of mortality, inbuilt numbering of our days, gains increasing importance in incidence and significance, and from here on our discourse will keep to the human context alone and consider in what sense mortality may be a blessing specifically for our own kind.

Reaching ripe old age and dying from mere attrition of the body is, as a common phenomenon, very much an artifact. In the state of nature, so Hobbes put it, human life is nasty, brutish, and short. Civil society, according to him, was founded mainly for protection from violent—and that means premature—death. This is surely too narrow a view of the motives, but one effect of civilization, this comprehensive artifact of human intelligence, is undeniably the progressive taming of the extraneous causes of death for humans. It has also mightily enhanced the powers of their mutual destruction. But the net result is that at least in technologically advanced societies, more and more people reach the natural limit of life. Scientific medicine has a major share in this result, and it is beginning to try to push back that limit itself. At any rate the theoretical prospect seems no longer precluded. This makes it tempting to hitch the further pursuit of our theme to the question of whether it is right to combat not merely premature death but death as such; that is, whether lengthening life indefinitely is a legitimate goal of medicine. We will discuss this on two planes: that of the common good of mankind and that of the individual good for the self.

The common good of mankind is tied to civilization, and this with all its feats and faults would not have come about and not keep moving without the ever-repeated turnover of generations. Here we have come to the point where we can no longer postpone complementing the consideration of death with that of birth, its essential counterpart, to which we have paid no attention so far. It was of course tacitly included in our consideration of individual mortality as a prerequisite of biological evolution. In the incomparably faster, nonbiological evolution the human species enacts within its biological identity through the transgenerational handing-on and accumulation of learning, the interplay of death and birth assumes a very new and profound relevance. "Natality" (to use a coinage of my long-departed friend Hannah Arendt) is as essential an attribute of the human condition as is mortality. It denotes the fact that we all have been born, which means that each of us had a beginning when others already had long been there, and this ensures that there will always be such who see the world for the first time, see things with new eyes, wonder where others are dulled by habit, start out from where they had arrived. Youth with its fumbling and follies, its eagerness and questioning, is the eternal hope of mankind. Without its constant arrival, the wellspring of novelty would dry up, for those grown older have found their answers and gotten set in their ways. The ever-renewed beginning, which can only be had at the price of ever-repeated ending, is mankind's safeguard against lapsing into boredom and routine, its chance of retaining the spontaneity of life. There is also this bonus of "natality": that every one of the newcomers is different and unique. Such is the working of sexual reproduction that none of its outcome is, in genetic makeup, the replica of any before and none will ever be replicated thereafter. (This is one reason humans should never be "cloned.")

Now obviously, just as mortality finds its compensation in natality, conversely natality gets its scope from mortality: dying of the old makes place for the young. This rule becomes more stringent as our numbers push or already exceed the limits of environmental tolerance. The specter of overpopulation casts its pall over the access of new life anyway; and the proportion of youth must shrink in a population forced to become static but increasing its average age by the successful fight against premature death. Should we then try to lengthen life further by tinkering with and outwitting the naturally ordained, biological timing of our mortality—thus further narrowing the space of youth in our aging society? I think the common good of mankind bids us answer "no." The question was rather academic, for no serious prospect is in sight for breaking the existing barrier. But the dream is taking form in our technological intoxication. The real point of our reflection was the linkage of mortality with creativity in human history. Whoever, therefore, relishes the cultural harvest of the ages in any of its many facets and does not wish to be without it, and most surely the praiser and advocate of progress, should see in mortality a blessing and not a curse.

However, the good of mankind and the good of the individual are not necessarily the same, and someone might say: Granted that mortality is good for mankind as a whole, and I am grateful for its bounty paid for by others, but for myself I still ardently wish I were exempt from it and could go on interminably to enjoy its fruit—past, present, and future. Of course (so we might imagine him to add) this must be an exception, but why not have a select few equally favored for companions in immortality? For *interminably* you are free to substitute "twice or triple the normal maximum" and qualify *immortality* accordingly.

Would that wish at least stand the test of imagined fulfillment? I know of one attempt to tackle that question: Jonathan Swift's harrowing description in *Gulliver's Travels* of the Struldbrugs or "Immortals," who "sometimes, though very rarely" happen to be born in the kingdom of Luggnagg. When first hearing of them, Gulliver is enraptured by the thought of their good fortune and that of a society harboring such fonts of experience and wisdom. But he learns that theirs is a miserable lot, universally pitied and despised; their unending lives turn into ever more worthless burdens to them and the mortals around them; even the company of their own kind becomes intolerable, so that, for example, marriages are dissolved at a certain age, "for the law thinks . . . that those who are condemned without any fault of their own to a perpetual continuance in the world should not have their misery doubled by the load of a wife"—or a husband, I hasten to add. And so on—one should read Gulliver's vivid description.

For the purposes of our question, Swift's fantasy has one flaw: his immortals are denied death but not spared the infirmities of old age and the indignities of senility—which of course heavily prejudges the outcome of his thought-experiment. Our test of imagined fulfillment must assume that it is not the gift of miraculous chance but of scientific control over the natural causes of death and, therefore, over the aging processes that lead to it, so that the life thus lengthened also retains its bodily vigor. Would the indefinite lengthening then be desirable for the subjects themselves? Let us waive such objections as the resentment of the many against the exception of the few, however obtained, and the ignobility of the wish for it, the breach of solidarity with the common mortal lot. Let us judge on purely egotistical grounds. One of Gulliver's descriptions gives us a valuable hint: "They have no remembrance of anything but of what they learned and observed in their youth and middle age." This touches a point independent of senile decrepitude: we are finite beings and even if our vital functions continued unimpaired, there are limits to what our brains can store and keep adding to. It is the mental side of our being that sooner or later must call a halt, even if the magicians of biotechnology invent tricks for keeping the body machine going indefinitely. Old age, in humans, means a long past, which the *mind* must accommodate in its present as the substratum of personal identity. The past in us grows all the time, with its load of knowledge and opinion and emotions and choices and acquired aptitudes and habits and, of course, things upon things remembered or somehow recorded even if forgotten. There is a finite space for all this, and those magicians would also periodically have to clear the mind (like a computer memory) of its old contents to make place for the new.

These are weird fantasies—we use them merely to bring out the mental side of the question concerning mortality and the individual good. The simple truth of our finiteness is that we could, by whatever means, go on interminably only at the price of either *losing* the past and therewith our real identity, or living *only* in the past and therefore without a real present. We cannot seriously wish either and thus not a physical enduring at that price. It would leave us stranded in a world we no longer understand even as spectators, walking anachronisms who have outlived themselves. It is a changing world because of the newcomers who keep arriving and who leave us behind. Trying to keep pace with them is doomed to inglorious failure, especially as the pace has quickened so much. Growing older, we get our warnings, no matter in what physical shape we are. To take, just for once, my own example: a native sensibility for visual and poetic art persists, not much dulled, in my old age; I can still be moved by the works I have learned to love and have grown old with. But the art of our own time is alien to me, I don't understand its language, and in that respect I feel already a stranger in the world. The prospect of unendingly becoming one ever more and in every respect would be frightening, and the certainty that prevents it is reassuring. So we do not need the horror fiction of the wretched Struldbrugs to make us reject the desire for earthly immortality: not even the fountains of youth, which biotechnology may have to offer one day to circumvent the physical penalties of it, can justify the goal of extorting from nature more than its original allowance to our species for the length of our days. On this point then, the private good does concur with the public good. Herewith I rest my case for mortality as a blessing.

Mind you, this side of it, which is perceived only by thought and not felt in experience, detracts nothing from the burden that the ever-present contingency of death lays on all flesh. Also, what we have said about "blessing" for the individual person is true only after a completed life, in the fullness of time. This is a premise far from being realized as a rule, and in all too many populations with a low life expectancy it is the rare exception. It is a duty of civilization to combat premature death among humankind worldwide and in all its causes—hunger, diseases, war, and so on. As to our mortal condition as such, our understanding can have no quarrel about it with creation unless life itself is denied. As to each of us, the knowledge that we are here but briefly and a non-negotiable limit is set to our expected time may even be necessary as the incentive to number our days and make them count.

Excerpt from
THE AUTOBIOGRAPHY
OF MARK TWAIN
by Mark Twain

In this excerpt from the final chapter of his autobiography, novelist Mark Twain confronts the most painful of all losses: the death of his own child. Yet despite his terrible grief, eloquently expressed, Twain avers that he "would not bring back" the daughter he lost.

At the time of its writing, Twain is old and has already buried many who were dear to him, including another child and his beloved wife; he has reached a stage of life, in fact, when his losses seem suddenly to be piling up, one upon the other. At this difficult time his adult daughter, Jean, has come home to live with him. Jean has suffered from ill health and her return brings him great joy. His joy turns to heartbreak, however, when he is awakened with the news that Jean has suddenly died.

Twain is so saddened by Jean's death that he cannot even attend her burial. Nonetheless he asserts, with little explanation, that even if he could, he would not "bring her back to life." Though his own life is now "a bitterness," death is a "precious" gift. It is "that gift which makes all other gifts mean and poor," and a "fortune" beside which all other fortunes are "poverty." How can he say this? What might he mean? What does it say about life if death is a precious gift?

Twain's last moments with Jean, though commonplace while she lived, acquire an exalted quality for him once she is gone. Does death sanctify life? Is this true only when death is sudden?

Stormfield, Christmas Eve, 11 A.M., 1909

Jean is dead!

Has any one ever tried to put upon paper all the little happenings connected with a dear one—happenings of the twenty-four hours preceding the sudden and unexpected death of that dear one? Would a book contain them? Would two books contain them? I think not. They pour into the mind in a flood. They are little things that have been always happening every day, and were always so unimportant and easily forgettable before—but now! Now, how different! how precious they are, how dear, how unforgettable, how pathetic, how sacred, how clothed with dignity!

Last night Jean, all flushed with splendid health, and I the same, from the wholesome effects of my Bermuda holiday, strolled hand in hand from the dinner table and sat down in the library and chatted and planned and discussed, cheerily and happily (and how unsuspectingly!)—until nine—which is late for us—then went upstairs, Jean's friendly German dog following. At my door Jean said, "I can't kiss you good night, father: I have a cold, and you could catch it." I bent and kissed her hand. She was moved—I saw it in her eyes—and she impulsively kissed my hand in return. Then with the usual gay "Sleep well, dear!" from both, we parted.

At half past seven this morning I woke, and heard voices outside my door. I said to myself, "Jean is starting on her usual horseback flight to the station for the mail." Then Katy entered, stood quaking and gasping at my bedside a moment, then found her tongue:

"Miss Jean is dead!"

Possibly I know now what the soldier feels when a bullet crashes through his heart.

In her bathroom there she lay, the fair young creature, stretched upon the floor and covered with a sheet. And looking so placid, so natural, and as if asleep. We knew what had happened. She was an epileptic: she had been seized with a convulsion and heart failure in her bath. The doctor had to come several miles. His efforts, like our previous ones, failed to bring her back to life.

It is noon, now. How lovable she looks, how sweet and how tranquil! It is a noble face and full of dignity; and that was a good heart that lies there so still . . . .

. . . I lost Susy thirteen years ago; I lost her mother—her incomparable mother!—five and a half years ago; Clara has gone away to live in Europe; and now I have lost Jean. How poor I am, who was once so rich! Seven months ago Mr. Rogers died—one of the best friends I ever had, and the nearest perfect, as man and gentleman, I have yet met among my race; within the last six weeks Gilder has passed away, and Laffan—old, old friends of mine. Jean lies yonder, I sit here; we are strangers under our own roof; we kissed hands good-by at this door last night—and it was forever, we never suspecting it. She lies there, and I sit here—writing, busying myself, to keep my heart from breaking. How dazzlingly the sunshine is flooding the hills around! It is like a mockery.

Seventy-four years old twenty-four days ago. Seventy-four years old yesterday. Who can estimate my age today?

I have looked upon her again. I wonder I can bear it. She looks just as her mother looked when she lay dead in that Florentine villa so long ago. The sweet placidity of death! It is more beautiful than sleep.

I saw her mother buried. I said I would never endure that horror again; that I would never again look into the grave of any one dear to me. I have kept to that. They will take Jean from this house tomorrow, and bear her to Elmira, New York, where lie those of us that have been released, but I shall not follow.

Jean was on the dock when the ship came in only four days ago. She was at the door, beaming a welcome, when I reached this house the next evening. We played cards and she tried to teach me a new game called "Mark Twain." We sat chatting cheerily in the library last night and she wouldn't let me look into the loggia, where she was making Christmas preparations. She said she would finish them in the morning and then her little French friend would arrive from New York—the surprise would follow; the surprise she had been working over for days. While she was out for a moment I disloyally stole a look. The loggia floor was clothed with rugs and furnished with chairs and sofas; and the uncompleted surprise was there: in the form of a Christmas tree that was drenched with silver film in a most wonderful way; and on a table was a prodigal profusion of bright things which she was going to hang upon it today. What desecrating hand will ever banish that eloquent unfinished surprise from that place? Not mine, surely. All these little matters have happened in the last four days. "Little." Yes—then. But not now. Nothing she said or thought or did is little now. And all the lavish humor!—what is become of it? It is pathos, now. Pathos, and the thought of it brings tears.

All these little things happened such a few hours ago—and now she lies yonder. Lies yonder, and cares for nothing any more. Strange—marvelous—incredible! I have had this experience before; but it would still be incredible if I had had it a thousand times.

"Miss Jean is dead!" . . .

. . . Would I bring her back to life if I could do it? I would not. If a word would do it, I would beg for strength to withhold the word. And I would have the strength; I am sure of it. In her loss I am almost bankrupt, and my life is a bitterness, but I am content: for she has been enriched with the most precious of all gifts—that gift which makes all other gifts mean and poor—death. I have never wanted any released friend of mine restored to life since I reached manhood. I felt in this way when Susy passed away; and later my wife, and later Mr. Rogers. When Clara met me at the station in New York and told me Mr. Rogers had died suddenly that morning, my thought was, Oh, favorite of fortune—fortunate all his long and lovely life—fortunate to his latest moment! The reporters said there were tears of sorrow in my eyes. True—but they were for *me*, not for him. He had suffered no loss. All the fortunes he had ever made before were poverty compared with this one.

FERN HILL

and

DO NOT GO GENTLE INTO THAT GOOD NIGHT

by Dylan Thomas

In both of these poems, Dylan Thomas expresses related thoughts about mortality. In the first, he considers the way we live ignoring it. The second concerns how we should react to death when it comes to us.

"Fern Hill" employs Edenic imagery to portray joyful youth, blind to the relentlessness of time. In the poet's youth, when time seems merciful, he is fruitful and glorious; nature seems to be at his command and he plays. Yet while he sleeps, and unbeknownst to him, all that he has is slipping through his hands. Daylight masks time's work and the poet runs his "heedless ways," not caring "that time allows / In all his tuneful turning so few and such morning songs / Before the children green and golden / Follow him out of grace."

Would youth be better spent if we were mindful that we will fall out of grace with time? Or does Thomas imply that it is precisely our obliviousness to time's finiteness that permits us to be happy? What would the speaker in "Fern Hill" answer to the question, "Why not immortality?"

Do Not Go Gentle Into That Good Night presents reasons why different men—the wise, the good, the wild, and the grave—rage at the approach of death.

Do you think, if we spent our lives more aware of our mortality, we would be less inclined to rage against the dying of the light?

Fern Hill

Now as I was young and easy under the apple boughs
About the lilting house and happy as the grass was green,
   The night above the dingle starry,
     Time let me hail and climb
   Golden in the heydays of his eyes,
And honoured among wagons I was prince of the apple towns
And once below a time I lordly had the trees and leaves
     Trail with daisies and barley
   Down the rivers of the windfall light.

And as I was green and carefree, famous among the barns
About the happy yard and singing as the farm was home,
   In the sun that is young once only,
     Time let me play and be
   Golden in the mercy of his means,
And green and golden I was huntsman and herdsman, the calves
Sang to my horn, the foxes on the hills barked clear and cold,
     And the sabbath rang slowly
   In the pebbles of the holy streams.

All the sun long it was running, it was lovely, the hay
Fields high as the house, the tunes from the chimneys, it was air
   And playing, lovely and watery
     And fire green as grass.
   And nightly under the simple stars
As I rode to sleep the owls were bearing the farm away,
All the moon long I heard, blessed among stables, the nightjars
   Flying with the ricks, and the horses
     Flashing into the dark.

And then to awake, and the farm, like a wanderer white
With the dew, come back, the cock on his shoulder: it was all
   Shining, it was Adam and maiden,
     The sky gathered again
   And the sun grew round that very day.
So it must have been after the birth of the simple light
In the first, spinning place, the spellbound horses walking warm
   Out of the whinnying green stable
     On to the fields of praise.

And honoured among foxes and pheasants by the gay house
Under the new made clouds and happy as the heart was long,
    In the sun born over and over,
        I ran my heedless ways,
    My wishes raced through the house high hay
And nothing I cared, at my sky blue trades, that time allows
In all his tuneful turning so few and such morning songs
    Before the children green and golden
        Follow him out of grace,

Nothing I cared, in the lamb white days, that time would take me
Up to the swallow thronged loft by the shadow of my hand,
    In the moon that is always rising,
        Nor that riding to sleep
    I should hear him fly with the high fields
And wake to the farm forever fled from the childless land.
Oh as I was young and easy in the mercy of his means,
    Time held me green and dying
    Though I sang in my chains like the sea.

Do Not Go Gentle Into That Good Night

Do not go gentle into that good night,
Old age should burn and rave at close of day;
Rage, rage against the dying of the light.

Though wise men at their end know dark is right,
Because their words had forked no lightning they
Do not go gentle into that good night.

Good men, the last wave by, crying how bright
Their frail deeds might have danced in a green bay,
Rage, rage against the dying of the light.

Wild men who caught and sang the sun in flight,
And learn, too late, they grieved it on its way,
Do not go gentle into that good night.

Grave men, near death, who see with blinding sight
Blind eyes could blaze like meteors and be gay,
Rage, rage against the dying of the light.

And you, my father, there on the sad height,
Curse, bless, me now with your fierce tears, I pray.
Do not go gentle into that good night.
Rage, rage against the dying of the light.

THREE JAPANESE POEMS

by Murasaki Shikibu, translated by Liza Dalby
by Sôku, translated by Donald Keene
by Dogen, as appears in *Japan, the Beautiful, and
Myself,* by Yasunari Kawabata, translated by Edward
Seidensticker

*Japanese artists and philosophers, perhaps more than those in other cultures,
have for many centuries perceived a connection between death and beauty.
This understanding is expressed in the concept* mono no aware, *which, while
difficult to translate, can be understood to mean a sensitivity to the transitory
nature of living beings, and an awareness that their beauty lies in this fleeting
quality.*

*A brief encounter with this ancient and complex idea, while not adequate to
understanding it fully, can nonetheless raise valuable questions about finitude
even for readers steeped in different philosophical traditions.*

Explorations of mono no aware *often make use of cherry blossoms, which
are both beautiful and short-lived (albeit recurring). Each of the three poems
translated below considers cherry blossoms and their relation to human life or
the life cycle.*

*Why might Shikibu see in the example of the mountain cherry an explana-
tion of our suffering? Does this make sense?*

*Sôku finds in the same image a model for noble self-sacrifice. How does this
differ from Shikibu's vision? Are the two poems at odds with one another or do
they share a common understanding?*

In Dogen's poem the cherry blossom does not simply fall, but takes its place in the whole cycle of the seasons, ending with winter. What might the title of this poem tell us about Dogen's view of time and mortality?

Why do we suffer so in the world? Just regard life as the short bloom of the mountain cherry.

   Murasaki Shikibu, eleventh century,
   translated by Liza Dalby

Yes, cherry blossoms,
I will fall along with you!
When once brief glory
Is past, better thus than let
Others see one's ugliness.

   Sôku, tenth century,
   translated by Donald Keene

"Innate Spirit"
In the spring, cherry blossoms, in the summer
the cuckoo.
In autumn the moon, and in winter the snow,
clear, cold.

   Dogen, thirteenth century,
   translated by Edward Seidensticker

SONNET 12

by William Shakespeare

Nothing can defend against death except having children, concludes Shakespeare in this twelfth, stark, sonnet.

The poet recalls the many sights, indicative of the relentlessness of time and decay, that remind him that even the beautiful must "die as fast as they see others grow." There is but one sure weapon against death: to "breed, to brave him when he takes thee hence."

Shakespeare says natural evidence of the inevitability of death causes him to question the beauty of the one to whom his sonnet is addressed. Why so? Is beauty that is destined for "the wastes of time" not truly beautiful? Must true beauty be enduring?

Is Shakespeare counseling defiance of death, or a way of reconciling oneself to it?

Might not the writing of the sonnet itself belie the poet's counsel?

When I do count the clock that tells the time,
And see the brave day sunk in hideous night,
When I behold the violet past prime,
And sable curls all silvered o'er with white:
When lofty trees I see barren of leaves,
Which erst from heat did canopy the herd
And summer's green all girded up in sheaves
Borne on the bier with white and bristly beard:
Then of thy beauty do I question make
That thou among the wastes of time must go,
Since sweets and beauties do themselves forsake,
And die as fast as they see others grow,
And nothing 'gainst Time's scythe can make defence
Save breed to brave him, when he takes thee hence.

SECTION III:
LIVING WELL

CHAPTER 8:
VULNERABILITY AND SUFFERING

READINGS IN THIS CHAPTER explore the most dreaded of experiences: suffering. Why do we suffer? Why should we? Is there anything to be said on its behalf?

Human beings are not the only creatures vulnerable to suffering. Yet although many animals can and do suffer, we are perhaps the only ones who suffer for the many reasons we do, and in our special way. Because no other creatures are capable of such complex awareness of suffering, our anguish no doubt has nuances and a poignance unmatched in the animal kingdom.

Yet human pain, while possibly more frequent and intense than animals', is also privileged in a way that that of animals never can be: Our suffering, and ours alone, may perhaps be redeemed. There is nothing to be gained for the animal, ever, from the bite of the trap on its leg (perhaps it is this that makes such spectacles so painful to witness). The same cannot always be said for a human being enduring physical torture, much as we deplore torture and strive to eliminate its practice. Nor need suffering be wrongly inflicted to offer redemptive possibilities. As the readings in this chapter illustrate, natural illnesses are also capable of elevating those they afflict, and those who love the afflicted, as well.

The relief of human suffering is one of the earliest and most cherished goals of science, especially medical science. No one can deny the importance of this undertaking and no one can fail to applaud, either, the extraordinary strides science and medicine have made. But does all human suffering call imperatively for a cure? The readings below may leave reason to wonder whether eliminating suffering would be wholly desirable. A life entirely free of suffering would be pleasanter, but would it be still be human? Is our vulnerability essential to our human identities and our human dignity?

We begin with perhaps the most famous and enigmatic sufferer in literature, the biblical Job, whose story, excerpted below, invites us to ponder both the meaning of suffering and how it is to be borne. We move to an excerpt from Homer's *Iliad*, where we see a man who is suffering from rage, grief, and guilt find peace after an appeal from the father of his vanquished enemy. Next, an excerpt from William Shakespeare's *King Lear* shows us the suffering of majestic old age. Poet W. H. Auden, in "Musée des Beaux Arts," then attempts to locate the "human position" of suffering, and finds it in everyday life.

The following pair of readings—two excerpts from Mary Webb's *Precious Bane*, and "On Deformity," by Francis Bacon—consider how suffering affects the character of the sufferer. Their conclusions contrast with each other.

Our last three readings present us with the hardest case to endure: sick and suffering children. The first two—"Witness," by Richard Selzer, and "People Like That Are the Only People Here," by Lorrie Moore—look at the effects of this suffering on those who love and care for afflicted children. Finally, in selected passages from her nonfiction essay "Introduction to a Memoir of Mary Ann," American writer Flannery O'Connor considers how the suffering of innocents is viewed in modern times: no longer through the lens of faith, which she describes as the "unsentimental eye of acceptance," but with "tenderness," a change, O'Connor argues, that has had dire consequences.

Excerpts from
THE BOOK OF JOB
translated by the Jewish Publication Society

The Book of Job *considers not just suffering itself, but whether suffering is merited or fair and, if it isn't, whether and how it is to be borne.*

The first of the two excerpts that follow relates the beginning and the main action of the story. Here Job is introduced as "blameless"—morally perfect—and prosperous in every way. As such he seems to embody the biblical promise that God will reward virtue. Yet he is stripped of everything.

At first Job continues to praise God, even after the calamities that befall him, and despite his wife's advice that he "blaspheme God and die." But in chapter 3, speaking to the friends who have come to comfort him, Job curses the days of his conception and birth and openly wishes to die.

In the next chapters, which are not reproduced here, Job argues with his "comforters" about whether he deserved what has happened to him. He insists that he did not. Although Job does not expect an explanation from God ("Who can say to him, 'What are you doing?'") he longs for one ("Indeed, I would speak to the Almighty; I insist on arguing with God.")

The second excerpt is the conclusion of The Book of Job. *Here God answers Job, not as the arbiter of what is fair and what is not, but as the maker and ruler of everything that is. God's catalogue of his works and powers takes the form of a series of ironic, belittling questions about Job.*

Although Job, humbled, replies that he will say no more, God speaks again (this time about the sea monster, Leviathan, in a passage that is not included here). When he is done, Job concedes. "I know that You can do everything," he says. "I recant and relent."

In the final verses of the book, God rebukes Job's comforters for failing to speak the truth about Him, "as did my servant Job." Job, on the other hand, is rewarded by the restoration of all that he had lost, and then some.

When bereft of all he has, Job maintains his "integrity" and praises God. Yet the Adversary (Satan) insists: "lay a hand on his bones and his flesh, and he will surely blaspheme you to your face." The subsequent inflammation of his flesh does, in fact, drive Job to confront God as he did not when he had lost only his children and all his wealth. What does this mean? Is there a hierarchy among afflictions with those of the body being worst and hardest to bear?

On the basis of Job's experience and God's reply, what are we to infer about the relation between suffering and justice?

In chapter 3, Job longs to die. Why does he not take his own life?

What can we learn from Job about the meaning of suffering and how it is to be borne?

Excerpt 1

Chapter 1

There was a man in the land of Uz named Job. That man was blameless and upright; he feared God and shunned evil. Seven sons and three daughters were born to him; his possessions were seven thousand sheep, three thousand camels, five hundred yoke of oxen and five hundred she-asses, and a very large household. That man was wealthier than anyone in the East.

It was the custom of his sons to hold feasts, each on his set day in his own home. They would invite their three sisters to eat and drink with them. When a round of feast days was over, Job would send word to them to sanctify themselves, and, rising early in the morning, he would make burnt offerings, one for each of them; for Job thought, "Perhaps my children have sinned and blasphemed God in their thoughts." This is what Job always used to do.

One day the divine beings presented themselves before the LORD, and the Adversary came along with them. The LORD said to the Adversary, "Where have you been?" The Adversary answered the LORD, "I have been roaming all over the earth." The LORD said to the Adversary, "Have you noticed My servant Job? There is no one like him on earth, a blameless and upright man who fears God and shuns evil!" The Adversary answered the LORD, "Does Job not have good reason to fear God? Why, it is You who have fenced him round, him and his household and all that he has. You have blessed his efforts so that his possessions spread out in the land. But lay Your hand upon all that he has and he will surely blaspheme You to Your face." The LORD replied to the Adversary, "See, all that he has is in your power; only do not lay a hand on him." The Adversary departed from the presence of the LORD.

One day, as his sons and daughters were eating and drinking wine in the house of their eldest brother, a messenger came to Job and said, "The oxen were plowing and the she-asses were grazing alongside them when Sabeans attacked them and carried them off, and put the boys to the sword; I alone have escaped to tell you." This one was still speaking when another came and said, "God's fire fell from heaven, took hold of the sheep and the boys, and burned them up; I alone have escaped to tell you." This one was still speaking when another came and said, "A Chaldean formation of three columns made a raid on the camels and carried them off and put the boys to the sword; I alone have escaped to tell you." This one was still speaking when another came and said, "Your sons and daughters were eating and drinking wine in the house of their eldest brother when suddenly a mighty wind came from the wilderness. It struck the four corners of the house so that it collapsed upon the young people and they died; I alone have escaped to tell you."

Then Job arose, tore his robe, cut off his hair, and threw himself on the ground and worshiped. He said, "Naked came I out of my mother's womb, and naked shall I return there; the LORD has given, and the LORD has taken away; blessed be the name of the LORD."

For all that, Job did not sin nor did he cast reproach on God.

Chapter 2

One day the divine beings presented themselves before the LORD. The Adversary came along with them to present himself before the LORD. The LORD said to the Adversary, "Where have you been?" The Adversary answered the LORD, "I have been roaming all over the earth." The LORD said to the Adversary, "Have you noticed My servant Job? There is no one like him on earth, a blameless and upright man who fears God and shuns evil. He still keeps his integrity; so you have incited Me against him to destroy him for no good reason." The Adversary answered the LORD, "Skin for skin—all that a man has he will give up for his life. But lay a hand on his bones and his flesh, and he will surely blaspheme you to Your face." So the LORD said to the Adversary, "See, he is in your power; only spare his life." The Adversary departed from the presence of the LORD and inflicted a severe inflammation on Job from the sole of his foot to the crown of his head. He took a potsherd to scratch himself as he sat in ashes. His wife said to him, "You still keep your integrity! Blaspheme God and die!" But he said to her, "You talk as any shameless woman might talk! Should we accept only good from God and not accept evil?" For all that, Job said nothing sinful.

When Job's three friends heard about all these calamities that had befallen him, each came from his home—Eliphaz the Temanite, Bildad the Shuhite, and Zophar the Naamathite. They met together to go and console and comfort him. When they saw him from a distance, they could not recognize him, and they broke into loud weeping; each one tore his robe and threw dust into the air onto his head. They sat with him on the ground seven days and seven nights. None spoke a word to him for they saw how very great was his suffering.

Chapter 3

Afterward, Job began to speak and cursed the day of his birth. Job spoke up and said:

> Perish the day on which I was born,
> And the night it was announced,
> "A male has been conceived!"
> May that day be darkness;
> May God above have no concern for it;
> May light not shine on it;
> May darkness and deep gloom reclaim it;
> May a pall lie over it;
> May what blackens the day terrify it.
> May obscurity carry off that night;
> May it not be counted among the days of the year;
> May it not appear in any of its months;
> May that night be desolate;
> May no sound of joy be heard in it;
> May those who cast spells upon the day damn it,
> Those prepared to disable Leviathan;
> May its twilight stars remain dark;
> May it hope for light and have none;
> May it not see the glimmerings of the dawn—
> Because it did not block my mother's womb,
> And hide trouble from my eyes.
>
> Why did I not die at birth,
> Expire as I came forth from the womb?
> Why were there knees to receive me,
> Or breasts for me to suck?
> For now would I be lying in repose, asleep and at rest,

With the world's kings and counselors who rebuild ruins for
    themselves,
Or with nobles who possess gold and who fill their houses
    with silver.
Or why was I not like a buried stillbirth,
Like babies who never saw the light?
There the wicked cease from troubling;
There rest those whose strength is spent.
Prisoners are wholly at ease;
They do not hear the taskmaster's voice.
Small and great alike are there,
And the slave is free of his master.

Why does He give light to the sufferer
And life to the bitter in spirit;
To those who wait for death but it does not come,
Who search for it more than for treasure,
Who rejoice to exultation,
And are glad to reach the grave;
To the man who has lost his way,
Whom God has hedged about?
My groaning serves as my bread;
My roaring pours forth as water.
For what I feared has overtaken me;
What I dreaded has come upon me.
I had no repose, no quiet, no rest,
And trouble came.

Excerpt 2

Chapter 28

Then the LORD replied to Job out of the tempest and said:

Who is this who darkens counsel,
Speaking without knowledge?
Gird your loins like a man;
I will ask and you will inform Me.

Where were you when I laid the earth's foundations?
Speak if you have understanding.

Do you know who fixed its dimensions
Or who measured it with a line?
Onto what were its bases sunk?
Who set its cornerstone
When the morning stars sang together
And all the divine beings shouted for joy?

Who closed the sea behind doors
When it gushed forth out of the womb,
When I clothed it in clouds,
Swaddled it in dense clouds,
When I made breakers My limit for it,
And set up its bar and doors,
And said, "You may come so far and no farther;
Here your surging waves will stop"?

Have you ever commanded the day to break,
Assigned the dawn its place,
So that it seizes the corners of the earth
And shakes the wicked out of it?
It changes like clay under the seal
Till [its hues] are fixed like those of a garment.
Their light is withheld from the wicked,
And the upraised arm is broken.

Have you penetrated to the sources of the sea,
Or walked in the recesses of the deep?
Have the gates of death been disclosed to you?
Have you seen the gates of deep darkness?
Have you surveyed the expanses of the earth?
If you know of these—tell Me.

Which path leads to where light dwells,
And where is the place of darkness,
That you may take it to its domain
And know the way to its home?
Surely you know, for you were born then,
And the number of your years is many!
Have you penetrated the vaults of snow,
Seen the vaults of hail,
Which I have put aside for a time of adversity,

For a day of war and battle?
By what path is the west wind dispersed,
The east wind scattered over the earth?
Who cut a channel for the torrents
And a path for the thunderstorms,
To rain down on uninhabited land,
On the wilderness where no man is,
To saturate the desolate wasteland,
And make the crop of grass sprout forth?
Does the rain have a father?
Who begot the dewdrops?
From whose belly came forth the ice?
Who gave birth to the frost of heaven?
Water congeals like stone,
And the surface of the deep compacts.

Can you tie cords to Pleiades
Or undo the reins of Orion?
Can you lead out Mazzaroth in its season,
Conduct the Bear with her sons?
Do you know the laws of heaven
Or impose its authority on earth?

Can you send up an order to the clouds
For an abundance of water to cover you?
Can you dispatch the lightning on a mission
And have it answer you, "I am ready"?
Who put wisdom in the hidden parts?
Who gave understanding to the mind?
Who is wise enough to give an account of the heavens?
Who can tilt the bottles of the sky,
Whereupon the earth melts into a mass,
And its clods stick together.

Can you hunt prey for the lion,
And satisfy the appetite of the king of beasts?
They crouch in their dens, Lie in ambush in their lairs.
Who provides food for the raven
When his young cry out to God
And wander about without food?

Chapter 39

Do you know the season when the mountain goats
   give birth?
Can you mark the time when the hinds calve?
Can you count the months they must complete?
Do you know the season they give birth,
When they couch to bring forth their offspring,
To deliver their young?
Their young are healthy; they grow up in the open;
They leave and return no more.

Who sets the wild ass free?
Who loosens the bonds of the onager,
Whose home I have made the wilderness,
The salt land his dwelling-place?
He scoffs at the tumult of the city,
Does not hear the shouts of the driver.
He roams the hills for his pasture;
He searches for any green thing.

Would the wild ox agree to serve you?
Would he spend the night at your crib?
Can you hold the wild ox by ropes to the furrow?
Would he plow up the valleys behind you?
Would you rely on his great strength
And leave your toil to him?
Would you trust him to bring in the seed
And gather it in from your threshing floor?

The wing of the ostrich beats joyously;
Are her pinions and plumage like the stork's?
She leaves her eggs on the ground,
Letting them warm in the dirt,
Forgetting they may be crushed underfoot,
Or trampled by a wild beast.
Her young are cruelly abandoned as if they were not hers;
Her labor is in vain for lack of concern.
For God deprived her of wisdom,
Gave her no share of understanding,
Else she would soar on high,

Scoffing at the horse and its rider.

Do you give the horse his strength?
Do you clothe his neck with a mane?
Do you make him quiver like locusts,
His majestic snorting [spreading] terror?
He paws with force, he runs with vigor,
Charging into battle.
He scoffs at fear; he cannot be frightened;
He does not recoil from the sword.
A quiverful of arrows whizzes by him,
And the flashing spear and the javelin.
Trembling with excitement, he swallows the land;
He does not turn aside at the blast of the trumpet.
As the trumpet sounds, he says, "Aha!"
From afar he smells the battle,
The roaring and shouting of the officers.

Is it by your wisdom that the hawk grows pinions,
Spreads his wings to the south?
Does the eagle soar at your command,
Building his nest high,
Dwelling in the rock,
Lodging upon the fastness of a jutting rock?
From there he spies out his food;
From afar his eyes see it.
His young gulp blood;
Where the slain are, there is he.

Chapter 40

The LORD said in reply to Job.

Shall one who should be disciplined complain against Shaddai?
He who arraigns God must respond.

Job said in reply to the LORD:

See, I am of small worth; what can I answer You?
I clap my hand to my mouth.
I have spoken once, and will not reply;

Twice, and will do so no more.

Then the LORD replied to Job out of the tempest and said:

Gird your loins like a man;
I will ask, and you will inform Me.
Would you impugn My justice?
Would you condemn Me that you may be right?
Have you an arm like God's?
Can you thunder with a voice like His?
Deck yourself now with grandeur and eminence;
Clothe yourself in glory and majesty.
Scatter wide your raging anger;
See every proud man and bring him low.
See every proud man and humble him,
And bring them down where they stand.
Bury them all in the earth;
Hide their faces in obscurity.
Then even I would praise you
For the triumph your right hand won you. . . .

Chapter 42

. . . Job said in reply to the LORD:

I know that You can do everything,
That nothing you propose is impossible for You.
Who is this who obscures counsel without knowledge?
Indeed, I spoke without understanding
Of things beyond me, which I did not know.
Hear now, and I will speak.
I will ask, and You will inform me.
I had heard You with my ears,
But now I see You with my eyes;
Therefore, I recant and relent,
Being but dust and ashes.

After the LORD had spoken these words to Job, the LORD said to
Eliphaz the Temanite, "I am incensed at you and your two friends,[1] for

---

[1] Job's comforters.

you have not spoken the truth about Me as did My servant Job. Now take seven bulls and seven rams and go to My servant Job and sacrifice a burnt offering for yourselves. And let Job, My servant, pray for you; for to him I will show favor and not treat you vilely, since you have not spoken the truth about Me as did My servant Job." Eliphaz the Temanite and Bildad the Shuhite and Zophar the Naamathite went and did as the LORD had told them, and the LORD showed favor to Job. The LORD restored Job's fortunes when he prayed on behalf of his friends, and the LORD gave Job twice what he had before.

All his brothers and sisters and all his former friends came to him and had a meal with him in his house. They consoled and comforted him for all the misfortune that the LORD had brought upon him. Each gave him one *kesitah* and each one gold ring. Thus the LORD blessed the latter years of Job's life more than the former. He had fourteen thousand sheep, six thousand camels, one thousand yoke of oxen, and one thousand she-asses. He also had seven sons and three daughters. The first he named Jemimah, the second Keziah, and the third Keren-happuch. Nowhere in the land were women as beautiful as Job's daughters to be found. Their father gave them estates together with their brothers. Afterward, Job lived one hundred and forty years to see four generations of sons and grandsons. So Job died old and contented.

Excerpt from

THE ILIAD OF HOMER

Meeting of Achilleus and Priam

translated by Richmond Lattimore

Homer's epic The Iliad *tells the story of the anger of the Greek hero Achilleus, which brought pains thousandfold upon his own men, as well as on their enemies, the Trojans. The passage below, taken from the end of the poem, describes the meeting of Achilleus and the old and broken King Priam, which cools Achilleus's anger and eases the suffering of them both.*

Earlier in the story, Achilleus's anger reaches its climax after Hektor, son of King Priam, kills his best friend, Patroklos. Even though Achilleus avenges his friend, and even though he buries Patroklos with all due ceremony, his anger is unabated. He continues to rage and mourn, periodically hitching the corpse of Hektor to his chariot and dragging it around the tomb of Patroklos. At last, the gods intervene: Achilleus is commanded to return the corpse of Hektor.

In the excerpt below, King Priam comes in person to Achilleus to retrieve the body of his beloved son, Hektor. The aged king appeals to Achilleus in the name of his father, Peleus: "Achilleus like the gods, remember your father," are the first words he utters.

As old King Priam presses his lips to the man who has killed his beloved son, as well as so many more of his people, a miracle appears to take place. Achilleus, hitherto locked in his own savage anger, seems to regain his humanity. Rather than shun the suppliant, Achilleus welcomes him with grace. The two men weep together, tell each other stories, eat together, and wonder at each other. In the end, Achilleus returns Hektor's body to Priam.

How and why does this come about? What brings about Achilleus's change of heart? Is it credible? Is it generalizable? Can the anger that is so closely connected to vulnerability and suffering really be abated?

Priam vaulted down to the ground from behind the horses
and left Idaios where he was, for he stayed behind, holding
in hand the horses and mules. The old man made straight for the
    dwelling
where Achilleus the beloved of Zeus was sitting. He found him
inside, and his companions were sitting apart, as two only,
Automedon the hero and Alkimos, scion of Ares,
were busy beside him. He had just now got through with his dinner,
with eating and drinking, and the table still stood by. Tall Priam
came in unseen by the other men and stood close beside him
and caught the knees of Achilleus in his arms, and kissed the hands
that were dangerous and manslaughtering and had killed so many
of his sons. As when dense disaster closes on one who has murdered
a man in his own land, and he comes to the country of others,
to a man of substance, and wonder seizes on those who behold him,
so Achilleus wondered as he looked on Priam, a godlike
man, and the rest of them wondered also, and looked at each other.
But now Priam spoke to him in the words of a suppliant:
'Achilleus like the gods, remember your father, one who
is of years like mine, and on the door-sill of sorrowful old age.
And they who dwell nearby encompass him and afflict him,
nor is there any to defend him against the wrath, the destruction.
Yet surely he, when he hears of you and that you are still living,
is gladdened within his heart and all his days he is hopeful
that he will see his beloved son come home from the Troad.
But for me, my destiny was evil. I have had the noblest
of sons in Troy, but I say not one of them is left to me.
Fifty were my sons, when the sons of the Achaians came here.
Nineteen were born to me from the womb of a single mother,
and other women bore the rest in my palace; and of these
violent Ares broke the strength in the knees of most of them,
but one was left me who guarded my city and people, that one
you killed a few days since as he fought in defence of his country,
Hektor; for whose sake I come now to the ships of the Achaians
to win him back from you, and I bring you gifts beyond number.
Honour then the gods, Achilleus, and take pity upon me
remembering your father, yet I am still more pitiful;
I have gone through what no other mortal on earth has gone through;
I put my lips to the hands of the man who has killed my children.'
    So he spoke, and stirred in the other a passion of grieving
for his own father. He took the old man's hand and pushed him

gently away, and the two remembered, as Priam sat huddled
at the feet of Achilleus and wept close for manslaughtering Hektor
and Achilleus wept now for his own father, now again
for Patroklos. The sound of their mourning moved in the house. Then
when great Achilleus had taken full satisfaction in sorrow
and the passion for it had gone from his mind and body, thereafter
he rose from his chair, and took the old man by the hand, and set him
on his feet again, in pity for the grey head and the grey beard,
and spoke to him and addressed him in winged words: 'Ah, unlucky,
surely you have had much evil to endure in your spirit.
How could you dare to come alone to the ships of the Achaians
and before my eyes, when I am one who have killed in such numbers
such brave sons of yours? The heart in you is iron. Come, then,
and sit down upon this chair, and you and I will even let
our sorrows lie still in the heart for all our grieving. There is not
any advantage to be won from grim lamentation.
Such is the way the gods spun life for unfortunate mortals,
that we live in unhappiness, but the gods themselves have no sorrows.
There are two urns that stand on the door-sill of Zeus. They are unlike
for the gifts they bestow: an urn of evils, an urn of blessings.
If Zeus who delights in thunder mingles these and bestows them
on man, he shifts, and moves now in evil, again in good fortune.
But when Zeus bestows from the urn of sorrows, he makes a failure
of man, and the evil hunger drives him over the shining
earth, and he wanders respected neither of gods nor mortals.
Such were the shining gifts given by the gods to Peleus
from his birth, who outshone all men beside for his riches
and pride of possession, and was lord over the Myrmidons. Thereto
the gods bestowed an immortal wife on him, who was mortal.
But even on him the god piled evil also. There was not
any generation of strong sons born to him in his great house
but a single all-untimely child he had, and I give him
no care as he grows old, since far from the land of my fathers
I sit here in Troy, and bring nothing but sorrow to you and your
     children.'

Excerpt from
KING LEAR
by William Shakespeare

One is vulnerable at every stage of life, but to be old is, perhaps, to be especially so. In this excerpt from Shakespeare's King Lear *we witness the terrible suffering of one "foolish fond old man." What is responsible for his suffering? Is such suffering inevitable?*

In the opening act of the play (not reproduced here), the aged King Lear announces his intention to divide up his kingdom, allegedly in order "To shake all cares and business from our age," by "conferring them on younger strengths." So "unburdened," he says, he will "crawl toward death." Thus, we know from the outset that the old king is acutely aware of his impending death and, seemingly, ready to make way for the next generation.

But the "younger strengths" on which he intends to bestow his largesse are those of his three daughters—Goneril, Regan, and Cordelia—and rather than give each her share outright, Lear makes his gifts contingent upon a test: Each must tell him how much she loves him.

Lear's first two daughters make fulsome—and false—declarations of love. They receive their portions of the kingdom. Cordelia, his youngest and favorite, increasingly perturbed by what she hears as well as by the evident self-humiliation of her beloved father, elects to "love, and be silent." In rage, Lear abruptly disclaims and disinherits her.

He divides Cordelia's portion between her sisters. In return for these dowries, Lear intends to retain one hundred knights, as well as "the name, and all th' addition to a king." He announces that he intends to live in each daughter's house for a month at a time, together with his retinue; in other words, he plans to maintain the authority of kingship without the responsibilities of being king. The ensuing tragedy reveals the terrible consequences of Lear's ambivalence and his own ill-advised decision.

Goneril, the first daughter to receive Lear and his retinue at her home, treats him disrespectfully and bars half his knights. Astounded and furious, Lear runs to Regan, who with her husband, Cornwall, is intentionally away from her own home, staying with the Earl of Gloucester. As we would antici-

pate, things go from bad to worse. Lear's servant arrives first and is promptly put into the stocks. And when Lear arrives and asks to see Regan and Corn- wall, instead of bringing them out, Gloucester tells the King that he has "in- formed" them of his request.

The excerpt below, taken from act 2, scene 2, begins as Regan and Corn- wall enter and greet King Lear. In the conversation that ensues, which Goner- il eventually joins, Lear tries desperately to beat down his anger and his rising madness, as his daughters try, steadily and deliberately, to force him to recog- nize his reduced estate and acquiesce to his own impotence. At the end, Lear runs off into a gathering storm, and madness.

Regan, defending Goneril, tells her father: "O, sir, you are old /. . . .You should be ruled, and led / By some discretion that discerns your state / Better than you yourself." In light of Lear's rashness in dividing his kingdom as he did, and in banishing the faithful Cordelia, is Regan right?

Later, Regan pleads with her father, "Being weak, seem so." In so saying, she is certainly disrespectful; is she also wrong? Is Lear weak? If he is, how ought he to "seem" (act)?

Sarcastically mimicking agreement with Regan, Lear replies that "Age is unnecessary." Is it? Why should one be old? Why should others tolerate age?

Repeatedly, Lear expresses his fear that he will go mad. Repeatedly, he insists, "I can be patient." Why does Lear fear madness? Why is it so difficult for him to be patient? To what extent are his subsequent madness and his ongoing impatience functions of his age?

What is the main cause of Lear's suffering? His age? His refusal to accept being old? Some other reason?

LEAR

	The King would speak with Cornwall. The dear father
97	Would with his daughter speak, commands—tends—
	service.
	Are they informed of this? My breath and blood!
	Fiery? The fiery Duke, tell the hot Duke that—
	No, but not yet. May be he is not well.
101	Infirmity doth still neglect all office
102	Whereto our health is bound. We are not ourselves

97   *tends* attends, awaits (?), tenders, offers (?)
101 *all office* duties
102 *Whereto . . . bound* to which, in health, we are bound

When nature, being oppressed, commands the mind
To suffer with the body. I'll forbear;
105   And am fallen out with my more headier will
To take the indisposed and sickly fit
For the sound man.—Death on my state! Wherefore
108   Should he sit here? This act persuades me
109   That this remotion of the Duke and her
110   Is practice only. Give me my servant forth.
Go tell the Duke and 's wife I'ld speak with them!
112   Now, presently! Bid them come forth and hear me,
Or at their chamber door I'll beat the drum
114   Till it cry sleep to death.

GLOUCESTER
I would have all well betwixt you. *[Exit.]*

LEAR
O me, my heart, my rising heart! But down!

117 FOOL Cry to it, nuncle, as the cockney did to the eels when
118   she put 'em i' th' paste alive. She knapped 'em o' th' cox-
119   combs with a stick and cried, 'Down, wantons, down!'
'Twas her brother that, in pure kindness to his horse,
121   buttered his hay.
[Enter Cornwall, Regan, Gloucester, Servants.]

LEAR
Good morrow to you both.

CORNWALL   Hail to your Grace.
[Kent here set at liberty.]

REGAN
I am glad to see your Highness.

LEAR
Regan, I think you are. I know what reason

105   *headier* headstrong
108   *he,* i.e., Kent
109   *remotion* remaining remote, inaccessible
110   *practice* trickery
112   *presently* immediately
114   *cry* pursue with noise (like a pack or 'cry' of hounds)
117   *cockney* city-dweller
118   *paste* pastry pie; *knapped* rapped
119   *wantons,* i.e., frisky things
121   *buttered his hay* (another example of rustic humor at the expense of cockney inexperience)

I have to think so. If thou shouldst not be glad,
126   I would divorce me from thy mother's tomb,
Sepulchring an adultress. *[to Kent]* O, are you free?
Some other time for that.—Beloved Regan,
Thy sister's naught. O Regan, she hath tied
Sharp-toothed unkindness, like a vulture, here.
I can scarce speak to thee. Thou'lt not believe
132   With how depraved a quality—O Regan!

REGAN

133   I pray you, sir, take patience. I have hope
You less know how to value her desert
135   Than she to scant her duty.

LEAR   Say? How is that?

REGAN

I cannot think my sister in the least
Would fail her obligation. If, sir, perchance
She have restrained the riots of your followers,
'Tis on such ground, and to such wholesome end,
As clears her from all blame.

LEAR

My curses on her!

REGAN   O, sir, you are old;
142   Nature in you stands on the very verge
Of his confine. You should be ruled, and led
144   By some discretion that discerns your state
Better than you yourself. Therefore I pray you
That to our sister you do make return;
Say you have wronged her.

LEAR   Ask her forgiveness?
148   Do you but mark how this becomes the house:
'Dear daughter, I confess that I am old.
[Kneels.]

126-27 *divorce . . . adultress,* i.e., refuse to be buried with your mother since such a
child as you must have been conceived in adultery
132   *how . . . quality,* i.e., what innate depravity
133   *have hope,* i.e., suspect
135   *scant* (in effect, a double negative; 'do' would be more logical though less
emphatic)
142-43 *Nature . . . confine,* i.e., your life nears the limit of its tenure
144   *some discretion . . . state* someone discerning enough to recognize your condition
148   *the house* household or family decorum

Age is unnecessary. On my knees I beg
That you'll vouchsafe me raiment, bed, and food.'
REGAN
    Good sir, no more. These are unsightly tricks.
    Return you to my sister.
LEAR [rises]   Never, Regan.
154   She hath abated me of half my train,
    Looked black upon me, struck me with her tongue
    Most serpent-like upon the very heart.
    All the stored vengeances of heaven fall
158   On her ingrateful top! Strike her young bones,
159   You taking airs, with lameness.
CORNWALL   Fie, sir, fie!
LEAR
    You nimble lightnings, dart your blinding flames
    Into her scornful eyes! Infect her beauty,
162   You fen-sucked fogs drawn by the pow'rful sun
163   To fall and blister—
REGAN   O the blessed gods!
    So will you wish on me when the rash mood is on.
LEAR
    No, Regan, thou shalt never have my curse.
166   Thy tender-hefted nature shall not give
    Thee o'er to harshness. Her eyes are fierce, but thine
    Do comfort, and not burn. 'Tis not in thee
    To grudge my pleasures, to cut off my train,
170   To bandy hasty words, to scant my sizes,
171   And, in conclusion, to oppose the bolt
    Against my coming in. Thou better know'st
173   The offices of nature, bond of childhood,
174   Effects of courtesy, dues of gratitude.
    Thy half o' th' kingdom hast thou not forgot,

154 *abated* curtailed
158 *ingrateful top* ungrateful head
159 *taking* infectious
162 *fen-sucked* drawn up from swamps
163 *fall and blister* strike and raise blisters (such as those of smallpox)
166 *tender-hefted* swayed by tenderness, gently disposed
170 *bandy* volley; *sizes* allowances
171 *oppose the bolt*, i.e., bar the door
173 *offices of nature* natural duties
174 *Effects* actions

        Wherein I thee endowed.

176 REGAN   Good sir, to th' purpose.

               [Tucket within.]

    LEAR

        Who put my man i' th' stocks?

    CORNWALL   What trumpet's that?

    REGAN

178   I know't—my sister's. This approves her letter,

        That she would soon be here.

        Enter Steward [Oswald].   Is your lady come?

    LEAR

180   This is a slave, whose easy-borrowèd pride

181   Dwells in the fickle grace of her he follows.

182   Out, varlet, from my sight.

    CORNWALL What means your Grace?

    LEAR

        Who stocked my servant? Regan, I have good hope

        Thou didst not know on't.

        Enter Goneril. Who comes here? O heavens!

        If you do love old men, if your sweet sway

186   Allow obedience, if you yourselves are old,

187   Make it your cause. Send down, and take my part.

               [To Goneril]

        Art not ashamed to look upon this beard?

        O Regan, will you take her by the hand?

    GONERIL

        Why not by th' hand, sir? How have I offended?

191   All's not offense that indiscretion finds

        And dotage terms so.

192 LEAR O sides, you are too tough!

        Will you yet hold?

176 *purpose* point
178 *approves* confirms
180 *easy-borrowèd* acquired on small security
181 *grace* favor
182 *varlet* low fellow
186 *Allow* approve
187 *Make . . . cause,* i.e., make my cause yours
191 *indiscretion finds* ill judgment detects as such
192 *sides* breast (which should burst with grief)

How came my man i' th' stocks?

CORNWALL

I set him there, sir; but his own disorders

195   Deserved much less advancement.

LEAR

                You? Did you?

REGAN

196   I pray you, father, being weak, seem so.

If till the expiration of your month

You will return and sojourn with my sister,

Dismissing half your train, come then to me.

I am now from home, and out of that provision

201   Which shall be needful for your entertainment.

LEAR

Return to her, and fifty men dismissed?

No, rather I abjure all roofs, and choose

204   To wage against the emnity o' th' air,

To be a comrade with the wolf and owl,

206   Necessity's sharp pinch. Return with her?

207   Why, the hot-blooded France, that dowerless took

Our youngest born, I could as well be brought

209   To knee his throne, and, squire-like, pension beg

To keep base life afoot. Return with her?

211   Persuade me rather to be slave and sumpter

212   To this detested groom.

GONERIL   At your choice, sir.

LEAR

I prithee, daughter, do not make me mad.

I will not trouble thee, my child; farewell.

We'll no more meet, no more see one another.

But yet thou art my flesh, my blood, my daughter;

Or rather a disease that's in my flesh,

---

195   *less advancement*, i.e., more abasement
196   *seem so*, i.e., act the part
201   *entertainment* lodging
204   *wage* fight
206   *Necessity's sharp pinch* (a summing up of the hardships previously listed)
207   *hot-blooded* choleric (cf. I, ii, 23)
209   *knee* kneel at; *squire-like* like an attendant
211   *sumpter* packhorse
212   *groom*, i.e., Oswald

Which I must needs call mine. Thou art a boil,
219   A plague-sore, or embossèd carbuncle
In my corrupted blood. But I'll not chide thee.
Let shame come when it will, I do not call it.
222   I do not bid the thunder-bearer shoot,
223   Nor tell tales of thee to high-judging Jove.
Mend when thou canst, be better at thy leisure;
I can be patient, I can stay with Regan,
I and my hundred knights.

REGAN   Not altogether so.
I looked not for you yet, nor am provided
For your fit welcome. Give ear, sir, to my sister;
229   For those that mingle reason with your passion
Must be content to think you old and so—
But she knows what she does.

LEAR   Is this well spoken?
REGAN
232   I dare avouch it, sir. What, fifty followers?
Is it not well? What should you need of more?
234   Yea, or so many, sith that both charge and danger
Speak 'gainst so great a number? How in one house
Should many people, under two commands,
Hold amity? 'Tis hard, almost impossible.

GONERIL
Why might not you, my lord, receive attendance
From those that she calls servants, or from mine?

REGAN
240   Why not, my lord? If then they chanced to slack ye,
We could control them. If you will come to me
(For now I spy a danger), I entreat you
To bring but five-and-twenty. To no more
244   Will I give place or notice.

219   *embossèd* risen to a head
222   *thunder-bearer*, i.e., Jupiter
223   *high-judging* judging from on high
229   *mingle . . . passion* interpret your passion in the light of reason
232   *avouch* swear by
234   *sith that* since; *charge* expense
240   *slack* neglect
244   *notice* recognition

LEAR
      I gave you all.
REGAN   And in good time you gave it.
LEAR

246   Made you my guardians, my depositaries,
247   But kept a reservation to be followed
      With such a number. What, must I come to you
      With five-and-twenty? Regan, said you so?
REGAN
      And speak't again, my lord. No more with me.
LEAR

251   Those wicked creatures yet do look well-favored
      When others are more wicked; not being the worst
253   Stands in some rank of praise.
      [To Goneril]   I'll go with thee.
      Thy fifty yet doth double five-and-twenty,
255   And thou art twice her love.
GONERIL   Hear me, my lord.
      What need you five-and-twenty? ten? or five?
      To follow in a house where twice so many
      Have a command to tend you?
REGAN   What need one?
LEAR

259   O reason not the need! Our basest beggars
260   Are in the poorest thing superfluous.
261   Allow not nature more than nature needs,
      Man's life is cheap as beast's. Thou art a lady:
263   If only to go warm were gorgeous,
      Why, nature needs not what thou gorgeous wear'st,
      Which scarcely keeps thee warm. But, for true need—
      You heavens, give me that patience, patience I need.

246 *depositaries* trustees
247 *kept . . . to be* stipulated that I be
251 *well-favored* comely
253 *Stands . . . praise*, i.e., is at least relatively praiseworthy
255 *her love*, i.e., as loving as she
259 *reason* analyze
260 *Are . . . superfluous*, i.e., have some poor possession not utterly indispensable
261 *than nature needs*, i.e., than life needs for mere survival
263-65 *If . . . warm*, i.e., if to be dressed warmly (i.e., for need) were considered
sufficiently gorgeous, you would not need your present attire, which is gorgeous rather
than warm

You see me here, you gods, a poor old man.
As full of grief as age, wretched in both.
If it be you that stirs these daughters' hearts
270   Against their father, fool me not so much
To bear it tamely; touch me with noble anger,
And let not women's weapons, water drops,
Stain my man's cheeks. No, you unnatural hags!
I will have such revenges on you both
That all the world shall—I will do such things—
What they are, yet I know not; but they shall be
The terrors of the earth. You think I'll weep.
No, I'll not weep.
                    Storm and tempest.
I have full cause of weeping, but this heart
280   Shall break into a hundred thousand flaws
281   Or ere I'll weep. O fool, I shall go mad!
                    Exeunt [Lear, Fool, Kent, and Gloucester].

CORNWALL
    Let us withdraw; 'twill be a storm.
REGAN
    This house is little; the old man and 's people
    Cannot be well bestowed.
GONERIL
285   'Tis his own blame; hath put himself from rest
    And must needs taste his folly.
REGAN
287   For his particular, I'll receive him gladly,
    But not one follower.
288 GONERIL   So am I purposed.

270   *fool* play with, humiliate
280   *flaws* fragments
281   *Or ere* before
285   *hath . . . rest,* i.e., he himself is responsible for leaving his resting place with her
(?), he is self-afflicted (?)
287   *particular* own person
288   *purposed* determined

Where is my Lord of Gloucester?
CORNWALL
Followèd the old man forth.
    [Enter Gloucester.]   He is returned.
GLOUCESTER
The King is in high rage.
CORNWALL   Whither is he going?
GLOUCESTER
He calls to horse, but will I know not whither.
CORNWALL
'Tis best to give him way; he leads himself.
GONERIL
My lord, entreat him by no means to stay.
GLOUCESTER
Alack, the night comes on, and the high winds

296   Do sorely ruffle. For many miles about
There's scarce a bush.
REGAN   O, sir, to willful men
The injuries that they themselves procure
Must be their schoolmasters. Shut up your doors.
He is attended with a desperate train,

301   And what they may incense him to, being apt
To have his ear abused, wisdom bids fear.
CORNWALL
Shut up your doors, my lord; 'tis a wild night.
My Regan counsels well. Come out o' th' storm. *Exeunt.*

---

296   *ruffle* rage
301-02   *apt . . . abused*, i.e., predisposed to listen to ill counsel

MUSÉE DES BEAUX ARTS
by W. H. Auden

According to the ancient legend, Daedalus, an architect, was held captive on the isle of Crete with his son, Icarus. To escape, Daedalus made them wings of wax, warning his boy not to fly too near the sun. Yet Icarus, exhilarated, forgot his father's warning and flew so high that the sun melted his wings. He fell into the ocean and drowned.

This catastrophe is the subject of a painting by an Old Master, Pieter Bruegel, called "Landscape with the Fall of Icarus." In the well-known poem reproduced below, Auden considers the lessons about suffering to be found in Bruegel's depiction of the tragedy.

The "human position" of suffering, writes Auden, is that it takes place within and alongside the ordinary flow of humdrum life. Tragedy occurs, but those not involved do not stop for it. The tragic coexists with the trivial. For the ploughman, who may have noticed, Icarus's fall is "not an important failure"; the ship "must have seen," but had somewhere to go; the sun went on shining, "as it had to." The name of Bruegel's painting tells the same story as the poem; it is "Landscape with the Fall of Icarus," and not the other way around.

Why might Auden call this the "human position" of suffering? Has it another position?

How ought one to respond to the truth Auden has identified? Is it reassuring or distressing? Does our recognition of this truth impose any obligation on us, beyond our "sailing calmly on"?

About suffering they were never wrong,
The Old Masters: how well they understood
Its human position; how it takes place
While someone else is eating or opening a window or just walking
    dully along;

How, when the aged are reverently, passionately waiting
For the miraculous birth, there always must be
Children who did not specially want it to happen, skating
On a pond at the edge of a wood:
They never forgot
That even the dreadful martyrdom must run its course
Anyhow in a corner, some untidy spot
Where the dogs go on with their doggy life and the torturer's horse
Scratches its innocent behind on a tree.

In Brueghel's *Icarus*, for instance: how everything turns away
Quite leisurely from the disaster; the ploughman may
Have heard the splash, the forsaken cry,
But for him it was not an important failure; the sun shone
As it had to on the white legs disappearing into the green
Water; and the expensive delicate ship that must have seen
Something amazing, a boy falling out of the sky,
Had somewhere to get to and sailed calmly on.

Pieter Bruegel (the Elder). *Landscape with the Fall of Icarus*. c. 1554-1555. Panel painting transferred to canvas. Musées Royaux des Beaux-Arts, Brussels.

Excerpts from
PRECIOUS BANE
by Mary Webb

Can a bane be precious? The narrator of Mary Webb's novel is afflicted with a facial deformity that threatens to rob her of all happiness. Yet it is the unexpected source of a rich gift, as well.

The novel takes place in rural England, at a time (unspecified) when Christianity was universal but pagan influences still colored it. It is narrated by Prue Sarn, who has a cleft palate. Prue, fifteen, lives by a lake called Sarn Mere with her old widowed mother and her elder brother, Gideon. Their father has recently died, and Gideon took over the farm at his death. Gideon is driven by a passion to make money, and improve the family's lot and his own standing in the world. He has made a pact with Prue that they will work as hard as humanly possible to achieve this goal. Her reward is to be a visit to a doctor, who will cure her cleft palate and make her "as beautiful as a fairy."

Prue's cleft palate never troubled her much before, as she was young, and loved, and lived a very isolated life. Now, however, she is gradually becoming aware not only of what she looks like but, more troublingly, that she should not expect to marry. Marriage and children have long been her dream. "I was," she says, "like a maid standing at the meeting of the lane-ends on May Day with a posy-knot as a favour for a rider that should come by. And behold! The horseman rode straight over me, and left me, posy and all, in the mire."

In the first of the selected chapters, the reader sees the usually patient Prue break down for the first time. In her distress she flees to the attic, where after a while an extraordinary feeling of peace comes to her, unsought.

In the second excerpt, Prue admires the beauty of the ripening corn, and then watches dragonflies emerge from their cocoons, an annual sight fraught with meaning for her.

What is responsible for Prue's revelation? What accounts for her special awareness of the richness and beauty of nature? Does Prue's vision or sensitivity redeem her suffering?

Should Prue's harelip be fixed? Could such surgery remove her scars?

Do these excerpts shed light on the novel's title?

Excerpt 1

. . . Now my thought was this: why shouldna I, that was in sore need of healing, do as the poor folk did here at Sarn in time past, and even now and again in our own day. Namely, at the troubling of the waters which comes every year in the month of August, to step down into the mere in sight of all the folk at the Wake, dressed in a white smock. It was said that this troubling of the water was the same as that which was at Bethesda, and though it had not the power of that water, which healed every year, and for which no disease was too bad, it being in that marvellous Holy Land where miracles be daily bread, yet every seventh year it was supposed to cure one, if the disease was not too deadly. You must go down into the water fasting, and with many curious ancient prayers. These I could learn, when I could read, for they were in an old book that Parson kept in the vestry. Not that he believed it, nor quite disbelieved it, but only that it was very rare and strange.

The thing I misdoubted most was it being such a public thing. I had need be a very brazen piece to make a show of myself thus, as if I were a harlot in a sheet, or a witch brought to the ducking-stool. And sure enough, when I spoke of it timidly to Mother and Gideon, they liked it not at all.

'What,' says Gideon, 'make yourself a nay-word and a show to three hundred folk? You met as well go for a fat woman at the fair and ha' done with it.'

'Only I amna fat,' I said.

'That's neither here nor there. You'd be making yourself a talked-about wench from Sarn to Lullingford and from Plash to Bramton. Going down into the water the like of any poor plagued 'oman without a farden! Folk ud say, "There's Sarn's sister douked into the water like poor folk was used to do, because Sarn's too near to get the Doctor's mon, let alone the Doctor." And when I went to market, they'd laugh, turning their faces aside. Never shall you do such a brassy thing! It ud be better, a power, if you took and made some mint cakes and spiced ale for the fair when the time comes, like Mother was used to do. You'd make a bit that way.'

'Yes, my dear,' said Mother, 'you do as Sarn says. It'll bring in a bit, and you'll see all as is to be seen, which you couldna, saving in the way of business, for it'll be scarce two months from Father's death. And come to think of it, what an unkind thing it would be for a poor widow to have it flung in her face afore such a mort of people that her girl had got a hare-shotten lip.'

She began to wring her little hands, and I knew she'd go back to the old cry in a minute, so I gave in.

'You've got to promise me you'll never do such a thing, Prue,' ordered Gideon.

'I promise for this year, but no more.'

'You've got a powerful curst will of your own, Prue, but promise or no, you shanna do such a thing, never in life shall you!'

'And in death I shanna mind,' I said. 'For if I do well and go to heaven I shall be made all new, and I shall be as lovely as a lily on the mere. And if I do ill and go to hell, I'll sell my soul a thousand times, but I'll buy a beautiful face, and I shall be gladsome for that though I be damned.'

And I ran away into the attic and cried a long while.

But the quiet of the place, and the loneliness of it comforted me at long last, and I opened the shutter that gave on the orchard and had a great pear tree trained around it, and I took my knitting out of my reticule. For it was on Saturday after tea that I had spoken of the troubling of the water, and the week's work being nearly done, I had my tidy gown on, and the reticule to match. Sitting there looking into the green trees, with the smell of our hay coming freshly on the breeze, mixed with the scent of the wild roses and meadowsweet in the orchard ditch, I hearkened to the blackbirds singing near and far. When they were a long way off you could scarcely disentangle them from all the other birds, for there was a regular charm of them, thrushes and willow-wrens, seven-coloured linnets, canbottlins, finches, and *writing-maisters*. It was a weaving of many threads, with one maister-thread of clear gold, a very comfortable thing to hear.

I thought maybe love was like that—a lot of coloured threads, and one maister thread of pure gold.

The attic was close under the thatch, and there were many nests beneath the eaves, and a continual twittering of swallows. The attic window was in a big gable, and the roof on one side went right down to the ground, with a tall chimney standing up above the roof-tree. Somewhere among the beams of the attic was a wild bees' nest, and you could hear them making a sleepy soft murmuring, and morning and evening you could watch them going in a line to the mere for water. So, it being very still there, with the fair shadows of the apple trees peopling the orchard outside, that was void, as were the near meadows, Gideon being in the far field making hay-cocks, which I also should have been doing, there came to me, I cannot tell whence, a most powerful sweetness that had never come to me afore. It was not religious, like the goodness of a text heard at a preaching. It was beyond that. It was as if some creature made all of light had come on a sudden from a great way off, and nestled in my bosom. On all things there came a fair, lovely look, as if a different air stood over them. It is a look that seems ready to come sometimes on those gleamy mornings after rain, when they say, 'So fair the day, the cuckoo is going to heaven.'

Only this was not of the day, but of summat beyond it. I cared not to ask what it was. For when the nut-hatch comes into her own tree, she dunna ask who planted it, nor what name it bears to men. For the tree is all to the nut-hatch, and this was all to me. Afterwards, when I had mastered the reading of the book, I read—

His banner over me was love.

And it called to mind that evening. But if you should have said, 'Whose banner?' I couldna have answered. And even now, when Parson says, 'It was the power of the Lord working in you,' I'm not sure in my own mind. For there was nought in it of churches nor of folks, praying nor praising, sinning nor repenting. It had to do with such things as bird-song and daffadown-dillies rustling, knocking their heads together in the wind. And it was as wilful in its coming and going as a breeze over the standing corn. It was a queer thing, too, that a woman who spent her days in sacking, cleaning sties and beast-housen, living hard, considering over fardens, should come of a sudden into such a marvel as this. For though it was so quiet, it was a great miracle, and it changed my life; for when I was lost for something to turn to, I'd run to the attic, and it was a core of sweetness in much bitter.

Though the visitation came but seldom, the taste of it was in the attic all the while. I had but to creep in there, and hear the bees making their murmur, and smell the woody, o'er-sweet scent of kept apples, and hear the leaves rasping softly on the window-frame, and watch the twisted grey twigs on the sky, and I'd remember it and forget all else. There was a great wooden bolt on the door, and I was used to fasten it, though there was no need, for the attic was such a lost-and-forgotten place nobody ever came there but the travelling weaver, and Gideon in apple harvest, and me. Nobody would ever think of looking for me there, and it was parlour and church both to me.

The roof came down to the floor all round, and all the beams and rafters were oak, and the floor went up and down like stormy water. The apples and pears had their places according to kind all round the room. There were codlins and golden pippins, brown russets and scarlet crabs, biffins, nonpareils and queanings, big green bakers, pearmains and red-streaks. We had a mort of pears too, for in such an old garden, always in the family, every generation'll put in a few trees. We had Worcester pears and butter pears, jargonelle, bergamot and Good Christian. Just after the last gathering, the attic used to be as bright as a church window, all reds and golds. And the colours of the fruit could always bring my visitation back to me, though there was not an apple or pear in the place at the time, because the colour was wed to the scent, which had been there time out of mind. Every one of those round red cheeks used to smile at poor Prue Sarn, sitting betwixt the weaving-frame and the window, all by her lonesome. I found an old locker, given up to the mice, and scrubbed it, and put a fastening on it, and kept my ink and quills there, and my book, and the Bible, which Mother said I could have, since neither she nor Gideon could read in it.

One evening in October I was sitting there, with a rushlight, practising my writing. The moon blocked the little window, as if you took a salver and held it there. All round the walls the apples crowded, like people at a fair waiting to see a marvel. I thought to myself that they ought to be saying one to another, 'Be still now! Hush your noise! Give over jostling!'

I fell to thinking how all this blessedness of the attic came through me being curst. For if I hadna had a hare-lip to frighten me away into my own lonesome soul, this would never have come to me. The apples would have crowded all in vain to see a marvel, for I should never have known the glory that came from the other side of silence.

Even while I was thinking this, out of nowhere suddenly came that lovely thing, and nestled in my heart, like a seed from the core of love.

Excerpt 2

. . . It was a great delight to me, apart from the thought of all this, to look at the standing corn and see it like a great mere under the wind. Times it was still, without a ripple; times it went in little waves, and you could almost think the big bosses of wild onion flowers under the far hedges were lilies heaving gently on the tide; and times there was a great storm down in those hollows, like the storm in Galilee Mere, that the King of Love did still. So I watched the grain week by week, from the time when it was all one green till it began to take colour, turning raddled or abron or pale, each in his kind. And it shone, nights, as if there was a light behind it, with a kind of soft shining like glow-worms or a marish light. I never knew, nor do I know now, why corn shines thus in the nights of July and August, keeping a moonlight of its own even when there is no moon. But it is a marvellous thing to see, when the great hush of full summer and deep night is upon the land, till even the aspen tree, that will ever be gossiping, durstna speak, but holds breath as if she waited for the coming of the Lord. I make no doubt that if any read this book it will seem strange to them that a farm woman should look at the things about her in this wise, and indeed it is not many do. But when you dwell in a house you mislike, you will look out of window a deal more than those that are content with their dwelling. So I, finding my own person and my own life not to my mind, took my pleasure where I could. There were things I waited for as a wench waits for her sweetheart at her edge of the forest. This rippling and shining of the corn was one, and another which came about the time of the beginning of the troubling of the water, was the marvellous sight of the dragon-flies coming out of their bodies. We had a power of dragon-flies at Sarn, of many kinds and colours, little and big. But every one was bound in due season to climb up out of its watery grave and come out of its body with great labour and pain, and a torment like the torment of childbirth, and a rending like the rending of the tomb. And there was no year, since the first time I saw it, that I missed to see this showing forth of God's power. . . .

. . . For though Sarn was an ill place to live, and in the wintry months a very mournful place, at this one time of the year it left dreaming of sorrow and was as other fair stretches of wood and water. All around the lake stood the tall bulrushes with their stout heads of brown plush, just like a long coat Miss Dorabella had. Within the ring of rushes was another ring of lilies, and at this time of the year they were the most beautiful thing at Sarn, and the most beautiful thing I'd ever seen. The big bright leaves lay calm upon the water, and calmer yet upon the leaves lay the lilies, white and yellow. When they were buds, they were like white and gold birds sleeping, head under wing, or like summat carven out of glistering stone, or, as I said afore, they were like gouts of pale wax. But when they were come into full blow they wunna like anything but themselves, and they were so lovely you couldna choose but cry to see them. The yellow ones had more of a spread of petals, having five or six apiece, but the white ones opened their four wider and each petal was bigger. These petals are of a glistering white within, like the raiment of those men who stood with Christ upon the mountain top, and without they are stained with tender green, as if they had taken colour from the green shadows in the water. Some of the dragon-flies look like this also, for their lacy wings without other colour are sometimes touched with shifting green.

So the mere was three times ringed about, as if it had been three times put in a spell. First there was the ring of oaks and larches, willows, ollern trees and beeches, solemn and strong, to keep the world out. Then there was the ring of rushes, sighing thinly, brittle and sparse, but enough, with their long trembling shadows, to keep the spells in.

Then there was the ring of lilies, as I said, lying there as if Jesus walking upon the water, had laid them down with His cool hands, afore He turned to the multitude saying, 'Behold the lilies!' And as if they were not enough to shake your soul, there beneath every lily, white and green or pale gold, was her bright shadow, as it had been her angel. And through the long, untroubled day the lilies and their angels looked one upon the other and were content.

There were plenty of dragon-flies about, both big and little. There were the big blue ones that are so strong they will fly over top of the tallest tree if you fritten them, and there were the tiny thin ones that seem almost too small to be called dragon-flies at all. There were rich blue kingfisher-flies and those we called damsels, coloured and polished in the manner of lustre ware. There were a good few with clear wings of no colour or of faint green, and a tuthree with a powdery look like you see on the leaves of 'rickluses. Some were tawny, like a fitchet cat, some were rusty or coloured like the copper fruit-kettle. Jewels, they made you think of, precious gems such as be listed in the Bible. And the sound of their wings was loud in the air, sharp and whirring, when they had come to themselves after their agony. Whiles, in some mossy bit of clear ground between the trees, they'd sit about like so many cats round the hearth, very contented in themselves, so you could almost think they were washing their faces and purring.

On a tall rush close by the bank I found one just beginning to come out of its body, and I leaned near, pretty well holding my breath, to see the miracle. Already the skin over its bright, flaming eyes was as thin as glass, so that you could see them shining like coloured lamps. In a little, the old skin split and it got its head out. Then began the wrostling and the travail to get free, first its legs, then its shoulders and soft wrinkled wings. It was like a creature possessed, seeming to fall into a fit, times, and, times, to be struck stiff as a corpse. Just afore the end, it stayed a long while still, as if it was wondering whether it durst get quite free in a world all new. Then it gave a great heave and a kind of bursting wrench and it was out. It clomb a little way further up the bulrush, very sleepy and tired, like a child after a long day at the fair, and fell into a doze, while its wings began to grow.

'Well,' I says, with a bit of a laugh and summat near a bit of a sob, 'well, you've done it! It's cost you summat, but you've won free. I'm in behopes you'll have a pleasant time. I suppose this be your Paradise, binna it?'

But of course it couldna make any sign, save to go on growing its wings as fast as might be. So there I stood, with my armful of wrathes, and there it clung, limp on the brown rush, in the golden light that had come upon Sarn like a merciful healer. I was wasting my time, which was deadly sin at our place, and I turned to go. But just as I turned, there was a bit of a rustle, and there stood Kester Woodseaves[1].

[1] The man Prue secretly loves.

ON DEFORMITY

by Francis Bacon

In this essay Bacon writes about one particular type of suffering: living with a physical deformity. Bacon attends, specifically, to the effects it produces in the character of the one deformed.

Bacon ends by acknowledging that there are exceptions to the pattern which "commonly" and "for the most part" he has observed. Nevertheless, he writes, it "seldom faileth" that deformed persons "have their revenge of nature." By this, Bacon means that the deformed lack natural affection and seek to free themselves from the scorn in which they are naturally held. Because the able-bodied tend to write them off as persons "they may at pleasure despise," the deformed often find their despisers disarmed and vulnerable. Thus "in a great wit," Bacon writes, "deformity is an advantage to rising."

This will happen if the deformed "be of spirit," and Bacon notes that "all deformed persons are extreme bold." He claims that the advancement they long for must be accomplished "either by virtue or malice," but he concerns himself mostly with the latter, noting that the deformed watch for the weaknesses of others, to take advantage of them, and that they make "good spials [spies]".

Prue Sarn, of Mary Webb's Precious Bane, *credits her deformity for her spirituality, love of beauty, and intense empathy. Bacon paints a very different picture. Can both accounts be right? Are they, in fact, compatible? Does Bacon regard deformity as a "precious bane?"*

Does what Bacon describes apply equally to those who suffer from pain and to those who suffer from other causes?

For whose benefit does Bacon write: for the deformed, or for those who know them? If Bacon is right, how should the able-bodied regard and act toward the deformed?

Deformed persons are commonly even with nature; for, as nature hath done ill by them, so do they by nature, being for the most part (as the Scripture saith) *void of natural affection*; and so they have their revenge of nature. Certainly, there is a consent between the body and the mind, and where nature erreth in the one, she ventureth in the other: *Ubi peccat in uno, periclitatur in altero.* But because there is in man an election, touching the frame of his mind, and a necessity in the frame of his body, the stars of natural inclination are sometimes obscured by the sun of discipline and virtue; therefore, it is good to consider of deformity, not as a sign which is more deceivable, but as a cause which seldom faileth of the effect. Whosoever hath anything fixed in his person that doth induce contempt, hath also a perpetual spur in himself to rescue and deliver himself from scorn; therefore, all deformed persons are extreme bold; first, as in their own defense, as being exposed to scorn, but, in process of time, by a general habit. Also, it stirreth in them industry, and especially of this kind, to watch and observe the weakness of others, that they may have somewhat to repay. Again, in their superiors, it quencheth jealousy towards them, as persons that they think they may at pleasure despise; and it layeth their competitors and emulators asleep, as never believing they should be in possibility of advancement till they see them in possession; so that upon the matter, in a great wit, deformity is an advantage to rising. Kings in ancient times (and at this present in some countries) were wont to put great trust in eunuchs, because they that are envious towards all are more obnoxious and officious towards one; but yet their trust towards them hath rather been as to good spials, and good whisperers, than good magistrates and officers; and much like is the reason of deformed persons. Still the ground is, they will, if they be of spirit, seek to free themselves from scorn, which must be either by virtue or malice; and, therefore, let it not be marvelled, if sometimes they prove excellent persons; as was Agesilaüs, Zanger, the son of Solyman, Aesop, Gasca, president of Peru; and Socrates may go likewise amongst them, with others.

WITNESS

by Richard Selzer

At the center of "Witness," a short story by Richard Selzer, is a child so disabled that he can reward the love he receives with absolutely nothing. The story poignantly asks us to ponder why and how this child is loved, and whether his life is "for the best."

As the story begins, the narrator, a surgeon, is presented with a severely disabled young patient who is in pain. The boy communicates his pain by striking his own face or grinding his teeth. He has never been known to utter an intelligible word. Surgery reveals his immediate problem to be caused by an undescended testicle, which has ceased to be viable and must be removed. After the surgeon removes it, the testicle appears to him like a witness, or testament, to "these events."

To what "events" is the testicle a witness? In biblical times oaths were sworn with a hand on the testicles, meaning, literally and symbolically on the existence and power of future generations. Might this custom help to illuminate Selzer's meaning? How do you understand the love—or the kind of love—that the boy's parents have for him? Can the suffering of the child be disentangled from the suffering of his parents?

At the outset, the narrator addresses his readers directly, asking us to consider whether the lives of infants who suffer and die, experiencing nothing but pain, are "for the best." Is there anything good to be said for unrelieved pain and suffering?

There are human beings who spend their infancy in pain. One, perhaps, is born lacking, and must be completed, or a pot of hot coffee is spilled and another must be grafted and grafted again, first with the skin of strangers and then, if any, his own. Still another becomes the toothsome morsel of a tumor. This baby must be cut and suffer and even die. What is one to think of that? When an old person dies, it is of his own achievements. But here was a body to which nothing had happened until this pain. If this body had lived, you say, it would have known no pleasure, remembered no comfort. It would have had only a heritage of pain upon which to base its life. It is for the best, you say! Then what of this?

The boy in the bed is the length of a six-year-old. But something about him is much younger than that. It is the floppiness, I think. His head lolls as though it were floating in syrup. Now and then he unfurls his legs like a squid. He has pale yellow hair and pale blue eyes. His eyes will have none of me, but gaze as though into a mirror. He is blind. The right cheek and temple are deeply discolored. At first I think it is a birthmark. Then I see that it is a bruise.

"Does he walk?" I ask.

"No."

"Crawl?"

"He rolls. His left side is weak," the mother tells me.

"But he has a strong right arm," says the father. I touch the dark bruise that covers the right side of the child's face where he has again and again punched himself.

"Yes, I see that he is strong."

"That's how he tells us that he wants something or that something hurts. That, and grinding his teeth."

"He doesn't talk, then?"

"He has never been heard to utter a word," says the mother, as though repeating a statement from a written case history.

I unpin the diaper and lay it open. A red lump boils at the child's groin. The lump is the size of a walnut. The tissues around it slope off into pinkness. Under the pressure of my fingers, the redness blanches. I let up and the redness returns. I press again. Abruptly the right arm of the child flails upward and his fist bumps against his bruised cheek.

"You're hurting him," says the father.

The eyes of the child are terrible in their sapphiric emptiness. Is there not one tiny seed of vision in them? I know that there is not. The optic nerves have failed to develop, the pediatrician has told me. Such blindness goes all the way back to the brain.

"It is an incarcerated hernia," I tell him. "An emergency operation will be necessary to examine the intestine that is trapped in the sac. If the bowel is not already gangrenous, it will be replaced inside the peritoneal cavity, and then we will fix the hernia. If the circulation of the bowel has already been compromised, we will remove that section and stitch the ends together."

"Will there be . . . ?"

"No," I say, "there will be no need for a colostomy." All this they understand at once. The young woman nods.

"My sister's boy had the same thing," she says.

I telephone the operating room to schedule the surgery, then sit at the desk to write the preoperative orders on the chart. An orderly arrives with a stretcher for the boy. The father fends off my assistance and lifts the child onto the stretcher himself.

"Is there any danger?"

"There is always danger. But we will do everything to prevent trouble." The stretcher is already moving down the corridor. The father hurries to accompany it.

"Wait here," I say to him at the elevator. "I will come as soon as we are done." The man looks long and deep at the child, gulping him down in a single radiant gaze.

"Take good care of my son," he says. I see that he loves the boy as one can only love his greatest extravagance, the thing that will impoverish him totally, will give him cold and hunger and pain in return for his love. As the door to the elevator closes I see the father standing in the darkening corridor, his arms still making a cradle in which the smoke of twilight is gathering. I wheel the stretcher into the operating room from which the father has been banished. I think of how he must dwell for now in a dark hallway across which, from darker doorways, the blinding cries of sick children streak and crackle. What is his food, that man out there? Upon what shall he live but the remembered smiles of this boy?

On the operating table the child flutters and tilts like a moth burnt by the beams of the great overhead lamp. I move the lamp away from him until he is not so precisely caught. In this room where everything is green, the child is green as ice. Translucent, a fish seen through murk, and dappled. I hold him upon the table while the anesthetist inserts a needle into a vein on the back of the child's left hand, the one that is weak. Bending above, I can feel the boy's breath upon my neck. It is clean and hay-scented as the breath of a calf. If I knew how, I would lick the silence from his lips. What malice made this? Surely not God! Perhaps he is a changeling—an imperfect child put in place of another, a normal one who had been stolen by the fairies. Yes, I think. It is the malice of the fairies.

Now the boy holds his head perfectly still, cocked to one side. He seems to be listening. I know that he is . . . listening for the sound of his father's voice. I speak to the boy, murmur to him. But I know it is not the same. Take good care of my son, the father had said. Why must he brandish his love at me? I am enough beset. But I know that he must. I think of the immensity of love and I see for a moment what the father must see—the soul that lay in the body of the child like a chest of jewels in a sunken ship. Through the fathoms it glows. I cup the child's feet in one hand. How cold they are! I should like to lend him my cat to drape over them. I am happiest in winter with my cat for a foot pillow. No human has ever been so kind, so voluptuous, as my cat. Now the child is asleep. Under anesthesia he looks completely normal. So! It is only wakefulness that diminishes him.

The skin has been painted with antiseptic and draped. I make the incision across the apex of the protuberance. Almost at once I know that this is no incarcerated hernia but a testicle that had failed to descend into the scrotum. Its energy for the long descent had given out. Harmlessly it hung in midcanal until now, when it twisted on its little cord and cut off its own blood supply. The testicle is no longer viable. The black color of it tells me so. I cut into the substance of the testicle to see if it will bleed. It does not. It will have to be removed.

"You'll have to take it out, won't you?" It is the anesthesiologist speaking. "It won't do him any good now. Anyway, why does he need it?"

"Yes, yes, I know. . . . Wait." And I stand at the table filled with loathing for my task. Precisely because he has so little left, because it is of no use to him . . . I know. A moment later I tie the spermatic cord with a silk suture, and I cut off the testicle. Lying upon a white gauze square, it no longer appears mad, threatening, but an irrefutable witness to these events, a testament. I close the wound.

I am back in the solarium of the pediatric ward. It is empty save for the young couple and myself.

"He is fine," I tell them. "He will be in the recovery room for an hour and then they will bring him back here. He is waking up now."

"What did you do to my son?" The father's eyes have the glare of black olives.

"It wasn't a hernia," I explain. "I was wrong. It was an undescended testicle that had become twisted on its cord. I had to remove it." The mother nods minutely. Her eyes are the same blue gem from which the boy's have been struck. There is something pure about the woman out of whose womb this child had blundered to knock over their lives. As though the mothering of such a child had returned her to a state of virginity. The father slumps in his chair, his body doubled as though it were he who had been cut in the groin. There in the solarium he seems to be aging visibly, the arteries in his body silting up. Yellow sacs of flesh appear beneath his eyes. His eyes themselves are peopled with red ants. I imagine his own slack scrotum. And the hump on his back—flapping, dithering, drooling, reaching up to hit itself on the cheek, and listening, always listening, for the huffing of the man's breath.

Just then the room is plunged into darkness.

"Don't worry," I say. "A power failure. There is an accessory genera-tor. The lights will go on in a moment." We are silent, as though the darkness has robbed us of speech as well. I cannot see the father, but like the blind child in the recovery room, I listen for the sound of his voice.

The lights go on. Abruptly, the father rises from his chair.

"Then, he is all right?"

"Yes," I nod. Relief snaps open upon his face. He reaches for his wife's hand. They stand there together, smiling. And all at once I know that this man's love for his child is a passion. It is a rapids roiling within him. It has nothing to do with pleasure, this kind of love. It is a deep, black joy.

PEOPLE LIKE THAT ARE THE ONLY PEOPLE HERE: CANONICAL BABBLINGS IN PEED ONK

by Lorrie Moore

In this short story, a proudly countercultural mother learns that her baby has a malignant tumor. She is staggered to discover, abruptly and horribly, that disaster and uncertainty can strike out of nowhere.

The mother, who is a writer, must ponder her helplessness before her unknown fate. She must learn how she is to protect her child, despite all that she is not given to know. As she and her husband see their son from diagnosis, to surgery, to discharge from the hospital, she is also forced to confront newly-revealed similarities between herself and "people like that"—others she had always considered very different.

After the mother and the husband learn that their baby has cancer, the mother tries to bargain with an unseen power for a guarantee for her child. An unbeliever, she imagines herself bargaining with the manager of a department store. In a moment of insight, she imagines the manager telling her that "What makes humans human is precisely that they do not know the future." What's more, "life's efforts" cannot produce stories if there it is no mystery as to how those efforts will turn out. The mother therefore realizes that the vulnerability with which she is struggling is not only the source of her humanity, but of her art as well.

While in the Pediatric Oncology Ward ("Peed Onk"), the mother observes among the other parents a "consuming and unquestionable obligation meeting illness move for move in a giant even-steven game of chess." She listens as these parents discuss whether this is courage. One father says it isn't, because "courage requires options," but another mother points out that there is always the option of giving up.

At the end of the story the mother is offered a choice of therapies for her child. Her husband is inclined toward the better-known and more aggressive choice, but she insists upon the experimental (less-known) and more passive treatment.

How are we to understand this choice? When she refused the husband's suggestion that they "stomp" on the cancer, "beat it, smash it to death," was she "meeting illness move for move" as the other parents had? Was she accepting her vulnerability to the unknowable, as the manager counseled?

Was she "giving up?"

As the family leaves the hospital at the end of the story, the husband feels uplifted by the good wishes expressed by the other parents in the ward. He is consoled by the thought that "we're all in the same boat."

"Woman overboard!" thinks the mother to herself, rejecting membership in the "club" of parents of cancer patients.

Does the mother truly understand the nature of this membership? Why does she reject it? Her son's illness has challenged her to see the superficiality of the differences she has always perceived between herself and others. Has she really seen it, by the end of the story?

Who are "people like that," and why are they "the only people" in Peed Onk?

A beginning, an end: there seems to be neither. The whole thing is like a cloud that just lands and everywhere inside it is full of rain. A start: the Mother finds a blood clot in the Baby's diaper. What is the story? Who put this here? It is big and bright, with a broken khaki-colored vein in it. Over the weekend, the Baby had looked listless and spacey, clayey and grim. But today he looks fine—so what is this thing, startling against the white diaper, like a tiny mouse heart packed in snow? Perhaps it belongs to someone else. Perhaps it is something menstrual, something belonging to the Mother or to the Babysitter, something the Baby has found in a wastebasket and for his own demented baby reasons stowed away here. (Babies: they're crazy! What can you do?) In her mind, the Mother takes this away from his body and attaches it to someone else's. There. Doesn't that make more sense?

Still, she phones the clinic at the children's hospital. "Blood in the diaper," she says, and, sounding alarmed and perplexed, the woman on the other end says, "Come in now."

Such pleasingly instant service! Just say "blood." Just say "diaper." Look what you get!

In the examination room, pediatrician, nurse, head resident—all seem less alarmed and perplexed than simply perplexed. At first, stupidly, the Mother is calmed by this. But soon, besides peering and saying

"Hmmmm," the pediatrician, nurse, and head resident are all drawing their mouths in, bluish and tight—morning glories sensing noon. They fold their arms across their white-coated chests, unfold them again and jot things down. They order an ultrasound. Bladder and kidneys. "Here's the card. Go downstairs; turn left."

In Radiology, the Baby stands anxiously on the table, naked against the Mother as she holds him still against her legs and waist, the Radiologist's cold scanning disc moving about the Baby's back. The Baby whimpers, looks up at the Mother. *Let's get out of here*, his eyes beg. *Pick me up!* The Radiologist stops, freezes one of the many swirls of oceanic gray, and clicks repeatedly, a single moment within the long, cavernous weather map that is the Baby's insides.

"Are you finding something?" asks the Mother. Last year, her uncle Larry had had a kidney removed for something that turned out to be benign. These imaging machines! They are like dogs, or metal detectors: they find everything, but don't know what they've found. That's where the surgeons come in. They're like the owners of the dogs. "Give me that," they say to the dog. "What the heck is that?"

"The surgeon will speak to you," says the Radiologist.

"Are you finding something?"

"The surgeon will speak to you," the Radiologist says again. "There seems to be something there, but the surgeon will talk to you about it."

"My uncle once had something on his kidney," says the Mother. "So they removed the kidney and it turned out the something was benign."

The Radiologist smiles a broad, ominous smile. "That's always the way it is," he says. "You don't know exactly what it is until it's in the bucket."

"'In the bucket,'" the Mother repeats.

The Radiologist's grin grows scarily wider—is that even possible? "That's doctor talk," he says.

"It's very appealing," says the Mother. "It's a very appealing way to talk." Swirls of bile and blood, mustard and maroon in a pail, the colors of an African flag or some exuberant salad bar: *in the bucket*—she imagines it all.

"The Surgeon will see you soon," he says again. He tousles the Baby's ringletty hair. "Cute kid," he says.

"Let's see now," says the Surgeon in one of his examining rooms. He has stepped in, then stepped out, then come back in again. He has crisp, frowning features, sharp bones, and a tennis-in-Bermuda tan. He crosses his blue-cottoned legs. He is wearing clogs.

The Mother knows her own face is a big white dumpling of worry. She is still wearing her long, dark parka, holding the Baby, who has pulled the hood up over her head because he always thinks it's funny to do that. Though on certain windy mornings she would like to think she could look vaguely romantic like this, like some French Lieutenant's Woman of the Prairie, in all of her saner moments she knows she doesn't. Ever. She knows she looks ridiculous—like one of those animals made out of twisted party balloons. She lowers the hood and slips one arm out of the sleeve. The Baby wants to get up and play with the light switch. He fidgets, fusses, and points.

"He's big on lights these days," explains the Mother.

"That's okay," says the Surgeon, nodding toward the light switch. "Let him play with it." The Mother goes and stands by it, and the Baby begins turning the lights off and on, off and on.

"What we have here is a Wilms' tumor," says the Surgeon, suddenly plunged into darkness. He says "tumor" as if it were the most normal thing in the world.

"Wilms'?" repeats the Mother. The room is quickly on fire again with light, then wiped dark again. Among the three of them here, there is a long silence, as if it were suddenly the middle of the night. "Is that apostrophe s or s apostrophe?" the Mother says finally. She is a writer and a teacher. Spelling can be important—perhaps even at a time like this, though she has never before been at a time like this, so there are barbarisms she could easily commit and not know.

The lights come on: the world is doused and exposed.

"S apostrophe," says the Surgeon. "I think." The lights go back out, but the Surgeon continues speaking in the dark. "A malignant tumor on the left kidney."

Wait a minute. Hold on here. The Baby is only a baby, fed on organic applesauce and soy milk—a little prince!—and he was standing so close to her during the ultrasound. How could he have this terrible thing? It must have been her kidney. A fifties kidney. A DDT kidney. The Mother clears her throat. "Is it possible it was my kidney on the scan? I mean, I've never heard of a baby with a tumor, and, frankly, I was standing very close." She would make the blood hers, the tumor hers; it would all be some treacherous, farcical mistake.

"No, that's not possible," says the Surgeon. The light goes back on.

"It's not?" says the Mother. *Wait until it's in the bucket,* she thinks. Don't be so sure. *Do we have to wait until it's in the bucket to find out a mistake has been made?*

"We will start with a radical nephrectomy," says the Surgeon, instantly thrown into darkness again. His voice comes from nowhere and everywhere at once. "And then we'll begin with chemotherapy after that. These tumors usually respond very well to chemo."

"I've never heard of a baby having chemo," the Mother says. *Baby* and *Chemo*, she thinks: they should never even appear in the same sentence together, let alone the same life. In her other life, her life before this day, she had been a believer in alternative medicine. Chemotherapy? Unthinkable. Now, suddenly, alternative medicine seems the wacko maiden aunt to the Nice Big Daddy of Conventional Treatment. How quickly the old girl faints and gives way, leaves one just standing there. Chemo? Of course: chemo! Why by all means: chemo. Absolutely! Chemo!

The Baby flicks the switch back on, and the walls reappear, big wedges of light checkered with small framed watercolors of the local lake. The Mother has begun to cry: all of life has led her here, to this moment. After this, there is no more life. There is something else, something stumbling and unlivable, something mechanical, something for robots, but not life. Life has been taken and broken, quickly, like a stick. The room goes dark again, so that the Mother can cry more freely. How can a baby's body be stolen so fast? How much can one heaven-sent and unsuspecting child endure? Why has he not been spared this inconceivable fate?

Perhaps, she thinks, she is being punished: too many baby-sitters too early on. ("Come to Mommy! Come to Mommy-Baby-sitter!" she used to say. But it was a joke!) Her life, perhaps, bore too openly the marks and wigs of deepest drag. Her unmotherly thoughts had all been noted: the panicky hope that his nap would last longer than it did; her occasional desire to kiss him passionately on the mouth (to make out with her baby!); her ongoing complaints about the very vocabulary of motherhood, how it degraded the speaker ("Is this a poopie onesie! Yes, it's a very poopie onesie!"). She had, moreover, on three occasions used the formula bottles as flower vases. She twice let the Baby's ears get fudgy with wax. A few afternoons last month, at snacktime, she placed a bowl of Cheerios on the floor for him to eat, like a dog. She let him play with the Dustbuster. Just once, before he was born, she said, "Healthy? I just want the kid to be rich." A joke, for God's sake! After he was born she announced that her life had become a daily sequence of mind-wrecking chores, the same ones over and over again, like a novel by Mrs. Camus. Another joke! These jokes will kill you! She had told too often, and with too much enjoyment, the story of how the Baby had said "Hi" to his high chair, waved at the lake waves, shouted "Goody-goody-goody" in what seemed to be a Russian accent, pointed at his eyes and said "Ice." And all that nonsensical baby talk: wasn't it a stitch? "Canonical babbling," the language experts called it. He recounted whole stories in it—totally made up, she could tell. He embroidered; he fished; he exaggerated. What a card! To friends, she spoke of his eating habits (carrots yes, tuna no). She mentioned, too much, his sidesplitting giggle. Did she have to be so boring? Did she have no consideration for others, for the intellectual demands and courtesies of human society? Would she not even attempt to be more interesting? It was a crime against the human mind not even to try.

Now her baby, for all these reasons—lack of motherly gratitude, motherly judgment, motherly proportion—will be taken away.

The room is fluorescently ablaze again. The Mother digs around in her parka pocket and comes up with a Kleenex. It is old and thin, like a mashed flower saved from a dance; she dabs it at her eyes and nose.

"The Baby won't suffer as much as you," says the Surgeon.

And who can contradict? Not the Baby, who in his Slavic Betty Boop voice can say only *mama, dada, cheese, ice, bye-bye, outside, boogie-boogie, goody-goody, eddy-eddy,* and *car.* (Who is Eddy? They have no idea.) This will not suffice to express his mortal suffering. Who can say what babies do with their agony and shock? Not they themselves. (Baby talk: isn't it a stitch?) They put it all no place anyone can really see. They are like a different race, a different species: they seem not to experience pain the way *we* do. Yeah, that's it: their nervous systems are not as fully formed, and *they just don't experience pain the way we do.* A tune to keep one humming through the war. "You'll get through it," the Surgeon says.

"How?" asks the Mother. "How does one get through it?"

"You just put your head down and go," says the Surgeon. He picks up his file folder. He is a skilled manual laborer. The tricky emotional stuff is not to his liking. The babies. The babies! What can be said to console the parents about the babies? "I'll go phone the oncologist on duty to let him know," he says, and leaves the room.

"Come here, sweetie," the Mother says to the Baby, who has toddled off toward a gum wrapper on the floor. "We've got to put your jacket on." She picks him up and he reaches for the light switch again. Light, dark. Peekaboo: where's baby? Where did baby go?

At home, she leaves a message—"Urgent! Call me!"—for the Husband on his voice mail. Then she takes the Baby upstairs for his nap, rocks him in the rocker. The Baby waves good-bye to his little bears, then looks toward the window and says, "Bye-bye, outside." He has, lately, the habit of waving good-bye to everything, and now it seems as if he senses an imminent departure, and it breaks her heart to hear him. *Bye-bye!* She sings low and monotonously, like a small appliance, which is how he likes it. He is drowsy, dozy, drifting off. He has grown so much in the last year, he hardly fits in her lap anymore; his limbs dangle off like a pietà. His head rolls slightly inside the crook of her arm. She can feel him falling backward into sleep, his mouth round and open like the sweetest of poppies. All the lullabies in the world, all the melodies threaded through with maternal melancholy now become for her—abandoned as a mother can be by working men and napping babies—the songs of hard, hard grief. Sitting there, bowed and bobbing, the Mother feels the entirety of her love as worry and heartbreak. A quick and irrevocable alchemy: there is no longer one unworried scrap left for happiness. "If you go," she keens low into his soapy neck, into the ranunculus coil of his ear, "we are going with you. We are nothing without you. Without you, we are a heap of rocks. We are gravel and mold. Without you, we are two stumps, with nothing any longer in our hearts. Wherever this takes you, we are following. We will be there. Don't be scared. We are going, too. That is that."

"Take Notes," says the Husband, after coming straight home from work, midafternoon, hearing the news, and saying all the words out loud—surgery, metastasis, dialysis, transplant—then collapsing in a chair in tears. "Take notes. We are going to need the money."

"Good God," cries the Mother. Everything inside her suddenly begins to cower and shrink, a thinning of bones. Perhaps this is a soldier's readiness, but it has the whiff of death and defeat. It feels like a heart attack, a failure of will and courage, a power failure: a failure of everything. Her face, when she glimpses it in a mirror, is cold and bloated with shock, her eyes scarlet and shrunk. She has already started to wear sunglasses indoors, like a celebrity widow. From where will her own strength come? From some philosophy? From some frigid little philosophy? She is neither stalwart nor realistic and has trouble with basic concepts, such as the one that says events move in one direction only and do not jump up, turn around, and take themselves back.

The Husband begins too many of his sentences with "What if." He is trying to piece everything together like a train wreck. He is trying to get the train to town.

"We'll just take all the steps, move through all the stages. We'll go where we have to go. We'll hunt; we'll find; we'll pay what we have to pay. What if we can't pay?"

"Sounds like shopping."

"I cannot believe this is happening to our little boy," he says, and starts to sob again. "Why didn't it happen to one of us? It's so unfair. Just last week, my doctor declared me in perfect health: the prostate of a twenty-year-old, the heart of a ten-year-old, the brain of an insect—or whatever it was he said. What a nightmare this is."

What words can be uttered? You turn just slightly and there it is: the death of your child. It is part symbol, part devil, and in your blind spot all along, until, if you are unlucky, it is completely upon you. Then it is a fierce little country abducting you; it holds you squarely inside itself like a cellar room—the best boundaries of you are the boundaries of it. Are there windows? Sometimes aren't there windows?

The Mother is not a shopper. She hates to shop, is generally bad at it, though she does like a good sale. She cannot stroll meaningfully through anger, denial, grief, and acceptance. She goes straight to bargaining and stays there. How much? she calls out to the ceiling, to some makeshift construction of holiness she has desperately, though not uncreatively, assembled in her mind and prayed to; a doubter, never before given to prayer, she must now reap what she has not sown; she must assemble from scratch an entire altar of worship and begging. She tries for noble abstractions, nothing too anthropomorphic, just some Higher Morality, though if this particular Highness looks something like the manager at Marshall Field's, sucking a Frango mint, so be it. Amen. Just tell me what you want, requests the Mother. And how do you want it? More charitable acts? A billion starting now. Charitable thoughts? Harder, but of course! Of course! I'll do the cooking, honey; I'll pay the rent. Just tell me. *Excuse me?* Well, if not to you, to whom do I speak? Hello? To whom do I have to speak around here? A higher-up? A superior? Wait? I can wait. I've got all day. I've got the whole damn day.

The Husband now lies next to her in bed, sighing. "Poor little guy could survive all this, only to be killed in a car crash at the age of sixteen," he says.

The wife, bargaining, considers this. "We'll take the car crash," she says.

"What?"

"Let's Make a Deal! Sixteen Is a Full Life! We'll take the car crash. We'll take the car crash, in front of which Carol Merrill is now standing."

Now the Manager of Marshall Field's reappears. "To take the surprises out is to take the life out of life," he says.

The phone rings. The Husband gets up and leaves the room.

"But I don't want these surprises," says the Mother. "Here! You take these surprises!"

"To know the narrative in advance is to turn yourself into a machine," the Manager continues. "What makes humans human is precisely that they do not know the future. That is why they do the fateful and amusing things they do: who can say how anything will turn out? Therein lies the only hope for redemption, discovery, and—let's be frank—fun, fun, fun! There might be things people will get away with. And not just motel towels. There might be great illicit loves, enduring joy, faith-shaking accidents with farm machinery. But you have to not know in order to see what stories your life's efforts bring you. The mystery is all."

The Mother, though shy, has grown confrontational. "Is this the kind of bogus, random crap they teach at merchandising school? We would like fewer surprises, fewer efforts and mysteries, thank you. K through eight; can we just get K through eight?" It now seems like the luckiest, most beautiful, most musical phrase she's ever heard: K through eight. The very lilt. The very thought.

The Manager continues, trying things out. "I mean, the whole conception of 'the story,' of cause and effect, the whole idea that people have a clue as to how the world works is just a piece of laughable metaphysical colonialism perpetrated upon the wild country of time."

Did they own a gun? The Mother begins looking through drawers.

The Husband comes back into the room and observes her. "Ha! The Great Havoc that is the Puzzle of all Life!" he says of the Marshall Field's management policy. He has just gotten off a conference call with the insurance company and the hospital. The surgery will be Friday. "It's all just some dirty capitalist's idea of a philosophy."

"Maybe it's just a fact of narrative and you really can't politicize it," says the Mother. It is now only the two of them.

"Whose side are you on?"

"I'm on the Baby's side."

"Are you taking notes for this?"

"No."

"You're not?"

"No. I can't. Not this! I write fiction. This isn't fiction."

"Then write nonfiction. Do a piece of journalism. Get two dollars a word."

"Then it has to be true and full of information. I'm not trained. I'm not that skilled. Plus, I have a convenient personal principle about artists not abandoning art. One should never turn one's back on a vivid imagination. Even the whole memoir thing annoys me."

"Well, make things up, but pretend they're real."

"I'm not that insured."

"You're making me nervous."

"Sweetie, darling, I'm not that good. I can't *do this*. I can do—what can I do? I can do quasi-amusing phone dialogue. I can do succinct descriptions of weather. I can do screwball outings with the family pet. Sometimes I can do those. Honey, I only do what I can. I do *the careful ironies of daydream*. I do *the marshy ideas upon which intimate life is built*. But this? Our baby with cancer? I'm sorry. My stop was two stations back. This is irony at its most gaudy and careless. This is a Hieronymus Bosch of facts and figures and blood and graphs. This is a nightmare of narrative slop. This cannot be designed. This cannot even be noted in preparation for a design—"

"We're going to need the money."

"To say nothing of the moral boundaries of pecuniary recompense in a situation such as this—"

"What if the other kidney goes? What if he needs a transplant? Where are the moral boundaries there? What are we going to do, have bake sales?"

"We can sell the house. I hate this house. It makes me crazy."

"And we'll live—where again?"

"The Ronald McDonald place. I hear it's nice. It's the least McDonald's can do."

"You have a keen sense of justice."

"I try. What can I say?" She pauses. "Is all this really happening? I keep thinking that soon it will be over—the life expectancy of a cloud is supposed to be only twelve hours—and then I realize something has occurred that can never ever be over."

The Husband buries his face in his hands: "Our poor baby. How did this happen to him?" He looks over and stares at the bookcase that serves as the nightstand. "And do you think even one of these baby books is any help?" He picks up the Leach, the Spock, the *What to Expect*. "Where in the pages or index of any of these does it say 'chemotherapy' or 'Hickman catheter' or 'renal sarcoma'? Where does it say 'carcinogenesis'? You know what these books are obsessed with? *Holding a fucking spoon*." He begins hurling the books off the night table and against the far wall.

"Hey," says the Mother, trying to soothe. "Hey, hey, hey." But compared to his stormy roar, her words are those of a backup singer—a Shondell, a Pip—a doo-wop ditty. Books, and now more books, continue to fly.

Take Notes.

Is *fainthearted* one word or two? Student prose has wrecked her spelling.

It's one word. Two words—*Faint Hearted*—what would that be? The name of a drag queen.

Take Notes. In the end, you suffer alone. But at the beginning you suffer with a whole lot of others. When your child has cancer, you are instantly whisked away to another planet: one of bald-headed little boys. Pediatric Oncology. Peed Onk. You wash your hands for thirty seconds in antibacterial soap before you are allowed to enter through the swinging doors. You put paper slippers on your shoes. You keep your voice down. A whole place has been designed and decorated for your nightmare. Here is where your nightmare will occur. We've got a room all ready for you. We have cots. We have refrigerators. "The children are almost entirely boys," says one of the nurses. "No one knows why. It's been documented, but a lot of people out there still don't realize it." The little boys are all from sweet-sounding places—Janesville and Appleton—little heartland towns with giant landfills, agricultural runoff, paper factories, Joe McCarthy's grave (Alone, a site of great toxicity, thinks the Mother. The soil should be tested).

All the bald little boys look like brothers. They wheel their IVs up and down the single corridor of Peed Onk. Some of the lively ones, feeling good for a day, ride the lower bars of the IV while their large, cheerful mothers whiz them along the halls. *Wheee!*

The Mother does not feel large and cheerful. In her mind, she is scathing, acid-tongued, wraith-thin, and chain-smoking out on a fire escape somewhere. Beneath her lie the gentle undulations of the Midwest, with all its aspirations to be—to be what? To be Long Island. How it has succeeded! Strip mall upon strip mall. Lurid water, poisoned potatoes. The Mother drags deeply, blowing clouds of smoke out over the disfigured cornfields. When a baby gets cancer, it seems stupid ever to have given up smoking. When a baby gets cancer, you think, Whom are we kidding? Let's all light up. When a baby gets cancer, you think, Who came up with *this* idea? What celestial abandon gave rise to *this*? Pour me a drink, so I can refuse to toast.

The Mother does not know how to be one of these other mothers, with their blond hair and sweatpants and sneakers and determined pleasantness. She does not think that she can be anything similar. She does not feel remotely like them. She knows, for instance, too many people in Greenwich Village. She mail-orders oysters and tiramisu from a shop in SoHo. She is close friends with four actual homosexuals. Her husband is asking her to Take Notes.

Where do these women get their sweatpants? She will find out.

She will start, perhaps, with the costume and work from there.

She will live according to the bromides. Take one day at a time. Take a positive attitude. *Take a hike!* She wishes that there were more interesting things that were useful and true, but it seems now that it's only the boring things that are useful and true. *One day at a time.* And *at least we have our health.* How ordinary. How obvious. One day at a time. You need a brain for that?

While the Surgeon is fine-boned, regal, and laconic—they have correctly guessed his game to be doubles—there is a bit of the mad, overcaffeinated scientist to the Oncologist. He speaks quickly. He knows a lot of studies and numbers. He can do the math. Good! Someone should be able to do the math! "It's a fast but wimpy tumor," he explains. "It typically metastasizes to the lung." He rattles off some numbers, time frames, risk statistics. Fast but wimpy: the Mother tries to imagine this combination of traits, tries to think and think, and can only come up with Claudia Osk from the fourth grade, who blushed and almost wept when called on in class, but in gym could outrun everyone in the quarter-mile fire-door-to-fence dash. The Mother thinks now of this tumor as Claudia Osk. They are going to get Claudia Osk, make her sorry. All right! Claudia Osk must die. Though it has never been mentioned before, it now seems clear that Claudia Osk should have died long ago. Who was she anyway? So conceited: not letting anyone beat her in a race. Well, hey, hey, hey: don't look now, Claudia!

The Husband nudges her. "Are you listening?"

"The chances of this happening even just to one kidney are one in fifteen thousand. Now given all these other factors, the chances on the second kidney are about one in eight."

"One in eight," says the Husband. "Not bad. As long as it's not one in fifteen thousand."

The Mother studies the trees and fish along the ceiling's edge in the Save the Planet wallpaper border. Save the Planet. Yes! But the windows in this very building don't open and diesel fumes are leaking into the ventilating system, near which, outside, a delivery truck is parked. The air is nauseous and stale.

"Really," the Oncologist is saying, "of all the cancers he could get, this is probably the best."

"We win," says the Mother.

"Best, I know, hardly seems the right word. Look, you two probably need to get some rest. We'll see how the surgery and histology go. Then we'll start with chemo the week following. A little light chemo: vincristine and—"

"Vincristine?" interrupts the Mother. "Wine of Christ?"

"The names are strange, I know. The other one we use is actinomycin-D. Sometimes called 'dactinomycin.' People move the *D* around to the front."

"They move the *D* around to the front," repeats the Mother.

"Yup!" the Oncologist says. "I don't know why—they just do!"

"Christ didn't survive his wine," says the Husband.

"But of course he did," says the Oncologist, and nods toward the Baby, who has now found a cupboard full of hospital linens and bandages and is yanking them all out onto the floor. "I'll see you guys tomorrow, after the surgery." And with that, the Oncologist leaves.

"Or, rather, Christ *was* his wine," mumbles the Husband. Everything he knows about the New Testament, he has gleaned from the sound track of *Godspell,* "His blood was the wine. What a great beverage idea."

"A little light chemo. Don't you like that one?" says the Mother. "Eine kleine dactinomycin. I'd like to see Mozart write that one up for a big wad o' cash."

"Come here, honey," the Husband says to the Baby, who has now pulled off both his shoes.

"It's bad enough when they refer to medical science as 'an inexact science,' " says the Mother. "But when they start referring to it as 'an art,' I get extremely nervous."

"Yeah. If we wanted art, Doc, we'd go to an art museum." The Husband picks up the Baby. "You're an artist," he says to the Mother, with the taint of accusation in his voice. "They probably think you find creativity reassuring."

The Mother sighs. "I just find it inevitable. Let's go get something to eat." And so they take the elevator to the cafeteria, where there is a high chair, and where, not noticing, they all eat a lot of apples with the price tags still on them.

Because his surgery is not until tomorrow, the Baby likes the hospital. He likes the long corridors, down which he can run. He likes everything on wheels. The flower carts in the lobby! ("Please keep your boy away from the flowers," says the vendor. "We'll buy the whole display," snaps the Mother, adding, "Actual children in a children's hospital—unbelievable, isn't it?") The Baby likes the other little boys. Places to go! People to see! Rooms to wander into! There is Intensive Care. There is the Trauma Unit. The Baby smiles and waves. What a little Cancer Personality! Bandaged citizens smile and wave back. In Peed Onk, there are the bald little boys to play with. Joey, Eric, Tim, Mort, and Tod (Mort! Tod!). There is the four-year-old, Ned, holding his little deflated rubber ball, the one with the intriguing curling hose. The Baby wants to play with it. "It's mine. Leave it alone," says Ned. "Tell the Baby to leave it alone."

"Baby, you've got to share," says the Mother from a chair some feet away.

Suddenly, from down near the Tiny Tim Lounge, comes Ned's mother, large and blond and sweatpanted. "Stop that! Stop it!" she cries out, dashing toward the Baby and Ned and pushing the Baby away. "Don't touch that!" she barks at the Baby, who is only a Baby and bursts into tears because he has never been yelled at like this before.

Ned's mom glares at everyone. "This is drawing fluid from Neddy's liver!" She pats at the rubber thing and starts to cry a little.

"Oh my God," says the Mother. She comforts the Baby, who is also crying. She and Ned, the only dry-eyed people, look at each other. "I'm so sorry," she says to Ned and then to his mother. "I'm so stupid. I thought they were squabbling over a toy."

"It does look like a toy," agrees Ned. He smiles. He is an angel. All the little boys are angels. Total, sweet, bald little angels, and now God is trying to get them back for himself. Who are they, mere mortal women, in the face of this, this powerful and overwhelming and inscrutable thing, God's will? They are the mothers, that's who. You can't have him! they shout every day. You dirty old man! *Get out of here! Hands off!*

"I'm so sorry," says the Mother again. "I didn't know."

Ned's mother smiles vaguely. "Of course you didn't know," she says, and walks back to the Tiny Tim Lounge.

The Tiny Tim Lounge is a little sitting area at the end of the Peed Onk corridor. There are two small sofas, a table, a rocking chair, a television and a VCR. There are various videos: *Speed*, *Dune*, and *Star Wars*. On one of the lounge walls there is a gold plaque with the singer Tiny Tim's name on it: his son was treated once at this hospital and so, five years ago, he donated money for this lounge. It is a cramped little lounge, which, one suspects, would be larger if Tiny Tim's son had actually lived. Instead, he died here, at this hospital and now there is this tiny room which is part gratitude, part generosity, part *fuck-you*.

Sifting through the videocassettes, the Mother wonders what science fiction could begin to compete with the science fiction of cancer itself—a tumor with its differentiated muscle and bone cells, a clump of wild nothing and its mad, ambitious desire to be something: something inside you, instead of you, another organism, but with a monster's architecture, a demon's sabotage and chaos. Think of leukemia, a tumor diabolically taking liquid form, better to swim about incognito in the blood. George Lucas, direct that!

Sitting with the other parents in the Tiny Tim Lounge, the night before the surgery, having put the Baby to bed in his high steel crib two rooms down, the Mother begins to hear the stories: leukemia in kindergarten, sarcomas in Little League, neuroblastomas discovered at summer camp. "Eric slid into third base, but then the scrape didn't heal." The parents pat one another's forearms and speak of other children's hospitals as if they were resorts. "You were at St. Jude's last winter? So were we. What did you think of it? We loved the staff." Jobs have been quit, marriages hacked up, bank accounts ravaged; the parents have seemingly endured the unendurable. They speak not of the *possibility* of comas brought on by the chemo, but of the number of them. "He was in his first coma last July," says Ned's mother. "It was a scary time, but we pulled through."

Pulling through is what people do around here. There is a kind of bravery in their lives that isn't bravery at all. It is automatic, unflinching, a mix of man and machine, consuming and unquestionable obligation meeting illness move for move in a giant even-steven game of chess—an unending round of something that looks like shadowboxing, though between love and death, which is the shadow? "Everyone admires us for our courage," says one man. "They have no idea what they're talking about."

I could get out of here, thinks the Mother. I could just get on a bus and go, never come back. Change my name. A kind of witness relocation thing.

"Courage requires options," the man adds.

The Baby might be better off.

"There are options," says a woman with a thick suede headband. "You could give up. You could fall apart."

"No, you can't. Nobody does. I've never seen it," says the man. "Well, not really fall apart." Then the lounge falls quiet. Over the VCR someone has taped the fortune from a fortune cookie. "Optimism," it says, "is what allows a teakettle to sing though up to its neck in hot water." Underneath, someone else has taped a clipping from a summer horoscope.

"Cancer rules!" it says. Who would tape this up? Somebody's twelve-year-old brother. One of the fathers—Joey's father—gets up and tears them both off, makes a small wad in his fist.

There is some rustling of magazine pages.

The Mother clears her throat. "Tiny Tim forgot the wet bar," she says.

Ned, who is still up, comes out of his room and down the corridor, whose lights dim at nine. Standing next to her chair, he says to the Mother, "Where are you from? What is wrong with your baby?"

In the tiny room that is theirs, she sleeps fitfully in her sweatpants, occasionally leaping up to check on the Baby. This is what the sweatpants are for: leaping. In case of fire. In case of anything. In case the difference between day and night starts to dissolve, and there is no difference at all, so why pretend? In the cot beside her, the Husband, who has taken a sleeping pill, is snoring loudly, his arms folded about his head in a kind of origami. How could either of them have stayed back at the house, with its empty high chair and empty crib? Occasionally the Baby wakes up and cries out, and she bolts up, goes to him, rubs his back, rearranges the linens. The clock on the metal dresser shows that it is five after three. Then twenty to five. And then it is really morning, the beginning of this day, nephrectomy day. Will she be glad when it's over, or barely alive, or both? Each day this week has arrived huge, empty, and unknown, like a spaceship, and this one especially is lit a bright gray.

"He'll need to put this on," says John, one of the nurses, bright and early, handing the Mother a thin greenish garment with roses and teddy bears printed on it. A wave of nausea hits her; this smock, she thinks, will soon be splattered with—with what?

The Baby is awake but drowsy. She lifts off his pajamas. "Don't forget, *bubeleh*," she whispers, undressing and dressing him. "We will be with you every moment, every step. When you think you are asleep and floating off far away from everybody, Mommy will still be there." If she hasn't fled on a bus. "Mommy will take care of you. And Daddy, too." She hopes the Baby does not detect her own fear and uncertainty, which she must hide from him, like a limp. He is hungry, not having been allowed to eat, and he is no longer amused by this new place, but worried about its hardships. Oh, my baby, she thinks. And the room starts to swim a little. The Husband comes in to take over. "Take a break," he says to her. "I'll walk him around for five minutes."

She leaves but doesn't know where to go. In the hallway, she is approached by a kind of social worker, a customer-relations person, who had given them a video to watch about the anesthesia: how the parent accompanies the child into the operating room, and how gently, nicely the drugs are administered.

"Did you watch the video?"

"Yes," says the Mother.

"Wasn't it helpful?"

"I don't know," says the Mother.

"Do you have any questions?" asks the video woman. "Do you have any questions?" asked of someone who has recently landed in this fearful, alien place seems to the Mother an absurd and amazing little courtesy. The very specificity of a question would give a lie to the overwhelming strangeness of everything around her.

"Not right now," says the Mother. "Right now, I think I'm just going to go to the bathroom."

When she returns to the Baby's room, everyone is there: the surgeon, the anesthesiologist, all the nurses, the social worker.

In their blue caps and scrubs, they look like a clutch of forget-me-nots, and forget them, who could? The Baby, in his little teddy-bear smock, seems cold and scared. He reaches out and the Mother lifts him from the Husband's arms, rubs his back to warm him.

"Well, it's time!" says the Surgeon, forcing a smile.

"Shall we go?" says the Anesthesiologist.

What follows is a blur of obedience and bright lights. They take an elevator down to a big concrete room, the anteroom, the greenroom, the backstage of the operating room. Lining the walls are long shelves full of blue surgical outfits. "Children often become afraid of the color blue," says one of the nurses. But of course. Of course! "Now, which one of you would like to come into the operating room for the anesthesia?"

"I will," says the Mother.

"Are you sure?" asks the Husband.

"Yup." She kisses the Baby's hair. "Mr. Curlyhead," people keep calling him here, and it seems both rude and nice. Women look admiringly at his long lashes and exclaim, "Always the boys! Always the boys!"

Two surgical nurses put a blue smock and a blue cotton cap on the Mother. The Baby finds this funny and keeps pulling at the cap. "This way," says another nurse, and the Mother follows. "Just put the Baby down on the table."

In the video, the mother holds the baby and fumes are gently waved under the baby's nose until he falls asleep. Now, out of view of camera or social worker, the Anesthesiologist is anxious to get this under way and not let too much gas leak out into the room generally. The occupational hazard of this, his chosen profession, is gas exposure and nerve damage, and it has started to worry him. No doubt he frets about it to his wife every night. Now he turns the gas on and quickly clamps the plastic mouthpiece over the baby's cheeks and lips.

The Baby is startled. The Mother is startled. The Baby starts to scream and redden behind the plastic, but he cannot be heard. He thrashes. "Tell him it's okay," says the nurse to the Mother.

Okay? "It's okay," repeats the Mother, holding his hand, but she knows he can tell it's not okay, because he can see not only that she is still wearing that stupid paper cap but that her words are mechanical and swallowed, and she is biting her lips to keep them from trembling. Panicked, he attempts to sit. He cannot breathe; his arms reach up. *Bye-bye, outside*. And then, quite quickly, his eyes shut; he untenses and has fallen not *into* sleep but aside to sleep, an odd, kidnapping kind of sleep, his terror now hidden someplace deep inside him.

"How did it go?" asks the social worker, waiting in the concrete outer room. The Mother is hysterical. A nurse has ushered her out.

"It wasn't at all like the filmstrip!'" she cries. "It wasn't like the film-strip at all!"

"The filmstrip? You mean the video?" asks the social worker.

"It wasn't like that at all! It was brutal and unforgivable."

"Why that's terrible," she says, her role now no longer misinformational but janitorial, and she touches the Mother's arm, though the Mother shakes it off and goes to find the Husband.

She finds him in the large mulberry Surgery Lounge, where he has been taken and where there is free hot chocolate in small Styrofoam cups. Red cellophane garlands festoon the doorways. She has totally forgotten it is as close to Christmas as this. A pianist in the corner is playing "Carol of the Bells," and it sounds not only unfestive but scary, like the theme from The Exorcist.

There is a giant clock on the far wall. It is a kind of porthole into the operating room, a way of assessing the Baby's ordeal: forty-five minutes for the Hickman implant; two and a half hours for the nephrectomy. And then, after that, three months of chemotherapy. The magazine on her lap stays open at a ruby-hued perfume ad.

"Still not taking notes," says the Husband.

"Nope."

"You know, in a way, this is the kind of thing you've *always* written about."

"You are really something, you know that? This is life. This isn't a 'kind of thing.' "

"But this is the kind of thing that fiction is: it's the unlivable life, the strange room tacked onto the house, the extra moon that is circling the earth unbeknownst to science."

"I told you that."

"I'm quoting you."

She looks at her watch, thinking of the Baby. "How long has it been?"

"Not long. Too long. In the end, maybe those're the same things."

"What do you suppose is happening to him right this second?"

Infection? Slipping knives? "I don't know. But you know what? I've gotta go. I've gotta just walk a bit." The Husband gets up, walks around the lounge, then comes back and sits down.

The synapses between the minutes are unswimmable. An hour is thick as fudge. The Mother feels depleted; she is a string of empty tin cans attached by wire, something a goat would sniff and chew, something now and then enlivened by a jolt of electricity.

She hears their names being called over the intercom. "Yes? Yes?" She stands up quickly. Her words have flown out before her, an exhalation of birds. The piano music has stopped. The pianist is gone. She and the Husband approach the main desk, where a man looks up at them and smiles. Before him is a xeroxed list of patients' names. "That's our little boy right there," says the Mother, seeing the Baby's name on the list and pointing at it. "Is there some word? Is everything okay?"

"Yes," says the man. "Your boy is doing fine. They've just finished with the catheter, and they are moving on to the kidney."

"But it's been two hours already! Oh my God, did something go wrong? What happened? What went wrong?"

"Did something go wrong?" The Husband tugs at his collar.

"Not really. It just took longer than they expected. I'm told everything is fine. They wanted you to know."

"Thank you," says the Husband. They turn and walk back toward where they were sitting.

"I'm not going to make it." The Mother sighs, sinking into a fake leather chair shaped somewhat like a baseball mitt. "But before I go, I'm taking half this hospital out with me."

"Do you want some coffee?" asks the Husband.

"I don't know," says the Mother. "No, I guess not. No. Do you?"

"Nah, I don't, either, I guess," he says.

"Would you like part of an orange?"

"Oh maybe, I guess, if you're having one." She takes an orange from her purse and just sits there peeling its difficult skin, the flesh rupturing beneath her fingers, the juice trickling down her hands, stinging the hangnails. She and the Husband chew and swallow, discreetly spit the seeds into Kleenex, and read from photocopies of the latest medical research, which they begged from the intern. They read, and underline, and sigh and close their eyes, and after some time, the surgery is over. A nurse from Peed Onk comes down to tell them.

"Your little boy's in recovery right now. He's doing well. You can see him in about fifteen minutes."

How can it be described? How can any of it be described? The trip and the story of the trip are always two different things. The narrator is the one who has stayed home, but then, afterward, presses her mouth upon the traveler's mouth, in order to make the mouth work, to make the mouth say, say, say. One cannot go to a place and speak of it; one cannot both see and say, not really. One can go, and upon returning make a lot of hand motions and indications with the arms. The mouth itself, working at the speed of light, at the eye's instructions, is necessarily struck still; so fast, so much to report, it hangs open and dumb as a gutted bell. All that unsayable life! That's where the narrator comes in. The narrator comes with her kisses and mimicry and tidying up. The narrator comes and makes a slow, fake song of the mouth's eager devastation.

It is a horror and a miracle to see him. He is lying in his crib in his room, tubed up, splayed like a boy on a cross, his arms stiffened into cardboard "no-no's" so that he cannot yank out the tubes. There is the bladder catheter, the nasal-gastric tube, and the Hickman, which, beneath the skin, is plugged into his jugular, then popped out his chest wall and capped with a long plastic cap. There is a large bandage taped over his abdomen. Groggy, on a morphine drip, still he is able to look at her when, maneuvering through all the vinyl wiring, she leans to hold him, and when she does, he begins to cry, but cry silently, without motion or noise. She has never seen a baby cry without motion or noise. It is the crying of an old person; silent, beyond opinion, shattered. In someone so tiny, it is frightening and unnatural. She wants to pick up the Baby and run—out of there, out of there. She wants to whip out a gun: No-no's, eh? This whole thing is what I call a no-no. Don't you touch him! she wants to shout at the surgeons and the needle nurses. Not anymore! No more! No more! She would crawl up and lie beside him in the crib if she could. But instead, because of all his intricate wiring, she must lean and cuddle, sing to him, songs of peril and flight: "We gotta get out of this place, if it's the last thing we ever do. We gotta get out of this place . . . there's a better life for me and you."

Very 1967. She was eleven then and impressionable.

The Baby looks at her, pleadingly, his arms splayed out in surrender. To where? Where is there to go? Take me! Take me!

That night, postop night, the Mother and Husband lie afloat in the cot together. A fluorescent lamp near the crib is kept on in the dark. The Baby breathes evenly but thinly in his drugged sleep. The morphine in its first flooding doses apparently makes him feel as if he were falling backward—or so the Mother has been told—and it causes the Baby to jerk, to catch himself over and over, as if he were being dropped from a tree. "Is this right? Isn't there something that should be done?" The nurses come in hourly, different ones—the night shifts seem strangely short and frequent. If the Baby stirs or frets, the nurses give him more morphine through the Hickman catheter, then leave to tend to other patients. The Mother rises to check on him in the low light. There is gurgling from the clear plastic suction tube coming out of his mouth. Brownish clumps have collected in the tube. What is going on? The Mother rings for the nurse. Is it Renée or Sarah or Darcy? She's forgotten.

"What, what is it?" murmurs the Husband, waking up.

"Something is wrong," says the Mother. "It looks like blood in his N-G tube."

"What?" The Husband gets out of bed. He, too, is wearing sweatpants.

The nurse—Valerie—pushes open the heavy door to the room and enters quietly. "Everything okay?"

"There's something wrong here. The tube is sucking blood out of his stomach. It looks like it may have perforated his stomach and that now he's bleeding internally. Look!"

Valerie is a saint, but her voice is the standard hospital saint voice: an infuriating, pharmaceutical calm. It says, Everything is normal here. Death is normal. Pain is normal. Nothing is abnormal. So there is nothing to get excited about. "Well now, let's see." She holds up the plastic tube and tries to see inside it. "Hmmm," she says. "I'll call the attending physician."

Because this is a research and teaching hospital, all the regular doctors are at home sleeping in their Mission-style beds. Tonight, as is apparently the case every weekend night, the attending physician is a medical student. He looks fifteen. The authority he attempts to convey, he cannot remotely inhabit. He is not even in the same building with it.

He shakes everyone's hands, then strokes his chin, a gesture no doubt gleaned from some piece of dinner theater his parents took him to once. As if there were an actual beard on that chin! As if beard growth on that chin were even possible! *Our Town! Kiss Me Kate! Barefoot in the Park!* He is attempting to convince, if not to impress.

"We're in trouble," the Mother whispers to the Husband. She is tired, tired of young people grubbing for grades. "We've got Dr. 'Kiss Me Kate,' here."

The Husband looks at her blankly, a mix of disorientation and divorce.

The medical student holds the tubing in his hands. "I don't really see anything," he says.

He flunks! "You don't?" The Mother shoves her way in, holds the clear tubing in both hands. "That," she says. "Right here and here." Just this past semester, she said to one of her own students, "If you don't see how this essay is better than that one, then I want you just to go out into the hallway and stand there until you do." Is it important to keep one's voice down? The Baby stays asleep. He is drugged and dreaming, far away.

"Hmmm," says the medical student. "Perhaps there's a little irritation in the stomach."

"A little irritation?" The Mother grows furious. "This is blood. These are clumps and clots. This stupid thing is sucking the life right out of him!" Life! She is starting to cry.

They turn off the suction and bring in antacids, which they feed into the Baby through the tube. Then they turn the suction on again. This time on low.

"What was it on before?" asks the Husband.

"High," says Valerie. "Doctor's orders, though I don't know why. I don't know why these doctors do a lot of the things they do."

"Maybe they're . . . not all that bright?" suggests the Mother. She is feeling relief and rage simultaneously: there is a feeling of prayer and litigation in the air. Yet essentially, she is grateful. Isn't she? She thinks she is. And still, and still: look at all the things you have to do to protect a child, a hospital merely an intensification of life's cruel obstacle course.

The Surgeon comes to visit on Saturday morning. He steps in and nods at the Baby, who is awake but glazed from the morphine, his eyes two dark unseeing grapes. "The boy looks fine," the Surgeon announces. He peeks under the Baby's bandage. "The stitches look good," he says. The Baby's abdomen is stitched all the way across like a baseball. "And the other kidney, when we looked at it yesterday face-to-face, looked fine. We'll try to wean him off the morphine a little, and see how he's doing on Monday." He clears his throat. "And now," he says, looking about the room at the nurses and medical students, "I would like to speak with the Mother, alone."

The Mothers heart gives a jolt. "Me?"

"Yes," he says, motioning, then turning.

She gets up and steps out into the empty hallway with him, closing the door behind her. What can this be about? She hears the Baby fretting a little in his crib. Her brain fills with pain and alarm. Her voice comes out as a hoarse whisper. "Is there something—"

"There is a particular thing I need from you," says the Surgeon, turning and standing there very seriously.

"Yes?" Her heart is pounding. She does not feel resilient enough for any more bad news.

"I need to ask you a favor."

"Certainly," she says, attempting very hard to summon the strength and courage for this occasion, whatever it is; her throat has tightened to a fist.

From inside his white coat, the surgeon removes a thin paperback book and thrusts it toward her, "Will you sign my copy of your novel?"

The Mother looks down and sees that it is indeed a copy of a novel she has written, one about teenaged girls.

She looks up. A big, spirited grin is cutting across his face. "I read this last summer," he says, "and I still remember parts of it! Those girls got into such trouble!"

Of all the surreal moments of the last few days, this, she thinks, might be the most so.

"Okay," she says, and the Surgeon merrily hands her a pen.

"You can just write To Dr.—Oh, I don't need to tell you what to write."

The Mother sits down on a bench and shakes ink into the pen. A sigh of relief washes over and out of her. Oh, the pleasure of a sigh of relief, like the finest moments of love; has anyone properly sung the praises of sighs of relief? She opens the book to the title page. She breathes deeply. What is he doing reading novels about teenaged girls, anyway? And why didn't he buy the hardcover?" She inscribes something grateful and true, then hands the book back to him.

"Is he going to be okay?"

"The boy? The boy is going to be fine," he says, then taps her stiffly on the shoulder. "Now you take care. It's Saturday. Drink a little wine."

Over the weekend, while the Baby sleeps, the Mother and Husband sit together in the Tiny Tim Lounge. The Husband is restless and makes cafeteria and sundry runs, running errands for everyone. In his absence, the other parents regale her further with their sagas. Pediatric cancer and chemo stories: the children's amputations, blood poisoning, teeth flaking like shale, the learning delays and disabilities caused by chemo frying the young, budding brain. But strangely optimistic codas are tacked on—endings as stiff and loopy as carpenter's lace, crisp and empty as lettuce, reticulate as a net—ah, words. "After all that business with the tumor, he's better now, and fitted with new incisors by my wife's cousin's husband, who did dental school in two and a half years, if you can believe that. We hope for the best. We take things as they come. Life is hard."

"Life's a big problem," agrees the Mother. Part of her welcomes and invites all their tales. In the few long days since this nightmare began, part of her has become addicted to disaster and war stories. She wants only to hear about the sadness and emergencies of others. They are the only situations that can join hands with her own; everything else bounces off her shiny shield of resentment and unsympathy. Nothing else can even stay in her brain. From this, no doubt, the philistine world is made, or should one say recruited? Together, the parents huddle all day in the Tiny Tim Lounge—no need to watch Oprah. They leave *Oprah* in the dust. Oprah has nothing on them. They chat matter-of-factly, then fall silent and watch *Dune* or *Star Wars,* in which there are bright and shiny robots, whom the Mother now sees not as robots at all but as human beings who have had terrible things happen to them.

Some of their friends visit with stuffed animals and soft greetings of "Looking good" for the dozing baby, though the room is way past the stuffed-animal limit. The Mother arranges, once more, a plateful of Mint Milano cookies and cups of take-out coffee for guests. All her nutso pals stop by—the two on Prozac, the one obsessed with the word *penis* in the word *happiness,* the one who recently had her hair foiled green. "Your friends put the *de* in *fin de siècle,*" says the husband. Overheard, or recorded, all marital conversation sounds as if someone must be joking, though usually no one is.

She loves her friends, especially loves them for coming, since there are times they all fight and don't speak for weeks. Is this friendship? For now and here, it must do and is, and is, she swears it is. For one, they never offer impromptu spiritual lectures about death, how it is part of life, its natural ebb and flow, how we all must accept that, or other such utterances that make her want to scratch out some eyes. Like true friends, they take no hardy or elegant stance loosely choreographed from some broad perspective. They get right in there and mutter "Jesus Christ!" and shake their heads. Plus, they are the only people who not only will laugh at her stupid jokes but offer up stupid ones of their own. *What do you get when you cross Tiny Tim with a pit bull?* A child's illness is a strain on the mind. They know how to laugh in a fluty, desperate way—unlike the people who are more her husband's friends and who seem just to deepen their sorrowful gazes, nodding their heads with Sympathy. How exiling and estranging are everybody's Sympathetic Expressions! When anyone laughs, she thinks, Okay! Hooray: a buddy. In disaster as in show business.

Nurses come and go; their chirpy voices both startle and soothe. Some of the other Peed Onk parents stick their heads in to see how the Baby is and offer encouragement.

Green Hair scratches her head. "Everyone's so friendly here. Is there someone in this place who isn't doing all this airy, scripted optimism—or are people like that the only people here?"

"It's Modern Middle Medicine meets the Modern Middle Family," says the Husband. "In the Modern Middle West."

Someone has brought in take-out lo mein, and they all eat it out in the hall by the elevators.

Parents are allowed use of the Courtesy Line.

"You've got to have a second child," says a different friend on the phone, a friend from out of town. "An heir and a spare. That's what we did. We had another child to ensure we wouldn't off ourselves if we lost our first."

"Really?"

"I'm serious."

"A formal suicide? Wouldn't you just drink yourself into a lifelong stupor and let it go at that?"

"Nope. I knew how I would do it even. For a while, until our second came along, I had it all planned."

"What did you plan?"

"I can't go into too much detail, because—Hi, honey!—the kids are here now in the room. But I'll spell out the general idea: R-O-P-E."

Sunday evening, she goes and sinks down on the sofa in the Tiny Tim Lounge next to Frank, Joey's father. He is a short, stocky man with the currentless, flatlined look behind the eyes that all the parents eventually get here. He has shaved his head bald in solidarity with his son. His little boy has been battling cancer for five years. It is now in the liver, and the rumor around the corridor is that Joey has three weeks to live. She knows that Joey's mother, Heather, left Frank years ago, two years into the cancer, and has remarried and had another child, a girl named Brittany. The Mother sees Heather here sometimes with her new life— the cute little girl and the new, young, full-haired husband who will never be so maniacally and debilitatingly obsessed with Joey's illness the way Frank, her first husband, was. Heather comes to visit Joey, to say hello and now good-bye, but she is not Joey's main man. Frank is.

Frank is full of stories—about the doctors, about the food, about the nurses, about Joey. Joey, affectless from his meds, sometimes leaves his room and comes out to watch TV in his bathrobe. He is jaundiced and bald, and though he is nine, he looks no older than six. Frank has devoted the last four and a half years to saving Joey's life. When the cancer was first diagnosed, the doctors gave Joey a 20 percent chance of living six more months. Now here it is, almost five years later, and Joey's still here. It is all due to Frank, who, early on, quit his job as vice president of a consulting firm in order to commit himself totally to his son. He is proud of everything he's given up and done, but he is tired. Part of him now really believes things are coming to a close, that this is the end. He says this without tears. There are no more tears.

"You have probably been through more than anyone else on this corridor," says the Mother.

"I could tell you stories," he says. There is a sour odor between them, and she realizes that neither of them has bathed for days.

"Tell me one. Tell me the worst one." She knows he hates his ex-wife and hates her new husband even more.

"The worst? They're all the worst. Here's one: one morning, I went out for breakfast with my buddy—it was the only time I'd left Joey alone ever; left him for two hours is all—and when I came back, his N-G tube was full of blood. They had the suction on too high, and it was sucking the guts right out of him."

"Oh my God. That just happened to us," said the Mother.

"It did?"

"Friday night."

"You're kidding. They let that happen again? I gave them such a chewing-out about that!"

"I guess our luck is not so good. We get your very worst story on the second night we're here."

"It's not a bad place, though."

"It's not?"

"Naw. I've seen worse. I've taken Joey everywhere."

"He seems very strong." Truth is, at this point, Joey seems like a zombie and frightens her.

"Joey's a fucking genius. A biological genius. They'd given him six months, remember."

The Mother nods.

"Six months is not very long," says Frank. "Six months is nothing. He was four and a half years old."

All the words are like blows. She feels flooded with affection and mourning for this man. She looks away, out the window, out past the hospital parking lot, up toward the black marbled sky and the electric eyelash of the moon. "And now he's nine," she says. "You're his hero."

"And he's mine," says Frank, though the fatigue in his voice seems to overwhelm him. "He'll be that forever. Excuse me," he says, "I've got to go check. His breathing hasn't been good. Excuse me."

"Good news and bad," says the Oncologist on Monday. He has knocked, entered the room, and now stands there. Their cots are unmade. One wastebasket is overflowing with coffee cups. "We've got the pathologist's report. The bad news is that the kidney they removed had certain lesions, called 'rests,' which are associated with a higher risk for disease in the other kidney. The good news is that the tumor is stage one, regular cell structure, and under five hundred grams, which qualifies you for a national experiment in which chemotherapy isn't done but your boy is monitored with ultrasound instead. It's not all that risky, given that the patient's watched closely, but here is the literature on it. There are forms to sign, if you decide to do that. Read all this and we can discuss it further. You have to decide within four days."

Lesions? Rests? They dry up and scatter like M&M's on the floor. All she hears is the part about no chemo. Another sigh of relief rises up in her and spills out. In a life where there is only the bearable and the unbearable, a sigh of relief is an ecstasy.

"No chemo?" says the Husband. "Do you recommend that?"

The Oncologist shrugs. What casual gestures these doctors are permitted! "I know chemo. I like chemo," says the Oncologist. "But this is for you to decide. It depends how you feel."

The Husband leans forward. "But don't you think that now that we have the upper hand with this thing, we should keep going? Shouldn't we stomp on it, beat it, smash it to death with the chemo?"

The Mother swats him angrily and hard. "Honey, you're delirious!" She whispers, but it comes out as a hiss. "This is our lucky break!" Then she adds gently, "We don't want the Baby to have chemo."

The Husband turns back to the Oncologist. "What do *you* think?"

"It could be," he says, shrugging. "It could be that this is your lucky break. But you won't know for sure for five years."

The Husband turns back to the Mother. "Okay," he says. "Okay."

The Baby grows happier and strong. He begins to move and sit and eat. Wednesday morning, they are allowed to leave, and leave without chemo. The Oncologist looks a little nervous. "Are you nervous about this?" asks the Mother.

"Of course I'm nervous." But he shrugs and doesn't look that nervous. "See you in six weeks for the ultrasound," he says, waves and then leaves, looking at his big black shoes as he does.

The Baby smiles, even toddles around a little, the sun bursting through the clouds, an angel chorus crescendoing. Nurses arrive. The Hickman is taken out of the Baby's neck and chest; antibiotic lotion is dispensed. The Mother packs up their bags. The Baby sucks on a bottle of juice and does not cry.

"No chemo?" says one of the nurses. "Not even a little chemo?"

"We're doing watch and wait," says the Mother.

The other parents look envious but concerned. They have never seen any child get out of there with his hair and white blood cells intact.

"Will you be okay?" asks Ned's mother.

"The worry's going to kill us," says the Husband.

"But if all we have to do is worry," chides the Mother, "every day for a hundred years, it'll be easy. It'll be nothing. I'll take all the worry in the world, if it wards off the thing itself."

"That's right," says Ned's mother. "Compared to everything else, compared to all the actual events, the worry is nothing."

The Husband shakes his head. "I'm such an amateur," he moans.

"You're both doing admirably," says the other mother. "Your baby's lucky, and I wish you all the best."

The Husband shakes her hand warmly. "Thank you," he says. "You've been wonderful."

Another mother, the mother of Eric, comes up to them. "It's all very hard," she says, her head cocked to one side. "But there's a lot of collateral beauty along the way."

Collateral beauty? Who is entitled to such a thing? A child is ill. No one is entitled to any collateral beauty!

"Thank you," says the Husband.

Joey's father, Frank, comes up and embraces them both.

"It's a journey," he says. He chucks the Baby on the chin. "Good luck, little man."

"Yes, thank you so much," says the Mother. "We hope things go well with Joey." She knows that Joey had a hard, terrible night.

Frank shrugs and steps back. "Gotta go," he says. "Good-bye!"

"Bye," she says, and then he is gone. She bites the inside of her lip, a bit tearily, then bends down to pick up the diaper bag, which is now stuffed with little animals; helium balloons are tied to its zipper. Shouldering the thing, the Mother feels she has just won a prize. All the parents have now vanished down the hall in the opposite direction. The Husband moves close. With one arm, he takes the Baby from her; with the other, he rubs her back. He can see she is starting to get weepy.

"Aren't these people nice? Don't you feel better hearing about their lives?" he asks.

Why does he do this, form clubs all the time; why does even this society of suffering soothe him? When it comes to death and dying, perhaps someone in this family ought to be more of a snob.

"All these nice people with their brave stories," he continues as they make their way toward the elevator bank, waving good-bye to the nursing staff as they go, even the Baby waving shyly, *Bye-bye? Bye-Bye?* Don't you feel consoled, knowing we're all in the same boat, that we're all in this together?"

But who on earth would want to be in this boat? the Mother thinks. This boat is a nightmare boat. Look where it goes: to a silver-and-white room, where, just before your eyesight and hearing and your ability to touch or be touched disappear entirely, you must watch your child die.

Rope! Bring on the rope.

"Let's make our own way," says the Mother, "and not in this boat."

Woman Overboard! She takes the Baby back from the Husband, cups the Baby's cheek in her hand, kisses his brow and then, quickly, his flowery mouth. The Baby's heart—she can hear it—drums with life. "For as long as I live," says the Mother, pressing the elevator button—up or down, everyone in the end has to leave this way—"I never want to see any of these people again."

There are the notes.
Now where is the money?

Excerpt from
INTRODUCTION TO A
MEMOIR OF MARY ANN
by Flannery O'Connor

The essay by novelist Flannery O'Connor that is excerpted below is an intro-
duction to a memoir of a disfigured and dying child, Mary Ann. The memoir
itself was written by the congregation of nuns who cared for Mary Ann during
her short life.

O'Connor's introduction addresses, among other matters, the modern ten-
dency not to wonder "why Mary Ann should die," but to ask instead "why she
should be born in the first place." In so doing, it considers the connections
among grotesqueness, suffering, and the potential for goodness. O'Connor
notes a modern tendency to respond to human suffering with "tenderness,"
and compares this reaction to its historical antecedent, faith, which she de-
scribes as "the blind, prophetical, unsentimental eye of acceptance."

O'Connor finds the solutions to these problems in Roman Catholic teach-
ings. Yet readers of any faith (or none), even if finding different answers to the
questions she asks, can appreciate the problems posed by the life and death of
Mary Ann, and may learn much from O'Connor's manner of addressing
them.

O'Connor begins by acknowledging how hard it is to write readably and
truthfully about good children. She recalls how the nuns who cared for Mary
Ann had originally invited her to write the memoir, and how she had shuddered
at the prospect. Still, the nuns sent her a picture of Mary Ann, and the child's
deformed face commanded her attention.

Because of the picture—and a connection, through his daughter, between
the American author Nathaniel Hawthorne and this order of nuns—O'Connor
found herself thinking of a passage from Hawthorne's "The Birth-Mark." It is
the passage in which Aylmer, the husband, expresses his "shock" at the mark
on his wife's cheek, calling it "the visible mark of earthly imperfection." His
wife declares, "You cannot love what shocks you!" O'Connor then relates
how this undertaking—loving what is shocking—recurs in the life of Haw-
thorne and in the order of nuns who raised Mary Ann.

When O'Connor finally reads the memoir the nuns write, she recognizes it as a document that, despite its faults, conveys the truth about Mary Ann. She then describes meeting with the nuns, the events of Mary Ann's funeral, and the "new perspective" on goodness and grotesquerie that she gained from these events.

Is it possible to "love what shocks you"?

How is human imperfection "the raw material of good"?

O'Connor writes that a tenderness for human suffering, when lacking in insight about human suffering, leads logically to terror. This is because, lacking insight, it is "wrapped in theory." What does she mean? In what theory or theories might it be wrapped? How might that theory—or "theory" in general—lead to terror?

Would the world be a better place if there were no deformed children? If we could prevent their being born?

Stories of pious children tend to be false. This may be because they are told by adults, who see virtue where their subjects would see only a practical course of action; or it may be because such stories are written to edify and what is written to edify usually ends by amusing. For my part, I have never cared to read about little boys who build altars and play they are priests, or about little girls who dress up as nuns, or about those pious Protestant children who lack this equipment but brighten the corners where they are.

Last spring I received a letter from Sister Evangelist, the Sister Superior of Our Lady of Perpetual Help Free Cancer Home in Atlanta. "This is a strange request," the letter read, "but we will try to tell our story as briefly as possible. In 1949, a little three-year-old girl, Mary Ann, was admitted to our Home as a patient. She proved to be a remarkable child and lived until she was twelve. Of those nine years, much is to be told. Patients, visitors, Sisters, all were influenced in some way by this afflicted child. Yet one never thought of her as afflicted. True she had been born with a tumor on the side of her face; one eye had been removed, but the other eye sparkled, twinkled, danced mischievously, and after one meeting one never was conscious of her physical defect but recognized only the beautiful brave spirit and felt the joy of such contact. Now Mary Ann's story should be written but who to write it?"

Not me, I said to myself.

"We have had offers from nuns and others but we don't want a pious little recital. We want a story with a real impact on other lives just as

Mary Ann herself had that impact on each life she touched . . . This wouldn't have to be a factual story. It could be a novel with many other characters but the outstanding character, Mary Ann."

A novel, I thought. Horrors.

Sister Evangelist ended by inviting me to write Mary Ann's story and to come up and spend a few days at the Home in Atlanta and "imbibe the atmosphere" where the little girl had lived for nine years.

It is always difficult to get across to people who are not professional writers that a talent to write does not mean a talent to write anything at all. I did not wish to imbibe Mary Ann's atmosphere. I was not capable of writing her story. Sister Evangelist had enclosed a picture of the child. I had glanced at it when I first opened the letter, and had put it quickly aside. Now I picked it up to give it a last cursory look before returning it to the Sisters. It showed a little girl in her first Communion dress and veil. She was sitting on a bench, holding something I could not make out. Her small face was straight and bright on one side. The other side was protuberant, the eye was bandaged, the nose and mouth crowded slightly out of place. The child looked out at her observer with an obvious happiness and composure. I continued to gaze at the picture long after I had thought to be finished with it.

After a while I got up and went to the book case and took out a volume of Nathaniel Hawthorne's stories. The Dominican Congregation to which the nuns belong who had taken care of Mary Ann had been founded by Hawthorne's daughter, Rose. The child's picture had brought to mind his story, *The Birthmark*. I found the story and opened it at that wonderful section of dialogue where Alymer first mentions his wife's defect to her.

> One day Alymer sat gazing at his wife with a trouble in his countenance that grew stronger until he spoke.
>
> "Georgiana," said he, "has it never occurred to you that the mark upon your cheek might be removed?"
>
> "No, indeed," said she, smiling; but perceiving the seriousness of his manner, she blushed deeply. "To tell you the truth it has been so often called a charm that I was simple enough to imagine it might be so."
>
> "Ah, upon another face perhaps it might," replied her husband, "but never on yours. No, dearest Georgiana, you came so nearly perfect from the hand of Nature that this slightest defect, which we hesitate whether to term a defect or a beauty, shocks me, as being the

visible mark of earthly imperfection."

"Shocks you, my husband!" cried Georgiana, deeply hurt, at first reddening with momentary anger, but then bursting into tears. "Then why did you take me from my mother's side? You cannot love what shocks you!"

The defect on Mary Ann's cheek could not have been mistaken for a charm. It was plainly grotesque. She belonged to fact and not to fancy. I conceived it my duty to write Sister Evangelist that if anything were written about this child, it should indeed be a "factual story," and I went on to say that if anyone should write these facts, it should be the Sisters themselves, who had known and nursed her. I felt this strongly. At the same time I wanted to make it plain that I was not the one to write the factual story, and there is no quicker way to get out of a job than to prescribe it for those who have prescribed it for you. I added that should they decide to take my advice, I would be glad to help them with the preparation of their manuscript and do any small editing that proved necessary. I had no doubt that this was safe generosity. I did not expect to hear from them again.

In *Our Old Home*, Hawthorne tells about a fastidious gentleman who, while going through a Liverpool workhouse, was followed by a wretched and rheumy child, so awful-looking that he could not decide what sex it was. The child followed him about until it decided to put itself in front of him in a mute appeal to be held. The fastidious gentleman, after a pause that was significant for himself, picked it up and held it. Hawthorne comments upon this:

> Nevertheless, it could be no easy thing for him to do, he being a person burdened with more than an English-man's customary reserve, shy of actual contact with human beings, afflicted with a peculiar distaste for whatever was ugly, and, furthermore, accustomed to that habit of observation from an insulated standpoint which is said (but I hope erroneously) to have the tendency of putting ice into the blood.
>
> So I watched the struggle in his mind with a good deal of interest, and am seriously of the opinion that he did a heroic act and effected more than he dreamed of toward his final salvation when he took up the loath-some child and caressed it as tenderly as if he had been its father.

What Hawthorne neglected to add is that he was the gentleman who did this. . . .

The Sisters write Mary Ann's story and send it to O'Connor. She realizes that "they had managed to convey" the "mystery of Mary Ann."

. . . She was an extraordinarily rich little girl.

Death is the theme of much modern literature. There is *Death in Venice, Death of a Salesman, Death in the Afternoon, Death of a Man.* Mary Ann's was the death of a child. It was simpler than any of these, yet infinitely more knowing. When she entered the door of Our Lady of Perpetual Help Home in Atlanta, she fell into the hands of women who are shocked at nothing and who love life so much that they spend their own lives making comfortable those who have been pronounced incurable of cancer. Her own prognosis was six months, but she lived twelve years, long enough for the Sisters to teach her what alone could have been of importance to her. Hers was an education for death, but not one carried on obtrusively. Her days were full of dogs and party dresses, of Sisters and sisters, of Coca Colas and Dagwood sandwiches, and of her many and varied friends—from Mr. Slack and Mr. Connolly to Lucius, the yard man; from patients afflicted the way she was to children who were brought to the Home to visit her and were perhaps told when they left to think how thankful they should be that God had made their faces straight. It is doubtful if any of them were as fortunate as Mary Ann. . . .

. . . I later suggested to Sister Evangelist, on an occasion when some of the Sisters came down to spend the afternoon with me to discuss the manuscript, that Mary Ann could not have been much *but* good, considering her environment. Sister Evangelist leaned over the arm of her chair and gave me a look. Her eyes were blue and unpredictable behind spectacles that unmoored them slightly. "We've had some demons!" she said, and a gesture of her hand dismissed my ignorance.

After an afternoon with them, I decided that they had had about everything and flinched before nothing, even though one of them asked me during the course of the visit why I wrote about such grotesque characters, why the grotesque (of all things) was my vocation. They had in the meantime inspected some of my writing. I was struggling to get off the hook she had me on when another of our guests supplied the one answer that would make it immediately plain to all of them. "It's your vocation too," he said to her.

This opened up for me also a new perspective on the grotesque. Most of us have learned to be dispassionate about evil, to look it in the face and find, as often as not, our own grinning reflections with which we do not argue, but good is another matter. Few have stared at that long enough to accept the fact that its face too is grotesque, that in us the good is something under construction. The modes of evil usually receive worthy expression. The modes of good have to be satisfied with a cliché or a smoothing down that will soften their real look. When we look into the face of good, we are liable to see a face like Mary Ann's, full of promise.

Bishop Hyland preached Mary Ann's funeral sermon. He said that the world would ask why Mary Ann should die. He was thinking undoubtedly of those who had known her and knew that she loved life, knew that her grip on a hamburger had once been so strong that she had fallen through the back of a chair without dropping it, or that some months before her death, she and Sister Loretta had got a real baby to nurse. The Bishop was speaking to her family and friends. He could not have been thinking of that world, much farther removed yet everywhere, which would not ask why Mary Ann should die, but why she should be born in the first place.

One of the tendencies of our age is to use the suffering of children to discredit the goodness of God, and once you have discredited His goodness, you are done with Him. The Alymers whom Hawthorne saw as a menace have multiplied. Busy cutting down human imperfection, they are making headway also on the raw material of good. Ivan Karamazov cannot believe, as long as one child is in torment; Camus' hero cannot accept the divinity of Christ, because of the massacre of the innocents. In this popular pity, we mark our gain in sensibility and our loss in vision. If other ages felt less, they saw more, even though they saw with the blind, prophetical, unsentimental eye of acceptance, which is to say, of faith. In the absence of this faith now, we govern by tenderness. It is a tenderness which, long since cut off from the person of Christ, is wrapped in theory. When tenderness is detached from the source of tenderness, its logical outcome is terror. It ends in forced labor camps and in the fumes of the gas chamber.

These reflections seem a long way from the simplicity and innocence of Mary Ann; but they are not so far removed. Hawthorne could have put them in a fable and shown us what to fear. . . .

CHAPTER 9:
LIVING IMMEDIATELY

IN THE PREVIOUS CHAPTER we examined human vulnerability and suffering. Readings there invited us to consider their essential qualities and to wonder whether, much as we fear them, a life without them might prove, though more secure, in some ways poorer.

In this chapter we consider human activities uncompromised by suffering: our appreciative awareness of the world and our fellow creatures, and our aspiring actions in the world and with our fellow human beings. When all goes well, we can be at work directly, wholeheartedly, and honestly, fully present and engaged in what we do: we can exercise our powers without mediation or intermediaries; we can live *immediately*. Yet human beings have always faced many possible impediments that threaten to disrupt our activities and our full and immediate engagement with the world. Of special interest to bioethics are those impediments that might arise, paradoxically, from those technological interventions that aim to alleviate suffering or to augment our native powers and improve our natural abilities.

To some extent, the problem of mediation and distortion is a hazard of technology itself, wherever we apply it. When we solve any problem technologically, we risk disconnecting our selves from our immediate experience. This is a risk we usually gladly run for the sake of the desired solution or benefit. Yet technological remedies for the weaknesses of our bodies and minds bring this risk home, as it were, to our very selves. On this terrain, the hazards of mediation for "real life" may become very significant.

To live immediately and genuinely is a challenge under the best of circumstances. Even without technology, it is hard for all of us, in much that we do, to experience life directly, wholly, and without distortion. Yet if living immediately is essential to living well, we should try to think about how we might accomplish it and how we might best defend its possibility against distorting intrusions, including those that accompany the great gifts of biotechnology.

We begin with an excerpt from Leo Tolstoy's *Anna Karenina*, in which an individual loses himself in productive physical labor. Next, an excerpt from Robert Louis Stevenson's "Child's Play" compares the way children play and adults fantasize. Stevenson, like Tolstoy, reminds us what it means to lose oneself in an experience, and reminds us, too, that this is a gift we tend to lose as we mature.

Our next six readings describe a variety of obstacles to living immediately. In "Pain Has an Element of Blank," poet Emily Dickinson shows us the problem posed by the constant intrusion of the body, in its most compelling form: pain. Walt Whitman ("When I Heard the Learn'd Astronomer") and Walker Percy (excerpts from "The Loss of the Creature") present us with the barriers caused by information and an intellectual detachment. Next, a pair of excerpts, one ancient and one modern, explore mediation by drugs; both a famous passage from *The Odyssey* of Homer and a contemporary passage from Malcolm Gladwell's "Drugstore Athlete" underscore the enduring nature of this temptation.

Finally, an essay from Jean Jacques Rousseau's *Reveries of a Solitary Walker* offers a vision—idealized? possible? attainable?—of a life free of these various barriers.

Excerpt from
ANNA KARENINA
Levin Mowing

by Leo Tolstoy, translated by Aylmer and Louise Maude

In these chapters from Leo Tolstoy's Anna Karenina, *Constantine Dmitrich Levin, a wealthy landowner in nineteenth-century Russia, decides to join his peasants in mowing hay. In this intense and productive physical labor he discovers a—for him—novel happiness.*

During the time Levin has this experience, he is playing host to his more cosmopolitan half-brother, Sergius Ivanich Koznyshev. Although he is fond of Koznyshev, Levin is becoming weary and frustrated with the contentious intellectual conversations into which they are drawn.

Levin has tried mowing before, but only for brief periods of time and as a remedy for his bad temper. This year, he decides to mow for several whole days. At first, he is distracted by anxiety about the impression he is making on his peasants, and by his conscious efforts to mow well. Soon, though, he begins to experience "unconscious intervals" in which "the scythe seemed to mow of itself." These moments are at first happy, and then "blessed."

Levin convinces himself to mow because mowing is physical exercise, without which "my character gets quite spoilt." Today we exercise for the health of our bodies. Why does Levin believe it is healthy for his character? Is he right?

Does Levin's satisfaction derive only from the physical exercise mowing offers? Would he be equally elated by exercise in a gym?

The state of "blessedness" Levin finds in mowing seems dependent on its being physical activity. Is it possible to attain such a state by losing oneself in activity that is not physical?

Levin understands that the joy of mowing is that, as he tells his brother, "one has no time for thinking." When Levin reaches that unthinking state, Tolstoy tells us he is happy. In general, must one be unconscious of one's own happiness to be completely and blessedly happy? Is consciousness necessarily an impediment to such happiness?

First published by Oxford University Press 1918. Anna Karenina, by Leo Tolstoy, Louise and Aylmer Maude, translators. Published by Oxford University Press. Reprinted by permission of Oxford University Press.

The personal matter that occupied Levin while he was talking with his brother was this. The year before, when visiting a field that was being mown, he had lost his temper with his steward, and to calm himself had used a remedy of his own—he took a scythe from one of the peasants and himself began mowing.

He liked this work so much that he went mowing several times: he mowed all the meadow in front of his house, and when spring came he planned to devote several whole days to mowing with the peasants. Since his brother's arrival, however, he was in doubt whether to go mowing or not. He did not feel comfortable at the thought of leaving his brother alone all day long, and he also feared that Koznyshev might laugh at him. But while walking over the meadow he recalled the impression mowing had made on him, and almost made up his mind to do it. After his irritating conversation with his brother he again remembered his intention.

'I need physical exercise; without it my character gets quite spoilt,' thought he, and determined to go and mow, however uncomfortable his brother and the peasants might make him feel.

In the evening Constantine went to the office and gave orders about the work sending round to the villages to tell the mowers to come next day to the Kalina meadow, the largest and finest he had.

'And please send my scythe to Titus to be sharpened, and have it taken to the meadow tomorrow: I may go mowing myself,' he said, trying to overcome his confusion.

The steward smiled and said, 'All right, sir.'

That evening, at tea, Levin said to his brother:

'The weather looks settled; to-morrow we begin mowing.'

'I like that work very much,' said Koznyshev.

'I like it awfully too. I have mown with the peasants now and then, and to-morrow I want to mow all day.'

Koznyshev looked up at his brother in surprise.

'How do you mean? All day, just like the peasants?'

'Yes, it is very pleasant,' replied Levin.

'It is splendid physical exercise, but you will hardly be able to hold out,' remarked Koznyshev, without the least sarcasm.

'I have tried it. At first it seems hard, but one gets drawn into it. I don't think I shall lag behind. . . . '

'Dear me! But tell me, how do the peasants take it? I expect they laugh at their crank of a master?'

'No, I don't think so; but it is such pleasant work, and at the same time so hard, that one has no time for thinking.'

'But how can you dine with them? It would not be quite the thing to send you claret and roast turkey out there?'

'No; I will just come home at their dinner-time.'

Next morning Constantine got up earlier than usual, but giving instructions about the farming delayed him, and when he came to the meadow each man was already mowing his second swath.

From the hill, as he came to his first swath, he could see, in the shade at his feet, a part of the meadow that was already mown, with the green heaps of grass and dark piles of coats thrown down by the mowers.

As he drew nearer, the peasants—following each other in a long straggling line, some with coats on, some in their shirts, each swinging his scythe in his own manner—gradually came into sight. He counted forty-two of them.

They moved slowly along the uneven bottom of the meadow, where a weir had once been. Levin recognized some of his own men. Old Ermil, wearing a very long white shirt, was swinging his scythe, with his back bent; young Vaska, who had been in Levin's service as coachman, and who at each swing of his scythe cut the grass the whole width of his swath; and Titus, Levin's mowing master, a thin little peasant, who went along without stopping, mowing his wide swath as if in play.

Levin dismounted and, tethering his horse by the roadside, went up to Titus, who fetched another scythe from behind a bush and gave it to Levin.

'It's ready, master! Like a razor, it will mow of itself,' said Titus, taking off his cap and smiling as he handed the scythe.

Levin took it and began to put himself in position. The peasants, perspiring and merry, who had finished their swaths came out on to the road one after another, and laughingly exchanged greetings with their master. They all looked at him, but no one made any remark until a tall old man with a shrivelled, beardless face, wearing a sheep-skin jacket, stepped out on to the road and addressed him:

'Mind, master! Having put your hand to the plough, don't look back!'

And Levin heard the sound of repressed laughter among the mowers.

'I will try not to lag behind,' he said, taking his place behind Titus and waiting his turn to fall in.

'Mind!' repeated the old man.

Titus made room for Levin, and Levin followed him. By the roadside the grass was short and tough, and Levin, who had not done any mowing for a long time and was confused by so many eyes upon him mowed badly for the first ten minutes, though he swung his scythe with much vigour. He heard voices behind him:

'It's not properly adjusted, the grip is not right. See how he has to stoop!' said one.

'Hold the heel lower,' said another.

'Never mind! It's all right: he'll get into it,' said the old man. 'There he goes. . . .'

'You are taking too wide a swath, you'll get knocked up.' . . . 'He's the master, he must work; he's working for himself!' . . . 'But look how uneven!' . . . 'That's what the likes of us used to get a thump on the back for.'

They came to softer grass, and Levin, who was listening without replying, followed Titus and tried to mow as well as possible. When they had gone some hundred steps Titus was still going on without pausing, showing no signs of fatigue, while Levin was already beginning to fear he would not be able to keep up, he felt so tired.

He swung his scythe, feeling almost at the last gasp, and made up his mind to ask Titus to stop. But just at that moment Titus stopped of his own accord, stooped, took up some grass and wiped his scythe with it. Levin straightened himself, sighed, and looked back. The peasant behind him was still mowing but was obviously tired too, for he stopped without coming even with Levin and began whetting his scythe. Titus whetted his own and Levin's, and they began mowing again.

The same thing happened at Levin's second attempt. Titus swung his scythe, swing after swing, without stopping and without getting tired. Levin followed, trying not to lag behind, but it became harder and harder until at last the moment came when he felt he had no strength left, and then Titus again stopped and began whetting his scythe. In this way they finished the swaths. They were long, and to Levin seemed particularly difficult; but when it was done and Titus with his scythe over his shoulder turned about and slowly retraced his steps, placing his feet on the marks left on the mown surface by the heels of his boots, and Levin went down his own swath in the same way, then—in spite of the perspiration that ran down his face in streams and dripped from his nose, and though his back was as wet as if the shirt had been soaked in water—he felt very light-hearted. What gave him most pleasure was the knowledge that he would be able to keep up with the peasants.

The only thing marring his joy was the fact that his swath was not well mown. 'I must swing the scythe less with my arms and more with the whole of my body,' he thought, comparing Titus's swath, cut straight as if by measure, with his own, on which the grass lay scattered and uneven.

As Levin was aware, Titus had been mowing this swath with special rapidity, probably to put his master to the test, and it chanced to be a very long one. The next swaths were easier, but still Levin had to work with all his might to keep even with the peasants. He thought of nothing and desired nothing, except not to lag behind and to do his work as well as possible. He heard only the swishing of the scythes and saw only the receding figure of Titus, the convex half-circle of the mown piece before him, and the grasses and heads of flowers falling in waves about the blade of his scythe, and in the background the end of the swath where he would rest.

Suddenly he was conscious of a pleasant coolness on his hot perspiring shoulders, without knowing what it was or whence it came. He glanced up at the sky whilst whetting his scythe. A dark cloud was hanging low overhead, and large drops of rain were falling. Some of the peasants went to put on their coats; others as well as Levin felt pleasure in the refreshing rain and merely moved their shoulders up and down.

They came to the end of another swath. They went on mowing long and short rows, good and poor grass. Levin had lost count of time and had really no idea whether it was late or early. His work was undergoing a change which gave him intense pleasure. While working he sometimes forgot for some minutes what he was about, and felt quite at ease; then his mowing was nearly as even as that of Titus. But as soon as he began thinking about it and trying to work better, he at once felt how hard the task was and mowed badly.

He finished a swath and was about to start another when Titus paused and went up to the old man, and both looked at the sun.

'What are they talking about, and why don't they start another swath?' thought Levin. It did not occur to him that the peasants, who had been mowing unceasingly for four hours, wanted their breakfast.

'Breakfast-time, master,' said the old man.

'Is it time? Well, then, breakfast!'

Levin handed his scythe to Titus and with the peasants, who were going to fetch the bread that lay with their coats, went across the swaths of the long mown portion of the meadow, slightly sprinkled with rain. Only then he remembered that he had not been right about the weather and that the rain was wetting the hay.

'The hay will be spoilt,' said he.

'It won't hurt, master. "Mow in the rain, rake when it's fine!" '

Levin untied his horse and rode home to his coffee.

By the time Levin had finished breakfast Koznyshev had only just got up, and Levin went back to the meadow before Koznyshev had come to table.

After breakfast Levin got placed between a humorous old man who invited him to be his neighbour and a young peasant who had only got married last autumn and was now out for his first summer's mowing.

The old man went along holding himself erect, moving with regular, long steps, turning out his toes, and with a precise and even motion that seemed to cost him no more effort than swinging his arms when walking, he laid the grass in a level high ridge, as if in play or as if the sharp scythe of its own accord whizzed through the juicy grass.

Young Mishka went behind Levin. His pleasant young face, with a wisp of grass tied round the forehead over his hair, worked all over with the effort; but whenever anyone glanced at him he smiled. Evidently he would have died rather than confess that the work was trying.

Between these two went Levin. Now, in the hottest part of the day, the work did not seem so hard to him. The perspiration in which he was bathed was cooling, and the sun which burnt his back, his head and his arm—bare to the elbow—added to his strength and perseverance in his task, and those unconscious intervals when it became possible not to think of what he was doing recurred more and more often. The scythe seemed to mow of itself. Those were happy moments. Yet more joyous were the moments when, reaching the river at the lower end of the swaths, the old man would wipe his scythe with the wet grass, rinse its blade in the clear water, and dipping his whetstone-box in the stream, would offer it to Levin.

'A little of my kvas? It's good!' said he, with a wink.

And really Levin thought he had never tasted any nicer drink than this lukewarm water with green stuff floating in it and a flavour of the rusty tin box. And then came the ecstasy of a slow walk, one hand resting on the scythe, when there was leisure to wipe away the streams of perspiration, to breathe deep, to watch the line of mowers, and to see what was going on around in forest and field.

The longer Levin went on mowing, the oftener he experienced those moments of oblivion when his arms no longer seemed to swing the scythe, but the scythe itself his whole body, so conscious and full of life; and as if by magic, regularly and definitely without a thought being given to it, the work accomplished itself of its own accord. These were blessed moments.

It was trying only when thought became necessary in order to mow around a molehill or a space where the hard sorrel stalks had not been weeded out. The old man accomplished this with ease. When he came to a molehill he would change his action, and with a short jerk of the point and then of the heel of his scythe he would mow all round the molehill. And while doing this he noted everything he came to: now he plucked a sorrel stalk and ate it, or offered it to Levin; now he threw aside a branch with the point of his scythe, or examined a quail's nest from which the hen bird had flown up, almost under the scythe; or he caught a beetle, lifting it with the scythe-point as with a fork, and after showing it to Levin, threw it away.

Levin and the young fellow on the other side of him found such changes of action difficult. Both of them, having got into one strained kind of movement, were in the grip of feverish labour and had not the power to change the motion of their bodies and at the same time to observe what lay before them.

Levin did not notice how time passed. Had he been asked how long he had been mowing, he would have answered 'half an hour', although it was nearly noon. As they were about to begin another swath the old man drew Levin's attention to the little boys and girls approaching from all sides along the road and through the long grass, hardly visible above it, carrying jugs of kvas stoppered with rags, and bundles of bread which strained their little arms.

'Look at the midges crawling along!' he said, pointing to the children and glancing at the sun from under his lifted hand. They completed two more swaths and then the old man stopped.

'Come, master! It's dinner-time,' said he with decision. All the mowers on reaching the river went across the swaths to where their coats lay, and where the children who had brought their dinners sat waiting for them. The men who had driven from a distance gathered in the shadow of their carts; those who lived nearer sheltered under the willow growth, on which they hung grass.

Levin sat down beside them; he did not want to go away.

All the peasants' restraint in the presence of the master had vanished. The men began preparing for dinner. Some had a wash. The young lads bathed in the river; others arranged places for their after-dinner rest, unfastened their bags of bread and unstoppered their jugs of kvas. The old man broke some rye bread into a bowl, mashed it with a spoon handle, poured over it some water from his tin, broke more bread into it and salted it, and then, turning to the East, said grace.

'Come, master, have some of my dinner,' said he, kneeling in front of his bowl.

The bread and water was so nice that Levin gave up all intention of

going home to lunch. He shared the old man's meal and got into conversation with him about his domestic affairs, taking a lively interest in
them and telling him about his own, giving him all the particulars which
would interest the old peasant. When the old man got up and, having
said grace, lay down beneath the willows with an armful of grass under
his head, Levin did the same, regardless of the flies, importunate and
persistent in the sunshine, and of the crawling insects that tickled his
perspiring face and body. He at once fell asleep, waking only when the
sun touched the opposite side of the willows and reached him. The old
man had already been long awake and sat setting the scythes for the
young men.

Levin looked round and hardly recognized the place, everything was
so altered. A wide expanse of the meadow was already mown, and with
its swaths of grass already giving off perfume, shone with a peculiar fresh
brilliance in the oblique rays of the descending sun. The bushes by the
river where the grass had been cut and the river itself with its curves,
previously invisible, were now glittering like steel; and the people getting up and moving about, the steep wall of yet uncut grass, and the
hawks soaring over the bare meadow, struck him as something quite
new. When he was fully awake Levin began to calculate how much had
been done and how much could still be done that day.

An extraordinary amount had been done by the forty-two men. The
larger meadow, which in the days of serfdom had taken thirty men two
days to mow, was all finished except some short patches at the corners.
But Levin wanted to get as much as possible done that day, and it was
vexatious to see the sun already declining. He was not feeling at all tired
and was only longing to work again and to accomplish as much as he
could.

'What do you think—could we manage to get Mashkin Heights mown
to-day?' he asked the old man.

'Well, God willing, we might! The sun is not very high though. Perhaps—if the lads could have a little vodka!'

At half-time, when they sat down again and those who smoked were
lighting their pipes, the old man informed the young fellows that if they
mowed the Mashkin Heights there would be vodka.

'What? Not mow that? Come along, Titus; we'll get it clear in no
time!'

'You can eat your fill at night. Let's begin!' shouted different voices,
and the mowers took their places, finishing their bread as they went.

'Now then, lads! Keep going!' said Titus, starting off ahead almost at
a trot.

'Go on, go on!' said the old man, hurrying after him and easily catching him up. 'Take care, I'll mow you down!'

And young and old vied with each other at mowing. But in spite of their haste they did not spoil the grass, and the swaths fell just as evenly and exactly as before. The small patch that was left in the last corner was mown in five minutes; and whilst the last mowers were finishing their swaths, those in front, carrying their coats over their shoulders, were already crossing the road toward Mashkin Heights.

The sun was already setting toward the trees when, with their tin boxes rattling, they entered the wooded ravine of the Heights.

The grass that in the middle of the ravine reached to their waists was delicate, soft, and broad-bladed, speckled here and there with cow-wheat.

After a short consultation as to whether they should mow the ravine across or lengthwise, Prokhor—a gigantic dark man and a famous mower—took the lead. He went in front, mowed a swath, turned round and restarted; following him all the others took their places, going downhill along the creek and back up to the very skirts of the wood. The sun had set behind the wood and now shone only on the mowers at the top of the hill, while in the valley, where the mists were rising, they were in cool, dewy shade. The work proceeded briskly.

The scented grass, cut down with a sound that showed how juicy it was, fell in high ridges. On the short swaths the mowers crowded together, their tin boxes clattering, their scythes ringing whenever they touched, the whetstones whistling upon the blades, and their merry voices resounding as they urged each other on.

Levin was again mowing between the old man and the lad. The old man, who had put on his sheepskin jacket, was still as jolly, witty, and easy in his movements as before. In the wood their scythes continually cut down wood mushrooms, grown plump amid the juicy grass. The old man stooped each time he came upon one, picked it up, and put it inside his jacket, saying, 'Another treat for my old woman.'

It was easy to cut the wet soft grass, but on the other hand it was very difficult to go up and down the steep slopes of the ravine. This, however, did not trouble the old man. Swinging his scythe just as usual, taking short steps with feet shod in large bark-plaited shoes, he slowly climbed the slopes; and though his whole body and his loosely-hanging trousers shook, he did not miss a single mushroom or a curious grass, and continued joking with the other peasants and with Levin. Levin followed, and often thought he would certainly fall when climbing a mound with his scythe in his hand—a mound so steep that it would have been hard to climb even unencumbered. Still, he managed to climb it and to do all that had to be done; and he felt as if some external force were urging him on.

Mashkin Heights were mown, and the peasants, having completed their last swaths, put on their coats and went home in high spirits. Levin, having regretfully taken leave of them, mounted and rode home. He looked back from the top of the hill. He could not see the men, for the mist rising from the hollow hid them; but he heard their merry rough voices, laughter, and the clanking of the scythes.

Koznyshev had long had his dinner, and was in his room drinking iced water with lemon, while looking over the papers and magazines just arrived by post, when Levin rushed in, his tangled hair clinging to his moist brow, his shirt saturated back and front and dark with perspiration, and cried out joyfully:

'We have finished the whole of the meadow! How delightful it is! And how have you got on?' Levin had quite forgotten the unpleasant conversation of the previous day.

'Dear me, what a sight you are!' said Koznyshev, turning to his brother with a momentary look of vexation. 'The door—the door! Shut it!' he exclaimed. 'You've certainly let in a whole dozen!'

Koznyshev could not bear flies, and opened the windows in his room only at night, keeping the door carefully closed.

'No, not one, I swear. And if I have, I'll catch it! . . . You would not believe what enjoyment it was! And how have you spent the day?'

'Quite well. But have you really been mowing all day? You must be as hungry as a wolf. Kuzma has everything ready for you.'

'No, I don't want to eat; I have had something there. But I'll go and wash.'

'Yes, yes, go; and I will come presently.' Koznyshev shook his head as he looked at his brother. 'Go, go, and be quick!' he added with a smile, as, gathering together his books, he prepared to go too. He also felt suddenly quite cheerful and did not wish to part from his brother. 'And where were you when it rained?'

'What rain was that? Only a few drops. . . . Well, then, I'll come back directly. So you have spent the day all right? That's good.' And Levin went off to dress.

Five minutes later the brothers met again in the dining-room. Though Levin had imagined that he was not hungry, and sat down to table only not to offend Kuzma, yet when he began eating he thought everything delicious. Koznyshev smiled as he looked at him.

Excerpt from
CHILD'S PLAY
by Robert Louis Stevenson

In this essay the poet and novelist considers the meaning of children's play, and some of the differences between childhood and adulthood. He finds that a child's experience is both more and less "mediated" than an adult's, in ways that leave the two ages moving "in different worlds," however their lives may appear to intersect.

Imagination, Stevenson observes, has a far greater power over children than it has over adults; a child's imagination is stronger even than his appetite. At the same time, the impressions of a child's senses are less compelling to him than those of an adult, and so he tends to use his senses directly, to serve utilitarian ends.

Stevenson asserts that as we age, we use our minds to create a medium of "theories and associations," within which we increasingly live. This medium is so compelling that we can "marry, fall and die; all the while sitting quietly by the fire or lying prone in bed." A child, on the other hand, can do none of these things without acting them out, with tangible props; this "testifies to a defect in the child's imagination which prevents him from carrying out his novels in the privacy of his own heart."

Stevenson asserts that children's play imitates perceived adult behavior almost exclusively, yet children are more interested in the imitations of other children than in the real adults they are copying. Is he right? Assuming so, do you think that a child playing one of these games of imitation is immediately connected to real life? Would you say he is happy?

Living immediately is crucial to adult happiness; is it equally crucial to the happiness of children?

Tolstoy's Levin lives immediately when he loses himself in an activity, becoming unconscious of how he is doing it. Are children at play or daydreaming adults similarly unconscious? Are they equally happy?

The regret we have for our childhood is not wholly justifiable: so much a man may lay down without fear of public ribaldry; for although we shake our heads over the change, we are not unconscious of the manifold advantages of our new state. What we lose in generous impulse, we more than gain in the habit of generously watching others; and the capacity to enjoy Shakespeare may balance a lost aptitude for playing at soldiers. Terror is gone out of our lives, moreover; we no longer see the devil in the bed-curtains nor lie awake to listen to the wind. We go to school no more; and if we have only exchanged one drudgery for another (which is by no means sure), we are set free for ever from the daily fear of chastisement. And yet a great change has overtaken us; and although we do not enjoy ourselves less, at least we take our pleasure differently. We need pickles nowadays to make Wednesday's cold mutton please our Friday's appetite; and I can remember the time when to call it red venison, and tell myself a hunter's story, would have made it more palatable than the best of sauces. To the grown person, cold mutton is cold mutton all the world over; not all the mythology ever invented by man will make it better or worse to him; the broad fact, the clamant reality, of the mutton carries away before it such seductive figments. But for the child it is still possible to weave an enchantment over eatables; and if he has but read of a dish in a story-book, it will be heavenly manna to him for a week.

If a grown man does not like eating and drinking and exercise, if he is not something positive in his tastes, it means he has a feeble body and should have some medicine; but children may be pure spirits, if they will, and take their enjoyment in a world of moon-shine. Sensation does not count for so much in our first years as afterwards; something of the swaddling numbness of infancy clings about us; we see and touch and hear through a sort of golden mist. Children, for instance, are able enough to see, but they have no great faculty for looking; they do not use their eyes for the pleasure of using them, but for by-ends of their own; and the things I call to mind seeing most vividly, were not beautiful in themselves, but merely interesting or enviable to me as I thought they might be turned to practical account in play. Nor is the sense of touch so clean and poignant in children as it is in a man. If you will turn over your old memories, I think the sensations of this sort you remember will be somewhat vague, and come to not much more than a blunt, general sense of heat on summer days, or a blunt, general sense of wellbeing in bed. And here, of course, you will understand pleasurable sensations; for overmastering pain—the most deadly and tragical element in life, and the true commander of man's soul and body—alas! pain has its own way with all of us; it breaks in, a rude visitant, upon the fairy garden where the child wanders in a dream, no less surely than it rules upon the field of battle, or sends the immortal war-god whimpering to his father; and innocence, no more than philosophy, can protect us from this sting. As for taste, when we bear in mind the excesses of unmitigated sugar which delight a youthful palate, "it is surely no very cynical asperity" to think taste a character of the maturer growth. Smell and hearing are perhaps more developed; I remember many scents, many voices, and a great deal of spring singing in the woods. But hearing is capable of vast improvement as a means of pleasure; and there is all the world between gaping wonderment at the jargon of birds, and the emotion with which a man listens to articulate music.

At the same time, and step by step with this increase in the definition and intensity of what we feel which accompanies our growing age, another change takes place in the sphere of intellect, by which all things are transformed and seen through theories and associations as through coloured windows. We make to ourselves day by day, out of history, and gossip, and economical speculations, and God knows what, a medium in which we walk and through which we look abroad. We study shop windows with other eyes than in our childhood, never to wonder, not always to admire, but to make and modify our little incongruous theories about life. It is no longer the uniform of a soldier that arrests our attention; but perhaps the flowing carriage of a woman, or perhaps a countenance that has been vividly stamped with passion and carries an adventurous story written in its lines. The pleasure of surprise is passed away; sugar-loaves and water-carts seem mighty tame to encounter; and we walk the streets to make romances and to sociologise. Nor must we deny that a good many of us walk them solely for the purposes of transit or in the interest of a livelier digestion. These, indeed, may look back with mingled thoughts upon their childhood, but the rest are in a better case; they know more than when they were children, they understand better, their desires and sympathies answer more nimbly to the provocation of the senses, and their minds are brimming with interest as they go about the world.

According to my contention, this is a flight to which children cannot rise. They are wheeled in perambulators or dragged about by nurses in a pleasing stupor. A vague, faint, abiding, wonderment possesses them. Here and there some specially remarkable circumstance, such as a water-cart or a guardsman, fairly penetrates into the seat of thought and calls them, for half a moment, out of themselves; and you may see them, still towed forward sideways by the inexorable nurse as by a sort of destiny, but still staring at the bright object in their wake. It may be some minutes before another such moving spectacle reawakens them to the world in which they dwell. For other children, they almost in-

variably show some intelligent sympathy. "There is a fine fellow making mud pies," they seem to say; "that I can understand, there is some
sense in mud pies." But the doings of their elders, unless where they
are speakingly picturesque or recommend themselves by the quality of
being easily imitable, they let them go over their heads (as we say)
without the least regard. If it were not for this perpetual imitation, we
should be tempted to fancy they despised us outright, or only considered us in the light of creatures brutally strong and brutally silly; among
whom they condescended to dwell in obedience like a philosopher at a
barbarous court. At times, indeed, they display an arrogance of disregard that is truly staggering. Once, when I was groaning aloud with
physical pain, a young gentleman came into the room and noncha-
lantly inquired if I had seen his bow and arrow. He made no account of
my groans, which he accepted, as he had to accept so much else, as a
piece of the inexplicable conduct of his elders; and like a wise young
gentleman, he would waste no wonder on the subject. Those elders,
who care so little for rational enjoyment, and are even the enemies of
rational enjoyment for others, he had accepted without understanding
and without complaint, as the rest of us accept the scheme of the universe.

   We grown people can tell ourselves a story, give and take strokes until
the bucklers ring, ride far and fast, marry, fall, and die; all the while
sitting quietly by the fire or lying prone in bed. This is exactly what a
child cannot do, or does not do, at least, when he can find anything else.
He works all with lay figures and stage properties. When his story comes
to the fighting, he must rise, get something by way of a sword and have
a set-to with a piece of furniture, until he is out of breath. When he
comes to ride with the king's pardon, he must bestride a chair, which he
will so hurry and belabour and on which he will so furiously demean
himself, that the messenger will arrive, if not bloody with spurring, at
least fiery red with haste. If his romance involves an accident upon a
cliff, he must clamber in person about the chest of drawers and fall bodily upon the carpet, before his imagination is satisfied. Lead soldiers, dolls,
all toys, in short, are in the same category and answer the same end.
Nothing can stagger a child's faith; he accepts the clumsiest substitutes
and can swallow the most staring incongruities. The chair he has just
been besieging as a castle, or valiantly cutting to the ground as a dragon,
is taken away for the accommodation of a morning visitor, and he is
nothing abashed; he can skirmish by the hour with a stationary coal-
scuttle; in the midst of the enchanted pleasance, he can see, without
sensible shock, the gardener soberly digging potatoes for the day's din-

ner. He can make abstraction of whatever does not fit into his fable; and he puts his eyes into his pocket, just as we hold our noses in an unsavoury lane. And so it is, that although the ways of children cross with those of their elders in a hundred places daily, they never go in the same direction nor so much as lie in the same element. So may the telegraph wires intersect the line of the high-road, or so might a landscape painter and a bagman visit the same country, and yet move in different worlds.

People struck with these spectacles cry aloud about the power of imagination in the young. Indeed there may be two words to that. It is, in some ways, but a pedestrian fancy that the child exhibits. It is the grown people who make the nursery stories; all the children do is jealously to preserve the text. One out of a dozen reasons why *Robinson Crusoe* should be so popular with youth, is that it hits their level in this matter to a nicety; Crusoe was always at makeshifts and had, in so many words, to *play* at a great variety of professions; and then the book is all about tools, and there is nothing that delights a child so much. Hammers and saws belong to a province of life that positively calls for imitation. The juvenile lyrical drama, surely of the most ancient Thespian model, wherein the trades of mankind are successively simulated to the running burthen "On a cold and frosty morning," gives a good instance of the artistic taste in children. And this need for overt action and lay figures testifies to a defect in the child's imagination which prevents him from carrying out his novels in the privacy of his own heart. He does not yet know enough of the world and men. His experience is incomplete. That stage-wardrobe and scene-room that we call the memory is so ill provided, that he can overtake few combinations and body out few stories, to his own content, without some external aid. He is at the experimental stage; he is not sure how one would feel in certain circumstances; to make sure, he must come as near trying it as his means permit. And so here is young heroism with a wooden sword, and mothers practice their kind vocation over a bit of jointed stick. It may be laughable enough just now; but it is these same people and these same thoughts, that not long hence, when they are on the theatre of life, will make you weep and tremble. For children think very much the same thoughts and dream the same dreams, as bearded men and marriageable women. No one is more romantic. Fame and honour, the love of young men and the love of mothers, the business man's pleasure in method, all these and others they anticipate and rehearse in their play hours. Upon us, who are further advanced and fairly dealing with the threads of destiny, they only glance from time to time to glean a hint for their own mimetic reproduction. Two children playing at soldiers are far more interesting to each other than one of the scarlet beings whom both are busy imitating. This is perhaps the greatest oddity of all. "Art for art" is their motto; and the doings of grown folk are only interesting as the raw material for play. Not Theophile Gautier, not Flaubert, can look more callously upon life, or rate the reproduction more highly over the reality; and they will parody an execution, a deathbed, or the funeral of the young man of Nain, with all the cheerfulness in the world.

The true parallel for play is not to be found, of course, in conscious art, which, though it be derived from play, is itself an abstract, impersonal thing, and depends largely upon philosophical interests beyond the scope of childhood. It is when we make castles in the air and personate the leading character in our own romances, that we return to the spirit of our first years. Only, there are several reasons why the spirit is no longer so agreeable to indulge. Nowadays, when we admit this personal element into our divagations we are apt to stir up uncomfortable and sorrowful memories, and remind ourselves sharply of old wounds. Our day-dreams can no longer lie all in the air like a story in the *Arabian Nights*; they read to us rather like the history of a period in which we ourselves had taken part, where we come across many unfortunate passages and find our own conduct smartly reprimanded. And then the child, mind you, acts his parts. He does not merely repeat them to himself; he leaps, he runs, and sets the blood agog over all his body. And so his play breathes him; and he no sooner assumes a passion than he gives it vent. Alas! when we betake ourselves to our intellectual form of play, sitting quietly by the fire or lying prone in bed, we rouse many hot feelings for which we can find no outlet. Substitutes are not acceptable to the mature mind, which desires the thing itself; and even to rehearse a triumphant dialogue with one's enemy, although it is perhaps the most satisfactory piece of play still left within our reach, is not entirely satisfying, and is even apt to lead to a visit and an interview which may be the reverse of triumphant after all.

In the child's world of dim sensation, play is all in all. "Making believe" is the gist of his whole life, and he cannot so much as take a walk except in character. I could not learn my alphabet without some suitable *mise-en-scene*, and had to act a business man in an office before I could sit down to my book. Will you kindly question your memory, and find out how much you did, work or pleasure, in good faith and soberness, and for how much you had to cheat yourself with some invention? I remember, as though it were yesterday, the expansion of spirit, the dignity and self-reliance, that came with a pair of mustachios in burnt cork, even when there was none to see. Children are even content to forego what we call the realities, and prefer the shadow to the substance. When they might be speaking intelligibly together, they chatter senseless gibberish by the hour, and are quite happy because they are making believe to speak French. I have said already how even the imperious appetite of hunger suffers itself to be gulled and led by the nose with the fag end of an old song. And it goes deeper than this: when children are together even a meal is felt as an interruption in the business of life; and they must find some imaginative sanction, and tell themselves some sort of story, to account for, to colour, to render entertaining, the simple processes of eating and drinking. What wonderful fancies I have heard evolved out of the pattern upon tea-cups!—from which there followed a code of rules and a whole world of excitement, until tea-drinking began to take rank as a game. When my cousin and I took our porridge of a morning, we had a device to enliven the course of the meal. He ate his with sugar, and explained it to be a country continually buried under snow. I took mine with milk, and explained it to be a country suffering gradual inundation. You can imagine us exchanging bulletins; how here was an island still unsubmerged, here a valley not yet covered with snow; what inventions were made; how his population lived in cabins on perches and travelled on stilts, and how mine was always in boats; how the interest grew furious, as the last corner of safe ground was cut off on all sides and grew smaller every moment; and how in fine, the food was of altogether secondary importance, and might even have been nauseous, so long as we seasoned it with these dreams . . . .

. . . One thing, at least, comes very clearly out of these considerations; that whatever we are to expect at the hands of children, it should not be any peddling exactitude about matters of fact. They walk in a vain show, and among mists and rainbows; they are passionate after dreams and unconcerned about realities; speech is a difficult art not wholly learned; and there is nothing in their own tastes or purposes to teach them what we mean by abstract truthfulness. When a bad writer is inexact, even if he can look back on half a century of years, we charge him with incompetence and not with dishonesty. And why not extend the same allowance to imperfect speakers? Let a stockbroker be dead stupid about poetry, or a poet inexact in the details of business, and we excuse them heartily from blame. But show us a miserable, unbreeched, human entity, whose whole profession it is to take a tub for a fortified town and a shaving-brush for the deadly stiletto, and who passes three-fourths of his time in a dream and the rest in open self-deception, and we expect him to be as nice upon a matter of fact as a scientific expert bearing evidence. Upon my heart, I think it less than decent. You do not consider how little the child sees, or how swift he is to weave what he has seen into bewildering fiction; and that he cares no more for what you call truth, than you for a gingerbread dragoon.

PAIN HAS AN ELEMENT OF BLANK

by Emily Dickinson

One barrier to self-forgetfulness is the near-constant intrusion of the body, with its needs, limitations, and unceasing sensations. In this brief poem, Emily Dickinson considers the most overwhelming of all bodily experiences: pain.

What is "the element of blank"? What is wiped out or concealed?

Pain is a direct experience that, according to Dickinson, seems to fill the present; nothing interposes itself between the poet and her pain. Does this mean that a person in pain is living immediately? If so, how might you square this with Tolstoy's view of living immediately as complete happiness?

Pain has an element of blank;
It cannot recollect
When it began, or if there were
A day when it was not.
It has no future but itself,
Its infinite realms contain
Its past, enlightened to perceive
New periods of pain.

WHEN I HEARD THE LEARN'D ASTRONOMER

by Walt Whitman

Scholarship can raise another barrier to living immediately. In these few lines, nineteenth-century American poet Walt Whitman shows how, and offers an alternative.

The poet recalls sitting in the "lecture-room" and listening as an astronomer transforms his celestial subject into proofs, figures, and measurables. Growing "tired and sick," he seeks solitude and the night, silence and the stars. Does the poet's reaction tell us more about his own poetic soul than about the adequacy or inadequacy of the astronomer's lessons? Is his response generalizable?

Whitman trades words for silence, an assembly for solitude, and "charts and diagrams" for the "mystical" night air. In so trading, what, if anything, does he lose or gain?

When I heard the learn'd astronomer,
When the proofs, the figures, were ranged in columns before
 me,
When I was shown the charts and diagrams, to add, divide,
 and measure them,
When I sitting heard the astronomer where he lectured with
 much applause in the lecture-room,
How soon unaccountable I became tired and sick,
Till rising and gliding out I wander'd off by myself,
In the mystical moist night-air, and from time to time,
Look'd up in perfect silence at the stars.

Excerpt from
THE LOSS OF THE CREATURE
by Walker Percy

Is it possible for social creatures such as ourselves to see with fresh eyes that which we know has already been "discovered"? Here novelist and essayist Walker Percy considers the many barriers to direct, sovereign perception in a world full of experts and packaged experiences.

Percy begins, in part 1 of this essay, with the problem a tourist faces if he wishes to see the Grand Canyon in its full majesty, as its discoverer, López de Cárdenas, first did. Because the canyon is now encrusted by a "symbolic complex," the task, he claims, is virtually impossible.

Moving to another example—that of a couple of tourists who stumble upon an "authentic" Mexican village—Percy points to a still deeper layer of difficulty. Even though the couple are themselves the discoverers, they "recognize a priority of title of the expert." They must seek an expert's approval of their experience; a direct experience of their own remains impossible for them. Nor is this the greatest difficulty they face. Even if a direct experience were possible for this couple, Percy writes, "with the onset of the first direct enjoyment, their higher consciousness pounces and certifies: 'Now you are doing it! Now you are really living!' And, in certifying the experience, sets it at nought."

In part 2, a portion of which is reproduced below, Percy considers the implications of his insights for education. How can a zoology student be made really to see a dogfish? How can a student of literature break through to a Shakespearean sonnet?

Throughout, Percy offers strategies for overcoming the many barriers to direct experience. He fears, however, that people "cannot escape their consciousness of their consciousness." Is he right? Is it really futile to try to live immediately? Are all of Percy's strategies doomed?

What is missing from the lives Percy describes? What are his searchers—the visitor to the canyon, the tourists in Mexico—seeking?

Percy says he is writing about "a radical loss of sovereignty over that which is as much [the tourist's] as it is [the experts']." What is "that"? Over what have they lost sovereignty? Is something really missing from the lives Percy describes?

Every explorer names his island Formosa, beautiful. To him it is beautiful because, being first, he has access to it and can see it for what it is. But to no one else is it ever as beautiful—except the rare man who manages to recover it, who knows that it has to be recovered.

García López de Cárdenas discovered the Grand Canyon and was amazed at the sight. It can be imagined: One crosses miles of desert, breaks through the mesquite, and there it is at one's feet. Later the government set the place aside as a national park, hoping to pass along to millions the experience of Cárdenas. Does not one see the same sight from the Bright Angel Lodge that Cárdenas saw?

The assumption is that the Grand Canyon is a remarkably interesting and beautiful place and that if it had a certain value P for Cárdenas, the same value P may be transmitted to any number of sightseers—just as Banting's discovery of insulin can be transmitted to any number of diabetics. A counterinfluence is at work, however, and it would be nearer the truth to say that if the place is seen by a million sightseers, a single sightseer does not receive value P but a millionth part of value P.

It is assumed that since the Grand Canyon has the fixed interest value P, tours can be organized for any number of people. A man in Boston decides to spend his vacation at the Grand Canyon. He visits his travel bureau, looks at the folder, signs up for a two-week tour. He and his family take the tour, see the Grand Canyon, and return to Boston. May we say that this man has seen the Grand Canyon? Possibly he has. But it is more likely that what he has done is the one sure way not to see the canyon.

Why is it almost impossible to gaze directly at the Grand Canyon under these circumstances and see it for what it is—as one picks up a strange object from one's back yard and gazes directly at it? It is almost impossible because the Grand Canyon, the thing as it is, has been appropriated by the symbolic complex which has already been formed in the sightseer's mind. Seeing the canyon under approved circumstances is seeing the symbolic complex head on. The thing is no longer the thing as it confronted the Spaniard; it is rather that which has already been formulated—by picture postcard, geography book, tourist folders, and the words *Grand Canyon*. As a result of this preformulation, the source of the sightseer's pleasure undergoes a shift. Where the wonder and delight of the Spaniard arose from his penetration of the thing itself, from a progressive discovery of depths, patterns, colors, shadows, etc., now the sightseer measures his satisfaction *by the degree to which the canyon conforms to the preformed complex.* If it does so, if it looks just like the postcard, he is pleased; he might even say, "Why it is every bit as beautiful as a picture postcard!" He feels he has not been cheated. But if it does not conform, if the colors are somber, he will not be able to see it directly; he will only be conscious of the disparity between what it is and what it is supposed to be. He will say later that he was unlucky in not being there at the right time. The highest point, the term of the sightseer's satisfaction, is not the sovereign discovery of the thing before him; it is rather the measuring up of the thing to the criterion of the preformed symbolic complex.

Seeing the canyon is made even more difficult by what the sightseer does when the moment arrives, when sovereign knower confronts the thing to be known. Instead of looking at it, he photographs it. There is no confrontation at all. At the end of forty years of preformulation and with the Grand Canyon yawning at his feet, what does he do? He waives his right of seeing and knowing and records symbols for the next forty years. For him there is no present; there is only the past of what has been formulated and seen and the future of what has been formulated and not seen. The present is surrendered to the past and the future.

The sightseer may be aware that something is wrong. He may simply be bored; or he may be conscious of the difficulty: that the great thing yawning at his feet somehow eludes him. The harder he looks at it, the less he can see. It eludes everybody. The tourist cannot see it; the bellboy at the Bright Angel Lodge cannot see it: for him it is only one side of the space he lives in, like one wall of a room; to the ranger it is a tissue of everyday signs relevant to his own prospects—the blue haze down there means that he will probably get rained on during the donkey ride.

How can the sightseer recover the Grand Canyon? He can recover it in any number of ways, all sharing in common the stratagem of avoiding the approved confrontation of the tour and the Park Service.

It may be recovered by leaving the beaten track. The tourist leaves the tour, camps in the back country. He arises before dawn and approaches the South Rim through a wild terrain where there are no trails and no railed-in lookout points. In other words, he sees the canyon by avoiding all the facilities for seeing the canyon. If the benevolent Park Service hears about this fellow and thinks he has a good idea and places the following notice in the Bright Angel Lodge: *Consult ranger for information on getting off the beaten track*—the end result will only be the closing of another access to the canyon.

It may be recovered by a dialectical movement which brings one back to the beaten track but at a level above it. For example, after a lifetime of avoiding the beaten track and guided tours, a man may deliberately seek out the most beaten track of all, the most commonplace tour imaginable: he may visit the canyon by a Greyhound tour in the company of a party from Terre Haute—just as a man who has lived in New York all his life may visit the Statue of Liberty. (Such dialectical savorings of the familiar as the familiar are, of course, a favorite stratagem of *The New Yorker* magazine.) The thing is recovered from familiarity by means of an exercise in familiarity. Our complex friend stands behind his fellow tourists at the Bright Angel Lodge and sees the canyon through them and their predicament, their picture taking and busy disregard. In a sense, he exploits his fellow tourists; he stands on their shoulders to see the canyon.

Such a man is far more advanced in the dialectic than the sightseer who is trying to get off the beaten track—getting up at dawn and approaching the canyon through the mesquite. This stratagem is, in fact, for our complex man the weariest, most beaten track of all.

It may be recovered as a consequence of a breakdown of the symbolic machinery by which the experts present the experience to the consumer. A family visits the canyon in the usual way. But shortly after their arrival, the park is closed by an outbreak of typhus in the south. They have the canyon to themselves. What do they mean when they tell the home folks of their good luck: "We had the whole place to ourselves"? How does one see the thing better when the others are absent? Is looking like sucking: the more lookers, the less there is to see? They could hardly answer, but by saying this they testify to a state of affairs which is considerably more complex than the simple statement of the schoolbook about the Spaniard and the millions who followed him. It is a state in which there is a complex distribution of sovereignty, of zoning.

It may be recovered in a time of national disaster. The Bright Angel Lodge is converted into a rest home, a function that has nothing to do with the canyon a few yards away. A wounded man is brought in. He regains consciousness; there outside his window is the canyon.

The most extreme case of access by privilege conferred by disaster is the Huxleyan novel of the adventures of the surviving remnant after the great wars of the twentieth century. An expedition from Australia lands in Southern California and heads east. They stumble across the Bright Angel Lodge, now fallen into ruins. The trails are grown over, the guard rails fallen away, the dime telescope at Battleship Point rusted. But there is the canyon, exposed at last. Exposed by what? By the decay of those facilities which were designed to help the sightseer.

This dialectic of sightseeing cannot be taken into account by planners, for the object of the dialectic is nothing other than the subversion of the efforts of the planners.

The dialectic is not known to objective theorists, psychologists, and the like. Yet it is quite well known in the fantasy-consciousness of the popular arts. The devices by which the museum exhibit, the Grand Canyon, the ordinary thing, is recovered have long since been stumbled upon. A movie shows a man visiting the Grand Canyon. But the moviemaker knows something the planner does not know. He knows that one cannot take the sight frontally. The canyon must be approached by the stratagems we have mentioned: the Inside Track, the Familiar Revisited, the Accidental Encounter. Who is the stranger at the Bright Angel Lodge? Is he the ordinary tourist from Terre Haute that he makes himself out to be? He is not. He has another objective in mind, to revenge his wronged brother, counterespionage, etc. By virtue of the fact that he has other fish to fry, he may take a stroll along the rim after supper and then we can see the canyon through him. The movie accomplishes its purpose by concealing it. Overtly the characters (the American family marooned by typhus) and we the onlookers experience pity for the sufferers, and the family experience anxiety for themselves; covertly and in truth they are the happiest of people and we are happy through them, for we have the canyon to ourselves. The movie cashes in on the recovery of sovereignty through disaster. Not only is the canyon now accessible to the remnant; the members of the remnant are now accessible to each other; a whole new ensemble of relations becomes possible—friendship, love, hatred, clandestine sexual adventures. In a movie when a man sits next to a woman on a bus, it is necessary either that the bus break down or that the woman lose her memory. (The question occurs to one: Do you imagine there are sightseers who see sights just as they are supposed to? a family who live in Terre Haute, who decide to take the canyon tour, who go there, see it, enjoy it immensely, and go home content? a family who are entirely innocent of all the barriers, zones, losses of sovereignty I have been talking about? Wouldn't most people be sorry if Battleship Point fell into the canyon, carrying all one's fellow passengers to their death, leaving one alone on the South Rim? I cannot answer this. Perhaps there are such people. Certainly a great many American families would swear they had no such problems, that they came, saw, and went away happy. Yet it is just these families who would be happiest if they had gotten the Inside Track and been among the surviving remnant.)

It is now apparent that as between the many measures which may be taken to overcome the opacity, the boredom, of the direct confrontation of the thing or creature in its citadel of symbolic investiture, some are less authentic than others. That is to say, some stratagems obviously serve other purposes than that of providing access to being—for example, various unconscious motivations which it is not necessary to go into here.

Let us take an example in which the recovery of being is ambiguous, where it may under the same circumstances contain both authentic and unauthentic components. An American couple, we will say, drives down into Mexico. They see the usual sights and have a fair time of it. Yet they are never without the sense of missing something. Although Taxco and Cuernavaca are interesting and picturesque as advertised, they fall short of "it." What do the couple have in mind by "it"? What do they really hope for? What sort of experience could they have in Mexico so that upon their return, they would feel that "it" had happened? We have a clue: Their hope has something to do with their own role as tourists in a foreign country and the way in which they conceive this role. It has something to do with other American tourists. Certainly they feel that they are very far from "it" when, after traveling five thousand miles, they arrive at the plaza in Guanajuato only to find themselves surrounded by a dozen other couples from the Midwest.

Already we may distinguish authentic and unauthentic elements. First, we see the problem the couple faces and we understand their efforts to surmount it. The problem is to find an "unspoiled" place. "Unspoiled" does not mean only that a place is left physically intact; it means also that it is not encrusted by renown and by the familiar (as is Taxco), that it has not been discovered by others. We understand that the couple really want to get at the place and enjoy it. Yet at the same time we wonder if there is not something wrong in their dislike of their compatriots. Does access to the place require the exclusion of others?

Let us see what happens.

The couple decide to drive from Guanajuato to Mexico City. On the way they get lost. After hours on a rocky mountain road, they find themselves in a tiny valley not even marked on the map. There they discover an Indian village. Some sort of religious festival is going on. It is apparently a corn dance in supplication of the rain god.

The couple know at once that this is "it." They are entranced. They spend several days in the village, observing the Indians and being themselves observed with friendly curiosity.

Now may we not say that the sightseers have at last come face to face with an authentic sight, a sight which is charming, quaint, picturesque, unspoiled, and that they see the sight and come away rewarded? Possibly this may occur. Yet it is more likely that what happens is a far cry indeed from an immediate encounter with being, that the experience, while masquerading as such, is in truth a rather desperate impersonation. I use the word *desperate* advisedly to signify an actual loss of hope.

The clue to the spuriousness of their enjoyment of the village and the festival is a certain restiveness in the sightseers themselves. It is given expression by their repeated exclamations that "this is too good to be true," and by their anxiety that it may not prove to be so perfect, and finally by their downright relief at leaving the valley and having the experience in the bag, so to speak—that is, safely embalmed in memory and movie film.

What is the source of their anxiety during the visit? Does it not mean that the couple are looking at the place with a certain standard of performance in mind? Are they like Fabre, who gazed at the world about him with wonder, letting it be what it is; or are they not like the over-anxious mother who sees her child as one performing, now doing badly, now doing well? The village is their child and their love for it is an anxious love because they are afraid that at any moment it might fail them.

We have another clue in their subsequent remark to an ethnologist friend. "How we wished you had been there with us! What a perfect goldmine of folkways! Every minute we would say to each other, if only you were here! You must return with us." This surely testifies to a generosity of spirit, a willingness to share their experience with others, not at all like their feelings toward their fellow Iowans on the plaza at Guanajuato!

I am afraid this is not the case at all. It is true that they longed for their ethnologist friend, but it was for an entirely different reason. They wanted him, not to share their experience, but to certify their experience as genuine.

"This is it" and "Now we are really living" do not necessarily refer to the sovereign encounter of the person with the sight that enlivens the mind and gladdens the heart. It means that now at last we are having the acceptable experience. The present experience is always measured by a prototype, the "it" of their dreams. "Now I am really living" means that now I am filling the role of sightseer and the sight is living up to the prototype of sights. This quaint and picturesque village is measured by a Platonic ideal of the Quaint and the Picturesque.

Hence their anxiety during the encounter. For at any minute something could go wrong. A fellow Iowan might emerge from a 'dobe hut; the chief might show them his Sears catalogue. (If the failures are "wrong" enough, as these are, they might still be turned to account as rueful conversation pieces: "There we were expecting the chief to bring us a churinga and he shows up with a Sears catalogue!") They have snatched victory from disaster, but their experience always runs the danger of failure.

They need the ethnologist to certify their experience as genuine. This is borne out by their behavior when the three of them return for the next corn dance. During the dance, the couple do not watch the goings-on; instead they watch the ethnologist! Their highest hope is that their friend should find the dance interesting. And if he should show signs of true absorption, an interest in the goings-on so powerful that he becomes oblivious of his friends—then their cup is full. "Didn't we tell you?" they say at last. What they want from him is not ethnological explanations; all they want is his approval.

What has taken place is a radical loss of sovereignty over that which is as much theirs as it is the ethnologist's. The fault does not lie with the ethnologist. He has no wish to stake a claim to the village; in fact, he desires the opposite: he will bore his friends to death by telling them about the village and the meaning of the folkways. A degree of sovereignty has been surrendered by the couple. It is the nature of the loss, moreover, that they are not aware of the loss, beyond a certain uneasiness. (Even if they read this and admitted it, it would be very difficult for them to bridge the gap in their confrontation of the world. Their consciousness of the corn dance cannot escape their consciousness of their consciousness, so that with the onset of the first direct enjoyment, their higher consciousness pounces and certifies: "Now you are doing it! Now you are really living!" and, in certifying the experience, sets it at nought.)

Their basic placement in the world is such that they recognize a priority of title of the expert over his particular department of being. The whole horizon of being is staked out by "them," the experts. The highest satisfaction of the sightseer (not merely the tourist but any layman seer of sights) is that his sight should be certified as genuine. The worst of this impoverishment is that there is no sense of impoverishment. The surrender of title is so complete that it never even occurs to one to reassert title. A poor man may envy the rich man, but the sightseer does not envy the expert. When a caste system becomes absolute, envy disappears. Yet the caste of layman-expert is not the fault of the expert. It is due altogether to the eager surrender of sovereignty by the layman so that he may take up the role not of the person but of the consumer.

I do not refer only to the special relation of layman to theorist. I refer to the general situation in which sovereignty is surrendered to a class of privileged knowers, whether these be theorists or artists. A reader may surrender sovereignty over that which has been written about, just as a consumer may surrender sovereignty over a thing which has been theorized about. The consumer is content to receive an experience just as it has been presented to him by theorists and planners. The reader may also be content to judge life by whether it has or has not been formulated by those who know and write about life. A young man goes to France. He too has a fair time of it, sees the sights, enjoys the food. On his last day, in fact as he sits in a restaurant in Le Havre waiting for his boat, something happens. A group of French students in the restaurant get into an impassioned argument over a recent play. A riot takes place. Madame la concierge joins in, swinging her mop at the rioters. Our young American is transported. This is "it." And he had almost left France without seeing "it"!

But the young man's delight is ambiguous. On the one hand, it is a pleasure for him to encounter the same Gallic temperament he had heard about from Puccini and Rolland. But on the other hand, the source of his pleasure testifies to a certain alienation. For the young man is actually barred from a direct encounter with anything French excepting only that which has been set forth, authenticated by Puccini and Rolland—those who know. If he had encountered the restaurant scene without reading Hemingway, without knowing that the performance was so typically, charmingly French, he would not have been delighted. He would only have been anxious at seeing things get so out of hand. The source of his delight is the sanction of those who know.

This loss of sovereignty is not a marginal process, as might appear from my example of estranged sightseers. It is a generalized surrender of the horizon to those experts within whose competence a particular segment of the horizon is thought to lie. Kwakiutls are surrendered to Franz Boas; decaying Southern mansions are surrendered to Faulkner and Tennessee Williams. So that, although it is by no means the intention of the expert to expropriate sovereignty—in fact he would not even know what sovereignty meant in this context—the danger of theory and consumption is a seduction and deprivation of the consumer.

In the New Mexican desert, natives occasionally come across strange-looking artifacts which have fallen from the skies and which are stenciled: *Return to U.S. Experimental Project, Alamogordo. Reward.* The finder returns the object and is rewarded. He knows nothing of the nature of the object he has found and does not care to know. The sole role of the native, the highest role he can play, is that of finder and returner of the mysterious equipment.

The same is true of the layman's relation to *natural* objects in a modern technical society. No matter what the object or event is, whether it is a star, a swallow, a Kwakiutl, a "psychological phenomenon," the layman who confronts it does not confront it as a sovereign person, as Crusoe confronts a seashell he finds on the beach. The highest role he can conceive himself as playing is to be able to recognize the title of the object, to return it to the appropriate expert and have it certified as a genuine find. He does not even permit himself to see the thing—as Gerard Hopkins could see a rock or a cloud or a field. If anyone asks him why he doesn't look, he may reply that he didn't take that subject in college (or he hasn't read Faulkner).

This loss of sovereignty extends even to oneself. There is the neurotic who asks nothing more of his doctor than that his symptom should prove interesting. When all else fails, the poor fellow has nothing to offer but his own neurosis. But even this is sufficient if only the doctor will show interest when he says, "Last night I had a curious sort of dream; perhaps it will be significant to one who knows about such things. It seems I was standing in a sort of alley—" (I have nothing else to offer you but my own unhappiness. Please say that it, at least, measures up, that it is a *proper* sort of unhappiness.)

A young Falkland Islander walking along a beach and spying a dead dogfish and going to work on it with his jackknife has, in a fashion wholly unprovided in modern educational theory, a great advantage over the Scarsdale high-school pupil who finds the dogfish on his laboratory desk. Similarly the citizen of Huxley's *Brave New World* who stumbles across a volume of Shakespeare in some vine-grown ruins and squats on a potsherd to read it is in a fairer way of getting at a sonnet than the Harvard sophomore taking English Poetry II.

The educator whose business it is to teach students biology or poetry is unaware of a whole ensemble of relations which exist between the student and the dogfish and between the student and the Shakespeare sonnet. To put it bluntly: A student who has the desire to get at a dogfish or a Shakespeare sonnet may have the greatest difficulty in salvaging the creature itself from the educational package in which it is presented. The great difficulty is that he is not aware that there is a difficulty; surely, he thinks, in such a fine classroom, with such a fine textbook, the sonnet must come across! What's wrong with me?

The sonnet and the dogfish are obscured by two different processes. The sonnet is obscured by the symbolic package which is formulated not by the sonnet itself but by the *media* through which the sonnet is transmitted, the media which the educators believe for some reason to be transparent. The new textbook, the type, the smell of the page, the classroom, the aluminum windows and the winter sky, the personality of Miss Hawkins—these media which are supposed to transmit the sonnet may only succeed in transmitting themselves. It is only the hardiest and cleverest of students who can salvage the sonnet from this many-tissued package. It is only the rarest student who knows that the sonnet must be salvaged from the package. (The educator is well aware that something is wrong, that there is a fatal gap between the student's learning and the student's life: The student reads the poem, appears to understand it, and gives all the answers. But what does he recall if he should happen to read a Shakespeare sonnet twenty years later? Does he recall the poem or does he recall the smell of the page and the smell of Miss Hawkins?)

One might object, pointing out that Huxley's citizen reading his sonnet in the ruins and the Falkland Islander looking at his dogfish on the beach also receive them in a certain package. Yes, but the difference lies in the fundamental placement of the student in the world, a placement which makes it possible to extract the thing from the package. The pupil at Scarsdale High sees himself placed as a consumer receiving an experience-package; but the Falkland Islander exploring his dogfish is a person exercising the sovereign right of a person in his lordship and mastery of creation. He too could use an instructor and a book and a technique, but he would use them as his subordinates, just as he uses his jackknife. The biology student does not use his scalpel as an instrument; he uses it as a magic wand! Since it is a "scientific instrument," it should do "scientific things."

The dogfish is concealed in the same symbolic package as the sonnet. But the dogfish suffers an additional loss. As a consequence of this double deprivation, the Sarah Lawrence student who scores A in zoology is apt to know very little about a dogfish. She is twice removed from the dogfish, once by the symbolic complex by which the dogfish is concealed, once again by the spoliation of the dogfish by theory which renders it invisible. Through no fault of zoology instructors, it is nevertheless a fact that the zoology laboratory at Sarah Lawrence College is one of the few places in the world where it is all but impossible to see a dogfish. . . .

. . . I wish to propose the following educational technique which should prove equally effective for Harvard and Shreveport High School. I propose that English poetry and biology should be taught as usual, but that at irregular intervals, poetry students should find dogfishes on their desks and biology students should find Shakespeare sonnets on their dissecting boards. I am serious in declaring that a Sarah Lawrence English major who began poking about in a dogfish with a bobby pin would learn more in thirty minutes than a biology major in a whole semester; and that the latter upon reading on her dissecting board

> That time of year Thou may'st in me behold
> When yellow leaves, or none, or few, do hang
> Upon those boughs which shake against the cold—
> Bare ruin'd choirs where late the sweet birds sang.

might catch fire at the beauty of it.

Excerpt from
THE ODYSSEY OF HOMER
The Lotus-Eaters

translated by Richmond Lattimore

Human beings are always tempted to seek refuge from sorrows and difficulties, rather than face such trials directly. This brief adventure, recounted by the ancient poet Homer in The Odyssey, *offers a rich account of the temptation to "mediate" painful experience.*

The Odyssey *is the story of the Greek king Odysseus's ten-year journey home after the ten-year Trojan War. Just before the adventure retold below, Odysseus relates the harsh trial he and his men endured immediately after leaving Troy, and how very dispirited they were; in "pain and weariness," they huddle[d] "together eating [their] hearts out."*

At this low moment, they are blown off course and come ashore in the land of the Lotus-Eaters. After the men have made camp and rallied to refresh themselves, Odysseus sends two scouts and a herald to see who lives in this still-unknown land. The three men discover the hospitable Lotus-Eaters and taste their "flowering food"; thereafter they long only to remain among the Lotus-Eaters and "forget the way home."

Despite the herald's apparent failure to return with a report, Odysseus finds his enthralled men. He takes all three back to their ships "by force," tying them under the benches. He and the remaining men hastily flee the island, lest someone else taste lotus and "forget the way home."

Odysseus's men go looking for "men, eaters of bread," and find instead a people who "live on a flowering food." Why are "men" (in Greek, anthropoi, human beings) characterized as "eaters of bread?" What does it mean to be eaters of flowers, instead? What can one assume about a people that eats bread? Or, more generally, to what extent does what we eat convey who we are?

The Lotus-Eaters had no "thoughts of destroying" Odysseus's men, "but they only gave them lotus to taste of." And yet, Odysseus acts as if their destruction was imminent. Is he right? What does it mean to "forget the way home?" Might such forgetting be tantamount to destruction? In general, is forgetting—memory loss—tantamount to destruction?

   Eaters of lotus live entirely and seemingly blissfully in the moment. Though they are living in the present, can they be said to be of the present? Can they be said to be living? Are they still themselves? Are they really happy?

'Nine days then I was swept along by the force of the hostile
winds on the fishy sea, but on the tenth day we landed
in the country of the Lotus-Eaters, who live on a flowering
food, and there we set foot on the mainland, and fetched water,
and my companions soon took their supper there by the fast ships.
But after we had tasted of food and drink, then I sent
some of my companions ahead, telling them to find out
what men, eaters of bread, might live here in this country.
I chose two men, and sent a third with them, as a herald.
My men went on and presently met the Lotus-Eaters,
nor did these Lotus-Eaters have any thoughts of destroying
our companions, but they only gave them lotus to taste of.
But any of them who ate the honey-sweet fruit of lotus
was unwilling to take any message back, or to go
away, but they wanted to stay there with the lotus-eating
people, feeding on lotus, and forget the way home. I myself
took these men back weeping, by force, to where the ships were,
and put them aboard under the rowing benches and tied them
fast, then gave the order to the rest of my eager
companions to embark on the ships in haste, for fear
someone else might taste of the lotus and forget the way home,
and the men quickly went aboard and sat to the oarlocks,
and sitting well in order dashed the oars in the gray sea.'

Excerpt from
DRUGSTORE ATHLETE
by Malcolm Gladwell

Technology increasingly mediates the natural relations among talent, effort, and achievement in many aspects of our lives. In his recent article, Malcolm Gladwell examines the use of performance-enhancing drugs in athletics. In the conclusion of this article, which is reproduced below, Gladwell presents some of the moral problems raised by this mediation.

The excerpt begins by comparing the training of Roger Bannister before he ran the first four-minute mile in 1954, with the training of a modern-day miler. Gladwell asserts that we are more "comfortable" with the relatively low-tech Bannister model, because "we want the relation between talent and achievement to be transparent." Yet he wonders, finally, whether there is any moral difference, in human competition, between availing oneself of natural and unnatural advantages.

Why might "animal" be a term of admiration, to an athlete?

What is "honest" about effort?

Does the seeming dishonesty of taking performance-enhancing drugs rest only in the refusal to disclose it? If an athlete were candid about taking such drugs, would his performance still seem to be "cheating"?

According to Gladwell, the "moral deregulation of social competition" has already been achieved, as "the distractable take Ritalin, the depressed take Prozac, and the unattractive get cosmetic surgery." Are natural advantages necessarily more "legitimate" than artificially derived ones? If so, why?

Does the reliance on artificial or auxiliary aids diminish or enhance the human meaning of the activity? Is there a difference between using, say, special shoes or a professional trainer or weight-training or special diets on the one hand and taking muscle-enhancing drugs or blood-doping medications on the other?

The first man to break the four-minute mile was the Englishman Roger Bannister, on a windswept cinder track at Oxford, nearly fifty years ago.

Bannister is in his early seventies now, and one day last summer he returned to the site of his historic race along with the current world-record holder in the mile, Morocco's Hicham El Guerrouj. The two men chatted and compared notes and posed for photographs. "I feel as if I am looking at my mirror image," Bannister said, indicating El Guerrouj's similarly tall, high-waisted frame. It was a polite gesture, an attempt to suggest that he and El Guerrouj were part of the same athletic lineage. But, as both men surely knew, nothing could be further from the truth.

Bannister was a medical student when he broke the four-minute mile in 1954. He did not have time to train every day, and when he did he squeezed in his running on his hour-long midday break at the hospital. He had no coach or trainer or entourage, only a group of running partners who called themselves "the Paddington lunch time club." In a typical workout, they might run ten consecutive quarter miles—ten laps—with perhaps two minutes of recovery between each repetition, then gobble down lunch and hurry back to work. Today, that training session would be considered barely adequate for a high-school miler. A month or so before his historic mile, Bannister took a few days off to go hiking in Scotland. Five days before he broke the four-minute barrier, he stopped running entirely, in order to rest. The day before the race, he slipped and fell on his hip while working in the hospital. Then he ran the most famous race in the history of track and field. Bannister was what runners admiringly call an "animal," a natural.

El Guerrouj, by contrast, trains five hours a day, in two two-and-a-half-hour sessions. He probably has a team of half a dozen people working with him: at the very least, a masseur, a doctor, a coach, an agent, and a nutritionist. He is not in medical school. He does not go hiking in rocky terrain before major track meets. When Bannister told him, last summer, how he had prepared for his four-minute mile, El Guerrouj was stunned. "For me, a rest day is perhaps when I train in the morning and spend the afternoon at the cinema," he said. El Guerrouj certainly has more than his share of natural ability, but his achievements are a reflection of much more than that: of the fact that he is better coached and better prepared than his opponents, that he trains harder and more intelligently, that he has found a way to stay injury free, and that he can recover so quickly from one day of five-hour workouts that he can follow it, the next day, with another five-hour workout.

Of these two paradigms, we have always been much more comfortable with the first: we want the relation between talent and achievement to be transparent, and we worry about the way ability is now so aggressively managed and augmented. Steroids bother us because they violate the honesty of effort: they permit an athlete to train too hard, beyond what seems reasonable. EPO[1] fails the same test. For years, athletes underwent high-altitude training sessions, which had the same effect as EPO—promoting the manufacture of additional red blood cells. This was considered acceptable, while EPO is not, because we like to distinguish between those advantages which are natural or earned and those which come out of a vial.

Even as we assert this distinction on the playing field, though, we defy it in our own lives. We have come to prefer a world where the distractable take Ritalin, the depressed take Prozac, and the unattractive get cosmetic surgery to a world ruled, arbitrarily, by those fortunate few who were born focussed, happy, and beautiful. Cosmetic surgery is not "earned" beauty, but then natural beauty isn't earned, either. One of the principal contributions of the late twentieth century was the moral deregulation of social competition—the insistence that advantages derived from artificial and extraordinary intervention are no less legitimate than the advantages of nature. All that athletes want, for better or worse, is the chance to play by those same rules.

---

[1] Erythropoietin, a hormone that stimulates the production of red blood cells. It is taken covertly by some endurance athletes, but is forbidden under the rules of most competitive sports.

Excerpt from
REVERIES OF A SOLITARY WALKER
by Jean-Jacques Rousseau, translated by Charles E. Butterworth

Jean-Jacques Rousseau was a paradoxical thinker, a key source both of the radical political program of the French Revolution and of the romantic movement's rejection of city life and civic engagement in favor of nature, solitude, and simplicity. Rousseau the solitary dreamer is most on display in his last book, the Reveries, *from which this excerpt is taken. In it we find a moving account of what Rousseau recalls as the happiest time in his life: living virtually alone on "a fertile and solitary island" in the middle of a lake, disengaged from the external world—and from all action, passion, memory, and care—he passes his days enjoying "the sweet sentiment of his own existence."*

Rousseau teaches that true happiness lies in fully embracing the immediacy of life, which involves primarily feeling, rather than thought or action. But the feeling he strives for is neither the fleeting ecstasy of intense pleasure nor the satisfaction of ambition achieved, but the calm and serene enjoyment of mere existence itself.

Is the blissful state Rousseau describes attainable at all times or only in idyllic natural surroundings? Is it a lasting state, or one that may be enjoyed only for brief periods? Is it available to all of us, or only to those suited to it by temperament and circumstances?

As Rousseau describes it, his happiest days are passed not only in idle reverie but also in energetic botanical pursuits (albeit only as a pastime); are both engagement and idleness then necessary for the full enjoyment of life?

Is the happiness recommended by Rousseau compatible with the commitments and connections that tie most of us to other people? Or does living in the moment necessarily mean detaching ourselves from responsibilities to family, community, and country?

Fifth Walk

Of all the places I have lived (and I have lived in some charming ones), none has made me so truly happy nor left me such tender regrets as St. Peter's Island in the middle of Lake Bienne. This small island, which is called Hillock Island in Neuchâtel, is quite unknown, even in Switzerland. As far as I know, no traveler mentions it. However, it is very pleasant and singularly placed for the happiness of a man who likes to cut himself off; for although I am perhaps the only one in the world whose destiny has imposed this on him as a law, I cannot believe myself to be the only one who has so natural a taste—even though I have not found it in anyone else thus far.

The banks of Lake Bienne are wilder and more romantic than those of Lake Geneva, because the rocks and woods border the water more closely; but they are not less cheerful. If the fields and vineyards are less cultivated, and if there are fewer towns and houses, there is also more natural greenery, more meadows, grove-shaded retreats, more frequent contrasts, and more variety in the terrain. As there are no large thoroughfares suitable for coaches on these happy shores, the countryside is seldom frequented by travelers; but it is interesting for solitary contemplators who like to delight in the charms of nature at leisure and collect their thoughts in a silence troubled by no noise other than the cry of eagles, the intermittent chirping of a few birds, and the rushing of torrents as they fall from the mountain. This beautiful basin almost circular in form has two small islands in its center, one inhabited and cultivated, almost half a league around; the other smaller, uninhabited, and uncultivated, and which will ultimately be destroyed because earth is constantly taken away from it to repair the destruction waves and storms make to the large one. Thus it is that the substance of the weak is always used for the advantage of the powerful.

On the island there is only a single house, but a large, pleasant, and comfortable one which, like the island, belongs to Bern Hospital and in which a tax collector lives with his family and servants. He maintains a large farmyard, a pigeon house, and fishponds. Despite its smallness, the island is so varied in its terrain and vistas that it offers all kinds of landscapes and permits all kinds of cultivation. You can find fields, vineyards, woods, orchards, and rich pastures shaded by thickets and bordered by every species of shrubbery, whose freshness is preserved by the adjacent water. A high terrace planted with two rows of trees runs the length of the island, and in the middle of this terrace a pretty reception hall has been built where the inhabitants of the neighboring banks gather and come to dance on Sundays during harvests.

This is the island on which I sought refuge after the stoning at Mô-tiers.[1] I found the sojourn on it so charming, I led a life there so suitable to my temper that, resolved to end my days there, I had no worry other than their not letting me execute this project which did not fit in with the one of transporting me to England[2]—a project whose first effects I was already feeling. Because of the forebodings that troubled me, I wanted them to make this refuge a perpetual prison for me, to confine me to it for life, and—removing every possibility and hope of getting off it—to forbid me any kind of communication with the mainland so that being unaware of all that went on in the world I might forget its existence and that it might also forget mine.

They let me spend scarcely two months on this island, but I would have spent two years there, two centuries, and the whole of eternity without being bored for a moment, even though besides my helpmate, I had no companionship there other than that of the tax collector, his wife, and his servants, who in truth were all very worthy people but nothing more; but that was precisely what I needed. I consider these two months the happiest time of my life, so happy that it would have con-tented me for my whole existence without the desire for another state arising for a single instant in my soul.

Now what was this happiness and in what did its enjoyment consist? From the description of the life I led there, I will let all the men of this century guess at it. The precious *far niente* [doing nothing] was the first and the principal enjoyment I wanted to savor in all its sweetness, and all I did during my sojourn was in effect only the delicious and necessary pursuit of a man who has devoted himself to idleness.

The hope that they would ask for nothing better than to leave me in this isolated spot where I had ensnared myself on my own, which it was impossible for me to leave without help and surely without being no-ticed, and where I could have communication or correspondence only by the assistance of the people who surrounded me, this hope, I say, led me to hope I would end my days there more peacefully than I had spent them until then. And the idea that I would have time to adapt myself to

[1] Rousseau fled France for Switzerland in 1762 after his book *Émile* was condemned by the Parliament of Paris. Soon afterwards *Émile* and *The Social Contract* were burned in Geneva; Rousseau then found refuge in the Swiss town of Môtiers until 1765 when his house was attacked by a stone-thowing mob.
[2] Faced with continued persecution on the Continent, Rousseau spent the year 1766 in England at the invitation of philosopher David Hume.

it in complete leisure caused me to begin by not adapting at all. Transported there abruptly, alone, and destitute, I had my housekeeper, my books, and my few furnishings brought over, one after the other. And I had the pleasure of unpacking nothing, leaving my boxes and my trunks as they had arrived and living in the abode in which I counted on finishing my days as in an inn I would have to leave on the following day. All things, such as they were, went along so well that to want to arrange them better would have been to spoil something. Above all, one of my greatest delights was to leave my books well packed up and to have no writing table. When wretched letters forced me to take up a pen to reply, I grudgingly borrowed the tax collector's writing table and then hastened to return it, in the vain hope of not needing to borrow it again. Instead of depressing papers and heaps of old books, I filled my room with flowers and dried plants; for I was then in my first botanical fervor for which Dr. d'Ivernois had given me an inclination and which soon became a passion. Wanting no more toilsome work, I needed something amusing which would please me and require only as much trouble as a lazy man likes to take. I set about doing the *Flora petrinsularis* and describing all the plants of the island, without omitting a single one, in sufficient detail to occupy myself for the rest of my days. It is said that a German did a book about a lemon peel; I would have done one about each stalk of hay of the meadows, each moss of the woods, each lichen that carpets the rocks; in short, I did not want to leave a blade of grass or a plant particle which was not amply described. As a result of this fine project, every morning after breakfast, which we all had together, I would go off, a magnifying glass in hand and my *Systema naturae* under my arm, to visit a district of the island, which I had divided into small squares for this purpose, with the intention of covering them one after the other in each season. Nothing is more singular than the raptures and ecstasies I felt with each observation I made on plant structure and organization, as well as on the role of the sexual parts in sporulation, which was then a completely new system for me. I was enchanted to discover generic features of which I previously had not the slightest idea and to verify them on common species, while waiting for rarer ones to offer themselves to me. The forking of the two long stamens of the self-heal, the spring of those of the nettle and the pellitory, the explosion of the fruit of the balsam and the pod of the boxwood, a thousand little games of sporulation which I observed for the first time, filled me with joy and I went around asking whether one had seen the horns of the self-heal plant like La Fontaine asking whether one had read Habakkuk. At the end of two or three hours I would come back laden with an ample harvest, a stock with which to amuse myself after lunch in the lodging in case of rain. I would use the rest of the morning to go with the tax collector, his wife, and Therese to visit their workers and their crops, quite often joining my hand with theirs in work; and often the residents of Bern who came to see me found me perched in large trees, girdled with a sack that I would fill with fruits and then lower to the ground with a rope. My morning exercise and the good temper which is inseparable from it made the pause for lunch very enjoyable. But when it took too long and good weather beckoned, I could not wait so long. While they were still at the table, I would slip away and go throw myself alone into a boat that I rowed to the middle of the lake when the water was calm; and there, stretching myself out full-length in the boat, my eyes turned to heaven, I let myself slowly drift back and forth with the water, sometimes for several hours, plunged in a thousand confused, but delightful, reveries which, even without having any well-determined or constant object, were in my opinion a hundred times preferable to the sweetest things I had found in what are called the pleasures of life. Often, warned by the setting of the sun that it was the hour of retreat, I would find myself so far from the island that I was forced to work with all my might to get back before nightfall. Other times, instead of heading out to open water, I took pleasure in gliding along the verdant banks of the island where the limpid waters and fresh shadows often induced me to bathe. But one of my most frequent sailings was from the large to the small island. There I would debark and spend the afternoon, sometimes in very limited promenades through great round-leaved sallow, alder-buckthorn, willow weed, shrubs of every sort, and sometimes setting myself on the summit of a sandy knoll covered with grass, common thyme, flowers, even cockscomb and clover that had most likely been sown there some time ago and were very suitable for housing rabbits which could multiply in peace there without fearing anything and without doing any harm. I passed this idea on to the tax collector who had male and female rabbits brought from Neuchâtel, and in great pomp his wife, one of his sisters, Thérèse, and I went to settle them on the small island where they began to breed before my departure and where they will undoubtedly have thrived, if they have been able to withstand the rigor of the winters. The founding of this little colony was a festival. The pilot of the Argonauts was no prouder than I, leading the company and the rabbits in triumph from the large island to the small. And I noted with pride that the tax collector's wife, who dreaded water excessively and always felt uncomfortable upon it, embarked under my leadership with confidence and showed no fear during the crossing.

When the lake was too rough for boating, I would spend my afternoon wandering over the island searching right and left for plants, sometimes sitting down in the most cheerful and solitary nooks to dream at my ease and sometimes on terraces and knolls to let my eyes wander over the superb and breathtaking view of the lake and its shores, crowned on one side by the nearby mountains and on the other spread out onto rich and fertile plains over which my sight extended all the way up to the more distant, bluish mountains which blocked it.

When evening approached, I would come down from the heights of the island and gladly go sit in some hidden nook along the beach at the edge of the lake. There, the noise of the waves and the tossing of the water, captivating my senses and chasing all other disturbance from my soul, plunged it into a delightful reverie in which night would often surprise me without my having noticed it. The ebb and flow of this water and its noise, continual but magnified at intervals, striking my ears and eyes without respite, took the place of the internal movements which reverie extinguished within me and was enough to make me feel my existence with pleasure and without taking the trouble to think. From time to time some weak and short reflection about the instability of things in this world arose, an image brought on by the surface of the water. But soon these weak impressions were erased by the uniformity of the continual movement which lulled me and which, without any active assistance from my soul, held me so fast that, called by the hour and agreed-upon signal, I could not tear myself away without effort.

After supper, when the evening was fine, we would all go for a little walk together on the terrace to breathe in the air and the freshness of the lake. We would relax in the pavilion, laugh, chat, sing some old song which was easily as good as the modern rigmarole, and finally go to bed content with our day desiring only a similar one the next day.

Leaving aside unexpected and importunate visits, this is the way I spent my time on this island during my sojourn there. Tell me now what is so alluring about it as to arouse such intense, tender, and lasting regrets in my heart that at the end of fifteen years it is impossible for me to think of that cherished abode without each time feeling myself carried away again by waves of desire.

In the vicissitudes of a long life, I have noticed that the periods of sweetest enjoyment and most intense pleasures are, nevertheless, not those whose recollection most attracts and touches me. Those short moments of delirium and passion, however intense they might be, are, even with their intensity, still only scattered points along the path of life. They are too rare and too rapid to constitute a state of being; and the happiness for which my heart longs is in no way made up of fleeting instants, but rather a simple and permanent state which has nothing intense in itself but whose duration increases its charm to the point that I finally find supreme felicity in it.

Everything is in continual flux on earth. Nothing on it retains a constant and static form, and our affections, which are attached to external things, necessarily pass away and change as they do. Always ahead of or behind us, they recall the past which is no longer or foretell the future which often is in no way to be: there is nothing solid there to which the heart might attach itself. Thus, here-below we have hardly anything but transitory pleasure. As for happiness which lasts, I doubt that it is known here. In our most intense enjoyments, there is hardly an instant when the heart can truly say to us: *I would like this instant to last forever*. And how can we call happiness a fleeting state which leaves our heart still worried and empty, which makes us long for something beforehand or desire something else afterward?

But if there is a state in which the soul finds a solid enough base to rest itself on entirely and to gather its whole being into, without needing to recall the past or encroach upon the future; in which time is nothing for it; in which the present lasts forever without, however, making its duration noticed and without any trace of time's passage; without any other sentiment of deprivation or of enjoyment, pleasure or pain, desire or fear, except that of our existence, and having this sentiment alone fill it completely; as long as this state lasts, he who finds himself in it can call himself happy, not with an imperfect, poor, and relative happiness such as one finds in the pleasures of life, but with a sufficient, perfect, and full happiness which leaves the soul no emptiness it might feel a need to fill. Such is the state in which I often found myself during my solitary reveries on St. Peter's Island, either lying in my boat as I let it drift with the water or seated on the banks of the tossing lake; or elsewhere, at the edge of a beautiful river or of a brook murmuring over pebbles.

What do we enjoy in such a situation? Nothing external to ourselves, nothing if not ourselves and our own existence. As long as this state lasts, we are sufficient unto ourselves, like God. The sentiment of existence, stripped of any other emotion, is in itself a precious sentiment of contentment and of peace which alone would suffice to make this existence dear and sweet to anyone able to spurn all the sensual and earthly impressions which incessantly come to distract us from it and to trouble its sweetness here-below. But most men, agitated by continual passions, are little acquainted with this state and, having tasted it only imperfectly for a few moments, preserve only an obscure and confused idea of it which does not let them feel its charm. It would not even be good in the present structure of things that, avid for these sweet ecstasies, they should become disgusted with the active life their ever recurring needs prescribe to them as a duty. But an unfortunate person who has been cut off from human society and who can no longer do anything here-below useful and good for another or for himself can find compensations for all the human felicities in this state, compensations which fortune and men could not take away from him.

It is true that these compensations cannot be felt by all souls nor in all situations. The heart must be at peace and no passion come to disturb its calm. The one who experiences them must be favorable to them, as must be the conjunction of the surrounding objects. What is needed is neither absolute rest nor too much agitation, but a uniform and moderated movement having neither jolts nor lapses. Without movement, life is only lethargy. If the movement is irregular or too strong, one is awakened. By reminding us of the surrounding objects, it destroys the charm of the reverie and tears us away from within ourselves, bringing us instantly back under the yoke of fortune and men and returning us to an awareness of our misfortunes. An absolute silence leads to sadness. It offers an image of death. Then the assistance of a cheerful imagination is necessary and comes naturally enough to those whom Heaven has favored. Movement which does not come from outside then occurs inside us. One rests less, it is true, but also more pleasurably, when light and sweet ideas only skim the surface of the soul, so to speak, without disturbing its depths. Only enough ideas are needed to remember our own self while forgetting all our troubles. This kind of reverie can be enjoyed wherever we can be quiet, and I have often thought that in the Bastille—even in a dungeon where no object would strike my sight—I would still have been able to dream pleasurably.

But admittedly that was done better and more pleasurably on a fertile and solitary island, naturally closed off and separated from the rest of the world, where nothing but cheerful images came to me; where nothing recalled depressing memories to me; where the society of the small number of inhabitants was gentle and sweet, without being so interesting as to occupy me continuously; where I could, in short, give myself up all day long to the preoccupations of my liking or to luxurious idleness, without hindrance and care. It was undoubtedly a perfect occasion for a dreamer who, knowing how to nourish himself with pleasurable fancies in the middle of the most unpleasant objects, could satiate himself with them at his ease by making everything which really struck his senses come together in them. Upon emerging from a long and sweet reverie, upon seeing myself surrounded by greenery, flowers, and birds, and letting my eyes wander in the distance on the romantic shores which bordered a vast stretch of crystal-clear water, I assimilated all these lovely objects to my fictions; and finally finding myself brought back by degrees to myself and to what surrounded me, I could not mark out the point separating the fictions from the realities; it was this thorough conjunction of everything which made the absorbed and solitary life I led during this beautiful sojourn so dear to me. If it could only occur again! If I could only go end my days on this beloved island without ever coming off it or ever seeing there any inhabitant of the continent to remind me of all the different calamities they have taken pleasure in heaping on me for so many years! They would soon be forever forgotten. Undoubtedly, they would not likewise forget me. But what would that matter to me, provided they had no way to come there to disturb my rest? Delivered from all the earthly passions the tumult of social life engenders, my soul would frequently soar up above this atmosphere and commune in advance with the celestial intelligences whose number it hopes to augment in a short while. I know men will be careful not to give me back such a sweet refuge when they did not want to leave me there. But at least they will not prevent me from transporting myself there each day on the wings of my imagination and from enjoying for a few hours the same pleasure as if I were still living there. The sweetest thing I would do would be to dream there at my ease. In dreaming that I am there, do I not do the same thing? I do even more: to the allure of an abstract and monotonous reverie, I join charming images which make it more intense. In my ecstasies, their objects often eluded my senses. Now the deeper my reverie is, the more intensely it depicts them to me. I am often more in the midst of them and even more pleasantly so than when I was really there. The misfortune is that to the extent that my imagination cools this comes with more labor and does not last as long. Alas! it is when we begin to leave our skin that it hinders us the most.

CHAPTER 10:
HUMAN DIGNITY

IN PREVIOUS CHAPTERS WE have considered both the unique character of human suffering and the special vitality of human engagement, with both life and the world. What is it about us, unique among the species, that enables our suffering to be (at least partially) redeemed? What is it about us, unique among the species, that enables us to strive upward against the downward pull of necessity or to meet the world and our fellow creatures fully and directly, actively and honestly, feelingly and truly? The name we give to this excellence is "human dignity." In examining it, with the help of the following readings, we may find that it is what we value most about our selves.

The religious among us may locate the origin of our special dignity in our God-given origin and God-like being. The secular may locate the source of it within our selves, whether seen as an unintended product of blind evolution, as a mysterious gift of nature, or as the result of law and custom—in any case, a power that sets us apart from everything else that lives. All of us, however, can see it expressed in the myriad ways we manifest our embodied humanity in living our individuated and finite lives. Although they emphasize different aspects of human dignity, the readings below illuminate this virtue that celebrates our full humanity: not just reason or will, not just strength or beauty, but our integrated powers of body, mind, and soul that express themselves in all our activities, large and small.

Our first two readings offer different views, religious and secular, of the source and ground of human dignity. The excerpt from *The Book of Genesis* suggests that it is bestowed upon us by divine gift, and that it rests in our being in God's image and likeness. The excerpts from Thomas Hobbes' *Leviathan* and Immanuel Kant's *Fundamental Principals of the Metaphysics of Morals* offer different philosophical accounts, the first suggesting that human dignity is not natural but a bestowal of society, the second suggesting that it is grounded in man's rational capacity to be moral.

The next two readings point to a primordial dignity that inheres in us as humans, by finding it in two inarticulate individuals: a corpse and an infant. An excerpt from The *Iliad* of Homer illuminates the need to respect the mortal remains of a human being. An excerpt from the *Histories* of Herodotus considers the inviolable quality of a baby.

In midlife, dignity inheres largely in behavior and character. Our fifth reading, consisting of excerpts from Willa Cather's *My Ántonia*, concerns a suicide, who retains his dignity despite taking his own life; this is appreciated even by those inclined to judge him for what he has done.

For most people, throughout most of history, the central and in many ways defining activity of life has been work. Our next four readings concern the dignity of labor. The special dignity of physical labor is expressed in Henry Wadsworth Longfellow's "The Village Blacksmith," and in the lyrics of the traditional song, "John Henry," with Paul Kaplan's contemporary parody, "Henry the Accountant." Victorian critic John Ruskin can be seen to challenge these readings in an excerpt from *Crown of Wild Olive*. A final dignified laborer, however, completes this quartet in Isaac Bashevis Singer's "The Washwoman."

Our last three readings present supreme examples of human dignity at its finest, displayed in acts of generosity, devotion, courage, self-knowledge, self-command, and bold defense of human freedom and human dignity itself. The first appears in a lighthearted work of fiction: O. Henry's "Two Thanksgiving-Day Gentlemen," in which two men suppress their own needs out of generosity to each other and out of devotion to a tradition they perceive to be larger than themselves. The next—from truth, not fiction, in an excerpt from his memoir *To Build A Castle*—is an attempt by former Soviet dissident Vladimir Bukovsky to identify the responsibilities that confront men and women living under tyrannies.

Our final reading is the story of one specific human being who resolves to live no more under the thumb of a tyrant. In this excerpt from his *Autobiography*, we learn that the self-liberation of former American slave Frederick R. Douglass must occur in mind and in body both, and by his own agency and effort. It results in a human being who has suffered and overcome suffering, and who stands resolved to suffer further, even to the point of death, if that is what it takes for him to live as a man, and not as a beast. It is a fitting end to our chapter on human dignity, and our volume about bioethics. It is a rich bioethics indeed that celebrates the birth into full humanity of such an individual.

THE BOOK OF GENESIS, 9:1-9

King James Translation

Although ideas about the basis of human dignity vary, an ancient and widely shared understanding of man's special standing in the world attributes it not to human merit but to divine gift, tied to God's creation of humankind. This idea is expressed in the Book of Genesis, first in the opening story of Creation and again in the following excerpt.

The reading begins just after the great Flood in which God, responding to pervasive evil, destroys all of creation but for the righteous Noah and his family and two of each animal species, from whom the world is to be repopulated. After the flood recedes, Noah—unbidden—offers animal sacrifices to God. Commenting on the sacrifice, God promises never again to curse the earth for man's sake, for "the imagination of man's heart is evil from his youth." Addressing the problem of man's evil inclination, God immediately gives Noah and his descendents laws, and human beings, separating themselves for the first time from the anarchic "state of nature," enter civil society and live under the rule of law.

Before the Flood, according to the Biblical account, men were to have been vegetarians. But under the Noahide law, they are granted permission to eat all animal flesh, save only the blood "which is the life." In contrast, the law establishes just punishment to restrain man's propensity for lethal violence against his own kind. God obliges man to requite all human bloodshed: "Whoso sheddeth man's blood, by man shall his blood be shed: for in the image of God made He man."

Man's blood should not be shed, says God, because man was made in the image of God: man is said to be "godlike," and made such by God. What does this mean, and in what does our "godlikeness" consist? How does it argue for the special dignity of human life, beyond that of animal life?

According to the Noahide code, every human life is equally to be requited, regardless of a person's special merit or social standing. Moreover, all human beings are equally charged with the duty of exacting justice for homicide. How are these aspects of radical human equality (under law) connected to man's godlikeness and God-given origins? Is it fitting that man learns that he is "godlike" only at the time when he begins to live under law?

According to this account, man's higher status among the creatures arises from his "godlikeness," from having an "image" relation to God. Yet his godlikeness requires special protection for his blood, for his "mere life." What does this suggest about the dignity also of man's physical being? What does it suggest about the origins of that dignity?

The beginning and the end of the Noahide law are commandments to "be fruitful and multiply." Can this injunction be linked to the special standing and dignity of human beings?

And God blessed Noah and his sons, and said unto them, Be fruitful, and multiply, and replenish the earth.

2 And the fear of you and the dread of you shall be upon every beast of the earth, and upon every fowl of the air, upon all that moveth *upon* the earth, and upon all the fishes of the sea; into your hand are they delivered.

3 Every moving thing that liveth shall be meat for you; even as the green herb have I given you all things.

4 But flesh with the life thereof, *which is* the blood thereof, shall ye not eat.

5 And surely your blood of your lives will I require: at the hand of every beast will I require it, and at the hand of man; at the hand of every man's brother will I require the life of man.

6 Whoso sheddeth man's blood, by man shall his blood be shed: for in the image of God made he man.

7 And you, be ye fruitful, and multiply; bring forth abundantly in the earth, and multiply therein.

8 And God spake unto Noah, and to his sons with him, saying,

9 And I, behold, I establish my covenant with you, and with your seed after you; . . .

Excerpts from

LEVIATHAN

by Thomas Hobbes

and

FUNDAMENTAL PRINCIPLES OF THE METAPHYSICS OF MORALS

by Immanuel Kant, translated by Thomas King Abbott

These two excerpts, from Hobbes's Leviathan *and Kant's* Fundamental Principles of the Metaphysics of Morals, *provide a quick introduction to the
problem of human dignity as it is treated in modern western philosophy.*

*One project of the Enlightenment was to show why we should still believe in
morality and human dignity if the world and everything in it are accurately
described by the blind laws of mathematical physics. For the seventeenth-cen-
tury English philosopher Thomas Hobbes, man has no intrinsic dignity: by
nature we are selfish, acquisitive, and belligerent; morality and respect for
human rights are entirely artificial, the result of a compact by which we flee
the state of nature for the relative tranquility of civil society. "Leviathan" is
Hobbes's name for the man-made state which provides the only available ground
for rights, justice, and human dignity. For Hobbes and other early modern
philosophers, the diminished status of human dignity (reduced to a mere convention) was a price worth paying in order to achieve the low but solid benefits
of peace, security, and mutual toleration.*

*A century later, German philosopher Immanuel Kant attempted to restore
human dignity to its exalted status, while accepting the Enlightenment principle that nature (including human nature) is utterly indifferent and even inhos-
pitable to morality. Kant's solution was to propose that reason, our unique
gift, elevates us out of the natural order and makes us members of the "kingdom of ends," able to resist natural impulses in favor of truly moral intentions.
For Kant, man is still subject to natural laws like any other being in the order*

FUNDAMENTAL PRINCIPLES OF THE METAPHYSICS OF MORALS by
Abbott, T. K. (translator) © Reprinted by permission of Pearson Education, Inc.,
Upper Saddle River, N.J.

of nature. But, in virtue of his rationality, man is also self-legislating: he obeys a moral law of which he himself is the author. And that law (the "categorical imperative," as Kant called it) commands that we treat every rational being with respect: treat him, that is, not merely as a means to our selfish desires but also as an end in himself.

Hobbes insists that there is no distinction between the dignity of an individual and the price others would pay for the use of his power. Is he right? Does Hobbes render human dignity meaningless, or does he succeed in setting human dignity on a realistic foundation?

Why does Kant insist that our natural inclinations are of such little worth that any rational being would wish to be wholly free of them?

Is Kant persuasive that it is because of our rationality that we human beings are responsive to moral considerations?

Can all moral intentions be understood as, at heart, a refusal to treat other people merely as means to the satisfaction of our desires?

For Kant, a "categorical imperative" is a moral obligation that binds us absolutely, without regard to consequences. Is it realistic to divorce morality from prudential considerations?

What does Kant mean by the difference between "value" and "dignity?"

How can Kant describe our obedience to the moral law as "freedom"?

Is he persuasive that respect for the moral law, and only that respect, gives us a dignity "infinitely above all value"?

From *Leviathan*

The value or worth of a man is, as of all other things, his price; that is to say, so much as would be given for the use of his power, and therefore is not absolute, but a thing dependent on the need and judgment of another. An able conductor of soldiers is of great price in time of war present or imminent, but in peace not so. A learned and uncorrupt judge is much worth in time of peace, but not so much in war. And as in other things, so in men, not the seller, but the buyer determines the price. For let a man, as most men do, rate themselves at the highest value they can, yet their true value is no more than it is esteemed by others.

The manifestation of the value we set on one another is that which is commonly called honouring and dishonouring. To value a man at a high rate is to honour him; at a low rate is to dishonour him. But high and low, in this case, is to be understood by comparison to the rate that each man setteth on himself.

The public worth of a man, which is the value set on him by the Commonwealth, is that which men commonly call dignity. And this value of him by the Commonwealth is understood by offices of command, judicature, public employment; or by names and titles introduced for distinction of such value. . . .

From *Fundamental Principles of the Metaphysics of Morals*

Supposing, however, that there were something whose existence has in itself an absolute worth, something which, being an end in itself, could be a source of definite laws; then in this and this alone would lie the source of a possible categorical imperative, i.e., a practical law.

Now I say: man and generally any rational being exists as an end in himself, not merely as a means to be arbitrarily used by this or that will, but in all his actions, whether they concern himself or other rational beings, must be always regarded at the same time as an end. All objects of the inclinations have only a conditional worth, for if the inclinations and the wants founded on them did not exist, then their object would be without value. But the inclinations, themselves being sources of want, are so far from having an absolute worth for which they should be desired that on the contrary it must be the universal wish of every rational being to be wholly free from them. Thus the worth of any object which is to be acquired by our action is always conditional. Beings whose existence depends not on our will but on nature's, have nevertheless, if they are irrational beings, only a relative value as means, and are therefore called things; rational beings, on the contrary, are called persons, because their very nature points them out as ends in themselves, that is as something which must not be used merely as means, and so far therefore restricts freedom of action (and is an object of respect). These, therefore, are not merely subjective ends whose existence has a worth for us as an effect of our action, but objective ends, that is, things whose existence is an end in itself; an end moreover for which no other can be substituted, which they should subserve merely as means, for otherwise nothing whatever would possess absolute worth; but if all worth were conditioned and therefore contingent, then there would be no supreme practical principle of reason whatever.

If then there is a supreme practical principle or, in respect of the human will, a categorical imperative, it must be one which, being drawn from the conception of that which is necessarily an end for everyone because it is an end in itself, constitutes an objective principle of will, and can therefore serve as a universal practical law. The foundation of this principle is: rational nature exists as an end in itself. Man necessarily conceives his own existence as being so; so far then this is a subjective principle of human actions. But every other rational being regards its existence similarly, just on the same rational principle that holds for me: so that it is at the same time an objective principle, from which as a supreme practical law all laws of the will must be capable of being deduced. Accordingly the practical imperative will be as follows: So act as to treat humanity, whether in thine own person or in that of any other, in every case as an end withal, never as means only. We will now inquire whether this can be practically carried out. . . .

. . . Looking back now on all previous attempts to discover the principle of morality, we need not wonder why they all failed. It was seen that man was bound to laws by duty, but it was not observed that the laws to which he is subject are only those of his own giving, though at the same time they are universal, and that he is only bound to act in conformity with his own will; a will, however, which is designed by nature to give universal laws. For when one has conceived man only as subject to a law (no matter what), then this law required some interest, either by way of attraction or constraint, since it did not originate as a law from his own will, but this will was according to a law obliged by something else to act in a certain manner. Now by this necessary consequence all the labour spent in finding a supreme principle of duty was irrevocably lost. For men never elicited duty, but only a necessity of acting from a certain interest. Whether this interest was private or otherwise, in any case the imperative must be conditional and could not by any means be capable of being a moral command. I will therefore call this the principle of autonomy of the will, in contrast with every other which I accordingly reckon as heteronomy.

The conception of the will of every rational being as one which must consider itself as giving in all the maxims of its will universal laws, so as to judge itself and its actions from this point of view—this conception leads to another which depends on it and is very fruitful, namely that of a kingdom of ends.

By a kingdom I understand the union of different rational beings in a system by common laws. Now since it is by laws that ends are determined as regards their universal validity, hence, if we abstract from the personal differences of rational beings and likewise from all the content of their private ends, we shall be able to conceive all ends combined in a systematic whole (including both rational beings as ends in themselves, and also the special ends which each may propose to himself), that is to say, we can conceive a kingdom of ends, which on the preceding principles is possible. For all rational beings come under the law that each of them must treat itself and all others never merely as means, but in every case at the same time as ends in themselves. Hence results a systematic union of rational beings by common objective laws, i.e., a kingdom which may be called a kingdom of ends, since what these laws have in view is just the relation of these beings to one another as ends and means. It is certainly only an ideal.

A rational being belongs as a member to the kingdom of ends when, although giving universal laws in it, he is also himself subject to these laws. He belongs to it as sovereign when, while giving laws, he is not subject to the will of any other.

A rational being must always regard himself as giving laws either as member or as sovereign in a kingdom of ends which is rendered possible by the freedom of will. He cannot, however, maintain the latter position merely by the maxims of his will, but only in case he is a completely independent being without wants and with unrestricted power adequate to his will.

Morality consists then in the reference of all action to the legislation which alone can render a kingdom of ends possible. This legislation must be capable of existing in every rational being and of emanating from his will, so that the principle of this will is never to act on any maxim which could not without contradiction be also a universal law and, accordingly, always so to act that the will could at the same time regard itself as giving in its maxims universal laws. If now the maxims of rational beings are not by their own nature coincident with this objective principle, then the necessity of acting on it is called practical necessitation, i.e., duty. Duty does not apply to the sovereign in the kingdom of ends, but it does to every member of it and to all in the same degree.

The practical necessity of acting on this principle, i.e., duty, does not rest at all on feelings, impulses, or inclinations, but solely on the relation of rational beings to one another, a relation in which the will of a rational being must always be regarded as legislative, since otherwise it could not be conceived as an end in itself. Reason then refers every maxim of the will, regarding it as legislating universally, to every other will and also to every action towards oneself; and this not on account of any other practical motive or any future advantage, but from the idea of the dignity of a rational being, obeying no law but that which he himself also gives. In the kingdom of ends everything has either value or dignity. Whatever has a value can be replaced by something else which is equivalent; whatever, on the other hand, is above all value, and therefore admits of no equivalent, has a dignity.

Whatever has reference to the general inclinations and wants of mankind has a market value; whatever, without presupposing a want, corresponds to a certain taste, that is to a satisfaction in the mere purposeless play of our faculties, has a fancy value; but that which constitutes the condition under which alone anything can be an end in itself, this has not merely a relative worth, i.e., value, but an intrinsic worth, that is, dignity.

Now morality is the condition under which alone a rational being can be an end in himself, since by this alone is it possible that he should be a legislating member in the kingdom of ends. Thus morality, and humanity as capable of it, is that which alone has dignity. Skill and diligence in labour have a market value; wit, lively imagination, and humour, have fancy value; on the other hand, fidelity to promises, benevolence from principle (not from instinct), have an intrinsic worth. Neither nature nor art contains anything which in default of these it could put in their place, for their worth consists not in the effects which spring from them, not in the use and advantage which they secure, but in the disposition of mind, that is, the maxims of the will which are ready to manifest themselves in such actions, even though they should not have the desired effect. These actions also need no recommendation from any subjective taste or sentiment, that they may be looked on with immediate favour and satisfaction: they need no immediate propension or feeling for them; they exhibit the will that performs them as an object of an immediate respect, and nothing but reason is required to impose them on the will; not to flatter it into them, which, in the case of duties, would be a contradiction. This estimation therefore shows that the worth of such a disposition is dignity, and places it infinitely above all value, with which it cannot for a moment be brought into comparison or competition without as it were violating its sanctity.

What then is it which justifies virtue or the morally good disposition, in making such lofty claims? It is nothing less than the privilege it secures to the rational being of participating in the giving of universal laws, by which it qualifies him to be a member of a possible kingdom of ends, a privilege to which he was already destined by his own nature as being an end in himself and, on that account, legislating in the kingdom of ends; free as regards all laws of physical nature, and obeying those only which he himself gives, and by which his maxims can belong to a system of universal law, to which at the same time he submits himself. For nothing has any worth except what the law assigns it. Now the legislation itself which assigns the worth of everything must for that very reason possess dignity, that is an unconditional incomparable worth; and the word respect alone supplies a becoming expression for the esteem which a rational being must have for it. Autonomy then is the basis of the dignity of human and of every rational nature.

Excerpt from
THE ILIAD OF HOMER
Achilleus Abuses the Body of Hektor

translated by Richmond Lattimore

Few writings in Western literature are more attuned to the dignity of the human body, both in life and in death, than Homer's Iliad, the story of heroes immersed in the war between the Achaians (Greeks) and the Trojans. The opening words of the poem introduce it as the story of "the anger of Peleus' son, Achilleus," an Achaian, an anger that "hurled . . . to the house of Hades strong souls of heroes, but left themselves [their bodies] to be the delicate feasting of dogs, of all wild birds."

The attached excerpt relates how the body of one such hero, the great Trojan warrior, Hektor, suffers and then is spared this indignity. As a result of the events described in this passage, Hektor is returned to his own people and given a fitting burial. In the final words of the epic he is once again named by the epithet he had as a living warrior: "So they buried Hektor, breaker of horses."

The anger of Achilleus, introduced in the opening words of The Iliad, *breaks in full force over Hektor. Hektor, son of the Trojan King Priam, kills Achilleus' best friend, Patroklos, on the battlefield. Although Achilleus avenges the death of his friend by killing Hektor, his rage and grief are not assuaged. Achilleus camps by the grave of Patroklos, hitches the body of Hektor to his chariot, and between bouts of weeping, drags it round and around the grave.*

Achilleus, son of a mortal father (Peleus) and an immortal mother (Thetis), is beloved by the gods. But the gods love Hektor, too, and this behavior offends their sense of justice. In this excerpt they intervene on Hektor's behalf.

The god Apollo says Achilleus is like a lion, without pity, shame, or justice, and that he "does dishonor to the dumb earth in his fury." This is not said because Achilleus took Hektor's life, but because of his treatment of what Apollo acknowledges is "only a corpse." Why does it matter what happens to the body of one who is, in the poet's words, "only a dead man?" Can one pity a corpse?

Achilleus, wanting to punish Hektor for the loss of his friend, drags his body

and leaves it in the dust. Why these particular insults? Why is dragging the
body an affront to one who has died? Why is leaving it exposed, and in the
dust? Can one insult a corpse?

    Apollo says Hektor's body should be returned so that his family can look
upon it, and the warrior can be given his "rites of burial." Is this rite owed to
his family, or to Hektor himself? Why?

    Why is Hektor not called "breaker of horses" in this passage, as he is in the
rest of the poem? How might this burial put him, so to speak, back atop the
horse?

And the games[1] broke up, and the people scattered to go away,
    each man
to his fast-running ship, and the rest of them took thought of their
    dinner
and of sweet sleep and its enjoyment; only Achilleus
wept still as he remembered his beloved companion, nor did sleep
who subdues all come over him, but he tossed from one side to the
    other
in longing for Patroklos, for his manhood and his great strength
and all the actions he had seen to the end with him, and the hardships
he had suffered; the wars of men; hard crossing of the big waters.
Remembering all these things he let fall the swelling tears, lying
sometimes along his side, sometimes on his back, and now again
prone on his face; then he would stand upright, and pace turning
in distraction along the beach of the sea, nor did dawn rising
escape him as she brightened across the sea and the beaches.
Then, when he had yoked running horses under the chariot
he would fasten Hektor behind the chariot, so as to drag him,
and draw him three times around the tomb of Menoitios' fallen
son,[2] then rest again in his shelter, and throw down the dead man
and leave him to lie sprawled on his face in the dust. But Apollo
had pity on him, though he was only a dead man, and guarded
the body from all ugliness, and hid all of it under the golden
aegis, so that it might not be torn when Achilleus dragged it.

---

[1] Funeral games for Patroklos.
[2] Patroklos.

So Achilleus in his standing fury outraged great Hektor.
The blessed gods as they looked upon him were filled with compassion
and kept urging clear-sighted Argeïphontes[3] to steal the body.
There this was pleasing to all the others, but never to Hera
nor Poseidon, nor the girl of the grey eyes, who kept still
their hatred for sacred Ilion[4] as in the beginning,
and for Priam and his people, because of the delusion of Paris
who insulted the goddesses when they came to him in his courtyard
and favoured her who supplied the lust that led to disaster.[5]
But now, as it was the twelfth dawn after the death of Hektor,
Phoibos Apollo spoke his word out among the immortals:
'You are hard, you gods, and destructive. Now did not Hektor
burn thigh pieces of oxen and unblemished goats in your honour?
Now you cannot bring yourselves to save him, though he is only
a corpse, for his wife to look upon, his child and his mother
and Priam his father, and his people, who presently thereafter
would burn his body in the fire and give him his rites of burial.
No, you gods; your desire is to help this cursed Achilleus
within whose breast there are no feelings of justice, nor can
his mind be bent, but his purposes are fierce, like a lion
who when he has given way to his own great strength and his haughty
spirit, goes among the flocks of men, to devour them.
So Achilleus has destroyed pity, and there is not in him
any shame; which does much harm to men but profits them also.
For a man must some day lose one who was even closer
than this; a brother from the same womb, or a son. And yet
he weeps for him, and sorrows for him, and then it is over,
for the Destinies put in mortal men the heart of endurance.
But this man, now he has torn the heart of life from great Hektor,
ties him to his horses and drags him around his beloved companion's
tomb; and nothing is gained thereby for his good, or his honour.
Great as he is, let him take care not to make us angry;
for see, he does dishonour to the dumb earth in his fury.'

---

[3] Argeïphontes, Hera, and Poseidon are gods. The "girl of the grey eyes" is a goddess,
Athene.
[4] Troy.
[5] In other words, because of the events that led to the war.

Excerpt from
THE HISTORIES OF HERODOTUS
translated by David Grene

There is something about a baby that confounds the determined intentions of soldiers of the king, in this passage from The Histories of Herodotus. *What is it?*

Ancient Corinth is ruled by the sons of Bacchis, and the members of this ruling family marry each other. To one of them, however, a lame daughter is born, and none of the others will have her. This daughter, Labda, is therefore married to a Lapith named Eëtion.

Two separate oracles then fortell that Eëtion will have a son who will overthrow the rulers of Corinth.

When Eëtion and his wife Labda give birth to a son, ten soldiers are sent to their home, so that the first to lay hands on the child may "dash it on the ground."

But the soldiers' plan goes awry, and in the conclusion of the story (not reproduced here), the oracles' prophecy does, indeed, come to pass.

Why might it be fitting that the lame woman they had rejected bears the child who overthrows the kings of Corinth?

Why are ten men sent to destroy a single baby in the care of a lame woman?

Why did the soldiers, after their first failure, decide to try acting together, instead of individually? Once they did, why could ten men not find a baby hidden in a chest?

Why does Herodotus note that the baby smiled? Had he not smiled, would things have turned out differently? Might things have turned out differently had the father been home?

Why could the soldiers not kill the baby? Would they have failed to kill any baby?

Where is human dignity, in this story?

"This is the story of Corinth's condition. There was an oligarchy, and those who were called the Bacchiadae administered the state and married and gave in marriage among themselves. Among these men there was one Amphion who had a lame daughter, whose name was Labda. None of the Bacchiadae would marry this girl, and she was finally taken by Eëtion, son of Echecrates, of the township of Petra. His remoter ancestors were of the Lapithae and Caenids. Eëtion had no children either by this wife or any other woman. So he went to Delphi about the matter of his issue. As he came in, the Pythia addressed him at once in these lines:

> Eëtion, you are rich in honor, yet none does you honor.
> Labda will still conceive, and a rolling rock shall she bear
>   you,
> Such as shall fall upon princes and deal out justice in
>   Corinth.

This oracle that was given to Eëtion was somehow reported to the Bacchiadae, who had not understood an earlier oracle about Corinth, which had the same purport as Eëtion's, and it ran thus:

> An eagle shall breed in the rocks and bring as offspring
>   a lion,
> A savage eater of raw meat; he shall loosen the knees
>   of many.
> Heed these things well, men of Corinth, you who around fair
>   Pirene
> Dwell, and also about the crag-crested city of Corinth.

This oracle had earlier been given to the Bacchiadae, but they had no clue to its meaning. When they heard of the new one for Eëtion, they immediately understood the former as in harmony with the latter.

"Although they understood this, they held their peace about it, because they wanted to make away with whatever child should be born to Eëtion. As soon as the woman gave birth, they sent ten of their own number to the district where Eëtion lived to kill the child. These men came to Petra and, entering the courtyard of Eëtion's house, asked for the child. Labda had no idea of why they had come there and thought that they asked for the child only out of good will toward the father. So she brought the baby and handed it to one of the ten. Now, when they had been on the way there, they had laid their plans that whoever of them first got his hands on the child would dash it to the ground. When Labda brought the baby and gave it over, it happened, by some stroke of providence, that the child smiled at the man who had taken it. The man noticed it, and a moment of pity held him back from the killing; he pitied it and handed it to a second man, and he to a third. So it was passed from hand to hand of the ten, and no one wanted to make away with it. So they gave it back to the mother and went out. But they then stood in front of the door and attacked one another with reproaches—especially the one who had got the child first, because he had not acted as they had determined, before, they would do. Eventually, as time went on, they resolved to go in again and all take a share in the murder. But fate had determined that evil should grow richly for Corinth from this child of Eëtion. For Labda, as she stood by the doors, heard everything. She was afraid that they would change their minds and the second time get hold of the child and kill it; and so she took and hid it in what seemed to her the most unlikely place to look, in a chest. For she knew that if they turned back to search, they would look everywhere. That indeed is what happened. They came and searched, but there was no sign of the child; and so they resolved to go away and to tell those who had sent them that they had done all they had been instructed to do. That was their tale when they came home."

Excerpts from
MY ÁNTONIA
by Willa Cather

My Ántonia *is a fictional memoir of a late-nineteenth century childhood on the great plains of Nebraska. It is narrated by Jim Burden, who came to the plains as a boy recently orphaned, to live with his grandparents.*

Jim's grandparents are comfortably settled and provide well for him. But Jim arrives on the same train with the Shimerda family. The Shimerdas have come from Bohemia, nearly destitute, knowing little about America, and dangerously ignorant about what it takes to farm in the harsh environment of the great plains.

Mr. Shimerda is a musician by training, and ill-equipped for his new life. A son, Marek, has been born physically and mentally handicapped. Nonetheless, Mrs. Shimerda has insisted on coming to America, placing her hopes in her eldest son, Ambrosch. The household also includes two daughters, Ántonia and Julka, and a cousin, Krajiek.

The first excerpt begins as the Burdens prepare to visit the Shimerdas at their dugout home in winter. Once there, they find the family in distress.

The Shimerdas are eating prairie dogs and their children are sleeping in a hole in the earth. Both practices sustain life effectively. Why is Jim's grandmother so disturbed by them?

Why is Mr. Shimerda dressed as he is, in the darkness of his hovel? Why does he seem at first to try to "hide," though he has taken pains to be clean and neat?

The second excerpt takes place at Christmas. The Burdens have delivered gifts to the Shimerdas, and Mr. Shimerda comes to their home for the first time, to thank them. The following week, Mrs. Shimerda visits with Jim's friend Ántonia, in a very different spirit.

Mr. Shimerda remains entirely dignified, even when utterly relaxed and passive, and even when he assumes a position—bowing before the tree—which looks strange to his hosts. In what does his dignity reside?

The Burdens, even young Jim, can tell that Mr. Shimerda is failing in important ways, yet he commands their respect. What do they respect about him?

Jim is annoyed because "even misfortune could not humble" Mrs. Shimerda. Is humility becoming, to one who is unfortunate?

The third excerpt begins the morning after Mr. Shimerda's suicide is discovered, as the agitated Burden household struggles to understand how a man they liked and admired could have abandoned his beloved children "in a hard world."

The fourth excerpt includes a discussion about where Mr. Shimerda is to be buried; as a suicide, he is unwelcome in at least one of the local graveyards. The Burdens are displeased by this, and shocked, too, at his own family's plan for his body.

The fifth and final excerpt describes the burial and the grave.

Why is there a local to-do over where Mr. Shimerda is to be buried? Why does Grandfather correctly predict that "the people of this country" will not make a crossroads over a grave? What about Mr. Shimerda does Grandfather seem to acknowledge in his words at the graveside?

Excerpt 1

For several weeks after my sleigh-ride, we heard nothing from the Shimerdas. My sore throat kept me indoors, and grandmother had a cold which made the housework heavy for her. When Sunday came she was glad to have a day of rest. One night at supper Fuchs[1] told us he had seen Mr. Shimerda out hunting.

'He's made himself a rabbit-skin cap, Jim, and a rabbit-skin collar that he buttons on outside his coat. They ain't got but one overcoat among 'em over there, and they take turns wearing it. They seem awful scared of cold, and stick in that hole in the bank like badgers.'

'All but the crazy boy,' Jake put in. 'He never wears the coat. Krajiek says he's turrible strong and can stand anything. I guess rabbits must be getting scarce in this locality. Ambrosch come along by the cornfield yesterday where I was at work and showed me three prairie dogs he'd shot. He asked me if they was good to eat. I spit and made a face and took on, to scare him, but he just looked like he was smarter'n me and put 'em back in his sack and walked off.'

Grandmother looked up in alarm and spoke to grandfather. 'Josiah, you don't suppose Krajiek would let them poor creatures eat prairie dogs, do you?'

'You had better go over and see our neighbours tomorrow, Emmaline,'

---

[1] Otto Fuchs and Jake are the Burdens' hired men.

he replied gravely.

Fuchs put in a cheerful word and said prairie dogs were clean beasts and ought to be good for food, but their family connections were against them. I asked what he meant, and he grinned and said they belonged to the rat family.

When I went downstairs in the morning, I found grandmother and Jake packing a hamper basket in the kitchen.

'Now, Jake,' grandmother was saying, 'if you can find that old rooster that got his comb froze, just give his neck a twist, and we'll take him along. There's no good reason why Mrs. Shimerda couldn't have got hens from her neighbours last fall and had a hen-house going by now. I reckon she was confused and didn't know where to begin. I've come strange to a new country myself, but I never forgot hens are a good thing to have, no matter what you don't have.

'Just as you say, ma'm,' said Jake, 'but I hate to think of Krajiek getting a leg of that old rooster.' He tramped out through the long cellar and dropped the heavy door behind him.

After breakfast grandmother and Jake and I bundled ourselves up and climbed into the cold front wagon-seat. As we approached the Shimerdas', we heard the frosty whine of the pump and saw Ántonia, her head tied up and her cotton dress blown about her, throwing all her weight on the pump-handle as it went up and down. She heard our wagon, looked back over her shoulder, and, catching up her pail of water, started at a run for the hole in the bank.

Jake helped grandmother to the ground, saying he would bring the provisions after he had blanketed his horses. We went slowly up the icy path toward the door sunk in the drawside. Blue puffs of smoke came from the stovepipe that stuck out through the grass and snow, but the wind whisked them roughly away.

Mrs. Shimerda opened the door before we knocked and seized grandmother's hand. She did not say 'How do!' as usual, but at once began to cry, talking very fast in her own language, pointing to her feet which were tied up in rags, and looking about accusingly at everyone.

The old man was sitting on a stump behind the stove, crouching over as if he were trying to hide from us. Yulka was on the floor at his feet, her kitten in her lap. She peeped out at me and smiled, but, glancing up at her mother, hid again. Ántonia was washing pans and dishes in a dark corner. The crazy boy lay under the only window, stretched on a gunny-sack stuffed with straw. As soon as we entered, he threw a grain-sack over the crack at the bottom of the door. The air in the cave was stifling, and it was very dark, too. A lighted lantern, hung over the stove, threw out a feeble yellow glimmer.

Mrs. Shimerda snatched off the covers of two barrels behind the door, and made us look into them. In one there were some potatoes that had been frozen and were rotting, in the other was a little pile of flour. Grandmother murmured something in embarrassment, but the Bohemian woman laughed scornfully, a kind of whinny-laugh, and, catching up an empty coffee-pot from the shelf, shook it at us with a look positively vindictive.

Grandmother went on talking in her polite Virginia way, not admitting their stark need or her own remissness, until Jake arrived with the hamper, as if in direct answer to Mrs. Shimerda's reproaches. Then the poor woman broke down. She dropped on the floor beside her crazy son, hid her face on her knees, and sat crying bitterly. Grandmother paid no heed to her, but called Ántonia to come and help empty the basket. Tony left her corner reluctantly. I had never seen her crushed like this before.

'You not mind my poor *mamenka*, Mrs. Burden. She is so sad,' she whispered, as she wiped her wet hands on her skirt and took the things grandmother handed her.

The crazy boy, seeing the food, began to make soft, gurgling noises and stroked his stomach. Jake came in again, this time with a sack of potatoes. Grandmother looked about in perplexity.

'Haven't you got any sort of cave or cellar outside, Ántonia? This is no place to keep vegetables. How did your potatoes get frozen?'

'We get from Mr. Bushy, at the post-office—what he throw out. We got no potatoes, Mrs. Burden,' Tony admitted mournfully.

When Jake went out, Marek crawled along the floor and stuffed up the door-crack again. Then, quietly as a shadow, Mr. Shimerda came out from behind the stove. He stood brushing his hand over his smooth grey hair, as if he were trying to clear away a fog about his head. He was clean and neat as usual, with his green neckcloth and his coral pin. He took grandmother's arm and led her behind the stove, to the back of the room. In the rear wall was another little cave; a round hole, not much bigger than an oil barrel, scooped out in the black earth. When I got up on one of the stools and peered into it, I saw some quilts and a pile of straw. The old man held the lantern. 'Yulka,' he said in a low, despairing voice, 'Yulka; my Ántonia!'

Grandmother drew back. 'You mean they sleep in there—your girls?' He bowed his head.

Tony slipped under his arm. 'It is very cold on the floor, and this is warm like the badger hole. I like for sleep there,' she insisted eagerly.

'My *mamenka* have nice bed, with pillows from our own geese in Bohe-mie. See, Jim?' She pointed to the narrow bunk which Krajiek had built against the wall for himself before the Shimerdas came.

Grandmother sighed. 'Sure enough, where *would* you sleep, dear! I don't doubt you're warm there. You'll have a better house after while, Ántonia, and then you will forget these hard times.'

Mr. Shimerda made grandmother sit down on the only chair and point-ed his wife to a stool beside her. Standing before them with his hand on Ántonia's shoulder, he talked in a low tone, and his daughter translated. He wanted us to know that they were not beggars in the old country; he made good wages, and his family were respected there. He left Bohemia with more than a thousand dollars in savings, after their passage money was paid. He had in some way lost on exchange in New York, and the railway fare to Nebraska was more than they had expected. By the time they paid Krajiek for the land, and bought his horses and oxen and some old farm machinery, they had very little money left. He wished grand-mother to know, however, that he still had some money. If they could get through until spring came, they would buy a cow and chickens and plant a garden, and would then do very well. Ambrosch and Ántonia were both old enough to work in the fields, and they were willing to work. But the snow and the bitter weather had disheartened them all.

Ántonia explained that her father meant to build a new house for them in the spring; he and Ambrosch had already split the logs for it, but the logs were all buried in the snow, along the creek where they had been felled.

While grandmother encouraged and gave them advice, I sat down on the floor with Yulka and let her show me her kitten. Marek slid cau-tiously toward us and began to exhibit his webbed fingers. I knew he wanted to make his queer noises for me—to bark like a dog or whinny like a horse—but he did not dare in the presence of his elders. Marek was always trying to be agreeable, poor fellow, as if he had it on his mind that he must make up for his deficiencies.

Excerpt 2

The Burden household has sent Christmas gifts to the Shimerdas. On Christmas Day, Mr. Shimerda comes to thank them. Soon after Christmas, his wife and daughter pay a visit of their own.

At about four o'clock a visitor appeared: Mr. Shimerda, wearing his rabbit-skin cap and collar, and new mittens his wife had knitted. He had come to thank us for the presents, and for all grandmother's kindness to his family. Jake and Otto joined us from the basement and we sat about the stove, enjoying the deepening grey of the winter afternoon and the atmosphere of comfort and security in my grandfather's house. This feeling seemed completely to take possession of Mr. Shimerda. I suppose, in the crowded clutter of their cave, the old man had come to believe that peace and order had vanished from the earth, or existed only in the old world he had left so far behind. He sat still and passive, his head resting against the back of the wooden rocking-chair, his hands relaxed upon the arms. His face had a look of weariness and pleasure, like that of sick people when they feel relief from pain. Grandmother insisted on his drinking a glass of Virginia apple-brandy after his long walk in the cold, and when a faint flush came up in his cheeks, his features might have been cut out of a shell, they were so transparent. He said almost nothing, and smiled rarely; but as he rested there we all had a sense of his utter content.

As it grew dark, I asked whether I might light the Christmas tree before the lamp was brought. When the candle-ends sent up their conical yellow flames, all the coloured figures from Austria stood out clear and full of meaning against the green boughs. Mr. Shimerda rose, crossed himself, and quietly knelt down before the tree, his head sunk forward. His long body formed a letter 'S.' I saw grandmother look apprehensively at grandfather. He was rather narrow in religious matters, and sometimes spoke out and hurt people's feelings. There had been nothing strange about the tree before, but now, with some one kneeling before it—images, candles . . . Grandfather merely put his finger-tips to his brow and bowed his venerable head, thus Protestantizing the atmosphere.

We persuaded our guest to stay for supper with us. He needed little urging. As we sat down to the table, it occurred to me that he liked to look at us, and that our faces were open books to him. When his deep-seeing eyes rested on me, I felt as if he were looking far ahead into the future for me, down the road I would have to travel.

At nine o'clock Mr. Shimerda lighted one of our lanterns and put on his overcoat and fur collar. He stood in the little entry hall, the lantern and his fur cap under his arm, shaking hands with us. When he took grandmother's hand, he bent over it as he always did, and said slowly, 'Good wo-man!' He made the sign of the cross over me, put on his cap and went off in the dark. As we turned back to the sitting-room, grandfather looked at me searchingly. 'The prayers of all good people are good,' he said quietly.

The week following Christmas brought in a thaw, and by New Year's Day all the world about us was a broth of grey slush, and the guttered slope between the windmill and the barn was running black water. The soft black earth stood out in patches along the roadsides. I resumed all my chores, carried in the cobs and wood and water, and spent the afternoons at the barn, watching Jake shell corn with a hand-sheller.

One morning, during this interval of fine weather, Ántonia and her mother rode over on one of their shaggy old horses to pay us a visit. It was the first time Mrs. Shimerda had been to our house, and she ran about examining our carpets and curtains and furniture, all the while commenting upon them to her daughter in an envious, complaining tone. In the kitchen she caught up an iron pot that stood on the back of the stove and said: 'You got many, Shimerdas no got.' I thought it weak-minded of grandmother to give the pot to her.

After dinner, when she was helping to wash the dishes, she said, tossing her head: 'You got many things for cook. If I got all things like you, I make much better.'

She was a conceited, boastful old thing, and even misfortune could not humble her. I was so annoyed that I felt coldly even toward Ántonia and listened unsympathetically when she told me her father was not well.

'My papa sad for the old country. He not look good. He never make music any more. At home he play violin all the time; for weddings and for dance. Here never. When I beg him for play, he shake his head no. Some days he take his violin out of his box and make with his fingers on the strings, like this, but never he make the music. He don't like this kawn-tree.'

'People who don't like this country ought to stay at home,' I said severely. 'We don't make them come here.'

'He not want to come, nev-er!' she burst out. 'My *mamenka* make him come. All the time she say: "America big country; much money, much land for my boys, much husband for my girls." My papa, he cry for leave his old friends what make music with him. He love very much the man what play the long horn like this'—she indicated a slide trombone. 'They go to school together and are friends from boys. But my mama, she want Ambrosch for be rich, with many cattle.'

'Your mama,' I said angrily, 'wants other people's things.'

'Your grandfather is rich,' she retorted fiercely. 'Why he not help my papa? Ambrosch be rich, too, after while, and he pay back. He is very smart boy. For Ambrosch my mama come here.'

Ambrosch was considered the important person in the family. Mrs.

Shimerda and Ántonia always deferred to him, though he was often surly with them and contemptuous toward his father. Ambrosch and his mother had everything their own way. Though Ántonia loved her father more than she did anyone else, she stood in awe of her elder brother.

After I watched Ántonia and her mother go over the hill on their miserable horse, carrying our iron pot with them, I turned to grand-mother, who had taken up her darning, and said I hoped that snooping old woman wouldn't come to see us any more.

Grandmother chuckled and drove her bright needle across a hole in Otto's sock. 'She's not old, Jim, though I expect she seems old to you. No, I wouldn't mourn if she never came again. But, you see, a body never knows what traits poverty might bring out in 'em. It makes a woman grasping to see her children want for things. Now read me a chapter in "The Prince of the House of David." Let's forget the Bohemians.'

Excerpt 3

On the morning of the twenty-second I wakened with a start. Before I opened my eyes, I seemed to know that something had happened. I heard excited voices in the kitchen—grandmother's was so shrill that I knew she must be almost beside herself. I looked forward to any new crisis with delight. What could it be, I wondered, as I hurried into my clothes. Perhaps the barn had burned; perhaps the cattle had frozen to death; perhaps a neighbour was lost in the storm.

Down in the kitchen grandfather was standing before the stove with his hands behind him. Jake and Otto had taken off their boots and were rubbing their woollen socks. Their clothes and boots were steaming, and they both looked exhausted. On the bench behind the stove lay a man, covered up with a blanket. Grandmother motioned me to the din-ing-room. I obeyed reluctantly. I watched her as she came and went, carrying dishes. Her lips were tightly compressed and she kept whisper-ing to herself: 'Oh, dear Saviour!' 'Lord, Thou knowest!'

Presently grandfather came in and spoke to me: 'Jimmy, we will not have prayers this morning, because we have a great deal to do. Old Mr. Shimerda is dead, and his family are in great distress. Ambrosch came over here in the middle of the night, and Jake and Otto went back with him. The boys have had a hard night, and you must not bother them with questions. That is Ambrosch, asleep on the bench. Come in to breakfast, boys.'

After Jake and Otto had swallowed their first cup of coffee, they began to talk excitedly, disregarding grandmother's warning glances. I held my tongue, but I listened with all my ears.

'No, sir,' Fuchs said in answer to a question from grandfather, 'nobody heard the gun go off. Ambrosch was out with the ox-team, trying to break a road, and the women-folks was shut up tight in their cave. When Ambrosch come in, it was dark and he didn't see nothing, but the oxen acted kind of queer. One of 'em ripped around and got away from him— bolted clean out of the stable. His hands is blistered where the rope run through. He got a lantern and went back and found the old man, just as we seen him.'

'Poor soul, poor soul!' grandmother groaned. 'I'd like to think he never done it. He was always considerate and un-wishful to give trouble. How could he forget himself and bring this on us!'

'I don't think he was out of his head for a minute, Mrs. Burden,' Fuchs declared. 'He done everything natural. You know he was always sort of fixy, and fixy he was to the last. He shaved after dinner, and washed hisself all over after the girls had done the dishes. Ántonia heated the water for him. Then he put on a clean shirt and clean socks, and after he was dressed he kissed her and the little one and took his gun and said he was going out to hunt rabbits. He must have gone right down to the barn and done it then. He layed down on that bunk-bed, close to the ox stalls, where he always slept. When we found him, everything was decent except'—Fuchs wrinkled his brow and hesitated—'except what he couldn't nowise foresee. His coat was hung on a peg, and his boots was under the bed. He'd took off that silk neckcloth he always wore, and folded it smooth and stuck his pin through it. He turned back his shirt at the neck and rolled up his sleeves.'

'I don't see how he could do it!' grandmother kept saying.

Otto misunderstood her. 'Why, ma'm, it was simple enough; he pulled the trigger with his big toe. He layed over on his side and put the end of the barrel in his mouth, then he drew up one foot and felt for the trigger. He found it all right!' . . .

. . . Grandmother told grandfather she meant to go over to the Shimerdas' with him.

'There is nothing you can do,' he said doubtfully. 'The body can't be touched until we get the coroner here from Black Hawk, and that will be a matter of several days, this weather.'

'Well, I can take them some victuals, anyway, and say a word of comfort to them poor little girls. The oldest one was his darling, and was like a right hand to him. He might have thought of her. He's left her alone in a hard world.'

Excerpt 4

The Burden household discusses where Mr. Shimerda will be buried.

At supper the men ate like vikings, and the chocolate cake, which I had hoped would linger on until tomorrow in a mutilated condition, disappeared on the second round. They talked excitedly about where they should bury Mr. Shimerda; I gathered that the neighbours were all disturbed and shocked about something. It developed that Mrs. Shimerda and Ambrosch wanted the old man buried on the southwest corner of their own land; indeed, under the very stake that marked the corner. Grandfather had explained to Ambrosch that some day, when the country was put under fence and the roads were confined to section lines, two roads would cross exactly on that corner. But Ambrosch only said, 'It makes no matter.'

Grandfather asked Jelinek[2] whether in the old country there was some superstition to the effect that a suicide must be buried at the cross-roads. Jelinek said he didn't know; he seemed to remember hearing there had once been such a custom in Bohemia. 'Mrs. Shimerda is made up her mind,' he added. 'I try to persuade her, and say it looks bad for her to all the neighbours; but she say so it must be. "There I will bury him, if I dig the grave myself," she say. I have to promise her I help Ambrosch make the grave tomorrow.'

Grandfather smoothed his beard and looked judicial. 'I don't know whose wish should decide the matter, if not hers. But if she thinks she will live to see the people of this country ride over that old man's head, she is mistaken.'

Excerpt 5

The coffin was put into the wagon. We drove slowly away, against the fine, icy snow which cut our faces like a sand-blast. When we reached the grave, it looked a very little spot in that snow-covered waste. The men took the coffin to the edge of the hole and lowered it with ropes. We stood about watching them, and the powdery snow lay without melting on the caps and shoulders of the men and the shawls of the women. Jelinek spoke in a persuasive tone to Mrs. Shimerda, and then turned to grandfather.

'She says, Mr. Burden, she is very glad if you can make some prayer for him here in English, for the neighbours to understand.'

---

[2] A Bohemian neighbor who had come to help.

Grandmother looked anxiously at grandfather. He took off his hat, and the other men did likewise. I thought his prayer remarkable. I still remember it. He began, 'Oh, great and just God, no man among us knows what the sleeper knows, nor is it for us to judge what lies between him and Thee.' He prayed that if any man there had been remiss toward the stranger come to a far country, God would forgive him and soften his heart. He recalled the promises to the widow and the fatherless, and asked God to smooth the way before this widow and her children, and to 'incline the hearts of men to deal justly with her.' In closing, he said we were leaving Mr. Shimerda at 'Thy judgment seat, which is also Thy mercy seat.'

All the time he was praying, grandmother watched him through the black fingers of her glove, and when he said 'Amen,' I thought she looked satisfied with him. She turned to Otto and whispered, 'Can't you start a hymn, Fuchs? It would seem less heathenish.'

Fuchs glanced about to see if there was general approval of her suggestion, then began, 'Jesus, Lover of my Soul,' and all the men and women took it up after him. Whenever I have heard the hymn since, it has made me remember that white waste and the little group of people; and the bluish air, full of fine, eddying snow, like long veils flying:

> 'While the nearer waters roll,
> While the tempest still is high.'

. . . .

Years afterward, when the open-grazing days were over, and the red grass had been ploughed under and under until it had almost disappeared from the prairie; when all the fields were under fence, and the roads no longer ran about like wild things, but followed the surveyed section-lines, Mr. Shimerda's grave was still there, with a sagging wire fence around it, and an unpainted wooden cross. As grandfather had predicted, Mrs. Shimerda never saw the roads going over his head. The road from the north curved a little to the east just there, and the road from the west swung out a little to the south; so that the grave, with its tall red grass that was never mowed, was like a little island; and at twilight, under a new moon or the clear evening star, the dusty roads used to look like soft grey rivers flowing past it. I never came upon the place without emotion, and in all that country it was the spot most dear to me. I loved the dim superstition, the propitiatory intent, that had put the grave there; and still more I loved the spirit that could not carry out the sentence— the error from the surveyed lines, the clemency of the soft earth roads along which the home-coming wagons rattled after sunset. Never a tired driver passed the wooden cross, I am sure, without wishing well to the sleeper.

THE VILLAGE BLACKSMITH

by Henry Wadsworth Longfellow

*Longfellow's famous tribute to a manual laborer offers a vision of a "worthy"
life. Is it a dignified life, as well?*

*The blacksmith's arms are like a machine ("iron bands") and their action is
like the ringing of the village bell, by the sexton. What might the poet mean by
linking the blacksmith both to something subhuman and to something lofty?*

*Longfellow admires the blacksmith not only for his physical power, but for
what he has attained: He "owes not any man," and earns his "night's repose."
The blacksmith knows that this entitles him to "[look] the whole world in the
face." Is the blacksmith entirely self-sufficient?*

*The blacksmith hears his daughter singing in the choir and is reminded of his
late wife. Remembering her, "With his hard, rough hand he wipes a tear out of
his eyes." Are you surprised by his reaction? Is the roughness of his hand a sign
of his character?*

*In his last stanza, Longfellow thanks the blacksmith "For the lesson thou
hast taught." He then asserts that our every "burning deed and thought" must
be shaped, "thus," on the "sounding anvil" of life. What is the meaning of the
lesson? Is it as generalizable as Longfellow would have us believe?*

Under a spreading chestnut-tree
    The village smithy stands;
The smith, a mighty man is he,
    With large and sinewy hands;
And the muscles of his brawny arms
Are strong as iron bands.

His hair is crisp, and black, and long,
    His face is like the tan;
His brow is wet with honest sweat,
    He earns whate'er he can,
And looks the whole world in the face,
    For he owes not any man.

596

Week in, week out, from morn till night,
    You can hear his bellows blow;
You can hear him swing his heavy sledge,
    With measured beat and slow,
Like a sexton ringing the village bell,
    When the evening sun is low.

And children coming home from school
    Look in at the open door;
They love to see the flaming forge,
    And hear the bellows roar,
And catch the burning sparks that fly
    Like chaff from a threshing-floor.

He goes on Sunday to the church,
    And sits among his boys;
He hears the parson pray and preach,
    he hears his daughter's voice,
Singing in the village choir,
    And it makes his heart rejoice.

It sounds to him like her mother's voice,
    Singing in Paradise!
He needs must think of her once more,
    How in the grave she lies;
And with his hard, rough hand he wipes
    A tear out of his eyes.

Toiling,—rejoicing,—sorrowing,
    Onward through life he goes;
Each morning sees some task begin,
    Each evening sees it close;
Something attempted, something done,
    Has earned a night's repose.

Thanks, thanks to thee, my worthy friend,
    For the lesson thou hast taught!
Thus at the flaming forge of life
    Our fortunes must be wrought;
Thus on its sounding anvil shaped
    Each burning deed and thought.

THE BALLAD OF JOHN HENRY

Traditional

and

HENRY THE ACCOUNTANT

by Paul Kaplan

There are many versions of this American folksong. All celebrate John Henry, the former slave who pitted himself against a machine and won, only to die of exhaustion.

Some historians believe there may have been a real John Henry. Most, though, believe truth and myth may both play a part in this beloved American legend. The legend is set in the nineteenth century, when thousands of laborers cleared a path for the railroad across the American continent, sometimes tunneling through solid rock to do so. At first, these tunnels were created by men with pickaxes and dynamite. Later, steam drills began to replace the pickaxes.

According to the legend, John Henry was a pickaxe man who learned that a steam drill was coming to do his work. As a matter of pride, he resolved to beat the steam drill. "A man ain't nothing but a man," he said, "But before I'd let your steam drill beat me down / I'd die with a hammer in my hand."

Machines are in many ways more powerful than people. Is there any indignity in being beaten by one?

Nearly every version of this song begins with John Henry's presentiment, as a baby, that his hammer would be his death. Yet as a man he clings to that hammer, and squarely faces the death he knows it promises. Why? What, for John Henry, does that have to do with being a man? Do you find this attitude frustrating? Admirable?

What does it mean to die with a hammer in one's hand?

The traditional lyric reproduced below is followed by a modern parody, "Henry the Accountant." Henry the Accountant is ridiculous and the parody is very funny. But there is nothing ridiculous about the original John Henry, and nothing whatsoever funny about his song.

Dying with a pencil in one's hand makes us laugh; dying with a hammer in one's hand makes us cry. Why?

Does physical labor have a dignity that pencil work lacks? Why?

The Ballad of John Henry

When John Henry was a little baby boy,
Sitting on his papa's knee
Well he picked up a hammer and little piece of steel
Said Hammer's gonna be the death of me, lord, lord
Hammer's gonna be the death of me

The captain said to John Henry
I'm gonna bring that steam drill around
I'm gonna bring that steam drill out on the job
I'm gonna whup that steel on down

John Henry told his captain
Lord a man ain't nothing but a man
But before I'd let your steam drill beat me down
I'd die with a hammer in my hand

John Henry said to his shaker
Shaker why don't you sing
Because I'm swinging thirty pounds from my hips on down
Just listen to that cold steel ring

Now the captain said to John Henry
I believe that mountain's caving in
John Henry said right back to the captain
Ain't nothing but my hammer sucking wind

Now the man that invented the steam drill
He thought he was mighty fine
But John Henry drove fifteen feet
The steam drill only made nine

John Henry hammered in the mountains
His hammer was striking fire
But he worked so hard, it broke his poor heart
And he laid down his hammer and he died

Now John Henry had a little woman
Her name was Polly Anne
John Henry took sick and had to go to bed
Polly Anne drove steel like a man

John Henry had a little baby
You could hold him in the palm of your hand
And the last words I heard that poor boy say
My daddy was a steel driving man

So every Monday morning
When the blue birds begin to sing
You can hear John Henry a mile or more
You can hear John Henry's hammer ring

Henry the Accountant
(Sung to the tune of "John Henry")

1. Henry was an accountant
He worked with a pencil in his hand
If you had something you needed added up, then
Henry, the Accountant, was your man, Lord, Lord
Henry, the Accountant, was your man
Henry, the Accountant, was your man, Lord, Lord
Henry, the Accountant, was your man.

2. When Henry was a little baby
Sitting on his daddy's knee
He picked up a crayon and a little piece of paper, and said
"Two plus one equals three, Lord, Lord
Two plus one equals three
Two plus one equals three, Lord, Lord
Two plus one equals three."

3. The man who bought the first calculator
He thought he was mighty fine
He walked up to Henry with a sneer on his lip and said
"Your job is gonna be mine, Lord, Lord
Your job is gonna be mine
Your job is gonna be mine, Lord, Lord
Your job is gonna be mine."

4. Henry stood up and drew his weapon
He said, "A man isn't anything but a man
We'll have ourselves a race and I'll put you in your place, or
I'll die with my pencil in my hand, Lord, Lord
I'll die with my pencil in my hand
I'll die with my pencil in my hand, Lord, Lord
I'll die with my pencil in my hand."

5. So each man grabbed a fifty-pound ledger
And Henry went to work with all his might
Though his hand was getting cramped and his shirt was getting
    damp, still
He swore that he would not give up the fight, Lord, Lord
He swore that he would not give up the fight
He swore that he would not give up the fight, Lord, Lord
He swore that he would not give up the fight.

6. After three long hours in battle
The man with the machine had moved ahead
He had Henry beat 'til on the final sheet
Suddenly his batteries went dead, Lord, Lord
Suddenly his batteries went dead
Suddenly his batteries went dead, Lord, Lord
Suddenly his batteries went dead.

7. So Henry beat that calculator
Now his powers could never be denied
But the terrible strain had been too much for his brain, so
He laid down his glasses and he died, Lord, Lord
He laid down his glasses and he died
He laid down his glasses and he died, Lord, Lord
He laid down his glasses and he died.

8. So they buried Henry in the graveyard
With his trusty pencil and his pad
And when their checks don't clear, they always shed a tear for
The last human being who could add, Lord, Lord
The last human being who could add
He was the last human being who could add, Lord, Lord
The last human being who could add.

THE CROWN OF WILD OLIVE

by John Ruskin

John Ruskin, the Victorian art critic and social commentator, here considers the comparative dignity of physical and mental labor. While acknowledging that either can be done badly or well, he asserts that when both are done equally worthily, "the head's is the noble work, and the hand's the ignoble."

Ruskin writes that the work of the hand is less "honorable" than the work of the head, because compared to mental labor it is "ignoble." Later, he notes that we hold days of rest to be "honorable, or 'holy.'" What does he mean by "honorable?" "Noble?" "Holy?" How are these terms related to one another? How do they relate to "dignity?" Is Ruskin right in his judgment?

John Henry and the Village Blacksmith do "rough work." Are they "rough men?" If not, what other words might you choose to describe them?

Ruskin cites the divine promise of eternal rest in support of his belief that physical labor is degraded. If that promise is offered equally to laborers of every class, as he seems to think, does it support or refute his argument?

Are some human activities and works more dignified than others? If so, what makes them so?

I pass now to our third condition of separation, between the men who work with the hand, and those who work with the head.

And here we have at last an inevitable distinction. There *must* be work done by the arms, or none of us could live. There *must* be work done by the brains, or the life we get would not be worth having. And the same men cannot do both. There is rough work to be done, and rough men must do it; there is gentle work to be done, and gentlemen must do it; and it is physically impossible that one class should do, or divide, the work of the other. And it is of no use to try to conceal this sorrowful fact by fine words, and to talk to the workman about the honorableness of manual labor, and the dignity of humanity. That is a grand old proverb of Sancho Panza's, "Fine words butter no parsnips," and I can tell you that, all over England just now, you workmen are buying a great deal too much butter at that dairy. Rough work, honorable or not, takes the life out of us; and the man who has been heaving clay out of a ditch all day, or driving an express train against the north wind all night, or holding a collier's helm in a gale on a lee-shore, or whirling white-hot iron at a furnace mouth, that man is not the same at the end of his day, or night, as one who has been sitting in a quiet room, with everything comfortable about him, reading books, or classing butterflies, or painting pictures. If it is any comfort to you to be told that the rough work is the more honorable of the two, I should be sorry to take that much of consolation from you; and in some sense I need not. The rough work is at all events real, honest, and, generally, though not always, useful; while the fine work is, a great deal of it, foolish and false as well as fine, and therefore dishonorable: but when both kinds are equally well and worthily done, the head's is the noble work, and the hand's the ignoble; and of all hand work whatsoever, necessary for the maintenance of life, those old words, "In the sweat of thy face thou shalt eat bread," indicate that the inherent nature of it is one of calamity; and that the ground, cursed for our sake, casts also some shadow of degradation into our contest with its thorn and its thistle; so that all nations have held their days honorable, or "holy," and constituted them "holy-days," or "holidays," by making them days of rest; and the promise, which, among all our distant hopes, seems to cast the chief brightness over death, is that blessing of the dead who die in the Lord, that "they rest from their labors, and their works do follow them."

Excerpt from
IN MY FATHER'S COURT
by Isaac Bashevis Singer

Singer's story, taken from a memoir of his boyhood in a Jewish ghetto in pre-war Poland, is a tribute to the dignity of labor and duty.

The author's family is poor, but not as poor as the washwoman who does its laundry. Of all the washwomen the family has known, the one remembered here is the best. Although the job appears to require more of her than a woman of her years could endure, endure it she does, just as she endures deep personal disappointment: abandonment by her wealthy son.

One day, the washwoman departs and does not return, leaving the family both fearful about what has become of her, and also without its much-needed laundry.

How do the washwoman's sacrifices on behalf of the work she has pledged to do compare to her own or the mother's sacrifices for her children? Are they of equal dignity?

The washwoman and the author's mother are from separate cultures, Gentile and Jewish. The author notes how very different these cultures are. Yet there is confidence and respect between the two women. What makes it possible for them to bridge their differences?

The washwoman repeatedly says: "I do not want to be a burden on anyone." Does she speak from humility or from pride?

The author says the washwoman's hands spoke of "stubbornness . . . of the will to work not only as one's strength permits but beyond the limits of one's power." In the end he praises her for her "effort." Is her effort unqualifiedly praiseworthy?

What does the author mean by calling the washwoman a "holy soul"?

The Washwoman

Our home had little contact with Gentiles. The only Gentile in the house was the janitor. Fridays he would come for a tip, his "Friday money." He remained standing at the door, took off his hat, and my mother gave him six groschen.

Besides the janitor there were also the Gentile washwomen who came to the house to fetch our laundry. My story is about one of these.

She was a small woman, old and wrinkled. When she started washing for us she was already past seventy. Most Jewish women of her age were sickly, weak, broken in body. All the old women in our street had bent backs and leaned on sticks when they walked. But this washwoman, small and thin as she was, possessed a strength that came from generations of peasant forebears. Mother would count out to her a bundle of laundry that had accumulated over several weeks. She would lift the unwieldy pack, load it on her narrow shoulders, and carry it the long way home. She also lived on Krochmalna Street, but at the other end, near Wola. It must have been a walk of an hour and a half.

She would bring the laundry back about two weeks later. My mother had never been so pleased with any other washwoman. Every piece of linen sparkled like polished silver. Every piece was ironed. Yet she charged no more than the others. She was a real find. Mother always had her money ready, because it was too far for the old woman to come a second time.

Laundering was not easy in those days. The old woman had no faucet where she lived but had to bring in the water from a pump. For the linens to come out so clean, they had to be scrubbed thoroughly in a washtub, rinsed with washing soda, soaked, boiled in an enormous pot, starched, ironed. Every piece was handled ten times or more. And the drying! It could not be done outside because thieves would steal the laundry. The wrung-out wash had to be carried up to the attic and hung on clotheslines. In the winter it would become as brittle as glass and almost break when touched. Then there was always a to-do with other housewives and washwomen who wanted the attic for their own use. Only God knew all she had to endure each time she did a wash!

The old woman could have begged at the church door or entered a home for the indigent aged. But there was in her a certain pride and a love of labor with which the Gentiles have been blessed. The old woman did not want to become a burden, and thus she bore her burden.

My mother spoke a little Polish, and the old woman would talk with her about many things. She was especially fond of me and used to say that I looked like Jesus. She repeated this every time she came, and Mother would frown and whisper to herself, her lips barely moving, "May her words be scattered in the wilderness."

The woman had a son who was rich. I no longer remember what sort of business he had. He was ashamed of his mother, the washwoman, and never came to see her. Nor did he ever give her a groschen. The old woman told this without rancor. One day the son was married. It seemed that he had made a good match. The wedding took place in a church. The son had not invited the old mother to his wedding, but she went to the church and waited at the steps to see her son lead the "young lady" to the altar. I do not want to seem a chauvinist, but I believe that no Jewish son would have acted in this manner. But I have no doubt that, had he done this, the mother would have shrieked and wailed and sent the sexton to call him to account. In short, Jews are Jews and Gentiles are Gentiles.

The story of the faithless son left a deep impression upon my mother. She talked about it for weeks and months. It was an affront not only to the old woman but to the entire institution of motherhood. Mother would argue. "Nu, does it pay to make sacrifices for children? The mother uses up her last strength, and he does not even know the meaning of loyalty."

And she would drop dark hints to the effect that she was not certain of her own children: Who knows what they would someday do? This, however, did not prevent her from dedicating her life to us. If there was any delicacy in the house, she would put it aside for the children and invent all sorts of excuses and reasons why she herself did not want to taste it. She knew charms that went back to ancient times, and she used expressions she had inherited from generations of devoted mothers and grandmothers. If one of the children complained of a pain, she would say, "May I be your ransom and may you outlive my bones!" Or she would say, "May I be the atonement for the least of your fingernails." When we ate she used to say, "Health and marrow in your bones!" The day before the new moon she gave us a kind of candy that was said to prevent parasitic worms. If one of us had something in his eye, Mother would lick the eye clean with her tongue. She also fed us rock candy against coughs, and from time to time she would take us to be blessed against the evil eye. This did not prevent her from studying *The Duties of the Heart*, *The Book of the Covenant*, and other serious philosophic works.

But to return to the washwoman: that winter was a harsh one. The streets were in the grip of a bitter cold. No matter how much we heated our stove, the windows were covered with frostwork and decorated with icicles. The newspapers reported that people were dying of the cold. Coal became dear. The winter had become so severe that parents stopped sending children to the heder, and even the Polish schools were closed.

On one such day the washwoman, now nearly eighty years old, came to our house. A good deal of laundry had accumulated during the past weeks. Mother gave her a pot of tea to warm herself, as well as some bread. The old woman sat on a kitchen chair trembling and shaking, and warmed her hands against the teapot. Her fingers were gnarled from work, and perhaps from arthritis too. Her fingernails were strangely white. These hands spoke of the stubbornness of mankind, of the will to work not only as one's strength permits but beyond the limits of one's power. Mother counted and wrote down the list: men's undershirts, women's vests, long-legged drawers, bloomers, petticoats, shifts, featherbed covers, pillowcases, sheets, and the men's fringed garments. Yes, the Gentile woman washed these holy garments as well.

The bundle was big, bigger than usual. When the woman placed it on her shoulders, it covered her completely. At first she swayed, as though she were about to fall under the load. But an inner obstinacy seemed to call out: No, you may not fall. A donkey may permit himself to fall under his burden, but not a human being, the crown of creation.

It was fearful to watch the old woman staggering out with the enormous pack, out into the frost, where the snow was dry as salt and the air was filled with dusty white whirlwinds, like goblins dancing in the cold. Would the old woman ever reach Wola?

She disappeared, and Mother sighed and prayed for her.

Usually the woman brought back the wash after two or, at the most, three weeks. But three weeks passed, then four and five, and nothing was heard of the old woman. We remained without linens. The cold had become even more intense. The telephone wires were now as thick as hawsers. The branches of the trees looked like glass. So much snow had fallen that the streets had become uneven, and on many streets sleds were able to glide down as on the slopes of a hill. Kindhearted people lit fires in the streets for vagrants to warm themselves and roast potatoes over, if they had any to roast.

For us the washwoman's absence was a catastrophe. We needed the laundry. We did not even know the woman's house address. It seemed certain that she had collapsed, died. Mother declared that she had had a premonition, as the old woman left our house the last time, that we would never see our things again. She found some torn old shirts and washed them, mended them. We mourned, both for the laundry and for the old, toilworn woman who had grown close to us through the years she had served us so faithfully.

More than two months passed. The frost had subsided, and then a new frost had come, a new wave of cold. One evening, while Mother was sitting near the kerosene lamp mending a shirt, the door opened and a small puff of steam, followed by a gigantic bundle, entered. Under the bundle tottered the old woman, her face as white as a linen sheet. A few wisps of white hair straggled out from beneath her shawl. Mother uttered a half-choked cry. It was as though a corpse had entered the room. I ran toward the old woman and helped her unload her pack. She was even thinner now, more bent. Her face had become more gaunt, and her head shook from side to side as though she were saying no. She could not utter a clear word, but mumbled something with her sunken mouth and pale lips.

After the old woman had recovered somewhat, she told us that she had been ill, very ill. Just what her illness was, I cannot remember. She had been so sick that someone had called a doctor, and the doctor had sent for a priest. Someone had informed the son, and he had contributed money for a coffin and for the funeral. But the Almighty had not yet wanted to take this pain-racked soul to Himself. She began to feel better, she became well, and as soon as she was able to stand on her feet once more she resumed her washing. Not just ours, but the wash of several other families too.

"I could not rest easy in my bed because of the wash," the old woman explained. "The wash would not let me die."

"With the help of God you will live to be a hundred and twenty," said my mother, as a benediction.

"God forbid! What good would such a long life be? The work becomes harder and harder—my strength is leaving me—I do not want to be a burden on anyone!"

The old woman muttered and crossed herself, and raised her eyes toward heaven. Fortunately there was some money in the house and Mother counted out what she owed. I had a strange feeling: the coins in the old woman's washed-out hands seemed to become as weary and clean and pious as she herself was. She blew on the coins and tied them in a kerchief. Then she left, promising to return in a few weeks for a new load of wash.

But she never came back. The wash she had returned was her last effort on this earth. She had been driven by an indomitable will to return the property to its rightful owners, to fulfill the task she had undertaken.

And now at last the body, which had long been no more than a broken shard supported only by the force of honesty and duty, had fallen. The soul passed into those spheres where all holy souls meet, regardless of the roles they played on this earth, in whatever tongue, of whatever creed. I cannot imagine Eden without this washwoman. I cannot even conceive of a world where there is no recompense for such effort.

TWO THANKSGIVING DAY GENTLEMEN

by O. Henry

O. Henry's two gentlemen face opposite physiological necessities. Both, however, reveal that there are things they value more highly than the needs of their own bodies.

Although the first Thanksgiving was celebrated by the Pilgrims at Plymouth Rock, the holiday itself was not enshrined in U.S. law until 1863. O. Henry's story takes place in New York City on Thanksgiving, when the holiday, though still young, had already become an occasion on which the charitably-minded feel especially bound to share with or give to the needy. The first of the two gentlemen in this story, Stuffy Pete, receives some of this largesse. The second is Stuffy Pete's "traditional" benefactor.

Is tradition equally important to both gentlemen? Why does the childless Old Gentleman sacrifice as much as he does for this tradition? Does the fact that he knows it will not be carried on when he is gone concern you?

O. Henry calls Stuffy a hero. Is he being ironic? Is Stuffy more or less heroic than his benefactor?

Both men end the story on hospital stretchers, each having subjected his body to an opposite form of excess. Is their plight ridiculous? For the reader, if not for the doctor, does either retain his dignity? Who is the real "gentleman" in this story? Why do you think so?

There is one day that is ours. There is one day when all we Americans who are not self-made go back to the old home to eat saleratus biscuits and marvel how much nearer to the porch the old pump looks than it used to. Bless the day. President Roosevelt gives it to us. We hear some talk of the Puritans, but don't just remember who they were. Bet we can lick 'em, anyhow, if they try to land again. Plymouth Rocks? Well, that sounds more familiar. Lots of us have had to come down to hens since the Turkey Trust got its work in. But somebody in Washington is leaking out advance information to 'em about these Thanksgiving proclamations.

The big city east of the cranberry bogs[1] has made Thanksgiving Day an institution. The last Thursday in November is the only day in the year on which it recognizes the part of America lying across the ferries. It is the one day that is purely American. Yes, a day of celebration, exclusively American.

And now for the story which is to prove to you that we have traditions on this side of the ocean that are becoming older at a much rapider rate than those of England are—thanks to our git-up and enterprise.

Stuffy Pete took his seat on the third bench to the right as you enter Union Square from the east, at the walk opposite the fountain. Every Thanksgiving Day for nine years he had taken his seat there promptly at 1 o'clock. For every time he had done so things had happened to him—Charles Dickensy things that swelled his waistcoat above his heart, and equally on the other side.

But today Stuffy Pete's appearance at the annual trysting place seemed to have been rather the result of habit than of the yearly hunger which, as the philanthropists seem to think, afflicts the poor at such extended intervals.

Certainly Pete was not hungry. He had just come from a feast that had left him of his powers barely those of respiration and locomotion. His eyes were like two pale gooseberries firmly imbedded in a swollen and gravy-smeared mask of putty. His breath came in short wheezes; senatorial roll of adipose tissue denied a fashionable set to his upturned coat collar. Buttons that had been sewed upon his clothes by kind Salvation fingers a week before flew like popcorn, strewing the earth around him. Ragged he was, with a split shirt front open to the wishbone; but the November breeze, carrying fine snowflakes, brought him only a grateful coolness. For Stuffy Pete was overcharged with the caloric produced by a super-bountiful dinner, beginning with oysters and ending with plum pudding, and including (it seemed to him) all the roast turkey and baked potatoes and chicken salad and squash pie and ice cream in the world. Wherefore he sat, gorged, and gazed upon the world with after-dinner contempt.

The meal had been an unexpected one. He was passing a red brick mansion near the beginning of Fifth Avenue, in which lived two old ladies of ancient family and a reverence for traditions. They even denied the existence of New York, and believed that Thanksgiving Day was declared solely for Washington Square. One of their traditional habits was to station a servant at the postern gate with orders to admit the first hungry wayfarer that came along after the hour of noon had struck, and banquet him to a finish. Stuffy Pete happened to pass by on his way to

[1] New York City.

the park, and the seneschals gathered him in and upheld the custom of the castle.

After Stuffy Pete had gazed straight before him for ten minutes he was conscious of a desire for a more varied field of vision. With a tremendous effort he moved his head slowly to the left. And then his eyes bulged out fearfully, and his breath ceased, and the rough-shod ends of his short legs wriggled and rustled on the gravel.

The Old Gentleman was coming across Fourth Avenue toward his bench.

Every Thanksgiving Day for nine years the Old Gentleman had come there and found Stuffy Pete on his bench. That was a thing that the Old Gentleman was trying to make a tradition of. Every Thanksgiving Day for nine years he had found Stuffy there, and had led him to a restaurant and watched him eat a big dinner. They do those things in England unconsciously. But this is a young country, and nine years is not so bad. The Old Gentleman was a staunch American patriot, and considered himself a pioneer in American tradition. In order to become picturesque we must keep on doing one thing for a long time without ever letting it get away from us. Something like collecting the weekly dimes in industrial insurance. Or cleaning the streets.

The Old Gentleman moved, straight and stately, toward the Institution that he was rearing. Truly, the annual feeding of Stuffy Pete was nothing national in its character, such as the Magna Charta or jam for breakfast was in England. But it was a step. It was almost feudal. It showed, at least, that a Custom was not impossible to New Y—ahem!—America.

The Old Gentleman was thin and tall and sixty. He was dressed all in black, and wore the old-fashioned kind of glasses that won't stay on your nose. His hair was whiter and thinner than it had been last years, and he seemed to make more use of his big, knobby cane with the crooked handle.

As his established benefactor came up Stuffy wheezed and shuddered like some woman's over-fat pug when a street dog bristles up at him. He would have flown, but all the skill of Santos-Dumont could not have separated him from his bench. Well had the myrmidons of the two old ladies done their work.

"Good morning," said the Old Gentleman. "I am glad to perceive that the vicissitudes of another year have spared you to move in health about the beautiful world. For that blessing alone this day of thanksgiving is well proclaimed to each of us. If you will come with me, my man, I will provide you with a dinner that should make your physical being accord with the mental."

That is what the Old Gentleman said every time. Every Thanksgiving Day for nine years. The words themselves almost formed an Institution. Nothing could be compared with them except the Declaration of Independence. Always before they had been music in Stuffy's ears. But now he looked up at the Old Gentleman's face with tearful agony in his own. The fine snow almost sizzled when it fell upon his perspiring brow. But the Old Gentleman shivered a little and turned his back to the wind.

Stuffy had always wondered why the Old Gentleman spoke his speech rather sadly. He did not know that it was because he was wishing every time that he had a son to succeed him. A son who would come there after he was gone—a son who would stand proud and strong before some subsequent Stuffy, and say: "In memory of my father." Then it would be an Institution.

But the Old Gentleman had no relatives. He lived in rented rooms in one of the decayed old family brownstone mansions in one of the quiet streets east of the park. In the winter he raised fuchsias in a little conservatory the size of a steamer trunk. In the spring he walked in the Easter parade. In the summer he lived at a farmhouse in the New Jersey hills, and sat in a wicker armchair, speaking of a butterfly, the *ornithoptera amphrisius*, that he hoped to find someday. In the autumn he fed Stuffy a dinner. These were the Old Gentleman's occupations.

Stuffy Pete looked up at him for a half minute. Stewing and helpless in his own self-pity. The Old Gentleman's eyes were bright with the giving pleasure. He face was getting more lined each year, but his little black necktie was in as jaunty a bow as ever, and his linen was beautiful and white, and his gray mustache was curled gracefully at the ends. And then Stuffy made a noise that sounded like peas bubbling in a pot. Speech was intended; and as the Old Gentleman had heard the sounds nine times before, he rightly construed them into Stuffy's old formula of acceptance.

"Thankee, sir. I'll go with ye, and much obliged. I'm very hungry, sir."

The coma of repletion had not prevented from entering Stuffy's mind the conviction that he was the basis of an Institution. His Thanksgiving appetite was not his own; it belonged by all the sacred rights of established custom, if not by the actual Statute of Limitations, to this kind old gentleman who had preempted it. True, America is free; but in order to establish tradition someone must be a repetend—a repeating decimal. The heroes are not all heroes of steel and gold. See one here that wielded only weapons of iron, badly silvered, and tin.

The Old Gentleman led his annual protege southward to the restaurant, and to the table where the feast had always occurred. They were recognized.

"Here comes de old guy," said a waiter, "dat blows dat same bum to a meal every Thanksgiving."

The Old Gentleman sat across the table glowing like a smoked pearl at his cornerstone of future ancient Tradition. The waiters heaped the table with holiday food—and Stuffy, with a sigh that was mistaken for hunger's expression, raised knife and fork and carved for himself a crown of imperishable bay.

No more valiant hero ever fought his way through the ranks of an enemy. Turkey, chops, soups, vegetables, pies, disappeared before him as fast as they could be served. Gorged nearly to the uttermost when he entered the restaurant, the smell of food had almost caused him to lose his honor as a gentleman, but he rallied like a true knight. He saw the look of beneficent happiness on the Old Gentleman's face—a happier look than even the fuchsias and the *ornithoptera amphrisius* had ever brought to it—and he had not the heart to see it wane.

In an hour Stuffy leaned back with a battle won.

"Thankee kindly, sir," he puffed like a leaky steam pipe; "thankee kindly for a hearty meal."

Then he arose heavily with glazed eyes and started toward the kitchen. A waiter turned him about like a top, and pointed him toward the door. The Old Gentleman carefully counted out $1.30 in silver change, leaving three nickels for the waiter.

They parted as they did each year at the door, the Old Gentleman going south, Stuffy north.

Around the first corner Stuffy turned, and stood for one minute. Then he seemed to puff out his rags as an owl puffs out his feathers, and fell to the sidewalk like a sunstricken horse.

When the ambulance came the young surgeon and the driver cursed softly at his weight. There was no smell of whiskey to justify a transfer to the patrol wagon, so Stuffy and his two dinners went to the hospital. There they stretched him on a bed and began to test him for strange diseases, with the hope of getting a chance at some problem with the bare steel.

And lo! An hour later another ambulance brought the Old Gentleman. And they laid him on another bed and spoke of appendicitis, for he looked good for the bill.

But pretty soon one of the young doctors met one of the young nurses whose eyes he liked, and stopped to chat with her about the cases.

"That nice old gentleman over there, now" he said, "you wouldn't think that was a case of almost starvation. Proud old family, I guess. He told me he hadn't eaten a thing for three days."

TO BUILD A CASTLE: MY LIFE AS A DISSENTER

by Vladimir Bukovsky, translated by Michael Scammell

*For more than twelve years beginning in 1963, dissident Vladimir Bukovsky
was held as a political prisoner in the former USSR. In 1976, following years
of international pressure, he was released to the west and freedom. In the
following excerpts from his autobiography, Bukovsky reflects on "the soul of
man under socialism," this "new type of man" who is subject to totalitarian
rule, often with a passivity that perturbs Bukovsky. In so reflecting, Bukovsky
considers what it means to retain one's human dignity as a citizen of a state.*

*In a part of the book not reproduced here, Bukovsky describes the chillingly
effective system that succeeds in keeping so many, so passive. Then, in the
first of the excerpts below, he compares people living under socialism to ants.*

*In the second excerpt, Bukovsky discusses the socialist dream of universal
equality, and its suppression and ultimate destruction of the individual, in
body and in spirit. He concludes by considering what it means to be alone, in
a tyrannical society bent on containing individuals in herds.*

*Of all animals, why might Bukovsky have chosen to compare socialist citi-
zens to ants?*

*Bukovsky describes the dream of universal equality as "inhuman." What
about humanity is sacrificed, for this dream? He also acknowledges that "it is
difficult for man to resist this dream and this noble impulse, particularly for
men who are impetuous and sincere." How can a dream that is essentially
inhuman be so beguiling? How can a dream born of noble impulse be inhuman?*

*Bukovsky asserts that to combat the transformation of human beings into
ants, we must "learn to respect the right of even the most insignificant and
repulsive individual to live the way he chooses." What does a concern for the
rights of the insignificant and repulsive have to do with the restoration of humanity? What are the implications for human dignity?*

*The defining characteristics of a socialist regime, Bukovsky writes, are that
it is "not responsive," that the individual may not possess "the least inalienable*

From TO BUILD A CASTLE: MY LIFE AS A DISSENTER by Vladimir Bukovsky.
Translated from the Russian by Michael Scammell. Published by Viking.

right," and that it requires "slaves," not "conscious citizens." Can one living at peace with such a state retain his dignity? Does dignity require merely the exercise of one's inalienable rights or also the assertion and defense of them? Must one be a conscious citizen to have dignity? What does the willingness to be alone have to do with dignity?

Excerpt 1

Once when I joined a geological expedition in Siberia, at one of our camp sites, I caught three ants and put them into a mug—I wanted to see to what degree ants were better than people. Naturally they tried to climb out, but I shook them down to the bottom again. They tried again, and again I shook them down. Overall they made about 180 attempts to climb out of the mug and every time, of course, were unsuccessful. They gave up, crawled toward one another, and settled in a circle. I watched them for a long time, but they made no more attempts to get away. The mug with the three ants in it stood there in the grass for almost three days. Several times it drizzled, the sun set and rose, but they simply stayed there in the mug, twitching their whiskers—probably telling one another jokes.

What else could they do? They had grasped the situation; they needed nothing more. They would have been happy to narrow their world to the confines of family and home, to live for their quiet antlike joys, to bask in the sun on warm spring days and have a drink together. And to savor the moment while it was still sunny, while it was still so cozy sitting there over their drinks in the alehouse, while every minute consisted of sixty blissful seconds, each of which could be stretched still further by the booze. . . .

Excerpt 2

The dream of absolute, universal equality is amazing, terrifying, and inhuman. And the moment it captures people's minds, the result is mountains of corpses and rivers of blood, accompanied by attempts to straighten the stooped and shorten the tall. I remember that one part of the psychiatric examination to which I was subjected as a prisoner was a test for idiocy. The patient was given the following problem to solve: "Imagine a train crash. It is well known that the part of the train that suffers the most damage in such crashes is the carriage at the rear. How can you prevent that damage from taking place?" The idiot's usual reply is expected to be: uncouple the last carriage. That strikes us as amusing, but just think, are the theory and practice of socialism much better?

Society, say the socialists, contains both the rich and the poor. The rich are getting richer and the poor poorer—what is to be done? Uncouple the last carriage, liquidate the rich, take away their wealth and distribute it among the poor. And they start to uncouple the carriages. But there is always richer and poorer, for society is like a magnet: there are always two poles. But does this discourage a true socialist? The main thing is to realize his dream; so the richest section of society is liquidated first; and everyone rejoices because everyone gains from the share-out. But the spoils are soon spent, and people start to notice inequality again— again there are rich and poor. So they uncouple the next carriage, and then the next, without end, because absolute equality has still not been achieved. Before you know it, the peasant with two cows and a horse turns out to be in the last carriage and is pronounced a kulak and deported. Is it really surprising that whenever you get striving for equality and fraternity, the guillotine appears on the scene?

It is all so easy, so simple, and so tempting—to confiscate and divide! To make everybody equal, and with one fell swoop to resolve all problems. It is so alluring—to escape from poverty and crime, grief and suffering, once and for all. All you have to do is want it, all you have to do is reform the people who are hindering universal happiness and there will be paradise on earth, absolute justice, and good will to all men! It is difficult for man to resist this dream and this noble impulse, particularly for men who are impetuous and sincere. They are the first to start chopping heads off and, eventually, to have their own chopped off. They are the first to put their head on the block or go to prison. Such a system is too convenient for scoundrels and demagogues, and they are the ones, in the final analysis, who will decide what is good and what evil.

You have to learn to respect the right of even the most insignificant and repulsive individual to live the way he chooses. You have to renounce once and for all the criminal belief that you can reeducate everyone in your own image. You have to understand that without the use of force it is realistic to create a theoretical equality of opportunity, but not equality of results. People attain absolute equality only in the graveyard, and if you want to turn your country into a gigantic graveyard, go ahead, join the socialists. But man is so constituted that others' experiences and explanations don't convince him, he has to try things out himself. We Russians now watch events unfolding in Cambodia and Vietnam with increasing horror, and listen sadly to all the chatter about

Eurocommunism and socialism with a human face. Why is it that nobody speaks of fascism with a human face?

Over the years we were often astounded by the idiotic stubbornness
of our authorities and their reluctance to look at the obvious facts, all of
which did them catastrophic harm. This self-destructive obstinacy may
strike us as incomprehensible, but that is because we forget that a regime of terror cannot behave otherwise. Where it differs from a democratic regime is precisely in not being responsive to public opinion. In
such a state, the individual cannot have any rights—the least inalienable right possessed by a single individual instantly deprives the regime
of a morsel of power. Every individual from childhood on must absorb
the axiomatic fact that never in any circumstances or by any means will
he be able to influence the regime one jot. No decisions can be made
other than on initiatives from above. The regime is immovable, infallible, and intransigent, and the entire world is left with no choice but to
accommodate itself to this fact. You may humbly beg its indulgence, but
never demand your due. It doesn't require conscious citizens demanding
legality, it requires slaves. In just the same way, it doesn't require partners, it requires satellites. Like a paranoiac, obsessed by a fantastic idea,
it cannot and will not recognize reality—it tries to realize its delirium
and to enforce its criteria on everybody else. We shall never be rid of
this terror, never acquire freedom and security, until we refuse categori-
cally to recognize this paranoid version of reality and oppose to it our
own reality and our own values.

Thousands of books have been written in the West and hundreds of
different doctrines created by the most prominent politicians to find a
compromise with this kind of regime. They are all evading the only
correct solution—moral opposition. The pampered Western democracies have forgotten their past and their essence, namely, that democracy
is not a comfortable house, a handsome car, or an unemployment benefit, but above all the ability and the desire to stand up for one's rights.
Neither atom bombs nor bloody dictatorships, nor theories of "contain-
ment" or "convergence" will save the democracies. We who were born
and have grown up in an atmosphere of terror know of only one remedy—the position of a citizen.

There is a qualitative distinction between the behavior of an individual and that of the human crowd in an extreme situation. A people,
nation, class, party, or simply crowd cannot go beyond a certain limit in
a crisis: the instinct of self-preservation proves too strong. They can
sacrifice a part in the hope of saving the rest, they can break up into

smaller groups and seek salvation that way. But this is their downfall.

To be alone is an enormous responsibility. With his back to the wall a man understands: "I am the people, I am the nation, I am the party, I am the class, and there is nothing else at all." He cannot sacrifice a part of himself, cannot split himself up or divide into parts and still live. There is nowhere for him to retreat to, and the instinct of self-preservation drives him to extremes—he prefers physical death to a spiritual one.

And an astonishing thing happens. In fighting to preserve his integrity, he is simultaneously fighting for his people, his class, or his party. It is such individuals who win the right for their communities to live— even, perhaps, if they are not thinking of it at the time.

"Why should I do it?" asks each man in the crowd. "I can do nothing alone."

And they are all lost.

"If I don't do it, who will?" asks the man with his back to the wall.

And everyone is saved.

Excerpts from
NARRATIVE OF THE LIFE OF FREDERICK DOUGLASS
by Frederick Douglass

Frederick Douglass was born a slave in Maryland in the early nineteenth century, but escaped to freedom as a young man. In his autobiography Douglass relates how, through the power of his will, he remained a human being under conditions intended to turn him into a beast.

Each of the two excerpts below concerns a key moment in Douglass' journey from enslavement to free manhood. The first occurs when he decides to liberate his mind. The second is his decision to defend himself against assaults on his body and will, or die trying. By these two supreme accomplishments he wins for himself the elementary human dignity of being "seated by my own table, in the enjoyment of freedom and the happiness of home, writing this narrative."

The first excerpt begins when the young Douglass is sent from the rural plantation where he began his life to a small home in Baltimore, where he is to care for the family's son, Thomas. The mistress of this household, Mistress Auld, has never owned a slave and greets Douglass with a kindness he has never before seen in a white face.

Douglass' new mistress is soon corrupted by her ownership of a human being. But first, and fatefully for him, she begins to teach him to read.

The second excerpt begins when Douglass is in his late teens. To his dismay, he has been sent back to the plantation. There his owner, Master Thomas, hires him out to a neighbor, Mr. Covey, for one year. Covey has a reputation for "breaking" slaves. He tries to break Douglass and succeeds, but only for a time.

Douglass writes of Mistress Auld: "Slavery proved as injurious to her as it did to me." How might her failure to respect the dignity of another have affected her own?

Douglass' masters, in Baltimore and on the plantation, are vicious. They lack humanity; do they lack dignity, as well?

Thanks to the events recounted in these two passages, Douglass claims self-emancipation. Given the fact that he is still, at that time, legally enslaved, does his claim make sense? Is one or the other of these two "emancipations" more crucial or essential to the attainment of human dignity?

Excerpt 1

My new mistress proved to be all she appeared when I first met her at the door,—a woman of the kindest heart and finest feelings. She had never had a slave under her control previously to myself, and prior to her marriage she had been dependent upon her own industry for a living. She was by trade a weaver; and by constant application to her business, she had been in a good degree preserved from the blighting and dehumanizing effects of slavery. I was utterly astonished at her goodness. I scarcely knew how to behave towards her. She was entirely unlike any other white woman I had ever seen. I could not approach her as I was accustomed to approach other white ladies. My early instruction was all out of place. The crouching servility, usually so acceptable a quality in a slave, did not answer when manifested toward her. Her favor was not gained by it; she seemed to be disturbed by it. She did not deem it impudent or unmannerly for a slave to look her in the face. The meanest slave was put fully at ease in her presence, and none left without feeling better for having seen her. Her face was made of heavenly smiles, and her voice of tranquil music.

But, alas! this kind heart had but a short time to remain as such. The fatal poison of irresponsible power was already in her hands, and soon commenced its infernal work. That cheerful eye, under the influence of slavery, soon became red with rage; that voice, made all of sweet accord, changed to one of harsh and horrid discord; and that angelic face gave place to that of a demon.

Very soon after I went to live with Mr. and Mrs. Auld, she very kindly commenced to teach me the A, B, C. After I had learned this, she assisted me in learning to spell words of three or four letters. Just at this point of my progress, Mr. Auld found out what was going on, and at once forbade Mrs. Auld to instruct me further, telling her, among other things, that it was unlawful, as well as unsafe, to teach a slave to read. To use his own words, further, he said, "If you give a nigger an inch, he will take an ell. A nigger should know nothing but to obey his master—to do as he is told to do. Learning would *spoil* the best nigger in the world. Now," said he, "if you teach that nigger (speaking of myself) how to read, there would be no keeping him. It would forever unfit him to be a slave. He would at once become unmanageable, and of no value to his master. As to himself, it could do him no good, but a great deal of harm. It would make him discontented and unhappy." These words sank deep into my heart, stirred up sentiments within that lay slumbering, and called into existence an entirely new train of thought. It was a new and special revelation, explaining dark and mysterious things, with which my youthful understanding had struggled, but struggled in vain. I now understood what had been to me a most perplexing difficulty—to wit, the white man's power to enslave the black man. It was a grand achievement, and I prized it highly. From that moment, I understood the pathway from slavery to freedom. It was just what I wanted, and I got it at a time when I the least expected it. Whilst I was saddened by the thought of losing the aid of my kind mistress, I was gladdened by the invaluable instruction which, by the merest accident, I had gained from my master. Though conscious of the difficulty of learning without a teacher, I set out with high hope, and a fixed purpose, at whatever cost of trouble, to learn how to read. The very decided manner with which he spoke, and strove to impress his wife with the evil consequences of giving me instruction, served to convince me that he was deeply sensible of the truths he was uttering. It gave me the best assurance that I might rely with the utmost confidence on the results which, he said, would flow from teaching me to read. What he most dreaded, that I most desired. What he most loved, that I most hated. That which to him was a great evil, to be carefully shunned, was to me a great good, to be diligently sought; and the argument which he so warmly urged, against my learning to read, only served to inspire me with a desire and determination to learn. In learning to read, I owe almost as much to the bitter opposition of my master, as to the kindly aid of my mistress. I acknowledge the benefit of both. . . .

. . . My mistress was, as I have said, a kind and tender-hearted woman; and in the simplicity of her soul she commenced, when I first went to live with her, to treat me as she supposed one human being ought to treat another. In entering upon the duties of a slaveholder, she did not seem to perceive that I sustained to her the relation of a mere chattel, and that for her to treat me as a human being was not only wrong, but dangerously so. Slavery proved as injurious to her as it did to me. When I went there, she was a pious, warm, and tenderhearted woman. There was no sorrow or suffering for which she had not a tear. She had bread for the hungry, clothes for the naked, and comfort for every mourner that came within her reach. Slavery soon proved its ability to divest her of these heavenly qualities. Under its influence, the tender heart became stone, and the lamblike disposition gave way to one of tiger-like fierceness. The first step in her downward course was in her ceasing to instruct me. She now commenced to practise her husband's precepts.

She finally became even more violent in her opposition than her husband himself. She was not satisfied with simply doing as well as he had commanded; she seemed anxious to do better. Nothing seemed to make her more angry than to see me with a newspaper. She seemed to think that here lay the danger. I have had her rush at me with a face made all up of fury, and snatch from me a newspaper, in a manner that fully revealed her apprehension. She was an apt woman; and a little experience soon demonstrated, to her satisfaction, that education and slavery were incompatible with each other.

From this time I was most narrowly watched. If I was in a separate room any considerable length of time, I was sure to be suspected of having a book, and was at once called to give an account of myself. All this, however, was too late. The first step had been taken. Mistress, in teaching me the alphabet, had given me the *inch*, and no precaution could prevent me from taking the *ell*. . . .

Douglass finds and reads books about slavery that "[give] tongue to interesting thoughts of [his] own soul."

. . . The reading of these documents enabled me to utter my thoughts, and to meet the arguments brought forward to sustain slavery; but while they relieved me of one difficulty, they brought on another even more painful than the one of which I was relieved. The more I read, the more I was led to abhor and detest my enslavers. I could regard them in no other light than a band of successful robbers, who had left their homes, and gone to Africa, and stolen us from our homes, and in a strange land reduced us to slavery. I loathed them as being the meanest as well as the most wicked of men. As I read and contemplated the subject, behold! that very discontentment which Master Hugh had predicted would follow my learning to read had already come, to torment and sting my soul to unutterable anguish. As I writhed under it, I would at times feel that learning to read had been a curse rather than a blessing. It had given me a view of my wretched condition, without the remedy. It opened my eyes to the horrible pit, but to no ladder upon which to get out. In moments of agony, I envied my fellow-slaves for their stupidity. I have often wished myself a beast. I preferred the condition of the meanest reptile to my own. Any thing, no matter what, to get rid of thinking! It was this everlasting thinking of my condition that tormented me. There was no getting rid of it. It was pressed upon me by every object within sight or hearing, animate or inanimate. The silver trump of freedom had roused my soul to eternal wakefulness. Freedom now appeared, to disappear no more forever. It was heard in every sound, and seen in every thing. It was ever present to torment me with a sense of my wretched condition. I saw nothing without seeing it, I heard nothing without hearing it, and felt nothing without feeling it. It looked from every star, it smiled in every calm, breathed in every wind, and moved in every storm.

Excerpt 2

If at any one time of my life more than another, I was made to drink the bitterest dregs of slavery, that time was during the first six months of my stay with Mr. Covey. We were worked in all weathers. It was never too hot or too cold; it could never rain, blow, hail, or snow, too hard for us to work in the field. Work, work, work, was scarcely more the order of the day than of the night. The longest days were too short for him, and the shortest nights too long for him. I was somewhat unmanageable when I first went there, but a few months of this discipline tamed me. Mr. Covey succeeded in breaking me. I was broken in body, soul, and spirit. My natural elasticity was crushed, my intellect languished, the disposition to read departed, the cheerful spark that lingered about my eye died; the dark night of slavery closed in upon me; and behold a man transformed into a brute!

Sunday was my only leisure time. I spent this in a sort of beast-like stupor, between sleep and wake, under some large tree. At times I would rise up, a flash of energetic freedom would dart through my soul, accompanied with a faint beam of hope, that flickered for a moment, and then vanished. I sank down again, mourning over my wretched condition. I was sometimes prompted to take my life, and that of Covey, but was prevented by a combination of hope and fear. My sufferings on this plantation seem now like a dream rather than a stern reality. . . .

. . . I have already intimated that my condition was much worse, during the first six months of my stay at Mr. Covey's, than in the last six. The circumstances leading to the change in Mr. Covey's course toward me form an epoch in my humble history. You have seen how a man was made a slave; you shall see how a slave was made a man. On one of the hottest days of the month of August, 1833, Bill Smith, William Hughes, a slave named Eli, and myself, were engaged in fanning wheat. Hughes was clearing the fanned wheat from before the fan, Eli was turning, Smith was feeding, and I was carrying wheat to the fan. The work was simple, requiring strength rather than intellect; yet, to one entirely unused to such work, it came very hard. About three o'clock of that day, I broke down; my strength failed me; I was seized with a violent aching of the head, attended with extreme dizziness; I trembled in every limb. Finding what was coming, I nerved myself up, feeling it would never do to stop work. I stood as long as I could stagger to the hopper with grain. When I could stand no longer, I fell, and felt as if held down by an immense weight. The fan of course stopped; every one had his own work to do; and no one could do the work of the other, and have his own go on at the same time.

Mr. Covey was at the house, about one hundred yards from the treading-yard where we were fanning. On hearing the fan stop, he left immediately, and came to the spot where we were. He hastily inquired what the matter was. Bill answered that I was sick, and there was no one to bring wheat to the fan. I had by this time crawled away under the side of the post and rail-fence by which the yard was enclosed, hoping to find relief by getting out of the sun. He then asked where I was. He was told by one of the hands. He came to the spot, and, after looking at me awhile, asked me what was the matter. I told him as well as I could, for I scarce had strength to speak. He then gave me a savage kick in the side, and told me to get up. I tried to do so, but fell back in the attempt. He gave me another kick, and again told me to rise. I again tried, and succeeded in gaining my feet; but, stooping to get the tub with which I was feeding the fan, I again staggered and fell. While down in this situation, Mr. Covey took up the hickory slat with which Hughes had been striking off the half-bushel measure, and with it gave me a heavy blow upon the head, making a large wound, and the blood ran freely; and with this again told me to get up. I made no effort to comply, having now made up my mind to let him do his worst. In a short time after receiving this blow, my head grew better. Mr. Covey had now left me to my fate. At this moment I resolved, for the first time, to go to my master, enter a complaint, and ask his protection. In order to do this, I must that afternoon walk seven miles; and this, under the circumstances, was truly a severe undertaking. I was exceedingly feeble; made so as much by the kicks and blows which I received, as by the severe fit of sickness to which I had been subjected. . . .

Douglass walks seven miles through the woods to his master's house, badly bloodying his body and feet. His appeal is rebuffed and he is sent back under threat of a whipping. He returns to Covey, where he expects to suffer revenge for having run away.

. . . All went well till Monday morning. . . . Long before daylight, I was called to go and rub, curry, and feed, the horses. I obeyed, and was glad to obey. But whilst thus engaged, whilst in the act of throwing down some blades from the loft, Mr. Covey entered the stable with a long rope; and just as I was half out of the loft, he caught hold of my legs, and was about tying me. As soon as I found what he was up to, I gave a sudden spring, and as I did so, he holding to my legs, I was brought sprawling on the stable floor. Mr. Covey seemed now to think he had me, and could do what he pleased; but at this moment—from whence came the spirit I don't know—I resolved to fight; and, suiting my action to the resolution, I seized Covey hard by the throat; and as I did so, I rose. He held on to me, and I to him. My resistance was so entirely unexpected, that Covey seemed taken all aback. He trembled like a leaf. This gave me assurance, and I held him uneasy, causing the blood to run where I touched him with the ends of my fingers. Mr. Covey soon called out to Hughes for help. Hughes came, and, while Covey held me, attempted to tie my right hand. While he was in the act of doing so, I watched my chance, and gave him a heavy kick close under the ribs. This kick fairly sickened Hughes, so that he left me in the hands of Mr. Covey. This kick had the effect of not only weakening Hughes, but Covey also. When he saw Hughes bending over with pain, his courage quailed. He asked me if I meant to persist in my resistance. I told him I did, come what might; that he had used me like a brute for six months, and that I was determined to be used so no longer. With that, he strove to drag me to a stick that was lying just out of the stable door. He meant to knock me down. But just as he was leaning over to get the stick, I seized him with both hands by his collar, and brought him by a sudden snatch to the ground. By this time, Bill came. Covey called upon him for assistance. Bill wanted to know what he could do. Covey said, "Take hold of him, take hold of him!" Bill said his master hired him out to work, and not to help to whip me; so he left Covey and myself to fight our own battle out. We were at it for nearly two hours. Covey at length let me go, puffing and blowing at a great rate, saying that if I had not resisted, he would not have whipped me half so much. The truth was, that he had not whipped me at all. I considered him as getting entirely the worst end of the bargain; for he had drawn no blood from me, but I had from him. The whole six months afterwards, that I spent with Mr. Covey, he never laid the weight of his finger upon me in anger. He would occasionally say, he didn't want to get hold of me again. "No," thought I, "you need not; for you will come off worse than you did before."

This battle with Mr. Covey was the turning-point in my career as a slave. It rekindled the few expiring embers of freedom, and revived within me a sense of my own manhood. It recalled the departed self-confidence, and inspired me again with a determination to be free. The gratification afforded by the triumph was a full compensation for whatever else might follow, even death itself. He only can understand the deep satisfaction which I experienced; who has himself repelled by force the bloody arm of slavery. I felt as I never felt before. It was a glorious resurrection, from the tomb of slavery, to the heaven of freedom. My long-crushed spirit rose, cowardice departed, bold defiance took its place; and I now resolved that, however long I might remain a slave in form, the day had passed forever when I could be a slave in fact. I did not hesitate to let it be known of me, that the white man who expected to succeed in whipping, must also succeed in killing me.